REVOLUTIONARY GOVERNMENT IN IRELAND

Dáil Éireann, 1919–22

ARTHUR MITCHELL

GILL & MACMILLAN

Gill & Macmillan Ltd
Goldenbridge
Dublin 8
with associated companies throughout the world
© Arthur Mitchell 1995
0 7171 1481 3 (hardback)
0 7171 2015 5 (paperback)
Print origination by
Seton Music Graphics Ltd, Bantry, Co. Cork
Printed by ColourBooks Ltd, Dublin

A catalogue record is available for this book
from the British Library.

REVOLUTIONARY GOVERNMENT IN IRELAND
Dáil Éireann, 1919–22

Do Mháire agus Gráinne

Contents

Preface

The question of Irish self-government has been a considerable political issue in the Western world since at least the middle of the nineteenth century. It could not have been otherwise, as the nationalists of Ireland were attempting political separation from what was then the most powerful state in the world. There was a large Irish population in the new colossus across the western ocean, as well as many Irish emigrants in the British dominions. The presence of Irishmen and Ireland in the midst of this powerful network of nations has meant that Irish affairs have been given much greater attention than those of almost any other small country. Even today, although three-quarters of Ireland has been self-governing for two-thirds of a century, Irish affairs not only directly and deeply involve Britain, but continue to attract attention from other countries as well, not least in the USA. The specific matter of international interest is, of course, the conflict in Northern Ireland that has now been boiling over for more than twenty years. It is not by chance that the Anglo-Irish Agreement of 1985 concerning the six north-eastern counties has been backed by a financial aid commitment from Australia, Canada, New Zealand and the United States.

Like many other small countries in Europe, Ireland achieved self-government after the First World War. Unlike all the others, however, Ireland had been a subordinate part, not of one of the defeated powers, but of a victorious one. Independence, therefore, did not drop into its lap in the aftermath of war; rather, it had to fight for it. In doing so, the supporters of self-government employed both military and political methods, with the two effectively complementing each other. The campaign started on a substantial foundation. The country had been part of the British parliamentary system for over a century, and Irish political organisation was well developed. A strong cadre of Irish nationalist members had been in the House of Commons since the 1880s, and they knew how to exert political pressure. One of them declared: 'There is no use in approaching an English minister unless you come to him with the head of a landlord in one hand and the tail of a cow in the other.'[1] Extensive experience in local government had been gained since it came under democratic control at the turn of the century. A limited form of self-government, 'home rule', had been approved by the British government, although its application had been delayed until after the war. This certainly was a good beginning to build on.

The movement that finally achieved effective self-government for the country employed all of the methods that were later used by national liberation movements throughout the colonial world. There is little evidence, however, that latter-day nationalist revolutionaries consciously modelled themselves on the Irish movement, though Ireland undoubtedly provided an example and inspiration for many. The Irish had succeeded in breaking away from Britain; others too could free themselves from British or other control.

The Irish movement employed open political agitation. It also organised a concerted campaign of boycott and obstruction of the existing administration. Intimidation and violence were provided by its military arm. To tie the whole campaign together there was the political leadership which created an alternative government. Thus almost anyone who supported Irish self-government was provided with an agency through which he or she could contribute towards attaining the chosen objective.

This book is about the creation of the alternative administration, that of Dáil Éireann, which was established in 1919 and carried the mandate of government for nationalist Ireland until the Anglo-Irish Treaty of December 1921. But since these other activities were related parts of a whole movement, they are also drawn into the story. Sinn Féin, indeed Ireland, divided on the issue of the Treaty; and the revolutionary government of Dáil Éireann, its achievements and failures, became caught up in the extended controversy about the period. When in 1930 the pro-Free State paper *The Star* asserted that the Irish Republic declared in 1919 had 'no existence at any time' and that it was only an elaborate humbug, a Republican journal, *The Nation*, took it to task: 'The truth is that the Government of the Irish Republic had all the authority a government can have and was gradually making that authority effective when the Truce [of July 1921] came. Otherwise there would have been no Truce, no negotiations and no Treaty.' This was the common fare of partisan combat in the inter-war period.[2]

One of the puzzling aspects of this period of Irish history is that while there are many memoirs by those involved on the military side in the Irish Republican Army, there is no extensive account by a major participant on the civil and political side. Part of the explanation for this may be that guns and violence are inherently more interesting and popular than apparently mundane activities like organising an underground government. Moreover, that strain of ebullience and imagination within the Irish character prefers drama and action; these certainly provide the basis for better stories. A more likely explanation is that those involved on the political side who survived the period continued with their political careers and had neither the time nor the inclination for writing books or articles about those times. They often spoke about the period in speeches and referred to it in campaign literature, but almost always for polemical purposes. The past provided ammunition for the political present; politicians operated in the realm of popular memory and belief. Reconstruction of the period was thus left to the historian. Having to rely on primary sources — the records, reports, notes and correspondence of the time — has proved, I am sure, to be an advantage in my study of the period.[3]

The work of three historians has been particularly valuable in providing me with an incisive view of the Irish situation in the decade from 1913 to 1923. In two short studies, *Nationalist Revolutionaries in Ireland* and *The Evolution of Irish Nationalist Politics*, Tom Garvin has excavated the roots of the nationalist leadership and examined the dynamics of Irish political society. David Fitzpatrick, in *Politics and Irish Life, 1913–1921*, has focused his attention on developments in Co. Clare, using it as a representative microcosm of what was happening in the country as a whole. Charles Townshend, in *The British Campaign in Ireland, 1919–1921*, has provided a rigorous analysis of the efforts of the imperial power to hold on to Ireland. In a work of wider scope, *Political Violence in Ireland: Government and Resistance since 1848*, Townshend employed the terms 'counter-state' and 'alternative government', and I have adopted them for use in this book. Since none of these excellent works gave centrality to the revolutionary government of Dáil Éireann, this study should fill that gap.

The story itself and the people involved were of great interest to me, but I hesitate to think what the result of my labours would be without the aid and encouragement of Pádraig Ó Snodaigh of the National Museum of Ireland. Invaluable assistance was also provided by T. P. O'Neill of University College, Galway, who read (and corrected) the manuscript. There are many others to whom I am grateful, including C. J. Woods, Colm Gavan Duffy, Séamas Ó Buachalla, Tom Garvin, Séamus Geraghty, John P. Feeney, Judson Lyon, Alan Greenberg, Liam Dalton, Mary Kotsonouris, Seán Ó Lúing, D. R. O'Connor Lysaght, Kevin O'Byrne, James R. Watson and Patrick Lane; also the Kilmainham Jail Museum, the Commissioners of Public Works, the Archives of University College, Dublin, the National Archives of Ireland (incorporating the former State Paper Office, Dublin Castle), the

Public Record Office, London, and, as always, the ever-helpful staff of the National Library of Ireland. My thanks also to Dr John J. Duffy, Chancellor, University Campuses, and the Research and Productive Scholarship Fund of the University of South Carolina. A year-long fellowship from the National Endowment for the Humanities was of great help in moving the research forward. A year spent as visiting professor at Trinity College, Dublin, was pure academic pleasure. I am deeply appreciative of those who contributed to a publication fund for this book. My thanks also to Fergal Tobin of Gill & Macmillan, and to my copy-editor, Colm Croker. Over many years Milton Harden of the USC Salkehatchie Campus has been my friendly guide in the arcane techniques of word-processing.

Arthur Mitchell

Introduction

That Irish nationalists would make a concerted effort to achieve self-government at the end of the first European war is hardly surprising. The wartime propaganda about the rights of small nations and self-determination might have found its origins in needs of Allied propaganda, but it was music to the ears of small, subject nationalities, not least the Irish.

The process of nation-building took place independently of wartime exigencies. Indeed, the cultural and intellectual foundation had already been laid by 1914. The political evolution was also impressive: a party dedicated to some form of national identity had won the allegiance of a majority of the Irish people, and local government was already controlled by supporters of nationalism. Even within the constraints of the British parliamentary system, the nationalist cause had advanced to the point that Home Rule had won legislative approval, with the act itself scheduled to be implemented after the war or whenever it suited the interests of the London government.

A major obstacle in this matter was the existence of a small but compact group in eastern Ulster that was determined to remain completely within the British state. As a result, some form of partition probably was inevitable. Time was to show that the real failure of nationalist leadership was not to prevent this, but to assure that the division of territory, when it came, would be based on the preferences of voters in specific areas, be they localities, parliamentary constituencies or counties. Had partition been implemented on this basis, it would at least have prevented large numbers of nationalists from being locked into a Unionist-controlled jurisdiction. Moreover, the Unionist-controlled area would have been drastically reduced, in fact by more than half of the area that was to become 'Northern Ireland'.

That was for the future. British involvement in the European war presented an opportunity for rebellion, and this opportunity was seized. The

1916 rising was a small and, from one point of view, unrepresentative affair, almost entirely restricted to Dublin. Yet this action struck a deep chord in the Irish psyche and turned Irish nationalists towards a more determined effort to attain political independence. The rising was called, incorrectly, the Sinn Féin rebellion, and almost all its participants were members of the Irish Volunteers and Irish Citizen Army; but the organisation that made it happen was the Irish Republican Brotherhood, which was to continue to have a vital if subterranean role in directing the course of events through the revolutionary period until after Anglo-Irish Treaty of 1921.

When the survivors of the revolt associated themselves with the Sinn Féin programme, political success seemed assured. Such a combination appealed to those who were prepared to use violence as well as to those who wanted to use non-violent means, and, of course, to those who wanted to use both. The position was stated in a party pamphlet of 1918:

> By embracing every branch of the administration, Sinn Féin pro-
> poses to paralyse the actions of a dominating power by the mutual
> co-operation of the community. Should suppression of the move-
> ment involve the use of physical force, Sinn Féin proposes to render
> it ineffectual by resorting to passive resistance, with as much active
> resistance as may be necessary.[1]

It was the position of the advanced nationalists within the revived Irish Volunteers and Sinn Féin that all means should be used. The political organisation emphasised that the way forward was through electoral success, appeal to world opinion, specifically at the post-war peace conference, the undermining of the existing British administration, and the creation of an alternative government. The general election of December 1918 presented Sinn Féin with an ideal opportunity to demonstrate that it was the dominant political force in Ireland.

Because it had achieved a broad base of support, Sinn Féin was able to push aside the small Irish Labour Party and demolish the atrophied remains of the Irish Parliamentary Party. Where it failed to establish significant support was in six of the nine counties of Ulster. Owing to their history of continuous political combat, both the Unionist and Irish Parliamentary Parties were in fine fighting form and repulsed Sinn Féin's efforts there.[2]

Sinn Féin won 73 of the 105 Irish seats, while the Unionists increased their representation from 18 to 26, and the Irish Parliamentary Party emerged with just 6 (four of these by agreement with Sinn Féin). This was a victory of great magnitude. The party won 25 seats unopposed. In 52 seats contested by both Sinn Féin and the Irish Parliamentary Party, it won 45 of them.

What did the outcome signify? To some Sinn Féiners the voters had given a mandate for the creation of an independent republic. To moderates the voters had simply rejected Westminster and had declared for self-determination. There was the certainty that those elected from Ireland would have nothing to do with the London parliament. There also was the certainty that a strengthened Ulster Unionist Party would be returning to a friendly parliament to seek protection from the rising tide of Irish nationalism. It must have been apparent to some Sinn Féiners that there was a price to be paid or at least real danger in abstention. The ultimate significance of the election was that the Irish people as a whole had resolved for full self-government; as time was to show, this decision was final and irrevocable.[3]

1

The Establishment of Dáil Éireann

(1) PRELUDE

Having achieved its overwhelming victory at the polls in December 1918, what course would Sinn Féin take? This was the question that preoccupied public opinion in the opening weeks of the new year. To judge from its election programme, three things could be expected: abstention from Westminster; the formation of a national council or constituent assembly; and an effort to secure recognition of Ireland's right to self-determination at the Versailles Peace Conference.

There was no question of the Sinn Féin members taking their seats at Westminster. John Dillon believed that many of them wanted to do so, and Thomas Harbinson, Nationalist M.P. for North-East Tyrone, argued that they would be forced to do so in order 'to avert disaster for Ireland'. Both Viscount French, the Lord Lieutenant of Ireland, and Walter Long, a member of the British cabinet, both of whom belonged to the Anglo-Irish landowning class, believed the Sinn Féiners would not be able to resist the lure of £400 per annum at Westminster. For his part, however, Sir Edward Carson argued forcefully that Sinn Féin would not and could not enter parliament: 'Their programme and policy is modelled on the Kossuth revolutionaries in Hungary. Therefore they must make some sort of a show in Ireland.' On the other side, the *Catholic Bulletin* was sure that Sinn Féin meant what it said about abstention: 'Ireland has just signalised the passing of the historic year just closed by deliberately turning her back for ever on London of the cocaine and the drugs, nursery of hypocrisy and infamy and of corruption that knows no end.'

The appeal to the Allied powers' conference was also certain. To Sinn Féiners, their victory was so impressive that no one could seriously challenge their party's right to speak for the country. There was, of course, no serious barrier that would prevent it from making an effort to present the claim in Paris, but how effective this campaign would be and what kind of a reception it would receive were completely different matters. Speculation centred on what Sinn Féin would do concerning a national assembly. The time period involved appeared to be short — the election results were announced on 28 December, and the new parliament was due to assemble on 4 February, a period of five weeks.

Dublin's Unionist newspaper prepared its readers for a period of tumult. The *Irish Times* (31 Dec.) believed that Sinn Féin had 'not the slightest chance' of gaining a hearing at the Peace Conference; nevertheless, 'the necessity of some sort of action is imposed on it'. It could summon its proposed constituent assembly, and then by means of strikes, disorder and lawlessness 'do its best to convince the world that British government is impossible in Ireland'. In the nationalist press, the *Irish Independent* celebrated the destruction of the Irish Party, while the *Freeman's Journal* raised the spectre of socialism and demanded to know when Sinn Féin would declare its republic. The Dublin *Evening Telegraph* (17 Jan.) not only passed on critical comment from the British press, but also observed that current Sinn Féin 'gloomy forebodings' afforded 'a piquant contrast to the resplendent rhetoric of pre-election days'.

Some of the provincial papers were prepared to attack Sinn Féin even before it acted. The *Dundalk Democrat*, a supporter of the vanquished Parliamentary Party, asserted that nothing could hold the discordant supporters of Sinn Féin together and that 'the Peace Conference will finish the sham unity of the congeries of forces know as Sinn Féin'. The Belfast *Irish News*, another supporter of the losing side, saw little future for any constituent assembly: 'We set aside cheap talk about Sinn Féin "MIPs" forgathering in Dublin and issuing decrees with an assumption of governmental authority.' People would not be satisfied with 'make-believes', and if the appeal to the Peace Conference failed, then Sinn Féin must rely on force. The *Belfast Newsletter* sought to reassure Unionists outside of Ulster that they had nothing to fear from Sinn Féin. When the Ulster Unionists were successful in gaining their new objective of partition, 'that of itself would make impossible the setting up of an Irish Republic'.

The English press demonstrated a keen but generally hostile interest in Sinn Féin intentions. The *Daily Telegraph* was quick to warn that 'if the Sinn Féiners resort to histrionics . . . and proclaim themselves to be an Irish Convention or Parliament or some such name, the Government must deal with them' with 'a resolute display of government and by no parleying with treason'. *The Star*'s Dublin correspondent reported that Sinn Féin would try to delay the establishment of an assembly, but 'sooner or later Sinn Féin will have to summon it, and its prospects are about as dismal as the ill-starred Chartist Convention of 1839'. To *The Globe* the policy of abstention was simply 'tomfoolery' because a few differential tariffs 'on pigs and butter would make Ireland bankrupt and raise in six months an overwhelming cry to be re-admitted into the British Empire on any terms'.

On 1 January 1919 the *Daily News* argued that Sinn Féin would not go so far as to set up a provisional government, 'reflection having shown the grave risks of such a movement ending in impotence and ridicule owing to its lack of force and funds'. But its Dublin correspondent, having discerned hints that Sinn Féin might resort to strikes, sabotage and 'wholesale passive resistance', counselled that although 'threats like these may sound foolish in London', in Dublin 'it is impossible not to admit that the great mass of the people are terribly earnest'. Two days later he concluded that Sinn Féin intended to set up a body similar to the 'Ulster Provisional Government' that Sir Edward Carson had threatened to establish in 1913. This would be a propaganda body, initially at least: 'This executive is not likely to try to assume authority or create trouble until or unless the attempt to get a hearing at the Peace Conference definitely fails.'

That Irish public sentiment currently was with Sinn Féin was granted by the Dublin correspondent of the London *Times* (15 Jan.), but he predicted that in six months 'all the material interests of the country will be hostile to it'. Moreover, he believed that an attempt to create a parliament would result in 'a hopeless fiasco'. *The Spectator* faced the prospect of a parliament without a large Irish contingent with optimism — the Sinn Féin policy of turning its back on Westminster 'may indeed be regarded as a blessing'. But a few days later both *The Star* and *The Times* reported that Sinn Féin members were preparing to descend on parliament before the swearing in of members and attempt, like an earlier generation of Irish obstructionists, to disrupt the proceedings. Confusion reigned in Fleet Street. Perhaps the most prescient view of the future was provided by Patrick Thompson, writing in the *Labour Leader*, who foresaw that 'a bitter conflict between the Irish Government *de jure* and the British Government *de facto* will be carried on, perhaps to the logical conclusion of another armed revolt'.[1]

The Sinn Féin press seemed unsure about what its party would do after the election. Even before the results were declared, *New Ireland* on 21 December commented that 'a National Council will have to meet in the early part of next year', one difficulty being that 'the machinery of the English Parliamentary representation is unsuitable' because of the small number involved, so that many who could contribute to 'the work of nation-building' were not included. It then fell silent about the future government of Ireland. It did, however, enjoy the spectacle of the Dillonite press and party being 'much exercised lest there be any undue delay in the production of the Irish Republic'; its view was that 'the Irish people can produce their Republic at whatever moment they like'. Neither *Nationality* nor *The Irishman* provided any clear indication of Sinn Féin's plans. The *Catholic Bulletin* acknowledged that the English press and 'the anglicised press in Ireland' were raising questions about Sinn Féin's intentions, but contented itself with the comment 'All this is in good time, as circumstances arise.' Only the *Irish World* had a clear view of what Sinn Féin should do: 'The first move is to summon the First Parliament of the Irish Republic.' This, it continued, should proceed to set up an administration which would take control of all public bodies. Even if the new government lacked tax power, it would be 'moral insurrection machinery'.

The public activity of Sinn Féin after the election was first directed at the promotion of public meetings to invite President Wilson to Ireland; these meetings took place during the last week of December. It also circulated petitions to be presented to the Peace Conference; these included a petition organised by Maurice Moore among Irishmen who had served as officers in the British army. Then, in the first week of January, it launched an agitation for the release of the 'German plot' internees, many of whom had won seats in the election.

When Sinn Féin spokesmen did refer to the future of Irish government, they sought to restrain the felt need for action. Father O'Flanagan told a meeting in the Mansion House on 31 December that he was not in 'hysterical impatience' to declare a republic; he wanted to see the Irish Republic postponed for months or years, as time would only increase the spirit of Sinn Féin among the people. In a speech on 12 January Eoin Mac Néill 'spoke despondently of the Republic becoming a reality "this year, next year or in ten year's time"'. Thomas Kelly warned the same meeting that the 'difficulties ahead are immense and the outlook is fairly dark'. Even Ireland's appeal to the Peace Conference was viewed as a doubtful venture: on the eve of the gathering at Paris Count Plunkett declared that it was a 'bogus peace conference'. To the *Evening Telegraph* the apparent wave of pessimism sweeping Sinn Féin was simply 'reality dawning at last'; furthermore, 'the Irish Republic that was almost immediately to have materialised through the Peace Conference grows more nebulous every day'.[2]

Meanwhile the Sinn Féin executive was quietly and privately preparing its scheme of government. On 19 December, five days before the results of the election were to be announced, it took the decision to 'convoke the Dáil Éireann' as had been agreed at the October 1918 *ard-fheis*. The first step in the process taken by the executive was to appoint a committee under the chairmanship of Seán T. O'Kelly to deal with the formation of the new assembly. The committee called a joint meeting of the available 'elected Republican members' for 1 January at the Mansion House, to be followed by a 'publicly announced' meeting of Sinn Féin members at Dublin City Hall. In launching the venture, the executive used proper parliamentary language: 'Messrs Béaslaí and Collins were deputed to issue the whip to the Republican members.'

It also explored the matter of the composition of the proposed body: 'The question as to whether the Carson members, members of the Irish Party and the Labour leaders should be invited to attend the deliberations of the Dáil Éireann was discussed and it was decided to leave the question over.' With Sinn Féin preparing to establish a national assembly, it would seem inevitable that all those elected to parliamentary seats would be invited, although Unionists and Home Rulers were sure to decline. One difficulty with an entirely Sinn Féin assembly was that it would have few participants. According to a Sinn Féin source, only twenty-six of the party's sixty-nine successful candidates were at liberty when the results of the election were announced. The *Evening Telegraph* (3 Jan.) believed the scarcity of members was one reason why Sinn Féin was slow to act. The Sinn Féin executive discussed the possibility of substitute members, but came to no decision. Michael Collins was 'very much against' forming a parliament while so many of those who had won seats in the election remained in prison.

There was speculation that Sinn Féin would attempt to overcome this scarcity and broaden the base of the assembly by extending membership to the leaders of national organisations, such as the Catholic Church, local government bodies and the labour movement. Most of the attention centred around the possibility of including some Labour leaders. The Dublin correspondent of the *Daily News* reported on 1 January that the Labour Party would be invited to send representatives to the new assembly and 'will almost certainly agree to do so, as its complexion is mainly republican'. A week later Thomas Johnson, one of the Labour leaders, told him that the Labour Party was 'willing to act as a Left-wing within the National Assembly'.

Sinn Féin faced obvious difficulties in widening the membership of its assembly. If the leaders of national organisations were included, the charge could be made that the assembly was less than a democratically elected body. If substitute members were selected or co-opted to replace those in jail, this practice would be attacked as being contrary to the generally accepted provisions of representative government. In the end it decided to include only those who had won seats in the election. As expected, members of other political parties did not accept invitations to the new assembly; indeed, only two replies were received from them.

The new body would therefore be composed solely of Sinn Féiners. What was the character of this group? It comprised sixty-eight men and one woman, predominantly young, urban middle-class, bred politically on a pure broth of simple nationalism and little more. There was not one of them who had been exposed to the wider learning about European political theory, social conditions, economics or technology. A few had some experience in local government, the Gaelic League and Sinn Féin. In terms of occupations, 65 per cent were in the professions or business, while only 10 per cent were in agriculture. Among those in the professions, there were nine journalists, seven in education, five doctors, and five lawyers. Many of the members of the group were fierce young men of no particular occupation who had been elected on the basis of their participation in the 1916 rising.

According to Hugh Martin of the *Daily News*, the Labour Party 'is piqued at not having received a direct invitation from the convening body, and has intimated, I understand, that it will not accept co-option as a compromise'. The result was 'distinctly strained relations' between Sinn Féin and the Labour executive. On the other hand, the same difficulties that arose in the proposal to withdraw a few Sinn Féin candidates in favour of Labour nominees also applied in this situation. Moreover, the Labour leaders made no public complaint, and in the event a few of them had an important but limited role in the launching of the new assembly.

At the same time the *Voice of Labour* freely advised Sinn Féin about what it should do. It declared that 'there is no obligation to draw up an elaborate programme and a national constitution' and that the body to be formed as a result of the December election should simply be a 'Constitutent Assembly'. The Dáil should concentrate its energies on gaining recognition abroad and disrupting the existing system of government at home. These policies, it held, are 'not only sufficient for its strength but possible with its resources'.[3]

(2) THE REVOLUTIONARY ASSEMBLY

The Principles of Government

Confident of a substantial victory, Sinn Féin began to prepare for the post-war conference even before the results of the election were announced. In fact its first step in this direction was taken immediately after the East Cavan by-election in June 1918. Following Arthur Griffith's success in this election, James O'Mara, one of the key Sinn Féin political operatives, concluded that his party would win the forthcoming general election. He asked Robert Brennan to select two men to go to the continent to prepare the way for presenting Ireland's case to the projected peace conference; he also provided £2,000 in cash and £2,000 in gold for this purpose. Brennan selected 'Jean Christophe' (a pseudonym of Roger Chaurive, a French lecturer at University College Dublin) and Mario Esposito (a Dublin-educated translator of medieval Latin manuscripts), who were duly dispatched across the water. Nothing useful appears to have resulted from the travels of the two, and Michael Collins complained that Esposito had not even submitted a report of his expedition.

The imminent prospect of the peace conference and post-war settlement required prompt action on the part of Sinn Féin, as President Wilson had arrived in Europe in mid-December on his first visit. At a meeting on

19 December the Sinn Féin executive appointed a special foreign affairs committee for this work, with its first task being the establishment of contacts with foreign sympathisers and governments. Seán T. O'Kelly, Michael Collins, George Gavan Duffy and Robert Barton were instructed to 'proceed immediately to London'. This committee undoubtedly was responsible for 'An Urgent Preliminary Note' dispatched to Wilson from the 'Irish Delegates' in late December which informed him that if the principle of self-determination, 'the cardinal doctrine of his Peace policy', was not applied to Ireland, 'the President will return to his own people with his mission made a mockery'. As it appeared out of the question that President Wilson would visit Ireland, the Sinn Féin members of the Dublin Corporation took action to prepare the way for sending a delegation to Paris. At a meeting on 3 January the corporation passed a resolution appointing a deputation to confer the freedom of the city on Wilson.

The meeting arranged by the Sinn Féin executive and the available elected members was duly held on 1 January. The attendance consisted of sixteen members of the executive, twelve of whom had won parliamentary seats, and six other successful candidates. At this time the Sinn Féin leaders changed the date of the calling together of the available elected members from 2 to 7 January, but for the first time they made clear what they proposed that the assembly was to do: it was to consider the issuing of a declaration of independence and a 'Message to the Free Nations of the World'. Harry Boland and Thomas Kelly, Sinn Féin joint secretaries, issued invitations, and a printed programme was prepared.

This preliminary gathering, although a private meeting of members of a single party, could be viewed as the first meeting of Dáil Éireann. The invitation issued to the Sinn Féin members stated this clearly: 'We have the honour to call you to the first meeting of the Dáil Éireann which will hold a private session . . .' It was attended by twenty-nine of the thirty-five members at liberty. As the senior Sinn Féin member, George Noble Plunkett, recently released from jail, took the chair. The meeting then declared itself the national assembly of the nation. With one dissenting vote (Thomas Kelly), it passed the following resolution:

> That we, the Republican Members of the Irish Constituencies, in accordance with the National Will, are empowered to call together the Dáil Éireann and proceed to act accordingly.

It also decided to invite all Irish members elected in December to attend the first public meeting. To prepare for this, it appointed two committees: one to prepare proposals for the procedures, standing orders and constitution of the new house, and the other to draft a declaration of independence. Those in attendence also made a declaration, which was presented to them on a large printed form:

> I hereby pledge myself to work for the establishment of an Independent Irish Republic; that I will accept nothing less than complete separation from England in settlement of Ireland's claims; and that I will abstain from attending the English Parliament.

According to Piaras Béaslaí, the men who prepared the fundamental documents and made the arrangements for the inauguration of Dáil Éireann were George Gavan Duffy, Seán T. O'Kelly, Con Collins, J. J. Walsh, James O'Mara and himself.

The committees were instructed to report at the next meeting, which was set for a week later. Before that time, however, on the night of 11 January a party of fifty members of the Dublin Metropolitan Police raided the Sinn Féin headquarters and carried away drafts of the Declaration of Independence, the constitution and other documents. As a result, Dublin Castle was in no doubt about what Sinn Féin was planning. At the scene of the raid were several of the key operators within Sinn Féin — O'Kelly, Boland, Tom Kelly, James Burke and Frank Gallagher. The Irish administration had the opportunity to arrest them, but did not do so.

One reason for its hesitancy in this matter was that the newly appointed Chief Secretary for Ireland, Ian Macpherson, had not yet arrived in Dublin. The *Catholic Bulletin* (25 Jan.) believed that Dublin Castle had concluded that any further action against Sinn Féin at this time would only attract unfavourable international attention. As if to further clear the way for Sinn Féin's public launching of the new assembly, Dublin Castle on 20 January removed the requirement that organisers of public meetings must first apply for and receive police permits. Thus, for the moment at least, the United Kingdom executive in Ireland had decided not to disrupt Sinn Féin's efforts to replace it as the political authority in the country.

On 14 January the Sinn Féin members held an all-day meeting at which they considered reports on the documents that were to be presented to the first public meeting of the new assembly, which, they said, was to meet 'at an early date'. They also appointed a committee 'to draw up a draft programme of constructive work on democratic lines in consultation with Labour leaders'. Two days later Sinn Féin announced that the new assembly would meet on 21 January. Two further preparatory meetings were held on 17 and 19 January.[4]

The new assembly was to called 'An Dáil Éireann'. This name was first publicly used by Sinn Féin at its *ard-fheis* in October 1918. According to James Burke, a member of the first Dáil, 'the ancient Irish word *Dáil*, which means a council or gathering of the elders, has the sanction of centuries of Gaelic history and tradition behind it'. The term *dáil* was occasionally used for special purpose meetings within the Gaelic League, but was not widely employed in the movement. The name 'Dáil Éireann' gave the new assembly an immediate identity; and, except for a feeble attempt to substitute the word 'parliament' during the early Free State period, the Assembly of Ireland has had this name ever since.

Why was the first public meeting set for 21 January? This was five weeks after the election, and it was time for Sinn Féin to act. It was on this date fifteen years before that the first of Arthur Griffith's articles on the Hungarian policies of abstention and alternative government first appeared in the *United Irishman*. It is not known, however, if anyone noted the coincidence of dates; at any rate, it was not publicly observed. A meeting of the Dáil on 21 January would mean that the new assembly would be in being before the gathering of the new parliament, due to meet at Westminster on 4 February. In addition, it would follow closely on the assembling of the Allied conference in Paris, which met on 18 January. This would give the Irish demand for independence maximum attention.

Preparation of the documents to be used for launching the Dáil continued until the morning of the inaugural meeting. Three of these were particularly important: the constitution, the Declaration of Independence, and the statement of social and economic objectives.

The constitution, drawn up by 'Committee A', provided for a democratically elected single legislative body and a cabinet dependent on majority support. The instrument was provisional, subject to simple legislative amendment, and made no mention of a republic. The original draft had included a preamble that explicitly stated that the new polity was indeed a republic, but this was missing from the final version. Both the Declaration of Independence and the 'Message to the Free Nations of the World', however, stated that the new body was housed in the framework of a republic. On the other hand, the pledge taken by the available Sinn Féin members at the meeting of 7 January committed them only to 'work for the establishment of an Independent Irish Republic'. In Basil Chubb's judgment, the constitution 'was intended to be a provisional constitution for a republic . . . which they hoped to make a reality'. Furthermore, it said nothing about the state; there was no provision for a head of state. These omissions demonstrate, Chubb concludes, that 'in 1919 the state did not exist in fact, though it may have existed in theory'. Thus there was ambiguity in the fundamental documents of Dáil Éireann; however, there was no uncertainty or confusion in the public perception of what took place: An Dáil Éireann had declared a sovereign, democratic, independent republic.

Why had Sinn Féin decided to declare a republic? Its election address had proposed to establish only a constitutent assembly. Michael Hayes, who was later to serve as Ceann Comhairle (chairman) of Dáil Éireann for ten years, believed that two factors were involved. First, the Irish demand for independence had been identified with a republican form of government since at least the Fenian rebellion of 1867. When Tom Clarke was asked in 1916 why the political entity declared by his revolutionary government was called a republic, he replied: 'What else could we call it?' The other factor was that it would not have been possible or creditable 'to appoint a government and purport to set up departments without purporting also to create a state and without giving the state a name, and what other name could it have been given except an Irish Republic?' According to Darrell Figgis, a Sinn Féin officer at the time, the party leaders had decided some time before the spring of 1918 that following the impending general election they would set up only a constituent assembly, on the basis of which they would appeal to the post-war peace conference If this appeal failed, then they would declare a republic. 'To declare a Republic before proceeding to Paris', he argued, 'would have been to snatch the very judgment in hope of which the court was to be prayed.'

If this was the strategy, why was it then abandoned? Darrell Figgis believed that the 'German plot' arrests changed the situation within the party. Its leaders — de Valera, Griffith, Plunkett, Mac Néill — all of them essentially moderate, politically astute men, were removed from the scene, and the vacuum was filled by bolder, more adventurous spirits, some of whom, like Collins, Harry Boland and Diarmuid O'Hegarty, were drawn from the Irish Republican Brotherhood, while others, such as Cathal Brugha and Seán T. O'Kelly, were former members of that body. These men wanted a republic immediately and were prepared to uphold it in arms, as they already had done in 1916. Figgis saw Brugha as the driving force in the situation: 'His life in the dream of the Republic — a Republic of name, without definition or constitution — was his reality. The public declaration of the name was all that to him was required to complete the reality that existed indivisibly in his mind.'

It was clear that it was this group of committed republicans that was in control of Sinn Féin at this time. If the jailed leaders had been on the scene, a different pattern of events would undoubtedly have ensued. Did the new leaders force a declaration of a republic in a fit of exuberance, because this was the best opportunity to do so since 1916? One factor they must have had in mind was the dismal prospect of gaining anything from the Peace Conference. By mid-January it must have been clear to them that the British government could easily block any consideration of the Irish case. Furthermore, it could privately advise one and all that it was in the process of preparing a new scheme for Irish government, so that there was no need to drag the matter in at this time. However, what the militant Sinn Féin leaders hoped to gain from an effort to present the Irish case was not a formal hearing, but world attention and support.

It is with these considerations in mind that the decision to launch a republic at this time should be viewed. Otherwise it is necessary to conclude that Collins, Brugha, Boland and the rest were simply irrepressible zealots without political sense. Audacity and more audacity had brought this group a long way, carrying along with them the IRB, Sinn Féin and the Irish Volunteers. A declaration of a republic at this time could be, and was, seen as a bold, dramatic act, but it was done without immediate political cost. As was then apparent, and as time was to prove, there was no need to be restrained in action, since there was no real hope of securing a hearing in Paris.

The emergence of the 'Democratic Programme' should also be seen within this context. The new Sinn Féin leadership, particularly Boland and O'Kelly, had been in close contact with the Labour Party leaders since mid-October, when they met to consider a deal to give Labour a few seats in Dublin. Major post-war labour and socialist conferences were pending. The Labour leaders wanted to have their movement attain full recognition in the international labour organisations; this would be dependent on Ireland being viewed as a separate country. This, of course, was something Sinn Féin also wanted to see happen. One obvious difficulty was that no Labour candidates had been elected in December 1918. This problem could be surmounted if the new government adopted a statement of social and economic principles that was progressive, indeed radical.

It has often been argued that since the principles incorporated in the Democratic Programme were far more radical than anything that Sinn Féin had ever supported previously, they did not represent an accurate statement of the party's socio-economic ideals. Its 1918 programme, for example, was almost wholly concerned with nationalism and culture; there was only one statement, urging a living wage for workers, that could be construed as recognising a need for socio-economic reform. It is also true that the Democratic Programme was thrown together hastily and at the last minute. The Sinn Féin members had set up a committee to formulate such a programme on 14 January. The only thing the committee had to work with was a draft proposal submitted by the Labour leadership, the principal author of which was Thomas Johnson with assistance from William O'Brien. According to Seán T. O'Kelly, there was wide disagreement within the Sinn Féin leadership concerning the Johnson draft, and, on the eve of the opening of the Dáil, Boland told him to take it home and overnight weave together an acceptable statement. In the process he modified but did not eliminate the strongly socialist assumptions in Johnson's draft.[5]

If by having the Dáil adopt an advanced social and economic statement of principles Sinn Féin could in return secure recognition of the separate status of Ireland by a major international organisation, then it was seen as a good investment. The programme was only a statement of principles and objectives; the Dáil would not actually have to do anything about it for the foreseeable future. Given the need to attract support from the Belfast Protestant working class — a matter of concern to the Sinn Féin executive — the adoption of such a programme could prove valuable.

Beyond all these considerations, just how radical was the programme? In the wake of the European war, most governments had pledged themselves, in the same general terms, to the extension of state responsibility for social and economic conditions. In Britain and the United States the term 'reconstruction' was bandied about. Lloyd George was talking about making his country 'a land fit for heroes'. In adopting this programme, the Dáil was following the political fashion of the day. What specific commitments were contained in the programme? One was 'to make provision for the physical, mental and spiritual well-being of the children, to secure that no child shall suffer hunger or cold from lack of food, clothing or shelter, but that all shall be provided with the means and facilities requisite for their proper education and training'. No one was in favour of hungry children, and the need to expand the educational system was obvious to almost everyone. The programme also committed the new state to replace the existing system of poor relief, but what it proposed as a replacement was described in the vaguest of terms: 'a sympathetic native scheme of the care of the Nation's aged and infirm, who shall not be regarded as a burden, but rather entitled to the Nation's gratitude and consideration'. The Democratic Programme was not a call for red revolution or anything like it; rather, as time was to prove, its socio-economic principles were simply in advance of the existing concerns of Irish political life.

The Inauguration of Dáil Éireann

Then arrived the day for the public unveiling of the Assembly of Ireland. The occasion attracted a large number — about seventy — of foreign journalists. This evidence of international interest, declared one Sinn Féin journal, 'widely shattered' the argument that abstention from Westminster would deprive the country of the 'only platform from which she could address the world'. To supporters of Irish independence this was a great event. 'No day that ever dawned in Ireland', asserted Máire Comerford, 'had ever been waited for, worked for, suffered for, like January 21, 1919. Standing in a queue that curled from the entrance to Dublin's Mansion House back to Kildare Street, men and women spoke softly of the dead, from the first coming of the English to Ireland.' 'There was an air of expectancy', said one observer, 'in every look and in every movement of the vast outside gathering.' Viewing the crowd from a building across the street were Colonel Wedgeworth Johnstone, Chief Commissioner of the Dublin Metropolitan Police, and Sir James Byrne, Inspector-General of the Royal Irish Constabulary. It was an interesting scene. As the Sinn Féin throng filed into the Round Room of the Mansion House they passed another group on their way out carrying Union Jacks. A reception for a group of Dublin Fusiliers who had been prisoners of war in Germany had just ended. The old order going out, the new coming in.

The crowd that packed the room found it without decoration save for a single tricolour above the lectern (the Union Jacks having departed with the old order). The audience contained about fifty priests, a large number of women, two US Navy officers and several soldiers from the dominions. Maud Gonne MacBride caused a stir as she entered the building. Tom Johnson sat in the balcony, eagerly waiting for the reading of the Democratic Programme.

Promptly at 3.30 p.m. the centre doors of the Round Room were opened and a small band of twenty-four deputies of the new assembly filed in. There were 'no robes, no mace, no velveted sergeant-at-arms, not even wigged Clerks of the House. The Deputies came through the great audience at the Mansion House richly clothed only in their associations.' Apart from translations of some of the documents presented and caution from Count Plunkett that there was to be no cheering, all the proceedings were in Irish. To begin the session, Father O'Flanagan read a prayer. The constitution of Dáil Éireann and the appointment of a delegation to the Paris Peace Conference were presented in Irish only, while the Declaration of Independence and the appeal for international support were translated into French and English. The Democratic Programme, 'hastily prepared', as Piaras Béaslaí noted in presenting it, was given only in Irish and English. The almost exclusive use of the Irish language was music to the ears of one witness: 'Never before did we so acutely feel the oneness of the Irish language and Ireland,' he commented, adding that this experience was 'worth a thousand propaganda books'.

The inaugural meeting, which lasted less than two hours, was without incident. Piaras Béaslaí claimed that he was responsible for the management of the proceedings: 'I was determined to leave nothing to chance. I had a long experience of producing plays, and I felt we must approach this public session in the same spirit.' Even Lord French's observer at the meeting, George Moore, was impressed by its orderliness and told French that the Dáil represented 'the general feeling in the country'. To another observer, 'the meeting was dull, but for us, the believers, it was electric, the fruition of many years of hard work'. Another reported: 'It is difficult to convey the intensity of feeling which pervaded the Round Room, the feeling that great things were happening, even greater things impending, and that in looking around the room he saw a glimpse of the Ireland of the future.' To an 'experienced observer' the significance of the event was to be found 'in the profound emotion of the spectators, that for many of them sitting absolutely quiet it was manifestly a day of their souls' consecration, a day that they had never expected to see but whose coming moved them profoundly'. One reporter noted 'quite a number' of people who seemed obsessed with the 'enormity' of the occasion. That evening a reception and dinner were held in the Oak Room in honour of the visiting journalists. The rebel government thus began what was to be one of most effective activities — the cultivation of foreign pressmen.[6]

The next morning the assembly met to organise its affairs. The most important business was the election of a cabinet, which was merely temporary, pending the eventual release of the interned members. Cathal Brugha was elected 'President of the Ministry *pro tem.*', whereupon he proposed and the Dáil approved of his ministers: Eoin Mac Néill as Finance Minister, Michael Collins as Home Affairs Minister, George Noble Plunkett as Foreign Affairs Minister, and Richard Mulcahy as National Defence Minister. The unanimity of the session was broken by what was to prove to be a rare event in the revolutionary Dáil — parliamentary opposition. Piarais Béaslaí voted against Mac Néill as Finance Minister. Mac Néill professed no expertise in finance, but this cabinet was merely designed to hold the fort until the release of the party leaders. The Dáil also approved standing orders, appointed a secretariat of four, and elected as Ceann Comhairle (chairman) Seán T. O'Kelly. With that the assembly adjourned and did not meet again until 1 April, by which time the political situation had changed considerably.

On the same day as the first session of the Dáil, 21 January, two policemen were killed by Irish Volunteers at Soloheadbeg in Tipperary. The two events were not coincidental. The physical-force men were asserting themselves. According to Séamus Robinson, he planned the raid for gelignite, which resulted in the shooting, as a demonstration that Ireland would need military as well as political action if it was to win independence. Dan Breen, another of the participants, held the same view. 'I was convinced that some sort of action was absolutely necessary', he said, to prevent the continued erosion of the military organisation in favour of the political movement. Archbishop Harty of Cashel condemned the killings as 'cold-blooded murder for which there was no justification'. Dáil Éireann said nothing. A 'Sinn Féin leader, relatively a moderate' told Charles Hathaway, the principal United States diplomat in Ireland at this time, that this act and 'similar and lesser outrages . . . were contrary to Sinn Féin orders and Sinn Féin policy'. When Hathaway asked him why Sinn Féin did not strongly and publicly denounce violent acts, 'he said he feared a disavowal would be taken as a sign of weakness'. The viceroy, Lord French, privately claimed that the killings had upset an attempt made through 'secret influences' to prevent such an occurrence.

As can be expected with any controversial event, the inauguration of Dáil Éireann attracted a wide range of press comment. The government press censor reacted immediately by banning the publication of the Declaration of Independence and the Democratic Programme. The Sinn Féin press, of course, was ecstatic. *The Irishman* (25 Jan.), for example, compared the proceedings to 'the Feis of Tara when the Prince Presidents of the communal clans met to make and revise the laws of ancient Éire'. On the moderate nationalist side, the *Freeman's Journal* was riven with doubt about the seriousness of the Sinn Féiners: 'The question which dominates all other issues is whether the declarations bear any relation to realities, and whether it is seriously proposed to take measures to give them practical effect.' If they were not serious, then the dignity of the national cause would suffer humiliation; if they were serious, then it feared that the country was 'on the eve of the one of the most tragic chapters in the history of Ireland'. Although it acknowledged that the position claimed by Dáil Éireann 'certainly did not err on the side of timidity or half-heartedness', it was sure that any attempt to bring it into effect 'inevitably must lead to defeat, disaster and ruin of the National hopes'.

The *Irish Times* (22 Jan.) viewed the proceedings, on one hand, as being 'futile and unreal'; on the other hand, they filled it with a sense of foreboding, as they constituted 'a solemn act of defiance of the British Empire, by a body of young men who have not the slightest notion of that Empire's power and resources and not a particle of experience in the conduct of public affairs'. It could distinguish two kinds of republicans — the idealists and the social revolutionaries — with the latter group proposing 'to apply the principles of Lenin and Trotsky to Irish affairs'. This development so alarmed the *Irish Times* that it returned to the attack the next day in an editorial entitled 'Cloud-Cuckoo Land': 'Will Ireland really allow her affairs to run to ruin while the young Republicans dream in their Nepheloccygia and Irish Bolshevism matures its plan for plunder and anarchy?'

The *Irish Independent* (22 Jan.) granted that the launching of Dáil Éireann was 'a bold move', but it warned the fledgling government that 'to draft and pass measures which it could not enforce would be to risk ridicule which would be more fatal than opposition'. To the *Cork Examiner* it was 'a political event of the first importance' which demonstrated, at the very least, that Ireland no longer placed any confidence in British government. The *Belfast Newsletter* saw the proceedings as merely a 'farce' and 'ridiculous', but claimed to have found a reference to religion as one of the differences between Ireland and England cited in the Message to the Free Nations of the World, which allowed for a burst of rhetoric: 'Thus Ireland is alleged to be a Celtic and Roman Catholic nation, and all who are not Celts and Romanists are regarded as foreigners. It is because Ulster knows that this is what Home Rule means that it will not have it.' (There was in fact no reference to religion — or indeed to Home Rule — in the document.) It also warned that nationalists would be encouraged to break the law if 'they see that the Rebel Assembly is not suppressed, and that a pretend "Cabinet" is allowed to issue orders and demand obedience to them in the name of the "Irish Republic"'. The American diplomat Charles Hathaway commented that the editorial hostility 'is not strange, for in Ireland Sinn Féin has no adequate press and practically all the newspapers whether Unionist or Nationalist are controlled by elements with small sympathy for the independence program'. He noted that 'to the press outside of Ireland the whole affair was naturally enough pretty nearly a blank incomprehensibility'.

Among English newspapers, the *Manchester Guardian* (22 Jan.) found the whole episode utterly ridiculous: 'The Republican theatricalism, which had its absurd climax in the gathering of the Irish "Constituent Assembly" will not be taken seriously in this country.' To the Dublin correspondent of the London *Times* the whole thing was just a 'stage play at the Mansion House'. The *Daily Mail*, as well, could not take the matter seriously: 'Whether Sinn Féin will perish either in a shriek of laughter or in a *De profundis* for the dead in a country where comedy and tragedy walk hand in hand none may prophesy.' One English paper, the *Daily News*, advised that is was 'very easy to laugh at the Sinn Féin Parliament, but it is not certain that it is wise'. It saw the Dáil as being 'a central gathering of well-meaning idealists' who were 'utterly unable to control the physical force men in the provinces'. The killing of the policemen at Soloheadbeg was probably 'a message deliberately sent by the new "invinvibles" to the "talking shop" in the capital'. The English journalist Richardson Evans later allowed that the Dublin event 'was a bold but well-conceived step; for, next to cunning, nothing impresses an Irishman more than bravado'. *The Leader* (25 Jan.) summed up most of the reaction of the Irish nationalist weeklies to the criticisms from across the water: 'The quips and jokes and threats and prophecies of the English press are, of course, of no interest to us.'

As soon as they were available, the *Freeman's Journal* presented its readers with a selection of the critical commentaries emanating from the American press. The general theme was that there was no need for concern, that England had matters well in hand. The New York *World* declared that the Sinn Féiners 'may fly their revolutionary flags, they may conduct their proceedings in Gaelic, as far as the delegates know how', but 'they are assured of full protection by the British Government', which (it said) had learned the value of restraint. The New York *Tribune* viewed the opening of the Dáil as 'an utterly Celtic proceeding', with England 'silently ignoring this most ideal and least real of all revolutions'. Lord French and the Chief Secretary for Ireland, reassured the New York *Times*, 'are not in the slightest degree disturbed by the event'. In Boston, however, the *Transcript* shared the alarm of the *Irish Times* about wolves in red clothing: 'Sinn Féin has become an insidious influence on the side of Bolshevism, outside of Ireland as well as within it. It passes as easily into affiliation with world-wide revolutionism as it did into the treasonable service of the Germans.'

The Irish Volunteer journal, *An tÓglach*, not surprisingly, had a completely different idea of the significance of the new assembly. Dáil Éireann, it declared, was 'a lawfully constituted authority, whose moral sanction every theologian must recognise, an authority claiming the same right to inflict death on the enemies of the Irish State as every free national Government claims in such case'.[7]

What did the Irish public think about the launching of the new assembly? The *Irish Independent* (22 Jan.) reported that there was 'keen public interest' in the event. On the other hand, the RIC Inspector-General's monthly report had a contrary view: 'According to reports from the several Counties the Dáil Éireann evoked little or no enthusiasm — by the majority of people apparently it is not taken seriously.' A major difficulty was that the new government was out of public view for the following two months. To many it must have seemed that the Dáil was just a novel Sinn Féin demonstration. The acting cabinet issued no public statements nor took any public action. When the *Freeman's Journal* criticised the effort to win support for Irish self-determination at Paris, Cathal Brugha responded by letter, but gave no indication that he was the acting head of a government; probably the censor would not allow this. Some Sinn Féin spokesmen appeared doubtful as to the reality of the new regime. At the end of February Seán Ó Muirthile declared that although the country was steadily marching towards the goal of a republic, the objective may be reached 'in our time or in the time of those to come after us'. On 1 March Piaras Béaslaí stated that it was the task of the people 'to make the *de jure* Irish Republic *de facto*'. A Cork woman believed this had already taken place. Charged in February with collecting for the prisoners' dependants' fund, she was asked if she 'had a permit from the Irish Government', to which she replied that 'she did not require one, that she had a permit from the "Irish Republic"'.

The RIC could find no evidence of activity by or on behalf of the Dáil. It was informed that Sinn Féin was simply 'marking time and still looking to the Peace Conference' while it was preparing a scheme for administration for the new government. It reported that at the first Sinn Féin executive meeting after the launching of the new government there was a sense of near dejection: 'The apathy with which the establishment of Dáil Éireann has been generally regarded was disappointing and the financial situation gave cause for considerable anxiety.' The meeting, however, had agreed to three proposals for action: the raising of a loan, prohibition of the use of existing courts by republicans, and the ending of the payment of taxes and annuities.

Some critics argued that time was showing that Dáil Éireann and its republic were sham devices concocted by political amateurs. In a letter to the *Freeman's Journal* (21 Feb.) 'Me Féin' maintained that 'The people's "mandate" will lose a good deal of its apparent force when the people realise later on that the Irish Republic is, like the Hy Brazil of the legend, "a beautiful spectre" only.' Overlooking the inactivity of the new government, *The Irishman* (8 Feb.) argued that the campaign of ridicule in the press was responsible for the fact that a section of the

Irish people did not 'fully realise' how the situation had changed as a result of the events of 21 January. Yet it was itself not entirely clear about what had actually taken place: it referred to Dáil Éireann as Ireland's 'Constituent Assembly'. As late as May 1919 *Nationality* did not believe there was a republic in being; an editorial in its 17 May issue declared: 'Nothing short of the establishment of an Independent Irish Republic will satisfy the aspirations of the people of Ireland.'

Arthur Griffith was full of ideas of what Dáil Éireann should be doing. He sent a long memorandum, dated 23 January, which he managed to smuggle out of Gloucester Prison. He first cautioned about trying to do too much: 'The Dáil should not commit itself to any scheme which it does not feel can be worked out with present resources.' He also argued that it was inadvisable 'to go into the details of an Irish Constitution at present'. In his view, primary attention should be given to the Peace Conference, and he warned about the negative effects that attacks on or even criticism of President Wilson would have on the Irish case. Then he proposed a programme of intense international propaganda combined with the initiation of a series of long-standing Sinn Féin proposals for local government and economic development. There was no immediate response from the acting leadership of Dáil Éireann, but Griffith's letter certainly gave them plenty of food for thought.

The Sinn Féin Abstentionist Policy
The election of candidates in seventy-three constituencies dedicated to the proposition that they should not take their seats at Westminster could not pass unnoticed in the wider world of British politics. Shortly after the results were announced the Dublin correspondent of *The Times* believed that the elections in twenty-three districts where Sinn Féin candidates were elected would be declared invalid because five of them were aliens and the other eighteen had been convicted of felony or treason. He also believed that if they were re-elected in subsequent by-elections, their opponents would be given their seats. A little later William O'Malley, an ex-Irish Party MP from Connemara, suggested in a letter to *The Times* that if the Sinn Féiners did not take their seats, then parliament should give them to their opponents. There was hope yet for the Irish Party. The Dublin *Evening Mail* predicted that the vacant seats would be handed over to the Irish Party candidates, but that they would not take their seats 'until the Irish Catholic Hierarchy calls on them to do so to defend Irish Catholic schools from new edu-cational legislation'. Such a large number of vacancies was unprecedented and not covered by statute, it noted, but the House of Commons could deal with the matter by order if it chose.

Despite the action of the Sinn Féiners in establishing their own legis-lature, there was concern at Westminster that they might unexpectedly arrive and seek admittance when parliament assembled on 4 February. Police were instructed to watch for the appearance of the Sinn Féin brigade and to arrest any wanted men in the group if they attempted to enter the House of Commons. Timothy Healy advised the Sinn Féin members that they 'could haunt Westminster without taking their seats', but he also commented that they 'did not understand the terrain' and 'could not forecast the effect of the tactics I recommended'.

The British government decided to ignore the gap in the composition of the house. When Horatio Bottomley proposed that the missing members be forced to attend by employing the device of 'the call of the house', last employed in 1836, Bonar Law replied that 'the Government did not propose to take any action in the matter'. The difficulty in dealing with the situation was obvious. If the seats were declared vacant, then by-elections would have to be held in nearly three-quarters of the seats in Ireland; these would present Sinn Féin with a new opportunity to demonstrate its popular support. The government did not want to provide such an occasion. Yet it remained concerned about what Sinn Féin was doing. In late January Lord Haldane arrived in Dublin as an emissary of Lloyd George. Although the Sinn Féin organisation denied there had been any meeting with him, he did confer with someone trusted by the party. Haldane stated that he was prepared to recommend full Dominion Home Rule if the Sinn Féin leaders would prevent an 'outbreak' before he had time to carry through the negotiations, which would take four to six weeks. Haldane was told that nothing could be done until all political prisoners were released, but was also referred to a speech of de Valera, made some time in 1918, in which he reportedly said that 'if a workable scheme were offered, he saw no reason why it should not be accepted as a payment on account'. After a few weeks Haldane returned to Dublin and informed the 'trusted person' that he had encounterd strong opposition but remained hopeful. Nothing more was heard of the Haldane proposal. If nothing came of this peace feeler, the American diplomat Charles Hathaway believed that a settlement was possible, as 'a large majority of all Irishmen — Sinn Féiners and others — would accept Dominion Home Rule with full control of Customs and Excise, but without army and navy'. As a result of what he had been told by the people he had spoken to in Dublin, it was his opinion that 'the majority of Sinn Féiners would not stand out for a republic — that in fact Sinn Féin in demanding independence is following the Irish practice of asking the most in order to get much'.[8]

Little attention has been given to the absence of the bulk of the Irish representatives from the Commons after 1918. Because of the lopsided result in the 1918 election, the seventy-three Irish seats held by Sinn Féin did not cause any constitutional dilemma, but most elections do not have so decisive an outcome. Surely the political history of the

United Kingdom in the 1920s would have been substantially different had there been a body of some seventy militant Irish nationalists in the Commons. Undoubtedly they would have generally voted with the Labour Party, and the ill-fated Labour administrations of 1923 and 1929 might have achieved more. Winston Churchill was aware of this possibility. He later expressed his relief that Sinn Féin had stayed out; the balance of power thus would not be turned 'against the main well-being of the State by an implacable enemy'. On the other hand, Sinn Féin or no Sinn Féin, Irish representation in the Commons was bound to be drastically reduced in the post-war period, as the British government was committed to some form of 'home rule' and Ireland was already over-represented in the Commons in terms of population.

Sinn Féin contested only one by-election to the Westminster parliament of 1918–22, and the vacancy was not caused by any action on its part; moreover, it ignored succeeding by-elections in Unionist districts. In a contest in North Derry in March 1919, caused by the resignation of the Unionist member, Patrick McGilligan stood as the Sinn Féin nominee and improved his 1918 vote.

*

The death of Pierce McCann, deputy for East Tipperary, on 6 March presented Dáil Éireann with its first vacancy. Sinn Féin and then the Dáil had been concerned about the necessity to appoint substitute members for the assembly, but the mass release of the internees had, at least temporarily, made this a largely irrelevant question. But what was to be done about the vacancy caused by the death of McCann? In April 1919 a select committee of the Dáil recommended that a vacancy 'shall be filled up by the body which selected the former member . . . until it is practicable to secure a poll of the people'. Arthur Griffith commented later that 'as this constituency was under Martial Law, this would appear to be the only course open to them'. This did not appear to be an entirely satisfactory mechanism, and the matter was put aside for a while. In June it was revived and a new select committee was appointed, but could not find a proper solution. The matter was buried with McCann: 'In view of the circumstances which occasioned the vacancy, it was due to the memory of the late Pierce McCann that his place should not be taken at present.' This was the first vacancy, but, as a result of death or imprisonment, there were to be many more. The problem of vacancies was not mentioned again until August 1920, and then without result. The Dáil with a full membership was a small parliament, but with many vacancies it looked still smaller, both numerically and politically.[9]

(3) BERNE AND PARIS

By-elections and vacancies were of little public interest in the period immediately after the establishment of the Dáil. Attention was focused almost entirely on the international scene, with anticipation by many, if not most, Irish nationalists of good things from Versailles.

Máire Comerford recalled that

It was impossible for youth, my age group then, to see how our request could be refused in the atmosphere of the time, when tyranny was supposed to have been forever broken by great and generous powers, like the USA, fighting for small nations. The experienced older men told us we were fools.

In his meetings with political figures in Dublin in January 1919, Charles Hathaway found that

Everybody seemed hopeful of the Peace Conference and full of confidence in the President [Wilson] — some suggesting that even if the Conference did not deal specifically with Ireland yet there was good hope that a League of Nations would be set up whose very nature would render impossible a long continuance of any government not based on self-determination.

Hathaway was told by an (unnamed) member of the Sinn Féin executive that his organisation was prepared to be patient, but if nothing was done for Ireland at the conference, 'they will obstruct'. He noted that 'one hears rumors as wild as that all the police barracks will be blown up'. In April he reported:

The dominant faction in the Sinn Féin organization headed by Mr de Valera is committed to passive methods and will probably control the situation even though the Peace Conference should break up without having done anything to give them hope.

The initial campaign for international recognition of a separate Irish identity began with a minor victory and ended with what was generally seen as a major failure. Thomas Johnson and Cathal O'Shannon, delegates from the Irish Labour Party and Trade Union Congress as well as the Socialist Party of Ireland, attended the first post-war socialist and labour conference which was held in Berne, Switzerland, in early February. They based their claim for a separate Irish identity within the international organisation upon the foundations of 'the historic nationality, separate and distinct, of the Irish people', a continuous and unceasing struggle of the Irish people for its manifestation in sovereignty' and 'the present . . . demand of the people of Ireland for independence under a Republican form of government'.

Despite some rumblings of dissent in the British delegation, Ireland was accorded the status of a national entity at the conference. The Irish delegation also succeeded in securing the passage of two important resolutions, one of which supported self-determination for Ireland, while the other urged the Paris conference 'to make good this rightful claim of the Irish people'. As part of its report, a delegation to the Allied meeting would present Ireland's claim.

Irish Labour's success at Berne, together with a similar success at a trade union international meeting two months later in Amsterdam, was given wide attention in the republican press. The significance of these achievements, however, was easily exaggerated. They had, in fact, no long-term significance either for Labour or Sinn Féin, as the Berne meeting did not lay the foundation for the creation of a united socialist international. This effort was frustrated by the ensuing conflict between constitutional and revolutionary socialists. When a follow-up meeting to Berne was held at Lucerne in August 1919, no Irish delegates attended and there was no mention of Ireland in its report. As was shortly demonstrated, the Paris conference was not swayed by the resolutions of the international socialist movement. Yet at Berne in February the effort to present Ireland's case to the Allied conference appeared to have moved ahead a notch.[10]

The campaign of militant Irish nationalism to win a hearing at the Peace Conference was beset by difficulties from the beginning. The three representatives selected by Dáil Éireann to the meeting — Count Plunkett, Griffith and de Valera — were refused passports by the British government; the freedom of movement of two of them, of course, was limited to the confines of a British prison. This being the case, the Dáil dispatched as 'envoy' its Ceann Comhairle, Seán T. O'Kelly, who earlier had been appointed a member of the committee of Dublin Corporation to make Woodrow Wilson a freeman of Dublin. He secured his passport on the basis of his mandate from the corporation. Dublin Castle certainly was aware that Seán T. was also a member and chairman of the rebel assembly. Apparently it estimated that O'Kelly's presence in Paris would not be significantly detrimental to the British position at the conference; otherwise it could easily have refused his application for a passport, Dublin Corporation resolution or not.

Then thirty-seven years old, O'Kelly had a long record in advanced nationalist politics. He had been a Sinn Féin member of Dublin Corporation long before many of that party held public office, and he had taken part in the 1916 rebellion. His experience abroad was limited to a sortie to the United States in 1915 to take collection of funds from the Clan na Gael to the IRB. He did have a knowledge of the French language, as did his wife, who accompanied him. A short-statured, ebullient professional politician of limited education and experience but good-hearted and dedicated, O'Kelly was at the beginning of a career in national politics that was to last for forty years, culminating in his election to the presidency of the Irish state in 1945. He was described in 1919 as 'slim, supple, with mobile face, easy gesture and Irish eyes of dancing blue'. By this time, as well, he had been in prison eight times. It was on the basis of these slender qualifications that O'Kelly carried the banner of Dáil Éireann into the arena of top-level international politics. To shore up his standing, he was accompanied by Michael MacWhite, who had served in the French army during the war and was well known to the Sinn Féin leaders, and who now took up his first assignment in a long diplomatic career.

The Sinn Féin press expressed unrestrained optimism concerning the outcome. *The Irishman* asserted that despite the claims of the Irish Parliamentary Party during the election, 'Ireland's claim cannot be kept out of the Peace Conference'. *Nationality* sarcastically commented: 'We await, with joy, the wreath of smiles which will mount the noble brows of the editors' of the newspapers hostile to Sinn Féin.

When he arrived in Paris on 10 February, O'Kelly slipped off the robe of alderman in the Dublin Corporation and revealed himself in a new, more exalted role. He sent a memorandum to the leaders of the conference informing them that he had been appointed by the 'Provisional Government of the Irish Republic to be their representative in Paris' and requested that Ireland be given a seat in the projected League of Nations. O'Kelly received no reply to this request. His action was, however, roundly attacked in the *Freeman's Journal* as crude, mendacious and ineffectual. It insisted that it was a grave blunder for O'Kelly to try to force himself on President Wilson and the conference as the envoy of an already existing and established independent Irish government: 'Such a pretension at that preliminary stage was calculated to invite and challenge a repulse.' Darrell Figgis, who was interned at this time, also believed that O'Kelly's 'pompous' letter was a grave error: 'That letter, I remember, was sent the week before the liberation of the prisoners, and it brought dismay to some of us. For it was not certain that President Wilson could not meet the envoy from Ireland. . . . A great opportunity was thus thrown away.'[11]

The Sinn Féin newspapers were surprised and upset by the initial reaction — or rather non-reaction — of the Peace Conference to Dáil Éireann's appeal. To at least one observer Sinn Féin was close to despair as it realised that nothing could be expected from the conference. The *Irish World* launched a bitter attack on President Wilson, while *The Irishman* urged support for Wilson 'on the assumption, which nothing has so far disproved, that he will at the proper time support us'. A small sop of encouragement was provided by *The Nation*, an American radical journal, which declared: 'Free Republic or Free Dominion it must be. All other ways are barred morally and even politically, since we accepted the principle of "self determination".' Britain might well be able to keep Ireland out of the Peace Conference, it said, but it could not exclude 'the spectre of Irish disaffection or evade the logic of the Irish case'.

Cathal O'Shannon provided a first-hand account of O'Kelly's efforts in Paris. Passing through the city on his way to the Berne conference, O'Shannon saw not a line about Ireland in the press. Upon his return, with O'Kelly now in operation, O'Shannon observed that 'each day brought its bundles of cuttings on Ireland from the whole French and European Press'. It was his judgment that the Irish delegation in Paris was doing excellent work and that O'Kelly 'has made Ireland a burning question in and around the Conference'. He concluded, however, that public attention would not be followed by any tangible gain: 'Ireland has nothing to hope for from the Peace Conference.'

The advocates of Irish independence refused to be discouraged by the lack of response from the conference. Their attention now shifted to the United States, where a major campaign was mounted to win over President Wilson, who returned there in February. As *Nationality* put it, 'We may not be able to get in touch with President Wilson, but our people in the United States can, and will.' Harry Boland declared that 'Ireland will be stuffed down his neck from the time he arrives in Long Island till he gets back to Paris.' The Irish Race Convention held another of its mass meetings in February and appointed a delegation to meet with the President before he returned to Paris. Patrick McCartan denied that there was 'a scheme to ram Ireland down President Wilson's throat'; on the contrary, he said, the Irish people believed in Wilson's sincerity.

The US House of Representatives passed a resolution on 4 March urging the Paris conference to 'favourably consider the claims of Ireland to self-determination'. Similar resolutions later followed from the US Senate, the American Federation of Labour, state legislatures and municipal bodies. Many in Ireland believed that this kind of pressure was bound to have an influence on Wilson. The *Irish Independent* (10 Feb.) commented: 'We do not see how President Wilson can ignore a resolution of Congress', a view echoed by the Irish correspondent of the *Manchester Guardian*, who added that Irish-American soldiers were so strongly supportive of Irish self-determination that Ireland was made off-limits for American soldiers on leave. Despite this pressure, Wilson was not swayed. His position was that he could do nothing directly and officially, but that he would work unofficially and privately with the British delegation to further Ireland's case. This mode of procedure was, however, deeply unsatisfactory to Sinn Féin, which was, of course, demanding direct and public recognition of Irish nationhood.

In order to survey the situation in Ireland, Wilson dispatched George Creel, head of the US wartime propaganda effort, who arrived in the country in late February. Creel met with the Dáil leadership, whom he told that the Paris conference was a gathering of victors to impose terms on the losers in the war, and not an assembly to give justice to subject nationalities. He also told them that Wilson's League of Nations would provide a forum for the presentation of Ireland's case for self-government. When he had finished addressing then, he relates, 'the disappointment in every face was plain to be seen, but except for one or two hotheads, there was general admission of the argument's force and logic'. In his report to the President, Creel stated that if dominion status was offered to Ireland immediately, it would be accepted; if this was not done, 'sentiment in Ireland and America will harden in favor of an Irish republic'. Obviously Creel did not take seriously the claims of the Dáil, but he did urge Wilson to put private pressure on Lloyd George to grant Ireland at least Home Rule. Shortly after his return to America Creel became an outspoken advocate of Irish independence and later worked for the Dáil's propaganda bureau in the United States.

Meanwhile in Paris, O'Kelly expressed his frustration in his efforts when he told an American journalist in early March that only one delegate had even acknowledged his memorandum, and that

> The others failed to grant me the courtesy usually bestowed by gentlemen when receiving a letter even from beggars. . . . It seems that the blacks and yellows, all colours and races, may be heard before the Conference, except the Irish.

Despite this, O'Kelly sent home this optimistic message:

> I still believe Wilson means business. He can put the screw on all the gang of old-time statesmen when he pleases. He is too heavily committed for even his courage to fail: an irate people in America is more to be feared than Clemenceau, Lloyd George and Balfour. If he declared 'off' they will be on their knees.

But as the months passed by and no opening was made to present the Irish case, hope began to die. A bare acknowledgment of O'Kelly's submissions by one member of the United States delegation, Henry White, was little solace. Before the conference came to an end in June and failure was made apparent to all, events at home brought Dáil Éireann back to public attention.

(4) DE VALERA AND THE REBEL GOVERNMENT

While O'Kelly and his small staff continued with their efforts in Paris during the spring of 1919, the government of Dáil Éireann began to crackle to life. In a dramatic rescue operation master-minded by Harry

Boland and Michael Collins, Eamon de Valera, together with two other important Sinn Féin figures, Seán Milroy and Seán McGarry, were spirited out of Lincoln prison on the night of 3 February. This was a sensational development, and the British and Irish papers were filled with speculation about Dev's whereabouts and plans for the future. The leader of the republican movement initially made no attempt to return to Ireland, but remained in hiding in Manchester for nearly three weeks. Cathal Brugha arrived in the city just four days after his escape and conferred with him there for a few days. De Valera's only public statement at this time was terse and vague, befitting an escaped prisoner: 'My message to the Irish people is — That I have escaped from Lincoln to do the country's work and am doing it.'

Because of this situation, de Valera realised that he could appear publicly neither in Paris nor Ireland. He decided the best thing to do was to proceed to the United States, where he could mobilise support among the large Irish-American community and beyond. He was persuaded by Brugha and others, however, to return first to Ireland and was smuggled into the country on 20 February. During only a few months in Ireland he managed to breathe the breath of political life into the government of Dáil Éireann. Just four days after his return he had an interview with an American journalist and with understandable exaggeration claimed that 'We have our Government completely organised. We can take over the administration of our country at a moment's notice.' Failing that, he warned, 'we are prepared for violence'. A few days later he returned to England and was in Liverpool awaiting a friendly ship when the other 'German plot' prisoners were suddenly released. The political situation was transformed.[12]

The immediate reason for the release of the internees was the death of Pierce McCann on the morning of 6 March; the gates swung open for all the others later that day. McCann, a large farmer and deputy for East Tipperary, was a victim of an influenza epidemic that was sweeping the prison. If they were not released promptly, more internees were likely to die. Having been hounded by Irish ghosts since 1916, the British government acted promptly. Moreover, these political prisoners, uncharged and untried after ten months in prison, would have to be released sooner or later, and the continued detention of most of the leaders of Ireland created a nagging public relations problem for the British government at home and especially abroad. In addition, there was speculation that Dublin Castle believed that the release would strengthen the hand of the moderates within the national movement.

De Valera, of course, was an escapee, not a released prisoner, and, as such, was liable to rearrest. After careful consideration, the Dáil leadership concluded that Dublin Castle would not attempt this; it decided it was safe to let the President-designate appear in public. To dramatise this act, a grand civic reception was planned for Dublin, with the Lord Mayor presenting the keys of the city at, appropriately, Mount Street Bridge. According to Darrell Figgis, Michael Collins took the initiative and in the name of Sinn Féin issued a press announcement that the reception would be held on 26 March. A massive demonstration of support was almost a certainty.

Not surprisingly, the Chief Secretary for Ireland banned the event. Troops and military vehicles filled the centre of the city. A controversy erupted within Sinn Féin as to the authority of Collins and his allies to issue his statement and what response should be made to the Chief Secretary's suppression of the reception. Collins declared himself eager to impose a situation of general disorder in the country in order to challenge British authority. Word of Collins's position evidently trickled out to the RIC; its monthly intelligence report noted that 'the physical force party has lately got the upper hand' in the independence movement. In fact de Valera eventually decided to cancel the reception, declaring in a public statement that he would not call on the people to endure any threat to their personal safety at that time. To the Sinn Féin executive he commented: 'England's proclamation with its accompanying military preparations will teach as much to those who are willing to be taught as would your demonstration.'

Some of the leaders viewed the cancellation as a major reverse. In a letter to Austin Stack, Collins expressed despair: 'We are having our Clontarf today. It may not be as bad, but it is bad and very bad.' He added that the Castle authorities 'have put up to us a challenge which strikes at the fundamentals of our policy and our attitude'. His position was shared by, among others, Erskine Childers and P. S. O'Hegarty. *The Irishman* (29 Mar.) declared that Volunteers and republicans generally were 'keenly disappointed' by the cancellation, which was only equalled by O'Connell's 'cowardly surrender at Clontarf'. De Valera took a more sensible view of the affair. It was not a major matter to him, and Robert Brennan related that 'he was rather cross at the fuss we made over him'. A week later he made an 'informal entry' into the city, was greeted by the Lord Mayor at the Mansion House, and was 'an amused spectator of the elaborate military precautions taken to prevent his state entry'.

A few days earlier he had given an interview to the *Daily Chronicle* in which he affirmed his commitment to a democratic decision on nationhood. He proposed a national plebiscite on this issue: 'Let her [England's] planted colonists and all be included, and if a decisive majority of the whole people declared not for a separate independent statehood, then we shall be silent.' Although he must have been confident that the outcome would be otherwise, he was taken to task by the *Catholic Bulletin* (Apr. 1919) for endangering the march to national freedom. In the realm of international opinion, de Valera was probably standing on firm ground when he argued Ireland's case for self-determination; the argument in favour of an independent republic would be more difficult to put across, but many republicans at home did not perceive this.

The leaders of Sinn Féin now turned from public relations gestures to the building of a government. The second session of Dáil Éireann was held on 1–4 April, and with an attendance of fifty-two was the largest meeting of the assembly during the entire revolutionary period. The first item of business was the election of Eamon de Valera as the President of the Council of Ministers.

Thus, at the age of thirty-seven, de Valera became the head of an Irish government. He was to remain the dominant figure in Irish politics for forty years; his national eminence was to last longer than that of any other political leader among democratic states. Brought up in rural Limerick, his birth in Brooklyn, New York, may have been a factor in saving him from execution in 1916. Raised in a farm labourer's cottage, he was a self-made man, winning scholarships up to and including university. He received a bachelor's degree in mathematics from the Royal University in 1904; but although he took some graduate courses, he did not pursue a postgraduate degree. Over the next dozen years he was a mathematics teacher and professor at several secondary schools and teacher training colleges, rising to the level of school inspector in that subject. Comfortably situated in the ranks of the nationalist middle class and with a young and large family, de Valera put all this in jeopardy when he took a prominent part in the 1916 rebellion.

As the senior surviving commandant, he was thrust into the forefront of the republican movement in the aftermath of the rising. His ascent was meteoric and almost effortless, enabling him to rise from being one of many officers in the Volunteers to the leadership of nationalist Ireland within little more than a year. For the first twenty years of his life he had been almost completely apolitical. Moreover, he had had no involvement with party activity before 1916; his first interest was in the Gaelic League and then in the Volunteers. In one important way this lack of political sophistication was to be an advantage, as he addressed national affairs with the simplicity, sincerity, almost naïvety, of one who was articulating his beliefs for the first time — as indeed he was. According to P. S. O'Hegarty, 'In those pre-American days of his he was a slow-moving, painfully uncouth, massive speaker, with a disarming habit of pouring forth as new discoveries things which had been for twenty years the commonplaces of separatist thought.' Here, it seemed, was the authentic voice of the common man, the representative individual of the nation. Frank O'Connor described him as 'tall, thin, sallow, with a drooping mouth set in firm lines and a colourless face which rarely smiled'. To Ernie O'Malley 'There was a sense of sternness about him, dignity, a definite honesty, and a friendly way of making one feel at ease.' O'Malley also noted that 'He had not the human qualities of Collins, the Big Fellow. Dev was more reserved, a scholarly type. He was cold and controlled.'

Sinn Féin seemed delighted with the personal impression made by de Valera at this time. One party paper declared that 'the effect of his melodious enunciation in the native language' was such that 'one could almost imagine hearing the heartbeats of those around as de Valera spoke'. Another said that the President 'sent off his sentences like bullets from a machine-gun, and in volley after volley there was sense as well as sentiment'.

His first act as Príomh-Aire was to appoint a new cabinet, which, in fact, was only the shifting of individuals from one ministry to another. The team of ministers (originally the American title 'secretary' was employed, but this did not take root) he appointed were to retain these positions, barring arrest, until after the truce of July 1921. Owing to the need for security and solidarity, as well as de Valera's long absence in America, there was no scope or desire for change. Ministers were replaced upon their arrest, but no one was dismissed, and only one was demoted (in June 1920 Plunkett's status was quietly reduced to that of Associate Secretary for Foreign Affairs).

The new ministers were: Griffith for Home Affairs, Count Plunkett for Foreign Affairs, Brugha for Defence, Collins for Finance, W. T. Cosgrave for Local Government, Constance Markievicz for Labour, and Mac Néill for Industries. Three non-cabinet directors were also appointed: Laurence Ginnell became Director of Propaganda (sometimes Publicity), Robert Barton Director of Agriculture, and Ernest Blythe Director of Trade and Commerce. The cabinet was soon expanded to eleven members with the addition in June 1919 of Seán Etchingham as Minister for Fisheries and J. J. O'Kelly as Minister for the National Language, and, in November, of Austin Stack as Minister for Home Affairs, replacing Griffith, who became Acting President while de Valera was in America.[13]

Here was the group that led the counter-state in the quest for national freedom. What kind of people were they? There were ten men and one woman. They ranged in age from twenty-eight (Collins) to sixty-eight (Plunkett), with the average age being 44.5 (though Plunkett's years elevates that figure considerably). Few of them had much education; three had university degrees: two (de Valera and Mac Néill) from the Royal University, and one (Plunkett) from Trinity College. They had a range of occupations. Three (Griffith, O'Kelly and Etchingham) were in journalism, while two (de Valera and Mac Néill) were in education. There was a publican (Cosgrave), businessman (Brugha), and a former actress and youth organiser (Markievicz). Two of them (Plunkett and Markievicz) had inherited wealth. All but three of them (Griffith, Mac

Néill and Plunkett) had taken part in the 1916 rebellion. Four of the eleven were natives of Dublin; only one was from Ulster, but all of them had long been living in the capital.

Not all of the effective leaders in the movement were in the cabinet or in the Dáil. The estimate of this writer is that the whole movement had a leadership of seventy-seven persons (listed in Appendix 1, p. 342). Included in this group are thirty members of the Dáil; of the other thirty-nine deputies, it is certainly the case that they were dutiful, courageous and committed, but they made no specific or distinctive contribution to their cause. Besides the eleven cabinet members, others in the leadership were the six substitute and assistant ministers, seven directors and substitute directors, nine leading officials, thirty-six military and civil leaders, and eight persons who provided significant support.

Of the seventy-three for whom the relevant information is available, twenty-two were from Dublin, nine from Co. Cork, but only one was from Belfast; ten were born outside Ireland, and the rest came from all around the country, with four each from Mayo and Limerick, three from Tipperary, and the rest widely scattered. Half came from urban areas, which meant a gross over-representation of cities and towns in the leadership. Of the total of seventy-seven, only two (Markievicz and Hanna Sheehy-Skeffington) were women; seven of the number were Protestants. The average age was almost forty (39.6)); 39 per cent were under 35, and 65 per cent were under 45, which is comparable to the age range for members of the first Dáil (33 per cent under 35 and 73 per cent under 45).

Only eleven of the seventy-seven came from prominent families (Maurice Moore and Robert Barton came from the landowning class; George Gavan Duffy and P. J. Little were sons of dominion provincial premiers) or had achieved public standing before 1916 (Griffith, Plunkett, Mac Néill, Ginnell, Childers, John Devoy and James O'Mara). The other sixty-six were unknown to the general public. Twenty-seven were university graduates or had professional training; this was a higher percentage (35 per cent) than of the Dáil as a whole (28 per cent). Eight were graduates of the Royal/National University (de Valera, Mac Néill, Kevin O'Higgins, Frank Fahy, Rory O'Connor, Conor Maguire, Ernie O'Malley and P. J. Little), two of Trinity College, Dublin (Art O'Connor and Count Plunkett) and one each of Oxford (Barton), Cambridge (Childers) and Sandhurst (Maurice Moore). Twenty-one of the seventy-seven had taken part in the 1916 rising (as well as Barton, who was an officer in the British army at the time).

In terms of occupations, thirty-seven (of the seventy-two for whom information is available) were in the professions: 51 per cent of the leadership, as opposed to 43 per cent for the members of the Dáil. Only seven were in commerce and business: 9 per cent, as opposed to 22 per cent for the Dáil. With five farmers and two landowners, 10 per cent of the leadership was in agriculture, which is the same as the percentage (10 per cent) for the Dáil. Twenty-one of seventy- two were in miscellaenous occupations: 29 per cent, which is only slightly more than the proportion (25 per cent) in the Dáil. The leading occupation was that of journalism, which was the profession of fourteen of the leaders. This was followed closely by civil servants/clerks (with fourteen), followed by lawyers (with nine). There were five each in farming, engineering and business. Four were in education, two each were doctors, labour leaders, landowners and Catholic clergy. Then there was a tailor (Boland), blacksmith (Mac Eoin), publican (Cosgrave), ex-actress and youth organiser (Markievicz), ex-soldier (Tom Barry), ex-student (Ernie O'Malley), building contractor (Seán Moylan) and scholar and museum administrator (Plunkett). The picture that emerges of the leadership is that it was young, lower middle class and predominantly urban, that is, Dublin-based. Only one of them, Seán MacEntee, came from Belfast. The great majority of them were relatively well educated, but lacking — largely on account of their youth — any substantial experience or personal achievement. The profile of the leadership of the movement was very similar to that of the members of the Dáil.

How effective was this mostly young and unseasoned leadership? Given the difficult conditions under which it operated, the Dáil government managed to maintain its cohension and organisation. There was considerable conflict and rivalry within the underground body, but not to an unusual degree, and the tensions were kept out of public view. One of the difficulties was that the leader of the government was out of the country for a year and a half. Some cabinet members proved to be more effective administrators than others, a natural enough situation. The leadership demonstrated surprising political skill, which enabled them to retain public support. Only two members of the first Dáil resigned. Even in a normal political situation, this would be a remarkable record of stability and continuity. Given the revolutionary situation, the civil side managed to maintain a reasonable control of most military activities. The movement as a whole maintained a united front until it was offered a proposal that would concede most, if not all, of what it was seeking. That this offer was so long in coming is due to the desire of the British government to offer as little as it could to meet the demands of Irish nationalism. Confronted by a resilient and resourceful movement, it was forced to concede much more than it had hoped. This is the measure of the effectiveness of the Irish leadership.

*

At the same session that it elected the new cabinet the Dáil also changed its rules in order to prepare for an imminent storm. The quorum for its meetings was reduced to one-half of the members in Ireland and free to attend, with a minimum of twenty members signing the roll. The constitution was amended to provide for a President-substitute and minister-substitutes. Having done this much, or this little, the Dáil took a break for some political activity.

On Sunday 6 April de Valera made his first public appearance for almost a year. Ignoring a proclamation banning such gatherings, a monster Gaelic football match was held at Croke Park, Dublin, to raise money for the prisoners' dependants' fund. When the new President made his appearance as guest of honour, the 30,000 spectators 'greeted him with tumultuous cheers'. The end of the match witnessed a display of mob enthusiasm: 'No sooner had the final whistle sounded than all present dashed for the line seats at the stand from which de Valera had watched the game.' The banning of the civic reception had received its reply. Nevertheless, de Valera made no attempt to address the public directly at this time — a matter which was puzzling to RIC intelligence.

The next event was a special Sinn Féin *ard-fheis* on 8–9 April, at which de Valera declared his opposition to violence against the RIC, a statement which a police informant said was 'well received by moderate members, resented by extremists'. He also proposed that with the coming into existence of Dáil Éireann, the Sinn Féin organisation should act as 'a sort of civil army' to carry out the decisions of the Dáil cabinet. In order to prevent the party being 'used as a political machine by members of the Dáil', only one-third of Sinn Féin's executive should be composed of deputies. Yet the party would have extraordinary influence: before putting a proposal to the Dáil, a minister would first submit it to the party executive to receive the reaction of 'a sample of the people'. To Seán MacEntee this procedure would result in the subordination of the Dáil to Sinn Féin; Griffith saw the relationship as running both ways: 'Sinn Féin was the servant and master of Dáil Éireann.'

The *ard-fheis* also elected a new executive. Darrell Figgis, for one, believed that the meeting was packed with IRB and IRA members who had been instructed to vote against those members of the executive, including Figgis, who supported purely political measures to attain self-government. In the contest for the position of secretary, Figgis was badly defeated by Harry Boland. It seemed to Figgis that the militants were now in control. But little more than a month later the leading militant, Michael Collins, was complaining that the political activists were squeezing out supporters of physical force in the party.

The Dáil returned to the task of nation-building in a two-day session on 10 and 12 April. The President provided a brief, vague statement of his government's intentions. He declared that it would continue to seek international support, co-ordinate the efforts of voluntary bodies in various national activities, and resist British efforts to impose harmful legislation on the country. In a curious statement, he touched obliquely on the relationship between the government and the Irish Volunteers: 'The Minister of National Defence is, of course, in close association with the voluntary military forces which are the foundation of the National Army.' Obviously there would need to be further definition of the relationship between the two bodies. The only concrete statement of action announced by de Valera was that his government would be issuing bonds for sale to the public, initially in the amount of £500,000, with half to be offered at home and half abroad.

The President also proposed the social ostracism of the police, who, he charged, were 'the main instruments' for keeping the country in subjection, 'spies in our midst' and 'the eyes and ears of the enemy'. His motion to impose such a ban was carried without objection. A second tangible decision had been made.

As the Dáil was preparing to adjourn after a day of light duties, Thomas Kelly, deputy for St Stephen's Green, asked de Valera what was being done to implement the Democratic Programme. Obviously unprepared for this query, the President responded, reasonably enough, that 'It was quite clear that the Democratic Programme . . . contemplated a situation somewhat different from that in which they actually found themselves.' The programme had not been shelved; what was needed first were consultations with organised labour and extended study of social conditions. Then action could be taken 'with a view to definite remedies that were immediately within their power'. The man to take this job in hand, said de Valera, was Griffith, 'who had twenty years' experience of effort in that particular department'. This was the first and almost last occasion when the question of implementing the programme was brought before the Dáil, but, as will be seen, the revolutionary government did bring forward a limited but specific programme of economic development. The atmosphere of self-congratulation and goodwill irritated one deputy. Speaking in Irish, Piaras Béaslaí gently criticised the President for providing the assembly with only a skimpy idea of what his government intended to do, but he was alone in his criticism.

Dáil Éireann now disappeared from public view for another month. The daily press had provided extensive if censored coverage of the session. In fact the account of the proceedings on 10 April was drawn from the *Irish Independent* when the official account was later confiscated by British forces. The RIC was not unduly concerned about the meeting; the Inspector-General reported that the session 'did not attract much attention in the Provinces'. Moreover, he believed that, despite the 'unabated energy' of Sinn Féin and the Irish Volunteers, the party did not seem to be making progress and attendance at meetings was 'often discouraging'.

It was obvious that the Dáil and its cabinet were cautiously feeling their way forward in the ways of government. They had need to be careful, as there were sixty-odd ex-MPs and thousands of supporters of the old Irish Party waiting for the first good opportunity to lead a caval-cade of ridicule. The chief intelligence officer of the RIC was almost surprised that the rebel government had not tried to do more in the first two months of its existence. 'Dáil Éireann which was to have usurped the government of Ireland has made no attempt to do so.' Yet a positive political impression had been made, especially by de Valera. Moreover, there was no visible impatience in the ranks of Sinn Féin about Dáil Éireann's pace of development.[14]

(5) THE IRISH-AMERICAN DELEGATION

Public attention once again shifted to the Versailles conference. Accord-ing to Seán T. O'Kelly, the escape of de Valera generated press interest in Paris about the Irish situation for the first time, and newspaper reporters sought out the Irish representative. This was just the oppor-tunity that he was seeking to develop relations with them, and 'from then on my difficulties with the Press decreased'. With a welcome increase in activity in his office, O'Kelly requested help from Dublin. The man dispatched was George Gavan Duffy, who would appear to have been an ideal choice. Then thirty-seven years old, he was the son of Charles Gavan Duffy, the Young Irelander and later premier of the Australian state of Victoria. A small-sized, serious and cultivated person, Duffy had been born in France and educated in that country and in England, where he practised law for a decade. He acted as one of Roger Casement's defence counsel in 1916. In the following year he moved to Ireland and won a parliamentary seat in the 1918 election. As has been seen, Duffy was a key figure in the launching of the Dáil. A fluent French speaker, he proved to be an effective spokesman for his government. The British government, obviously confident about how things were going in Paris, made no attempt to prevent him from going there.

Another valuable addition to the Paris staff at this time was the writer Yann Goblet, who, under the pen-name of Louis Trequiz, had written about wartime Ireland in *L'Irlande dans la crise universelle*, which was published in 1917. An updated version of the book, appearing under his own name, was released in 1921. Duffy declared that Goblet was 'our best asset with the French press' because of his standing with 'impor-tant papers like the *Debates* who would not otherwise look at Ireland and who do not care to take things direct from this Delegation'. Erskine Childers shared Duffy's high opinion of Goblet's services. There was also Annie Vivanti, the wife of John Chartres (of whom more later). A poetess and novelist, she was able to address a wide audience of readers in

France, Switzerland and Italy. Duffy declared that her work was 'really invaluable and beyond praise'. After her return to Italy in mid-1919 she continued to write and speak for Irish self-government.

Hard on the heels of Duffy came a much more potent force in the struggle to secure a hearing for the Irish cause — a delegation of three Irish-Americans representing the Irish Race Convention. The idea of such a delegation probably originated with the resourceful Griffith, who from prison proposed a top-level representation — Cardinal O'Connell of Boston and two senators or congressmen, one from each party. Such a delegation, he believed, would be 'impossible to keep from being heard at the Conference'. In the name of the Dáil ministry, Cathal Brugha and Michael Collins sent the proposal to Diarmuid Lynch, a member of the Dáil who had earlier been deported to the United States. The Irish Race Convention, which met for the third time in six months on 22–23 February 1919, appointed a committee to meet with President Wilson. When this encounter proved unproductive, the committee appointed a delegation of three to proceed to Paris.

The three men selected were not, as Griffith had hoped, from the highest level of American political life, but they were successful, experienced men in their own right, with solid credentials in Woodrow Wilson's political party. Frank P. Walsh (1864–1939) was a noted labour lawyer who had served as joint president of the War Labour Conference Board. Edward F. Dunne (1853–1937) was a former Mayor of Chicago and Governor of Illinois. Michael J. Ryan (1862–1943) of Philadelphia had served for many years as national president of the United Irish League of America. Of the three men, it was Walsh who demonstrated the greatest commitment to the Irish cause.

In sharp contrast to the treatment afforded to O'Kelly and other unimportant supplicants, the Irish-American delegates were given open access to leading American officials at the conference. Within a week of their arrival, on 17 April, they met with President Wilson, who declared that he would inform Lloyd George of the intense feeling among the Irish in America for the movement for Irish self-government and of the necessity for the British government to satisfy this demand if it wanted to avoid troubled relations with the United States. Lloyd George agreed to meet with them, and there were indications that he would allow the delegates appointed by Dáil Éireann to come to Paris. The delegation was making progress. Perhaps contrasting their achievement with his own ineffectiveness, Seán T. O'Kelly believed that 'their work has been as fruitful and successful as we could expect under the circumstances'. But then, pleading the pressure of conference affairs, Lloyd George twice cancelled meetings with the American trio.[15]

It was at this point that the idea was put to them that they should visit Ireland. Frank Walsh believed the visit had been proposed by Lloyd

George, who later said that he understood that the idea had originated with Colonel Edward M. House, a key American adviser. Sir William Wiseman of the British delegation thought that Wilson wanted them to go. The idea of inviting the delegation to Ireland apparently originated with the Limerick Sinn Féin branch and was unanimously approved by the national executive on 27 March. De Valera obviously agreed: a month later a message was sent to the Paris office declaring that the delegates 'ought to visit Ireland immediately'. In any case, the British government provided the delegation with diplomatic visas for the visit.

Their ten-day sojourn in Ireland was dramatic, indeed explosive, in its consequences. When the delegation arrived at Kingstown (Dún Laoghaire) on 4 May, it was met by representatives of the Dáil government and was driven to Dublin in a car flying American and Irish flags. Frank Walsh announced: 'We have come to confer with President de Valera on the question of securing international recognition of the Irish Republic at the Peace Conference.' This was to be no mere fact-finding mission. Travelling under the auspices of Sinn Féin, the delegates traversed the country, conferring only with supporters of that party. Everywhere they broadcast their support for Irish independence and the republic whose establishment had been ratified by Dáil Éireann. Such statements generated an apopletic reaction from the *Irish Times*. On 7 May it declared: 'Their message has given an enormous stimulus to Sinn Féin [and has come] as a dose of oxygen to a patient whom the absurd policy of abstention from the House of Commons in favour of a mock Parliament at home had reduced to a very critical state.'

The delegates were received almost everywhere as conquering heroes. The climax of their visit came with their presentation to Dáil Éireann on 9 May. This was 'a great moment', said Máire Comerford, as 'no foreigner had addressed an Irish Parliament since Benjamin Franklin was received in the old Irish House on College Green'. De Valera later told Walsh that his speech convinced him that the republic was a living reality. Yet privately the delegation gave him a most pessimistic assessment of the chances of success at Paris. As if to confirm charges that Ireland was subjected to a campaign of suppression, the police and military invaded a reception that followed the session. To Tim Healy this occurrence was providential: 'The stars in their courses fight in favour of the Sinn Féiners'; the raid was 'sheer folly'. As the visit of the Americans drew to a close, the attitude of the *Irish Times* shifted from anger to apprehension. On 10 May it declared that 'three weeks ago none save fools and fanatics believed in the possibility of an Irish Republic', but that as a result of the American tour the hopes of a large number of nationalists had been stimulated to believe that a republic was coming. The *Belfast Newsletter* commented that the 'Irish Government . . . would have been within its right if it ordered these foreign mischief-makers out of the country'.

The visit also set off reactions in both the British press and in parliament. The London *Times* on 13 May held that the effect of the visit was the submergence of 'every policy of moderation, so that a full Republic is now the irreducible minimum of hundreds of thousands of Nationalists, and it has shaken grievously the prestige and influence of the Irish Executive'.[16]

When the delegation left to return to Paris in the second week of May, it left behind a reinvigorated Sinn Féin movement. The RIC Inspector-General reported that the visit 'gave a fresh impetus to republican aspirations'. Sinn Féin speakers were now boasting that they would compel the Peace Conference to hear the Irish case, with the result being that 'the whole community is restless and apprehensive'. It was also being said that, if perchance the conference declined to hear the Irish case, Sinn Féin had plans to launch 'a spectacular revolution' that 'apparently would be general if it only lasted twenty-four hours'.

On their return to Paris, the Irish-Americans plunged back into their intensive activities on behalf of the Irish cause. This cause further annoyance to Wilson, who privately declared that he was nearing the point where he would have to condemn their 'miserable mischief-making', adding: 'They see nothing except their own small interest.' Neither resolutions from the US Senate nor from the American Federation of Labour urging a hearing for Ireland had any effect on Wilson.[17]

When the delegation again met Wilson, on 11 June, the report of the Peace Conference had already been published; it said nothing about Ireland. Wilson informed them that their statements in Ireland had been wholly counterproductive, as they had merely served to inflame British opinion. As a result of his own efforts, he told them, 'we were well on our way of getting Mr de Valera and his associates over here . . . when you made it so difficult by your speeches in Ireland that we could not do it'. When Walsh challenged him to explain why the principle of self-determination was not being applied to Ireland, Wilson responded philosophically:

> You have touched on the great metaphysical tragedy of today. My words have roused hopes in the hearts of millions of people. . . . When I gave utterance to those words I said them without the knowledge that nationalities existed who are coming to us today.

Yet both as a professor and later as a politician Wilson must often have heard of the Irish claim to nationhood.

As far as Wilson was concerned, this was the end of the matter. George Gavan Duffy told the Dáil cabinet:

> Wilson will do nothing (and apparently never intended to do anything) beyond politely persuading [Lloyd] George that he should do something, no matter what, to drown the pestilential clamour of the pestilential Irish and so give Wilson a respite.

The journalistic opponents of Sinn Féin celebrated its defeat. Both the *Freeman's Journal* and the Belfast *Irish News* repeated their view that no other result could have been anticipated. The RIC Inspector-General noted that the party was 'at present in a position of embarrassment'. According to one observer, the campaign of denunciation was not sustained, 'apparently because the editors concluded that the hoped for revulsion from Sinn Féin had after all not yet arrived'.[18]

If the advocates of Irish independence could foresee almost inevitable failure at the Peace Conference, why did their representatives persist in their efforts? In the first place, it was something that Sinn Féin had to go through with. According to O'Kelly, the Paris mission was 'a forlorn hope, almost a concession, made by fiercer spirits among the Sinn Féin leaders to those of their comrades who urge that every possible instrument of peaceful negotiation should at least be tried'.

Some in Sinn Féin had been looking beyond the Peace Conference all along. O'Kelly, who had hoped for more from Paris, was now ready to go on to the next round: 'As things have turned out here, it looks as if the fight will have to be very vigorously pushed in the States.' He wrote to de Valera on 24 May that 'American friends are satisfied the fight must be transferred to the US' and 'We are of the opinion you should go to the States as soon as we have been definitely turned down here.' There was already a powerful American organisation, the Friends of Irish Freedom, which was being developed under its secretary, Diarmuid Lynch, and Harry Boland had been sent to America in May. At the end of that month Eamon de Valera disappeared from Dublin and began a secret journey to the land of his birth. While its opponents probed the depths of its failure at Paris, Sinn Féin enthusiastically rose to the challenge of moving the game forward.[19]

2

Building the Counter-State

While the government of Dáil Éireann was being organised in the spring of 1919 there was considerable public discussion about the nature of the new institution. Some observers hoped and believed that the new Irish government would drastically or at least substantially deviate from the British model. Others anticipated that Sinn Féin might adopt a radical or revolutionary system. Liam O'Flaherty has given us this picture of that time:

> A new spirit had taken possession of the Irish people, and it seemed at last that the kingdom of heaven had descended upon the earth, naturally choosing the island of saints and scholars as its resting place. In their enthusiasm the Irish writers of pamphlets and propaganda sheets talked of a wonderful Paradise in Ireland when the Peace Conference in Paris should take away the superimposed British Empire and allow the Irish to rule themselves in peace. There was wild talk of a Gaelic Communist Society. There was to be no more poverty, no more social conflict, no more hatred, no more ugliness.

Much of the speculation about the future form of government had been fuelled by Sinn Féin declarations that the world would be a substantially different place once it had won the election. The first few meetings of Dáil Éireann, however, did not show any apparent departure from the British parliamentary model — though of course the assembly's policies and organisation were not yet clearly established. This allowed for speculation about what might be in store for the Irish people. When in January one Dáil member, J. J. Walsh of Cork, declared that the 'Irish people were really revolutionary' and that there was a 'new-born spirit' in the country towards the 'emancipated democracies of Russia', the *Irish Times* (21 Jan.) warned that the republicans might be moving towards a liaison with Bolshevism. Furthermore, with the Sinn Féin spokesmen proclaiming that the Dáil would be a working, legislative body rather than just a propaganda organ, the Unionist paper concluded that, whether its programme was feasible or not, one thing was certain: 'It will mean ruin and misery for all classes of the Irish people.'

Canon J. O. Hannay (better known as a writer under the pen-name George A. Birmingham) was also alarmed about the relationship between Sinn Féin and Bolshevism. He argued that since it was Irish Labour that had given Sinn Féin its victory, the labour movement would be looking for 'substantial and tangible results'. If the appeal to the Peace Conference failed, Sinn Féin idealism would be swept aside and it 'may degenerate into Bolshevism'. In March Cardinal Logue, alarmed by the spread of socialism in Ireland, advised in his Lenten pastoral that this doctrine 'in any of the forms in which its advocates propound it, is inconsistent with Catholic teaching'. Another prelate, Bishop Kelly of Ross, criticised the leaders of the Dáil, particularly Constance Markievicz, for their extremist tendencies, while Sylvia Pankhurst, the English socialist, proposed the redrawing of the Dáil's constitution 'on Soviet lines', as the American type of republic was outdated. An RIC intelligence report related that church leaders had warned Sinn Féin to avoid violence and 'urged them not to allow Liberty Hall (the Citizen Army) to get control as they were irreligious and socialistic'. An orator of the United Irish League viewed the radical current with alarm:

> Nowadays the watchword of Sinn Féin was the 'gospel of James Connolly', and not Republican America but Bolshevist Russia was hailed as the land of hope and freedom. Did many who voted Sinn Féin support land nationalisation and secularisation of education?

The Irish Unionist Alliance was convinced that Bolshevism had penetrated the Irish labour movement and would soon spread to Sinn Féin. A Unionist deputation told members of parliament in May 1919 that the Irish Labour leadership sought not only complete Irish independence 'but also the overthrow of British civilisation through the establishment of a Bolshevist State in Ireland'. Since Sinn Féin was dependent on Labour support, it was the Bolshevists who were calling the tune.[1]

The early months of 1919 was a period of unusual labour strife, with a large number of strikes taking place throughout the country, the most notable of which was the Belfast general strike of February 1919. The May Day demonstrations organised by city labour bodies were the largest ever. Reporting on the rapidly swelling ranks of the Irish Transport and General Workers' Union, the RIC Inspector-General asserted that a majority of its members were Sinn Féiners, 'but they have not so far exhibited Bolshevist tendencies'; nevertheless, 'Labour is in a very unsettled state'. These developments undoubtedly stirred the belief that a new day had dawned. Social change was in the air.

The Irish Labour Party and Trade Union Congress naturally supported sweeping changes in social and economic institutions. The *Voice of Labour*, edited by Cathal O'Shannon, provided weekly incitement. The leading advocates of this among those of a Sinn Féin bent were Darrell Figgis, Aodh de Blacam and P. J. Little, editor of the Sinn Féin weekly *New Ireland*. Their views probably derived from and were consistent with those of George Russell (AE), whose book on the subject, *The National Being*, had been published in early 1916. All of these proposed the reorganisation of Irish economic and political institutions along co-operative lines inspired by their view of Gaelic social organisation in the ancient past.

De Blacam's book *Towards the Republic*, published in 1918 (with a revised edition appearing in February 1919), probably had the greatest impact. De Blacam was a self-appointed Sinn Féin seer and critic; he held no position in either party or state and had no direct involvement in politics. In a chapter entitled 'Away with Parliaments' he confidently declared that 'Ireland had no use for corrupt, inefficient and decivilising institution called Parliament' because the country 'has different conception of the right way to conduct a state'. What was this different conception? 'The Irish State', he asserted, 'will make the agricultural industry, the education profession, and all other great agencies of public service self-directing (and thus free from being the sport of parties).'

A rash of articles by de Blacam, Father Patrick Gaynor and others, as well as pamphlets by Jack White and Selma Sigerson, celebrated the advent of the communal organisation of Irish society. This brought a rejoinder from P. S. O'Hegarty. In an article, 'The Socialist Pistol', in the *Irish World* (5 July) he charged that these ideologues were trying to ram socialism down the people's throats. In his view, Sinn Féin was neither socialist nor capitalist, and 'all attempts to commit it now to any particular policy of economic reconstruction are attempts which can do nothing but injury to the cause'.

What exactly had Dáil Éireann done so far in this area? The Democratic Programme had recommended the organisation of the economy along co-operative lines. But de Valera had refused to be drawn out on the matter when questioned about it in the Dáil in mid-April. At the following *ard-fheis* there had been no mention of the programme, an omission which was noted in the pages of *New Ireland*.

The lack of innovation on the part of the rebel government brought a response from 'Lector' (Alfred O'Rahilly) in that journal: 'Even Dáil Éireann can be overdone. I suspect some of our TDEs would scent Anarchy if they were told that the people of Ireland are the ultimate sovereign.' 'How many of them', he asked, 'know anything about the Referendum? About decentralisation of government?' He hoped that the new state 'is not going to start on the career of parliamentary autocracy and despotism of which England (so rich in democratic phraseology) has become a notorious example'. Another correspondent was convinced that Sinn

Féiners would do things differently: they 'have come to understand the weakness of the old parliamentary system' and were in the process of developing a 'new economic formula'. He observed that 'Efforts are being made to build up the country administratively, and to strengthen the co-operative system, so that when the proper time comes the parliamentary organisation can be abandoned without friction or disaster' — a kind of Marxist withering away of the state when the Promised Land had been reached.

Aodh de Blacam, despite the Dáil's lack of interest, told advocates of co-operatives: 'We must organise and keep our aims before the Dáil members.' If the Dáil failed to respond, he proposed, 'then and not till then, we must condemn the present members as parliamentary fossils'. Another critic of the parliamentary system was Hanna Sheehy-Skeffington, who declared that the Dáil had taken 'its machinery from its worst enemy'. She objected to 'all the tosh and piffle' of Westminster being employed in the new assembly. The *Irish Citizen*, of which she was editor, congratulated the Dáil for its progressive action in appointing a woman, Constance Markievicz, as a cabinet member (a half-century was to pass before another woman attained this position). It added, however: 'We cannot help wishing that the Dáil would cast off the whole system of British Cabinet making and British Parliamentary methods, a system that has strangled true democracy.' It urged the Sinn Féin government to model itself on that of the 'progressive small nations' of Sweden, Norway, Finland, Denmark, Holland and Switzerland.[2]

Mrs Sheehy-Skeffington was not alone in deprecating the London model. A Father Lynch held that the Dáil was 'at present a ramshackle copy of the British Parliament'. J. J. Walsh, a member of the Dáil, wrote to Mrs Sheehy-Skeffington that he strongly supported her views and gave this picture of the nature of the assembly:

> The Dáil members are called together once every two or three months to hear reports from these Dictators. They are then dispersed to mooch around amongst their constituents as if they were the most insignificant of ciphers. In the eyes of the framers of our constitution any single 'Cabinet Minister' knows more than half a dozen such men. Evidently their functions end with election and the endorsing of pious resolutions.

He announced his intention of proposing the establishment of a committee system within the Dáil, and he urged Mrs Sheehy-Skeffington to propose a resolution advocating this in the Sinn Féin national executive.

Walsh was as good as his word. At the next Dáil session, on 19 June, his resolution was read to the assembly: 'That a committee be set up to draft a constitution suitable to the democratic needs of this country.' Walsh himself was not present, and no action was taken on the matter. The Dáil did consider a motion by Joseph MacDonagh to alter its constitution by shifting executive power from the ministers to 'Committees composed of all members of the Dáil', but he was persuaded to accept the idea of consultative committees to work with each ministry. The committees were formed, but, largely owing to the circumstances of the times, did not prove to be effective agents in either shaping policy or directing its execution.

The revolutionary assembly, in any case, was not wholly composed of quiescent party loyalists. The sudden and unexplained departure of de Valera to the United States resulted in the first outburst of objection at a Dáil session. At the meeting of 17 June both Seán MacEntee and Joseph MacDonagh called for an explanation, MacEntee adding that 'no member of the Dáil had been consulted' about de Valera's mission and that 'it was neither right nor fair to them that they should be unable to say whether the President had gone away and where he was'. Later, in January 1921, he again took the ministry to task for not consulting with the Dáil.

Darrell Figgis recalled that several members of the Dáil were dissatisfied about the lack of authority that they possessed and had urged him to allow his new weekly paper to be a platform for opposition to cabinet domination of the new government. He also asserted that Griffith played no part in the decision of de Valera to go to America. There were, therefore, substantial grounds for objection within the Dáil concerning the way its infant government was evolving, but the action of Dublin Castle in driving the Dáil underground largely submerged this opposition.[3]

If nothing was done to restructure Irish government along directly democratic and decentralised lines, many of the leaders lent their support to the idea that the economy should be shaped by co-operative organisation. Ernest Blythe, Director of Trade and Commerce, showed marked support: 'The co-operative movement seemed to be the only feasible method of combating foreign trusts and combines.' He was aware, however, of the controversial nature of his position. 'They should handle the matter with care', he advised, 'so as not to endanger the unity of the people and so as to retain the support of the Labour Movement.' Blythe's statement was echoed by Eoin Mac Néill, his nominal superior, who declared that the development of co-operatives, both distributive and productive, was 'the only way to fight the Trust policy'. Blythe prepared a circular on co-operative organisation that Sinn Féin in June agreed to distribute. On 3 July Michael Collins presented three circulars on 'proposed industrial activities for Cumainn' which the party also undertook to send out.

Sinn Féin had shown a modest but increasing interest in co-operatives. When the party set up a variety of departments in November 1917, in anticipation of forming a government, one of these dealt with 'co-operative effort'. The department left no apparent mark, but in the early months of 1919 Sinn Féin actively supported the development of the co-operative movement. In April the party executive established a sub-committee of Father Michael O'Flanagan, Harry Boland, Laurence Ginnell and Arthur Griffith to create a plan for co-operative 'land acquisition and working' and the defining of a proper land policy. This group, upon the prodding of Collins, prepared a plan for a co-operative bank.

A meeting of the full party executive on 6 May took a strong position on co-operative enterprise, urging *cumainn* to form co-operative societies 'in every district in Ireland, having as their purpose the development for the benefit of all the people of the district of all latent natural resources . . . and for the more efficient development of such resources as are at present only imperfectly developed'. Lest it be accused of being against capitalism, the executive added a note declaring that it was only advocating co-operative activity in regard to resources 'that are at present undeveloped either by co-operation or individual enterprise'. It proceeded to appoint a commission, headed by Father O'Flanagan and including George Russell, Edward (Mac)Lysaght and Robert Barton, to study 'the whole question of Co-operation in Ireland'. O'Flanagan, a member of the executive of the Irish Agricultural Organisation Society, spent several weeks in the spring of 1919 stumping the countryside urging the formation of co-operatives. He told a meeting at Athlone that 'if the shopkeeper did not co-operate he would go down before the co-operative movement and the Trusts'. An RIC report in June noted that this effort was 'perhaps the only practical scheme receiving Sinn Féin support'.[4]

Griffith produced a pamphlet, approved by the Dáil cabinet, urging the formation of distributive co-operatives. Then in August word arrived that President de Valera had endorsed the idea of a co-operative commonwealth for Ireland. On 26 September the Dáil cabinet went on record as favouring co-operative production. The recently established National Land Bank, funded by the Dáil, envisioned lending money to co-operatives of landless farm labourers. Furthermore, the Dáil's programme for the development of the fishing industry was based on the formation of co-operatives of fishermen.

Sinn Féin interest in co-operatives, however, was not sustained. An RIC report in June stated that Father O'Flanagan was 'getting the cold shoulder from Sinn Féin extremists'. Perhaps both the supporters of political action and physical force feared that the independence movement would be diverted from the task of destroying and supplanting the British administration to the pursuit of social and economic causes. In any case, when the Dáil Loan campaign was launched in September, some merchants objected to Sinn Féin support for co-operative stores. A Galway informant, Father O'Kelly, wrote to Michael Collins: 'This Co-operative Store business is destroying our efforts in the constituency. Not being a businessman, I have nothing to say for or against them. They are in our way in any case.' O'Flanagan's commission failed to produce a report.

The co-operative idea in Ireland probably drew added inspiration at this time from the social and economic proposals adopted by the American Conference of Catholic Bishops, copies of which were sent to Ireland by Dr W. J. A. Maloney. The idea met with little response from the laity in the United States and presented a variety of difficulties in Ireland. None of the Sinn Féin *cumainn* acted on the proposals for co-operative activity. It was clearly not regarded as a significant or likely future development. Sinn Féin, very much an electoral organisation, turned its attention to the forthcoming local government elections. In future some party leaders occasionally expressed collectivist beliefs. Collins supported public ownership of mineral and coal deposits 'so that they could not be exploited by private syndicates, as had happened in other countries'. W. T. Cosgrave proposed a state insurance monopoly: 'There was a good deal of money in the business if run economically by the State.'

The RIC intelligence unit seemed puzzled that the Dáil, 'which was to have usurped the government of Ireland, has made no attempt to do so'. The *Irish World* voiced its concern: 'On all sides, in recent weeks, men and women have been wondering and asking one another what was being done.' In fact the Dáil ministry had been busy preparing a legislative programme. Joseph McGrath told his constituents on St Patrick's Day to 'be patient for a while', as the Dáil was working in committee day and night. Diarmuid O'Hegarty wrote to George Gavan Duffy in July: 'We are slave-driving here — Committees on all conceivable form of project, floatation of loans, etc.' The programme was presented to the Dáil at its session of 17–19 June 1919. This 'constructive programme' proposed to create a consular service, stimulate fishing and forestry, provide for land redistribution, establish a system of arbitration courts, and launch a commission of inquiry into the nation's resources. All proposals of the ministry passed by the Dáil were described as 'decrees'. The decree concerning land, undoubtedly the most important of these, was certainly broad in scope but equally vague:

> The provision of land for the agricultural population now deprived thereof is decreed, and a Loan Fund under the authority of the Dáil may be established to aid this purpose.

The Dáil heartily approved of all of these very general measures. How exactly any of these proposals would be implemented was not revealed, but they did represent a set of propositions which, with a bit of embellishment, could be seen as a set of achievements. The enthusiasm of O'Hegarty was apparent when he wrote to Duffy in Paris:

> I am personally very glad that this side of the business is being taken up in a definite fashion. Actual constructive work will leave a bigger mark on people than political work. It makes them think more, and besides, it invests the Government with tangibility as such. It means

that the Dáil has stepped away from the beaten path of political parties and their shibboleths, and that it is functioning as any progressive Government would be expected to function.

Liam de Roiste held the Dáil had to contend with two sets of critics: 'those who said it can do nothing, and those who expected it to do wonders'. If press censorship did not exist, he declared, 'the public would understand that the Dáil had done more than any political party in Ireland'. The *Irish World* voiced relative satisfaction: 'We are glad to see a lifting of even a portion of the veil that shrouds the proceedings of the Dáil.'[5]

(2) AN UNUSUAL ADMINISTRATION

When President de Valera departed for the United States in June 1919, Arthur Griffith became Acting President. Then forty-eight years old, he had by far the most political experience of anyone in the leadership of the movement. It was he who had propounded the basic idea of Sinn Féin over twenty long and apparently fruitless years — the proposition that the people of Ireland could achieve self-government simply by practising it. He rejected violence as counterproductive; rather, he stressed political action, including civil disobedience, the refusal to acknowledge the governing power of the existing administration.

Griffith was a Dubliner, born in 1871, of fairly ordinary origins. A printer by trade, he became a journalist. Except for two years spent in South Africa when he was a young man, Griffith knew only Ireland — though not rural Ireland or indeed anywhere else but Dublin. Like many other self-educated people, Griffith had formed rigid beliefs. He had a singular mind; he was prejudiced, puritanical and extremely partisan, but also determined, courageous and unselfish. Having weathered disappointment and opposition for many years, Griffith now saw his great idea of the counter-state come into its own, but this was in conjunction with the physical-force approach rather than with the non-violent methods which he advocated. There was to be a race, a contest, as to which outlook would predominate. It was Griffith's task to propel the civil side of the movement into the ascendant. This was his great challenge.

In many ways he was not an impressive public figure. Short and stocky, he made no attempt to be a popular orator; he was not a politician in so far as he had not sought elected office. He was, however, a political being; almost all of his proposals called for political action. Frederick Dumont, the new United States consul in Dublin, formed a strongly negative view of him:

He is a man of the Irish lower middle class and has a good deal of the Irish air of mysticism. He is badly groomed, almost ungroomed — dour, sullen, unenthusiastic — a man with bitterness seemingly engendered by brooding over disappointments, defeats and wrongs.

Dumont on another occasion concluded that Griffith 'has not great ability. He expresses his ideas badly in speech and in writing, betraying a lack of fundamental knowledge.'

When Sinn Féin was reorganised in 1917, Griffith's original idea of Sinn Féin was merged with the belief in the efficacy of physical force. He took part in the revived movement, but in a subordinate position. He was not committed to the achievement of a republic and was in an English jail when the establishment of the Irish Republic was formally ratified in January 1919, yet he enthusiastically greeted the establishment of an Irish national assembly and became a leading minister in the new government on his release in April.

Now he was to be in charge of the new administration during what was anticipated as a lengthy absense of de Valera. No one knew how long de Valera would be gone or even if he would be able to return to Ireland. In fact Griffith was to be Acting President for nearly a year and a half, until his arrest in November 1920. If he was not a supporter of physical force, he apparently had come to terms with its use by the time he took de Valera's place. Up to June 1919 and for long after neither the Dáil ministry nor the assembly itself had taken a clear position on this matter. Yet violent actions were being taken by the Irish Volunteers, under at least the nominal authority of the Minister for Defence.

Despite all that was going on around him, Griffith continued to lead a normal life: he lived at home, walked and bicycled around the city, visited offices. He also resumed his former occupation of journalist, editing *Young Ireland* at 204 Great Brunswick Street throughout the period. Apparently he had no other office from which he directed the work of the government of the Republic of Ireland. It also meant that he was a part-time President. He continued to frequent his favourite pubs — the Bailey in Duke Street and the Ship in Abbey Street — where messages were delivered to him from Dáil departments by couriers. This caused embarrassment to some Sinn Féin supporters. Máire Comerford related that she was shocked 'the day when I found A.G. in a city centre pub with a glass of whiskey in front of him'. She added: 'I did not know then, or for long, how much of the work of the Republic was done in bars and public houses.' He was able to carry on this style of life as a result of the policy of the British administration, which, viewing him as a moderating force within the independence movement, ordered that he was not to be arrested.[6]

As the head of the ministry, Griffith was the key factor in how the new government would proceed in making good its claims. It is hard to estimate his importance in what followed. Very little material about his role is available today. This may be due to the loss of most of his papers after his death in 1922. Yet he not does figure prominently in the correspondence of other Dáil ministers. It appears, however, that he dealt with the business of the ministry briefly and orally. He was always at cabinet meetings and sessions of the Dáil. Except for a few brief speaking trips to Britain and a very occasional sortie outside of Dublin, he was in the city every day, always available, working in his office, walking the streets. No one complained of any lack of attention to duty. He appears as being constantly in touch with events. But there is little direct evidence of his giving instructions or directing the development of the alternative government. Because of this, he remained the public man, readily available for press statements, the publicist, the spokesman, but not the administrator, the director of events or the constructor of a state. He was an effective public spokesman. One of his associates later said that he 'had a way of making incisive statements, very short, and not too frequent, which cleared the air like a flash and a thunderclap'.

There was not a single Dáil scheme with which he was closely identified, yet everything the national assembly did was part of the programme he had developed many years before. When Nevil Macready became commander of the British army in Ireland in April 1920, he kept a copy of Griffith's *The Resurrection of Hungary* on his desk and marked in it the dates on which the measures proposed in it were carried out.

It was during Griffith's time as head of the executive that the term 'Saorstát Éireann' came into general use as the name of the state, rather than 'Poblacht na hÉireann', which had been used in 1916. In fact *saorstát* had been used to describe the Republic in the Irish-language version of the Declaration of Independence. Eoin Mac Néill has been given credit for it being employed in that document. Griffith supported the use of *saorstát* as a way to bridge the gap between the Irish desire for complete independence and the British insistence that a constitutional link be maintained. To the Irish it would mean *republic*; to the English *free state*. It did not matter what the English called the Irish state, he argued, as long as the Irish were satisfied that they got what they wanted. When 'Saorstát Éireann' began to appear as the heading on stationery and proclamations, there were some who objected to the elimination of the term *poblacht*. The use of the new name was raised by the British side during the Treaty negotiations. De Valera told the Dáil in December 1921:

> When I was over with the British Prime Minister he looked at my notepaper and he said, 'You need not change the name of your state'. That was very simple for him. So the Irish Republic as a name being repugnant to them, it was suggested, I think by Mr Griffith, that the Irish Free State was a good name. . . . If the name mattered I would have chosen, for instance, the Free State of Ireland.[7]

Another key person in the development of the counter-state, who has been largely overlooked, was Diarmuid O'Hegarty (1893–1958). Like Michael Collins, he was a native of West Cork, had been in the 1916 rebellion, and was a leader in the IRB. He had gained administrative experience as private secretary to the head of the Department of Agriculture and Technical Instruction. At the age of twenty-six he became not only Director of Organisation for the IRA but also Secretary to the Ministry. He was, indeed, 'the civil servant of the revolution'. Ernie O'Malley remembered him well:

> Hegarty's long cow's lick fell over his right eye; he had an untidy collar, an angled tie and a dishevelled appearance. He seemed to take life easy, but he worked hard. He had a muttered rapid speech; his mind worked quickly, shrewdly and surely. . . . He used clear, clever imagery, often biting. I admired his type of quick intellect, often disguised by a surface implication of casualness.

Kathleen McKenna judged him as 'one of the most able and intelligent men on the work'. Although he avoided all public attention, there is a wealth of evidence that his efficient and energetic administration of the business of the Dáil government was a crucial factor in the development of the counter-state.[8]

(3) Locating The Underground Government

In the first half of 1919 the ministers of the rebel government worked out of the Sinn Féin offices at 6 Harcourt Street, which the English journalist Hugh Martin characterised as an 'extraordinarily shabby and mean-looking headquarters'. No government, not even a rebel one, could operate for very long in a few rooms, so in July 1919 the ministry purchased a building up the road at 76 Harcourt Street for £1,130. As was the case of many Dáil offices, Batt O'Connor, a master builder and carpenter, was dispatched to survey the premises and prepared hiding places for important documents. The Dáil was informed at its August meeting that 'new and spacious premises' had been secured, but was urged 'not to make this matter public until they were actually in possession'. The name of the occupant given to the post office was that of 'The Irish Club', which deceived not the members of the CID at Dublin Castle, who censored the mail going to both No. 6 and No. 76, while in turn the IRA's intelligence section rifled the mail going to the Castle.[9]

The Dáil leadership clearly anticipated that its administration would be allowed to operate openly for a considerable period of time. However, this was not to be the case. In response to the Dáil Loan campaign, Dublin Castle declared Dáil Éireann to be an illegal organisation on 11 September. The Dáil cabinet advised nineteen members not to attend the session in October. Yet its offices were undisturbed for exactly two months, when the British military finally staged a raid. Two weeks later, on 26 November, the Castle authorities banned Sinn Féin, the Irish Volunteers, the Gaelic League and Cumann na mBan, and three days later ordered the closure of Sinn Féin and Dáil Éireann headquarters on Harcourt Street. This order being ignored, the police responded by clearing the buildings and nailing up the front doors at the beginning of January 1920. This action, reported the RIC Inspector-General, 'has administered a severe check to the pretensions and prestige of Dáil Éireann'. Henceforth the revolu-. tionary government would operate underground.

By this time the ministry had already established a confidential office for central administration and communications, presided over by Diarmuid O'Hegarty in rooms on the first floor of a building at the corner of O'Connell and Abbey Streets. It remained unknown to the police until February 1920, when it was raided and following which O'Hegarty was sentenced to three months in jail for 'illegal assembly'. The Dáil secretariat thereupon moved around the corner to Middle Abbey Street, where it was undisturbed and where O'Hegarty resumed his work upon his release.

The dozen offices established by the Dáil were spread around Dublin, most of them being located in places convenient to the city centre. A few years later Free State army intelligence drew up a list of locations used during the 1919–21 period. With additions, this is the picture that emerges: the Department of Fisheries and the Industrial Resources Commission used one office each, while the Labour and Irish Language departments had two each; Foreign Affairs and Agriculture used three locations, and Trade and Commerce four; Home Affairs and Local Government had six different offices, and Defence seven. Finance used ten locations, and Propaganda fourteen. In addition to No. 76, the Dáil ministry purchased four other buildings, which were used for meetings, offices and hideouts. Most of the departments, however, rented office space, using various plausible front names. Nineteen residences and one hotel — Vaughan's in Parnell Square (now the head office of the Workers' Union of Ireland) were used for meeting places. On the few occasions when the Dáil convened after its proscription it met mostly in Alderman Walter Cole's large house in Mountjoy Square, but it also met at least once in the Oak Room of the Mansion House and in Fleming's Hotel in Gardiner Place, which was owned by Seán O'Mahony, T.D. In all, about eighty-five addresses were used to conduct the business of the counter-state. Very few of these were discovered by Castle authorities, although Dáil officials had to be constantly on guard.[10]

Ministers and officials of the Dáil circulated freely in the city. The best disguise was to present the appearance of ordinary citizens going about their business; it worked. This was, indeed, a 'government by bicycle'. 'It may be impossible to calculate', remarked Kathleen McKenna, 'what the bicycle meant to the great majority of those engaged in the conflict. Wherever one went, one encountered hunted men such as Collins, Mulcahy, Béaslaí, etc. pedalling along on high noisy "grids".' Máire Comerford recalled:

I soon knew the look of some of the bicycles ridden by the men we were trying to protect. Desmond FitzGerald seemed to have the same bit of string hanging from his carrier all the time I knew it. Mick Collins rode a very big, high framed black Lucania. Cathal Brugha's green Pierce was a sign that he was present in his office when one saw it in the corridor leading there. De Valera's very high machine with a strengthened frame was not, I think, ridden by him after 1916.

In fact de Valera continued to use a bicycle frequently when he was in Dublin. At the height of the Black and Tan period, in February 1921, he informed Diarmuid O'Hegarty that 'I will go on my bicycle to the usual house this evening for the meeting.' One night he was stopped for not having a lamp by a member of the Dublin Metropolitan Police, who addressed him by name and urged him to avoid being out at night in those dangerous times. 'It was a very common thing', a French journalist related, 'to recognise an Irish "Minister" in a cheerfully juvenile figure which flits past on a muddy bicycle, in a faded waterproof and a little cleft hat dripping under the pelting rain.' The scene, he added, was 'odd and delightful'. David Neligan had a bicycle story:

Collins had an old bicycle and the chain was faulty on it; it used to rattle against the frame. And one night a bloody awful fog came down. It was like a London peasouper, you couldn't see a shagging thing. So I was walking along Nassau Street minding my own business, you see, and I heard a rattle, this old banshee wail from the chain. 'Christ,' I said, 'that's Mick's old bicycle', and I stood in the middle of the tramline. So along comes Collins from Grafton Street corner with his dust coat flying, and when he sees me he says, 'Jesus, where did you come out of?' 'I heard the old bicycle,' says I. 'By Christ, that'll get you shot yet.' So he roared laughing.[11]

Communications between the departments in Dublin and with other parts of the country were maintained by a group of couriers or messengers. Each department had at least one of these, and most of the traffic went to the general communications centre, colloquially known as 'The Dump'. According to Robert Brennan, 'These couriers were of tremendous importance to the organisation and they had great responsibilities, though they seemed hardly to realise this. They were seemingly carefree messenger boys, flitting here and there on bicycles.' Despite the danger involved, 'there was no instance of even an accidental leakage of information on the part of any of the couriers'. Kathleen McKenna agreed with him that the messengers, all members of Fianna Éireann, were impervious to the offers of huge rewards for information about Dáil ministers and operations. 'Our lads carried, day after day,' she related, 'stones of paper, ink, envelopes to our "hideout" and day after day consigned this material in the form of seditious literature to the care of His Majesty's postal service.'

Two couriers, Dáithí Ó Donnchadha and Seán McGrath, were particularly important, as it was they who carried the funds of Dáil Éireann around the streets of the capital. Ó Donnchadha was the secretary of the Dáil trustees. A 'bowler-hatted, formally dressed businessman', he paraded with aplomb down the roads to the banks and Dáil offices carrying thousands of pounds. Máire Comerford related: 'He had to be ready at all times to be held up and searched, so he tried to keep the documents he carried in a form which would mislead the enemy. The Home Affairs Dept was entered as "Arthur Holmes" and so on.' An unflappable man, on one occasion when his office was being searched by the police he 'lit the cigar he kept for emergencies and joined other interested spectators of the raid who dawdled in the street outside'. In contrast, Seán McGrath was a man of ordinary appearance and demeanour, but he was equally important as he carried the wages to the scattered employees of the Republic in Dublin. They called him 'Bainc ar Siubhall' ('the Walking Bank'), and, appropriately, his signature later appeared on Free State paper money. Neither of these two couriers was arrested nor lost a penny — and this in a city supposedly filled with spies, touts and intelligence agents of the *ancien régime*!

Members of the Cumann na mBan were used mainly for communications with other parts of the country. This organisation, founded in 1913 and with about 3,000 members by 1920, provided other support services, including intelligence gathering. Seán Harling, the President's messenger, later described his method for summoning members of the Dáil for a meeting: each deputy had a girl assigned to him to whom Harling would write a letter, as from a boyfriend, asking her to visit him in Dublin on a certain date; she would then inform the deputy. Not until he got to Dublin was he informed where and exactly when the meeting would be held. The general secretariat dispatched the following message to deputies on one occasion: 'The meeting will take place on Tuesday morning at the usual hour, and the place will be notified to you verbally.' As the Dáil administration developed, however, the efforts of Cumann na mBan were increasingly supplemented by the IRA network, a burden which was objectionable to that body. Members of the Volunteers had more important things to do than deliver mail for the civil side of the movement. Mrs Tom Clarke advised Diarmuid O'Hegarty in June 1921 that Volunteer messengers should 'avoid all appearances of military training'.[12]

Being driven underground certainly had an effect on Dáil Éireann: it met only eight times between September 1919 and July 1921. At its first meeting after being declared illegal, that of 27 October, nineteen members were advised not to attend. The assembly did not meet again until eight months later, on 29 June 1920. Joseph MacDonagh, TD, wrote to O'Hegarty in February 1920 to find out what had happened to the Assembly of Ireland. Not having been summoned to a meeting since August, he was 'being forced to the conclusion that private members are to abstain from Dublin as well as Westminster'. O'Hegarty replied that 'The difficulty is, of course, to prevent the enemy from discovering that a meeting is being held.' MacDonagh had to wait five months for the next meeting of the Dáil. Yet only a few deputies were arrested during 1919.

Repression also had an effect on the Dáil leadership. In the middle of 1919 one minister, three department directors and two propagandists were arrested. These were Constance Markievicz, Robert Barton, Laurence Ginnell, Ernest Blythe, Piaras Béaslaí and Frank Gallagher. None of them were in prison for long. Barton and Béaslaí escaped, Blythe was released after twenty days, and Markievicz, Ginnell and Gallagher served four months. These actions by the Castle authorities had only a slight effect on the developing Dáil administration; it was in the following year that they were to have a serious impact. By March 1920, of the sixty-nine members of the Dáil, all but nine had been or were in prison or were being sought by the RIC; six of the nine were then outside Ireland.[13]

(4) FINANCING THE COUNTER-STATE

By the middle of 1919 the emerging counter-state had mounting financial commitments. First there were the ministerial salaries, which cost about £4,100 a year. The salary of the President was set at £500 per annum; the seven ministers received £350 each, and the three directors of departments got the same amount. Although they received no salary, deputies did receive transportation and hotel expenses. Later, in September 1920, deputies were given up to £250 annually for expenses. Then there were eight officials, ranging from the Secretary to the Ministry (£500 per annum) to a messenger (£52 per annum), whose salaries amounted to about £1,700 annually. There was also the cost of the Paris office, which had a staff of four, with salaries amounting to £1,100 a year and other expenses ranging up to several thousand pounds. Over £6,000 was approved by the cabinet for this operation between February and June 1919. The Dáil voted £10,000 annually for the new consular service and another £10,000 for the fisheries programme. Even if its operations remained at this level (and excluding the American campaign), the new government would need £25,000 annually. The American operation would be costly, and the 'constructive programme' would plunge the new state into much greater expenditure. The need for income was now predominant.

Despite some hopeful prognostications, the ministry clearly believed that an attempt to divert revenue — particularly income tax — from the British exchequer to the Dáil government would have scant results. Arthur Griffith told the Dáil that of the £23 million collected in 1918 only £6 million was from income tax, £4 million of which was paid by 'people out of sympathy with them'. That left £2 million, of which not more than half a million was paid directly. He argued that the only other area in which they could stop revenue flowing to the British treasury was excise tax, principally on beer, spirits and tobacco, which amounted to £3 million. This might reduce British revenue, but it would also affect the Irish producers of such products. Moreover, it would not provide funds for Dáil Éireann. However, the arguments against trying to tap income and excise taxes were not conclusive, as Michael Collins later proposed to tackle the matter; in the end nothing came of this.

The new government would not be able to do very much without money, and it had been in a financial bind from the beginning. Sinn Féin had provided a loan of £1,300 to cover the expenses of launching the Dáil. A few individuals also lent money. Anna O'Rahilly made a loan of £2,000, and Sheila Humphries lent £1,000. But even a very small government body could not be financed on that basis. When Michael Collins became Minister for Finance at the beginning April 1919, a source of income was tantalisingly close at hand — the £250,000 that had been subscribed to the anti-conscription fund in mid-1918 and which was being disbursed in the spring of 1919.[14]

When the custodian of the money, the Mansion House Committee, announced that local public meetings would be held on 2 March to decide on the disposition of the funds, there was a scramble between Sinn Féin and the Catholic Church, with the church winning hands down. Most of the money was held by parish priests, who were the local trustees of the fund. Despite the pleas of Sinn Féin collectors, the great majority of the meetings gave nothing to Dáil Éireann. According to the RIC Inspector-General, £164,000 was returned to subscribers or 'applied to ecclesiastical charities' (no further breakdown), £21,000 went to the Mansion House Committee (for what purpose?), £50,000 was unclaimed, and only £17,000 went into the party's 'Self-Determination Fund'.[15]

What this episode demonstrated was that if Dáil Éireann was going to finance its programme, it would have to appeal directly to the people. At the same time another possible source of funding appeared. In the USA the Friends of Irish Freedom had launched an 'Irish Victory Fund' which had collected a million dollars by February 1919. Michael Collins responded with alacrity when he learned this. Together with Cathal Brugha, he wrote to Diarmuid Lynch, a member of the Dáil now resident in America, where he held the post of secretary of the FOIF: 'We want £5,000 at once.' The money had been collected, however, not to support the independence movement in Ireland, but for American political purposes. After considerable reluctance and delay, the organisation finally sent $10,000.[16]

At his first public appearance in America, Eamon de Valera announced the establishment of a loan fund, the goal initially being to raise $5 million dollars, but quickly increased to $25 million. Now that it had a programme before the public and with a loan campaign being organised in the USA, the Dáil appealed to the Irish people for money. On 4 April the Dáil voted to authorise the ministry to 'issue Republican Bonds to the value of £250,000'. To Stephen Gwynn this was an ambitious goal. He recalled that when the Irish Parliamentary Party had raised £10,000 'we thought it was a big achievement'. He noted, however, that there was a popular expectation that the Dáil appeal would succeed, commenting: 'If this forecast proves to be true, Sinn Féin would need to be taken very seriously indeed. Money talks! It would mean that the peasant farmers are really in it.'

The man who was to lead the loan drive was Michael Collins. With little or no interest in platform oratory or nationalistic journalism, Collins, in addition to being a man of energy and action, was also a skilful organiser and superlative administrator. He was indeed, a 'wonder man'. Eamon de Valera said of him that he was one of the two men (the other was Seán Lemass) he had known who always wanted to take immediate action once a decision had been reached. His impatience and outspokenness aroused resentment and hostility among some of his associates, but he drove the movement forward. A country boy from Co. Cork, he had been ten years in London as a post office clerk. Having taken part in the 1916 rising, he gained administrative experience in the prisoners' dependants' organisation. His principal activity from 1917 onwards was in reviving the Irish Republican Brotherhood and expanding the Irish Volunteers. But as the result of the massive loan campaign, his name became a household word. Although he was to achieve fame for his other activities, it was through his financial leadership that he reached the first rank of Irish politics, a position he retained and reinforced until his death just three years later.[17]

Collins first organised a finance committee composed of sixteen members of the Dáil which met in the summer of 1919; then four

provincial organisers were appointed in October. At this juncture
Collins wanted speed: 'The work must go ahead rapidly. It will be
essential to get on with a rush.' He anticipated opposition from Dublin
Castle, including press censorship, during the campaign. This was all
the more reason 'for increased individual effort on the part of all
members of the Dáil'. He told the fund-raisers:

> It is urgent that you should get the painting squads who did such
> service during the General Election at work. . . . The dead wall, etc.
> should be covered with such inscriptions as 'England fears the Loan',
> 'Buy Dáil Éireann Bonds', 'Put your money on Ireland', etc.

He personally held a public meeting in his constituency of South Cork
and subscribed £25.[18]

A short film about the loan, which showed Collins receiving
applications, was produced by the Irish Film Company at the cost of
£600. Members of the Irish Volunteers arranged that the film have
unscheduled showing in cinemas around the country. Copies were sent
to the USA, Collins being informed that 'they have been of very great
service there', and another was sent to Australia.

The loan campaign was launched in early September. Progress initially
was slow. An RIC intelligence report noted that although the country 'was
flooded with Loan literature' and that 'no pains have been spared to
obtain subscriptions', there was considerable resistance to the drive. On
the other hand, the Dáil's *Irish Bulletin* reported that 'All over Ireland
police were engaged in tearing down posters advertising the Irish National
Loan.' Reflecting the confidence of the Dáil leadership, Diarmuid
O'Hegarty, the Secretary to the Ministry, declared privately: 'Feeling in
Ireland is very sound and we expect to get the full amount subscribed.' He
recognised that it would require a concerted effort: 'It means getting
everybody's coat off.' By the end of October £19,160 had been subscribed.

Collins decided to risk advertising the loan in newspapers. Of course, it
would be at their risk, not his. He prepared an appeal that made no
mention of Dáil Éireann. The two Dublin nationalist dailies, on being
informed by Dublin Castle that publication of the prospectus was illegal,
declined to print it. The only daily paper in which it appeared was the *Cork
Examiner*. It was also published in twenty-two separatist and provincial
weekly papers. Darrell Figgis, himself the editor of a nationalist print,
recognised Collins's strategy: 'All of us who owned journals were to be
thrown cheerfully into the conflagration, the blaze of which would prove
a much more successful advertisement than any mass of printed matter.'
Injured party that he was, Figgis had to admire Collins's audacity: 'It had
the touch of largeness that, with his new responsibilities, he was now
beginning to acquire.'[19]

When these papers printed the loan prospectus, they were closed
down. The provincial papers were allowed to reopen after a few days,

but seven Dublin partisan papers were permanently banned. As a result, the Sinn Féin press virtually disappeared for almost two years. Griffith's *Young Ireland* did not publish the loan advertisement and was the only Sinn Féin paper to operate in Ireland during that period. *New Ireland* circumvented its suppression by changing its name to *Old Ireland* and by being printed in Scotland.

By this time the British government had concluded that Dáil Éireann and its infant administration would not disappear in a wave of Irish satire and cynicism; a new feeling was abroad. People were beginning to take the emerging institution seriously, or at least it took itself seriously. Dublin Castle decided to act against its impudent rival. On 11 September it issued a proclamation suppressing Dáil Éireann. Ian Macpherson, the Chief Secretary, privately explained why he acted at this time: 'We had to allow these members to sit together in consultation if they wished', but when 'they conspired by executive acts . . . to overthrow the duly constituted authority, then we could act'.

The newly established headquarters of Dáil Éireann at 76 Harcourt Street was raided by police and military on the night of the 11th, and nine staff members were arrested. The reaction of Griffith and other Dáil leaders was that Dublin Castle had not moved until it saw that the Irish assembly meant business. Griffith viewed this act of repression with contempt: 'Neither their goals nor their bullets nor their bayonets will prevent us from carrying on the trust the Irish people gave us.' He affirmed that the loan campaign would go forward and that the suppression of the Dáil 'would be worth a million votes to Sinn Féin in America'. 'The more extreme section of Sinn Féin and the leaders of the Volunteers', related the Dublin correspondent of an English paper, 'are jubilant at the action of the Government in giving the public this further proof of the virility of their organisation.' The *Manchester Guardian* believed that Dublin Castle had 'saved Sinn Féin from the consequences of a first-class blunder'. Supporters of the parliamentary party were awaiting the results of the loan campaign 'with amused expectancy', it said, but the suppression 'ensured a first-class subscription, irrespective of the prospects of a dividend'.

The actions did not mark the end of Dáil Éireann or its loan campaign. The small Dáil administration went underground, establishing a network of disguised offices throughout the city, mostly in the quays area on both sides of the Liffey. When Griffith was asked in November 1919 what would happen if all the members of the Dáil were arrested, he commented that plans had been made for that possibility and that 'there is a second line of defence and a third'.

The attacks on the fledgling counter-state and the republican press were a stimulus to the promotion of the loan, to which the small farmers — a vital element — were already subscribing in large numbers. Bryan Cooper, a former press censor, believed that the policy of suppressing newspapers was futile, as Sinn Féin had secret printing-presses; it was his opinion that Dublin Castle's action had given the loan campaign 'the best advertisement it could possibly desire'. Diarmuid O'Hegarty wrote to Seán T. O'Kelly:

> The British are out after the Loan — neck or nothing. . . . But the loan gets merrily on. They appear to have got into a blue funk about it, but they cannot stop its progress. Their activities so far have been an asset.

In the view of the ex-parliamentarian Stephen Gwynn, 'Things have got to the point that the Government cannot check the growth of Sinn Féin: any repressive action can only increase its power.' The London *Times* man in Dublin was doubtful about these actions: 'The purpose is, no doubt, to prove that Sinn Féin does not "pay"'; yet no countervailing effort was 'being made to win back to the support of law and order the great number of moderate Irishmen who have become only too ready to excuse, though not commend, the actions of the extremists'. The correspondent of the *Daily Herald* was deeply impressed by the rebel government's resilience: 'Suppressed though it may be, the Republic . . . commands the unforced obedience of the Irish people.' 'This invisible Republic', he observed, 'exists in the hearts of the men and women of Ireland and wields a moral authority which all the tanks and machine-guns of King George cannot command.'[20]

The Catholic hierarchy generally did not provide support, but three prelates did publicly back the drive — Bishop Fogarty of Killaloe, of course; Archbishop Harty of Cashel, who declared that 'Ireland is in a state of political and industrial bondage' and who hailed de Valera as 'the trusted representative of the Irish people'; and, most importantly, Archbishop Walsh of Dublin, who wrote to Cardinal O'Connell of Boston: 'None of our newspapers dare publish the fact that I have subscribed. We are living under martial law.'

The Minister for Finance carefully monitored progress. In one constituency his anger boiled over concerning 'the bloody pack down there and their casual, meaningless, purposeless way of carrying on'. Collins told Harry Boland: 'This enterprise will certainly break my heart. I never imagined there was so much cowardice, dishonesty, hedging, insincerity and meanness in the world.' In March Griffith sent a letter to deputies 'whose constituencies are bad', and Collins sent out a 'black list' of laggard constituencies. Although he regretted this action, Diarmuid O'Hegarty argued that 'If it only succeeds in shaming the slackers into some sort of activity, it will have served a useful purpose.'[21] A number of loan workers were arrested, including Alex McCabe, T.D. for South Sligo, who was sentenced to nine months' hard labour for his activities.

Dublin Castle asserted that Sinn Féin and, more particularly, the IRA were pressuring wealthy Unionists to subscribe. Captured lists of subscribers included the names of individuals who were strongly opposed to Irish separatism. It is conceivable but unlikely that some Unionists purchased bonds as insurance for the future. Stephen Gwynn declared that the republicans were employing the methods of a 'regime of forced levy, effectively carried out and producing large sums'. Recollecting this period in Co. Clare, Edward MacLysaght saw the matter differently: 'If any further proof of the whole-hearted support of the people were wanted it would be furnished by the remarkable response on the part of the small farmers — never too eager to subscribe to sentimental causes — when Michael Collins launched the First Dáil Loan.'

Denied access to Irish newspapers, the Minister for Finance looked abroad. The European edition of the *Chicago Tribune* published a full-page advertisement for the loan (at the cost of 8,400 francs). Seán T. O'Kelly admitted privately that 'the result of the advertisement so far has not been very encouraging'. Loan notices also appeared in Catholic weeklies in Britain. Again the response was discouraging. The Dáil's representative in London, Art O'Brien, noted: 'Not one of our monied people here in London gave any support.' Collins called it 'a bad all-round performance'. The total amount raised in Britain and France was £11,719 8s.[22]

Just as the campaign reached high gear, Dublin Castle took measures that threatened to destroy the effort. At the end of January 1920 police raided a thousand houses and arrested eighty-six persons, including six members of the Dáil and several local office-holders. Then, at the beginning of March, the Castle administration launched an effort to find out where the loan subscriptions were being lodged. First came a raid on the Sinn Féin Bank, in which about £11,116 in cash and £7,204 in deposits (later returned) were confiscated. Then officials of the major banks received summonses to bring their records of depositors to an inquiry that opened on 8 March.

The two Dublin nationalist daily newspapers vehemently opposed this action, while the Dáil publication, the *Irish Bulletin*, centred its attention on the man who was conducting the inquiry. In a series of articles it denounced Alan Bell as a secret service agent whose record of opposition to Irish nationalism extended back to the Land League days. It quoted a London paper that described Bell as 'a man utterly unscrupulous and a perfect liar'. The inquiry came to an abrupt end when Bell was killed by members of the IRA on 26 March 1920. Collins reported to the Dáil in the following June that the load funds 'are perfectly safe as the non-success of the bank inquiry will assure you all'. In the same month funds of the Sinn Féin Bank that had earlier been seized by the British forces were returned.

On the only occasion when the crown forces managed to get hold of a substantial amount of Dáil money it was not in the form of subscriptions to the Dáil Loan, although the funds very likely were derived from that campaign. Some papers of Richard Mulcahy captured on 26 October during a raid conducted by Ormonde Winter, the new head of British intelligence, led to the seizure of funds in a Dublin bank. Winter's associate, Mark Sturgis, noted in his diary that Winter 'had been pinching M.C.'s "war chest" from the Munster and Leinster Bank — quite illegally I expect — brought in about £4,000. £15,000 more to come.' This money was undoubtedly the £18,732 reported as seized in an auditor's report on Dáil finances for the last half of 1920. The amount impounded in the period up to the truce of July 1921 was £23,000, of which £20,000 plus £2,000 interest was repaid to the Provisional Government in 1922. This was the only money that British forces managed to secure of the hundreds of thousands of pounds that passed through the hands of the Department of Finance.[23]

Collins set 17 July as the closing date of the campaign. He told the Dáil that by making this the firm closing date he wanted 'to dispel the idea that the Loan Fund was going to drag on indefinitely'; it would, he maintained, help to assure the success of a new loan appeal in the future. Funds continued to be collected until September, the final figure being £371,849 1s. Approximately 150,000 individuals had suscribed to the loan; this represented about 15 per cent of the approximately one million households in the country. Collins declared that loan expenses were 2 per cent of the money raised. In addition, the Self-Determination Fund (contributions to the cause, not money loaned) had raised £55,770 9s 3d, of which £22,607 6s had come from supporters in the United States.

By this time money from the loan drive in America began to arrive. The amount received in Dublin by mid-1920 was £58,880 14s. This was only a small part of the funds collected in the USA; the head office in New York reported that it had received $2,995,643.27 (approximately £750,000) by 17 May 1920. Although there were reports of considerable sums being collected in Australia, up to this time only £175 had been received. Final figures show that the early lead provided by Mid-Cork and West Limerick was surpassed by Cork City (£12,067) and East Limerick (£32,285, the largest amount raised in any constituency). The constituency leader in Connacht was South Mayo (£7,057); in Leinster, Leix and Offaly together gave £10,030; and in Ulster the leading contributor was South Monaghan (£5,705). Subscriptions were lowest, naturally, in areas of Unionist domination. Mid-Antrim contributed £162, while East and North Antrim together gave only £196, and West Down £199. The nine Belfast constituencies averaged £261. Pockets of Parliamentary Party strength also were niggardly: Waterford City (£636), East Wicklow (£819) and Dublin's Harbour Division — Alfie Byrne's former constituency — (£1,058). Not one of the eleven constituencies in Dublin city and county contributed funds that reached the national average (£3,629). Michael Collins's own constituency of South Cork raised £4,875, which was well below the average for Munster (£7,501).

The results were a strong endorsement of Dáil Éireann by the south and west, a weaker response in the midlands and the metropolis and pronounced rejection in most of Ulster. The loan drive followed the local election returns, and a substantial body of people backed their votes with their money. The English *Daily Sketch* (17 May 1920) drew this lesson from the effort: 'The financing of revolutionary activities is secured for some years to come and unpaid service is so general in the organization that funds are not being extravagantly spent.'

The Dáil's finance committee had also proposed to set up a gold reserve. Collins wrote to the local Sinn Féin bodies: 'I ask you to get all the Gold you can', as it was one and a half times as useful as English paper money in international exchange. Only £800 in gold was received by late October 1919, but this rose to £10,105 10s by the end of April 1920. Batt O'Connor, who secreted the metal, subsequently revealed that it eventually totalled a value of £25,000; in August 1921 Collins told the Dáil that there was 'a sufficient Gold Reserve'.[24]

The Dáil had secured the financial foundation it needed to create an alternative administration; now it was faced with the challenge of doing just that.

(5) DÁIL ÉIREANN AND THE IRISH VOLUNTEERS

Questions of Authority and Allegiance

The campaign to secure tangible public support and a financial base for the alternative government did not take place in a void; rather, it took place side by side with a growing campaign of violence conducted by the Irish Volunteers. It should be recalled that the reorganisation of separatist forces in 1917 involved three different bodies. The new or revived Sinn Féin was a coalition of republicans and those who would settle for less than complete independence. There was also the Irish Volunteers; this was not a coalition but a united body committed to an independent republic and the employment of physical force to achieve it. Lastly, there was the Irish Republican Brotherhood, a secret, conspiritorial society with the same objectives as the Volunteers.

The by-elections of 1917–18, the conscription crisis and the general election all emphasised political activity; the physical-force organisation was in the background, and membership of the Volunteers declined sharply. To the supporters of violence the imminent establishment of Dáil Éireann probably was viewed as a development that would further reduce the position of the physical-force party. A group of the Volunteer leaders in Tipperary — Dan Breen, Séamus Robinson, Seán Treacy and Seán Hogan — decided to make a demonstration of their belief that Ireland would not secure self-government by peaceful means alone. On the day of the opening of the Dáil the exuberant gunmen of South Tipperary led an attack on a police convoy at Soloheadbeg in which two policemen were killed. That these two events were not merely coincidental was later made clear by both Dan Breen and Séamus Robinson, two of the principal participants in the attack.

At the initial public meetings of the Dáil no reference was made to the Soloheadbeg incident or to the new government's relationship to the Irish Volunteers. But according to Richard Mulcahy, Assistant Minister for Defence, at the first private meeting of the Dáil he made a statement on the condition of the Volunteers and their relationship to the parliamentary assembly. 'There was no explicit authority from the Executive of the Volunteers to do so, but the implication must be accepted' that the Dáil had authority over this force, 'as the Volunteers put themselves entirely at the disposal of the Dáil once the Dáil was elected'. In the Dáil proceedings for 1 April there is a bare notation that Mulcahy had given a report.[25]

There was a close connection between the Volunteers and the new assembly and government. Several leaders of the Volunteers were also members of both the Dáil and the cabinet. Indeed, the Chief of Staff of the military force, Cathal Brugha, was the first President of the Dáil. When he left this position in April upon the return of de Valera to Ireland, Brugha assumed direct responsibility for military matters as Minister for Defence. The new Chief of Staff, Richard Mulcahy, was both a member of the Dáil and Assistant Minister for Defence. De Valera, already President of both the Volunteers and Sinn Féin, became President of the Dáil.

The fact that the Volunteers now constituted a force that was under the authority of the Dáil was not stated publicly until much later, in the spring of 1921. That it was not done from the beginning or early on, Mulcahy has commented, 'was no embarrassment to members of the Dáil or Government', implying that it suited the new assembly and cabinet to evade this responsibility. He has also argued that this position was taken to protect members of the cabinet should they be arrested: 'We could not send the Members of the Cabinet into their Captors' hands with a rope tied round their necks.' The Volunteers' publication *An tÓglach* in its issue of 1 April 1919 sought to give the impression that the military force was coming under civil authority: 'The Volunteers are the right arm of the Irish Republic, the men who can be trusted to carry out the will of the Irish Government with the readiness and effectiveness of disciplined men.' This assertion, however, did not necessarily mean that what it said was true, that the Volunteers would be controlled and directed by the Dáil government. In fact, as time was to show, both the government and the army executive had difficulty imposing their control over the scattered units of the IRA.

On his election as head of the government on 10 April, de Valera referred to the relationship between state and army, informing the Dáil that the Minister for Defence was 'in close association with the Voluntary military forces which are the foundation of the National Army' — a statement which did not actually place the Volunteers under Dáil authority. Following de Valera's statement, and speaking in Irish, Piaras Béaslaí addressed the matter: the Volunteers 'are the army of Ireland and if they are under the control of the government, they must be loyal to the Assembly'. What he was proposing was a loyalty oath. Brugha, also speaking in Irish, made a general statement that gave the impression that the Volunteers were under his authority.

Brugha obviously saw that the situation was ambiguous, as he proceeded to get cabinet approval of an oath of allegiance that would be mandatory for all Volunteers, Dáil deputies and employees. At its August meeting the Dáil supported this position. The Volunteer executive accepted the oath, as well as the appointment of the Minister of Defence as its chairman. There appeared to be some reluctance to take the oath on the part of some Volunteers, particularly Collins and his IRB group. Yet Ernie O'Malley relates that Collins spoke approvingly of the oath: 'That will give us more status and it'll help some to realise that they're not joining us for fun.' Within the Volunteer organisation the proper method to amend its constitution was to hold a general convention, but since this was too dangerous a proceeding at that time, the change was secured through a mail poll and unit meetings held around June 1920 (though many Volunteers had already taken the oath as individuals long before this date). Collins wanted to make sure that all available deputies also took the oath, and twenty-six of them who had not been present at the October meeting did so at the June Dáil session.[26]

A more important matter was the question of who controlled the actions of the Volunteers. Neither the Dáil nor the cabinet ordered or supported an offensive policy by the army at this time. Nor did the headquarters staff. The army's publication, *An tÓglach*, urged that Volunteer units simply train and prepare for eventual action. Yet violent actions, at first scattered and spasmodic, were taken by Volunteer units. P. S. O'Hegarty, a Sinn Féin journalist, commented that the Volunteers 'had drifted into a guerrilla war, without conscious impulse. It just happened.' But it didn't just happen; at the local level unit commanders took the initiative in launching attacks, initially centred on the RIC, while the Dáil looked the other way.

Formally the Volunteer units were under the authority of an executive, renamed the 'headquarters staff', which was subordinated to the Ministry of Defence. On the other hand, these units were organised locally, were in existence before the creation of the Dáil, and elected their own officers. Yet the hand of national authority was not lacking even in mid-1919. In June 1919 the Sligo Brigade issued an order which declared that 'No officer or non-commissioned officer is to make any public speech' because 'the expression and spreading of political doctrine belongs to the Civil Power. Soldiers have no politics.' When a Sinn Féin organiser in Meath reported in August that 'prominent Volunteers seem to encourage amongst their men a feeling of contempt for the political side of the movement, and put it down as constitutionalism', the Volunteer executive reprimanded the local leaders. Later, in May 1920, Collins, as Adjutant-General, issued an order which stipulated that 'No Volunteer shall take upon himself the issue of any public proclamation in the name of the Irish Volunteers or of the Irish Republic without formal authority from Headquarters Staff.' The executive also asserted its authority by collecting affiliation fees from local units.

Then there was the Irish Republican Brotherhood, a secret organisation that continued in existence after the establishment of Dáil Éireann. It had been revived after the 1916 rebellion, although some former members, such as Cathal Brugha and Eamon de Valera, believed that it had outlived its usefulness. In May 1919 Michael Collins became its President, a position he retained until his death in August 1922. In response to the creation of the rebel republic and the mandatory oath of allegiance, the IRB amended its constitution in September 1919 to provide for these. The continued existence of the organisation, now under the vigorous direction of Collins, eventually created suspicion and conflict within the independence movement; the IRB was seen by its critics, particularly Brugha and eventually de Valera, as something like a government within a government. Yet during his long stay in the United States de Valera was aware of the activities of the organisation and its representative in America, Harry Boland, and did nothing to stop them; on the contrary, he viewed Boland's IRB work as a confidential matter and respected his need for secrecy.[27]

The War against the Royal Irish Constabulary

Rather than address the matter of the relationship between itself and the Volunteers or pronounce on the question of physical force, the revolutionary government turned to a campaign to isolate and render ineffective the Royal Irish Constabulary. But even here the Dáil and cabinet could not avoid the question of the relationship with the physical-force adherents.

The police force was widely disliked and even hated by many. Although its ranks were composed mainly of Catholics, almost all the county inspectors were Protestants; Kevin O'Shiel declared that conversion to Protestantism was the key to advancement to that level. Pádraic Colum believed that the part played by the RIC in the general round-up after the 1916 rebellion cast the police in the role of 'the most active and ubiquitious of the forces of repression'.

The Dáil decreed a peaceful boycott of the RIC on 10 April 1919; two weeks later Diarmuid O'Hegarty sent out a circular letter directing that the police should be treated as 'persons who, having been adjudged guilty of treason to their country, are regarded as unworthy to enjoy any of the privileges or comforts which arise from cordial relations with the public'. Sinn Féin and Cumann na mBan provided the enforcement. The party issued specific instructions to all its *cumainn*: 'Avoid all social intercourse. No salutations. No social contact. If they attend, you leave. Avoid places where police known to visit, particularly public houses which they frequent.' Members were instructed to report the names of persons having social contact with the RIC to *cumann* officers, who should keep a list of such persons. But when this non-violent campaign was accompanied by Volunteer attacks on the police, the Dáil leadership said nothing.

Even before the Dáil acted, the organ of the Irish Volunteers had taken the initiative. In its issue of 26 February 1919 *An tÓglach* declared that: 'Any policeman, warder, judge or official must be made to realise that it is not wise for him to distinguish himself by undue zeal in the service of England.' Kevin O'Shiel later explained that because of the RIC's local knowledge and influence, action against that body was imperative: 'There was obviously no alternative for the Dáil Government but to strike at it in the first place and render it innocuous before the RIC had time to destroy that Government as, otherwise, it certainly would and could have done.' De Valera told the Dáil that the members of the RIC 'are spies in our midst. They are England's janissaries. . . . They are the eyes and ears of the enemy.' He indicated that the boycott was to be social in nature; he said nothing about violence. Later, addressing the Sinn Féin *ard-fheis*, he was reported to have opposed the shooting of policemen.[28]

The campaign against the RIC obviously had become effective within weeks of its inauguration in April. According to Kevin O'Shiel, most people supported the boycott 'with remarkable unanimity and in a remarkably short space of time'. Joseph Byrne, the Inspector-General of the police, reported that by August 1919 'in a large area the police without the assistance of troops would be totally unable to maintain any semblance of order'. In the following month Dublin Castle announced that RIC would be supplied with hand-grenades. By the end of the year the breakdown of law enforcement was apparent to others. The president of the Under-Sheriffs' Association complained in December that his members 'found it impossible to carry out their duties under present conditions'. In order to shore up the RIC, civil servants were asked to serve as special constables; however, there were few volunteers, and the idea was dropped, but not before the *Freeman's Journal* suffered temporary suspension for denouncing the proposal. The *Irish Statesman* saw in this action the hand of tyranny: 'It has come to this — that in the eyes of the law under which we live any criticism of the Executive Government is an offence.' The London *Daily News* reported:

> Both the official Sinn Féin Party and the unofficial groups of gunmen have their spy service in the very heart of the Government machine. The old position, where there was always a traitor among the Irish revolutionaries, has been completely reversed. The conspirators are now well informed and the Government utterly in the dark.

That the situation had indeed changed substantially can be discerned from a number of contemporary reports and comments. On 4 November the commandant of the Mid-Clare Brigade of the IRA wrote to Michael Collins: 'We failed to decode police wires this month. Will you please let me have this month's code as soon as possible.' The code was promptly dispatched. Frederick Dumont, the American consul in Dublin, was impressed with the rebel intelligence network: 'Nothing occurs in Ireland that the wonderful espionage system organized by Sinn Féin does not cover. This very espionage system, supposedly unpaid, shows the hold that Sinn Féin has either through fear or affection.' He told his superiors in Washington that 'No conversation can be conducted over the public telephone without it being known or reported to Sinn Féin.' With this all-encompassing system, he concluded, the leaders of the political side of the movement must have known who was conducting the campaign of the assassination of policemen.[29] What Dumont did not realise was that the intelligence network was supplying information to Michael Collins in his capacity of GHQ Director of Intelligence, not to the cabinet or officials of Dáil Éireann.

The boycott of the RIC was accompanied by violent attacks on the police by Volunteer units. There is evidence that both the cabinet and the Volunteer executive tried to curb the desire of many of the Volunteers for action. In Tipperary Seán Treacy and Dan Breen sought authority to issue a proclamation ordering all British forces out of the county, but the Volunteer executive and the Dáil leaders refused to give permission. As a substitute for this, the Tipperary units (followed by those in Clare and Cork) issued a proclamation denouncing the RIC as 'traitors as well as spies and shall be treated as traitors deserve' and forbidding citizens of the Irish Republic to answer 'any question whatsoever to representatives of the enemy or assist them in any way'. The proclamation issued by the IRA Western Command in Cork declared:

> This is not an appeal, but an Order from the Irish Republican Government. To those who ignore it will be meted out the punishment of traitors. Fraternising with the enemy cannot be tolerated.

Physical assaults on the police apparently received popular support. Following an attack on police in Co. Cork in the same month, the RIC district officer reported that 70 per cent of the people were 'in sympathy with the attackers' and that 'the police had been attacked, boycotted and impeded in every possible way'. When an RIC inspector was shot dead in the street of Thurles, Co. Tipperary, in June, one witness declared: 'The crowd jeered, and there were cries "Up the Republic". There was not the least sympathy for the unfortunate man. Public bodies did not pass a resolution. Scarcely a blind was drawn on the day of the funeral.'

Hugh Martin, a perceptive English journalist, reported that 'the people's acute hatred of the police' was due 'to the fact that the police have been turned by the Irish Administration into a band of political spies and tale-bearers'. Lord French, the Lord Lieutenant, took most seriously this campaign to destroy the RIC. He told an English audience that the Dáil was a 'so-called, self-constituted, illegal, insane Government' which possessed a 'secret army, which they call the Irish Volunteers'. The army contained 'a body of assassins'; 'the result is a complete system of intimidation throughout the whole population', while police efforts to track down the assassins 'are rendered absolutely abortive'.

Not everyone agreed that the Dáil stood behind the campaign of violence. Charles Hathaway informed the US State Department in April 1919 that 'The dominant faction in the Sinn Féin organization headed by Mr de Valera is committed to passive methods and will probably control the situation even though the Peace Conference should break up without having done anything to give them hope.' In July he reported that the violence was 'presumably the work of a small coterie of Sinn Féin supporters, perhaps the Irish Republican Brotherhood', but that no nationalist politician dared to take a stand against them. The Dublin correspondent of the *Manchester Guardian* commented: 'One still believes that a system of private assassination is no part of the Sinn Féin campaign, and that these crimes are reprobated by Dáil Éireann itself.' He added that the *Irish Times*, 'the most influential Unionist newspaper in Ireland, seems to share this belief'. Most newspapers condemned the campaign. The *Dundalk Democrat*, for example, commented: 'The shooting of policemen, the raids for arms . . . are all attributed, rightly or wrongly, to the revolutionary or "active" wing of the movement of which the Dáil is the political head. We do not think these things can serve the cause of Sinn Féin in the long run.' Roger Sweetman, the only member of the Dáil to address this matter, was critical of the campaign of violence. He declared in a letter to the London *Times* that 'Ireland was fighting for the moral case of the freedom of nations' and that those who supported that great cause ought not to degrade or spoil it by employing violence.[30]

RIC intelligence reported in July 1919 that Father O'Flanagan and Eoin Mac Néill were strongly opposed to physical force and were threatening to resign from Sinn Féin unless it stopped its campaign. In August police intelligence related that a conference was held between the physical-force advocates and the Dáil executive at which 'the former agreed to be guided by the advice of the Dáil until the return of de Valera, on the assurance that the Dáil, if its methods fail, would fall back on the organised manhood of their organisations to rid the country of their enemies'. Darrell Figgis, a supporter of the old, non-violent Sinn Féin, viewed the campaign against the police as part of a cunning ploy on the part of the Volunteers to condition the Irish public to the use of physical force:

> The ground was well chosen, and the gains were many. The first gain was that the civil work of the RIC practically ceased. . . . The second gain, from the point of view of those who planned this campaign, was that the people were being attuned to the thought of the appeal to armed force. The third gain was that the RIC were steadily withdrawn from all isolated barracks and concentrated in the larger, more central barracks, leaving large tracts of county to be controlled and policed completely by IRA.

In fact Figgis was right. According to Richard Mulcahy, it was the policy of the Volunteer executive to lead the Irish people gradually to accept the use of violence to attain self-government.[31]

If there was support for the campaign of violence, there was also widespread opposition. The press was generally critical, while the county councils of Leitrim, Meath and Westmeath and the Dublin and Cork city councils passed resolutions against the campaign of violence. The *Irish Independent* condemned the killing of people in the cause of Irish freedom in December 1919 — only to have its premises invaded by a body of fifty men who wrecked its printing works.

Leaders of the Catholic Church also joined the chorus of opposition. Cardinal Logue repeated his Lenten denunciation of secret societies, and the three other archbishops, Walsh of Dublin, Harty of Cashel and Gilmartin of Tuam, rejected murder as a political weapon. There was also opposition at parish level. Father Nicholas Lawless, parish priest of Faughart, Co. Louth, proclaimed:

> Today Ireland is a political Sahara, littered with the dry bones of Sinn Féin pledges. Germany is down, and Paris gone. America is arranging treaties and alliances with England, and yet there are Irishmen mad enough to think that Britain trembles when a young policeman is shot in Connaught.

In October 1919 Dr Walter McDonald, a Maynooth professor, published *Some Ethical Questions of Peace and War, with special reference to Ireland,* in which he denied that anyone had the moral right to use physical force to secure national independence.

Standing alone among the hierarchy was Bishop Fogarty of Killaloe, who refused to condemn 'outrages': 'Why should I?' he asked. 'Why should Bishops be asked to become police agents? . . . I will not permit myself to become a tool of any political agitation.' A Sinn Féin journalist, Frank Gallagher, asserted that 'The Irish people no longer take seriously pulpit denunciations of political activities, however extreme these activities may have been.' After three years, he said, the people 'realise that the heads of their church are either unable or unwilling to see the death-struggle of a nation in its proper perspective, and that these dignitaries prefer to defame rather than to aid those prominent in the struggle'. The Inspector-General of the RIC privately shared Gallagher's view on weakened clerical influence. In his report for August 1919 he commented that 'There is good reason to believe that already the priests have to a considerable extent lost influence over their parishioners.'

Those in the leadership of the Protestant fold reiterated their opposition to Irish nationalism. Archbishop Crozier of Armagh declared that he 'could not conceive how anyone who worshipped in the form provided by the prayer book of the Church of England or the Church of Ireland could be anything but loyal'. The Provost of Trinity College, Dr John Bernard, offered a hard-hitting assessment of the activities of Dáil Éireann: 'A conspiracy of crime organised on behalf of a mad and impossible project of an Irish Republic existed, but it would never come.'

After Soloheadbeg the idea was floated around Sinn Féin circles in Dublin that the exuberant gunmen of South Tipperary should follow the example of others who had done some shooting and then slipped away to the the United States. Michael Collins is said to have made arrangements for this. They refused to go. Seán Treacy declared: 'Any fool can shoot a peeler and run away to America.' The action at Soloheadbeg forced the question of what policy the Dáil and the Volunteers should follow in dealing with the police and military. The Dáil leadership obviously was opposed to a policy of violence, hence its programme of peaceful ostracism of the RIC. What about the official position of the Volunteers? No clear policy position can be discerned in early 1919. Its executive neither condemned nor supported the shooting of policemen; it certainly did nothing to initiate similar action. Its policy at this time seems to be one of watching and waiting. Perhaps it is significant that when the executive was developing its staff structure, it did not establish an operations section.[32]

No major violent event took place for two months after Soloheadbeg, although there was a series of minor events — beatings of policemen, seizures of a few weapons, hunger-strikes, spectacular prison escapes. Prison breakouts became a familiar and important occurrence during 1919, stimulating to Sinn Féin morale and demoralising to Dublin Castle and its servants. Among those who escaped were many of the top rank of Sinn Féin: Eamon de Valera, Seán McGarry, Seán Milroy, Robert Barton, Piaras Béaslaí and Austin Stack. According to Máire Comerford, 'these rescues were the first official service performed by the Volunteers for elected constitutional government'.

Then, on 29 March, a resident magistrate in Westport, Co. Mayo, was shot and later died. This could be treated as an isolated incident, as it was not the policy of either the Volunteers or the Dáil to kill magistrates. On 6 April an attempt to rescue an imprisoned Volunteer in Limerick led to the deaths of two policemen; repressive measures by British forces initiated a two-week general strike in the city. The group of activists in South Tipperary were once again in action on 13 May, when Robinson, Breen and Treacy rescued Seán Hogan at Knocklong, Co. Limerick, and in doing so killed two policemen. This was followed by a wave of killing of policemen, eighteen of whom died violently from May to December 1919.

The Dáil and Volunteer leaderships responded to this development by trying to restrict or restrain actions by local Volunteer units. The IRA executive banned all attacks on police barracks without its prior approval. Then in the late autumn of 1919 it decreed that all Volunteer actions must be designed to avoid police casualties. This policy was adopted, according to Séamus Robinson, 'because the Government was anxious that no military action should be traced to its authority or to the IRA'. As we have seen, at the conference held in August between representatives of the Volunteers, Citizen Army and the Dáil executive, the military bodies agreed to be guided, for the time being, by the Dáil, while continuing nevertheless to keep their organisations in readiness for immediate action.[33]

But the Volunteer GHQ was not opposed to all action; it merely wanted selected action. In countermanding a plan of the East Clare Brigade for a general onslaught on the RIC in the late summer, Mulcahy maintained that 'the people had to be educated and led gently into open war'. According to Michael Hayes, Mulcahy was following the advice of Arthur Griffith, who urged that there should be no violence unless and until Dublin Castle proscribed Dáil Éireann. Fifty years later Mulcahy stated that this position was agreed to by both the Dáil cabinet and the army leadership, adding: 'It would not have been reasonable or useful to encourage an attitude of aggression as long as the Dáil was there for propaganda appeal purposes.' Following the suppression of the Dáil in September 1919, the Volunteer headquarters staff began to take the initiative. It launched a scheme to kill the viceroy, Lord French, and, after many false alarms, an abortive effort was made on 19 December 1919. GHQ was also responsible for the campaign of assassinating members of the political detective force in Dublin. Yet according to Mulcahy, provincial units were not given authority to attack police barracks until January 1920.

Bryan Cooper, perceptive Unionist observer of the Irish scene, commented in December 1919 that the gunmen had transformed the situation:

Six months ago Sinn Féin was a losing game, its leaders having staked their reputation on the recognition of Ireland's independence by the Peace Conference. The Government wisely turned a blind eye to the doings of Dáil Éireann, with the result that Ireland was amused rather than impressed by its somewhat farcical proceedings. Seeing the danger, the most extreme section of the Republican party determined to force the Government's hand by a campaign of assassination, and from that time the Irish Government has done precisely what the extremists wished them to do.

The unleashing of the local units of the IRA reinvigorated the organisation, and membership swelled. The executive, however, continued to keep a tight rein on its boisterous country cousins. It was not until July 1920 that it gave permission to attack British military facilities — provided there were no casualties on either side. How long this impractical policy was maintained or adhered to is unknown, but unrestricted attacks on police barracks and military patrols were common occurrences by the autumn of 1920. One of the principal advocates and practitioners of such action was Liam Lynch, commandant of the 2nd Cork Brigade, who held that 'The Army has to hew the way to freedom for politics to follow.'[34]

There were some in the Dáil leadership who were not in favour of physical force. The man who was on the spot in this matter and who bore the burden of public concern was Arthur Griffith, the Acting President of the Dáil. For many years he had advocated the policy of active, vigorous but non-violent resistance to British government in Ireland and the creation of alternative institutions. What was he to say, and what to do, about the IRA campaign? Publicly Griffith blamed all violence on the repressive actions of the RIC and British forces. He told a French journalist in February 1920: 'It is only natural that Sinn Féiners should defend themselves against the provocations and outrages to which they have been subjected.' He said the same thing to an Albert Hall audience at that time. Earlier — in November 1919 — he made a terse acknowledgment that the Dáil had an army, but otherwise said nothing on the subject. In private, as well, he usually kept his own counsel.

Eoin Mac Néill took the same public position as Griffith in regard to violence. In May 1919 he told a Scottish newspaper: 'As to the shooting of policemen, in all cases, as far as I know, these acts were committed in resistance to policemen engaged on purely repressive activities.' Darrell Figgis, another of the non-violent Sinn Féin element, commented on the outbreak of shooting:

Sinn Féin in remaining silent is simply pursuing what I may call the traditional foreign policy of Nationalist Ireland. When Parnell was asked what he was going to say in condemnation of the early agrarian outrages, he replied that if he and his followers had the government of the country in their hands, they would know how to stop them very soon, but that while others usurped that government Irishmen would refuse any measure of responsibility.

In making such a comment, Figgis conveniently overlooked the existence of the Dáil government, of which he was one of the highest-salaried employees.

In his memoirs, Figgis, a close associate of Griffith, argued that although Griffith was opposed to the IRA taking offensive action, he did not try to stop it, as the physical-force element had achieved so much in advancing the cause of self-government. P. S. O'Hegarty also held that Griffith was against the action of the IRA. When O'Hegarty informed him about a particularly alarming action that the Volunteers were planning in Cork city some time in 1920, Griffith commented: 'The military mind is the same in every country. Our military men are as bad as the British. They think of nothing but their own particular end, and cannot be brought to consider the political consequences of their proceedings.' On another occasion he said: 'I am old enough to remember the tail-end of the Fenians — the Invincibles. The danger of an armed movement is always that of turning the guns on one another.' He was greatly upset by the killing of a dozen British officers in Dublin in November 1920. These were occasional, private responses, not public ones. Richard Mulcahy related that in his frequent meetings with the Acting President, Griffith never gave him the impression that he opposed the methods being employed by the IRA. On the other hand, he never encouraged such action.

Griffith has been given credit for preventing at least three offensive actions by the Volunteers. One proposed operation was to assassinate Lord French during an Armistice Day parade in November 1919; another was Cathal Brugha's idea to shoot up the House of Commons; and the third was the one in Cork that O'Hegarty told him about. Just a month after Griffith prevented one of the attempts on French, however, there was an another, almost successful effort made to kill the Lord Lieutenant. He obviously knew nothing beforehand of the action that took place on 'Bloody Sunday' in November 1920. What emerges is a picture in which Griffith knew about some of the plans of the leadership of the IRA, but not about all of them. It would appear that in the early days he was generally consulted concerning these, but by the middle of 1920 this was not the case; the campaign had taken on a momentum of its own.

In the United States Eamon de Valera openly endorsed the use of physical force. In February 1920 he declared: 'Can we, struggling for our freedom, afford to fling away any weapon by which nations in the past achieved their freedom? We in Ireland hold today that we may not.' It is interesting that he made this statement to a group of Indian nationalists, whose leader, Gandhi, was an advocate of non-violent civil disobedience. In June 1920 de Valera requested that the Dáil appropriate a million dollars for the Department of Defence, a clear commitment to the programme of violence pursued by the IRA.

It should be recalled that for long neither the Dáil nor the cabinet assumed responsibility for Volunteer actions. A strange game of make-believe was being played; the situation was ludicrous and illogical. Cathal Brugha, as Minister for Defence, had achieved at least nominal control of the IRA, and yet the government of which he was a prominent member did not stand behind the deeds of the 'citizen-soldiers' of its army. How long the Dáil could dodge this matter, and what purpose was being served in not facing up to it, became a topic of concern in the ranks of the IRA. Ernie O'Malley told Frank Gallagher, editor of the *Irish Bulletin,* around December 1920: 'It's time for you to acknowledge the IRA at last, Frank.'[35]

Cathal Brugha and Richard Mulcahy

The military organisation of the independence movement was headed by Cathal Brugha, Minister for Defence, and Richard Mulcahy, Chief of Staff of the Irish Volunteers. Brugha, a native of Dublin and forty-five years old in 1919, was small and sallow, determined and fearless, and when he spoke he did so 'with directness and finality as if the matter had been thought out and was now finished'. A notable participant in the 1916 rebellion, he had for long been in the top leadership of the Volunteers, having served as its Chief of Staff from its reorganisation in October 1917 until March 1918, when he became head of its national executive. Thus he was the obvious choice to become the minister to deal with this organisation. As has been seen, he moved in August 1919 to draw this body into direct allegiance to the Dáil, and, over a period of months, its members conformed. Unlike almost all the other ministers, he maintained outside employment; he worked for Lalor's, a supplier of church candles.

Born in Waterford in 1886, Richard Mulcahy was a post office worker before his participation in the 1916 rebellion. He rose quickly in the revived Volunteers and succeeded Brugha as Chief of Staff in the spring of 1918. He was a successful candidate in Clontarf in the general election. He has been described as withdrawn, thoughtful and monkish. Frank O'Connor called him a 'born dreamer', but he also possessed intelligence, administrative ability and determination. His restraint served him well in dealing with superiors, principally Brugha, as well as with IRA commanders. Ernie O'Malley said of him that he 'could not be flurried or rushed. He had a quiet strength that was impressive.'[36]

Brugha's supervision of the IRA has often been characterised as loose and distant. Piaras Béaslaí said of him: 'He was hopelessly out of touch with our Army, and the realities of its situation. He hardly ever came into direct contact with any of the officers or men, except the heads of departments.' A minister in a government is supposed to formulate and direct policy and be responsible for all personnel within his jurisdiction, rather than direct actual operations. This was Brugha's conception of his responsibilities. He did not attend meetings of the Volunteer executive; rather, he received reports from its Chief of Staff and other members of the executive. What is not entirely clear is the extent to which he actually formulated policy for the IRA and, if he did, how much effect this policy direction had on operations. The IRA journal published no pronouncements from him, and the Dáil's official report almost always simply noted that he had given only an oral report about his department. Apparently there were no written reports. None have survived, and it is most unlikely that, given the need for security and Brugha's reticent nature, any ever existed.

There were several occasions when Brugha asserted his authority over the guerrilla force. When Collins's special 'squad' was preparing to wipe out a body of British secret intelligence agents in November 1920, Brugha vetted the evidence against each of the projected victims, rejecting evidence as insufficient in several cases. A pet project of his was to send a group of gunmen to London to shoot hostile British politicians. This operation was eventually aborted, its only tangible result being the capture of Seán Mac Eoin who who had been summoned by Brugha from his Longford hideout to Dublin to become part of the proposed group. At the beginning of 1921 he assumed a highly officious stance in demanding total accountability for funds expended when Michael Collins handed over the position of Director of Purchases to Liam Mellows.

There is no disagreement about Brugha being completely committed to the cause of the Republic, or concerning his experience, energy and intelligence. Throughout the period he was always readily available, either at work or at home. Thus it seems very doubtful that he was in any way slack or vague in the direction of his ministry. Mulcahy's typed reports to him were quickly returned with hand-written comments and orders. Yet he obviously did not have anything like full control of the actions of the Volunteers. In the first place, there were the members of the general staff, especially Michael Collins, who often carried on as though there was no Minister for Defence. Brugha's authority was necessarily limited by the political standing of several members of the headquarters staff. Ernie O'Malley commented on this situation: 'Why didn't the Staff pay attention to pure staff work, leaving the political field to the others?' The answer was that Collins and Mulcahy were both deputies and ministers. O'Malley thought it would have been better if Brugha had been a full-time minister, but it is difficult to see what more he could have done. After all, he was a minister, not a chief of operations, and the IRA was very much a decentralised organisation, operating effectively at the local or county levels. This characteristic of the IRA, in fact, constituted a further constraint on Brugha's authority. Many of the local units carried on as though there was neither an executive nor a minister. The difficulties of co-ordinating a guerrilla campaign go a long way towards explaining the lack of consistent, commanding authority at the top of the organisation. Decentralisation and local initiative were vital ingredients in the successes of Sinn Féin, Dáil Éireann and the IRA.

One of the most remarkable things about the period from January 1919 to July 1921 is that Cathal Brugha sat in his office in Lalor's candle works on Ormond Quay day after day, regularly receiving Volunteer personnel and reports from GHQ, and yet Dublin Castle did nothing about it. This situation can only be viewed as testimony to the ineffectiveness of the police intelligence system.

The activities of the Ministry of Defence and its army have only a shadowy presence in the official report of Dáil proceedings and in departmental reports. Brugha addressed the Dáil on military matters only seven times, and in only two instances was any information included in the record. The Dáil did not appropriate any funds for the military until November 1919. The previous June the cabinet had voted to provide £2,000 to the department, but this money was intended to pay for legal representation of imprisoned Volunteers. Not until the Dáil session of 29 June 1920 was there any open, direct appropriation of funds for Brugha's ministry. At that time the Dáil appropriated £10,175, as well as one million dollars (the dollars upon de Valera's request). Brugha informed the assembly on 6 August that he would use the smaller amount to carry out a complete reorganisation of his department (the results of which are not apparent). The million dollars was merely a grand political gesture; no attempt was made to spend this money for military purposes in Ireland. When the Dáil voted to create the office of accountant-general, Collins, as Minister for Finance, noted that 'The Department of Defence would in the nature of things be free from an examination of its accounts by the officer.'

It is obvious that during the first year and a half of its existence the Dáil and its defence ministry were not financing the activities of the IRA. During this time Collins, as Director of Purchases, was spending money to purchase weapons in Britain, while local Volunteer units financed their own activities. From June 1920 the Dáil began appropriating gradually increasing sums for the military. In the decisive six-month period preceding the truce of July 1921 the Ministry of Defence estimated expenses at £32,750 and spent £39,350. By any standard, this was revolution on the cheap.[37]

(6) The First Initiatives in Civil Government

While the Ministry of Finance was busy collecting the loan and the IRA was harassing the RIC, the government of Dáil Éireann launched its programme of constructive action. Among its first initiatives in civil government were the creation of a commission to survey the country's resources, a land bank, an afforestation scheme, a programme to stimulate fisheries, and an Irish language department. None of these projects were directly related to the core task of forging an alternative government, but they were activities that would demonstrate initiative and would rally public support. In addition, they were actions that could be taken with initially modest costs and where there was a lack of interest on the part of Dublin Castle. This was as much as the Dáil leadership believed it could do until it had adequate finances for more ambitious undertakings in assuming the government of Ireland.

Probing the Resources of Ireland

On the suggestion of Dr Brian Cusack, TD, the Dáil on 18 June 1919 voted to create a commission to investigate the resources and industries of the country. The proposal was one of long standing with Sinn Féin and had the present attraction of giving the appearance of activity and concern without committing substantial funds or of directly challenging the British regime. Who could object to such a beneficial activity? Darrell Figgis claimed that the commission was 'the first act of a constructive character' undertaken by the new government. He also noted that this was work that could be undertaken immediately, while 'other civil tasks had to wait before they could be effective till the network of the organisation of the Royal Irish Constabulary had been torn beyond recovery over large tracts of the country'.

The mandate of the commission was not only to investigate existing resources and industries but also to report on how they might be further developed. With £5,000 provided by the Dáil, Arthur Griffith issued invitations to sixty businessmen, scientists, industrialists and others asking if they would serve as unpaid members of the inquiry. Out of necessity as well as political wisdom, invitations were sent to persons who were not Sinn Féin supporters. Seán MacEntee, TD, an engineer by profession, regretted that the invitees were composed 'almost entirely of business men to the exclusion of representatives of manufacturing industries and of practical engineers'. Forty-nine persons accepted, including eight members of the Dáil, two professors, two Labour leaders (Thomas Johnson and William O'Brien) and one priest (Rev. Murtagh Farragher of the Aran Islands, who had started a fishing co-operative); there were no women members.

As secretary of the commission Griffith selected Darrell Figgis. Then thirty-seven years old, 'with a red pointed beard, green eyes and a commanding manner', Figgis had already lived an eventful life. Born in Dublin, he grew up on a tea plantation in India. On his return to Ireland in 1914, he became a writer and political activist. He was a key figure in the Howth gun-running, and, although he was in Achill at the time, was arrested in the wake of the 1916 rebellion. A prolific writer, he wrote about twenty books over a period of ten years, including novels and studies of other men of literature, all of which are now long out of print and almost forgotten. He rose quickly in the ranks of Sinn Féin and was elected one of the joint secretaries of the party in 1917; as such he represented the pre-1916 or non-violent rump that was merged with the militaristic group at that time. He was interned in the 'German plot' of the spring of 1918 and remained in prison until the general release of prisoners almost a year later. Almost alone among the leading figures in Sinn Féin, he was not selected as a party nominee for the general election. The men who controlled the selection process at the national level — Collins and Boland — sought to keep the opponents of violence out of nominations. Griffith and Mac Néill could not be overlooked; men of lesser stature like Figgis could be. Moreover, Figgis was widely disliked. Robert Brennan has said of him that 'Despite untiring efforts to turn on charm, he made enemies more easily than any man I knew. His assertive manner and his unbounded egotism had a lot to do with this, but he had, in addition, a trait which, in Ireland, would damn a much greater man. His meanness in money matters was so pronounced and so obvious that it became almost proverbial.' Ernie O'Malley and Pádraic Colum reported similar views of Figgis.[38]

At the special Sinn Féin *ard-fheis* held shortly after the release of the internees in the spring of 1919, Figgis was defeated for re-election as joint secretary but remained a member of the executive. At this time he clashed with Michael Collins over the public welcome being planned for de Valera, with Figgis accusing Collins and other militants of trying to use the party executive as a catspaw. To butt heads with Collins was hardly the best way to secure preferment in the movement. Being outside both the Dáil and the government, Figgis turned to journalism. In June 1919 he established his own weekly paper, *The Republic*, which only lasted until September, when it was banned together with all the other Sinn Féin papers. Figgis declared that his paper would 'be concerned mainly with the constructive work before the country', and he opened his columns to discussion of a wide range of social and economic proposals. With these kinds of interests and his initiative, writing skills and organisational ability, he was well suited to direct the secretariat of the new commission.

The first meeting of the new body was held on 19 September 1919, at which time Griffith told its members that the Dáil government viewed the commission as a 'responsible, autonomous and independent body'. In organising its work, the commission decided to give primary attention to the matters of food, power, textiles and minerals. As time was to show, the last two of these received no investigation during the nearly three years of the commission's existence. John O'Neill, a Dublin businessman, was elected chairman, and he in turn appointed two sub-committees. That on food supplies, presided over by the ever-serviceable Thomas Johnson, set its priorities as being dairying, fisheries and meat supply. The power sub-committee, headed by Dr Hugh Ryan, a UCD professor of chemistry, decided to first investigate coal resources, then peat, industrial alcohol and water power.

The initial effort of the commission to hold public hearings proved abortive. When members of the commission, led by Figgis and O'Neill, arrived at the offices of the Monaghan County Council on 24 November, they were told by the RIC that the commission was illegal, whereupon the council chairman adjourned the meeting in protest. The action of the police gave rise to a considerable amount of adverse comment in the press: it was widely regarded as grossly unfair, since the commission, rather than acting in the interests of Sinn Féin, was simply trying to assess the country's resources. Buoyed by this favourable public opinion, the commission proceeded to stage hearings in Dublin a week later. Dublin Castle decided to handle the matter differently this time: there would be no police interference, but accounts of the hearings could not be printed in Irish newspapers, though they could appear in English papers, which were readily available in Ireland. *The Statist*, a London economic journal, in announcing that it would print a weekly synopsis of the proceedings of the commission, commented:

> If we acquit the Irish Government of the accusation that it is bent on deliberately checking the encouragement and extention of the industries of the very country from which its highly paid members draw their salaries, then the only conclusion we can arrive at is that it is wholly unable to discriminate between bodies with 'political' and economic ends in view.

For six days a wide range of persons presented statements to the body at meetings held in Dublin City Hall. With that success behind it, the commission announced that it would hold hearings in Cork the next month. At this juncture the Castle administration shifted its policy once again — there would be no further hearings, public or private. The *Irish Stateman* (10 Jan. 1920) responded with a satirical account of a commission hearing held in a diving-bell beyond the territorial limits, 'unaffected by the proclamations of a Government which condemns us in its ignorance as Sinn Féiners'.

Ban or no ban, the commission went ahead with the Cork hearings. While the police occupied the City Hall, the commission met in the School of Art, then in the Chamber of Commerce building and elsewhere during its three-day session. On one of the days Figgis 'was within an ace of being hanged out of hand by an English officer hopelessly drunk and irresponsible', according to a French journalist, who added: 'A sergeant was actually bringing up a rope when Colonel Moore, a veteran of the Transvaal war, and now a member of the Commission of Inquiry, fortified by his rank as ex-Colonel of the Connaught Rangers, providentially intervened just in the nick of time.' The same hide-and-seek procedure was employed in Limerick a few days later. The Dublin *Evening Telegraph* (23 Jan.) complained that the members of the commission were 'harried from pillar to post by police, but no Irish paper dare print a line dealing with their proceedings under the penalty of bringing down upon itself the mailed fist of the Competent Military Authority'. A British Labour delegation, which had observed the police actions in Cork, commented that it could not understand official opposition to the commission 'unless it be part of a deliberate policy, calculated to hinder the development of Irish industries'. The affair had turned into a propaganda coup for Sinn Féin.

If the commission was to do serious work, however, it would have to put an end to the running battle with the RIC. Therefore it decided to shift from public hearings to staff consultations with interested parties. A series of meetings was arranged with county councils. At one of these, at Carrick-on-Shannon, Figgis and the commission chairman were arrested — an action which served to provide yet more grist to the propaganda mill. As a result of all this activity, Figgis gained considerable public attention. Pondering the question of who was in control of Sinn Féin in August 1920, Lloyd George included Figgis with Griffith, Mac Néill and de Valera among the possibilities.[39]

While all this was going on there was trouble within the commission. After a period of 'constant and continual friction' between Chairman O'Neill and a majority of the commission, O'Neill resigned in September 1920. The point at issue was O'Neill's belief that the commission should do no more than report on the existing resources, while the majority held that they should propose how best these should be developed. He was replaced by Colonel Maurice Moore (1854–1939), a much-respected ex-professional soldier, Redmondite and pre-1916 Volunteer officer.

Meanwhile a burning sense of impatience about the slow pace of the commission's work had developed in both the cabinet and the Dáil. The commission had only issued a single report — an interim report on milk production. This impatience was evident at the Dáil session of 29 June when Griffith proposed that Figgis's salary be increased from £350 to £500 (backdated to 1 March!) and told the assembly that the commission could go on for another two years. Roger Sweetman, a commission member, declared that the body 'would sit for five years at least, or more likely for ten years' and that it had assumed 'semi-ministerial powers'. The Minister for Finance was not impressed. With the country calling for action, he said, the body had issued no general interim report, and, further, 'he would undertake to do in one year what the Commission was going to take five years to do'. Moreover, the commission had not kept the departments informed of its progress. Collins was particularly keen for a speedy investigation of mineral resources.

Two other ministers were also discontented. Austin Stack commented that the milk report 'did not contain any practical suggestions', while Cathal Brugha remarked that 'some of the Commissioners and their Secretary did not quite understand what their functions were' and that apparently they saw the commission becoming a ministry in itself. After a spirited defence of Figgis by Griffith, the Dáil very reluctantly approved the salary increase by a vote of 17 to 15, the closest vote on any matter brought before the first Dáil.

The cabinet itself was partially responsible for the slow work of the commission. When it produced the interim report on milk production in the early summer of 1920, the government asked for a detailed scheme on its recommendations. A special committee for this task did not report until March 1921. On the other hand, the quality of the material produced by the commission and its staff received high praise. When in December 1920 the commission issued a report of evidence on milk production and fisheries, *Old Ireland* (4 Dec.) viewed the product with special pleasure: 'The selection of witnesses, the arrangement of the evidence, the accompanying tables, etc., were, to some extent, we presume, the work of Mr Darrel[1] Figgis; the selective taste of the whole document is recognisably his.' Warre B. Wells, an English socialist observer, praised the commission's first reports as 'models of industry in the collection of information, of lucidity in the collation and arrangement, and of suggestiveness in its applications to economic problems' and gave credit to Figgis for the results.

Anticipating a request for more operating funds in December 1920, Collins told Griffith: 'I'm afraid the Dáil will make an awful "rumpus" if we give them this further amount — at any rate until more results are shown.' In the following month the Department of Trade and Commerce was made responsible for the work of the commission. The department's director, Ernest Blythe, told the Dáil in May 1921 that he thought it was a mistake to have set up a commission with such a wide field of inquiry. He later argued that the body was grossly understaffed: while the commission had four or five committees, there was only one staff of three or four. He held that 'a great deal of valuable information has been assembled and collated' and that many commission members had attended meetings two or three times a week, 'without fee or reward', for weeks on end. It was Blythe's opinion that 'the impatience shown by the Dáil was not justified'. Seán MacEntee believed that the main problem with the commission was that Figgis tried to keep all of its activities 'too completely under his own control' and had not made use of the help of experts in compiling reports.

At the Dáil session of May 1921 there was a general consensus that a deadline be set to the commission's activities. This was later established as the end of October; at that time the committees were to hand in their reports, finished or unfinished. Once again, however, the cabinet decided to allow more time for the work to be completed, and the commission did not wind up its proceedings until 1922. Eight reports were eventually published: on dairying, coal, industrial alcohol, milk production, peat, fisheries, stock breeding and water power.

The whole difficulty with the idea of a commission of inquiry was the times in which it operated. Both the cabinet and the Dáil were under enormous political pressure to demonstrate that they constituted a real government; they needed timely, if not rushed, results to shown this. While the members of the underground government were hunted men, the commissioners proceeded with what seemed to be an air of scholarly detachment. If the commission had rushed through its work, however, the results would have done more harm than good. The Dáil got great value, in propaganda alone, for the £6,000 it spent on the commission. In Warre B. Wells's view, the inquiry 'was an enterprise of a kind hitherto almost completely neglected in Ireland, and planned on a scale which few other countries have yet rivalled'. In the process of nation-building under the first Dáil, he asserted, 'perhaps the most important part of this work was that undertaken by the National Commission on the Resources and Industries of Ireland'.[40]

Land and the Land Bank
One of the objectives of Sinn Féin was to assert national control over the financial resources of the country. Another was to achieve a broader distribution of land. Following the establishment of Dáil Éireann, its supporters anticipated at least some action in both of these concerns. What the Dáil produced was probably its most innovative programme.

Finance and land had been the staples of public discussion for years, but they were given renewed attention in the early months of 1919. In a series of articles in *The Irishman* M. Byrne advocated the creation of a network of Sinn Féin banks (a small one existed in Dublin) to begin the process of breaking the financial chain linking Ireland with Britain. In the issue of 5 April Byrne claimed that the Dáil was about to take action to stop the outflow of Irish money for the sole enrichment of foreigners. The Dáil was indeed preparing to act and at its session of 18 June approved a decree which stated that 'The provision of land for the agricultural population now deprived thereof is decreed.' The government also announced that a loan fund scheme to finance the measure would be presented to the assembly. A land mortgage bank committee under the direction of the new Director of Agriculture and with guidance from the Irish Agricultural Organisation Society had been at work since April.

Robert Childers Barton (1881–1975), who became director in the cabinet realignment in April, was an unusual kind of republican. An Anglo-Irish landowner in Wicklow, he was serving in the British army in Dublin when the 1916 rebellion broke out. Thereafter he moved from being a Home Ruler to a separatist, and was elected as a Sinn Féiner to the West Wicklow parliamentary seat in 1918. Arrested in February 1919, he escaped from captivity in the following month and was then appointed Director of Agriculture. Barton had direct, practical experience of agriculture, and he knew something about banking as well, having been chairman of a co-operative bank upon its establishment in 1908.

At the Dáil session of 20 August the land bank committee submitted a report calling for the formation of a state-financed National Co-operative Mortgage Bank (in Irish, Banc na Talmhan). Based on models in Germany, Austria and Hungary, the bank would loan money to land purchase societies as well as to individuals; it would also conduct general banking business after it had been firmly established. This proposal differed from the existing land acts in that 'its primary object is not to provide funds to enable occupying tenants to purchase the Landlord's interest in their holdings, but rather to settle upon the land, either as owners or occupying tenants, persons who at present neither own nor occupy any land' or who had uneconomic holdings. Loans to individuals would require a 25 per cent deposit; commercial banks usually required 50 per cent. No deposit would be needed for loans to co-operative land societies, but the land purchased would only be leased to such organisa-tions or their members until the deposit was paid. The bank, moreover, 'will undertake the organisation of the necessary society'.

Initial funding of the bank was to be in the form of a covert investment of £200,000 by Dáil Éireann, with the control of the bank to be substantially in its hands: its president was to be a member of the cabinet, and four of eight directors would be appointed by the government. The Dáil would be asked to provide £10,000 for initial expenses. The government viewed the scheme as a simple but effective means of land redistribution: 'The Irish people will do for themselves at a minimum cost to Irish Public funds what the English are unable to do for them.' The plan received an enthusiastic response from the Dáil. Barton told his wife: 'It had a very good reception, but largely due to the suddenness of its appearance, lack of time to criticise and sympathy for me on the run producing anything . . . . It is only a preliminary draft issued to curb criticism.'

The Sinn Féin executive asked its local organisations,to estimate the potential for deposits in the proposed bank. The Dáil was told on 27 October that preliminary arrangements were almost complete. Several deputies favoured starting land purchases immediately. J. N. Dolan proposed that the Dáil provide £200,000 to the bank, provided the money was available. That, of course, was the problem; there was no money as yet. Declaring that 'the Land question is the biggest question we have', Arthur Griffith urged restraint, arguing that it would be several months before the necessary funds would be available and that 'if we start this Bank on a small basis it will be a failure'.[41]

The bank was organised in December 1919 and, according to the Department of Agriculture, 'began to deal with Land advances immediately'. In the following April it began ordinary banking operations. The directors of the new body were eminently respectable: the managing director was Lionel Smith Gordon, who came over from the IAOS, and the other directors were Sir Henry Grattan-Bellew, a Galway landlord who had sold most of his land to the Land Commission, Robert Erskine Childers, James MacNeill (later Governor-General of the Irish Free State) and E. M. Stephens (who was soon afterwards replaced by Henry Dixon). Of this group, the one who was to be the most important in Irish affairs was Childers. Cousin and intimate friend of Barton, he had already been deeply involved in political and military events in both Ireland and Britain. After the founding of Dáil Éireann, however, he had eyes only for Ireland; he told Art O'Brien in June 1919 that he intended 'to devote the rest of his life to forwarding the cause of Ireland' — which is precisely what he did. He was involved with the revolutionary government from its beginning. His London address was one of the first used as a conduit for American funds. In the summer of 1919 he served on the Paris staff, dealing with press relations. While the bank was being organised he advised his cousin on land purchase schemes.

As money from the loan campaign began to accumulate, the government injected funds into the bank. The sum of £102,000 was transferred by 30 April 1920, and the remaining £98,000 was remitted by 24 June. There was a considerable clamour for the money. Michael Collins wrote to de Valera in February 1920: 'The Bank can absorb an enormous amount, as quite apart from its Land activities other enterprises are making applications which might with great advantage and success be granted.' Smith Gordon pointed out that there were 'several hundred urgent cases pending, involving hundreds of thousands of pounds'. To meet this demand, de Valera committed $500,000 (approximately £125,000) of American loan funds to the bank, and this money was received by the bank apparently in late 1920 or early 1921.[42]

Barton was again arrested in January 1920, but the work went forward under his successor, Art O'Connor. Then came the land agitation of the spring of 1920. The bank's solicitors issued a statement declaring that the 'influence of the Land Bank has been most vigorously directed against any form of violence, and that in no case where money had been advanced has any such violence taken place'. The link between the bank and the

Dáil must have been widely known; Barton later said that 'it was fairly well known in Dublin Castle' that the bank 'had a connection with the Dáil'. Banc na Talmhan had to live with the threat of suppression, but, strangely enough, this never happened. Crown forces raided the bank and arrested staff members, but went no further. This was probably due, commented Smith Gordon, to 'something in English psychology which inspires a respect for financial institutions'.

In an unusually expansive frame of mind, Griffith told the Dáil in June 1920 that 'perhaps their greatest achievement was the establishment . . . of the Land Bank', which he believed had 'enabled them to settle the land crisis that arose in the West of Ireland'. At this time the Dáil provided £25,000 for the creation of six branches of the bank, which Collins declared were necessary if it was to attract deposit and current account customers. In September he proposed that £500,000 of the loan funds in the United States should be used to provide capital for the branches. There was no open opposition to this idea; but although this amount was set aside for this purpose, the money was not sent over. Collins undertook to form a society to gather share capital for the expanding institution. At the beginning of 1921 branches were established in Cork, Athlone, Ennis, Waterford, Limerick and Tralee, but they failed to attract much business or money. Ernest Blythe later commented: 'When the branch was opened, the people who had been most urgent in asking that it should be opened gave a very small amount of business indeed to the bank.' Barton asserted that 'some important personages' who wanted a branch set up in their part of the country promised that the bank would 'be snowed under by money', but this did not happen. Although the bank claimed at the end of 1920 that £406,011 had been subscribed, only £203,011 had in fact been paid up, almost exactly the amount provided by the Ministry of Finance.

The control that the Dáil government exerted over the bank was direct: the cabinet voted approval of at least most of the loans made by the bank. The cavalier actions of some deputies presented problems to both the cabinet and the bank. In March 1920 Con Collins informed the ministry that he had been buying and distributing land and requested £1,000 for this project, adding that 'If I get this . . . it will mean a few more thousands to the loan in West Limerick.' Being a champion loan-collector, Collins undoubtedly got the money. The bank lent money not only to groups buying land, but for other purposes as well. With cabinet approval, it provided £29,930 to five fishing co-operatives and made a few loans to manufacturers and one for a local government housing scheme. After April 1920 the cabinet decided that all loans would be for land purchase. By January 1921 the bank had dealt with 11,000 acres, for 6,882 of which it had advanced £178,485; for the other 4,000-odd acres it had committed £95,000, making a total of over £273,000.

At this juncture the Department of Agriculture warned that the bank would not be able to continue financing land purchase at the current rate and complained that deputies and other public representatives had not supported the bank as they should have. It also objected to cash payments for land. The 'Lords of the Soil', it asserted, 'are delighted to get an opportunity to clear out of the country with their pockets well-lined with Irish money'. Smith Gordon had high ambitions for his infant institution:

> The ideal is to create co-operative communities of men who will work in harmony with one another and help one another to get the highest possible yield out of the land, to standardise the produce, to brighten the life of the countryside, and to do away with the existing class distinctions and feelings of bitterness which arise from unequal distribution of wealth and opportunity.

In this as in as many other instances, soaring aspirations were borne down by grim reality. The intensification of British action against the Dáil government and the IRA, combined with a sharp decline in agricultural prices at the beginning of 1921, resulted in a dramatic reduction in demand for loans. The bank, nevertheless, weathered the storm and financed the acquistion of an additional 5,500 acres in the first six months of that year. By that time time a total of £316,590 had been lent to thirty-five societies, with a combined membership of about 800, for the purchase of 15,750 acres, mostly in the midlands, 'where the greatest area of untenanted land remains'. Moreover, the bank achieved modest profits in 1920–21 and claimed total assets of £846,755 on 30 June 1921.

Both Barton and Smith Gordon later claimed that the bank played no small part in saving the national movement from the disastrous effects of a violent land agitation. But surely the land courts and the IRA were much more effective in dealing with this upheaval. Moreover, owing to its modest finances, the bank only toyed with the continuing demand for land. As Michael Collins later commented, 'It only just reddened the surface, and it only dealt with the thing in the smallest possible way.' On the other hand, it was a concrete expression of the Dáil's commitment to tackling this problem.[43]

An Attempt at Afforestation
One of the earliest activities of the Department of Agriculture was to encourage tree-planting. This, it said, was a matter which the British administration had totally ignored. The deforestation of the country had long been an issue with Arthur Griffith. In June 1919 he declared that 'It will be the duty of the Dáil to find a remedy for this condition of things.' The assembly responded by passing a decree to stimulate afforestation. Robert Barton appointed a forestry committee which presented a scheme at the August session. It called for a voluntary tree-

planting programme assisted by Dáil financial aid, with the campaign to culminate with a 'National Arbour Day' in November. Walter Cole, a Dublin businessman and Sinn Féin city councillor, agreed to serve as the temporary and unpaid national forestry inspector.

Cole proceeded to organise a campaign that included illustrated lectures and the distribution of 50,000 leaflets. He also ordered 80,000 plants (at the cost of £450) to be ready for delivery at the end of October. Sinn Féin *cumainn* were urged to participate in a circular sent from headquarters in August. The Sinn Féin Clubs were asked to seek participation of local bodies and schools, as well as the 'collaboration of local corps of Irish Volunteers in carrying out planting'. The Department of Agriculture proposed that every farmer plant sixteen trees — one for each man executed in 1916. National Arbour Day was observed on 29 November, with Griffith planting a ceremonial tree in Dublin. Cole estimated that between 250,000 and 300,000 trees were planted during the campaign.

That was the end of the Dáil's afforestation effort. Thereafter Cole had to give his full attention to his business and political work. Although the Dáil in August 1920 voted to provide for a salaried, professional forestry inspector, Art O'Connor, the Acting Minister for Agriculture, was unable to find a suitable person to appoint. By this time his department had its hands full in dealing with the land agitation. O'Connor later said that the problem he had concerning trees was not to get them planted but the opposition of local people and Volunteers to any effort to harvest the timber commercially. Of course, the Volunteers did chop down lots of trees — for the purpose of obstructing police and British army patrols.[44]

The Fisheries Programme
The revitalisation of the Irish fishing industry was another long-standing proposal in the Sinn Féin programme, and the Dáil proceeded to make a start in the process. Arthur Griffith told his outlaw parliament on 17 June 1919 that fishery yields had 'been steadily decreasing' and that 'the English Department is not going to help our Fisheries; it was bent on destroying them'. He proposed that £5,000 be appropriated for this industry and that a fisheries inspector be appointed; the Dáil subsequently raised the amount to £10,000.

A committee appointed to survey the industry reported to the Dáil meeting in August, with E. J. Duggan submitting a study of urban markets and Frank Fahy recounting his visits to Connemara and the Aran Islands. The committee asked each deputy from a maritime district for assistance in gathering information about fisheries and in the formation of local advisory committees of fisherman. In November the committee recommended the creation of a Department of

Fisheries. This was agreed to by the cabinet on 28 November, and it appointed Seán Etchingham as director.

A lively and humorous native of Wexford, Seán Etchingham (1870–1923) was a noted journalist with the *Enniscorthy Echo* for many years. He was first elected to the Sinn Féin national executive in 1910 and was also active in the Gaelic League. A leader in the 1916 rising in Wexford, when brought before a court martial he inquired if the 'first offender act' applied in this instance. The reply was no, and he spent a year in prison. He was again imprisoned at the time of the 'German plot' and was elected for East Wicklow at the general election of 1918. Two years later he became the first republican chairman of the Wexford County Council.

His first action as head of the new department was to appoint four officials, who were to be both inspectors and organisers; they were to work closely with the Irish Agricultural Organisation Society. The department launched a programme to stimulate the industry by providing loans to groups of fisherman, organised in co-operatives, for vessels, equipment and facilities. Michael Collins told a spokesman for a group of fishermen in Skibbereen that he hoped 'we shall be able to give them the help they want. Of course the first thing they have to do is to form a Society, as we deal with Societies only, not with individuals.' Over the next few months Etchingham's organisers fostered the establishment of eight fishing co-operatives, five of which received loans totalling £19,930 from the National Land Bank upon the approval of Etchingham; these were in Baltimore, Dingle, Ring, Gorumna in Connemara, and Tory Island in Co. Donegal.

The underground government was taking action in an area that had been neglected by the Dublin Castle administration. *Old Ireland* (18 Dec. 1919) charged that the Congested Districts Board 'has at all times shown a vicious dislike of co-operative methods' for the fishing or any other industry. In August 1920 General Macready sent on to Dublin Castle a captured memorandum from Griffith which claimed that the British government had done nothing for Irish fisheries; he suggested that a new programme should be initiated, 'as it would cut the ground from under these people's feet'.

The Dáil's fisheries scheme soon ran into problems. In the spring of 1920 controversy erupted in Dingle, and the ministry dispatched Erskine Childers, Eoin Mac Néill and Conor O'Brien to investigate. In their report they recommended that the Dingle co-operative be given a loan of £40,000. The cabinet baulked at this large amount; the society received a loan of £1,630 in March 1920. In Baltimore a situation developed that became a minor scandal. The society there had received the largest loan — £12,000. Most of the money had been used to buy a boat to ship fish to England. This caused an outcry from local fish factors, many of whom, it was claimed, were 'good republicans'. The boat sank, but was covered by insurance. The manager fled, and a lot of money disappeared. Seán Hayes, TD, charged that the organiser for that area 'knew nothing about fishing'. A Dáil investigation, initiated in August 1920, was told by local supporters that the Department of Fisheries was guilty of 'gross carelessness in the disposal of public money'. They further claimed that the fishermen in the local co-operative had contributed only £3 to the Dáil Loan and had paid in only £667 to their society. Trouble also occurred elsewhere. The boat purchased by the Tory co-operative 'was destroyed by enemy forces' (but was also covered by insurance). Members of the Gorumna society came into conflict with others in that community; in addition, they were accused by Austin Stack of refusing 'to work the boat they got as a free gift' from a fund collected by the *Irish Independent.*[45]

On 22 July the cabinet voted to halt payments to the fisheries co-operatives until the Dáil committee had reported on the 'condition of each society to which money has been advanced'. As a result of this inquiry, the cabinet decided that fishing societies would have to 'put down one pound for one pound of any money to be advanced' by the bank.

The commission of inquiry's sub-committee on food, chaired by Thomas Johnson, issued a report on the fishing industry in December 1920, but its proposals were not to be of any help in the existing circumstances. In March 1921 the issuing of loans to fishing societies was officially ended. Seán MacEntee told the Dáil at that time: 'Most of the fishery schemes had been disastrous to the reputation of the Dáil.' Collins argued that 'the failures all arose from dishonesty on the part of the fishermen'. He proposed that the department should restrict itself to giving expert advice (of which there must have been very little), as 'it was too big a problem to tackle successfully in present conditions'. If two or three of the co-operatives had mismanaged their funds, he declared, 'the other Fishing Societies, from the financial point of view, were working well enough'. However, a report issued in early 1922 stated that only one of the five organisations financed by the Dáil had been successful. It attributed the lack of success primarily to the violence of the time, but also to depressed fish prices.

With the ending of the loan scheme, the department restricted itself to the 'organisation of existing home markets and an attempt to establish new markets in Irish centres'. Its staff was reduced to one organiser, who was given the task of advising fishermen on the preparation, grading and packing of fish. The department also issued a pamphlet on this matter, sought support from public bodies, attempted to get the railways to provide better transport facilities, and mediated in two disputes among fishermen. In August 1921 the department asked for an appropriation of only £650, with Etchingham explaining that the amount 'was very small as it was only for organising the existing markets and trying to establish new ones'. The department had survived in little more than name only.[46]

Education Policy and the Irish Language

Education was not a high priority with Sinn Féin. Its 1917 constitution supported 'reform of education', but referred specifically only to the need to include instruction in the Irish language and in 'Irish agricultural and manufacturing potentialities' at the primary level. It said nothing about secondary education, but did advocate the elevation of agriculture and economics 'to the position of dominance in the University system'. The party's 1918 election manifesto was silent on the subject of education, and no Sinn Féin leader, unlike Patrick Pearse, had anything to say about it. There were seven teachers among the Sinn Féin candidates, but these were people leaving that field for political life; not one of them addressed the question of change in the system of education or showed any interest in the matter at all. The 1919 Democratic Programme had a strong statement on education (thanks to the concern of Thomas Johnson): 'the first duty of the Government of the Republic' would be to provide all children 'with the means and facilities requisite for their proper education and training as Citizens of a Free and Gaelic Ireland'. Fine words, indeed; but, realistically, much needed to be done before such important matters as education could be tackled. The Dáil and its government first had to survive.

In the first few weeks of its existence the Dáil established a working committee on education and the Irish language. When de Valera took office as Príomh-Aire and appointed a new cabinet in April, the subject of education was not mentioned. A week later, when questions about education arose in the assembly, Cathal Brugha (speaking in Irish) assured the deputies: 'Education is being taken care of, but that Department is not ready yet. Nobody need have any fear that we will not take care of Education, as will be seen shortly. . . . We will have a minister for education.' But in fact there was not to be a minister for education.

The Catholic Church had built up a broadly-based system of education of its own and was contending with Dublin Castle for ultimate control of the field. It is apparent that Sinn Féin decided that it would lose support if the Dáil sought to establish a major claim in the area at the beginning of its existence. The underground government was in the process of seeking support, open or tacit, from church leaders. Already the violent acts of some members of the IRA were causing strenuous objections from bishops and priests. Moreover, there is no evidence that Dáil leaders or deputies objected to church domination of education; all the evidence is to the contrary.

There could be little objection if the Dáil stood up for the Irish language. With so many members with backgrounds in the Gaelic League, there was strong support in the Dáil for efforts to strengthen the language. The matter was first brought up by Brugha at the session of August 1919, when he proposed the creation of a committee for this purpose. He argued that the efforts of the Gaelic League were inadequate, a contention that was strongly endorsed by J. J. O'Kelly, the new president of the League, who pointed out that the organisation had been without a general secretary for two years (Seán T. O'Kelly, its last secretary, had been preoccupied with political work) and that Eoin Mac Néill, president for the previous three years, 'had not attended three meetings' of the League executive.

At its October session the Dáil supported the proposal of the League that a minister for the national language be appointed. It also briefly addressed the matter of having a ministry of education. Among those supporting the creation of such were Brugha (again), Collins, Liam de Roiste and Terence MacSwiney. Educational matters were at last receiving attention. The Dáil had already agreed to subsidise the Limerick Technical School, whose director was in conflict with the Dublin Castle authorities. One of the major concerns of the language ministry would be the expansion of Irish in primary schools. Two Irish-speaking summer 'colleges' were seeking 'recognition' by the Dáil. An education bill before the British parliament had roused passionate opposition from the Catholic bishops. How could education be ignored?

The Dáil decided to avoid a decision on the matter of an education ministry. Brugha 'thought President de Valera had some definite reason for not appointing a Minister of Education when he was constituting his Ministry'. The problem would be addressed when de Valera returned, whenever that would be. Brugha's vague statement satisfied everyone present. Not a word was said about the role and aspirations of the Catholic Church in this field.

The man selected to be Minister for the National Language was, appropriately, J. J. O'Kelly (*alias* 'Sceilg'), president of the Gaelic League. O'Kelly (1872–1957) was born on Valentia Island, Co. Kerry, facing Sceilg Mhichil, and was for many years editor of the *Catholic Bulletin*, a monthly journal owned by the Gill publishing company; in spite of its name, its primary purpose was to promote Irish nationalist ideals, and it only addressed religious matters when the interests of the church were threatened. O'Kelly was a strong supporter of the revival of Irish, but he had no discernible experience or interest in education. Furthermore, he was essentially a propagandist of a few immutable ideas, not a scholar or intellectual. At the time of his appointment he was already Leas-Ceann Comhairle (deputy chairman) of the Dáil. In keeping with the principles of the Gaelic League, O'Kelly, like Brugha, served without pay.

The new ministry got off to a slow start, as O'Kelly was sentenced to three months' imprisonment a few days after his appointment on 7 November 1919. On his release in February 1920, he organised a committee composed of representatives of national organisations and four members of the Dáil. The group produced a four-part programme:

financial encouragement to Irish-speaking societies (a 2 per cent grant towards loans); encouragement to public bodies and national institutions to use the language; formation of parish support committees; and a scheme for competitions in primary schools, with prizes awarded by the ministry. Moreover, it would 'take over the direction and financing of the language revival in the Irish-speaking districts'. Eight organisers would be appointed: one each for the Gaeltacht areas in Donegal, Mayo, Galway, Clare, Kerry and Waterford, and two for Cork. The annual cost was estimated at £10,000.

In June 1920 the Dáil appropriated £5,000 to launch the programme. There was an administrative problem within the ministry: because he devoted so much time to journalism, O'Kelly was of necessity a part-time minister. To back him up, Frank Fahy was appointed assistant minister in August 1920. According to Michael Hayes, O'Kelly was quite invisible as minister. An active member of the Gaelic League at the time, Hayes later commented that he had 'no recollection of anything that Sceilg did as Minister for Irish'. Moreover, although he had 'several conversations with Cathal Brugha regarding schemes for the Gaeltacht', he could not remember O'Kelly's name being mentioned. Brugha, of course, made a principle out of reticence. Yet there must have been considerable opposition to O'Kelly. In August 1920 he was very nearly defeated for the presidency of the Gaelic League by Piaras Béaslaí, the editor of *An tÓglach.* In defending his tenure in the presidency, O'Kelly declared that he gave all his time outside of his job at Gill's to the work of the League; he said nothing about his position of minister. In any case, O'Kelly was active in directing the implementation of his programme, stimulating support from clergy and county councillors, and addressing 'great hostings' at public meetings around the country.[47]

Despite its failure to appoint a minister for education, there was no way that the Dáil government could avoid the question of education — if for no other reason than that its rival was already busying itself in that field. In March 1919 two commissions (one on primary and the other on secondary education) established by Ian Macpherson, the Chief Secretary for Ireland, presented their reports. Their recommendations were accepted by Macpherson and were incorporated in a bill presented to parliament in the following November. These proposals included the setting up of locally elected school committees with power to finance school maintenance through local rates and, most importantly, supervise school management; the creation of a centralised system under a department of education; and the granting to lay teachers of security of employment, improved salaries and pension rights. All of these measures would dilute church power in education in the name of expanded educational opportunities for the Irish people.

The Protestant churches and the Unionist press joined the Irish National Teachers' Organisation in supporting the bill, but this was inadequate support when weighed against the adamant opposition of the Catholic Church. A protracted debate concerning the merits of the proposal was carried on in the correspondence columns of the newspapers and in public forums, with T. J. O'Connell, general secretary of the INTO, being the principal advocate of the bill. Hanna Sheehy-Skeffington declared that she was opposed 'to the autocratic managerial control of the schools' and believed that the people ought to get more representation in connection with education. A 'Catholic Parent' commented: 'I have never known or heard of a school manager who either wanted or encouraged parents to take an active interest in educational matters. I have never heard of a school manager calling together a committee consisting of parents to help him in the working of a single national school, although some of these national schools are as cold, dreary, cheerless and unattractive as a prison.' 'Cú Uladh' held that the exclusion of parents 'from all responsibility in the practical work of education seems to have atrophied their educational faculties'.

To its opponents the bill seemed to be the Antichrist at hand. They denounced it as a Protestant, Carsonite plot to further anglicise the historic Irish nation. Their slogan was simple: back the bishops; Faith and Fatherland. The Catholic Clerical School Managers' Association opposed the bill because, it said, it would result in an increased burden on the ratepayers — a curious concern on the part of members of the clergy. It did not mention the proposed school committees. Cardinal Logue, never one to overlook a threat to the Faith, opposed the bill because he saw it as the thin end of the wedge of secularisation and 'godless education'. He warned his flock that the bill was likely to pass as 'we have been left almost completely unrepresented in Parliament'. This situation, declared the *Freeman's Journal* (6 May 1920), was clear evidence of the foolishness of Sinn Féin's policy of ignoring Westminster. Another paper believed that this issue would force Sinn Féin to take its seats in parliament. But *Old Ireland* (7 Feb. 1920) argued that the Dáil should simply ignore the Castle's educational machinations by 'turning to the resources of energy in the Irish people to build up our own system'.

The Catholic bishops assembled in January 1920 to denounce Macpherson's bill root and branch. With what could be perceived as a sidelong glance at the Dáil, which they had otherwise ignored, they declared that 'The only Department which the vast majority of the Irish people will tolerate is one which shall be set up by its own Parliament.' How did they know that the vast majority of the Irish people felt this way? For one thing, the Dáil cabinet decided to support the bishops, though it did so in a secretive fashion. Despite pressure to condemn publicly 'both the Bill itself and those who had the termerity to give it countenance', it made no official statement on the matter. Collins, who took a lively interest in the controversy, as well as in just about everything else, was the minister who privately communicated the cabinet's opposition to the bishops. On the other hand, Austin Stack privately encouraged the teachers to persist in their support of the bill: 'Let you collar the money; we will run the machinery later on.' No prominent Sinn Féiner said anything about the bill, and the Dáil did not discuss it.

This was not the case with local government bodies, many of which were now controlled by Sinn Féin, who competed in rhetorical denunciations of the bill. The height of hyperbole was probably reached by Chairman McNally of the Edenderry No. 2 RDC, who characterised the bill as 'but the prelude to the most odious and diabolical system which had ever threatened the moral, religious and national character of the Irish race'. Novenas were held throughout the country to pray for the defeat of the bill. Macpherson had found out that Ireland was not Scotland, and, frustrated and overwrought, he resigned in April 1920. That also was the end of the bill; it was quietly dropped in the following December.[48]

The Dáil government thus found that its hand had been forced: it now had to do something about education. What it did, of course, was to form a committee. The group appointed by O'Kelly in February 1920 was given the assignment of formulating 'a general scheme of National Education'. It did produce a report, but its scheme has apparently fallen through the cracks of history. Occasional reference was made to the proposed plan, but that was all.

The first attempt of the Dáil to take action on an educational matter outside of the Irish language revival proved abortive. In November 1920 a cabinet committee was appointed to investigate the possibility of bringing the technical education system under Dáil control. If this happened, the local committees of technical instruction would be deprived of funds from Dublin Castle, but the cabinet thought the system could get by with less money, claiming that 'a large proportion of the expenditure is not justified by results'. However, since the membership of the technical instruction committees were appointed by the county councils, almost all of which had Sinn Féin majorities, there seemed no good reason to alter the existing arrangement. Accordingly, the cabinet decided to leave well alone.

Another cabinet action proved to be more fruitful. In February 1920 it authorised O'Kelly's department to join with the Irish National Teachers' Organisation in sponsoring a conference to draw up a programme for primary education. The terms of reference for the conference included an examination of educational administration, school facilities and textbooks. The conference, which held meetings from January to March 1921, recommended university degrees for national teachers, enforcement of school attendance and improvements in curricula, but said nothing about structural alterations, such as changing from clerical to public control. T. J. Corcoran, SJ, Professor of Education at University College, Dublin, and an associate of O'Kelly on the *Catholic Bulletin*, has been credited with having great influence on the course of the conference. Neither O'Kelly, the cabinet nor the Dáil took any action on or even mentioned the conference's recommendations, but the first half of 1921 was a time of extreme pressure for the alternative government. This set of proposals became the basis of the new primary school programme the next year.

The department, meanwhile, worked at implementing its programme for promoting the spread of the Irish language. O'Kelly reported in January 1921 that the scheme for primary schools had been widely adopted. He noted the problem, not just for this scheme but for education in general, of irregular school attendance in the Gaeltacht: 'Parents laugh at the foreign law. They know . . . that the Óglaigh have no time to act as school attendance officers just now.' Two months later he told the Dáil that he had secured wide support from the Catholic bishops for his scheme. He noted, however, that 'the Church alone could restore and perpetuate the national language if only it so willed'. He claimed that the language competitions in the primary schools had been enthusiastically embraced by students, teachers and managers, and the Department of Local Government had succeeded in getting local bodies to employ the language in their communications. Furthermore, the lack of suitable texts in Irish was being overcome: 'Practically every available writer of Irish is now at work to remedy this want.' Two months later the Dáil provided £2,000 for an authors' guarantee scheme to encourage the publication of books in Irish. One publication which resulted was Seoirse Mac Cluin's two-volume glossary of Irish words and expressions from Dunquin and the Blasket Islands. Earlier the cabinet had voted £200 for a new edition of the *Táin Bó Cuailgne* by Dr Rudolf Thurneysen, a German scholar. The grant was eventually used by Dr Thurneysen in the preparation of his monumental study of the early Irish hero and king tales (*Die irische Helden- und Königsage*, 1921). The results in higher education were mixed: although college authorities in Galway and Cork had agreed to provide evening lectures in Irish, those in Dublin had remained unmoved, despite the fact that a Sinn Féin slate had swept a recent election for the UCD senate.

As was the case in all Dáil operations, the department's activities were circumscribed by enemy action. O'Kelly reported that three of his eight organisers were arrested in the spring of 1921. In addition, 'all Irish speakers are treated similarly and seized by the Army of Occupation'. O'Kelly himself was again arrested in March. Even before then, however, he appeared to be completely out of touch with what was happening in the Dáil government. He failed to attend the Dáil session of 25 January, claiming that he had not been notified, which was strongly denied by Diarmuid O'Hegarty. The Gaelic League failed to send a draft statement requested by de Valera, who had to demand that O'Kelly produce a departmental report. To Dáil complaints in August about the inactivity of his officials, O'Kelly described the intense repression under which his department operated:

> There was no man in Ireland that the enemy was more against than the Irish inspector, and many of them had been arrested. For the past year if a piece of paper written in Irish was found on a person he was immediately arrested, and now no one was writing Irish. This year competitions at the Oireachtas fell to the ground.

Some members of the IRA might have taken exception to this statement, but in any case counter-insurgency had effectively put paid to the programme.[49]

(7) The Propaganda War

Arthur Griffith often made the point that England had put a paper wall around Ireland; on the inside she told Ireland what she wanted the Irish to believe about the world, and on the outside she told the world what she wanted the world to believe about Ireland. To break through that barrier, whether deliberately or casually constructed, the government of Dáil Éireann developed a broadly-based campaign to win international support for Irish self-government. This effort was based on a tripod of the Department of Propaganda, the Department of Foreign Affairs and the Irish mission in the United States. Because the Irish Republic was not recognised by any other state, both the Foreign Affairs Department and the American mission gave priority to their efforts to influence public opinion rather than to developing relations with foreign governments.

Bridging the Paper Wall: the Propaganda Department
The Department of Propaganda (later Publicity) was responsible for the gathering and dissemination of all public information about the civil activities of the Dáil government, as well as those actions of the Castle regime that would put it in a bad light. Already working in the field of foreign propaganda were a pioneering handful of diplomats. In early 1919 the Dáil cabinet established two offices outside Ireland.

The first of these was in London. At the end of 1918 Art O'Brien (1872–1949) was asked by a group of Sinn Féin leaders to become the London 'envoy' of the government they intended to establish. Born in London of Irish parents, O'Brien was forty-seven years old when he took up this position. A civil engineer, he had for long been active in Irish cultural and political organisations, serving as head of the Gaelic League in Britain since 1914 and as the president of the Sinn Féin Council of Great Britain since 1916.

Using the cover of the office of the *Music Trade Review*, of which he was manager, O'Brien's operation had many responsibilities: spreading propaganda both in England and abroad, organisation of Irish nationalists in England, gathering intelligence for Dublin, and securing and shipping armaments to Ireland. O'Brien was not directly involved in the last activity — this was the responsibility of his long-time associate Seán McGrath — but O'Brien later acknowledged that 'I supplied the cash for purchases'. His first major undertaking was the formation of the Irish Self-Determination League of Great Britain, an organisation whose membership was restricted to Irish people (Englishmen sympathetic to Irish self-government later formed their own group, the Peace with Ireland Council). For all his other experience, O'Brien knew nothing of professional journalism.

This was also true of the top men who were in charge of the Paris office. Both Seán T. O'Kelly and George Gavan Duffy were essentially politicians. They devoted themselves to trying to influence the French government, but after a few unsuccessful efforts they secured professional assistance. When *Le Temps* in August 1919 proposed that the British evacuate Ireland, Duffy credited Erskine Childers with bringing about this position. Childers's continuing success with the French press, declared Duffy, was 'due, apart from his abilities and wide knowledge, to the fact he fought in the war, that he was well-known as a literary man'.

The Sinn Féin party in 1918 was able to combine effective political propaganda with an extremely favourable shift in national feeling to win a sweeping victory for the cause of self-government. A press bureau under Robert Brennan had been established in March 1918, and he continued to direct press relations for a time after the creation of Dáil Éireann. His principal activity was to write a weekly column, 'Sinn Féin Notes', which appeared in forty provincial papers. With the cabinet realignment of April 1919, Laurence Ginnell was appointed Director of Propaganda. Brennan continued to work in both the Sinn Féin and Dáil press organisations until early 1921, when he became Under-Secretary for Foreign Affairs.

The only Nationalist MP to switch to Sinn Féin after 1916, Ginnell was a seasoned journalist and politician of sixty-five years of age when he took up this position. Although he was elected treasurer of the Sinn Féin executive, he was not a key figure in the party leadership. It was assumed, however, that his literary and oratorical abilities could be effectively employed in the new department.

The first task of the department was to rally public support for Dáil Éireann. In the early months of 1919 it issued a series of fourteen pamphlets explaining the purposes and objectives of the rebel government. It was also responsible for the production of a film, *Sinn Féin Review*, which was shown around the country. It is not clear what further efforts Ginnell had planned at the time of his arrest in May 1919. After serving four months in prison, he went on paid sick leave for about a year and then went to the United States, where he became head of the Chicago-based Labour Bureau for Irish Independence; in 1921 he went on a mission to Argentina.[50]

The man chosen to replace Ginnell was Desmond FitzGerald (1889–1947). Just thirty years old at this time, FitzGerald was born in London and, a cultivated, intellectual person, was part of the literary world there until he moved to Ireland in 1913, where he became a Gaelic League official in Kerry. A participant in the 1916 rebellion, he rose in the ranks of Sinn Féin and was elected to a Dublin seat (a very marginal one at that) in 1918. His literary and journalistic contacts in London, as well as his linguistic attainment (he reportedly could speak six languages), were valuable qualifications for his new position. He was to serve in this post until his arrest in February 1921.

He was described in an English newspaper as 'a young, good-looking man, with a boy's face, but with a knowledge of Irish history which would be worthy of an up-to-date Methuselah'. Frederick Dumont found him to be 'a well-educated young man, with an excellent address and most pleasing manners' who was 'always on hand to see that each correspondent arriving in Dublin gets the proper viewpoint'. What later impressed Frank Pakenham about the man was 'his youth, his looks, his combination of literary grace and wit with ferocious activity and endurance, of gaiety with fixed resolve'. On the other hand, Robert Barton, also years later, had a negative recollection: 'His watery, flat eyes gave me the impression of a snake in the grass.' FitzGerald was ably assisted by his wife Mabel, of Ulster Presbyterian stock, of whom Kathleen McKenna said: 'There was no more tireless worker in the Republican cause. She worked all day. . . . She never walked; she went always at a trot.'[51]

When FitzGerald took over the department, he quickly expanded its scope and impact. The day of the brief pamphlet distributed to country towns was past. FitzGerald directed his attention at assisting and influencing visiting journalists and transmitting political propaganda to the opinion-formers of Europe. His department generally made the most of the weapons it possessed in the propaganda war. It had the advantage of representing a nation fighting for self-government; it had the attraction of the underdog confronting and sometimes besting the bigwig, the brasshat and the bully. It possessed the Irish capacity for the ready welcome, for making visiting journalists feel like accepted companions in a common venture. It skilfully revealed and proclaimed excesses on the part of the old regime, yet was selective in the material it supplied: while almost always avoiding lies and fabrication, it said little about the IRA and its acts of violence. Its business was to generate the greatest possible degree of foreign support for Irish independence.

According to Warre B. Wells, FitzGerald 'was on intimate terms with every visiting Pressman. At times when the hue and cry was not too close after him a regular visitor to the offices of the *Freeman's Journal* where they usually congregated, at other times to be found in more discreet quarters, he contrived to keep himself in close and constant touch with the newspaper world of Europe and America.' The Director of Propaganda regularly produced leaders of the Dáil and the underground army for interviews. Ernie O'Malley was one of these: 'I met foreign journalists and labour men who were getting angles from either side. It was a mild adventure for some, an exciting thrill for others, to talk to men of the hidden government, for whom Castle officials, seen earlier in the day, were hunting.'

FitzGerald was always very keen to be informed in advance of any journalists coming to Ireland. He urged Art O'Brien in London to provide close, continuing contact with newsmen who were *en route* to Dublin. Because of his interest in French literature and his knowledge of the language, FitzGerald was particularly effective in working with French journalists. Among those given the FitzGerald treatment were Maurice Bourgeois, Joseph Cassell and Salvador de Madariaga.[52]

FitzGerald made frequent visits to London, where he met with a wide range of journalists. He noted that because many journalists were 'very chary of anything in the nature of propaganda, I endeavoured to meet them through introductions of a non-propaganda nature'. He urged O'Brien to maintain personal contact with these journalists, which O'Brien believed could only be done with an expanded London staff.[53]

The Dáil propagandists worked under considerable difficulties. They had to work underground, always facing the danger of arrest and the threat to their office (it moved thirteen times in two years and was discovered only once). When he took office, FitzGerald requested Sinn Féin Clubs and other nationalist organisations to send immediately to his office all accounts of raids and other actions of the police and army, but in May 1920 he declared that up to that time 'we might have received one reply, but no more'. This was to be a repeated complaint; however, he had other, very good sources of information, the intelligence network of the IRA being the best of these.[54]

Another difficulty faced by FitzGerald was that much of the news about Ireland was transmitted by English wire services which, because they derived much of their information from Dublin Castle, presented the news in a manner consistently hostile to Irish nationalism. To deal with this situation, FitzGerald set out to establish a telegraphic news service that would send news from Ireland to Britain by wire. The operation was launched in June 1920, but was 'discontinued after a few weeks' without explanation. At the same time FitzGerald announced that his department was about to create a central news office 'for the whole of the Continent'. A scheme for such an office, based in Paris, was prepared by FitzGerald and Michael MacWhite of the Paris staff and was approved by the cabinet in November 1920. Nothing further was heard of this project.[55]

News and Views: the *Irish Bulletin*

As the alternative government developed, various publications were created that were directed at particular audiences, but there was no single agency or publication that communicated with the people of the country as a whole. Perhaps the Sinn Féin leaders simply assumed that after two years of massive campaigning, culminating with the loan effort and concrete endorsements both in votes and money, they could be confident that they had the Irish people behind them and that the best communication for the Dáil would be its own initiatives. When the assembly was established, it voted to have its proceedings published, but apparently only the proceedings of the session of April 1919 were printed at the time. After the Dáil was declared illegal by Dublin Castle and the Sinn Féin papers were suppressed, the general public would have almost no direct knowledge of what the Dáil was doing. A committee looked into the possibility of buying the ailing *Freeman's Journal*, but decided against it.

The Irish Volunteers, being an older organisation, already had a publication. *An tÓglach*, begun in March 1918, was a monthly journal that overcame every obstacle in providing information and direction to local IRA units. Its editor was Piaras Béaslaí (1881–1965), 'a nervous little man who had a horrible habit of "ahem-ing" incessantly'. Like FitzGerald he was English-born (Liverpool) and had been active in the Gaelic League and the IRB.

Shortly after FitzGerald's appointment the department began issuing a weekly list entitled *Acts of Aggression by the Enemy*. Some of the reports in its early issues were not exactly of the type that would ignite world indignation. Its issue of 3 October reported that 'W. O'Grady, Hairdresser, Wicklow, having failed to remove a full-page advertisement of the Dáil Éireann Loan which was adhered to the window, the constabulary raided the premises and completely defaced it with their penknives.' This is the genesis of the *Irish Bulletin*, which first appeared in November 1919.[56]

The *Irish Bulletin* was issued five times weekly, and despite all difficulties was able to maintain this schedule for the next two years. It initially had a mailing list of only thirty, but this eventually grew to 2,000. It was intended primarily for foreign consumption. Although both FitzGerald and, for a time, Arthur Griffith were involved, its principal editor was Frank Gallagher (1893–1962), a twenty-six-year-old native of Cork who joined the Sinn Féin press office in March 1918.

Kathleen McKenna, who typed almost all of its issues, claimed that the *Bulletin* never published anything 'which could not be substantiated by inconfutable proofs'. For most of its first year it concentrated on the wrongdoings of the British regime in Ireland; Dáil Éireann and the IRA were ignored. In its first direct reference to the IRA, it had an article about the Volunteers being a 'dry force'. Dáil Éireann received no notice until mid-1920. Perhaps the people behind the *Bulletin* did not want to draw attention to the two organisations for fear that it would lead to questions about their relationship with each other.

The *Bulletin* had an obvious impact in England. By early 1920 its reports were being cited in the London *Times* and other papers. Information it related led to questions in the House of Commons. In May FitzGerald credited it with helping to achieve a 'friendly spirit' towards Irish self-government in the English press.

For all of this, the cabinet was not satisfied with the publication. In February 1920 it suggested to FitzGerald that 'Rather than just lists and bare details of incidents, specific selected occurrences should be fully investigated and written up in considerable detail.' Accordingly, the *Bulletin* soon included long articles about particular events. In addition, there were internal problems affecting the administration of the department. In May 1920 the secretary of the cabinet instructed FitzGerald to deal with his printing bills, 'some a year old'. At the same time he informed FitzGerald that the cabinet wanted a report 'about the activities of your Department during the past six months'. It also decided that the *Bulletin* should be distributed to the domestic press, an obvious oversight.

Art O'Brien in London was the sharpest critic of the department and its director. O'Brien was adamantly opposed to FitzGerald's proposal to establish a separate London news bureau. Moreover, he had a long list of complaints about FitzGerald. In September he wrote to Michael Collins that FitzGerald had endangered security by communicating with O'Brien's office through the public postal service rather than by using Dáil couriers. Worse still, 'he leaves papers and things about all over the place, and never knows where they are. One of these days, his carelessness will probably land himself and perhaps others in trouble.' After a talk with FitzGerald about propaganda, 'I found his ideas in the matter quite hopeless'. O'Brien declared his intention to 'draw up a complete report of the needs of propaganda and the lines upon which it should be conducted'. George Gavan Duffy in Paris joined O'Brien in criticising FitzGerald's department.[57]

Collins fully shared the views of O'Brien and Duffy. When in September 1920 copies of the *Bulletin* were put, unwrapped, in the wrong letter-box in the building where his department had an office, Collins wrote to FitzGerald: 'I have received complaints from numbers of people regarding the manner in which communications and parcels are sent out from your department.' He added that 'A careless mistake of this kind might —

and in fact does — involve my whole Department, as well as placing your own Department in jeopardy.' When similar incidents occurred, Collins's anger boiled over in a letter to O'Brien: 'It is simply heart-scalding the way this carelessness is allowed, and the effect it has. It is only a waste of time pointing out these things to the Department, consequently I am drawing Mr Griffith's attention to the matter.' The department touched a raw nerve when, without consulting Collins, it issued an inaccurate statement about the results of the Dáil Loan. This was the last straw: 'The Propaganda Department is positively extraordinary. . . . It is just the sort of thing that would make a friendly foreigner get sick of us.'

Despite all these problems, the course of events presented the Dáil publicists with a plethora of opportunities for swaying public opinion. Commenting on the public impact of the long hunger-strike of Terence MacSwiney in the autumn of 1920, FitzGerald said that 'foreign journalists thought that the Irish Government spent millions of money on propaganda in other countries'. In fact it was an extremely low-cost operation. FitzGerald added: 'The value of the advent of so many journalists to Ireland lay in the fact that they returned firmly convinced of the iniquity of the British occupation.' If the efforts of FitzGerald and his department were sometimes, or even frequently, confused and disorganised, this was only apparent to those within the hidden government. Much more importantly, they obviously had a strongly positive effect on those they sought to influence — the foreign press and public opinion.[58]

(8) FOREIGN AFFAIRS: PROPAGANDA UNDER ANOTHER NAME

The first Minister for Foreign Affairs was George Noble Plunkett (1851–1948), Count of the Papal Court. At the age of sixty-eight, he was a well-travelled gentleman and scholar. Literary man, advocate of the Irish language and antiquarian, Director of the National Museum from 1907 to 1916, he was dragged into revolutionary politics by his son's execution in 1916. A man of principle and intelligence, Plunkett left little mark on his ministry. He demonstrated neither a sense of purpose nor eagerness to initiate action. He was promptly subordinated: at the Dáil session of June 1919 he was listed as the 'Associate Secretary for Foreign Affairs'. Griffith later claimed that he himself had acted as Foreign Minister while de Valera was away; yet it was Plunkett who reported to the Dáil and, apparently, administered the little department, although there are no papers to indicate that he did very much of anything. Soon after his return to Ireland in late December 1920, de Valera quickly moved to strengthen the department with the appointment of Robert Brennan as Under-Secretary for Foreign Affairs. When the cabinet was reorganised during the truce period, all the released ministers resumed their former positions, while Plunkett was appointed to head the new Ministry of Fine Arts.

The department initially concentrated on four countries: Britain, of course, the United States, France and Italy (and the headquarters of the international church that was located there). Art O'Brien already was at work in London, and de Valera was mounting a massive campaign for support in America; the Dáil government did not send a representative to Rome until mid-1920. Because of the Versailles conference, there had been a Dáil presence in Paris since the beginning of 1919. When the conference ended, the Dáil representatives remained in place.

Helping the Egyptian and Indian Nationalists
One valuable activity carried on by the Dáil government was the development of relationships begun earlier in the year with representatives of independence movements in other countries, principally Egypt and India, within the British empire. An active anti-imperialist foreign policy had been advocated by Frank Gallagher on several occasions.

The relationship with the Egyptian group was particularly close. Seán T. O'Kelly later claimed that Saad Zagloul, the leader of the Egyptian movement, and himself became 'great personal friends', but O'Kelly, a genuinely good-natured and warm-hearted man, was a professional politician to whom ties of friendship and regard were tools of the trade. 'Zagloul seldom sent any communication to the English that he did not submit to me beforehand,' commented O'Kelly, 'for, as he frequently said, we Irish had good reason to know the English better than they did.'

The Egyptian situation was acute, as Egyptian nationalists were moving towards negotiations with the British government about self-government. To complicate the situation, mass rioting, amounting to an insurrection, broke out in the spring of 1919. This event was hailed in the Sinn Féin press. In mid-June came an announcement that the Irish representatives had joined with Egyptian, Indian and South African nationalists in a joint-action agreement. The Irish agents told the Dáil cabinet that the purpose of the pact 'was for propaganda and to alarm the English', that, in fact, the South African nationalists had quietly departed, and that there were no Indian nationalist representatives in Paris, only an 'official delegation'. The Egyptians, however, 'are genuine and keen on any co-operation that can hurt or appear to hurt'. The agreement was welcomed by *The Irishman* (14 June) as furthering an objective it had supported for years and whose 'advantages are incalcuable'. The government of Dáil Éireann, however, was alarmed. Griffith told the Dáil on 14 June that 'There was no alliance between India, Egypt and Ireland.They were working in co-operation.'[59]

O'Kelly and Duffy in Paris were informed of the position of the cabinet: the other victims of empire 'have our full sympathy and any mutual assistance that can be rendered without definitely aligning our position with theirs is very desirable.' It was argued that all-encompassing resolutions denouncing England at international conferences 'would be less helpful to us in the eyes of the world than definite demands for the recognition of Ireland's elected Government'. In other words, take care of yourself first and the rest of the world will benefit in the long run.

At about the same time Art O'Brien was approached by 'Egypt's leading man in London' who sought help in organising and directing a nationalist movement. O'Brien was very pleased to provide advice, but he shared the view of Dublin about the nature of these relationships: 'I think [it] is a really important point for them all to recognise that our triumph will be the triumph of all and consequently it is really, therefore, more in their interests in one way to work hard for our success.' The cabinet decided that a 'sympathetic message' to the Egyptians would be a sufficient gesture at this time. The message that it dispatched in late July declared its hope that Egypt would regain its independence 'in the near future' and denounced English domination of the country.

Despite the cabinet's position, Frank P. Walsh accepted Zagloul's offer to become counsel for the Egyptian movement in the United States. Walsh used some of the money he received for his services to establish the League of Oppressed Peoples, obviously a purely propagandist forum. Later, in the summer of 1921, Joseph Folk, his former law partner, presented the Egyptian case to a US Senate committee.[60]

The Irish-Egyptian relationship was renewed in the spring of 1920 with the advent of Egyptian nationalist negotiations with the British. While Duffy maintained contact in Paris, Art O'Brien became a key if covert adviser to the Egyptian negotiators in London. When offered less than effective self-government, O'Brien knew what they should do: they should accept merely the first article of the agreement, which recognised independence, 'then proceed to establish their independent Government, [and] let that Government proceed to discuss any necessary terms with the English Government'. He also urged that the negotiations should not take place in London but in a neutral country. When an agreement was signed on 6 July 1920 which gave only nominal independence to Egypt, Gavan Duffy commented: 'England is throwing away a big sprat in a desperate attempt to keep hold of the whale.'

When neither of the two major American parties supported Irish independence in the presidential election of 1920, Frank Gallagher concluded: 'We have no allies except our brothers in pain. The Indians and Egyptians will be true to us.' A month later Seán T. O'Kelly in Rome joined forces with Egyptian and Indian representatives to launch a new co-operative organisation — the Roman Committee of Subject Nations. In the United States de Valera cast doubt on the reality of any British offer of Egyptian self-government: 'You will be independent, but you must not do so and so, and so and so, and so and so, and when all the Egyptians must not do is subtracted from nominal independence not much would be left.' This kind of offer, he said, would be the kind that Britain would offer Ireland.

Among his many activities, O'Brien assisted Ibrahim Rashid, an Egyptian student, to write a book about his experiences in Ireland. Under O'Brien's severe guidance, Rashid published the book in 1921. *An Egyptian in Ireland,* interesting as a period piece, was strongly sympathetic to Irish nationalism. Rashid remarked that 'My fellow-countrymen tell me I must have some distant ancestor, probably in the pre-historic days, who was Irish.' A leader in the nationalist movement among Egyptian students in England, he warned Irish nationalists about the dangers of being offered an agreement like that extended to his country. His most notable achievement was to join two Irishmen in running onto the field waving tricolours at the 1921 Ireland–France rugby match in Paris; up to this time, of course, the Union Jack was the 'official' flag of Ireland.[61]

The representatives of Dáil Éireann worked with other groups seeking self-government for their countries. In the United States de Valera clearly aligned his government with the nationalist causes in India, Egypt and Persia. 'The great moral forces of the world are with India and with Ireland today,' he declared in February 1920. 'We must use them to the full, but we must never forget that we must ultimately rely upon ourselves if we are to be successful.' In October of that year O'Brien, after conferring with a Burmese nationalist group, told Michael Collins that because 'their views and outlook with regard to their political position seems to be similar to our own . . . we should give them full information on the constructive side of our work, both before and after the estab-lishment of the Republic'. In response, Collins said that he had asked the Propaganda Department to prepare 'a Treatise on the achievements of the Irish Republic up to the present and sketch a programme of reconstruction for the future. . . . This would be the best guide for our friends.'

In January 1921 a Turkish revolutionary, 'favourably impressed with [the] manner in which the Advanced Party in Ireland are conducting their struggle against Great Britain', requested that the Dáil government provide a group of ten or twelve men 'who are acquainted with the military and political aspects of our movement and capable of applying their information to the circumstances in Turkey and Egypt'. De Valera's response was that 'the sending of men is out of the question'. This matter was to arise again. But the Dáil representatives continued their advisory services to Indian and Egyptian nationalists to the end of 1921.[62]

Conflict within the Paris Mission

For a time in the latter half of 1919 the Irish mission in Paris did not have much to do. According to O'Kelly, Duffy frequently remarked that 'our work here just now is *not* serious, that we can do little more than mark time till we are recalled, that we are wasting money. . . .' Probably to fill this void, the members of the mission squabbled among themselves. Victor Collins, a former Paris correspondent of an American newspaper, decided to return to Ireland, but not before denouncing O'Kelly and Duffy 'for treating him as an office boy'. In any case, this minor controversy soon subsided and Collins continued to work in the new foreign service.

Then O'Kelly and Duffy came into conflict. When the Versailles conference ended, it was assumed that both men would shortly return to Dublin. On 15 June 1919 Duffy wrote to the cabinet to recommend reduction in office space and the appointment of Ernest Boyd, a Dublin literary critic, as consul. The cabinet, however, decided that both its existing envoys should remain in Paris. Trouble soon developed. O'Kelly had been working under great pressure from the beginning of the year and now suffered what was obviously a nervous breakdown. On 3 September Duffy accused O'Kelly of not showing him the reports he was sending to Dublin. While expressing his sympathy for O'Kelly in his present affliction, he nevertheless complained: 'I do protest against your treating matters of business in this way, for your methods can only result in making our supposed co-operation an unpleasant farce.' In his good-natured way, O'Kelly immediately agreed to joint dispatches and the employment of 'strict business methods if you think that would alleviate the woes of our exile'.[63]

The cabinet decided that O'Kelly should return to Dublin at the end of November 1919, but his illness returned; on his recovery, he was dispatched to Rome, where he 'was again taken very ill'. Anticipating O'Kelly's return to Paris in February 1920, Duffy wrote to Dublin: 'It is a waste having the pair of us here and we are not a good team to work together, as you may have surmised ere now.' But in the following month O'Kelly received a letter from de Valera in which he declared that he 'was strongly of the opinion that we should both stay on in Paris until further notice'. The President's judgment came as 'something of a shock' to Duffy, who informed Dublin that it was 'perfectly certain' that there would be 'no loyal co-operation between us if Seán T. returns here'. He sent a similar message to de Valera in July.

Having met with Duffy in Paris and O'Kelly in Rome during June, Art O'Brien strongly advised that both of them should not be based in Paris. He also saw the need 'to have someone in Dublin to deal with [the] Foreign Service promptly'. The man nominally in charge, Count Plunkett, told the Dáil in June 1920: 'The strain of the past year and a half is telling on them, and it may be necessary for them both to take an extended vacation.' In the summer the cabinet at last grasped the nettle and decided to keep both men where they were.

It was just at this time that the Paris office became busy again. From the beginning of 1920 Duffy had noted 'a great change from last summer and early autumn when no one here or very few wanted to have anything to do with us or to hear anything about Ireland'. He attributed the 'keen revival of interest' to French resentment concerning a series of British political and economic actions. To counter the influence of 'English effort and English gold', he urged a variety of measures, including the establishment of a Paris press bureau, an expanded propaganda campaign and an association with a French press agency. Both Sylvain Briollay and O'Brien also noted the improved press and political climate in France. This was a good omen for Dáil Éireann's propaganda efforts on the continent.[64]

(9) THE AMERICAN CAMPAIGN: THE FIRST PHASE

The revolutionary government of Dáil Éireann made a major commitment of personnel and resources to a campaign in the United States. During 1919 a miniature government in exile was assembled in New York. Sinn Féin was compelled to make such an effort because America presented the best opportunity for gathering support abroad. In addition, funds collected in the United States were absolutely vital for the development of an alternative government. The loan campaign in Ireland eventually raised £370,000, but that feat could not be expected to be repeated in the near future, and the amount raised would not be enough to create a substantial counter-state. Thus the United States became a key factor, both politically and financially, in the conflict. The most notable advocate of Irish self-government to cross the Atlantic was the head of the executive of the rebel republic, but Eamon de Valera was only the best known of the group dispatched from Dublin.

The process of establishing a presence in America began just over a year after the 1916 rising. Dr Patrick McCartan (1878–1966), a veteran of the rebellion, arrived in May 1917 with the title of 'Envoy of the Provisional Government of the Irish Republic'; in fact he represented the Irish Republican Brotherhood. Already in place was Clan na Gael, financier of militant nationalism in Ireland and the American counterpart of the IRB. It was led by the indomitable John Devoy and had as its front organisation the Friends of Irish Freedom, which was then largely a New York body but which developed a nationwide membership through its sponsorship of a series of Irish Race Conventions from 1916 to 1919.

McCartan was in an anomalous position for fully two years. Devoy and his colleagues did not acknowledge him as the spokesman of Irish republicanism, preferring instead to deal directly with the IRB in Dublin. There was a splinter group within the Clan led by Joseph McGarrity

(1874–1940), a Tyrone-born Philadelphia businessman who had been in the USA since 1892 and who established a republican newspaper, the *Irish Press*, in May 1918. McCartan and McGarrity were old friends, having been born in the same parish, and it is therefore not surprising that McCartan aligned himself with McGarrity's faction. As a result, he also developed a close relationship with Dr William Maloney (1882–1952), a former British army physician and war veteran, who proved to be the most innovative and effective propagandist for the Irish cause in America. Already he had launched a picket of the British embassy in Washington, had shipped a quantity of copies of the American Catholic bishops' programme for social and economic reconstruction to Sinn Féin leaders in Ireland, and had written a large number of articles supporting Irish independence. Later he was to propose the establishment of commissions to investigate British actions in Ireland and to provide relief to the victims of violence. He must have been a man of remarkable acuteness and insight. De Valera said that he could not meet and discuss anything with Maloney 'without revealing what was in his mind'. The trio of McCartan, McGarrity and Maloney soon became locked in conflict with the Devoy organisation in New York.

John Devoy, the senior citizen of the Irish revolutionary tradition, was seventy-eight years old in 1919. Fenian and felon, he had lived in the United States for nearly fifty years, where he had fought a long battle to control the Clan and where he edited the *Gaelic American*, probably the most influential Irish-American newspaper. Devoy had played an important role in initiating the 1916 rebellion, and his prestige among Irish republicans was, accordingly, at its zenith. He was a determined, domineering man who devoted his life to the cause and took violent exception to anyone who threatened his authority. When challenged by the Philadelphia group, he was mortally offended and received support from a group of Irish-American political leaders.

Foremost among these was Daniel F. Cohalan (1865–1946), a New York lawyer and Tammany Hall figure who had risen to be a member of the New York state supreme court. As a member of the bar and bench, his record appears to have been without distinction, but within the politics of Irish-American organisations he had attained real power by the end of the world war. A member of Clan na Gael for many years, Cohalan gained a predominant influence over the aged, sedentary Devoy and was the leader of the Friends of Irish Freedom. He was also anathema to the Wilson administration for his opposition to Wilson's re-election in 1916 and for his association with a pro-German faction within the Irish-American community.

Joining forces with Devoy and Cohalan was Diarmuid Lynch (1878–1950), who had earlier become an American citizen and was a 1916 veteran. After being expelled from Ireland as a result of his leadership of the Sinn Féin food control campaign in 1918, Lynch became the secretary of the FOIF and initiated the rapid expansion of that organisation.[65]

What was the basis of the conflict between the two factions? It appears to have been simply a matter of power — of who would control the organisation and resources of the campaign for Irish self-government in the United States. One group sought control because it was exclusively interested in Irish independence; the other group primarily wanted to use the movement to further its quest for power in American politics. It is worth noting that this conflict existed before de Valera set out on his mission and was one which he had no part in originating.

An Irish Race Convention, organised by the FOIF, met on 22–23 February 1919; it voted to raise $2 million for an 'Irish Victory Fund' and dispatched a three-man delegation to the Paris Peace Conference (at the cost of $21,500). It viewed itself as being separate from but equal to the republic whose establishment had been ratified a month earlier; its demand was for self-determination for Ireland. Sinn Féin newspapers assumed that events in Paris and Ireland were having a considerable impact on American opinion. *The Irishman* (7 June 1919) declared that the work done in Paris 'means a great achievement in the coming struggle in America'. When the Irish-American delegation issued its report on conditions in Ireland, the paper held that its conclusions would create 'such a hostile attitude in America that an alliance or entente' between the United States and Britain 'will become . . . impossible'. It was generally assumed that the funds collected for the Victory Fund would be used in Ireland in the struggle for national freedom.

There were problems in the American camp. The million dollars that had been collected for the Victory Fund by September 1919 were controlled by the FOIF, which clearly intended to use the money to fight Woodrow Wilson and the League of Nations. When Dáil Éireann sought some of this money, Cohalan was ill-disposed to accede to its request, and only $10,000 was initially provided; this was not dispatched directly to the government in Dublin, but was transmitted through a FOIF employee in Paris. The complexity and intensity of the internal feuding in America can be seen in the reports Gavan Duffy dispatched to Dublin. For his part, Devoy wrote to Seán T. O'Kelly that William Maloney was 'the most dangerous British agent' who attacked the loyalty and misrepresented the nature of men who had been working all their lives for the cause. O'Kelly assured him all would be put right shortly, as the Dáil government was dispatching a representative to New York.[66]

The Dáil leadership was aware of the division of forces in the United States. Michael Collins commented in October 1919: 'From the very beginning and indeed prior to anyone going out I knew well what to expect from the people in command in the US. However, the best, not the worst, must be made of them, and there is little doubt that eventually things will be all right.' 'To straighten matters', Harry Boland, who was one of the leading figures in the IRB, was sent as Dáil representative. Arriving in mid-May, he was told by the Devoy–Cohalan group that their opponents were seeking to disrupt an effectively organised movement. After considering the situation, however, Boland gave his support to the McGarrity–McCartan group and issued fresh credentials to McCartan as the envoy of the Republic of Ireland. Diarmuid O'Hegarty, for one, believed that Boland was having 'good success' in dealing with the division and that 'his presence and that of the President will, we think, obviate any recurrence of the difficulty'. But peace was not at hand. When challenged by Boland about the Irish Victory Fund, Cohalan declared that he was opposed to sending any money to Ireland. After 'a very, very stiff fight to get any money for home', the FOIF executive agreed to send the Dáil $250,000.

On 11 June, less than a month after Boland's arrival, de Valera landed in New York. The President had three objectives before him: to gain American support for Irish independence; to seek diplomatic recognition of the Irish Republic and its national parliamentary assembly; and to raise money to finance the alternative government. At his first public appearance, on 23 June, he announced that he would be leading a loan campaign in the USA. The idea for such an undertaking is credited to M. J. Ryan, a member of the Irish-American delegation, who broached the subject during his visit to Ireland. On his return to the USA, however, he declared that he could not see how the Dáil could spend more than $50,000 a year, an opinion which may be explained by the fact that the underground government was only in its infancy at the time of his visit.[67]

De Valera's loan drive would cut across the campaign under way for the Irish Victory Fund. 'At the urgent request of President de Valera' and despite Cohalan's objection that the issuing of bonds by a non-recognised government was almost certainly illegal, the FOIF at length agreed to end its campaign in September. Moreover, it also agreed to provide a loan of $100,000 to launch the new effort and provide funds for de Valera's travel expenses. These expenses were heavy, as de Valera almost immediately began a national speaking tour. He also asked the three Irish-American delegates to continue as members of the American Commission on Irish Independence, which would become the initial custodian of the loan funds. To preclude criticism that this effort was just another Irish collection device, the Dáil government agreed to accept financial responsibility for the $500,000 of Fenian bonds issued in the later 1860s. In order to accept direct contributions, a Self-Determination Fund was established. A publicity campaign for the loan was begun in August, and a prospectus was issued in October; the actual sale of bonds did not take place until January 1920.

Thus far de Valera had been received by the Devoy–Cohalan group with studied respect and deference, in spite of their initial difficulty in recognising his status as the head of a government in being. (Patrick McCartan had the same problem: 'I know it sticks in one's throat for a while in the beginning to gravely speak of President de Valera, but he had to stand for it here and did it magnificently with good results.') Conversely, for their part Cohalan and his likes were impressive figures to the newly arrived band of young Irishmen. Seán Nunan, a member of the Dáil staff in New York, wrote to Collins in September 1919:

> I thought at one time that we had some politicians at home, but believe me they are nothing to the brands over here. Harry's hair is falling out with worry. Your remarks to him at Vaughan's on the night of his American wake he often repeats, 'I'm a poor lonesome whore'.

Nunan added that 'The GWC [Great White Chief, i.e. de Valera] is beating them and in spite of a lot of trouble and jealousy will come out on top.' In the same month Liam Mellows, another staff member, wrote home:

> Gang not pulling with de Valera. Want to run him. He won't run. He has seen through them. . . . Never saw a sicker man. Disillusionment isn't the word.

Devoy informed O'Kelly that 'de Valera has fallen into the wrong hands' and that a public rupture was likely. Both O'Kelly and Art O'Brien were hopeful that de Valera would be able to avoid an open split. De Valera told his colleagues in Dublin of his difficulties which he believed to be so serious 'that I was actually considering the question of whether it would not be better for our cause that I should return, or go elsewhere'.[68]

He did not leave the United States; instead he remained there for a year and a half. It was a tumultuous time for everyone who was part of the Irish mission. If relations with the Devoy–Cohalan group did not improve, an effort was made on both sides to keep their differences out of the public eye. De Valera believed there was a crying need to educate the American public about Ireland: 'It is astonishing how little is really known about the true situation even by our friends. The ABC has to be learned.' Within a month of his arrival the President began a public speaking tour in the north-eastern states, with their large Irish-American populations, as a prelude to the launching of the loan campaign. The public response was nothing short of electrifying. Introduced to a massive crowd of 70,000 at Fenway Park in Boston by Senator David I. Walsh as the 'Lincoln of Ireland', de Valera rose to the occasion with a speech that had an extraordinarily powerful impact. His 'passionate sincerity and utmost simplicity', commented the *Boston Herald*, 'burn their way into the consciousness of everyone who sees and hears him'. According to *The Nation* (12 July 1919),

Governors, Senators and mayors pay court to him and do him honor. He issues a presidential statement of Irish republican policy, and the newspapers print it in full. He proposes to pay off the $500,000 issue of Fenian bonds put out in 1866 to finance an invasion of Canada, and the same jealous guardians of our national honor roar as gently as the sucking dove. He gets a front-page spread whenever he wants it, with unexampled editorial kindness thrown in.

Dr Maloney might have overestimated de Valera's public standing, but *Current Opinion* (Aug. 1919) commented that he 'has made himself an interesting world figure, whose passionate pleas and political adroitness have in a few weeks turned a joke into a topic of serious discussion on both sides of the Atlantic'.

Many Irishmen naturally were prepared to believe the flood of news-paper reports about the progress of the American campaign. To the Sinn Féin executive this was 'the most momentous American news concerning Ireland for a century', but owing to 'the weak-kneed policy of the Irish Daily press the full tide of American feeling on the Irish question is not recorded here'. It appeared that de Valera and his colleagues were sweep-ing all before them. Arthur Griffith echoed this belief at the Sinn Féin *ard-fheis* of November 1919, adding: 'If they remain steadfast here, de Valera would do the rest in America.' The French journalist Sylvain Briollay observed that many Irish people were certain that 'great things were happening or were about to happen in America'. Statements to this effect were repeated 'and in such trenchant tones', he related, 'that one is on the point of accepting them as obvious. One must have lived in Ireland to understand the spell cast, in the long run, by the endless repetition of gratuitous statements.' It was, however, the view of the English journalist and historian H. N. Brailsford that the enthusiastic reception accorded to de Valera did not mean that the Irish question would be an important factor in the next year's election, because the American people were eager to get away from involvement in Europe.[69]

During the summer and autumn of 1919 a fully-fledged Irish mission was assembled in the United States. This included seven members of the Dáil. Liam Mellows, the leader of the 1916 rising in Galway, had been in the USA since 1917. James O'Mara, a prominent Dublin businessman, arrived in July to become the financial director of the loan campaign. James A. Burke, deputy for Mid-Tipperary, arrived in November and became New York state director of that effort. Other deputies in the USA, either then or later, were McCartan, Boland, Ginnell and, of course, de Valera. Diarmuid Lynch, secretary of the FOIF, was also a member of the Dáil and was working in co-operation with the Irish mission at that time. Other Irishmen involved were Seán Nunan, Clerk of the Dáil, Diarmuid Fawsitt, consul in New York city, and Captain Robert Monteith, another 1916 veteran, who also worked in the loan drive. In the following year de

Valera asked the cabinet to send Robert Brennan to direct publicity and Erskine Childers to be ambassador. During the latter half of 1919 a campaign organisation was assembled, although the effort was not launched until the following January.

Communication with Ireland was generally secure; some important messages were sent in code by telegram, but the rest were carried by friendly seamen. The arrest of one of these in July 1920 at Southampton led to the seizure of some dispatches about the conflict within the Irish ranks in the USA. Michael Collins was unconcerned: 'The Mail was the least important one that was ever dispatched from New York. . . . They must have been disappointed.' The Irish mission sent more than reports. Seán Nunan was a principal participant in the shipping of small amounts of arms and ammunition. When in October 1919 the head of the Dublin Metropolitan Police issued an order that 'the sailors on all American ships are now suspect, and all their belongings must be searched', Collins secured a copy which he hoped could be used to rouse public opinion in America. The British administration had little success in stopping this small flow of arms. In December 1920 the British ambassador to the United States requested 'any available evidence to prove that munitions and money reach Sinn Féiners from the US'. Obviously little or no such evidence was then at hand.

De Valera was concerned about likely British efforts to counter his efforts. When Horace Plunkett, leader of the new Irish Dominion League, arrived in the United States in mid-1919, he was viewed by the Irish mission as little more than a British agent. The response of the British government to the Irish agitation was low-keyed. A few government-financed lecturers were dispatched, but it was the official view that a direct effort to combat the Irish campaign would be counter-productive at this time. Members of the Irish mission, however, charged that British agents preceded and followed de Valera on his speaking tours, seeking to influence public officials not to receive him and spreading the view that religion was the basis of the Irish conflict. They had some successes: 'On four occasions they succeeded in inducing bodies of clergymen to adopt resolutions giving the colour to this impression.'

The only open attempt to battle the Irish agitation was initiated by Max Aitken, Lord Beaverbrook. Drawing on his Canadian origins and his experiences in wartime propaganda in the USA, Beaverbrook used the pages of his *Daily Express* in July and September to propose the sending of an Ulster Unionist/Protestant delegation to rouse American Protestant feeling against the Irish nationalist effort. 'The Methodist Church . . . regards a politico-religious crusade preached by the Irish with small favour,' he declared, 'but it might take no practical action on the other side unless its interest was suddenly roused. Then it would act and it would crush the American Sinn Féiners as a cartwheel crushes a toad.' The need, then, was for an Ulster counter-force, and 'if they make the appeal in loud enough accents the feelings of those Presbyterian and Methodist Churches will move them. Let it be agitated and fought out for a time on the other side of the Atlantic.'[70]

Such a delegation, sponsored by the Ulster Unionist Council, was dispatched in November. It was led by William J. Coote, journeyman MP for South Tyrone and businessman of a clouded background. It included six Belfast clergymen — three Methodists, two Presbyterians and an Anglican — none of whom was prominent. Ernest Blythe, the only Ulster Protestant in the Dáil, pointed out that none of them had been officially appointed by their churches. This was indeed a low-level delegation. But Edward Carson sent a telegram, the Church of Ireland Bishop of Down and Connor saw it off, and Thomas Moles, MP, made a departure speech in which he remarked that, while several American presidents were of Ulster descent, 'the people they were going to antagonise had left no better impress upon public life in America than that of Tammany Hall'.

Immediately upon the delegation's arrival in New York, de Valera challenged Coote to a public debate, with the issues in contention to be judged by an all-American commission of inquiry. Coote replied that he would not debate with a man 'the hands of whose followers are dyed in the blood of my countrymen'. As the Coote delegation toured the country it was pursued by a group of Protestant ministers and laymen organised in the Protestant Friends of Ireland. This group was led by Lindsay Crawford, an Ulster-born journalist, formerly a leading figure in the Independent Orange Institution and then editor of the *Toronto Statesman*, and included Dr Maurice F. Murphy, a Methodist minister formerly of Dublin. One of Coote's group called them 'a lot of renegade Protestants who are being financed, backed and supported by the Roman Catholic Church', a charge repeated by Coote himself. The Rev. Louis Crooks, a Church of Ireland clergyman, told a Detroit audience that the cause 'of all the trouble and dissatisfaction in Ireland' was

the division of authority between two powers. . . . Side by side with the civil power, there is another which is dark and tortuous in its workings — even when you are in your bed at night. I mean the Vatican (*applause. A voice from the audience:* We have it here!). When these two powers come into conflict, take it from me, the civil power always goes under.

Lindsay Crawford returned these salvoes: 'Could there be a more striking example of rampant Clericalism than the spectacle presented by Mr Coote's troupe of Clerical nomads in their visit to the US, as the apostles of sectarian hate and bigotry?'

De Valera sought to refute the charges of nationalist sectarianism by offering to 'put a clause in the Irish Constitution granting full religious freedom to every citizen'. He also began appearing before gatherings in Protestant churches. After addressing an open forum at the Grace Methodist Church in Denver, he was praised by its minister for presenting a forthright, manly statement. He was accompanied on some of his travels by the Rev. J. Grattan Mythem, an Episcopal clergyman and descendant of Henry Grattan. To further shore up the non-sectarian position, the Rev. Dr J. A. H. Irwin, a Presbyterian minister from Killead, Co. Antrim, travelled from Ireland to support de Valera's campaign. He was, said Harry Boland, 'just the type of man we require'. He was unique among Ulster ministers in that he had taken a Ph.D. at University College, Dublin. During the several weeks he spent in the USA Irwin joined de Valera on an extensive speaking tour in the south. The chemistry between the two was good, and they became lifelong friends. Irwin's message was that, based on his experience, there was no sectarianism among Irish nationalists, and that the Coote delegation did not represent the views of a majority of Ulster Protestants. After his return to Ireland he was sentenced to a year in prison on a clearly nebulous charge. He then served as one of the Dáil government's advisers on Ulster. Years later he moved to Dublin and was awarded an honorary D.Litt. by the National University in 1950.

A later recruit was the Rev. Herbert Dunnico, an English evangelist with an Irish father. Michael Collins believed that 'a non-conformist in America could unquestionably be of advantage to us'. Supplied with £250, Dunnico toured the USA and Canada in the autumn of 1920, visiting over seventy communities. Through his efforts, he reported, 'prejudices and fears, genuinely held by many, were dissipated and the movement, particularly in Canada, received a great impetus'. At the express desire of de Valera, he declared his support for Irish self-government 'before he planned doing so', as a result of which several speaking engagements were cancelled. To cover his excess expenses, Dunnico was given an additional £150; he later became a Labour MP.

At the end of four months the Coote delegation 'left with a sense that they had not been given a full hearing in print'. Owing to its blatant sectarianism, and the counter-measures put into effect by the Sinn Féin mission, the delegation was ineffective in generating opposition to Irish self-government. There was strong anti-Catholic feeling in many parts of the USA, as a presidential election a few years later was to demonstrate, but this was primarily an internal phenomenon and could not be directed at situations in other countries.[71]

During the period from his arrival until the end of 1919, indeed for almost the first year he was in the United States, de Valera went from strength to strength. He was met with an overwhelming popular reception. His cause gained enormous attention in the press: every daily newspaper had to address the question of Ireland in its editorials. A hugely successful loan campaign had been organised. Much of the success of the Irish mission was due to de Valera's powerful personality and platform presence — the public knew a dynamic political figure when it saw one. All of this had a major impact in Ireland — and this undoubtedly was the most important result of his American sojourn. Sinn Féiners were greatly encouraged to persevere, while the uncommitted were swayed towards the belief that Irish independence was an emerging reality.

*

As 1919 drew to a close the two sides in the struggle for Ireland had reason for both satisfaction and apprehension. Dublin Castle had maintained effective control of the country and had forced its impudent rival underground. A new plan for Irish government was being prepared in London. Yet the existing administration had to face the fact that it had little public support and was unlikely to secure more, while the strength of Sinn Féin was increasing. The Castle government's principal arm of control, the police force, was being stripped of its authority.

The insurgents, on the other hand, had brought about the inauguration of a new assembly and fledgling government, though they had experienced an early disappointment at Paris. This had been followed by the success of the loan campaign and de Valera's impressive activities in America. The process of destroying the RIC as a police and intelligence-gathering body was well under way. Several domestic programmes had been launched, and an effective propaganda effort had been mounted. Public opinion was volatile, however, and the new Home Rule Bill might swing the electorate away from support for full independence; the public might sicken of the campaign of violence. Nor could Dáil Éireann yet claim that it had effectively supplanted the British administration. This was to be the task for the new year of 1920.

3

The Year of Revolution

Sinn Féin anticipated the new year of 1920 with relish. The long-delayed local government elections were to be held — for urban areas in January and for county councils in June. The process of destroying the RIC could be carried to completion. Continued and growing support from America was a reasonable expectation. But 1920 was to see more than platform oratory and barrack attacks: the burden of government was to be shifted onto the shoulders of Dáil Éireann. It was the year in which British domination of Ireland ended. This was brought about not primarily by the IRA, Sinn Féin or Dáil Éireann, but by the will and choice of a majority of the politically involved people of the country. All the fury of British counter-revolution would not alter this fundamental change. On the other hand, Dáil Éireann would be challenged to live up to its claim to be the government of Ireland.

(1) Capturing Local Government: the Elections of 1920

Local government elections had not been held in Ireland since before the outbreak of the European war. They were due to be held in 1917, but the rise of the new militant nationalism persuaded the British government to postpone them repeatedly. Sinn Féin looked forward to the elections and during 1919 taunted Dublin Castle for not being prepared to face another plebiscite on self-determination. Party activists were urged to revive their campaign organisations. Seán Milroy, the Sinn Féin Director of Organisation, informed the Dáil in August 1919 that there was 'considerable reluctance' on the part of some deputies to get to work on this task.

There appeared to have been a general relaxation of party organisation in the euphoric period after the general election. Of the 1,822 Sinn

Féin *cumainn* that had existed in November 1918, only 60 per cent were affiliated by mid-1919 and only 4 per cent had paid membership fees. In August the party executive took action to revive the local branches by appointing eighteen sub-organisers to assist the four provincial organisers — five for Ulster, Munster and Connacht, and three for Leinster. Milroy announced that special attention was being given to Ulster in order 'to discover what is the most effective means of overcoming antagonism to the Nationalist idea where such exists in the Province'.

In an action obviously designed to limit the scope of an anticipated Sinn Féin victory, the British government changed the method of election in Irish local government from the traditional simple first-past-the-post system to that of proportional representation (with the single transferable vote). This change was not applied to any other part of the United Kingdom. To gauge the effect of the new method, it was employed in a special municipal election held in Sligo in January 1919. Emboldened by the failure of Sinn Féin to win a majority of seats, the British government set elections for borough and urban district councils for the following January, and elections for county councils and rural district councils for June.

Proportional representation struck no terror into the ranks of Sinn Féin. With its overwhelming public support, the party could anticipate winning the elections under any system. De Valera welcomed the change: 'Whether it benefited us or not I would be in favour of the principle because it is founded on justice. We know the object for which it was designed. It was a crooked object. . . .' Moreover, as Arthur Griffith pointed out, the party had supported proportional representation since 1907. It reaffirmed its support at the *ard-fheis* of April 1919. This position was baffling to the London *Daily News* (6 Jan.): 'That Sinn Féin, instead of opposing a change declaredly designed to cripple its power, should willingly help in its development is more than remarkable.'

If Dublin Castle and Home Rulers were encouraged by the Sligo result, their reassurance was to be short-lived. In October 1919 the National University held its senate election in which Eoin Mac Néill endorsed a slate of Sinn Féin candidates who swept the boards, defeating several distinguished incumbents, including Dr Douglas Hyde, Father Tom Finlay and Dr George Sigerson. One of the successful Sinn Féiners was labelled a 'Bolshevik bosthoon'. When another university election was held in January 1920, the result was the same — another Sinn Féin sweep.

Dáil Éireann created a local government department at the beginning of its existence; its minister since April 1919 was William T. Cosgrave (1880–1965), who had served for ten years as a member of Dublin Corporation. There was considerable support for Sinn Féin in many local bodies, with many incumbents shifting over to the new power in the land, but the party was not in a majority in any major council. Thus in its first year the department could not do much; Cosgrave investigated the possibility of organising a municipal milk service and the purchase of the *Freeman's Journal,* both without result. His department advised local government bodies to apply for all possible British grants while time allowed, anticipating that things would change after the next elections. In particular it urged the councils to proceed 'full steam ahead' in applying for funds for public housing.

In October 1919 the department reported that it was preparing a local government programme for use in the elections, but its contents would not be revealed at that time 'as it might be subject to piracy'. A month later Joseph McGuinness, as Sinn Féin Director of Elections, informed *cumainn* that all party candidates would be required to take a pledge to support Dáil Éireann and make a commitment 'to carry into effect the democratic programme approved by the elected representatives of Ireland'. The official oath declared: 'I recognise the Republic established by the will and vote of the Irish People as the legitimate Government of Ireland.' A specific party programme for local government, if produced, has not come to light, but the whole thrust of the Sinn Féin campaign was not based on a concrete programme but rather on a simple appeal for support for Dáil Éireann by voting for party candidates.[1]

Another party was also making vigorous preparations for the local elections. Since its withdrawal from the 1918 parliamentary election the Labour Party had turned its attention to the local level. It developed a comprehensive programme of municipal reform which could be described as 'gas and water' socialism, emphasising public housing and education. Not surprisingly, it made no mention of the national question. This position was not satisfactory to the leadership of the Irish Transport and General Workers' Union, and in Dublin and Cork the union put forward slates of 'Republican Labour' candidates. This action, in Dublin specifically, was partly based on a power struggle for control of the union: since their opponents were in control of the Dublin Trades Council, the union leaders decided to launch a separate campaign. At the same time, this position would not force the national party into any particular stance on the national question, which would be a handicap to a lively campaign being waged by Labour in Belfast. Beyond the factor of personal power struggles, the Transport Union did contain a strong nationalist element, since the republican movement had provided the impetus for the rapid expansion of the organisation. The Sinn Féin paper *Old Ireland* commented: 'There is an understanding between Sinn Féin and Labour that, provided the Labour candidates take the necessary pledge, complete harmony will exist between both parties.' The Republican Labour nominees together with the Labour candidates in Wexford made that commitment.

Agreements between Labour and Sinn Féin were worked out at the local, not national level. In addition, Home Rule candidates in marginal Ulster areas were not required to take the oath in order to receive Sinn

Féin support. These agreements probably account for the relatively small number of Sinn Féin candidates that went forward. Excluding some minor offices, there were 1,816 seats at stake, with 717 Sinn Féin nominees, 595 Labour, and 436 Unionist; there were also 588 independents, of whom three-fifths were, in effect, Home Rulers. The *Irish Times* (16 Jan.) reported that in the matter of campaign literature the Sinn Féin candidates in Dublin were 'well ahead of their opponents, and in some of the areas issued quite elaborate documents' giving biographical details, 'a wise inspiration, seeing that most of the candidates are hitherto virtually unknown to the Dublin public'. On the other hand, the party claimed it was working under grave handicaps — its headquarters were raided and closed on 7 January, its election addresses were not delivered in the mail, police tore down its posters, and de Valera's election telegram was not transmitted until after the election. Moreover, it charged that several British newspapers — the *Guardian, Daily Mail* and *Daily News* — 'threatened the Irish people with intensified military repression if Sinn Féin carried a majority'.

Polling day was 15 January 1920. Dublin Castle's Local Government Board did not issue instructions concerning the new voting system, but, in any case, with few spoiled ballots, the voters showed they could figure it out without official assistance. The voter turnout was much higher than in 1918: 72 per cent nationally, with Connacht leading the way with an astounding 78 per cent. The election took place relatively peacefully, with the exception of Cork city, where on election eve the Lord Mayor was assaulted by some Sinn Féin supporters and polling day featured a riot between Volunteers and ex-soldiers. 'The wonder is that life was not lost,' commented the *Irish Times* (16 Jan.), 'considering the deadly weapons employed — revolvers, hand-grenades, iron bars and hurling-sticks.' The *Irish Bulletin* (17 Jan.) claimed that in Dublin and elsewhere 'soldiers with trench helmets and fixed bayonets paraded the streets while the voters were going to the polls'.

The results showed a Sinn Féin victory that was as substantial as had been generally anticipated. Of the 1,816 seats up for election, Sinn Féin candidates won 560, Labour 394, Unionists 355, Home Rulers 238, independents 161, and municipal reformers 108. The first-preference votes were closer, with Sinn Féin polling only 1,400 more votes than Unionists (87,311 to 85,932), while Labour got 57,626, Home Rulers 47,102, and independents 44,273. Arthur Griffith overstated the case when he declared that the Irish people 'have repeated — if possible — more emphatically in 1920 the verdict of 1918'. His paper, *Old Ireland* (7 Feb.), acknowledged Sinn Féin failure in some urban districts of Co. Dublin, where it attributed 'the very unsatisfactory returns' to the survival of a 'factional remnant of the Irish Party'. The *Irish Times* (19 Jan.) was not impressed with the Sinn Féin showing, commenting that its 'failure to sweep the country is, indeed, from the political point of view, the outstanding feature of the elections'.

Given that it greatest strength was in rural areas, Sinn Féin could rightly claim a solid victory: it had a majority in nine of eleven corporations (in Dublin and Cork with its Republican Labour allies; in Wexford its ally Labour held the majority) and sixty-two of ninety-nine urban councils.[2]

The Ulster results were most significant. In numbers of seats won, Sinn Féin (with 93) trailed both Labour (109) and Home Rulers (94). In Derry city the two nationalist parties combined to take control of the corporation for the first time. In Belfast, however, in a city council of sixty members, Sinn Féin won only five seats, the same number as the Home Rulers; it was the election of thirteen Labour members that was impressive. The *Irish Bulletin* (23 Jan.) noted that of the 573 seats up for election in the province, 318 had been won by non-Unionists, while the Unionists secured 255. The *Irish Times* (19 Jan.) commented: 'In Unionist Ulster the ancient order of things has felt something like an earthquake', while the Dublin *Evening Telegraph* (19 Jan.) asserted that the results 'destroyed for ever the arguments of a homogeneous "Ulster"'. According to Andrew Wilson (Belfast) of the Proportional Representation Society, the lesson of it all was that

> the six counties alleged to be homogeneous were shown to be divided most deeply, and the apparent solidarity of old had been proved to rest upon their false method of registering public opinion. But then neither was the apparent solidarity elsewhere a true picture.

No wonder the Ulster Unionists got rid of PR at the earliest opportunity. Above all, however, if Unionism was shown not to be monolithic in six of the counties of Ulster, the Sinn Féin poll indicated that over a two-year period the party had failed to make any substantial progress there.

At the end of January Sinn Féin was installed in control of the great majority of urban government bodies. The *Irish Times* (31 Jan.) noted the significance of the development:

> Yesterday Sinn Féin entered into possession of most of the Boroughs and Urban Councils in Ireland. . . . In other words, the local administration of the South and West of Ireland is now in the hands of a party which publicly repudiates British government alike in political and in municipal affairs.

The Dáil Local Government Department promptly sent the new councils resolutions to be adopted: for those with Sinn Féin majorities a resolution pledging allegiance to Dáil Éireann, and for those with mixed nationalist majorities a resolution supporting self-determination. The Cork and Limerick corporations swiftly pledged allegiance to the Dáil, actions which the *Irish Times* (31 Jan.) termed 'deliberate and audacious declarations of war', but most of the other bodies held back. The Local Government Department noted that 'the response to both of these resolutions was only fair', the reason being that the councils did not want to be put in a position where 'they stood alone in the realm of local administration'. Breaking with Dublin Castle was bound to have serious consequences, including the loss of central funds. Playing safe, many of them waited until after the county council elections in June. The only thing all of the Sinn Féin-controlled councils did at this time was to refuse to nominate candidates for the position of High Sheriff.

Among those who delayed pledging allegiance (they did not take this step until 3 May) was the militant republican majority in the corporation of the capital city. They did provide plenty of oratorical fireworks, however. When the council clerk refused to accept Mrs Wyse Power's signature in Irish, he was suspended. The council voted to fly the tricolour on top of the City Hall, restore Dr Kuno Meyer (deceased) as an honorary burgess, dismiss a knighted Home Ruler from the war pensions committee, and, on the motion of William O'Brien, remove the municipal mace, symbol of a rejected imperialism, from the council chamber. The fact that the man they had nominated as Lord Mayor was in a British prison probably restrained them from further action at this time.

Thomas Kelly, Dáil deputy and veteran member of the corporation, was a moderate Sinn Féiner of the pre-1916 school. He had been arrested on 11 December and sent to Wormwood Scrubs prison in London. His imprisonment created a storm of public and press objection and he was unanimously nominated as Lord Mayor by the new corporation. In failing health, he was released to a nursing home in mid-February and returned to Dublin on 28 April.

The Dáil Local Government Department had been busy issuing instructions to the councils. Included in these were orders to impede the efforts of the Dublin Castle administration 'to repair the damage and loss sustained by them owing to raids on Income Tax offices' and to refuse to strike rates to meet malicious and criminal injury claims. It also recommended that all labour and contract disputes should be submitted to the conciliation boards created by the Dáil government. On 4 March the cabinet required all Sinn Féin members of local bodies to sign undated letters of resignation 'to be available in case of wholesale arrest of members'. The work of the department was disrupted by the arrest of its minister on 25 March. Cosgrave was replaced a month later by Kevin O'Higgins, who was already serving as assistant minister.

*

The elections for county councils in June 1920 resulted in a crushing victory for Sinn Féin. Its candidates and allies, standing on a platform of expanded public housing, health services and education, won majorities in twenty-nine of the thirty-three county councils. These included Tyrone and Fermanagh, wrested from the Unionists for the first time. Although the Dáil cabinet had declared that it would not tolerate voter intimidation, Volunteers stood guard at the polls in rural areas in the south and west. Many seats fell to Sinn Féin without contest, and almost all of its nominees were elected. The *Irish Bulletin* claimed that ninety per cent (325 of 362) of the Labour candidates stood as Republican Labour. In assessing the Sinn Féin victory, *The Nation*, the English liberal journal, commented: 'With this extension of its fighting front a new phase of the struggle is entered upon, with many subtle complexities and far-reaching ramificiations. It is not a situation in which the army and fleet can be of much assistance.' The London *Daily News* (9 June) was impressed by the magnitude of the victory: 'Without firing a shot the Republican forces have got control of all the effective machinery of government in the entire area of the proposed Southern Parliament and in a greater part of the area of the proposed Northern Parliament.' The Dáil government could rightly claim that the voters had endorsed its policies.[3]

(2) Outrages and Repression

The urban elections took place in a period of intense activity on the part of both the IRA and the RIC. The IRA had been increasing its actions against the police and other symbols of British authority since the summer of 1919. At that time Dublin Castle claimed that a wave of outrage and crime was sweeping the country, which drew a comment from 'J.H.C.' (*Irish Independent*, 22 Aug.): 'The Bolsheviks must tear their hair on learning how far they fall short of us. We are the nth power of brutality and barbarism.' Counter-measures seemed to be counterproductive. When in the same month the police banned fairs and *aeridheachta* in various parts of the country, Seán Etchingham commented: 'Sinn Féiners were delighted with the raids and proclamations. It would be a grand thing for the world to see how England treated the elected representatives of the Irish people.' In December Lord Chief Justice Maloney took the people of Clare to task for falling into 'moral degradation' by not opposing crime; Bishop Fogarty saw the situation from a completely different perspective: the people of Clare and other Sinn Féin counties 'had the manliness to stand up against tyranny and flourish the flag of independence in the face of Castle hacks'. After examining the condition of Ireland in a series of articles, a special correspondent of the London *Times* (13 Dec.) came to the conclusion that there were two coercions operating in the country, and 'the serious part is that on the whole Sinn Féin has more moral authority'. During its first year of operation forty of its sixty-nine members had spent some time in jail.

Then came the attempt to assassinate Lord French on 19 December 1919; this action demanded a strong response from the Castle administration. As a new year's present to the rank and file, the Volunteer leadership approved attacks on police barracks in January 1920. Local IRA units took full advantage of this approval, and the month was filled with assaults on police stations. That the British administration was under physical as well as political assault is seen in the act of closing Dublin Castle yard to the public. Moreover, there appeared to be a void in the Dublin Castle administration. With Ian Macpherson obviously on his way out as Chief Secretary, Lord French and Sir Henry Wilson, CIGS, were free to employ a policy of military repression. The London correspondent of the *Irish Independent* (2 Feb.) claimed that Wilson was operating a 'sinister dictatorship' in Irish military affairs and that the British army commander in Ireland 'is responsible not to the Irish Executive but to the Carsonite Field Marshal', that is, Wilson. According to the London *Daily News*, 'prominent members of the Irish Executive were in total ignorance of what was happening'.

Immediately after the urban elections the armed forces of state and counter-state returned to action. To meet the IRA offensive, the RIC mounted a series of arrests which netted a couple of cabinet members, several Dáil deputies, a few newly elected local officials and many Sinn Féin supporters. A major round-up was conducted on 31 January, when about sixty persons were arrested. This action did not impress the *Irish Independent* (2 Feb.): 'The net was flung wide, but the meshes were too big. It may have been seen coming. And the result is that once more the prestige of the Government has had a fall, while everyone is speaking of the ability of the Sinn Féin intelligence staff.' Three days later came 'an extraordinary and inexplicable Military display' in which parties of military paraded the principal thoroughfares of Dublin and Limerick, which activity the *Independent* (5 Feb.) characterised as 'a needless, irritating and stupid proceeding, but it is just what we might expect from rulers animated by spleen and not guided by reason and commonsense'. It saw a connection with the Sinn Féin victory in the local elections: 'The intention cannot have been to treat the Irish municipal councils to a latter-day "Pride's purge" — unless, indeed, Alderman O'Brien's mace motion suggested the unhappy idea to Lord French.' Lord Monteagle, president of the Proportional Representation Society, commented that the acts of repression 'will be inevitably regarded' as an attempt to reverse the results of the elections. He too drew on history: 'What did his attempt to arrest the five members profit Charles I?. . . . The immediate result of Charles's action was to precipitate civil war.'

The *Irish Statesman* (28 Feb.) declared that the country had become 'the New Belgium' in which the English were 'almost as much foreigners as the Germans' had been in Belgium: 'They have their curfew in Dublin, their tanks and patrols. They have our Lord Mayor deported, our jails full, they have substituted trial by soldiers for trial by jury, they have broken every part of the Constitution into as many pieces as their Ministers have broken every pledge they ever gave us.' At the end of March Erskine Childers launched a series of articles in the London *Daily News* which were a general assault on British policy in Ireland. The Irish people, he declared, had been 'bludgeoned into silence by the law, driven underground to preserve its national organisation, and too often forced under intolerable provocation into desperate reprisals'. No regime can long survive this kind of criticism, but Dublin Castle was oblivious to Irish public opinion.

Despite the barrage of opposition, the police round-ups were not without result. Among the couple of hundred persons arrested between January and March were a Dáil minister (Cosgrave), two directors (Barton and Blythe) and four deputies (McGrath, Ginnell, Maloney and Sweeney). To 'Serena' in the *Irish Statesman* (27 Mar.) 'catching an MP in Ireland is rather like lassoing wild cattle in other parts of the world'. The outburst of police and military activity may well have been employed to cover the retreat of the RIC from over 500 barracks and police huts which had taken place from the beginning of the year. Another factor was the belief that the IRA was planning a special effort to mark the anniversary of the Easter Rising. The London press seemed to be convinced that something was in the works. The American ambassador, John W. Davis, was one who believed this. He informed his State Department that the Volunteers had available a force of between 110,000 and 200,000 armed men. Ian Macpherson estimated the number at 200,000.

Sinn Féin spokesmen argued that Dublin Castle was deliberately trying to provoke an outbreak; Arthur Griffith himself made this specific charge. The *Daily Herald* claimed that 'There are people in high places who want a massacre. "To get Sinn Féin into the streets", that is their pleasant phrase, and when Sinn Féin has been got into the streets, the tanks and machine guns and reliable old soldiers will get their chan[c]e.' Such an event would discredit the movement for Irish self-government in British and American eyes, which would allow the British administration to proceed to impose a new 'home rule' scheme on a demoralised, complaisant Irish public.

The IRA did, in fact, have plans for the Easter weekend. While British soldiers and barbed-wire entanglements were spread around Dublin, the Volunteers struck at an obvious target — the newly evacuated barracks. About three hundred 'tombstones of British prestige in Ireland' were destroyed by fire or explosives. This nationwide assault, declared the *Irish Times* (5 Apr.), 'illustrates the startling progress of the Republican Party's guerrilla campaign during the last three months. During those months a large number of police barracks and huts have been abandoned, and on Saturday night the armies of revolution "cleaned up" the job." Beyond torching empty barracks, the Volunteers also burnt twenty-two tax offices and other government offices. The Irish Attorney-General, Denis Henry, estimated that 25,000 men took part in the attacks.

Destruction of the abandoned stations continued for the next two months; there was no need for haste, though it was undoubtedly a waste of valuable public facilities that could have been used for other purposes. Frederick Dumont, the United States consul in Dublin, reported an IRA action on 1 June which he characterised as 'perhaps the most sensational raid that has taken place in Ireland':

> Shortly after the raids on the Income Tax Offices, early in April, troops were sent to a number of Government offices where records are kept, among which were the King's Inn, the offices of the Registry of Deeds, where documents relating to titles to land and other property, dated back to 1702, are kept. The raiders, who were young men, undisguised and without masks, entered the gates quietly with a number of other people. Once inside, the gates were closed by some of the party while others held up and disarmed the sentry. Some twenty others rushed into the guard room and, presenting revolvers at the soldiers there, disarmed them. The Chief Registrar and his staff were dealt with in a similar manner. After a rapid and thorough search of the premises, the raiders withdrew, taking with them all the arms, ammunition and other equipment that could be found, including one Lewis gun.

During the first six months of the year the Volunteers destroyed 424 empty barracks, as well as forty-seven courthouses; the underground army also destroyed sixteen occupied police stations and damaged twenty-nine others. All told, it was a sizeable offensive. The *Irish Times* (14 Apr.) charged that the English people 'do not realise the full extent — or one-half of the extent — to which the government of the country has been snatched from the hands of the British Crown and of the Imperial Parliament. . . . The House [of Commons] does not seem to know that the whole South of Ireland has fallen under the government of Sinn Féin.' Returning to the theme the next day, it insisted that the Volunteer attacks 'are revolution's bold and resolute challenge to the last strongholds of the King's authority in Ireland'.

The British government once again found itself with a large number of Irish political prisoners, but not for long. On 5 April the 200 of them lodged in Mountjoy Jail went on hunger-strike. Demonstrations of support were soon mounted around the jail. Resolute, Lord French declared that the strikers could die if they chose to do so. As political emotions soared, on 13 April the Irish Labour Party and Trade Union Congress began a general strike for the release of the prisoners which was almost totally observed around the country with the exception of north-east Ulster. At the end of that day, with the Labour executive already having issued orders for the strike to continue the next day, Dublin Castle suddenly announced its decision to release the men. It was, it said, an act of clemency designed to create the opportunity for a fresh start for the newly appointed Chief Secretary, Sir Hamar Green-wood, and commander of the British forces, Sir Nevil Macready. The *Irish Times* (15 Apr.) saw it differently: the sudden collapse of the government's resolve 'is slightly ridiculous and will weaken the Government's authority on both sides of the Irish Sea. It will be claimed as a great triumph by Sinn Féin and the Irish Labour Party.' Taking an even darker view of the situation, the London *Morning Post*, no friend of Irish nationalism, char-acterised it as 'a situation of unparalleled ignominy and painful humiliation'.

A total of 172 Irish prisoners responded by going on hunger-strike at Wormwood Scrubs prison in London on 20 April. Lacking the support of an aroused public, the London strikers did not achieve a mass release, but in dribs and drabs those prisoners thought to be in danger of death were moved to hospitals, from where, apparently, they were free to leave when recovered. Austin Stack informed the London office that the released men 'are anxious to oblige the British Government by paying their own fares back to Ireland — or allowing us to do so for them'. Collins believed 'it was a great mistake on their part to come out'. Yet he saw a positive side to the episode: the violence employed against the Irish demonstrators 'will tend to greatly increase the members of the various Irish Organisations. "Wormwood Scrubs" will form the rallying point for the hitherto lost or unknown members of our exiles abroad.'[4]

(3) A New Land War

Incredible as it may seem, all of these events of early 1920 were of less significance than a development that was taking place at the same time in rural areas — the creation of a popularly based system of justice and the subsequent collapse of the existing courts. It began in mid-March with a spontaneous land agitation in the western counties. Land agitations, complete with cattle-drives, levelling of walls, demonstrations, etc., were nothing new in Ireland, but had been generally absent for many years. There was tension in rural areas annually leading up to 1 May, when new eleven-month leases were made. In 1918 there was a spirited land agitation in the western counties, directed by local leaders of the Volun-teers and Sinn Féin. In ordering Volunteers to stay away from the movement, the army executive declared that 'these questions are neither of a national nor a military character'. The Sinn Féin executive, while granting that most of the cattle-drives taking place were justifiable, ruled that no *cumann* could get involved without the approval of its constituency organisation. There was no recurrence of land trouble in the following year, probably because of the anticipation that the Dáil would address the land question.

The land agitation of 1920 was an eruption that 'made the worst of previous years seem positively tame'. The movement was centred in the Connacht counties of Galway, Mayo and Roscommon, as well as Kerry, Clare and the midlands counties of Westmeath and Longford, but its effects were felt around the country, particularly in Dublin.

The precondition for the upheaval was the withdrawal of the RIC from hundreds of rural stations in the early months of the year, a retreat caused by the pressure of the Volunteers. But the IRA, Sinn Féin and Dáil Éireann had no direct or official role in initiating the new land war. The Dáil had, however, in June 1919 passed a decree declaring that 'The provision of land for the agricultural population deprived thereof is decreed' and had established a land bank to facilitate the transfer of at least a small amount of land. When the Dáil failed to do any more than this, others took action. The agitation was apparently generated by the local branches of the Irish Transport Union (without any encouragement from their head office), surviving units of the Land and Labour organisation and local Sinn Féin activists.

Newspaper reports spoke of hundreds of people involved in the agitation, complete with public humiliation of landowners and forced agreements to sell land. One of the earliest reports, however, describes a peaceful movement. At two farmers' meetings near Athlone co-operative societies were formed for land purchases, with the landowners apparently agreeing to sell and with promised financing from the National Land Bank. The bank stated that it was opposed to violence and noted that 'in no case where money had been advanced [by it] has any such violence taken place'. The funds at the disposal of the bank were tiny, however, compared with the size of the demand. Moreover, most of the agitators seemed to want immediate and forceful action. The Kilbride, Co. Galway, *cumann* took possession of land. Mrs Mary Waller Sawyer later wrote to Griffith to report that after she had been asked to sell her land local agitators 'attacked with a large mob with sticks and threatened to drown me — though I had decided to sell'. Looking back on the period three years later, Patrick Hogan insisted that land confiscation had been justified: 'Illegal action of that sort while the English were here was necessary, absolutely necessary. It was, I might say, virtuous.'

The Irish Unionist Alliance provided accounts of dramatic incidents. When Lynch Staunton refused to give up his demesne land, 'he was dragged to the shores of Lough Corrib, and there, under threat of drowning, signed a document handing over his estate'. Mrs Palmer of Glenloe Abbey, Co. Galway, a widow, was ordered to sell eighty acres in front of her house. Under threat of death, she 'offered to take £4,000, but finally sold under compulsion for £1,000, much below the value of the land'. In Tubber, Co. Westmeath, an armed band entered the house of a farmer named Flynn and 'dragged the family from bed, and compelled the father, mother and daughter to sit in the yard while they shot the son. They took £156 16s from Flynn, and made him promise to give up the farm.' The London *Sunday Times* (20 June) reported an even more alarming incident: 'An unfortunate mother who had two daughters was waited upon one night by thirty Sinn Féiners, who demanded that she should give up a certain farm. She refused, and in the presence of the horrified mother her daughters were outraged by the thirty scoundrels.' Arthur Griffith rejected the report as 'obviously a vile, infamous and malicious falsehood'; to the *Irish Independent* (22 June) it was 'an outrageous libel upon this country'.

Despite the operation of the land purchase acts, there still remained many large estates. According to Kevin O'Shiel, 'Landlordism, though badly broken, still survived — mainly in the west and in parts of the south of Ireland.' He estimated that thirty per cent of estate lands remained unsold. When finance was stopped owing to the European war, the Congested Districts Board ceased purchases, although it had thousands of acres in its control, which it leased on an annual basis. When armed crowds proclaiming 'The land for the landless and the road for the bullocks' interfered with its activities, the board ceased operations altogether. O'Shiel dated the beginning of the 1920 upheaval to the shooting dead of Shawe-Taylor, a large Galway landowner. 'Then, of a sudden, all bonds were burst and the fever swept like a prairie fire over Connacht' and beyond. According to Art O'Connor, the land agitation was a mere symptom of a much wider development. Thrust into the position of Dáil Director of Agriculture at this time, O'Connor surveyed the situation: 'During the winter of 1919 in Ireland government seemed to stand stock-still', but in the springtime 'power, actual and moral, was passing from the British Authorities in Ireland into the hands of the Government of the Republic, but in those days it was in a state of flight and had not yet taken definite rest in its new home'.

The agitation shook the remnant of the old landed ascendancy to the core. The *Irish Times* (7 Apr.) argued that the victims of the agitation were not the big landowners, but the small ones, though 'these had only themselves to blame because of the tacit consent they gave' when 'the whole machinery of law has been thrown on the scrap heap'. There was 'a wave of Bolshevism, before which Sinn Féin itself stands appalled'. Art O'Connor believed that the attacks on smaller landowners were based on a 'policy of the line of least resistance'. Among those subjected to pressure were landowning priests, publicans and shopkeepers. On the other hand, Denis Henry told the British cabinet that it was the big landowners who were most threatened, while Hamar Greenwood was of the opinion that this 'part of this movement is not doing the Government any harm'.

When the landowners turned to the RIC for protection, they were informed that the police 'had neither the men nor the time to spare for police work, especially on a scale so intensive'. Some troops were used to protect farm property and stock, but there were not enough of them to have a wide effect. Nor could the Catholic Church stem the tide. Referring to the agitation which had been 'feverishly active within the past few weeks', Bishop O'Dea of Galway denounced all land-grabbing. The Bishop of Clonfert declared that the chief victims of the campaign of plunder were the nationalist farmers. The episcopal sermons had no apparent effect.

The landowners had one option left — to appeal to the alternative government. According to Kevin O'Shiel, 'East-bound trains brought to Dublin large numbers of terrified landowners, who came beseeching the Dáil Government for protection.' Arthur Griffith was astonished by the number and class of people who appealed to him for help. 'It is a curious anomaly', noted Art O'Connor, 'that those aggrieved landholders, mostly persons with strong British sympathies and hence opposed to the Republic, were actually the first section of the community to advocate strongly the setting up of a Judiciary responsible to An Dáil.' Both Darrell Figgis and Conor Maguire informed Griffith of the situation in Mayo and urged him to take action. Taking the 'gravest possible view of the outbreak', Griffith decided after long consideration that his government would have to respond to the challenge.

During the previous two years the Sinn Féin leadership had discouraged land agitation. In 1918 it instructed the party in Clare to exercise strict control over cattle-drives, 'some of which were unjustified'. Now, in the spring of 1920, the Dáil cabinet voiced its disapproval. Responding to the part played by the Kilbride, Co. Galway, Sinn Féin Club in a land occupation, it issued a directive on 25 April: 'Sinn Féin Clubs should not take steps of this nature until a fair offer had been made to owner.' At the same time the party executive repeated its instruction that constituency leaders 'are to be consulted in all cases before action is taken'. They should, if necessary, pass the matter through the national executive to the Dáil government (a fine recipe for doing nothing). The only deputy known to be involved in cattle-driving was James Lennon of Carlow; on 4 March the cabinet voted to 'ask Art O'Connor to see him'.

There had been a change in the leadership of the Dáil's Department of Agriculture. Robert Barton, rearrested in January 1920, was replaced two months later by Art O'Connor (1888–1950), a thirty-two year old engineering graduate of Trinity (1911) from Elm Hall, Celbridge, Co.

Kildare, who belonged to a well-known farming family. According to Daniel Hoctor (later a department official), 'Like Barton, he was well versed in agricultural affairs and he brought boundless energy, ability and enthusiasm to his work.' Elected for South Kildare in 1918, O'Connor began his work for the department in early February 1920, when Griffith dispatched him to Kerry to deal with a localised but violent land conflict. At a conference of farmers and labourers held on 8 May O'Connor secured support for the formation of a land commission and the use of the Dáil Loan fund to finance land transfer. As a result of this achievement, O'Connor was appointed acting director of the department.

In response to the explosion in the west, the Dáil cabinet decided to establish a land tribunal. It had authorised the formation of 'arbitration courts' in June 1919, and these were set up in West Clare (under the leadership of Brian O'Higgins, TD) and probably in Galway, but not much was done elsewhere. O'Connor claimed that 'they gradually spread to other parts of the West as the need demanded' and that 'at first their operations were small'. Apparently many supporters of Sinn Féin preferred to wait for a national initiative, while others saw no need for action. According to Kevin O'Shiel, there was no popular demand to replace the existing local courts. Moreover, with all of its other responsibilities, the Dáil government was not anxious to act: 'It would have suited it admirably to have turned a Nelsonian blind eye on that side of things and leave well enough alone.'

With the outbreak of the agitation, arbitration courts sprang up, notably in Galway, Mayo and Roscommon. But more than arbitration was needed to contain the land war. On 21 April the four deputies from Kerry issued a manifesto to their constituents which urged them not to disrupt the national cause and recommended that aggrieved persons should 'file their claims with the courts now being set up'. They warned that 'The forces of the Republic will be used to protect the citizens against the adoption of high-handed methods.' As Volunteer Adjutant-General, Michael Collins informed the commander of the Kerry Brigade that the unit 'will of course be rigidly bound by the manifesto' and that those who did not do so should be suspended and court-martialled. These actions, said Art O'Connor, 'finally calmed the trouble, and thus a danger to the State was fortunately removed'. At least as important was the fact that in many areas the trouble came to an end when the new annual land leases came into effect on 1 May. As the RIC Inspector-General reported, 'The season for cattle-driving is past now.'

But Kerry was not Connacht, and the flames still burned in that province. On 12 May O'Connor travelled to the west to deal with the problem. At this time Arthur Griffith called in Kevin O'Shiel (1892–1970), a thirty-eight-year-old solicitor who was a native of Omagh, Co. Tyrone. He had practised law on the Western Circuit since 1913 and had stood as a Sinn Féin candidate in two Ulster constituencies in 1918. 'Taking the gravest possible view of the situation', Griffith recruited O'Shiel to join forces with O'Connor.

At this time O'Connor was planning simply to extend the arbitration courts, but at a conference held at Ballinasloe, Co. Galway, he met with a demand for stronger measures. On the urging of Conor Maguire, among others, he decided to establish an emergency land commission, with O'Shiel and himself as commissioners. The first sitting of this body was held a few days later — on 17 May — at Ballinrobe, Co. Mayo. O'Connor then returned to Dublin to secure cabinet approval for his action. A conference of Connacht deputies, Volunteer commandants and cabinet ministers was held on 29 May which concluded that 'Passivity or attempt to drive the Land Movement under would be not merely futile but dangerous and unjust to the young men whom circumstances of the war had compelled to remain in Ireland.' Reporting to the Dáil in June, O'Connor told the deputies: 'We should be worse than fools if we let the opportunity pass of righting the wrongs of ages.' The cabinet obviously hoped that the land tribunal would stop the upheaval. On 31 May it decided that 'clergymen and others of influence to be asked to advise people that Dublin is dealing with the matter, to tell them they must abide by decisions and keep quiet meanwhile'.[5]

For three months O'Shiel was left as a one-man commission. His first land decision, given at Ballinrobe on 26 May, was in favour of those who held legal title to land, as 'they had barely economic holdings'. Those who had occupied the land publicly declared that they would not abide by the decision. This was a test of the new system. O'Shiel turned for advice to O'Connor, who sent him to Griffith, who, in turn, sent him to Cathal Brugha. The Minister for Defence declared his opposition to any involvement that diverted the Volunteers from military activity. Griffith told O'Shiel not to worry, and a few days later four of the principal objectors were arrested and taken away by the local IRA unit. O'Shiel later commented: 'No event did us, or our courts, more good.'

During his tour of thirteen counties O'Shiel spent more time in Roscommon — three weeks — than in any other. The situation there was most difficult, with 'an aggressive, "bolshie" spirit' about the litigants. According to Graham Sennett, a local auctioneer, 'The most vile hooligans that did the dirty work against us in the General Election are marching, with the Tricolour, to commandeer lands.' On the other hand, the county party organisation, led by Father O'Flanagan, the 'Sinn Féin priest', had formed a complete court organisation, including a land commission.

O'Shiel's sessions there received great attention, 'surpassing the public interest displayed in the Assize Court of the British system in the period of its heyday. . . . The court was crowded with the general public who took the greatest interest in the proceedings, and from the start the people's courts were everywhere enthusiastically welcomed by all classes of the community, and their awards were, with a few exceptions, loyally accepted and carried out.' During this period O'Shiel dealt with sixty-nine cases involving 11,575 acres. In some instances O'Shiel ordered the transfer of ownership, but 'in a great many cases the claimants could not raise the money required', so the land remained with the original occupant. In addition, high land prices made many landowners agreeable to sale. Stephen Gwynn commented: 'In a sense this makes matters easy for the Sinn Féin courts. . . . Of course there is an element of duress in the transaction; many men will come before these courts as sellers who would never have thought of sale but for the agitation.'

The new land commissioner proved to be an effective pioneer for the counter-state's judicial system, winning respect for his honesty, fairness and good judgment. In one case brought before him a father had left his farm to his two sons. 'The elder, being married, worked the farm, and the younger lived with him — till he, too, desired to marry. Then the elder brother refused to divide the farm; and the younger brother sued him in the Republican land courts.' O'Shiel's judgment was that the elder brother should divide the farm in two halves as and how he wished, but that the younger brother should have first choice which he should take for his portion. Darrell Figgis, who related the story, commented: 'Truly a judgment that Solomon might envy — and with the touch of humour well beloved of all honest folk.' O'Shiel carried on single-handed until 17 September 1920, when the Dáil established a land settlement commission. O'Shiel became the leading official in the organisation and, indeed, was to spend the rest of his public service career in this capacity. At the end of September O'Connor paid tribute to O'Shiel's 'great ability and sense he has displayed in handling very difficult cases', as well as to the readiness 'with which he took the Big Risk', professionally speaking.

The matter of the land upheaval confronted the Dáil when it met, for the first time in eight months, on 29 June 1920. Art O'Connor said of this encounter: 'The Dáil itself seemed overwhelmed by the suddenness with which the responsibility of Government had been thrust upon it and for a while it seemed to shrink from its duties as one shrinks from the fulfilment of an unexpected joy.' In fact the Dáil leadership seemed to be irritated and angry that others should take any initiative in the affairs of the country without direction of itself; but what else could it expect to happen during the best part of a year when the Dáil was out of sight and mind? It lashed out at the land agitators, accusing them of stirring up strife among 'our fellow-countrymen' and threatened to set the IRA on them. It asserted that the land claims were 'for the most part, of old date, and while many of them may be well-founded, others seem to be of a frivolous nature, and are put forward in the hope of intimidating the present occupiers'. In the decree denouncing the agrarian movement a clause was deleted (on Griffith's suggestion) that promised that after independence was secured the Republic would take steps 'to do justice and equity to all those who have suffered wrong in the past through the power and operation of England's unjust laws'. Apparently Sinn Féin was determined not to get involved in a programme of the Land League type. In the years ahead it was to be a source of bitter regret to Peadar O'Donnell and others on the left wing of the republican movement that the IRA had been employed to control and curtail the land agitation. In retrospect, they saw that the Dáil leadership had simply revealed its capitalist, bourgeois orientation.

At the same June session the Dáil took the momentous decision to create a national court system. These courts, however, would not consider any land cases without a written licence from the Minister for Home Affairs. Rural hotheads could amuse themselves by filing 'particulars of their claims with the Registrar of the District Court in which the property is situate'. What of the work of O'Shiel and the special emergency land tribunal? The published record of the Dáil proceedings does not mention, it, but O'Connor said that he proposed the creation of a permanent land settlement commission at this session and that the matter was referred to a committee for consideration. Would the Dáil's decree establishing the new courts put a stop to all land claims? No, said Austin Stack; people would still be able to pursue 'claims to lands which were being used as ranches and demesne lands', apparently through O'Shiel's ministrations.

What was the lesson of this chain of events? Frank Gallagher saw it clearly:

> Galway, Clare and Kerry have shown the entire nation that its purpose is two-fold — to break down and to build up. The period of breaking down is almost over; the period of building up is merely beginning.[6]

(4) The People's Courts

The history of extra-legal, popularly based courts in Ireland is an interesting one. During the Repeal campaign Daniel O'Connell proposed that arbitration courts should be established to frustrate the operation of the crown courts (he also proposed the creation of a national council of 300 leading citizens — a national assembly, in fact). The courts operated briefly in 1843. Later, in the early 1880s, a wide network of courts were established under the auspices of the Land League. In the second decade of the twentieth century the United Irish League established arbitration boards to deal with local disputes. When Sinn Féin was reorganised in October 1917, the party established eleven departments, none of which apparently had responsibility for settling disputes or providing justice. Further, there is no clear indication when or if the organisation made a policy commitment to provide this service. On the other hand, Sinn Féin, on occasions and at the local level, did form a few arbitration bodies from late 1917 onwards. Probably the earliest report of such activity is found in the 3 October issue of *The Irishman*. Following a decision of the national executive, the party set up 'arbitration courts' in many parts of the country, particularly in the south and west, in the latter part of 1918 and early 1919. When a Sinn Féin court in Galway tried to adjudicate a land dispute in January 1918, its efforts resulted in a slander suit being filed against the adjudicators in the district crown court.

At the beginning of 1919 Griffith pointed to courts operating in Cavan and Kilkenny, which certainly had been given no national attention, as models for the rest of the country. The central Sinn Féin *cumann* was told in February 1919 that the courts had been very successful and that they should be extended to every district. *The Irishman* declared on 31 May that although not much had been heard about them, these bodies 'continue to discharge their duties with marked success. The latest striking example of this comes from Rochestown, Co. Cork, where a twenty-seven-year-old land dispute has been satisfactorily settled, the evicted tenant being restored to occupation with the full consent of the owners.' There were other reports of arbitration courts during that spring.

Sinn Féin had long advocated the creation of an alternative, Irish-inspired court system. A committee to study the establishment of Dáil-sponsored courts was formed shortly after the assembly came into being. At its session on 4 April, 1919 the Dáil was told that the committee was still working on its report. On 18 June the ministry presented the body with a decree which called for the creation 'in every County of National Arbitration Courts, and the appointment of National Magistrates'. The proposal to appoint magistrates was dropped (too much of a commitment there) and the amended decree passed. This measure, of course, simply ratified the position taken by the Sinn Féin executive the previous year and based on which a few party activists proceeded to create judicial bodies. Alone among the deputies, Brian O'Higgins showed initiative in organising a system of arbitration courts in his West Clare constituency. This was also done in parts of Galway, although less is known about developments there. Pending the approval of a general plan, however, 'each constituency was left free to pursue its own course in carrying the decree into operation'. The cabinet itself become immediately involved in the matter and during 1919 appointed several arbitration 'tribunals' or courts to probe disputes upon the request of both parties. Yet in its report for the period from

August to October 1919, the Department of Home Affairs made no mention of the activities of Dáil-sanctioned courts in the provinces.

A new committee was formed after the Dáil session of June, and a week before the next session, on 31 July, it held a meeting under the chairmanship of Griffith. Reporting to the session of 6 August, the committee recommended the formation of an arbitration system which would have not only local courts but also district courts and a supreme court; the Dáil approved the report. On 27 October it was told that 'the necessary preliminary arrangements' were being made for setting up the courts, but in fact the committee had not met since the last session of the Dáil, over two and a half months previously. This omission was noted by deputies, and the committee held a meeting three days later. It then decided that there should also be circuit courts for each province, an idea approved by the cabinet on 7 November, subject to cost estimates. This effort was carried through to the new year, when an estimate for a full court system was put at £112,000, with £5,000 for the supreme court and court of appeal, £40,000 for district courts, and £67,000 for local courts. The local courts would have the following membership: 'Three justices per parish might be elected if possible, and the local Clergy of all denominations and the chairman of the County Councils and Urban and District Councils should be entitled to adjudicate as ex-officio Magistrates.'

A fine plan, to be sure, and thoroughly investigated and exhaustively discussed — but nothing was done by the Dáil government to put it into effect. One of the problems was that Griffith, the Minister for Home Affairs, was also Acting President. Moreover, he never showed any particular interest or ability in matters of administration; he was a talker, writer, leader. He was not replaced in Home Affairs until late November 1919, when Austin Stack, suffering from the effects of a long spell of imprisonment, was appointed. Stack, for his part, however, was a professional rebel, not an administrator. Then, in the spring of 1920, came the explosion in the west. The local people knew what to do: they quickly set up arbitration courts. The Dáil government, viewing developments with something like injured dignity covering neglect of duty, was forced to act.[7]

So far in its brief existence Dáil Éireann had had two Ministers for Home Affairs: Michael Collins, serving briefly and nominally from January to April 1919, and Arthur Griffith. Now it was to have its third and last until the passage of the Anglo-Irish Treaty at the beginning of 1922: Austin Stack (1879–1929). Then forty years of age, Stack was a native of Kerry and a famous Gaelic footballer. His occupation was that of solicitor's clerk. A leader in the Kerry IRB and Volunteers, he was in charge of the bungled attempt to land arms there in 1916. He spent most of the next three years in prison, where he organised a series of notable demonstrations, hunger-strikes, etc. He escaped from prison in October 1919. His advent to the Dáil leadership had been eagerly anticipated. De Valera had left an opening for him in the cabinet, and Collins had a very high opinion of him. On the other hand, there was nothing to suggest that he would be an able minister. Furthermore, his long imprisonment had drained him. He proved to be the least effective of the leaders of the first Dáil. He lacked nothing in terms of courage, honesty, sincerity and dedication, but he did not possess the aggressiveness, confidence and organisational ability to direct successfully a vital government activity.

When he became minister in November 1919, he provided no impetus for the arbitration court scheme; the work proceeded at a leisurely pace. In January 1920 a suggestion was made in the cabinet that the courts should have full civil powers, and Stack was asked to prepare a scheme. He was very doubtful about the idea and in seeking Diarmuid O'Hegarty's advice, declared: 'I do not see how this could be made to work.' His doubts remained in his subsequent departmental report: 'I cannot see how this could be successfully carried out for the moment, and as the Dáil decree provides only for Arbitration Courts, I do not propose to deal with the suggestion now.' If the arbitration courts scheme worked successfully 'for some time', then he might consider asking the Dáil to extend their powers. But the arbitration courts were already in operation in many counties, and they mushroomed in the spring of 1920. The people *en masse* turned to these bodies, and they wanted more than mere arbitration; they wanted courts of justice with full powers. Stack continued to nurse his arbitration scheme, with papers passing back and forth to the cabinet. The cabinet itself took a cautious view of the matter. In approving a plan for parish and district courts on 13 May, it recommended that Stack concentrate on only one or two counties; on 10 June it gave him authority 'to organise in any counties where he thinks it advisable'. But eventually the need for a fully-fledged court system became overwhelming.

By the time the Dáil met at the end of June it was necessary for the leadership to recognise the emergence of the popular bodies. Stack now proposed that the courts assume civil authority, with the cabinet reserving the right to extend criminal powers to the courts if and when 'they deem fit'; the cabinet agreed to this at its meetings of 10 and 16 June, and the Dáil followed suit at its session of 29 June. In this report to the Dáil, Stack revealed what was already known to most people: 'In some parts of the country the Courts have on their own initiative undertaken work in excess of the power granted by the Decree of An Dáil', that is, they had assumed civil and criminal authority. He foresaw all the problems of sanctioning this authority — enforcement of decisions, modes of punishment, British army and police interference, etc. — but he seemed to be unaware of the power of public opinion and of the strong arm of the IRA. Stephen Gwynn addressed this matter in an article in *The Observer* (23 May):

If the individual Sinn Féiner is discontented with the award, will he submit? I think he will. Under the old Bre[h]on law, public opinion was the only sanction: the judge pronounced findings which he had no power and obligation to enforce. But if the Court's findings are disregarded by Sinn Féiners, Sinn Féin *pro tanto* breaks up.

The government of Dáil Éireann had been trailing public events by a long measure. Sinn Féin courts sprang to life on a broad scale from mid-March. By the time the Dáil acted, courts had been formed in twenty-eight counties. It appears there was a rough division of labour in the new system of justice — the courts dealt with civil matters, and the IRA with criminal cases; in addition there was the O'Shiel land tribunal making the rounds in the west. The courts appeared to sweep all before them. Both British and Irish newspapers had frequent reports of the revolutionary courts in operation. Foreign journalists flocked into the country to observe the phenomenon. Desmond FitzGerald was in his glory making arrangements for newsmen to attend court sessions. He made sure that John Steele of the *Chicago Tribune* was at one of the earliest sessions of the land tribunal. Steele wrote an article about the event in the *Sunday Times*, which received much attention in England.

The popular tribunals first received major press attention when the *Manchester Guardian* published an article about them on 17 April; on 10 May, in judging the new courts to be fair, popular and effective, it said that they had 'sprung up spontaneously on the west coast of Ireland' and that they were 'the natural result of the strong common will for national independence and national responsibility'. The *Daily Mirror* on 1 May reported on a court held in Galway:

> Seven appeals from decisions of the lower Sinn Féin Land Court were heard, and to one like myself, accustomed to the devious subtlety of the Irish witness in land cases, there followed an extraordinary exhibition of despatch, efficiency and, if the truth must be told, a fairness bordering on Quixotism. Many of the witnesses were not Sinn Féiners, and one man, who obtained his appeal, was in 1916 a deadly enemy of the organisation.

As the movement grew, so did the press coverage. In the end almost every major newspaper carried accounts of the effectiveness of the new system. These results could not have been achieved by sleight of hand or through the ingenuity of FitzGerald's Propaganda Department; they had to have the reality of experience.

The *Irish Times* declared on 2 June that confidence in the sanctions of British law and order 'vanished long ago, and whole countrysides now bring their rights and wrongs to the courts of Sinn Féin'. It returned to this theme in the following month (7 July), when it commented: 'Of course, every Irishman is well aware that the King's writ runs no longer in many parts of the country. . . . The Sinn Féin tribunals are jostling British law into oblivion, as a fast motor-car jostles foot-passengers off the road.' Robert Lynd reported in the London *Daily News* that 'Sinn Féin has accomplished an amazing work in producing law and order in those parts of Ireland in which it is in power. Sinn Féin law has a sanction behind it such as no other law in Ireland has had for generations.' His judgment was based on personal experience: 'I have attended a number of Sinn Féin courts in the north of Ireland, and the more I see of them the more I feel convinced that nothing so marvellous has grown up out of the ground of Ireland since the coming of the Normans.' Writing in *The Observer* (11 July), Stephen Gwynn declared:

> Sinn Féin deserves the credit of having created its greatest success out of what seemed to be its gravest peril. Nothing has brought it so much genuine prestige as the courts in which it administers justice: nothing goes so far to give reality to the claim that there is an Irish Republic in being. Yet these courts were an improvisation to meet a need.

The Kerryman held that the most important aspect of the creation of the new court system was that it demonstrated to the Irish people 'that they can run their own country in their own way in spite of alien interference'.[8]

Testimony to the success of the experiment was provided by a variety of figures who had not been associated with the cause of Irish nationalism. Lord Monteagle asserted in the *Irish Times* (5 July) that the new courts were 'dispensing justice even handed between man and man, Catholic and Protestant, farmer and shopkeeper, grazier and cattle drover, landlord and tenant'. Lord Kilmaine told the House of Lords that 'What I have seen of the Sinn Féin Courts and government in the west . . . has extremely changed my opinion. They have shown extraordinary fairness and have been extremely just.' Mr Godfrey Fetherstonhaugh, KC, a former Unionist MP, took it upon himself to write a letter to the London *Times* (16 July):

> The Government in more that three-quarters of Ireland appears to have abandoned all its functions except demand of taxes. The Sinn Féin courts are crowded, and if the system of law they administer leaves much to be desired, they can and do enforce their orders.

The Anglican *Church Times* pointed out that

> The Sinn Féin courts of justice are resorted to, not only by Republicans, but also by Unionists and Protestants, for the easily understood reason that in them justice is administered promptly and damages are recovered expeditiously.

In his report of 15 June, Frederick Dumont, the United States consul in Dublin, took a cautious view of the development:

If the anomaly of the existence and claims of these courts be accepted, it must be granted that, judging not only from the *Irish Bulletin* but from newspaper reports, they appear to act impartially and try to do rough justice between man and man. . . . The whole matter of the establishment of Sinn Féin courts is too recent to enable one to pass judgment as to whether or not the people will abide by their decisions.

Sinn Féin leaders, however, told Dumont that they were 'much elated by the sympathy with which the decisions of their courts have been received by the people'. They also informed him that the courts 'to date have operated under temporary rules and are people's courts where perhaps the local carpenter or some other mechanic acts as judge', but also that Sinn Féin had in process of preparation rules governing court procedure and that when completed 'a copy is to be furnished this office'. He added an ominous note: 'Every successful revolution began by making the tenancy of the "usurping" Government an impossible one; from which point revolutionary governments have proceeded to chain up and control the forces they have unloosed.'

The new courts required judges. In rural areas these were drawn from the ranks of Catholic priests, local lawyers and persons of standing in the community. Women and former magistrates and justices of the peace were eligible. In Dublin many well-known persons served in this capacity, including Maud Gonne MacBride, Mrs Tom (Kathleen) Clarke, Darrell Figgis, Erskine Childers and Mrs Alice Stopford Green. The selection process was initially based on party co-option, but the Dáil decree provided for election. Given the circumstances, however, it is most likely that the elections, where held, were perfunctory affairs. In several counties conventions were held to select justices. The local organisation in Queenstown decided to advertise for judges and posted notices on the walls of the courthouse: 'Three persons are required by the L[ocal] G[overnment] Board of Dáil Éireann to act as judges of the Republican Courts to be set up in the district.' Applicants were required to speak Irish, pledge allegiance to Dáil Éireann, and acknowledge the authority of the Dáil Minister for Home Affairs.

The need for rules and regulations for the courts was obvious. Austin Stack assembled an able group of young lawyers for the task. Arthur Clery had already done valuable work in the matter. Conor Maguire could rightly claim to be one of the founding fathers of the whole scheme. James Creed Meredith and Hector Hughes (later a Scottish MP) had the distinction of being Protestants. The others were Diarmuid Crowley and Kevin O'Shiel. Drawing on the experience of the West Clare courts, the group prepared a booklet which in simple language set out procedures, rules and regulations, and the publication was widely distributed sometime after September 1920. Stack also appointed several court organisers and registrars; one of the registrars was Seán O'Duffy, the general secretary of the electricians' union, who served in south Leinster.

The new courts and their proceedings initially drew rapt public attention, an obvious reason being that they were by far the best show in town. Robert Lynd reported that at one court an old farmer who had lost his case marched out of the room expostulating: 'To hell with these courts. I don't care a snap of the fingers for any of them.' 'He was at once put under arrest, accused of contempt of court and sharply fined.' He apologised for his remarks and thereafter had no further difficulties with the judicial system of Dáil Éireann. In North Clare a man charged with larceny was brought before the court. Turning the usual republican position on its head, he refused to recognise the authority of the court, to which the president of the panel of judges replied: 'That being so, will you kindly inform us which court you do recognise. We shall be pleased to hand you over immediately.' The man changed his mind, pleaded guilty, was heavily fined and ordered to replace the stolen property, and released. In West Galway a court fined a Sinn Féiner who had abused an ex-soldier because he had cut turf for the RIC. A Cork priest was charged with slander, but the plaintiff could not make up his mind as to which court he should bring his case. In the end he opted for the Dáil court, and before a packed house in Cork City Hall he won his case and damages of one shilling. On one occasion in Longford the two court systems operated within the same courthouse: 'While the sessions were in progress in one room an arbitration Court sat in another courtroom, and disposed of one of the biggest cases of the session to the satisfaction of all parties.'

Behind the court decisions stood the agency of enforcement. The Volunteers were present as court officers from the beginning, but they did much more than that. When a West Clare magistrate refused to obey the finding of a Dáil court, he was arrested and imprisoned. Three tenant farmers in Ballinrobe, Co. Mayo, were arrested for defying a decision of the local land tribunal. In Kilkenny the Volunteers arrested a man for damaging a Protestant church. 'He was tried by a Republican Court, confessed his guilt and was heavily fined. He was subsequently brought before the principal Protestant inhabitants to whom he publicly apologised.' Westmeath County Council, having voted to close all courthouses, called upon the Volunteers 'to see to it that no judges are allowed to enter these buildings for the purposes of holding courts which are not recognised by Dáil Éireann'. In its issue of 15 May the IRA journal *An tÓglach* declared that not only had the Volunteers assumed responsibility for law and order, but the force had 'also been entrusted with the duty of enforcing the decrees of courts established by Dáil Éireann. As long as the state of war continues, the Army of the Irish Republic must remain the chief executive instrument of the Irish Republic.' Cathal Brugha told the Dáil at the end of June that 'the Department of Defence would provide such protection and assistance as was necessary to enforce' court decisions, but he hoped that this 'portion of the work of the Volunteers would be made as light as possible, so as not to take up the time which must be devoted to their military duties'.

The rise of the alternative court system created a dilemma for the gentlemen of the legal profession. In many cases the new courts began operations without the services of lawyers, who noted the decline in requests for their assistance. A *Times* correspondent declared that 'The simple truth is that the Bar and the solicitors' profession are confronted with the near prospect of an almost total loss of normal business.' In fact most solicitors decided to follow their clients into the new courts. The council of the Incorporated Law Centre found no objection to this practice. Most barristers refused to follow suit, and the Bar Council declared that any member who appeared in the upstart courts was guilty of professional misconduct. Only a handful of barristers practised in the Dáil courts, but in the rough-and-ready brand of justice dispensed therein, the absence of the barrister was hardly noticed.[9]

The rapid growth of the judicial system was celebrated by the *Irish Bulletin*, which on 8 July reported that in the period from 16 June to 8 July forty-seven courts were held, 115 persons were arrested, and that the courts and police 'are operating effectively in twenty-one counties'. Austin Stack asserted in August that courts had been set up 'in almost every County with the exception of Antrim and Derry'. Derry city soon had its courts, but apparently none were ever established in Belfast. While various kinds of courts were busily at work around the country, Stack proceeded to establish higher courts, as provided by the decree. On 15 August he appointed James Creed Meredith and Arthur Clery to the supreme court, and Cahir Davitt (son of Michael Davitt) and Diarmuid Crowley to the appeal court. Conor Maguire joined Kevin O'Shiel as a judicial commissioner. In fact all six jurists served, as circumstances required, on both the supreme and circuit courts. Six persons, however, cannot constitute the higher judiciary of any country, however small. More judges were supposed to have been appointed, but they never were. To deal with the pressure of cases, temporary circuit judges were later appointed. The Dáil courts eventually grew to a peak of forty-four district and 900 parish courts, rendering more than 5,000 decisions.

Meanwhile the courts of the old regime were almost empty except in eastern Ulster and Dublin. The recently appointed Joint Under-Secretary, Sir John Anderson, informed the British cabinet on 25 July that 'The machinery of the Courts has been brought virtually to a standstill and rival Courts are functioning openly, and, where forcibly suppressed, will continue to function in secret.' On the urging of a Dáil proclamation, there was a mass resignation of magistrates and justices of the peace. District judges of the crown courts were often presented with white gloves, meaning that there were no cases on the docket. Angry and embarrassed, perhaps frightened about their livelihoods, they harangued the empty courtrooms about the people's lawlessness and other sins. But they had to endure more than being ignored. Many courthouses had been attacked and destroyed. Those that survived were surrounded by barbed wire, sandbags and troops. In some towns judges were refused their usual accommodations in hotels. Some circuit judges had to move from place to place in convoys of troops and armoured cars. Some were shot. In the capital the high court, with its specialised functions, remained in operation and was used by republicans to bring suit for damages caused by the RIC and the British army and to create a variety of other legal difficulties. The Dáil did not attempt to replicate courts dealing with probate, contracts and related matters.

When persons were summoned to appear as jurors in the crown courts, they were warned off by the IRA. In Waterford prospective jurors were told that 'To obey such summons will be considered an act of treason against the Irish Republic, and you are hereby warned that you will do it at your peril.' Very few appeared, whereupon the court imposed heavy fines on the absentees. Following cabinet approval of the plan on 22 July, magistrates and justices of the peace were urged to resign. Large numbers of them did so — some for nationalist reasons, others in opposition to British repression, and some others out of fear; a few who refused were killed. Over three hundred magistrates had resigned by early August 1920. On 28 September Frederick Dumont reported to the US State Department that 'resignations of police, justices of the peace, commissioners of oaths, etc. continue on a heavy scale'. He estimated that three-quarters of them had done so because 'they or their families are terrorised and intimidated by Sinn Féiners'. He also reported that 'there have been several resignations of Deputy Lieutenants and one or two Privy Councillors'.

The initial response of Dublin Castle to the rebel courts was to do nothing. Arbitration courts were legal in British law. When asked in the Commons on 3 June if there were many illegal courts being held in Ireland, Hamar Greenwood replied that this was not the case: 'There have been meetings of men under various names for various purposes', many of which were not illegal. Frederick Dumont reported on 15 June that the Castle administration had at first taken a conciliatory view of the courts and other Sinn Féin activities; its policy was to 'step softly and carry a big stick'. A week later he reported that because Sinn Féin had viewed this policy as a sign of weakness, the Castle had decided to change to a policy of action against them. To Conor Maguire 'it was quite amazing that the Dublin Castle's British authorities ignored our activities for so long'. In July policemen were ordered to attend Dáil court meetings to observe what was going on. When a policeman asked the president of a Thurles court by what authority the proceedings were being conducted, he was told: 'By the people's authority.' After being informed that no criminal cases were being heard, he let the court proceed.

Several leaders involved in the new court system, including Kevin O'Shiel, believed that the old regime had not acted against the courts because they expected them to fail, thereby discrediting the Dáil government. This was the position taken by H. A. L. Fisher, a member of the British cabinet's Irish Situation Committee. At a meeting on 6 August he advised that the best thing to do was to ignore the Sinn Féin courts because they would not last long. Owing to their mild sentences and the lack of courage in imposing severe penalties, they would end in ridicule. According to the Lord Chancellor, however, it was the British courts that had become the object of ridicule. He urged attacks both on the Dáil courts and the IRA because 'the latter [was] trying to break the power of the British government through terrorism and the former through ridicule'. General Decie, the head of the RIC in Limerick, stated confidentially on 5 June that 'his office had full knowledge of all Sinn Féin courts, where they were held, who attended and who conducted them, the records of the courts and the places to which convicted prisoners were sent, but that he was not allowed to enforce order in his district'. He believed that his men 'could easily defeat these forces if protected and backed up properly by the Government'.[10]

(5) The Collapse of the RIC and the Rise of the Republican Police

The RIC had been under mounting pressure from Sinn Féin from mid-1919 when the Dáil ordered a boycott of the force. In January 1920 the IRA was unleashed against police barracks. The *Morning Post* that month asserted: 'It is now common knowledge that the whole of the Royal Irish Constabulary in the South and West are marked down for attack, and in suitable circumstances (that is, when the assailant incurs no risk) for death.' The campaign so effective that the RIC was withdrawn from six hundred small barracks and huts. The countryside was surrendered to the guerrillas. Its prestige and power shattered, the force began to crumble. In an effort to prevent recruitment, the IRA on 14 February issued a proclamation, distributed widely in the south and west, in which it solemnly warned prospective recruits that 'they join the RIC at their own peril. All nations are agreed as to the fate of traitors.' A few weeks later it extended its threats to anyone who did business with a supplier of the RIC. The campaign against the force took a new turn in the spring when pressure was applied to the families of constables. In April an elderly farmer and his wife were brought out of their house and made to promise to withdraw their son from the police force. The same month in Leitrim an RIC recruit was dragged from his bed and made to swear on his knees that he would not continue in police training. Another recruit was shot in the leg. In May the Adjutant-General declared that recruits to the force were 'to be made unfit for carrying out the duties of the RIC'.

Here was a force of 15,000 men, many of whom had served for twenty or more years and were approaching retirement. For the younger men it was the only job they knew. Some took the view that Sinn Féin and Dáil Éireann would be ephemeral, like the Young Irelanders and the Fenians. Another consideration was that with any change in government, Home Rule or whatever, the force would be abolished and everyone pensioned off. The natural inclination was to hold on until that time. Most of them stuck it out; as Kevin O'Shiel later noted, 'These RIC men were no cowards.' It was obvious, however, that those who stayed on did not do so in order to fight the IRA.

The Dáil had, of course, decreed a peaceful ostracisation of the force. From the United States, President de Valera proposed in early 1920 that the members of the RIC should be approached individually through their families in order to get them to leave the force. Those with over thirty years of service should retire. Young single men, 'the prop of the police system', should resign. All those who resigned would be organised in a Free Men's Association. Moreover, 'whilst a very large sum of money is available in America to take all these men to USA and give them very good employment now, it is . . . highly desirable to keep them in Ireland'. In July Sinn Féin headquarters issued instructions that members of *cumainn* should organise deputations to approach the families of policemen, 'and the relatives should be requested to communicate with them urging them to resign their membership of the English-controlled police and return home where they will be welcomed to live and act as good Irish citizens'. But how would they live? Sinn Féin would provide, first through local efforts to secure employment, and secondly through a national fund which was being raised 'to assist in cases of special hardship'. There were also promises of assistance from the Irish in America, some of whose organisations 'have already expressed their desire to help ex-policemen from Ireland, and to secure them employment as soon as they land in America'. Michael Collins went so far as to tell Art O'Brien on 20 September that 'in certain circumstances assistance would be given to get them to USA where employment would be absolutely certain in accordance with arrangements we have made'. On the same day, however, he wrote to the wife of a constable contemplating resignation that 'it is absolutely impossible to give a promise' of employment.

The men who did resign found that very little was done to get them jobs. Harry Boland told the Secretary to the Ministry on 19 November that the promised employment in the United States, along with the men who made the commitments, had disappeared, 'like so many promises made in this country'. A Free Men's Association was formed under the leadership of Jeremiah Mee, a resigned policeman, but failed to gain employment for its members. Mee declared that those still in the force 'are nearly all willing to come out, but having in their mind's eye some comrade or acquaintance who has done so and is yet unemployed, they point to him as an example of what they themselves would expect to get from Sinn Féin'. If employment was given to those who had resigned, he said, 'police would resign by the hundred, [and] the Volunteer ranks would be greatly strengthened by good fighting material'. Without a guarantee of employment, 'any attempts at organisation will be absolutely futile'. Nothing was done about the matter, probably because of the difficulties involved. If ex-policemen were guaranteed jobs, what about the men of the IRA, loyal supporters of Sinn Féin, or dedicated members of Cumann na mBan?

The IRA continued its pressure against the RIC. On 21 June it reiterated its boycott order. The boycott was extended to anyone who associated with the police, 'and the fact of their association with and toleration of this infamous force shall be kept public in every possible way'. Specifically, 'business people must take their choice of the custom of their neighbours or the cowardly ruffians of the RIC. A sensible business man will be able to judge which pays the best in the long run.' Some girls who were keeping company with constables 'suffered the loss of their tresses'. In Galway in May four men were sentenced to six months' imprisonment for assaulting Bridget Keegan: 'It was alleged that the girl was taken out of bed, forcibly placed in a chair, and taken into the yard, where two of the men held her while another clipped her hair with sheepshears.' The Adjutant-General ordered the expulsion of a Volunteer who associated with members of the RIC; if this action was repeated, 'he would be dealt with in a most severe manner without court martial or any notice'. When he was informed that in Leitrim the 'enemy was taking goods at the point of a revolver', Michael Collins advised that no counter-measures be taken: 'When we have driven them to this position our boycott is a success.'

The Dublin Metropolitan Police, the companion force of the RIC, had been almost completely neutralised. Its unit to investigate political crimes had been shattered by assassinations. In May 1920 the uniformed branch of the service had been disarmed at its own request. According to Michael Hayes, by this time a great part of the civil administration, including particularly the uniformed section of the DMP, was 'either neutral or favourable. Some were neutral through fear, some through a natural disinclination to be involved in activities against their fellow-countrymen'. The *Daily Herald* (25 Sept.) declared: 'The authority of the DMP is nil. Nobody pays the slightest attention to them.' At a meeting of the Dublin Port and Docks Board it was suggested that the DMP should be replaced on the docks by police appointed by the counter-state.

Many policemen looked for a way out of their dilemma. In the summer of 1920 organised groups of them advocated the abolition of the force and the immediate application of pension rights. During his investigation of the Irish situation in March, Sir Warren Fisher, the leading civil servant in charge of the United Kingdom Treasury, was told that the RIC was 'on the verge of a breakup, at all events in the South'. General Tudor, who had become head of the force two months earlier, reported in June that his men 'were living behind sandbags and wire entanglements; they were boycotted and life was altogether intolerable'. Hamar Greenwood told the British cabinet that the force had been 'cruelly tried by the callous indifference shown towards their unjust persecution by the general body of the public'.

The RIC appeared to be finished as an effective force. Resignations mounted month by month, totalling almost 2,000 by mid-June 1921. Although there were a lot of replacements, these men did not have the knowledge and experience of the men who had left. At this point the IRA stepped forward with its 'Republican Police'.[11]

The Volunteers, in fact, had been involved in police work, in Dublin at least, since mid-1919. In June of that year Simon Donnelly, vice-commandant of the 3rd Dublin Brigade, gathered together a small group of Volunteers to form a unarmed police force whose purpose was 'to encourage the people to ignore the British courts' and turn to the alternative courts. There were very few of the latter until early 1920. Seán Condron, one of the pioneering force, found that there was very little in the way of supervision, guidelines, records or money, but once the public became aware of its existence, information — often inaccurate and with malicious intent — poured in. 'We could not understand', he recalled, 'why lies were so often told to us by our own people in the fight against the British.' He also observed that 'The importance of the work was not explained to us. . . . Nearly twelve months passed before it dawned on some of us that the successful outcome of our work was even more important than an occasional ambush.'

Elsewhere the Volunteers had already been involved in major criminal investigations. The Millstreet, Co. Cork, bank robbery of 17 November 1919 was the most notable episode. On that day cars transporting £18,000 from two banks were stopped and robbed. The robbers gave the impression that they were Volunteers, an impression, said the *Irish Bulletin*, that Dublin Castle readily accepted and broadcast. The RIC failed to solve the crime. Finally on Sunday 25 April a force of between 100 and 200 Volunteers occupied the village of Millstreet, with the police retreating to their barracks. After a massive but quick investigation, six men were arrested, including three brothers and a driver of one of the cars, and about half of the funds were recovered. At this point the Volunteer commander was uncertain as to what action to take. Detain the robbers and turn them over to the RIC? Return the money to the bank? Mulcahy suggested handing over the robbers to the bank officials; he also said that the Volunteers could provide testimony by written statement, which, of course, entailed involvement with the crown courts. This advice did not appeal to the IRA in Cork, so the robbers were court-martialled and ordered out of the district, a sentence enforced by an armed escort.

During May 1920 the IRA was reported to be involved in dealing with crime in various parts of the country. In Tipperary a house break-in 'was brought to the notice of the commandant of the Volunteers, and the local corps mobilised and directed to search for the thieves. In the evening a young man was placed under arrest and charged with the offence. He protested his innocence, but he was taken away to an unknown destination, where he awaits trial before a Volunteer court martial.' In Ballybunion, Co. Kerry, the windows of many Sinn Féiners having been smashed, the urban district council 'asked the officer commanding the troops there to allow the local Irish Volunteers to be used for the protection of the citizens' property'. The officer's reply was not noted. The Volunteers in Co. Dublin first became involved in crime detection a month later when they arrested several people after some gold was stolen from a postman.

The success of the Volunteers' campaign against the RIC had driven most of the police off the streets and into fortified barracks. There was a yawning gap in ordinary law enforcement, and the IRA had stepped in to fill the void. Brugha told the Dáil on 29 June that his department 'had now to do work which it should not have to do, namely, to perform police duties, capture criminals, and put down crime and offences and so forth'. The IRA leadership and rank and file were obviously reluctant to do police work. As late as 26 May Mulcahy as Chief of Staff instructed all units to avoid assuming police powers, but he saw the obvious need: 'They were advised, however, that because of their organisation and efficiency, public opinion, regardless of their primary function as Volunteers, would at times look to them as a body to interfere in certain matters.' He told them that in such cases they should urgently report to GHQ, use foresight, seek advice and act prudently.

At the same time as the Dáil government decided to assume full judicial powers it also decided to assume full police authority. On 19 June Mulcahy issued an order for the army to form a police force: 'A police officer would be appointed at company, battalion and brigade level, and a police force voluntar[il]y recruited from the ranks of the Volunteers.' Until the Dáil developed a criminal code (which it never did) and the courts had developed further, the army would also assume judicial powers. Offenders would be brought 'before a court of enquiry appointed by the brigade commandant on the requisition of the brigade police officer. However, no punishment will be inflicted but persons convicted will be publicly paraded after the principal Mass on Sunday.'

The position of the police was further defined by a Dáil government order of 1 November which set up the police force as a separate body within the army. 'When members of the army were taken into the police force, they would be placed on the army reserve and relieved of all routine army service.' On the other hand, not only the Republican Police but also the IRA as a whole was to be available, if necessary, to enforce court orders: 'No battalion commandant would refuse assistance additionally requisitioned by the police for the execution of court orders.' The position of national Chief of Police was created, and Simon Donnelly was appointed to this office. The Dáil government announced that the police were a separate force 'under a Chief of Police, who will administer them as a section of the Home Affairs Department', but there was no effective separation from the army, and this caused great difficulties until the truce of July 1921. In July 1920 General Macready found the situation intolerable:

> Nearly every day one sees in the papers that the Sinn Féin Police are able to round up malefactors where the RIC are powerless, and that of course is merely because the Sinn Féiners have now at their disposal the very men who formerly were used by the RIC to get their information, that is, the loafers and hangers-about in the various towns and villages.

In December 1920 Bishop Cohalan of Cork declared that 'The Volunteer police are now universally and deservedly popular and esteemed.'

The IRA originally dealt with criminal offenders by means of courts martial; as the court system developed, the army increasingly turned over to it defendants charged with criminal offences. The policing activities of the force also drew favourable press attention. In Dingle, Co. Kerry, two men charged with theft were tried by court martial. 'During the sitting a large crowd, among whom six policemen stood helpless, gathered in the street. It was stated that all the missing property had been recovered by the Sinn Féin secret service.' Two men in Co. Cork were arrested on bank robbery charges, were tried by court martial and aquitted. They had nothing but good to say about their treatment: 'They were supplied with excellent food, and an abundance of cigarettes, were allowed two daily newspapers every day and were given two hours exercise daily.' Three men charged with robbing a Co. Roscommon post office were even more fortunate. Although they were to be held while the case was investigated further, they told the court that 'they had no complaint to make about their treatment while in custody. They were informed that they could write home to their friends, and were removed to an unknown place of captivity. . . . The prisoners were given four meals a day, cigarettes, and a glass of whiskey if desired.' A Co. Cavan publican had quite a different experience. Charged with breaching the local Volunteer licensing regulations, he was 'kept in close confinement and without food for several days, and . . . had to keep the rats off with a stick'.

Illicit whiskey distilling attracted Volunteer attention in some localities. There was a report that in the mountains of Donegal some residents were taking advantage of the withdrawal of the RIC to distil 'Republican Whiskey', that is, untaxed poteen, but generally the Volunteers cracked down on this venerable activity. The *Irish Independent* (12 June) reported: 'A complete poteen still and accessories were discovered at the house of a Unionist farmer and a quantity of poteen at the house of a prominent Sinn Féiner in County Monaghan. Both still and poteen were confiscated and the owners arrested and fined £10 each on liberation.' The IRA disapproval of poteen-making received a patriotic response in Co. Longford. The Adjutant-General informed the county brigade commandant: 'There is open permission to deal with poteen stills in your area if they interfere with the discipline of your force.' This was followed by a report that 'Several of the delinquents . . . who had for years eluded the vigilance of the RIC handed over their stills to the Republican police and retired from business. A limited time was given them to dispose of stock already in hands.' Poteen-making seemed to have achieved a mighty renaissance at this time. In April 1920 the cabinet voted to examine the possibility of a tax on spirits that by British law were illicit. Austin Stack raised the matter in the Dáil in August 1920, and Pádraic Ó Máille, a deputy from Connemara, proposed that the government should regulate the process and 'a tax should be imposed upon its manufacture rather than that the stills should be broken up'. In the event, the Dáil took no action on the matter.

The IRA also assumed other police responsibilities, including the regulation of hours of public houses. The *Irish Bulletin* (9 May) asserted that 'The young men who are most active in the political and military wings of the Republican cause are determined that the reproach of drunkenness shall no longer be brought against Ireland.' In Longford 'notices by the IRA Commandant ordering public houses to close at 9 p.m. were torn down by the RIC, but were enforced by Volunteers'. On 17 June the cabinet decided that local bodies 'may if necessary take action suiting local requirements but must not mention D[áil] É[ireann] as no decree has been issued'. Another duty assumed by the Volunteers was stewarding both Gaelic sports matches and race meetings. They succeeded in ousting bookmakers from Croke Park and other Gaelic fields and won commendation for their success in maintaining order at the races. Lord Dunraven noted 'the excellent order that IRA police administered at race meetings and the like'. They also gained a great deal of visibility. This is one of the first public functions of the IRA that was stopped when Dublin Castle decided to respond to the challenge to its authority. A deputation of English Quakers reported in November:

> It is plausibly maintained that if the English garrison and armed police were to withdraw, the Sinn Féin Government could and would run the country, and that at present order and safety are only found in districts from which they have been withdrawn. . . . The English Government has ceased to function over at least eighty per cent of Ireland.[12]

(6) THE HIGH-WATER MARK OF THE COUNTER-STATE

Problems and Perspectives

The alternative government of Dáil Éireann blossomed in the summer of 1920; its growth was rapid and the season short. Its successes with the courts, police, army and local government created a public demand for its services far beyond these areas of administration. It was now seen by many, if not most, people as the *de facto* government of the country. To put it more modestly, it was now viewed by many people as being at least one of the governing forces in Ireland. To meet this demand for its services, the underground state had to expand quickly, and there were severe growing pains.

Until the summer of 1920 the existence of a counter-state had been almost completely ignored by the Irish press, but this situation changed dramatically at that time. The activities of Dáil Éireann received greater coverage not only in the daily press but also in such strong Sinn Féin supporters as *The Kerryman*, which filled its pages with a wide range of reports about the new administration. One reason for the increased attention was that the Dáil government was doing more, but it was also due to the fact that the press perceived that it was gaining wider support. The rash of favourable press coverage, not only in Ireland but also in Britain, was a sore trial to British officials. When an interview with Arthur Griffith in a London newspaper was reported by the Dublin press, General Macready was ruefully realistic: since they could not do anything about a publication in the English press, 'it would be childish to do anything in regard to Irish papers'. On the other hand, he observed that 'day after day scandalous and lying statements appear' in the Irish press 'which goaded and exasperated the police and troops'. He demanded action to stop this litany of falsehoods. 'Sinn Féin is making every effort', reported Frederick Dumont in June, 'to prove its claim that it has established its own government in all Ireland except a few counties inside the Ulster "pale".' A month later the *Irish Times* asserted that 'An Irish

Republic is very nearly in being', noting that 'The Sinn Féin flag flies already over the whole province of Munster, and soon will fly over the whole of Leinster and Connaught and over a large part of Ulster.' The London *Nation* went further; in August it stated: 'The central fact of the present situation in Ireland is that an Irish Republic exists.'

The reality of the counter-state and its army were clearly perceived by Ernie O'Malley: 'Throughout the city were [the army's] offices and duplicate offices, and those of government departments of Dáil Éireann, houses where ministers and staff officers could be met; others in which they ate and slept. They carried on their work as if they controlled the city.' Charles Grastly, a visiting American journalist, was astounded to find the leaders of the rebel government in open view:

> There is no fear of interruption or punishment. If one saw them through the window he would not dare reveal their identity. These men can sit together, chat, smoke their cigars, and do their work tranquilly. They are not only protected by their 'intelligence', but they undoubt-edly have a well-organised business machine, with executive and clerical help down to card-indexes, to make systematic the carrying out of a definite policy planned in every detail and understood by all.

This view was not shared by one knowledgeable insider. Michael Collins told Art O'Brien on 18 June:

> We are carrying an absolute dead weight. . . . To me it is nothing short of a disaster. For instance, I get many matters through you for other Departments. I tell you I receive them, and hand them over, and there, as a rule, the matter ends. Important communications are left unanswered. Important actions are delayed, with all the consequent disadvantages and dangers.

Collins had long been dissatisfied with the efficiency of Desmond FitzGerald and the Propaganda Department. A new object of frustration and contempt had now emerged — Austin Stack and the Home Affairs Department. With the rise of the Dáil courts, Stack's department had turned to the IRA for use of its communications system. This brought strong objections from Cathal Brugha and Richard Mulcahy. But Collins's criticisms were much broader and stronger. In his view, Stack and his department were guilty of administrative incompetence, which he con-sidered to be a cardinal sin. This was the beginning of a rift within the Dáil government that threatened to become an open breach.

The communications system remained a problem throughout the period. The IRA had created an effective system, and every department of the Dáil government wanted to use it. In October 1920 the Volunteers' Director of Communications asked each department for proposals to deal with the matter. When asked 'What aid can your Department give?',

Austin Stack replied: 'At present nil till the Court System is in full being.' Kevin O'Higgins had an eminently sensible idea — create an alternative Dáil-sponsored communications system. This was not done, on a broad scale at least, and the IRA continued to bear this burden until the end. Terror or repression notwithstanding, the civilian mail had to go through, in many cases 'by hand'.

With new responsibilities came an avalanche of work for Dáil Éireann. Never again were eight months to pass between meetings; nine weeks became the average, even during the height of the campaign of repression by its rivals in Dublin Castle. After the session of June 1920 Collins wrote to Art O'Brien: 'You will be pleased and interested to hear that we had a full meeting of the Dáil yesterday for the whole day, from early morning until late at night.' O'Brien told Gavan Duffy: 'It is indeed heartening to see the dreams of one's life gradually evolving into actual and solid fact.' Naturally the pressure of time resulted in rushed legislation. Roger Sweetman spoke for many deputies when in September 1920 he told the Dáil that it was 'very undemocratic to have to dispose of important questions in the few minutes that could be devoted to them under the circumstances'. Seán MacEntee agreed with Sweetman's position, adding that 'under the present circumstances there could be no real opposition to the Ministry'. But J. J. Walsh's latest and last effort to shift responsibility for legislative approval to Dáil committees was once again brushed aside. At the Dáil meeting held in the following January, Michael Collins pointed to the fact that the committees created a year and a half earlier had been poorly supported by deputies; but, of course, these were only advisory bodies. He also rejected the charge that members had not been kept informed of matters between Dáil sessions. He noted that deputies had been in easy communication with the ministry in land cases and 'they would have as little difficulty getting into touch on any occasion as they would have on such occasions if they put themselves to the very small trouble of sending a letter or paying a visit to Dublin'. 'Ignorance on the part of the Deputies', he charged, 'of anything the Ministry was doing was very much the fault of the Deputies themselves.'

The number of full-time employees grew to about 300. An estimated 2,000 persons provided voluntary labour, particularly in the court system. This was much too small a number, however, to administer a country the size of Ireland; by comparison, the Castle regime had about 12,000 employees, excluding the police. How seriously could the public view the claim of an organisation with so few public servants to be the real government? How seriously did the officials themselves take their role and that of the Republic of Ireland? On his visit to Ireland in March 1920 Patrick McCartan was struck by the lack of seriousness with which the operations of the Republic were taken by some of the leaders. He pointed out to them that in America members of the Irish mission always tried to observe a publicly respectful attitude towards their position and functions; de Valera was always addressed and referred to as 'President de Valera'. He recommended that the same practices be observed at home. 'Eunan' in *Old Ireland* (4 Sept. 1920) raised the same matter:

A question to members and officials of the Republican Government and public representatives. How often during the past week have you been guilty of something approaching seditious utterances?. . . Since January 1919 there has been only one Government in Ireland — the Government of the Irish Republic. Yet how many of those who speak for us nowadays remember this fact when they open their mouths? . . . Such terms as 'the Government', 'the military', 'the police', when referring to the enemy forces are symbols of the slave mind.

Art O'Brien reported that members of Irish support groups in Britain had difficulty grasping the idea that the Dáil government was a real government; but of course, that was across the water, not at home.[13]

The Department of Local Government
The department that was called upon for immediate action in the summer of 1920 was that of Local Government. Already hanging over the heads of the county councils was £3 million in malicious injuries assessments that had been made the responsibility of local government by British law in October 1919; the Dáil's Department of Local Government had declared that county councils must not increase rates to meet the cost of these assessments, and this instruction was generally followed. As we have seen, the county council and rural district council elections held in June 1920 resulted in a crushing victory for Sinn Féin.

The county councils and other local bodies now looked to the Dáil government for direction. The Department of Local Government was not prepared to respond. Although for the past year and a half all signs pointed to a major Sinn Féin victory in the county council elections, very little had been done in anticipation of this development. The minister, W. T. Cosgrave, had been arrested on 25 March, and although he was released at the end of April, he was in hospital in mid-May and did not resume his duties until July. To fill the void, Kevin O'Higgins, a twenty-eight-year-old solicitor from Co. Leix, was appointed his substitute on 19 April. He had first gained local attention for his opposition to con-scription, as a result of which he served six months in prison. This propelled him into a nomination as a Sinn Féin candidate in the 1918 election. What he lacked in political and administrative experience he made up for in intelligence and initiative.

Looking beyond the pending elections, O'Higgins organised a conference on local government on 11 May. The meeting recommended that after the election local bodies with Sinn Féin majorities should have nothing further to do with the Local Government Board of Dublin Castle. This proposal filled O'Higgins with alarm, as the new councils would be dominated by persons with little experience who 'would be unable to carry such a policy to success'. He believed that 'before we break we should be sure that we are not rushing the Boards and Councils into a hopelessly false position and imposing on them a super-human task'. A break would mean the end of hundreds of thousands of pounds in grants from the British government. Many of the new councils wanted an immediate break, but some of members believed that they could pledge allegiance to Dáil Éireann and still work with the Castle's Local Government Board — a form of having your cake and eating it too. This attitude drew forth a reprimand from the Dáil department on 17 July: 'It has been reported to the Department that some Councils are willing to obey instructions re political matters, but that outside of this they should have free scope. There would be little use in having a Department of Local Government unless the general business of the Local Authorities were under supervision.'

There was no clear direction from the cabinet. On 10 June it instructed the councils to pass resolutions of allegiance to Dáil Éireann, and on 17 July it ordered them to stop 'passing foolish resolutions'. Left in this position, O'Higgins could not give the local bodies a definite statement of policy. He did instruct them to provide neither income tax information nor funds for criminal and malicious injury claims to the Castle. He told the Dáil meeting of 29 June that the best thing to do was to delay the break until the Dáil government had prepared a uniform scheme, including financial provisions, for dealing with the matter. Some councils had already acted, and Terence MacSwiney believed the situation should be faced squarely: 'By adopting the Declaration of Allegiance to Dáil Éireann the Councils had put themselves in the position of declaring war. It was only a question of time when the crisis would arise. It was now for the British Local Government Board to make the next move.' On O'Higgins's advice, however, the Dáil shifted the whole matter to a commission, which was given little more than a month to report. A year and a half of indolence was to be made up by the hurried work of eighteen local officials and deputies sitting in Dublin, with no time for hearings outside the capital. While the commission was considering the situation the Castle authorities decided to act. The Local Government Board in the Custom House issued a circular on 29 July which decreed that no grants would be paid to councils 'without a definite assurance that they will submit their accounts to audit and be prepared to conform to the rules and orders of the Local Government Board as heretofore'.

Pushed into the position of having to fight or surrender, the Dáil department on 10 August instructed the local bodies to affirm their support for the underground republic and turn forever away from their former allegiance; this was followed by a Dáil decree to this effect on 17 September. In a circular to the councils Cosgrave declared: 'The stoppage of grants in aid of local taxation by the enemy government is a last despairing attempt to bribe the people of Ireland back into slavery.' Only a handful of local bodies complied with the requirement set down by the Custom House board; the vast majority followed the policy laid down by the Dáil department. Even then, the break was not complete and uniform. An exception was made in the case of local committees of agriculture, which had representation on a central committee. Art O'Connor advised the Dáil that there was £200,000 involved and that 'the English Department did not wish that anything in the nature of a break should occur'. The Dáil commission had not even considered this matter.

The other local bodies faced a financial crisis, with almost one-fifth of their funds now in the process of being lost. The commission's report, submitted to the Dáil session of 17 September, recommended sweeping economies. The proposal to end free school lunches in the slums of Dublin at the cost of £8,000 was dropped only upon the vigorous protest of Seán MacEntee, while Joseph McGrath failed to have the projected plan for closing tuberculosis hospitals deleted. The commission also suggested the consolidation of all workhouses into one institution in each county. Cosgrave had a strong aversion to what he saw as the effect of workhouse life on able-bodied persons. He later declared that 'these institutions had bred a peculiar race, peculiar to themselves — people who had got no civic pride or sense of civic responsibility'. The Democratic Programme of January 1919 had denounced the existing poor law system and had proposed the creation of 'a sympathetic native scheme for the care of the Nation's aged and infirm'. The old poor law system was largely demolished, but there was no alternative scheme to take its place. In many counties aged, infirm and mentally ill persons were turned out into the street or rescued by religious orders and private groups.

The proposed economies would only save about £280,000 for the next half-year, which still left a deficit of over £200,000. The commission proposed that the Dáil begin collecting the huge payments going to the British exchequer in the form of land purchase annuities, income tax and all other sources of income — licensing fees, motor tax, estate duty, etc. It also warned of the difficulty of collecting rates once the break with the British government had been made. One member of the commission, Denis Rushe, stated that in twenty-three counties Unionists paid most of the local taxation and that 'the Protestants are already being advised not to make any payment to the Dáil or to any of the County Councils with non-Unionist majorities'.

Meanwhile the department had its own problems. Having assumed authority over local government, it now had to provide supervision.

This required a large staff. The Dáil approved the immediate appointment of thirty-three new employees (nineteen auditors, ten clerks and four inspectors), and over the next year the staff grew to over sixty, thus becoming the largest department in the Dáil government. Cosgrave had his office in the General Council of County Councils building in Parnell Square. The department advised local bodies on 19 November to take stern action against officials who refused to carry out council instructions. In Dublin the corporation had suspended the City Clerk and his assistant for failing to withhold records from the Custom House auditor as instructed. Kevin O'Higgins anticipated that there would be 'many cases' in which employees would not follow the directives of local bodies, especially if the instructions originated from the Dáil department. 'Officials are reminded', warned the department, 'that their pensions are paid from the rates, not by the English Government, and no pension from public money can be granted to any official who is dismissed for endeavouring to thwart the will of the people of Ireland.'

It was not only the local employees who were a problem, but also some of the republican councils themselves. Some of them did not clearly grasp the implications of the shift of allegiance to the Republic. When Fermoy Urban District Council sent a resolution demanding a sworn inquiry into the destruction of property in the town to British military headquarters, it was informed that since it had placed itself under the authority of Dáil Éireann, 'it would be neither seemly nor proper for an official of the British Government to take any steps in the direction referred to'. In a circular to county council chairmen on 20 December, O'Higgins charged that 'Owing to the imprisonment or enforced absence of Republican members, some public bodies are failing to comply in all particulars with instructions issued by this Department.' Overall, the councils followed instructions: 'The exceptions are not greater than were anticipated from the beginning and are confined to certain Urban Districts and Joint Bodies whose personnel is unsuited to the responsibilities of public administration in the present strenuous times.' A month later he painted a much more serious picture for the Dáil. 'One thing struck him forcibly', he declared, '— the hollowness of the Declaration of Allegiance.' At both the county council and urban district levels there were many members elected as republicans, together with officials, who 'were not carrying out the instructions of the Dáil and were in full communication with the British Local Government Department'. What was needed, he believed, was authority from the Dáil 'to deal with men on public bodies who did not act according to their pledge, and against officials who directly or indirectly were trying to scuttle the ship'.

Collecting rates was the principal headache for local councils. Rate-collectors were caught in a limbo between the Custom House and Parnell Square. The Dáil cabinet decided in January 1921 that negligent rate-collectors should be fired; it also ordered that a list of tax defaulters should be forwarded to the Local Government Department and that those listed should 'be dealt with by the Defence Department where necessary'. Up to this point the Dáil government had done nothing to provide any financial support for local government. Now it adopted a different tack. The sum of £100,000 was appropriated for a loan fund to county councils who had collected three-quarters of their rates. Cosgrave believed that this amount of money 'could retrieve the position of the local bodies entirely'. Moreover, 'the moral effect of it would inspire the people throughout the country where the "money-backing" would have a great effect'.[14]

Other Departments

Two other departments of the first Dáil government deserve attention here. A Ministry of Labour had been established at the beginning, its minister being the remarkable Constance Markievicz (1868–1927). Born into the Sligo ascendancy Gore-Booth family, she had married a Polish count. Drawn into Irish nationalism in the early years of the century, She established the Fianna Éireann, a boys' junior army, in 1909. She also developed strongly socialist views and supported James Larkin and the Transport Union during the 1913 lock-out struggle and become an officer in the Citizen Army. After taking part in the 1916 rising, she became prominent in Sinn Féin. In 1918 Arthur Griffith is said to have been displeased by her flamboyant rhetoric and would have liked to silence her, 'but such a thing would be taken as a division in the camp, so she is allowed to go on making idiotic revolutionary speeches'. She won a seat at the general election of 1918, thereby becoming the first woman to be elected to the United Kingdom parliament.

At the time of her appointment as minister she was president of Cumann na mBan, the women's republican organisation. The Countess, as she was known, had a theatrical flair. Máire Comerford related that Madame (another name) went about the streets of Dublin disguised as an old woman 'and she used to pop up here and there at street corners. She would hold a brief meeting and disappear.' Kathleen McKenna often observed her in the Propaganda Department office: 'She would sit for hours on a corner of a table smoking cigarette after cigarette and discussing in her musical voice the most varied and fascinating topics.'

She had time for these activities because the Labour Department initially had little to do. It got involved in labour mediation, but handled few cases. It requested an appropriation of only £400 for the second half of 1920. In July of that year the cabinet strengthened the labour relations machinery. If agreement could not be reached through the conciliation boards, then the ministry would appoint an arbitrator. A group of pro-minent supporters were nominated to act in this capacity. The department also became involved in assisting in the formation of a new Irish-based engineering union. The cabinet agreed to cover an overdraft of the union up to £2,000, and it attracted 1,100 members in the summer. The department was given two new functions at this time: to seek employment for resigned policemen and unemployed Volunteers, and to manage the boycott of goods from Belfast.

Madame was arrested several times and spent extended periods in jail. When she was arrested for a minor vehicle offence in September 1920, Mark Sturgis, a British official in Dublin Castle, noted: 'I believe she's a thorn in the flesh of Sinn Féin, so it may be a pity to take her away from them.' He favoured letting her go, 'which might, I think, discredit her with everybody'. She was released. When she was again arrested in November, Frederick Dumont reported that he had been 'told by Sinn Féiners that her arrest is a relief to them; that she was a firebrand and dangerous, even to them'. As Minister for Labour, she made no effort to establish standards for employment or anything of the sort. In December she was sentenced to two years in prison. She was succeeded by Joseph McGrath, but his tenure lasted only a month before he too was arrested. In January 1921 Joseph McDonagh became acting minister.

The Dáil government also had a Department of Trade and Commerce, whose director was Ernest Blythe (1889–1975), the only Ulster Protestant in the Dáil. A 'big, lanky, soft-spoken Ulsterman' from Lisburn, Co. Antrim, he was active in the Gaelic League, the IRB and the Volunteers and had been in prison both before and after 1916. Blythe became director in April 1919 and, at de Valera's request, was included in the cabinet in June. Eoin Mac Néill, who had been nominal Minister for Industries, became minister without portfolio at that time.

Given the conditions under which the Dáil government operated, it is not surprising that Blythe's department achieved little. It provided assistance, including a staff member, to the formation of a co-operative society to produce butter and cheese in Waterford. Although £200,000 was raised, construction of a plant was postponed to quieter times. After the Moore–McCormack Line established direct shipping from Ireland to America in 1919 the department created the Irish Overseas Shipping Trading Company to generate Irish exports to the US market. It also explored the feasibility of forming an import/export firm, complete with warehousing in Ireland, the creation of an investment company and various other schemes, but nothing came of them. This kind of activity probably did not seem urgent during the prosperous year of 1920, and after the economy went into recession in the following year the Dáil government was not in a position to act.

The department had supervisory authority over the Industrial Resources Commission and also the National Economic Council formed in September 1920. At that time Blythe proposed a bill to encourage Irish manufacturing by requiring retailers to stock approved Irish goods, with fines for failing to comply. Moreover, when an Irish product was available in sufficient quantity and variety, his department could 'prohibit retailers from taking into stock any foreign makes of such goods'. Several deputies objected that the proposal would interfere with the rights of shopkeepers; J. J. Walsh suggested what was really needed was a 'buy Irish' campaign as 'the Irish people were asleep as regards their duty to support Irish manufacture'. The bill was handed over to a special committee and was heard of no more. In the spring of 1921 the department imposed a selective boycott of British goods, which had the same effect as Blythe's bill.

For its first year the department was flooded with requests for loans for industrial capital. Blythe commented: 'Many of the projects came under my notice through the promoters coming forward with proposals that the Dáil should lend or give them sums ranging downwards from £3,000,000, which was asked for by one gentleman who previously held a fairly important position in a Belfast shipyard and who submitted elaborate plans for the development of a great dockyard in the neighbourhood of the Alexandra Basin.' The cabinet, after providing a few small grants, decided against any further loans or grants. Blythe agreed with this policy: 'It would be impossible to discriminate amongst the hundreds of applicants without giving offence to many good Republicans, and moreover the giving of loans direct would be an incentive to applicants to apply political pressure to members of the Dáil.' Yet there remained a persistent problem: 'Our industrial backwardness is partly due to the reluctance of people to invest in home enterprises.' The National Land Bank had proposed the creation of a state-financed Industrial Loan Guarantee Fund, an idea supported by Blythe, which would provide security to economic development loans made by the bank. The scheme could not be undertaken until the bank had acquired more capital. Since this did not happen, nothing more was heard from Blythe concerning the provision of state stimulation for industrial development.[15]

Finance

The operations of the Dáil government through the summer of 1920 had been financed from the proceeds of the Dáil Loan in Ireland; when the campaign ended in September 1920, £380,000 had been collected. As the counter-state gained momentum, more and more money was needed. The government spent only £30,000 to the end of October 1919; in the next eight months £76,000 was expended; for the last half of 1920 the figure rose to £109,000. For the first half of 1921 £185,900 was appropriated, although only £111,000 was spent. Impressive stories about the success of the loan drive in the USA had wide circulation, with the figure of $3,000,000 being the informed total; in fact $5,123,640 were eventually raised. About $1,400,000 was spent on the various activities of the

American mission, leaving approximately $3,700,000. Little of this money came into the hands of the government until mid-1920. On 5 June the cabinet proposed that £500,000 be sent over 'at once'. In July Collins told Gavan Duffy that $200,000 had been received and that 'probably four to five times this sum will be transferred during the coming quarter'. By September $300,000 (approximately £75,000) had been received. In fact this was all that was sent.

With the rapid expansion of its services, the alternative state was in need of money. When the Local Government Department sought a considerable expansion of its staff in September, Collins declared that the money was not available. By aligning with Dáil Éireann, local government units lost hundreds of thousands of pounds in grants. Collins wanted to pour half a million pounds of the money raised in America into the Land Bank, but these funds were not to hand.

The financial picture was changing. If the Dáil programmes continued their growth, the funds collected in Ireland would soon be exhausted. This would make the counter-state totally dependent on the money raised in America. Admittedly, almost all this money came from people born in Ireland or from Irish-Americans, but it would still mean that the government had to rely on external funding. What if the United Kingdom government found an effective means to cut off this source? What if the United States government impounded the funds?

There was a huge amount of money within tantalising reach. Fifteen million pounds in Irish income tax went into the British exchequer annually. In addition, there were several millions paid in land annuities. There were also a few millions paid in various fees. In 1918 Sinn Féin had proposed that the payment of all annuities and taxes should cease if conscription was imposed. Now Collins committed himself to getting possession of some of this money. He had been urged to follow this course by Terence MacSwiney and Cork Corporation. He moved first on income tax when on 29 June he asked the Dáil to establish an income tax department. Payment of such tax to the department would apparently be voluntary, with the government providing indemnity against legal action by the Treasury. His motion was widely supported. He had earlier declared that 'the creation of this taxation department would be an easy matter, and would strike the imagination of all'.

A cabinet committee had been considering such action since May 1919. Collins was confident that income could be derived from this source: 'There is a very popular feeling in favour of paying to the Dáil, and it is equally certain that with good organisation, an understanding with Labour, and a vigorous campaign, we can get a very considerable revenue, amounting, possibly, to £500,000 annually.' In October 1920 the cabinet carried the matter further when it decided that the counter-state should assess income tax at 60 per cent of the British rate up to £500, and 75 per cent above that level. The great difficulty was that most income tax payers were Unionists. Collins claimed that progress was being made in preparing to secure income tax and fees for auctioneer's licences, but the programme was never put into effect.

Collins sometimes talked about the need to tackle the matter of revenue from land annuities. Art O'Connor later explained that although he had been urged many times to propose the stoppage of land annuity payments as a response to British actions, he was always opposed. He held that such a measure would kill the credit of the nation. 'The Irish people had contracted to borrow a certain sum of money on certain terms'; the contract should be fulfilled. And so it was that while the IRA attacked and destroyed many tax offices, the Dáil government never ordered or even advised that patriotic Irishmen should stop payment of taxes and land annuities to its British rival.

Another possible source of money was licence fees, particularly those paid by publicans. An anonymous flyer was distributed in 1920 which declared that on the basis of a 'Resolution of National Appeal' owners of licensed premised henceforth would pay their fees to the Dáil government 'and no longer act as tax-gathering agencies for the aggressor and oppressor of our nation'. Consumers of alcoholic beverages were asked to 'abstain from all intoxicants on which tax is being paid' to the United Kingdom government. There was no discernible response to either appeal. Perhaps Collins was just testing the waters.

The Minister for Finance continued to raise the matter of revenue. He told the Dáil in September 1920: 'During the next few months the machinery to run the Income Tax Proposal will be brought into existence, and I have every reason to anticipate great success.' In a press interview at the beginning of 1921 he announced: 'This year we shall begin to collect income taxes. . . . One half of the Income Taxes of Ireland will be paid to our Government in a year or two.' De Valera and Collins reviewed the matter in June. The practical difficulties proved to be insurmountable. A large staff and secure records would be required. In addition, there was the danger of public rejection, the danger that people might vote for Sinn Féin, relate stories of Volunteer heroics and throw a few coins into party collection pails, but would not be prepared to risk their land, licences and money in a conflict with British authorities. For someone of Collins's temperament, it must have been difficult to admit, at least to himself, that he could not succeed in this vital matter. It must have dawned on him and others that the counter-state was reaching the limit of its development.[16]

(7) FACING NORTH

The existence of a large Unionist population in north-east Ulster had been given little attention by either Sinn Féin or the Dáil government. Sinn Féin had been primarily concerned with first winning and then maintaining domination in nationalist Ireland. Its demand for complete independence was at the opposite pole to the Unionist position. In the 1918 election Sinn Féin had failed miserably in Belfast; Joe Devlin and his political organisation remained dominant in mainly Catholic west Belfast. There was no Sinn Féin member of the Dáil elected from within twenty miles of Belfast. As a result, the party did not have very favourable feeling towards that grim industrial city.

With all the difficulties of setting up an alternative state, the Dáil government apparently believed that a few minor measures would deal with the Ulster problem, at least for the time being. In any case, it could not overlook the fact that it had a problem there. A couple of extra party organisers were appointed for the province. The way Sinn Féin basically saw the matter was that the northern Unionists would have to accept being incorporated into a united, independent Ireland. P. S. O'Hegarty stated the case clearly at the beginning of 1919: 'Ulster would be Irish whether she liked it or did not like it.' For his part, Griffith refused to accept the proposition that economic self-interest tied industrial Ulster to the British connection, arguing that 'most of the province had experienced a decline in population'. National self-government and the development of a distinctive Irish culture would be as good for Ulster as for the other three provinces.

Another approach was proposed: the adoption of a labour programme to appeal to the Belfast Protestant industrial workers. The Belfast general strike of early 1919 had demonstrated that Unionism was by no means monolithic. 'The important lesson which Sinn Féin in Belfast must learn', declared *Old Ireland* (8 Nov. 1919), 'is that Sinn Féin cannot afford to ignore social justice.' It argued that 'The best service both in the interests of Sinn Féin and the people would be to tackle the enemy with the labour weapons with which he can be beaten.'

Sinn Féin decided to have the northern situation looked at through fresh eyes when in June 1919 it commissioned W. Forbes Patterson to investigate. An Ulster Protestant who had served in the Canadian army during the war, Patterson had publicly declared his support for Sinn Féin. Patterson advised against counter-demonstrations to those addressed by Edward Carson in the name of militant Unionism. He attended a conference of Ulster Sinn Féiners in October that stressed that the province was suffering from the same political and economic evils as a result of British rule as the rest of the country. This view was reflected in the conclusion drawn by the conference: 'The issue in Ulster was identical with the issue in Leinster, Munster and Connacht — the issue of the freedom of the whole Irish Nation.'

In a report submitted later that month Patterson proposed that Sinn Féin adopt a strong labour position. He noted that Unionism was steadily being broken up by the advance of Labour, but the Labour Party in the north 'retains an English outlook'. He also found that republicanism was weak and was not advancing. To deal with this situation, he suggested the setting up of a newspaper, based on the principles of the Democratic Programme, that would weld labour interests and Irish nationalism together. The party executive did not give the report a warm welcome. At a meeting presided over by Griffith it decided the report should be considered by the Dáil cabinet. Yet at another meeting, also presided over by Griffith, the Dáil cabinet decided that it was a matter to be considered by the party.

Patterson would not be put off, and in November he was employed by the Dáil government to retrace his steps through Unionist Ulster. In April 1920 Patterson submitted a report that was very much the same as the one he had produced for Sinn Féin. There was also a report from Eoin Mac Néill. When, in the autumn of 1920, the Dáil government decided to launch a continuing propaganda effort in the north, it established an Ulster Information Bureau, which distributed leaflets proclaiming the advantages of Irish self-government. Patterson became editor of a short-lived (Sept.–Dec. 1920) magazine, *The Red Hand,* which presented itself as a journal of literary and political commentary, but whose underlying purpose was to demonstrate that the northern industrial workers would be better off in an independent Irish state rather than in the grasp of British capitalism. This was the end of Patterson's involvement with Irish nationalism.

Why did the Dáil government not adopt Patterson's plan? None of the leaders of Sinn Féin had any experience concerning Belfast or the labour movement. Only one member of the cabinet, Constance Markievicz, had even a fleeting involvement with unions. The ministers were middle-class people with a middle-class outlook. They were adamant nationalists and apprentice politicians. If they adopted a strong labour programme, not just a vague statement of principles as in the Democratic Programme, they would open themselves up to charges, or confirm charges already being hurled at them, that they were crypto-Bolsheviks, left-wing extremists, enemies of Christian civilisation, etc. How would the grocer, the priest and the farmer react to such a programme? Negatively, without a doubt: flaming nationalism had got them this far, and flaming nationalism would see them the rest of the way.

When the local elections of January and, particularly, June 1920 demonstrated a decline in Unionist support, sundry loud hurrahs were sounded in Dublin. These results, however, did not show any dramatic growth in support for Sinn Féin alone, but also for non-Unionist candidates, particularly Labour nominees. The outcome was a severe jolt to the Unionist Party. In Protestant working-class areas Labour and other socialist candidates polled well, while only one of the eight Ulster Unionist Labour Association candidates was elected. In the summer Sinn Féin appointed five sub-organisers to assist Eamonn Donnelly in the province.

Then in July came a vicious counter-attack by the Unionists. During the European war there had been a large influx of Catholic workers into industries which formerly had been almost entirely Protestant. Using the argument that reprisals were the necessary response to the murders of policemen and other by Sinn Féiners, Protestant workers, aided and abetted by the Orange Order, drove 8,000 Catholic workers out of their jobs in industrial Belfast, particularly in the shipyards. The expulsions were extended to some Protestant workers of socialist views, whom Unionist leaders claimed to be little more than disguised republicans. The expulsions were followed by bloody riots in which thousands of Catholics were driven out of their homes. Many of these fled to Dublin, where they made their presence felt. There was also rioting in Derry city, but because of the different population balance, the Catholic population was able to give as good as it got.

The response of the British government to the upheaval in Belfast was almost minimal. Appeals for military assistance were only reluctantly met. No serious effort was made to employ the military to do more than stop the rioting. Nothing was done to restore the thousands of Catholics to their homes and jobs. The blow struck in Belfast suited the British government's policy of crushing the rebellion in Ireland with any and all means. Much has been made of the utter irresponsibility of that government in its employment of the Black and Tans in the rest of Ireland, but its indifference to what happened in Belfast is an even more serious blot on its record. The government of the fledgling Irish Republic could not ignore the situation. It was forced to make some kind of response: that general response, inaugurated in August 1920, was the 'Belfast boycott'.

Anger and opposition to Unionist violence and repression in Ulster had been growing in nationalist Ireland for many years. Ulster Unionist opposition to Home Rule was clearly engraved in the minds of many republicans. Sectarian rioting at times of political tension were common occurrences in both Derry and Belfast. The British government's new Government of Ireland Bill provided for the separation of the six north-eastern counties of Ulster from the rest of the country.

The boycott was a weapon that had long been in use in Ireland. It had been effectively employed in the land agitations of the late nineteenth century. The Dáil had already decreed one boycott — that of the RIC. The boycott of Ulster Unionist economic interests originated in Galway in December 1919. On 2 December the Tuam Traders' Association called for a boycott of Belfast products and services, which it believed would make for 'a speedy solution of the so-called "Ulster question"'. It believed that a boycott would be effective:

We submit that the most effective, as it is the most expeditious, method of dealing with the still reactionary remnant is to leave them to themselves, and cease from all economic relations with them. They declare they will never abide with us as one political unit. Let us retort, neither then shall you share our economic life.

Belfast was the commercial capital of the country, and most consumer goods were distributed from there to the northern half of the country. If Belfast goods were boycotted, then the required goods would come from somewhere else, that other place being Dublin. Dublin commercial travellers would replace Belfast commercial travellers; Dublin commissions and services would replace those of Belfast. In such considerations, personal economic self-interest was surely a factor.

The campaign began to spread in the west in the early weeks of 1920. The Dáil government made no statement on this development; the Sinn Féin executive informed one of its *cumainn* on 5 February that the party did not initiate the boycott 'and the matter has not yet been discussed'. *Old Ireland* (21 Feb.) commented: 'At present Sinn Féin does not encourage the economic boycott, but if Sinn Féin were forced to use that weapon it could smash Belfast in a month.' In the same issue P. S. O'Hegarty argued that the boycott accepted partition, that it was somehow dishonourable to employ economic weapons, and that the general effect would be to reinforce the Ulster Unionist identity. How far the boycott spread before July is difficult to determine, but the events in Belfast that month made it a major national issue.

In the wake of the upheaval of the summer of 1920, a Belfast Expelled Workers' Fund was established and an appeal for funds was made. However, more than money was needed: 'The only way to meet this is to arraign the wrongdoers at the bar of Public Opinion, and to frustrate this manoeuvre by economic action.' The question of the boycott was promptly raised in the Dáil. At its session of 6 August Seán MacEntee, the only Belfastman in the assembly, presented a statement from Sinn Féin members of the Belfast Corporation and other republican activists which advocated a ban on dealing with Belfast distributors and banks. They argued that 'The chief promoters of Orange intolerance here are the heads of the distribution trade throughout Ireland.' The Dáil would be hard-pressed to reject a call for help from the spokesman of the victims of the Unionist pogrom. Ernest Blythe opposed a general blockade of Belfast, as it would 'destroy for ever the possibility of any union'; instead he proposed a boycott of specific individuals and firms. Both Constance Markievicz and Desmond FitzGerald held that a general boycott would be a vote for partition. In Griffith's view, 'the resolution was practically a declaration of war on one part of their own territory', but he believed that a boycott of Belfast banks would be an effective measure: 'If they held up the banks it would bring the Unionist gentlemen to their senses very quickly.' Terence MacSwiney believed that, rather than imposing a boycott, the Dáil could achieve a permanent improvement of the situation in Belfast if it sponsored alternative employment: 'The establishment of co-operative factories to provide employment for Republicans who could be induced to settle in Belfast would be a big step towards the solution of the problem.' In the end the Dáil passed a motion proposed by Griffith that religious tests for industrial employment should henceforth be illegal 'and that action be taken by the Ministry to prevent such tests being imposed in Ireland'. So the decision to impose the boycott was handed to the cabinet. The Dáil also voted to establish a commission to investigate 'Organised Opposition to the Republic'.

The cabinet, with obvious reluctance, on 11 August voted for a limited boycott, confined to banks and insurance companies having headquarters in Belfast. The campaign was to be co-ordinated by the General Council of County Councils — a move to demonstrate grassroots support. In September Griffith appointed Michael Staines, a Dublin TD, to direct the effort. By this time the boycott had become a general ban, although there is no evidence that such an broad application had been supported by the Dáil or the cabinet. The boycott obviously struck a chord among party activists. Sinn Féin-controlled local government bodies quickly supported the boycott, as did the Irish Labour Party and Trade Union Congress at its September conference. The effort had the support of many Catholic prelates and priests. The Rev. N. Lawless, PP, Faughart, Co. Louth, took a completely different point of view. The Belfast upheaval, he declared, was due to IRA violence: 'It is those crimes that enraged — and no wonder — the workers of Belfast, who have said they will let Catholics workers back when the shooting of RIC men and others stops.'[17]

Although the campaign had a drastic effect on Belfast distributors, some of them did not believe the boycott would last long. They based 'their hopes for better times on the anticipation that what they called "the characteristic lack of tenacity" on the part of the Southerners will induce them very soon to bring the boycott to an end'. Far from this happening, the campaign intensified. This was due in part to the failure to reinstate expelled workers and the continuing flow of refugees from Belfast.

The Belfast ban drew attention to Unionists in other parts of the country. Although some Church of Ireland bishops had condemned the intolerance and violence of Orangemen in Belfast, this was not enough for T. Costello of the Tuam Board of Guardians: 'Why then, when Catholics are hounded from their work in Belfast did not Protestants of the West and South, who were never insulted by the Catholic majority because of their creed, speak out and condemn the conduct of the North?' Protestants were soon speaking out in condemnation of the Belfast expulsions and offering testimonials to the tolerance and goodwill of their Catholic neighbours.

In the autumn of 1920 an advisory committee was formed in Belfast and enforcement committees were established around the country. The Volunteers provided assistance in policing the effort, and at the beginning of 1921 the Dáil government appointed eight inspectors to further enforcement. At least some people were concerned about the effect of the boycott. A midlands farmer claimed that the 'No Belfast goods cry' had resulted in high prices for cattle feed now that Dublin suppliers had replaced those from Belfast. The response of an expelled worker was that the farmer should confer with the Dublin suppliers 'instead of rushing into print to give heart to "Ulster" bigots'. He predicted that 'Long before Easter Belfast will be ready to make peace with Ireland on the latter's terms.' On 17 December Erskine Childers presented a statement signed by a group to the Dáil government which argued that a general ban was inappropriate and counterproductive. The Belfast advisory committee responded: 'The boycott of Belfast was made general because the city of Belfast as a Corporate community acting through its responsible civic authority endorsed the savage persecution to which Republican and Catholic workers were subjected.' There were to be no second thoughts about the campaign; rather, there was general confidence in Sinn Féin ranks that the campaign would prove effective. At the Dáil meeting of January 1921 Michael Collins predicted that, properly organised, 'this boycott would have far-reaching effects. It would make a Vienna of Belfast if it remained outside Ireland.' According to Seán MacEntee, 'They could not reduce Belfast by force of arms, but they could bring her to reason by economic force.' At this time Joseph McDonagh was appointed Acting Minister for Labour and director of the boycott, replacing Constance Markievicz and Michael Staines, both of whom were in prison. The Dáil also voted funds to support the boycott — £1,500 to hire a dozen organisers and £1,000 for advertising. In March McDonagh claimed that Belfast was facing bankruptcy.

At the same time General Macready believed that a counter-offensive was needed: 'It would be a good thing for the Government to say they have had enough of this nonsense and that unless it ceases they will put an embargo on coal for Southern Ireland.' Although Sir John Anderson, the recently appointed Joint Under-Secretary, found the boycott 'most annoying', he argued that it was simply a response to the expulsion of Belfast Catholics about which the administration in Dublin Castle had done nothing effective.

Ulster Unionist leaders attempted to downgrade the impact of the boycott. They could hardly admit that it was being effective, because, of course, this would provide grist to the mills of their opponents. But it was effective. Belfast distributors lost almost all of their trade with the rest of the country. Belfast-based banks were forced to close most of their branches outside north-east Ulster. On the other hand, despite the efforts of some employers and British trade unions, none of the expelled workers got back their jobs. 'Vigilance committees' were set up in the affected industries to ensure that this did not happen.

All of this led to hardening of opinion in the rest of the country. The view grew that what the bigots of Belfast needed was punishment. In rejecting the idea of Ulster home rule within an Irish state, *Old Ireland* in February 1921 voiced that attitude: 'When she has learnt by painful experience that Belfast depends on Ireland for its existence, when she has come to see that the English connection only means financial loss and isolation, then it will be time enough to deal with her.' In the following month Seán MacEntee urged the Dáil to issue a warning to voters in the six-county area about what would happen to them if they supported partition. He proposed the extension of the economic boycott to the entire region, expulsion of the supporters of partition from the rest of the country, and imposition of a system of passport control for anyone coming from the six counties. After the general election to the new parliament of Northern Ireland *Old Ireland* was filled with outrage towards the majority who had voted against Irish unification.[18]

(8) Triumvirate: the Catholic Church, Labour and Sinn Féin

The most powerful organisations in Ireland were the Unionist Party and its auxiliaries, the Catholic Church, the labour movement, the Irish Volunteers, and Sinn Féin and its offspring, the Dáil Éireann government. The last five bodies completely dominated nationalist Ireland. The relationships between them were of vital importance in shaping the outcome of the campaign for self-government.

There was considerable public interest in how the three powerful organisations of Sinn Féin, the Catholic Church and Labour would relate in the difficult circumstances of the time. An English observer commented in May 1919:

> Sinn Féin is not a homogeneous force. It represents a temporary conjunction of incompatible elements. Even today the difficulties of maintaining the semblance of union are apparent. The leaders of the revolutionary Socialist and Labour element have little in common with the believers in the possibility of reviving the mythical glories of Gaelic romance. The Roman Catholic Church is becoming uneasily aware of the need of escape from its compromising relations with those who serve under the red flag.

Church and Counter-State

The relationship of the Catholic Church and Sinn Féin evolved with the rise of the new political movement. In 1917 the few comments of the bishops were generally critical. On the other hand, many of the younger priests lent their support. In June 1918 the church and Sinn Féin were partners with the labour movement in defeating conscription. This was the first — and last — occasion when leaders of the three movements actually met together. Church leaders made no acknowledgment of the establishment of Dáil Éireann. When the Dáil Loan campaign was launched, Bishop Fogarty of Killaloe became a trustee of the funds collected, while a handful of bishops made subscriptions. Throughout the revolutionary period, however, the hierarchy provided no recognition of the rebel republic. Rather, it issued fiery denunciations of British policies and practices in Ireland, while also offering generally muted criticism of attacks on police and soldiers.

In one of its earliest pronouncements — that of 23 June 1919 — it condemned the British regime for employing 'the rule of the sword, utterly unsuited to a civilised nation and extremely provocative of disorder and chronic rebellion'. The view of the London *Times* (26 June) was that this statement 'will be widely regarded as an endorsement of the Republican claims. One fears that it will do much harm in the United States, where it is likely to be accepted as a verification of the preposterous charges of the Irish-American delegates.' As a result of the popularity of Dáil Éireann, moderate bishops 'find themselves forced, now, to shout with the largest crowd, and actually to provide material for the advancement of the very movement which they fear and distrust'.

At a later gathering of the bishops — that of January 1920 — a statement was issued that clearly supported Irish self-determination:

> The one true way to terminate our historic troubles and establish friendly relations between England and Ireland, to the advantage of both countries, is to allow an undivided Ireland to choose her own form of Government.

Yet it was the position of Sinn Féin that the Irish people had already chosen their form of government. In October the bishops issued a stronger statement:

> If there is anarchy in Ireland, the Ministers of the British Crown are its architects. Not by inhuman oppression will the Irish question be settled, but by the recognition of the indefeasible right of Ireland, as of every other nation, to choose the form of government under which its people are to live.

The Dáil government avoided all controversy with church leaders. Attacks on church spokesmen were left to Dáil members and Sinn Féin journals. When the church opposed the Macpherson bill for educational reform, Sinn Féin county councils vied with each other in denouncing the measure. The Dáil government studiously avoided the question of the public control of education. The alarm of some church spokesmen concerning the land agitation was calmed when the counter-state acted to stem and regulate the movement. When Dr Walter McDonald of Maynooth published a booklet in 1920 which denied that the Volunteers or anyone else had a moral right to use violence to attain independence, none of the bishops gave any immediate support to his position. The gathering of bishops and Dáil representatives in Rome on the occasion of the beatification of Oliver Plunkett in June 1920 provided a good opportunity for church leaders to show muted support for the counter-state. Art O'Brien believed that 'It is the general impression that certain of the Hierarchy and some well-known laymen have, as a result of these meetings in Rome, considerably advanced in their opinions with regard to political matters in Ireland.' The hierarchy raised no objections to priests serving as judges in the Dáil courts. In December Bishop Cohalan of Cork, rejecting the legitimacy of the Dáil government, imposed excommunication on any of his flock who killed police or soldiers. No other member of the hierarchy followed his example.

If the Dáil leadership said nothing to conflict with the church, some of the Sinn Féin journals were not so reticent. Archbishop Gilmartin of Tuam was critical of the campaign of violence, and two bishops — Kelly of Ross and Hoare of Ardagh — denied that Dáil Éireann had a moral right to function as a government. These views met a response in *Old Ireland* (8 Jan. 1921): 'If Ireland is defeated after its heroic struggle, after the agony of its heroes, it will be defeated by men like Dr Cohalan and Dr Gilmartin. A few more pronouncements like the recent statements' would undermine the morale of the Irish people. When some of the bishops deplored the use of violence on both sides in their Lenten pastorals, the Sinn Féin journal again responded: 'The Pastorals of the Irish Bishops show how completely out of touch they are with the people. The same old abuse is hurled at them and the same kind of statements as were made in the famine times.'[19]

The bishops undoubtedly helped to prevent a Vatican pronounce-ment on violence in Ireland. Yet Dr John Hagan, rector of the Irish College in Rome, declared that he was the only Irish priest there to give active support to the Irish cause. With the Dáil government's assumption of civil power in many parts of Ireland, clerical criticism disappeared. Some opponents of Irish self-government now became apprehensive. Provost J. H. Bernard of Trinity College declared that the bishops 'were more powerful people than anyone else in this country, and, on the whole, they had been in the past a steadying force'. He did not want to deprive them of their power, 'because he would be very much afraid of the consequences of doing so'. Frederick Dumont viewed the church as an ally of the independence movement. In November 1920 he reported to Washington: 'The deaths of hunger strikers and the hanging of Kevin Barry have served to force the Church out into the open. Their funerals as well as the numerous funerals of Irish volunteers killed in attempts to ambush or assassinate members of the British forces, have been remarkable for the numbers of bishops and priests in attendance.' Further evidence of clerical support for the rebel cause was found in raids on Dáil courts, 'where it is and usually has been the case in very many instances that a priest is sitting as judge. More and more the Church is suspected of supporting the Sinn Féin movement and keeping the people irreconcilable to any connection with Great Britain.'

In fact almost all the bishops favoured a political settlement far short of an independent republic. The terms Cardinal Logue would have accepted were no partition and fiscal control, the latter apparently being important to maintain church control of education. Some of the bishops were prepared to discuss all sorts of political settlements with envoys of the British government. More than once Cardinal Logue told British agents that the Irish people would accept what was, in effect, glorified Home Rule, thus undercutting the negotiating position of the Dáil government. At the height of the negotiations for a truce in December 1920 some Dáil leaders considered raising with the hierarchy 'the question of the Governmental Status of Dáil Éireann'. Griffith prepared a draft of an appeal to the bishops, but Collins had 'very great doubts' about the timeliness of the proposal. Several months passed before the bishops were asked to recognise the Dáil government as the legitimate authority in Ireland; this they declined to do.

One of the interesting aspects of the situation was the role of Australian bishops. Four of them (all Irish-born) became directly involved with the struggle. The most noteworthy of these was Archbishop Daniel Mannix of Melbourne, a former President of Maynooth, who travelled, via the USA, to Europe to promote the cause of Irish self-government. Denied entry into Ireland, he carried on a campaign of support in England from August 1920 until May 1921. The Irish hierarchy made a muted protest concerning his exclusion — in Collins's words, a 'rather colourless' statement. The other three Australian bishops were allowed into the country. Archbishop Barry of Hobart, visiting his native Midleton, Co. Cork in July 1920, 'gave the Irish Republic his blessing and good wishes and hoped it would continue to grow in unity, in strength and wisdom'. Another Australian bishop, Dr Hayden, a native of Kilkenny, gave his full support to the independence movement. Archbishop Clune of Perth arrived in August and spent the next few months as an intermediary in the negotiations for a truce.

Surprisingly, very few American bishops came to Ireland in this period. Most of them were not Irish-born but were of Irish parentage.

On the other hand, many of them provided support for the Irish move-ment in the United States, which was probably of greater importance.

The Catholic hierarchy in Britain was in favour of Home Rule, but nothing more than that. Sinn Féin attention centred on Cardinal Bourne. *Nationality* (3 May 1919) charged that Bourne had become a press agent for the British government on the continent, where he supplied state-ments hostile to Sinn Féin. 'The real object of Sinn Féin', he declared, 'is to set up a Republic of a communistic and godless type, and Sinn Féiners are using the Irish Catholic prelates as pawns.' Art O'Brien believed that Bourne had 'accepted a definite Alliance with the Foreign Office'. In February 1921 Bourne warned that some Catholics in Britain 'are unwarily allowing themselves to become implicated, by active sympathy or even actual co-operation in societies and organisations which are in opposition to the law of God and of the Catholic Church'. On behalf of the Irish Self-Determination League, O'Brien struck back, charging that the cardinal 'has never definitely raised his voice against any of the acts of barbarism and repression' by British forces in Ireland. In fact Bourne had proposed the withdrawal of British forces from the country.

That the Catholic bishops as a group did not recognise the Dáil gov-ernment is not surprising. After all, even in Ireland it is not the business of the leaders of a church to judge political matters that do not directly bear on religious concerns. Furthermore, the Catholic Church was very much an international body, and the Irish hierarchy was not prepared to suffer a reproach from the Vatican for supporting violence and revol-ution. The bishops were prepared to face political facts, but as far as they were concerned the Republic was not a fact, and they would not directly and publicly help to make it a fact. The counter-state would have to prove that it was viable without their assistance.[20]

Labour and Dáil Éireann
Labour and Sinn Féin rocketed to prominence together. The pre-war labour movement was well-developed only in Dublin and Belfast. In the northern city the great majority of industrial workers were in British-based unions and had almost nothing to do with the Irish Trade Union Congress; neither did they support the candidates of the Irish Labour Party. From 1917 both trade unionism and Sinn Féin spread rapidly in nationalist Ireland.

What was the reason for this rapid growth in union membership? It was a European phenomenon arising from the need for wartime labour mob-ilisation. Irish trade unionism had been underdeveloped before the war and had a lot of scope for expansion. Some of the growth was more appar-ent than real — workers transferring from British-based unions to Irish ones. Milo McGarry later attributed the rise of the Irish trade unions to 'the fire of a nation at war, not the warmth of a creative social force springing upwards into flames from the wage-earning masses'. Most Irish trade union-ists seemed to be motivated by nationalist as well as economic objectives.

What of Labour's commitment to socialism, the nationalisation of transportation and industry? This caused considerable concern among conservatives, including some Catholic clergymen. The *Voice of Labour*, edited by Cathal O'Shannon, provided ammunition to the alarmists. In November 1919 it proclaimed: 'The workers of this country can erect in this island the Workers' Republic they admire in Russia.' O'Shannon and a few other Labour spokesmen were enthusiastic about a workers' state, but there is no evidence that this met with a substantial response from ordinary trade unionists. Since its establishment by James Larkin in 1909 the Irish Transport and General Workers' Union had been strongly influenced by syndicalism — the idea that the continued growth of unions would eventually lead to worker control of industry. This approach would shun conventional political power in favour of real power — economic control. Some people believed that the labour movement had now attained that position of strength. Darrell Figgis proposed the creation of a Irish National Council of Labour which would 'do real constructive work, and do it as a matter of self-government'. Richard Dawson, an Eng-lish journalist, published a collection of newspaper articles under the title *Red Terror and Green*, whose message was that Sinn Féin had been drawn into an alliance with a labour movement dominated by Bolshevism. Sir Edward Carson and the Duke of Northumberland were active in raising the alarm in London. An event that appeared to confirm these fears was the action of a group of striking workers at a creamery at Knocklong, Co. Limerick, who in May 1920 seized control of the premises, whereupon 'they immediately hoisted a red flag and a Sinn Féin flag. Next the name of the company was removed from the principal door, which was painted a bright red, with, in white letters, "The Soviet Creamery".' The strike was settled a few days later.

What had occurred, however, was a danger signal to the defenders of the status quo. Father Peter Finlay, SJ (brother of Father Tom Finlay, a supporter of the co-operative movement) took upon himself the res-ponsibility of demonstrating that no good Catholic could support socialism. In March 1920 a heated correspondence took place in the *Irish Independent* between Father Finlay and spokesmen for the ILP and TUC. In *Old Ireland* (20 Mar.) Frank Gallagher voiced his impatience with clerical opponents of social and economic reform:

> For a generation the Catholic clergy and the lay publicists of the Catholic Church in Ireland have had the opportunity to develop a Catholic social policy. . . . Nothing was done. . . . Not one Irish worker in a hundred realises that the Catholic doctrine permits of State ownership of all the resources of a country if such ownership is desired by the people and is necessary to the life of the State.

But what of the radical labour influence on Sinn Féin? The London *Times* (9 Aug.) decided that its earlier stated alarm had been mistaken: 'Irish Labour, it is true, has some affinity with Continental Socialism of an extreme type, and, at the moment, Irish Labour is in a not wholly comfortable alliance with Sinn Féin. But there, in our view, the political connection ends.' Sinn Féin, *The Times* admitted, was popular and democratic and 'its economic policy has hitherto borne no relation to that of Lenin and Trotsky'.

The two key leaders of Labour in this period were William O'Brien (1881–1968) and Thomas Johnson (1872–1963). O'Brien was the chief administrator in the Transport Union, and Johnson had a similar position in the ILP and TUC. Their leadership was not based on popular support or a mass personal following. Neither of them had risen to the top as leaders of industrial actions; rather, they had climbed the administrative ladder. A hard, aloof man from Dublin, O'Brien was both a republican and a socialist. As the most powerful figure in the Transport Union, he kept that huge organisation from any friction with the Dáil government. An articulate but colourless figure, Johnson was a transplanted Englishman of Liverpool origins and socialist beliefs. He was not a republican, but, from his early days as a Home Ruler in Belfast, his views evolved to the point where he would accept the largest measure of self-government that could be obtained. Johnson was the ideal contact man in all dealings with British Labour. After all, he was one of them and spoke their language.

Both these men — indeed, the entire Labour executive — could be relied on absolutely by the Dáil leaders. A close working relationship existed between their two organisations. Disagreement or division would have been a grave threat to the emerging counter-state. This did not happen simply because of the co-ordination between the leadership of the two movements, but also because most of the members of Irish unions strongly supported Irish independence. O'Brien told the Dáil in 1922 that 'At many critical periods within the past couple of years great inducements were held out to his party to break the national solidarity but they resisted every effort.' But the Labour leaders had political ambitions for their movement, and they recognised that Sinn Féin, then in the ascendant, was a friendly but nevertheless separate political entity.

In 1919 the power of Labour seemed to be as great as that of militant nationalism. Strikes were more prevalent than ever before. In an article entitled 'The Rock in the Road' a correspondent of the London *Times* in January warned that there was the danger that the radicals in the labour movement 'will push aside the middle-class intelligentsia' of Sinn Féin, just as Lenin and Trotsky pushed aside Kerensky and the other speechmakers'. The RIC Inspector-General reported in July 1919 that the leaders of the Transport Union 'hold strong Communistic and revolutionary principles and the majority of its 68,000 members are Sinn Féiners'; the union, therefore, 'may be regarded as the left wing of Sinn Féin'. Frederick Dumont reported in January 1920 that the Transport Union, 'an extremely powerful syndicalistic organization', was 'the only real menace to the Sinn Féin movement, and Sinn Féin knows this thoroughly and acts accordingly'. In the following April Arthur Griffith was confident that the two forces would remain united: 'Labour stood down for Sinn Féin at the General Election and worked in harmony with it at the local elections. If our enemies are relying on a breach in our forces in that direction they will be disappointed.' Dumont continued to see the over-whelming power of the labour movement. In September he reported that 'Sinn Féin acknowledges tacitly, if not officially, the One Big Union idea, the probable reason being that Sinn Féin must have the support of Irish Labour at any price.' Basil Clarke, an experienced English journalist, told one of his colleagues around this time that the alliance between Sinn Féin and Labour was 'an *affaire de convenance* because Labour hold Sinn Féin's strongest weapon — the transport strike'.

At the beginning of Dáil Éireann Labour secured the Democratic Programme and used this to gain recognition as a national entity at the first major post-war international labour conference. For the next two years the labour movement asked for nothing else from the revolutionary government. With prosperity and expanding union membership, the Labour leaders obviously believed they could achieve their ends on their own. For their part, Dáil ministers declared their strong sympathies with Labour. De Valera told an American journalist in the spring of 1919: 'The worker is unfairly treated. Whether it is bolshevistic or not, Sinn Féin hopes to bring about a government in which there will be juster conditions for the labouring classes.' The Dáil government established a policy of refusing to purchase goods made by 'sweated labour' (without actually defining that term). Furthermore, the unions were consulted in all matters affecting their interests.

If Labour wanted nothing from Dáil Éireann, the supporters of Irish independence did anticipate getting something from Labour. *Nationality* in January 1919 declared that as a means of disrupting the British regime the general strike was 'a good way, and will be adopted in due course'; the *Voice of Labour* was unenthusiastic about the idea. There were several instances when strike action was used to further the cause of Irish self-government. In all but one of these occasions, however, the national Labour leadership did not initiate the action.[21]

The first instance was in Limerick in February 1919, when the local Trades Council staged a general strike as a protest against British military actions. For a few days the council was in control of the city. Thomas Johnson went to Limerick and, rather than supporting the continuation of the strike, suggested that the population should evacuate the city. His advice was not followed. The strike lasted for one week, during which it was termed the 'Limerick Soviet' by journalists. One informant told the United States consul in Cork that this action 'was not a trade dispute strike, not a strike against the Military, but purely a Labour demonstration of Bolshevism served out with a flavour of Sinn Féin'. The London *Times* (2 May) commented: 'The Limerick strike broke down, but the collapse did not come before it demonstrated the power of Labour to an impressionable degree.'

The next strike grew out of the effort of Dublin Castle in December 1919 to control road transportation by requiring motor permits. The resistance to this order was led by a small new union, the Irish Automobile Drivers' Union. Its huge rival, the Transport Union, was not amused, and support was only reluctantly given by the ILP and TUC. Once the issue was joined, however, it decided to fight hard. The executive issued a directive: 'In no case can motor driven traffic or vehicles be handled or repaired by members of any union.' Union members held up cars in Dublin, and dockers refused to unload vehicles, motor fuel or parts. The Dáil cabinet contributed £1,000 to the strike fund. The strike had effect throughout the country. 'An Irishwoman' gave an exciting account in *Blackwood's Magazine*.

> The Government having decreed that permits signed by the British Executive were obligatory, and Sinn Féin having declared that such permits were an insult to the 'Republic', the motorist ventured on the road at his peril. Should he fall in with a Sinn Féin picket he might merely be turned back with a caution and his permit torn to shreds. But the chances were that his car would be wrecked under his eyes while a revolver was held against his head.

After first urging that the action be extended to a general strike throughout the country, the drivers' union, without consulting the Labour executive, abruptly ended the strike in early February.

In mid-April the labour movement staged a general strike to secure the release of political prisoners on hunger-strike. At the end of the first day the prisoners were released, just as the new (and last) Chief Secretary for Ireland was taking the oath of office. In Waterford the Trades Council, obviously anticipating an extended struggle, took control of the town for two days. It orders 'were enforced by "Red Guards", who were followed by a mischievous rabble'. The mayor afterwards congratulated the 'Soviet government of Waterford on a very effective, masterly and successful administration'.

Three days later Labour launched an action to lower food prices. At that time the British government removed price controls on butter and bacon, which resulted in a rapid rise in the prices of these goods. The Labour executive proceeded to impose a boycott of the export of live pigs, bacon and butter. Sinn Féin had opposed the export of pigs in

1917. The Irish Farmers' Union protested, but, after negotiations, the prices of bacon and butter were reduced. The *Irish Times* (21 Apr.) drew a serious lesson from the affair, viewing the rise of Labour as a dangerous threat both to Sinn Féin and to the propertied classes:

> Irish Labour does not propose to use its one-hundred-ton steam-hammer merely for the cracking of nuts. The clever men who lead it have a very definite programme — far more definite, indeed than that of Sinn Féin. Labour, for instance, not only is Republican, but knows exactly the sort of Republic that it wants. It proposes gradually to capture many of the essential functions of government. A continuance of the fight which ended yesterday might have witnessed the establishment, or attempted establishment, of soviets of working men in all parts of Ireland. . . . The Sinn Féin farmers are as little in love with Labour's claim to control food prices as are the Unionist farmers of North-East Ulster. The agrarian agitation in the West — wholly a Labour movement — is viewed with intense alarm by the shopkeeping proprietors of grazing land. We imagine that a good deal of unpleasant thinking is being done in Ireland today by people who were content hitherto to shout with the largest crowd.

The major Labour effort in support of self-government was the boycott of the transport of munitions and armed soldiers and police. This action was not initiated by the Labour leadership but by ordinary dockers. British dockers had refused to load munitions on a British ship scheduled to bring supplies to the anti-communist forces in Poland. The Dublin dockers saw a parallel with Ireland. The railwaymen soon joined in, and a major struggle, lasting from May to December 1920, ensued. Its effect was to disrupt the movement of British troops and supplies at a critical period. General Macready told an Irish situation conference on 31 May: 'The troops are now stationary except the cavalry. The War Office is fulfilling my demands as fast as they can but they are held up by the strike.' The method he employed to root out rebellion — large-scale military sweeps — had little effect, and he later commented that the strike had been 'a serious set-back to military actions during the best season of the year'.

The Labour executive decided to adopt a policy by which individual railwaymen and dockers would refuse to move armed servicemen and munitions, thus allowing the bulk of their fellow-workers to remain in employment. All Irish railway employees were members of British-based unions, principally the National Union of Railwaymen. The NUR executive, led by J. H. Thomas, refused to support the actions of its Irish members. Rather, it attempted to get them to resume normal operations while it negotiated with Lloyd George. Appeals from the Irish Labour executive to its British counterparts for aid fell on deaf ears.

A call to the Irish public for assistance found a ready response. The Dublin correspondent of the London *Times* claimed that the objectives of labour and Sinn Féin 'in this case are identical, and the coffers of Sinn Féin are well filled'. All Sinn Féin *cumainn* were instructed to organise collections in their areas. About £120,000 was contributed to the strike fund, with the Dáil government providing £5,000. By 10 June 400 men had been dismissed, and this figure rose to nearly 1,000 a month later. *The Times* saw the political purpose behind the strike: 'At least a section of Irish working men has thus not merely declared its alliance with those endeavouring to institute an Irish Republic, but has become accessory to those monstrous methods of outrage and assassination which the Irish secret societies have adopted.' The Belfast area branches of the NUR refused to support the industrial action, but it received strong backing from the Irish Volunteers, who, where necessary, used force and intimidation; sometimes they provided car transport in areas where rail service had ceased.

The danger that the conflict might lead to a general strike of all railwaymen or the closing of whole rail lines was averted by the British army headquarters at the end of July when it restricted the shipment of munitions by rail. Even when the army attempted to use rail transport on a limited basis, however, the railwaymen refused to co-operate. The dispute dragged on until mid-October, when the British government, which had legal control of and was subsidising the railway companies, decided to force the issue. The British army once again attempted to make full use of the railways. Confronted again with the railwaymen's opposition, London responded by ordering the Midland Great Western Railway, which ran from Dublin to the west, to suspend operations on 14 November; other rail companies were to follow suit later. Michael Collins saw what was at stake. Writing to James Burns, he pointed out: 'The greatest danger in the Railwaymen giving in now is that the English would regard it as typical of the whole situation and might (in fact, would) feel much stronger in their efforts against the entire national cause then.' He said he was certain that the country would support the continuation of the boycott and promised that 'we'll put our organisation everywhere working to help them'.

The prospect was of a shut-down of the entire rail system, with 20,000 men being thrown out of work. Although it wanted the strike to continue, the Dáil cabinet decided on 4 December to 'leave matters in hands of labour to get out as best they can'. On the advice of the Labour executive, the railwaymen decided to end their action just before Christmas. As a result of a campaign which had lasted over six months, British military organisation had been severely disrupted. Thousands of Irish railwaymen made a direct, tangible contribution — their lost wages — to the cause of self-government; in doing so, they did more than most of their countrymen.

This was the end of industrial actions with political objectives; there were to be no such strikes in 1921. By that time a recession had begun and union members had to be concerned about their jobs. Nevertheless, the British authorities always had to face the possibility of a return to the strike weapon.

Neither the ILP and TUC nor its affiliated unions recognised the government of Dáil Éireann. In order to serve the interests of their members, the unions had to operate legally and openly. Irish unions continued to take advantage of British labour legislation at the same time as they employed the conciliation and arbitration schemes set up by the Dáil's Department of Labour. Because the union organisation was not officially aligned with the revolutionary government, Dublin Castle was unable to place any effective curb on its activities, many of which, particularly at the local level, provided more than aid and comfort to the opponents of British rule. Moreover, an independent labour movement was in a strong position to appeal to the British movement for support of Irish self-government. Johnson was an ideal envoy. He told the 1920 meeting of the Scottish TUC that 'The only alternative to absolute self-determination in Ireland is the extermination of its people.' Irish Labour was also positioned to issue ringing denunciations of British actions in Ireland. In August 1920 the Labour executive used the pages of the *Daily Herald* for this purpose: 'Your military forces are suppressing our democratic institutions, interfering day by day with the municipal government of our towns and cities, dispersing by force our courts of law, and imprisoning our civic administrators.' Sinn Féin had a stalwart ally.[22]

(9) WORLD VIEW

The Dáil's Campaign in Europe

While the Dáil's domestic programmes were springing to life in mid-1920, the activities of its foreign campaign were intensifying. Not only was there greater energy expended, but the story was coming right. British policy and actions were writing the script. This was clear to the *Irish Independent*: 'English Ministers are betraying uneasiness at the accuracy and extent of the information which is reaching the world Press on the struggle in Ireland. In the new world and the old every phase of that conflict is discussed with overflowing sympathy for Ireland.'

Since early 1919 the Irish Republic had had four envoys: Seán T. O'Kelly in Paris and later Rome, George Gavan Duffy in Paris, Art O'Brien in London, and Patrick McCartan in the United States; each had the support of a small staff. At its session of June 1920 the Dáil authorised the cabinet to appoint a wide range of officials abroad, including appointment of 'Consuls and Diplomatic Agents' in France, Germany, Italy, Spain, Austria, Denmark, Switzerland and Russia. Griffith told the assembly that as many as thirty persons might be employed. A year earlier the Dáil had voted to establish a consular service, and during the summer of 1919 several consuls had been appointed. These were Eamon Bulfin in Argentina, Leopold Kerney in Paris, Donal M. Hales in Genoa, Gerald O'Kelly, a papal count, in Switzerland, and Diarmuid Fawsitt in New York. All but Fawsitt were paid only small salaries and worked as consuls only part-time. Following the Dáil action, additional consuls were appointed, including Frank W. Egan in Chile in August 1920; others were to follow.

No consuls were appointed in Scandinavia, but the government had two part-time press agents: Seán Dunne in Norway, and Gearóid O'Loughlin in Denmark. They reported that the Danish press was generally pro-British, but that the newspapers in Norway and Sweden, being outside the British orbit, 'write mainly and freely about the Irish case'. When C. J. Humbro, a Norwegian editor, published a short book about the conflict in Ireland, Dunne commented: 'If Arthur Griffith wrote the above, he couldn't present our case better.' The widespread sympathy for Terence MacSwiney during his long hunger-strike Dunne viewed as a sharp reverse for British propaganda and its agents: 'The wrigglers and liars are squelched everywhere; they haven't as much as a straw to keep them afloat.' As a result of British repression in Ireland, he reported in late 1920, 'the tide has begun to turn here in Scandinavia in our favour'.

At the time of the expansion of the consular service George Gavan Duffy advised that he was doubtful if there were suitable people available. Because of the small salaries being offered, he suggested the appointment of 'a man already established in a business of his own and allow him to continue it together with your representative as consul'.

An obvious problem of an underground government was the creation of an efficient system of overseas communications. The system developed by the Dáil's representatives appears to have been seriously deficient. Gavan Duffy, for one, was scathing in his criticism. In his view, the system 'was as bad as bad could be'. In some instances, he declared, one or two months elapsed between the sending of a message and a reply being received. De Valera also recognised the serious defects, but the obvious remedy, a cadre of couriers, would require such a degree of expenditure that 'they would have to curtail their essential work'. The problem was not merely one of the movement of dispatches; it also sprang from the lack of a sensible administration of the department in Dublin. There is no systematic flow of information from Dublin. Egan had been appointed consul in Chile in August 1920, yet eight months later Gavan Duffy did not know if he was fully accredited in an official capacity. Art O'Brien told Michael Collins in July that there was a 'need to have someone in Dublin to deal

with [the] Foreign Service promptly'. On the other hand, the Dáil government tried to keep a tight reign on its politically influential envoys. On
26 June it issued an order that all communications between representatives
abroad 'must be sent through [the] Home Government'.

Despite these problems, the fledgling Irish diplomatic service received
a ringing commendation from the *Irish Independent* in September 1920:

> During the past twelve months the Continent has been enlightened
> on Ireland as it never was before. Formerly the people of Europe
> heard nothing about our country except the perverted views sent
> them through English sources. Through the activities of Mr Gavan
> Duffy in Paris and Mr Seán T. O'Kelly in Rome the exact facts have
> been given to continental readers.[23]

Feste da Roma

O'Kelly, who had been temporally shifted to Rome only a short time
before, was the right man in the right place in June 1920. At that time the
Catholic Church held a ceremony, attended by a large Irish contingent, to
beatify Oliver Plunkett, the seventeenth-century Irish martyr. The timing
could not have been better, as the British government had been actively
seeking a papal denunciation of Sinn Féin and the IRA. Arthur Balfour
had conferred with Pope Benedict xv shortly before. Having met with
many Irish and American bishops in Paris on their way to Rome, Gavan
Duffy informed Dublin that the British government was mounting 'a
desperate effort' to achieve this end. Now was the opportunity for the
advocates of Irish independence to make their case in Rome. O'Kelly had
audiences with the pope both before and after the Plunkett ceremonies.

The Dáil government appointed a delegation consisting of Count
Plunkett, a collateral descendant, Professor Stockley, Art O'Brien and
Count O'Byrne. O'Kelly and Donal Hales organised a large reception,
with the Irish tricolour prominently displayed. The gathering was attend-
ed by all but two of the Irish bishops, as well as by ecclesiastics from the
United States and Australia. 'The youngest bishop, Dr O'Doherty of
Clonfert, mounted the platform and sang "Wrap the Green Flag Round
Me, Boys".' At a subsequent gathering the Bishop of Limerick declared
that just as Oliver Plunkett had died for moral right, so they in Ireland
were now fighting for the principle of freedom. Both Count Plunkett and
O'Kelly had private audiences with the pope, whom Plunkett said 'showed
an acute and lively interest in the affairs of Ireland'.

These activities raised hackles in London. Questions were 'asked in the
House of Commons, *The Times* was upset, and the Rome correspondent
of the *Daily Chronicle* observed: 'Mr Ó Ceallaigh has been very prominent
in political demonstrations here connected with the sojourn of the
Hibernian Episcopate.' The Dáil's Department of Foreign Affairs believed
that the work of the Irish representatives, both lay and clerical, had

dashed the hopes of the British government for a papal pronouncement and that 'very great disappointment has been felt by the enemy at its failure'. On his return to Ireland, Bishop O'Doherty made the same point, adding: 'Our people have their ambassadors there — priests and laymen working unceasingly for the Irish cause. . . . The visit of the Irish bishops was calculated to strengthen the efforts of our representatives.' He also stressed the frank and outspoken nature of the bishops' contribution: 'We didn't keep our mouths closed regarding the rights and wrongs of Ireland.'

Several Irish priests recommended the establishment of a permanent Dáil presence in Rome. Art O'Brien noted a much-improved attitude towards Irish nationalism: 'Italy is getting more and more friendly to Ireland; the Italian press correspondents have given us a very good showing in their papers.' In December 1920 one *Irish Independent* correspondent noted that in northern Italy 'a continued and most successful Press campaign has for many months been kept going by Mr Hales, the Irish consul in Genoa', while another reported that 'Italian sympathy in the Irish struggle grows more and more articulate'.[24]

France and Belgium

Meanwhile in France the situation had greatly improved. Gavan Duffy reported on 3 July that 'the French press generally continues to be excellent'. The cause of Irish self-government began to win support on the French left. Albert Thomas, the leader of the socialist party, supported this position in September 1919. When in June 1920 Marc Sangnier, of the Christian Social Democrats, 'came out openly for the Republic and nothing less than the Republic, to the great astonishment of some of his colleagues', Gavan Duffy reported that his group was the 'only one with us wholeheartedly'. The socialists 'are with us but do not like our religion and many of them pin their faith to English Labour and are fearful of offending it by championing Ireland'. Sangnier was invited to Dublin for a week.

Duffy now found himself overwhelmed by work. He claimed: 'I have more to do than any one man can get through.' He not only dealt with French journalists and politicians, but he also carried on a large correspondence with Dáil representatives in Germany, Switzerland, Italy, Belgium and Scandinavia. In fact Paris had become the communications centre for the entire continental campaign.

Sylvain Briollay observed the change in the press: 'The Paris Press which had always refused to accept the communiqués of the *Irish Bulletin* ceased to pin its faith to the accuracy of Reuter's versions of events in Ireland.' In August Duffy urged Dublin to establish a central news bureau in Paris, particularly as he foresaw that its 'envoy will sooner or later be evicted'. This happened, in fact, sooner rather than later. In the wake of the arrest of Terence MacSwiney, he wrote a public letter to the French President demanding action for MacSwiney's release. On 31 August the French government informed him that he had twenty-four hours to leave the country; he removed to Brussels, where he pursued 'flaming publicity'. Briollay believed that this action showed that the British government was now taking a serious view of Irish diplomatic and propaganda efforts in Europe. For his part, Duffy asserted: 'There is a very real feeling for us throughout France in nearly all quarters.'

The expulsion of Duffy astounded Art O'Brien, but he quickly saw its positive side: 'I think this move of the English Government will do us a lot of good in France and America.' Count Plunkett told the Dáil in September that, with French popular opinion being aroused in Duffy's favour, the French government and the semi-official press 'realised that a most serious blunder had been committed'. On the other hand, Arthur Griffith took strong exception to Duffy's public demand to the French President, which he later condemned as 'a great error of judgment'; henceforth he was a determined critic of Duffy.

Michael MacWhite, a member of the Paris staff and a decorated officer in the French army during the war, stepped into the breach until O'Kelly, who again had been seriously ill during the summer, was shifted from Rome in mid-September. The long hunger-strike of Terence MacSwiney generated widespread support and sympathy both for the man and his cause. When his struggle came to its fatal end, O'Kelly reported that 'The French press on the whole has been remarkably good on the death of Terry.'

In early September Duffy proposed that he go to London, 'which would create some excitement in France and the general effect would be excellent', but Griffith instructed him to remain in Brussels for the present. He remained there until November, when he 'found the English too strong for him in Belgium which has not recovered its political independence'. From there he made an inspection tour of Irish offices in Denmark, Germany, Switzerland and Spain before taking O'Kelly's place in Rome in February 1921.[25]

Germany

In contrast to France and Italy, the situation in Germany was unsatisfactory. With its very limited resources, the Dáil government could only afford a few overseas representatives, and Germany in the immediate post-war period was a low priority. There was a scattering of people there who had been involved in the German-financed propaganda campaign during the war. One of these was Dr Georges Chatterton Hill, who was secretary of the German-Irish Society during the war and had been one of those who represented Ireland at the Stockholm conference sponsored by European socialist parties in June 1917. In early

1919 he informed the Dáil government that he was actively working on its behalf with the German press. On his request for funds, the cabinet decided to send him £100 but not to encourage his further involvement. In July 1920 he requested £200 for a lecture tour. George Gavan Duffy was doubtful about the man: 'The suggestion against Hill was that he was capable of behaving like Mr Pim [a Sinn Féin apostate] if he had any sort of falling out with Dublin.' Collins told Art O'Brien to forward £50 to Hill, adding: 'No further payment; this payment an act of grace in recognition of services which have been rendered in the past.' Hill, however, was not to be discouraged, and he eventually became head of the press section of the Berlin office when it finally was set up in 1921.

When a man named Hamilton was proposed as a representative in Germany in November 1919, adamant opposition emerged. O'Kelly declared himself 'strongly opposed'. O'Brien was 'astounded' to hear of the possibility of the appointment, adding that he would 'use all my influence to have it stopped'. Hamilton apparently had been involved in some secret matters concerning German-Irish relations during the war. This is the only construction that can be placed on O'Brien's statement in June 1920 that Hamilton had 'handed over his black book' to him and that he had then sent it to Collins, who in turn gave it to Griffith. On 3 September the cabinet concluded that Hamilton was 'not considered suitable for [a] post of official nature'.

There was also Thomas St John Gaffney, an Irish-born American politician who served as United States consul in Munich until he was forced to resign in 1915 because of his pro-German activities. He remained in Germany and was the spokesman on behalf of Irish self-government at the 1917 Stockholm conference. He was active in the Irish cause after the war, and in May 1920 sent a memorandum to Dublin urging the dispatch of missions to Moscow, Afganistan, Turkey and South Africa, declaring that 'it is in the power of the Irish to take the chief part in the destruction of Imperial England'. He was appointed a Dáil agent for Switzerland and proposed that payment should be made to Debrit, editor of the Swiss socialist paper *La Feuille*, 'the only Swiss organ that had given us a fair show'. Refused entry into Switzerland, Gaffney was in and out of Germany in some capacity until the truce of July 1921. Aubrey Stanhope offered his services as Irish minister to Germany in January 1920. Among his qualifications was his editorship of the anti-British *Continental Times* during the war, his acquaintance with Casement and his inclusion on a British black list. He proposed the use of 'my fine big apartment as legation and consulate' and offered to work for nothing until 'funds were in running order'.

To add comedy to confusion, a Mr Ryan appeared in Irish circles in Germany. Apparently a British agent, 'Ryan' flourished an extravagant Irish brogue and threw himself in the way of anyone Irish. Eventually he made his way to Dublin and met Michael Collins, who regarded him 'as a man who was out to make money without working for it. We are, however, dropping him altogether. Our friends should "give him a wide berth".' There was another Mr Ryan in Germany who was quite a different sort. This was John T. Ryan, an Irish-American lawyer who had fled the United States during the war and, as 'Mr Jetter', was the principal arms procurer in Germany for the IRA. During his arms purchase sorties there he contacted Charles McGuinness, the Derry-based gun-runner for the IRA; he, however, was not impressed by Ryan and did not seek his assistance.

An attempt to bring direction to the German campaign was the appointment of Gerald Count O'Kelly de Gallagh as head of the mission in March 1920, but for some reason he was eventually posted not to Germany but to Switzerland. For another year the German effort remained disorganised. The most that the Foreign Affairs Department could say about the position in Germany in mid-1920 was that the situation 'has hitherto been such that it is very difficult to make much headway', although a few pamphlets had been translated into German and distributed. Occasionally one of the party newspapers denounced British repression in Ireland, but most of the press, reflecting the view of the German government, looked to Britain for help against a vengeful France. Count Plunkett told the Dáil in June that 'the news from that country was very discouraging but latterly they appeared to be regaining their old discipline'. In December 1920 the situation had reached such a state that Diarmuid O'Hegarty privately declared: 'Almost everyone in Germany who purports to be working for Ireland's interest is more concerned in blackening the character of everyone else than in doing any useful work.'[26]

Mission to Moscow

From the seizure of power by the Soviets in 1917, the new government of Russia had been consistently supportive of the cause of Irish national freedom. This was acknowledged by the *Irish Nation* (27 Apr. 1918): 'New Russia has been wholly disinterested in the appeal she has made to the civilised world for Ireland.' In 1918 the Russian representative in London told an Irish Labour delegation that the Russian movement would support the establishment of a separate Irish identity in the international labour movement, and at the Berne conference of February 1919 the Russians made good their promise. Gratified by this support, Thomas Johnson and Cathal O'Shannon told their Labour colleagues at home: 'We have grown still stronger in our conviction that the Soviet Government of Russia is Ireland's best and most disinterested friend.' Both the *Voice of Labour* and the left-wing Sinn Féin paper *New Ireland* gave considerable and favourable attention to developments in the communist

state. The Russian Foreign Minister declared in June 1919 that his government would provide special protection to Irishmen, Egyptians and
'any other nationality oppressed by the Allies'; the *Voice of Labour*
considered this a 'special mark of honour'.

Two outlaw governments, one of Dáil Éireann and the other of the
Bolsheviks, were both seeking friends and support, and they made contact
in the United States. Patrick McCartan, the Dáil envoy, and Dr William
Maloney had discussions with the Russian agents early in 1919. They
believed that the governments of Russia and Mexico were the most likely
to accord recognition to the new Irish Republic. In May an exchange of
letters between McCartan and Ludwig Martens, the Russian representative, shows the emergence of a close relationship. The letters were
published and were used to demonstrate that the Irish revolutionaries
were falling into the clutches of the communists. It was at this time, as well,
that a story went around that the Soviets had contributed 250 or 500
million roubles to Sinn Féin. This was denied by both McCartan and
Harry Boland, but similar stories about Russian gold being sent to Ireland
were floated from time to time. In fact there was no Russian gold involved,
only jewels.

One of de Valera's primary objectives in his American mission was to
secure recognition of the Irish Republic by the United States government.
He told McCartan that this came before recognition by Russia, Mexico or
any other state. Nevertheless, two months after his arrival in the USA de
Valera was moved to declare that the 'Irish Republic is a friend to the
Soviet Union'. The American radical journalist Lincoln Steffens told Art
O'Brien in January 1920 that 'it would be advantageous for us' to establish
relations with Soviet Russia 'as quickly as possible'; O'Brien saw great value
in this proposal. In the spring of 1920 Boland and de Valera had lengthy
discussions with Russian representatives in Washington. When the United
States government cut off financial relations with Russia, Boland, without
conferring with de Valera, offered to loan the Russians $20,000 in
exchange for some Russian 'crown jewels'. De Valera decided that he had
to stand behind the commitment, and the loan was made. He then turned
over negotiations to McCartan, with the instruction that he wanted an
agreement to be secured. The resulting accord provided for mutual
recognition by the two governments and important advantages for Dublin
in trade and religious matters. The Irish Republic would be entrusted with
'the interest of the Roman Catholic Church within the territory of the
Russian Republic'; to McCartan 'this clause gives us a good grip on the
Vatican and makes them less impressionable by British agents'.[27]

When McCartan showed the draft agreement to de Valera, he observed
that the President 'showed surprise at it but no enthusiasm. It seemed as
if he got more in a treaty than he really wanted.' Nevertheless, de Valera
instructed McCartan to send the proposed agreement to Dublin; he also

informed the cabinet that he was 'very anxious' that a delegation 'should proceed at once to Russia'. Heeding his advice to approach Russian relations with caution, the cabinet agreed to the sending of a delegation, but decided that a firm commitment to seek Russian recognition should only come after the attempt had been made in the USA and simultaneously with other countries. At its June 1920 session the Dáil gave unanimous approval to a resolution which authorised the dispatch of 'a Diplomatic Mission to the Government of the Russian Socialist Federal Republic with a view to establishing diplomatic relations with that Government'. (It was on the basis of this resolution that the Republic of Ireland began diplomatic relations with the Soviet Union fifty-four years later.) The proposed treaty was not mentioned. The only comment on the resolution was that of J. J. Walsh, who wondered why it had taken so long to get in touch with the Soviets. The cabinet agreed to leave it to de Valera to decide exactly when the mission should depart.

The possibility of close ties with the communists was most alarming to George Gavan Duffy. He wrote from Paris on 8 July that if a delegation was sent to Russia, 'we may as well at once give up all further political effort on the Continent', adding that 'the real gain from the move is problematical and the loss certain'. Although he was doubtful about the Russian connection, Collins asked O'Brien to get into contact with the Russian representatives in London. Seán T. O'Kelly reported that a French wire service report about the Dáil resolution 'proved we are allied with the Bolshies; I cannot exaggerate the harm done by this kind of thing which is believed'.

At this stage de Valera wanted McCartan to go to Russia (which had been McCartan's original destination when he left Ireland as an IRB envoy in 1917). McCartan now sought plenary powers to conclude a treaty, arguing that 'an Irish Commission in Moscow without plenary powers would be a mere Russian shuttlecock' and that 'if the mission is suspended in Moscow, the enemy press of the world will say we are innocent tools, or victims of the Bolsheviki'. If a treaty was concluded, he would ask the Russians to ship 50,000 rifles to Ireland. De Valera refused to grant this power, and the project of the mission languished. In September 1920 Count Plunkett told the Dáil that the Soviets were 'manifesting the most friendly feelings towards Ireland and were anxious to come to an understanding with the Republic and with Irish Labour'. Lincoln Steffens, returning from a visit to Russia, told Art O'Brien in October that 'everybody there is very favourable to the Irish Republic and that they are quite willing to recognize if necessary'. A month later two Irish communists, Roderick Connolly, the son of James Connolly, and Eamon McAlpine, returned from Moscow as representatives of the Third or Communist International. In a 'secret' message to the Dáil cabinet they declared that they were the 'only accredited agents empowered to negotiate for the initiation of diplomatic negotiations'. The cabinet responded that the Irish government would only deal with representatives of the Russian government and ordered that the documents submitted to it by Connolly and McAlpine be destroyed. Nevertheless, these were all indications that the Soviets remained interested in developing a relationship with Dublin. By late 1920 there was no chance of American recognition. Just before he left the United States in December, de Valera instructed McCartan to proceed to Moscow.

When McCartan arrived in the Russian capital in February 1921, Maxim Litvinoff told him that the situation was now much less favourable for a Russo-Irish agreement than it had been six months or even four months previously. He was informed by other officials that a trade agreement with Britain was now their primary objective, and such an agreement was in fact signed in March. Despite this new development, McCartan remained in Moscow.

The whole matter of Sinn Féin–Soviet contacts exploded into headlines in June when the British government published as a white paper the proposed treaty between the Dáil government and the Soviets and related correspondence. To those who wanted to believe, this demonstrated that Sinn Féin and the communists were hand in glove. A newspaper report that month declared that Sinn Féin had opened an embassy in Moscow with a staff of six, including 'a Mr Connolly and an ex-Abbey actress'. The Foreign Affairs Department had told the Dáil in May that McCartan remained 'very optimistic' about his prospect in Moscow despite the fact that the Russian Foreign Office 'had got the impression that Ireland would compromise, and that this affected their readiness to recognise'. In any case, McCartan returned home empty-handed in July.[28]

The United States

By the start of the year 1920 the Irish campaign in the United States was going from strength to strength. In early February Horace Plunkett, then on a tour of America, was convinced that the Irish agitation was succeeding in turning American opinion against Britain. The only way to avoid permanent damage to Anglo-American relations was the 'speediest possible settlement of the Irish question'. To the *Irish Times* (9 Feb.) 'the encouraging whoops of Mr William Randolph Hearst, the guttural "bravos" of the hyphenated Teuton, and the massed oratory of the Irish-American vote hunters, who, with the disappearance of the drink trade, have been compelled to look elsewhere for political ammunition' did not constitute American public opinion on the Irish question.

The Irish mission was preparing a major campaign to influence American opinion in this election year. The Dáil had given de Valera permission to spend half a million dollars on the elections and a million to try to secure recognition of the Republic. During the course of the year the mission's staff was expanded, and between the loan campaign and political expenses the million and a half dollars were expended. De Valera sought the services of Robert Brennan for publicity and Erskine Childers as ambassador, but neither could be spared. In June the cabinet did, however, authorise the appointment of diplomatic agents for Chicago, New Orleans, San Francisco and Boston.

A minor project of the mission was to finance the research of W. H. Joyce. A former Dublin Castle employee, he had gained Griffith's enthusiastic support for an exposé of British efforts to discredit Griffith's hero, Charles Stewart Parnell. De Valera gave his consent to paying Joyce to do this work, and, despite efforts get rid of him, Joyce continued his labours for the next three years. In mid-1922 he produced an 1,150-page manuscript, largely composed of material taken from public sources, whereupon he returned to Ireland and attempted to interest the Free State government in his project.

Another unusual undertaking was the experiment in black propaganda by Dr William Maloney, who prepared a fake dossier which purported to demonstrate that the British government was trying to draw the United States into political alignment with Britain. This material was sent to newspaper editors throughout the country, some of whom swallowed it whole. This project was Maloney's own doing; in fact he never was an employee of the Irish mission.

Reports of the activities of the Irish campaign, particularly the speeches and tumultuous receptions of de Valera, were regular items in the nationalist-orientated newspapers in Ireland. Frederick Dumont noted in January: 'The movement is kept very much alive by reports of the great progress the cause of Irish freedom is making in the United States.' This was a delusion: 'Most Irishmen take it for granted that the American people are all greatly interested in seeing Ireland obtain its freedom and cannot realize what a large percentage of them have no interest in or thought of Ireland.' P. S. O'Hegarty warned in *New Ireland* (18 Mar.): 'It would be a great mistake to count too much on America. . . . If an Irish Republic is to be established it will have to be established by us here.'

The Dáil leadership publicly affirmed its belief that the campaign in the United States was gaining significant political influence. Arthur Griffith declared that de Valera had become a 'vital factor in the American political situation; that the Irish-American vote is the backbone of the Democratic Party; and that the Catholic Church in America, dominated as it is by Irish', would secure official American support for Irish self-government. As he was about to depart on a southern speaking tour in March, de Valera told his colleagues in Dublin that 'the Democrats will bid high for the Irish vote now'; otherwise there was no hope for them. Now that the propaganda campaign of the Ulster delegation had clearly failed, Sir Edward Carson bemoaned the lack of the counter-force to the Sinn

Féin campaign. With a presidential election due later in the year, the supporters and opponents of Irish nationhood, both foreign and domestic, anticipated a turbulent period of politics in which almost anything could happen.[29]

In January 1920 the Dáil Loan campaign was launched in the United States. There were some last-minute objections within the US government about the propriety and legality of such an undertaking, but no official action resulted. The drive began on 17 January and met with an immediate response. Huge public meetings provided momentum, and the loan organisers declared that nearly a million canvassers were involved. The New York *Evening World* asserted that every bona fide Irishwoman in New York was a subscriber, and from the outset the campaign was described as 'on the top wave, rolling strong'. There was probably some exaggeration in these reports, but an English journalist was impressed by the scope and intensity of the campaign in New York. S. K. Ratcliffe wrote in *The Nation* (20 Mar.):

> Posters in the shop windows along the New York avenues invite you to purchase the bonds of the Irish Republic. Catholic priests announce from the pulpit that they are on sale at the close of the service. One day in January when I was in New York, the steps of the Public Library in Fifth Avenue were occupied by a bevy of girls in the dress of colleens, singing and dancing for the loan, while an Irish policeman, in the employ of New York City, offered bonds for sale — a service in which, I was informed, the police of other cities are engaged — while in stores and offices, in churches and private homes, the financial business of the Irish Republic is systematically pressed.

Much of the credit for the efficient organisation of the campaign belongs to James O'Mara, who provided the executive leadership for the drive, but its success was due to the enthusiasm of Irish-Americans, particularly the Irish-born, stimulated by de Valera's rhetoric and personality. As a result of the fund drive, the sum of $5,500,000 was raised in a six-month period.

At this point de Valera decided, entirely on his own initiative, to employ a different political tactic. In an interview with a reporter of the *Westminster Gazette*, published on 6 February, he stated that the Irish people were prepared to accept a form of the Monroe Doctrine for the Irish Republic in order to reassure the British government that Ireland would never be used as a base for foreign attacks. To the *Irish Times* (9 Feb.) his position 'is indicative of nothing but the instability that afflicts the supposititous Republic's master-mind, and his evident desire to recede from a position regarded as hopelessly fantastic by every sane American'. The opinion of this particular paper was of little account, but when John Devoy's *Gaelic American* criticised de Valera's statement as a retreat from full Irish independence, the long-simmering conflict between the two factions within the Irish movement erupted into public view. Both de Valera and Devoy defended their positions, de Valera claiming that his views had been distorted in the press, and Devoy claiming that he was only offering constructive criticism. The row was on.

The most disturbing aspect of de Valera's statement was that he had apparently confided with no one beforehand. This caused dismay among his staff, leaving them no alternative except to support their chief. Moreover, it provided all the evidence the Devoy–Cohalan group needed to show that de Valera was an impulsive, headstrong individual who had rejected the mature, experienced guidance of their group.

His statement initially was received by his colleagues at home with public silence. Only Arthur Griffith, a week later, 'reaffirmed Mr de Valera's assertion that Ireland was willing to accept a British Monroe Doctrine if she were granted full independence'. Father O'Flanagan privately voiced his fear that de Valera was retreating from the republican position. Art O'Brien later told de Valera: 'There was a great deal of misunderstanding amongst our people here [in London], and I had to explain your point on many occasions.' As the controversy developed, de Valera wrote to the cabinet on 17 February that he was dispatching Patrick McCartan to explain the matter and asked for statements of full confidence from both the cabinet and the Dáil. What was behind the affair, he declared, was that the Devoy–Cohalan group was trying to ruin the bond campaign and 'drive me home or make me a rubber stamp'. He would put no more in writing, because 'if captured and published such a letter might blow our work here sky-high'.

McCartan, who arrived in Dublin in March, found that after he told the cabinet his explanation Constance Markievicz, Cathal Brugha and Count Plunkett remained dissatisfied, but Griffith and Collins closed down the discussion and secured approval of McCartan's explanation. McCartan himself commented: 'The Cabinet had acted on the problem of de Valera, in his Cuban role, practically as we had acted on it in the United States, and for the same compelling reason: de Valera had usurped the right to speak and act for Ireland, and the situation left us without the power to challenge him.' As the controversy rolled along, Collins refused to be unduly alarmed. He wrote to Seán Nunan on 20 March: 'I am fully aware of all the little troubles you have had in the New World, but the little troubles here are so absorbing that one is inclined to forget them.'

The public posture of Sinn Féin at this time was that the conflict had been or was being patched up, that the great majority of the Irish in the United States supported the President, and that both Sinn Féin and the Dáil government stood solidly behind him. *Old Ireland* (13 Mar.) reassured its readers that there was 'no possibility of the enemies of Ireland magnifying the discussion into a split'. It argued that de Valera 'would be the last person in the world to resent healthy criticism' and that there was 'much wisdom' in Devoy's comments.

The cause of Irish nationhood was given a boost in late March when the US Senate voted to include a reservation to the Versailles treaty that the USA 'adheres to the principle of self-determination, and to the resolution of sympathy with the aspirations of the Irish people for a Government of their own choice, adopted by the Senate on June 6, 1919'. The vote had been close: 45 for, 38 against. De Valera claimed that as a result of this vote his mission to the United States had been crowned with success. Yet when the Senate a few weeks later failed to ratify the Versailles treaty, de Valera saw this also as a positive factor in the struggle for Irish nationhood.[30]

After an emotional agreement on 19 March to end the conflict, the infighting soon resumed. James O'Mara, director of the loan campaign, demanded a financial accounting of the Irish Victory Fund, since 'such money morally belongs to Ireland'. This demand was rejected by the Friends of Irish Freedom, who declared that 'we are under no obligation to submit statements to any other organization'. O'Mara's staff had already come into conflict with Diarmuid Fawsitt, the Irish consul in New York. In early March O'Mara decided to resign, a decision de Valera urged him to postpone for two months, by which time most of the loan would have been collected. His immediate resignation 'would be misrepresented and misconstrued' as 'certain persons . . . are but waiting for a vantage point to attack'. Back in Dublin Collins was dismayed: 'What on earth is wrong with Mr O'Mara? There always seems to be something depressing coming from the USA.' After further pleas from Griffith and Collins, O'Mara withdrew his resignation.

With the reports of great success in the loan campaign in America, Collins decided to try to get some of the funds sent to Ireland. On 9 February he wrote to de Valera that 'the necessity for the money is now beginning to press'. At the end of April he told Seán Nunan that he was very anxious 'to get some idea of the results to date, or at any rate to get some idea of the results up to a certain date'. On 5 June the cabinet authorised Collins to arrange for the transmission of '£500,000 at once'. Obviously the Minister for Finance was not being kept informed by his colleagues across the ocean. By the summer of 1920 only relatively small sums had been transmitted; yet $3 million was available. At this point de Valera became 'particularly anxious that you at home be satisfied that you can safeguard the money'. He also was involved in a nit-picking dispute with Collins about the appropriate date from which interest should accrue on the bonds that had been sold.

Gearing up for a confrontation with the Devoy–Cohalan group during the season of the American political conventions, Harry Boland returned to Dublin in May, where he reported on the situation to the Dáil cabinet.

He also secured the approval of the Irish Republican Brotherhood to break affiliation with the Clan na Gael if necessary. Collins, who by now was the leader of the IRB, told Art O'Brien on 22 June: 'Those who ought to be our friends are not faithful to the Republic.' The next day Griffith sent a message from the Dáil cabinet to Devoy and Cohalan urging them to 'give your loyal support to our President in his great work'.

An American political convention was a forum where Cohalan was in his element and de Valera was not. Cohalan was deeply involved in supporting a candidate for the Republican nomination and had obviously done a lot of preparation for the resolution calling for Irish self-determination that he presented to the platform committee when the Republican convention assembled in Chicago in June. De Valera, apparently believing that the cheering crowds of the past year gave him considerable political influence, presented his own resolution, which advocated recognition of the Irish Republic. After bitter infighting, both resolutions failed. Having burnt his bridges with that party, Cohalan did not attend the Democratic convention in San Francisco three weeks later. De Valera did, but had little success. The platform committee rejected his resolution, though it did secure substantial support from the body of the convention (400 for, 700 against). The Democratic Party could not accept the de Valera position without rejecting Woodrow Wilson; this it would not do. The platform only supported Irish national aspirations.

The anticipated national conventions had come and gone, and de Valera and company had come away empty-handed. In frustration, both groups turned to recrimination. Gavan Duffy wrote to Diarmuid O'Hegarty in July: 'Anything to equal the barging match now proceeding at full tilt between McCartan and Devoy I have never seen; the fury of the Parnellite split is not in it' — to which O'Hegarty replied: 'There is no doubt that they are having a great passage of arms in the States, but something like this was bound to occur.'

Action against Clan na Gael and its Irish-American adherents was mounted from Dublin. Collins told Griffith that it was 'absolutely essential' to stop the *Irish Bulletin* being sent to the Friends of Irish Freedom, as it gave the Devoy–Cohalan group 'a power out there to use against the President'. Diarmuid Lynch, national secretary of the FOIF, rejected overtures to give up this position and join the Irish mission. Faced with the prospect of a demand that he give up his seat in the Dáil, he anticipated this development by resigning. On 17 July he sent a long letter justifying his role in the whole affair. At the August Dáil meeting, at which the letter was read, Griffith announced that he had been informed that 'the friction was for all effective purposes at an end, as 99 per cent of the people there had rallied to Mr de Valera'.[31]

There was an effort at a truce, but it did not last. In September de Valera attempted to take control of the FOIF executive. Failing in this endeavour, in the following month he established a rival organisation, the American Association for the Recognition of the Irish Republic — a long name but with a clear objective. The new body quickly eclipsed the Friends, which soon sank to insignificance. It was also in October that Harry Boland publicly announced that the IRB had broken affiliation with Clan na Gael; together with McCartan, he attempted to create a rival Clan, though with little success.[32]

Just when it would appear that the work of de Valera and the Irish mission had come to a virtual dead-end, there was a reversal of fortune. The new organisation blossomed, with de Valera later claiming that it grew to half a million members. Then Dr William Maloney stepped forward with more of his creative ideas. He first proposed the creation of a commission to investigate British actions in Ireland; his other idea was to form a body to raise money to provide aid to the victims of British repression. Both ideas were to be implemented with great success; neither of them would require more than the initial involvement of de Valera. His mission had obviously run its course; in fact it had probably outlasted its usefulness. The cabinet on 9 October instructed him to remain until a formal demand for recognition had been submitted; this was done on 20 October.

When Maloney first proposed the idea of a commission of inquiry, de Valera was concerned that a body composed solely of Americans might not produce a report that supported the assertions of Sinn Féin. His misgivings were soon overcome, and the project went forward. Maloney's ties with the intellectual community proved invaluable. He got Oswald Garrison Villard, a relation by marriage, to sponsor the project in *The Nation*, a prestigious periodical owned and edited by Villard. Following the announcement of the establishment of the commission on 17 September, invitations to join the organising committee were issued to 150 political, religious and cultural leaders. Most accepted, and the committee elected a commission of eight. Only one of the members, Senator David I. Walsh of Massachusetts, was an Irish-American, but all of the members were of a liberal, progressive persuasion and thus were favourable towards self-determination and national freedom. At this point de Valera became enthusiastic about the project. He told Harry Boland on 21 October: 'As regards the Inquiry Commission, we must take it as it is. Half-heartedness would be simply ruinous. We can make it give good returns if we throw ourselves into it.' He saw the need for a guiding hand to direct the commission to the desired conclusions: 'If the wrong men get hold of that and give the evidence a British complexion, we are ruined.' The President need not have worried; Maloney managed the matter. Furthermore, the Irish mission secretly provided most of the commission's financing.

Both the *Gaelic American* and the *Irish World*, usually at daggers drawn, united in their initial hostility to the idea, which undoubtedly helped to elevate the project above the level of Irish-American internal feuding.

The British government also provided assistance by refusing to let the commission come to Ireland and by not submitting evidence. It also discouraged witnesses from Ireland, with the disingenuous statement that it could not guarantee that reprisals would not be imposed by Sinn Féin extremists upon hostile witnesses. Arthur Griffith charged that potential witnesses were being arrested and denied passports. After the cabinet had approved the proposal Desmond FitzGerald urged all deputies to collect full particulars about British actions. When his request 'had practically no response', a solicitor, James O'Connor, was employed to gather evidence and recruit witnesses.

The commission held hearings in Washington from mid-November until January, during which time it heard testimony from eighteen Irish men and women (including Michael O'Callaghan, Mayor of Limerick, who was smuggled into the country), eighteen Americans, fifteen of whom had recently been in Ireland, and two English women, representing the English branch of the Women's International League. It also drew evidence from British reports on Ireland, including those of the Labour Party, the Society of Friends Committee and the Women's International League. It received cordial co-operation from Cardinal Logue, Horace Plunkett, George Bernard Shaw, George Russell and the Irish Labour leaders. Frederick Dumont grumbled that, as usual, the Irish national press was guilty of exaggeration: the commission 'is always spoken of as the "American Commission of Inquiry" and the fact that it sits in Washington is used to fool ignorant people. The only witnesses from Ireland who are to give testimony before the Commission are convinced Sinn Féiners.'

Transcripts of the hearings were published weekly in *The Nation*, and the proceedings attracted widespread coverage in the American, British and Irish press. In March 1921 the commission issued an interim report, written by Maloney, which denounced British actions root and branch and declared that a majority of Irish people supported the government of Dáil Éireann. The *Manchester Guardian* acknowledged the validity of the commission's conclusions, adding: 'We may as well keep our tempers and take our pelting with any dignity that is left us.'

The second Maloney commission, to provide assistance to the victims of the conflict in Ireland, was organised in November 1920; on 6 November the cabinet approved of the proposal, and Griffith wrote to de Valera to urge him to proceed. Most of the work of this body took place in 1921, and the undertaking raised $5 million.[33]

The situation in Ireland had become increasingly difficult for the underground government and its military arm. The British counter-attack was having effect, and on 26 November Griffith was arrested. It was time for de Valera to return. Before he left the United States, however, there was the matter of the disposition of money to be dealt with.

By mid-October the proceeds of the loan campaign came to $3,762,588, of which only $650,000 had been sent to Ireland. What was to be done with the bulk of the funds? There were dangers in sending it over — so was it simply to be spent in America on flamboyant publicity campaigns? Was this to be just another Irish Victory Fund? Michael Collins favoured keeping $500,000 in the United States so that funds 'would be always available for carrying on the Government if anything extraordinary happened'. This still would have left about $3 million for Ireland. Without any apparent cabinet authority, de Valera decided to keep this money in the USA, at least for the time being. With the agreement of James O'Mara, he divided the funds between bank deposits and government bonds. He gave Joseph McGarrity power of attorney for the money. Further, in an extraordinary letter, he informed McGarrity that should the Irish people vote against full independence, the money could be used to finance a future republican movement. De Valera, therefore, appears to have had personal control of a large sum of money that was the property of Dáil Éireann.

In March Collins told the Dáil that the government would be running an 'apparent deficit' but that the funds in America would be used to finance its activities. At the same time he wondered if the expenditures of the American campaign would be covered by receipts. The Minister for Finance obviously was displeased to find that he had no control over the only sizeable quantity of money that the government had left.[34]

When de Valera left for Ireland in early December 1920, he could look back on a year and a half of intensive, highly emotional activity. The Irish mission had achieved a great deal. On the other hand, he had fallen into an ugly, brawling quarrel with the Devoy–Cohalan group, which did damage to the Irish cause. His American experiences had provided him with a crash-course in partisan politics and public relations. His successful apprenticeship in both areas must have given him confidence to face the dire situation that awaited him at home.

(10) DUBLIN CASTLE RESPONDS

During the first half of 1920 British administration in Ireland suffered a near collapse. Government employees continued to appear at their posts, but there was less and less for them to do. Whole areas of government — particularly the courts, police and local government — had been stripped from Dublin Castle and transferred to the Dáil government. None of them were to return to their former allegiance. The old regime initially had watched the rise of its rival with patronising amusement, but as the alternative government gained strength and Dublin Castle discovered that it was the object of ridicule, the amusement turned first to anger and then to violence. Now it would be the counter-state that would be on the defensive.

The British government had been preoccupied with other, more pressing matters elsewhere in the immediate post-war period. After all, it had to deal with the settlement of the war and the affairs of a great empire. But it did come up with a new Home Rule Bill, introduced in December 1919. The act passed in 1914 had been immediately suspended because of the war and was never implemented. Lloyd George and his ministers declared in favour of a new, improved bill. This would result in considerable delay before any form of Irish self-government would become a reality. In fact two and a half years were to pass from the end of the war until the new bill became an act.

How was the new bill different from the 1914 act? The principal difference concerned the Unionist part of Ulster. Under the 1914 act this area would have simply continued, administratively and constitutionally, as it was, simply as part of the unitary state called the United Kingdom. Under the new bill it was to have its own parliament, equal in status and powers with that of the parliament for the southern part of the country, with a Council of Ireland to provide some bare linkage between the two jurisdictions. Obviously the British government hoped to defeat the separatists before implementing the act. By doing so it would force Sinn Féin or at least a large number of Irish nationalists to agree to settle for what the act had to offer — internal autonomy and partition. In any case, some form of self-government was coming to Ireland, and those who carried on the administration of the existing structure did so in an atmosphere of impending doom.

The leadership of the existing regime was not impressive. Field-Marshal Viscount French had served as Lord Lieutenant since March 1918. Then sixty-six years of age and of an Anglo-Irish background, he was a failed general, combative and blustery, of befogged outlook and no political experience. As a symbol of the old regime, he was a gift to Sinn Féin and an attractive target for the Volunteers, who almost succeeded in shooting him in December 1919. The Volunteers captured some indiscreet correspondence with one of his female friends, and the Propaganda Department printed a choice selection of it in an unattributed flyer. To add to his discomfort, his sister, Charlotte Despard, was a prominent figure in many of the demonstrations against the Castle regime. The IRA also attacked his country home in Frenchpark, Co. Mayo, so often that he was unable to visit it. Since he had no other home except the viceregal lodge, he remained on, an aged irrelevancy who could only venture outside the Phoenix Park in an armed convoy.

Ian Macpherson, who served as Chief Secretary for Ireland from January 1919 until April 1920, resigned in a state of frustration and shock. He was succeeded by Lieutenant-Colonel Sir Hamar Greenwood, a fifty-year-old Canadian, bluff and obdurate. Another nominal Home Ruler, Greenwood previously had served in minor office. His first trip to Ireland was not auspicious: he arrived by destroyer and was escorted to his residence in the Phoenix Park by 'a strong force of military and police'. He did not make a favourable impression on some of his colleagues. Alfred Cope, his Assistant Under-Secretary, told his Irish girlfriend in September 1920 that Greenwood 'was no good and was out for a big job and did nothing'. Lloyd George told an Irish visitor in November that Greenwood 'knows nothing at all about Ireland'.

The second member of the new team, also appointed in April, was Sir Nevil Macready (1862–1946), an ex-general and Commissioner of the London Metropolitan Police before becoming commander-in-chief in Ireland. A new head of the RIC was appointed two months later. Major-General H. H. Tudor had no police experience, but time was to show that he had no intention of running a police force. In any case, the RIC as a police force was already shattered by the time he arrived. The army and the police were not under one command, and this proved to be a crippling disability. There was an obvious need to create a unified intelligence system. The man appointed for this task was Brigadier-General Ormonde Winter, reputedly a very clever chap but without any experience of intelligence work. Partly because of his lack of administrative ability, and partly because of the internal squabbling within Dublin Castle, he failed to develop a combined intelligence organisation. He saw his role as that of chief detective, and in fact it was only as a detective that he had any success — locating Dáil Loan bank accounts, and digging up a report that Collins was sleeping with a girl once a week. His operation seemed to be an unhappy one; there were at least five suicides among his staff.

There was an urgent need for the reorganisation of the existing structure of administration. In order to bring order out of confusion, a new team of top English civil servants was brought to Dublin Castle. The group, with not one member having experience in Irish affairs, was headed by Sir John Anderson, said to be the most brilliant civil servant of his time. In Ireland he spent most of his time occupied with administrative business while the Black and Tans roared up and down through the countryside. Two junior members were Mark Sturgis, who wrote a witty account of events in his diary, and Alfred ('Andy') Cope, who took on the role of energetic handyman. Sturgis wrote of him: 'Old Andy is like an octopus grasping everything with his tentacles and when he has got hold of more than he can digest he sinks to the bottom of the tank.' Cope told his Irish girlfriend, who reported all to Collins, that he was part of a group that 'made sorties all over the country. When they got outside Dublin or any other big town they put a Sinn Féin flag on the bonnet of the car. Thought this a great joke.' He further told her that 'he wished he was on the other side (meaning ours), that it must be a great adventure and very exciting'. His principal task appeared to be to make contact with the leadership of the Dáil government.

The flow of paperwork probably was smoothed, but the group Anderson headed was basically in a holding operation, struggling to keep an administration from disintegrating while waiting to hand over control to the natives. The apparent lack of effort to stem the tide of nationalism was alarming to the imperialist press in England. The *Morning Post* saw a plot:

> The position is wholly inexplicable, except upon the hypothesis we have already mentioned that the Government intend to allow the Irish Republic to be established, and then explain to the British public that they are very sorry, but they have been unable to prevent that consummation.

The new administration failed to achieve acceptance by public opinion. Rather, it was subjected to a torrent of abuse — and not just from Sinn Féin. A 'Victim of Terror' wrote to the London *Times* in April 1920: 'There is no indication of any brains in Ireland except on the side of the revolution.' Tim Healy declared: 'Out of Bedlam no such councillor of the King as Greenwood could have been selected. His lies alone would have set the hearts of the people ablaze.' The two major Dublin newspapers — the *Irish Independent* and the *Freeman's Journal* — were almost constantly critical of practically every Castle policy and action.

The public naturally compared the leadership of the British regime with that of Dáil Éireann, and all the advantages appeared to be with the latter. The Sinn Féin leaders were Irish; those in Dublin Castle were not. The leaders of Dáil Éireann were young, fresh personalities seeking to carve out a new age for their country. Dublin Castle was staffed by stuffy, middle-aged Englishmen, some of dubious pasts and most with no knowledge of the country, who pontificated on law and order while reluctantly moving towards a minimum grant of national autonomy. One insider saw the administration as being filled with 'sticky old Irish officials with cold feet and nowt in their hearts but jealousy of their colleagues and care for their salaries'.

The new team set out to restore the authority of its government. It faced a daunting task. In late June in Derry and then in the second week of July in Belfast bloody clashes took place between unionists and nationalists, to be followed by the expulsion of thousands of Belfast Catholics from their jobs and homes. At a meeting of the cabinet's Irish Situation Committee on 15 July, Lord Midleton, Lord Dysert and William Jellett, MP for Dublin University, agreed that the loyalist population of the south and west 'felt the time had come when they must know whether the Government intended to master the country or they would be forced to make terms with Sinn Féin'. A week later the committee was given an even stronger message by W. E. Wylie, Dublin Castle's Law Adviser. He gave it as his opinion that 'within two months the Irish Police Force as a Police Force would cease to exist' and that in regard to the courts 'the entire administration of the Imperial Government had ceased'. Local government bodies were defying all instructions from the Castle; and as for the campaign of violence sanctioned by Sinn Féin, 'things had become worse than they had ever been before'. He had even more amazing things to tell them: the murderers of policemen 'were not real criminals', but political fanatics, and 'after seeing the marvellous organisation which Sinn Féin had build up, he was of the opinion that the Irish were capable of governing themselves'. General Tudor offered a note of despair: 'The Government was up against a well-organised body, and to restore order would be a very lengthy business, which he ventured to think could not be done in the time at their disposal.' Time had become a factor.[35]

One of the first actions was to prop up the RIC, not with new recruits from Ireland, for by now there were few of these, but with thousands of men enlisted in Britain — the so-called Black and Tans. The remodelled body would no longer be a police force, but a purely military force employed to suppress violence with violence. There also was the Auxiliary force, composed of former British army officers, that was originally to have been incorporated in the new RIC, but was in fact kept separate as an elite body. Sinn Féin spread the story that the new special constables were the dregs of the British prisons — useful propaganda, though untrue. They were, however, a rough, violent group. Who else would have volunteered for such dangerous duty? The IRA journal, *An tÓglach* (1 May), appeared to relish their advent:

> The new recruits are mostly Englishmen, physically and morally degenerate and inefficient and with small knowledge or understanding of the country. When the IRA comes to deal with these men it will make short work of them.

Then there were the regular soldiers of the British army in Ireland. It had a strength of 36,000 men in April 1920. Reinforcements were promised, but a year later it had risen to only 40,000. It did receive some new equipment, principally armoured cars. On the other hand, its system of communications was in disarray. During the first ten months of 1920 the Volunteers had conducted 250 mail raids. A particularly damaging seizure took place in early March when the IRA captured the Castle mail. According to the *Sunday Chronicle*, 'The organisers of the affair have scored more effectively over the Government than by any number of raids on police barracks. The strategic value of knowing what the other fellow is thinking of lies with the revolutionaries.' In June Volunteers seized mail

on a train in Cork and, after removing the military and police correspondence, delivered the mail to the Bantry post office. 'Practically all the
parcels had been opened and some were marked "Censored by Irish
Republic".' The most spectacular mail raid took place in July 1920 when
the Volunteers carried away a huge haul from the Dublin GPO. The *Pall
Mall Gazette* commented that if the central post office in the country was
not secure, 'it would really save time if official correspondence were forwarded direct to Sinn Féin', while the *Irish Times* remarked glumly: 'We
seem to be approaching the day when British authority in Ireland will be
shaken to its base by the laughter of two hemispheres.'

Many post office workers not only supplied information to Collins's
intelligence unit, but also used post office facilities to transmit messages
and materials for the alternative state and its army. Because of the ever-
present danger of mail seizures, the British army was forced in September
1920 to use aeroplanes for normal communications. At Bantry five
Volunteers disguised as British soldiers stood around a white circle drawn
on the ground, and a military plane dropped a bundle of communications in their midst. Michael Collins investigated the use of small, portable
planes for his communications system. Scotland Yard believed that Art
O'Brien was trying to arrange for the training of aviators and purchase of
planes in order to create a Sinn Féin air force.

The Castle intelligence service failed to penetrate the apparatus of its
opponents. On the other hand, Collins's agents were operating within the
Castle organisation. After Archbishop Clune conferred with Collins in
December 1920 Mark Sturgis wondered how Clune could have easy access
to Collins while 'our own intelligence fails to find him after weeks of
search'. His only explanation was that 'Dublin is a terrible warren of a
place'. Art O'Brien told Collins in the same month that he had learned
that, owing to the 'keen scrutiny of the IRA, the enemy secret service
found it impossible to keep spies in any one place for very long'. When
O'Brien informed him in January 1921 that he had been approached by
what appeared to be another agent posing as a friend of Ireland, Collins
replied: 'The details are correct down to the "Michael Collins" without
whose name no such conversation is complete. My advice would be to call
a policeman and get him thrown down the stairs.'

The British army's system of supply and movement of troops was in
even worse condition. In an industrial action that lasted from May to
December 1920, Irish dockers and railwaymen refused to move military
supplies and armed policemen and troops. The army had to employ
men and energy in simply maintaining routine supplies and normal
troop transfers. One of the immediate problems was the shortage of
lorries; another was that convoys of trucks, travelling along the twisting
Irish roads, became enticing objects of Volunteer ambushes. The
embargo continued to the point where the British government seemed

to be about to close most of the major rail lines in retaliation. The campaign was generally a voluntary one, but the Volunteers used intimidation and force to deal with the few railwaymen who did not support the effort. Mark Sturgis, who directed the Castle's efforts to defeat the strike, saw the effort weakening in early November. At the end of the month the Dáil cabinet decided that it did 'not feel justified in interfering to the extent of calling upon the men to carry on. They wish the strike prolonged in its present condition as far as possible.' On 21 December a conference of railwaymen voted to end the boycott. With IRA attacks and sporadic work stoppages, however, the railway system remained an unreliable means of military transportation.

There also was a lack of Irish recruits for the army. The *Irish Times* (5 Jan. 1920) reported that 'Officers and NCOs are disheartened beyond measure at the reception they received from their own countrymen after the war.' The troops sent to Ireland were ill-prepared for the situation there. An army pamphlet issued to the troops in 1919 was widely propagandist and lacking in any sober appreciation of the prevailing political situation. It declared that Sinn Féin had 'used every means to substantiate the fallacy that the Irish were a separate nation'. Another pamphlet issued to the troops in the following year was less propagandist and more realistic. Service in Ireland was difficult and unattractive for many soldiers. Frederick Dumont reported in July: 'The Irish public dislikes them and shows its dislike openly.'

A relatively small action by a group of Irishmen in the British army gained a lot of public attention. At the end of June 350 soldiers in the Connaught Rangers regiment stationed in India staged a rebellion in protest against British actions in Ireland. The revolt was short-lived; seventy-five soldiers were court-martialled, and fourteen of them were sentenced to death, though only one, James Daly, a member of the IRB, was executed. The rest of them were given long prison sentences; forty-two of them were still in prison two years later. Gavan Duffy wrote from Paris that 'the news from India sent a thrill of joy through all our friends here'. He proposed that the *Freeman's Journal* mount 'a rampageous campaign' for the immediate release of every Irish soldier in the British army who wanted to be discharged. Although this incident was embarrassing to the British government, this is the only protest among the many thousands of Irishmen in the British military. In the following year, however, the army authorities became concerned about Irish soldiers serving at home.

Hamar Greenwood faced the situation with determined optimism. He was a heavy, blunt instrument, obviously just what Lloyd George wanted. He paid no heed to the pessimistic but realistic view of the London *Times* (2 June): 'If the Government of Ireland bill goes into operation the Sinn Féiners of today will exercise constitutionally many of those powers which they now arbitrarily assume. . . . For the moment, Sinn Féin is all-powerful, and it is virtually synonymous with the Irish people.' He told a London audience on 13 July: 'I believe the vast majority of the Irish people hate and loathe the campaign of terror and murder now carried on in certain parts of their country. (*Cheers*)' In September the Irish Office announced: 'The military in Ireland are in no sense an army of occupation. . . . That the intervention of armed forces is welcomed by the responsible body of Irish opinion has been proved abundantly.'

In July 1920 Greenwood and his organisation tackled their tasks with enthusiasm. First came the attack on the Dáil courts. A British army order of 13 July declared that troops and RIC should attend all popular courts being held to see if they exceeded the powers of the arbitration tribunals. If admittance was denied or if the courts exceeded their authority, then they should be dispersed. Five courts were broken up in that month. On the 25th, however, Sir John Anderson took a gloomy view of the effort to eradicate the popular courts: 'The machinery of the Courts has been brought virtually to a standstill and rival Courts are functioning openly, and where forcibly suppressed, will continue to function in secret.' The press reported that during the month eighty Dáil courts were held in twenty-seven counties. In August the RIC Inspector-General reported: 'The toleration extended to republican courts and the directions that police are to attend these courts, but not otherwise interfere, is undoubtedly doing harm and steadily undermining the authority of Government. They could be easily dispersed in most instances.' He believed the great mass of the population 'would be relieved to see an end to them'. The RIC district inspectors favoured 'not the arrest of persons holding Courts but the breaking up and kicking out policy'. In September there was a general suppression of the courts, but, as Anderson had predicted, they soon resumed their proceedings away from the view of the RIC and British army.

At the same time the RIC acted against the Republican Police. The Inspector-General instructed the constabulary to prohibit the assumption of police functions by Irish Volunteers and where necessary to invoke military aid for this purpose. This order did not impress the Dublin correspondent of the London *Times* (19 July), who commented that the order 'will serve no useful purpose unless the Executive give definite proof of its ability to fulfil the functions which these Sinn Féin Volunteers are beginning to usurp'.[36]

During the summer of 1920 the remodelled police force and the British army sought to destroy the IRA and had what appeared to be a fair measure of success. Yet danger was always present. General Macready informed all units on 19 May of a new procedure for billeting troops in private residences: 'Cases have arisen where the very fact of a reconnaissance being made . . . has resulted in the house being burned.' Therefore loyalist owners of property 'have asked that permission not be requested; rather the OC merely announce his intention to occupy'. Two months later all officers were told that they must possess pistols and that it was important that they 'are proficient in the use of their weapon, are good and above all quick shots'. They were, however, also informed that there was no need to carry the weapon at all times, as this might be dangerous or it might be captured by the rebels.

The 'small band of picked English civil servants' who had come over with Anderson had initially decided that it would be 'fatal to any prospect of success either in restoring the Civil machinery or in influencing public opinion if they allowed themselves to be besieged in the Castle'. But on 7 August a Castle memorandum concluded that 'the lives of these men will henceforth no longer be safe', and two days later they were ordered to move from their outside accommodation into the Castle. Mark Sturgis, who was one of these, noted in his diary that he 'must try to get something in the papers to shew we are on the move and not shut up in spite of our orders. It would be madness to live inside like moles.' He obviously was suffering from a 'siege mentality', as he celebrated a Sunday-afternoon drive in a Crossley tender to Mullingar and Athlone as 'eighty miles into the enemy's territory'. On 28 August a 'confidential and urgent' order was issued: 'Officers living out of barracks are to wear plain clothes when going to and from their work.' Three days later officers were advised that, 'owing to the present situation', they should send their wives and families to England. In September civilian clothes were issued to chauffeurs and 'individuals engaged on Intelligence duties'. There was also a query sent to all units: 'Are there any Irishmen now serving in your command who you consider should be transferred to commands outside Ireland in view of the present political situation?' In the following month British officers stationed in Kerry were told they would not be allowed to hunt, as it presented too obvious a target for the Volunteers. The British 6th Division decided to take an aggressive and retaliatory stance on the matter. If hunting was interfered with, 'a terrible penalty' would follow: all sport — fox-hounds, harriers, racing, hurling and athletic meetings — would be prohibited.

The situation in the capital was deeply disturbing to Ormonde Winter, who told Sturgis at the end of July that their opponents were learning that 'they can act in Dublin, which is full of soldiers and police, with as complete impunity as elsewhere and they're bound to have a good try shortly to disorganise by one means or another the seats of so-called Government'. Frederick Dumont noted that 'both the Government and Sinn Féin act with vindictiveness' and that the latter 'take delight in acts that tantalize the Government'. He took a dim view of the British army's displays of power: 'The driving of armoured "Tanks" through the streets of Dublin after any except great outrages in order to awe a peaceful population seems childish. . . . The marching of troops in steel trench helmets, fully armed, seems equally foolish and needlessly exasperating to the Irish people.' He also observed a race for privately held weapons: 'During the past five weeks, both the Government and Sinn Féin have been raiding on a wholesale scale and it has been nip and tuck between them to see who could get the arms first, Sinn Féin usually anticipating the Government.'

General Macready both privately and publicly voiced his understanding of unofficial reprisals by British troops. In July British forces began, without orders or authorisation, the destruction of creameries in areas of IRA attack. Both Horace Plunkett and George Russell vigorously protested at these acts, but without effect. Stephen Gwynn told Mark Sturgis in December 1920: 'Dáil Éireann no more controls the gunman than you control the police.'

Michael Collins was puzzled by his opponent's violent activity. On 30 September he wrote to Seán Nunan in New York that the British 'are losing the last few friends they had here. Positively some of the things they do are almost inconceivable, even to those who thought they knew them well.' The fact that advertisements for the Black and Tans continued to appear in British newspapers through the autumn indicated to him that 'their recruiting in spite of all their talk is not so brisk as they would like it to be'.

The leaders of the British forces believed they were making substantial progress. At the beginning of September General Tudor said he thought Sinn Féin was beaten and that the people 'were sick of it', but, as Mark Sturgis observed, 'it's the same old story and precious little good to us if nobody will up and say so'. Brigadier-General J. Brind of the general staff sent a secret message on 23 September in which he claimed that things were getting better. The leaders of the RIC strongly urged that the winter concentration of troops be postponed from 1 October to 1 December. Now was the time to press ahead with the knock-out blow; if the troops went into winter quarters at the end of September, 'Sinn Féin will flourish in abandoned districts which will have to be reconquered in the Spring'. A postponement order was issued. On 4 November Sturgis recorded his belief that the police 'were getting a bit of their own back and morale is improving'. Yet he remained uneasy about how things were going. On Armistice Day, observing Union Jacks along Dame Street and Grafton Street, he noted: 'Could not have been more beflagged if it had been Bond Street. What a queer country!'

Frederick Dumont believed that 'Sinn Féin is desperate. The Administration is beginning to get the upper hand.' On the other hand, he believed that the insurgents were fully prepared for any onslaught: 'This time Sinn Féin is thoroughly organized and its leaders tell me that any man taken can be replaced six or seven deep before the organization will fail to function.' Notwithstanding the hectic activity of the enemy, Collins remained confident. On 3 October he commented to Gavan Duffy that

British 'repressive measures are becoming more and more marked, but their evacuations are becoming more marked also'. He told Art O'Brien on 17 November: 'In spite of all their terrorism, things are going pretty well here. For the moment outwardly they are doing their best to make it appear they are winning, but they know very well this is not so.' It was the latter-day view of Richard Mulcahy that if the British military had been used earlier and widely, the IRA would have been crushed, and that it was the refusal of the British authorities to admit the seriousness of the situation that prevented this from happening.

The pace of repression increased in the autumn of 1920. In mid-October the Sinn Féin executive voted to abandon regular meetings; none were held until February. RIC inspectors in five counties reported in November that the police boycott was breaking down, and fourteen of them reported general improvement in conditions in their counties. At the same time Hamar Greenwood declared: 'We are succeeding. The Sinn Féin Court has disappeared, except in back rooms where it is held for the purposes of propaganda, especially in the American press.' The *Irish Bulletin* heatedly rejected this assertion. Although in a few cases courts had been dispersed, it said, 'there is no difficulty in selecting venues safe from such interruption'. As evidence of this activity, it cited only the work of the land tribunal. Both Kevin O'Shiel and Conor Maguire recalled that they carried on their work during the whole period of repression. Only one of the major judges (Diarmuid Crowley) was arrested, and this did not take place until November. Maguire was another who believed that the Castle had waited until too late to act effectively: 'The blow had been too long delayed to be effective. The courts were established so firmly that, although their activities were necessarily restricted, they continued to function.'

The evidence strongly points to the effective disruption of most of the Dáil courts. The *Irish Bulletin* became silent about their activities by the end of the year. This might have been for reasons of security, but that seems unlikely. The most that the Dáil Department of Propaganda would later claim was that 'District Courts sat regularly in the martial law areas of Cork, Kerry, Limerick and Tipperary. Clare, first in the field with republican tribunals, refused to relinquish them. In other parts of the country the courts continued to function sporadically.' In August 1921 Austin Stack paid a 'special tribute to a few districts which never for a day ceased to carry on their work . . . North and South Longford, North City of Dublin, Cork City and parts of Cork County, East Limerick, and East and West Clare'. At that time Alex McCabe said that the courts in Sligo survived, despite the loss of the district courts, by reverting 'to the old system of getting Parish Courts together'.

The new civil structure of the Dáil government certainly was a frail child; it had so little time to develop. In this it had none of the advantages of the Volunteer organisation, building steadily since its reorganisation in 1917, or the local government structure, which had been in place since 1898. The courts attracted many sunshine patriots in the summer of the year, most of whom remained out of sight in the cold, dark days of winter. If many of the Dáil courts disappeared, this did not mean the public returned to the old courts; it seems for the most part that they did not use any courts. In November, in what could be seen as a desperate effort to revive its judicial system, the Castle administration divided the entire country into two districts, with courts to sit in the fortified pales of Dublin and Belfast.[37]

Dublin Castle had a serious public relations problem. Categorical denial of all charges by British ministers turned many journalists away from official sources of information. According to Nevil Macready, 'the English attitude was that the Government was always right and needed no defence'. There also seemed to be some attempts at black propaganda. Arthur Griffith had told Frederick Dumont in January 1920 that 'Dublin Castle was "cooking" up a charge of moral turpitude against him with an ex-soldier'. An order from the Dáil government's 'Ministry of War' ordering railwaymen not to move troops was an obvious forgery.

The Castle initially had made no attempt to develop good press relations. Warre B. Wells said that 'inquiring journalists had been treated as at best a necessary evil'. Dumont declared that the approach was 'coldly polite' but uninformative. He cited specifically the failure to bring to the attention of journalists that fact that Terence MacSwiney, the Lord Mayor of Cork, who was arrested on 12 August, was a commandant of an IRA unit. 'No efforts were made to explain the real reasons for his arrest until public sentiment in England compelled the Premier to speak.'

The leaders of the crown forces keenly felt that the army was working under attack from the press. One of these commented: 'We have been greatly handicapped . . . owing to the fact that almost the only reports appearing in the Press have been written entirely from the other point of view and have been wilfully misleading and untrue.' Years later Major Hervey de Montmorency was still puzzled by the situation:

> For some obscure reason, which I have never seen explained, we had a very bad press; to read the *Daily Mail* or *Daily News* one might have supposed that we, who were risking our lives to keep the Union Jack flying in Ireland, were the foe, and that the treacherous, bloodthirsty cut-throats of Sinn Féin were noble heroes, suffering persecution at our hands.

Although J. J. Walsh had urged Sinn Féin to 'disseminate Bolsheviki literature to the military in this country' at the beginning of 1919, there was little direct attempt to appeal to British soldiers. One such effort, an unsigned handbill, probably dating from 1920, asked 'fellow trade unionists' in the British army: 'How long will you be the tools of your Masters, the Government of the capitalists, who think they own you, body and soul?'

The need for effective counter-propaganda was clearly seen by Nevil Macready upon his appointment in April 1920. Two months later he appointed a press officer to his staff, and in September press officers were appointed in all regional headquarters. Dublin Castle followed suit in the same month. The man appointed was Basil Clarke, who brought with him a wealth of experience in journalism. He claimed to be interviewing thirty journalists a day in his new position. He found it a difficult job and within weeks considered resigning, as he could provide no justification for the rampages of the crown forces. Furthermore, Clarke's authority was not unchallenged, and there was competition and contention among the Castle publicists. If the books later written by two of them, H. B. C. Pollard and C. J. C. Street, are indicative of the publicity work they did at the time, the Castle propaganda office remained locked in that myopic state of mind which was receptive only to reports of one outrageous atrocity after another.

The first publication to attempt to present the Castle point of view was the *Summary of Official Reports*, which began on 3 May 1920. In Erskine Childers's view, 'These Summaries became the laughing-stock and the scandal of Ireland, though they probably served their purpose as defamatory propaganda against her for the consumption of the outside world.' The *Irish Statesman* termed the material it presented 'the propaganda of lies'. This was followed by a publication designed specifically for the RIC/Black and Tans, which first appeared on 13 August. The *Weekly Summary* was designed to bolster morale and encourage aggressiveness in the police. Both Hamar Greenwood and General Tudor claimed parentage. It received universally critical reviews from its competitors. *An tÓglach* (15 Sept.) commented: 'This dope, aided by rum, they hope will restore the morale of their "RIC".' The *Irish Bulletin* (9 Nov.) claimed the publication had the 'deliberate intention of inciting the English armed forces in Ireland to acts of outrage and violence against the Irish people'. One of its intended readers, Douglas Duff, was similarly unimpressed: 'When has there ever been a more fatuous, childish and lying government publication than the *Weekly Summary*?'

In October 1920 the Castle's press office began producing *An Official Survey of Irish Affairs*. This also met with disapproval from the *Irish Bulletin*, which remarked that the Castle publicists only began issuing the publication when they believed 'they had broken the Republican Movement and could from week to week supply the supporters of repression with proof of the wisdom of "stern measures"'. However, events had not turned out as Dublin Castle had expected, it said, and the survey had been forced to acknowledge that the situation was not improving.

Something always seemed to happen to spoil the efforts of the Castle press officers. In October 1920 some Volunteers captured military messages 'dropped by aerial post in the wrong place by incredible stupidity'. Shortly afterwards, when London refused to allow the arrest of Griffith, who had charged that the Castle regime had been involved in the killing of Sinn Féin leaders, Mark Sturgis wrote in his diary: 'So we are uncontradicted murderers', adding: 'It seems to matter not one damn whether we contradict lies or not — interest dies if we don't, and nobody believes us if we do.' Efforts to curb the relentless opposition of the nationalist press were unsuccessful and counterproductive. As a result of a decision in September to prosecute any newspapers that encouraged opposition or published false statements, General Macready in the following month demanded that charges be brought against the *Freeman's Journal*, in which 'day after day, scandalous and lying statements appear'. Although the proprietor and chief editor were convicted of 'spreading false reports', the reaction in the British press was so heated that they were released after a few weeks.

Meanwhile the publications of the other side continued to appear without any apparent difficulty. *An tÓglach* was distributed to some police barracks along with the *Weekly Summary*. Excerpts from the *Irish Bulletin* appeared in the London *Times* and other newspapers, which, according to General Macready, caused great irritation among his troops. The circulation of the *Irish Bulletin* in the House of Commons in November 1920 roused Hamar Greenwood to fury: 'I consider it a loathsome alliance that men whose hands are red with the blood of gallant soldiers and policemen should come into the lobby of this House and be allowed to circulate their hideous documents of falsehood.' Frank Gallagher commented that 'When we of the *Bulletin* staff read that speech, we knew how fearful the British Government had grown, and we bowed to our work with a new devotion.'[38]

(11) BITTER ENDING

In the autumn of 1920 the full effect of the British military response was felt throughout Ireland. At the same time a great episode of resistance unfolded. Terence MacSwiney, Lord Mayor of Cork, had been arrested on 12 August. Convicted by a military court of having seditious documents and a key to a police code, he was sentenced to two years' imprisonment. Thereupon he joined eleven other Cork prisoners who had gone on hunger-strike three days before his arrest. This was the beginning of a dramatic battle of wills that lasted until the

early part of November. In September the British government asked
Dublin Castle if MacSwiney should be released; the answer was no.
Mark Sturgis recorded his belief that his release 'would not affect
soldiers much either way, but it would take the heart right out of the
police'; it would show that the government was only bluffing and
'would make our job impossible'.

As international attention mounted, the struggle went on. As early as
26 August Cardinal O'Connell of Boston had written to the US State
Department: 'I implore you in the name of humanity that our government do everything it can' to prevent MacSwiney's death. The London
Times (30 Aug.) declared: 'We can recall no parallel in the history of this
country to the duel now reaching its climax in Brixton Prison.' The end
came on 25 October. The day of MacSwiney's funeral was declared a
national day of mourning by the Dáil government, and the country came
to a standstill for two hours.

MacSwiney's long hunger-strike had brought more international attention to the situation in Ireland than any other event. Frederick Dumont
was not unmoved: 'One cannot help regretting the loss of a man brave
enough to die for his ideals but it must be remembered that the Lord
Mayor was one of the great leaders of a revolutionary movement which
has plunged Ireland into industrial and political chaos.' One of the other
hunger-strikers died before MacSwiney, and one after; on 12 November
Griffith asked the other nine to end their demonstration. Art O'Brien
reported an incident involving the painter Sir John Lavery and Winston
Churchill. When Churchill visited Lavery's studio, the painter, without
comment, put a portrait of MacSwiney on his easel.

> Churchill studied it and then said to Lavery, 'Well, what could we
> do?' Lavery remained silent, and Churchill after a while continued
> looking at the picture, 'He was a brave man! They are a fine people,
> we cannot afford to lose them. We shall be shaking hands together
> in three months.'

Six days after the death of MacSwiney came the first execution of a
member of the Volunteers. The American consul reported to Washington:

> On the morning of November 1, 1920, there was hanged at Mountjoy
> Jail in Dublin, one Kevin Gerald Barry, a student at the National Uni-
> versity (Catholic), Dublin, aged a few months over eighteen years. . . .
> Intense feeling was exhibited by Irish partisans over this hanging,
> although it was neither denied that he was guilty nor that he was a
> member of the Irish Volunteers.

Sturgis recorded in his diary: 'Barry hanged this morning in Mountjoy.
Would have been better to have shot him as a rebel after drumhead Court
Martial at the time rather than hanging him as a murderer after a month.'

On 17 November a raiding party almost caught Richard Mulcahy and did seize important papers that showed that Mulcahy was considering extreme actions against his opponents, including the spreading of disease among troops and army horses and industrial sabotage in Britain. Mark Sturgis was delighted with the seizure: 'The papers collected in the Mulcahy raid are absolutely smashing and should practically kill the English support of Sinn Féin.' The leaders of Dáil Éireann, faced with a failing transport struggle and now the Mulcahy revelations, 'look like getting their tails down again'. Dublin Castle publicists had a field day with this material, which demonstrated, they said, that the IRA was on its last legs. In December Bishop Cohalan observed a turn in the tide:

> Some Republicans used to speak of the receding authority of England and of the occupation of the deserted districts by the advancing author-ity of the Republic. . . . He would be a bold Republican who would talk now, in city or county, of districts delivered from British rule.[39]

As attack and counter-attack increased, so did a sense of danger. Griffith had not slept at home since August. On 1 October he charged that Dublin Castle had initiated a campaign to assassinate the leaders of the Dáil. According to Dumont, the documents that Griffith showed him about this plan 'would not have been accepted by a child'. British authorities had told him that 'they regarded the moderates as com-parative friends and I know of my own knowledge that under no circumstances would the authorities have anything happen to Mr Griffith'. The real danger, he believed, was that the 'physical force' section of Sinn Féin might kill him; the authorities had considered giving him a guard. The situation concerning Collins was quite different: 'It is quite probable that should Michael Collins, Sinn Féin Minister of Finance and head of the Irish Republican Brotherhood, and reputed leader of assassins, be captured in a night raid, he would be shot at once by his capturers.'

On 12 November Dumont believed that things had taken a turn in favour of the old regime:

> The Irish Administration is slowly but surely resuming control of Ireland. Ulster is being put in a position to take over its own govern-ment. The courts of justice for the country will function in Dublin and Belfast. Sinn Féin's secret service has been matched by the organisation of a superior one which has in its possession enough to condemn the society.

But nine days later Collins's 'squad' struck. On 21 November fourteen undercover British agents were killed at their residences. The British organisation, according to Lloyd George, had been beaten by counter-hoppers. In response, Black and Tans that afternoon surrounded Croke Park, where a huge crowd was attending a Gaelic football match, and proceeded to fire into the stadium for several minutes, as a result of which fourteen people died. Among those killed was one of the goalkeepers. The British force later claimed it had been fired on first, but there were no casualties in that group. Later than day a mixed group of Auxiliaries and RIC first searched a group of civilians in Lincoln Place, beside Trinity College, and then ordered them to run and shot down seven of them, of whom one later died. Three IRA prisoners were shot to death 'while trying to escape' in Dublin Castle. The *Irish Independent* (23 Nov.) commented: 'Dublin has just passed through a week-end the like of which it has not experienced since 1916.' The London *Times* was appalled: 'An army already perilously indisciplined and a police force avowedly beyond control have defiled by heinous acts the reputation of England.'

Over the next few days there were wholesale arrests, which mounted to 500 in a month. Caught in the dragnet were Arthur Griffith, Eoin Mac Néill and Eamonn Duggan. The arrest of Griffith was ordered by General Boyd, the British commander in Dublin, not by Dublin Castle or the British government; Boyd said he did it to protect Griffith and others from angry regimental officers who were in the mood to commit murder. Despite Lloyd George's irritation about this action, Griffith and the others were to remain in prison until the truce of July 1921. Mrs Griffith found her husband in great spirits, although the arrest had been a great surprise to him. In Mountjoy he was the centre of a court. He easily communicated with his cabinet. Important visitors came and went and he 'was treated with great defence by warders and prison officers'. Obviously they had decided who was going to win. Mac Néill wrote a little poem about the situation:

> Imprisoned, we are their jailors,
> On trial, their judges,
> Persecuted, their punishers,
> Dead, their conquerors.

Six days after 'Bloody Sunday' came the first of the arson attacks launched by the IRA in England; seventeen warehouses were destroyed by fire in Liverpool. Sturgis saw the arson as helpful: 'Great value to have all we claimed for the Mulcahy disclosures proved true so soon.' A round-up of Irish activists in England followed, which disrupted Collins's network there. One of those arrested, Edward Brady, conceded that this response 'had a most demoralising effect on the military side of the movement'. In addition, the public gallery of the House of Commons was closed, and a police boat patrolled the Thames. Already barricades had been erected in Downing Street, which Sturgis viewed as 'a tribute to Sinn Féin prowess'. Scottish police conducted a series of arms searches at the end of December. On 27 November the British army headquarters informed all officers that they must be always 'prepared to offer resistance to any attempt against their persons'. The next day a group of Volunteers wiped out a British motor patrol at Macroom, Co. Cork.[40]

Feelers for Peace

Incredibly, it was in these inauspicious circumstances that the first serious efforts to bring about a cessation of hostilities took place. Mark Sturgis wondered how there could be any real contact between the two sides 'with the bodies of the week-end crop of murdered police including another District Inspector hardly cold'. In fact there had been a spate of contact and correspondence about a truce during the summer of 1920. The British government had a variety of agents exploring the ground. The most active of these was the irrepressible Alfred ('Andy') Cope, who since his appointment as Assistant Under-Secretary for Ireland in July had been travelling around Dublin 'talking loosely to everybody'. Collins wanted to know all about the background of this man 'of a most engaging personality'. Cope told his Irish girlfriend that no one in Dublin Castle counted at all and that the whole British effort was 'a great spoof'; he 'hoped he would be there to hand over'.

Since March Art O'Brien had been receiving visits at his London office from a variety of British political figures, including Alfred T. Davies, a Unionist MP, who told him that the great majority in the House of Commons wanted to see peace between their two countries. Serious discussions took place in July as a result of which Davies invited Griffith to come to London for an informal meeting with the Prime Minister. Another person who talked with O'Brien at this time was Sir Charles Russell, friend of Lloyd George and lawyer for Irish political prisoners, who had the premier's authority to approach Sinn Féin.

Meanwhile Thomas Jones, an assistant secretary to the British cabinet, had had several hours of consultation with Desmond FitzGerald in early August. According to Jones, FitzGerald believed the following would be an acceptable settlement: ports — Cuban model; north-east Ulster — any constitutional safeguards that an impartial tribunal might devise; Dominion Home Rule — past associations were anathema; any *bona fide* offer should be considered seriously; and finally, 'To refuse to recognise the Dáil is as futile as to refuse to recognise the Soviet.'

On 2 August James MacMahon, one of the Castle Under-Secretaries, reported that Cardinal Logue had 'assured me confidentially that if a firm offer, not a promise or Bill that might be revoked or reduced, is made by the Government, the Bishops would unanimously accept and support it'. Griffith told the Dáil on 6 August that press reports about negotiations 'were altogether without foundation'. Of course, discussions, not negotiations, were taking place, but Griffith made no mention of these. Ten days later Lloyd George told the House of Commons that he was prepared for discussions 'with anyone who can claim to represent Irish opinion', on three conditions: separate treatment for Ulster; no seccession from the United Kingdom; and provision for British national security. No one took up his offer at this time. Mark Sturgis mused on 15 August that although various groups said they would enthusiastically support dominion Home Rule, 'it's by no means certain that we shan't find that all the fine talkers and plotters have underrated the young Republicans' power in the Councils of Sinn Féin'.

In mid-September the leaders of the independence movement publicly stated that they were ready for a settlement. Both de Valera, who spoke on 16 September, and Griffith, two weeks later, advocated a treaty that would provide self-government for Ireland as well as meet the security needs of Britain. Pádraic Colum later pointed out that both men used the word 'treaty' and neither used the word 'republic'. Shortly after de Valera's statement Griffith asked for a secret meeting with Sir John Anderson to discuss the possibility of a truce. The meeting, arranged for 26 September, proved to be abortive owing to the condition Griffith demanded — a signed statement that the British government would treat with Dáil Éireann as an equal. Although 'it all came to nothing', Sturgis believed the episode demonstrated a shift in position for the Dáil government: 'It looks as if the pressure on the Quiet Side of Sinn Féin to break away from the Gunmen was increasing.' The *Philadelphia Public Ledger*, often a conduit for British government information, carried a report that a certain leading member of Dáil Éireann was threatening Griffith and his moderate group that if they adopted 'the policy of accepting less than complete independence', he would break away from the body, 'carrying with him the Irish Volunteers and the Irish Republican Brotherhood, both of which he controls'. The *Irish Bulletin* (21 Oct.) retorted that this story was simply part of a campaign to prepare British public opinion for the murder of Michael Collins.

Meanwhile another avenue of contact was being developed. The intermediary this time was Patrick Moylett, a businessman from Ballina, Co. Mayo, and a leading figure in the IRB. At Griffith's request, Moylett met John Steele, an Irish Protestant who was the London correspondent of the *Chicago Tribune*. On 7 September the two proceeded to London, where they conferred with H. A. L. Fisher, chairman, and C. J. Phillips, secretary, of the Irish Situation Committee of the British cabinet. When Moylett returned to Dublin on 15 October, he told Griffith that 'the British were as hard up for a settlement as we were'.

Returning to London, Moylett extracted a written statement that both sides would appoint representatives after the Dáil had met; this statement, the first in which British officials used the term 'Dáil Éireann', was taken by Moylett and Griffith to be a recognition that the Dáil constituted the representative assembly of Ireland. When Moylett showed Griffith the statement, he 'actually broke down with emotion. While writing a reply Griffith was visibly affected by high-wrought emotion, so much so that he could not refrain from laughing whilst the tears coursed down his cheeks.' Matters had reached a point where Griffith was thinking about an Irish negotiator. Moylett returned to London in early November to meet with Sir William Tyrrell, the permanent head of the Foreign Office, who told him: 'If Sinn Féin takes advantage of half of our mistakes we are ruined.' After Bloody Sunday C. J. Phillips transmitted through Moylett an urgent message for Griffith: 'Ask Griffith for God's sake to keep his head; and not to break off the slender link which had been established. . . . These men were soldiers, and took a soldier's risk.' Griffith replied that he 'will do his best [to] stop shootings, but afraid he will lose control if reprisals continue. "Let them do their part — I'll do mine."' By the end of November, with Moylett and Phillips holding daily meetings, an agreement seemed near. At this point the Castle administration threatened to resign *en bloc* if matters went any further. With Moylett's efforts having come to a dead end, Collins told Griffith that he considered Moylett to be 'an unutterable fool'. In a note to Art O'Brien on 15 December he distanced himself from the Moylett affair: 'I had no doubt at all about the class of busybodies who were humming around with all sorts of claims of their own importance, and all sorts of suggestions for the settlement of Ireland, as well as every place else.' When John Steele published his account of the negotiations, Griffith denied to Collins that he had indicated any weakening on the demand for a republic.[41]

A new intermediary was Archbishop Patrick Clune of Perth in Western Australia, a uncle of Conor Clune, who had been killed in Dublin Castle on 'Bloody Sunday'. On 2 December Clune met Art O'Brien and, relating that Lloyd George and other British officials 'are desperately anxious' for peace, told him of Lloyd George's terms for a truce. In reporting to Griffith, O'Brien thought a truce was a good idea, even if negotiations led nowhere immediately, because it would 'open up possibilities of our making a big score in the game which would considerably hasten settlement and recognition'. Joseph McDonagh, who had conferred with Bishop MacRory of Down and Connor, also supported a truce. When Clune met with Griffith, he transmitted a definite proposal for a truce, the terms of which were acceptable to Griffith: reprisals to be called off; cessation of arrests and pursuits; the Dáil be free to meet; and no espionage. These terms were also in general agreement with those proposed at the Dáil cabinet meeting of 4 December. An agreement for a truce seemed very near.

By this stage there were others who wished to take a hand in the matter. On 5 November Archbishop Thomas Gilmartin of Tuam proposed that the British government should initiate a truce to be followed by a 'full measure of home rule including fiscal control'. Later, on 26 November, he told an English newspaper that a 'truce of God' was needed. He also 'wrote a few letters to Mister Churchill pressing for a truce'. His position was endorsed by Cardinal Logue and Archbishop Walsh of Dublin. Another supporter was John Sweetman, ex-MP and Sinn Féin supporter, whose letter appeared in the press on 27 November. Then, three days later, came a public letter from Sweetman's son, Roger Sweetman, TD, who stated that he was 'absolutely convinced that the methods of warfare now being employed are deplorable in their results to our country'. He proposed that a conference should be convened, including the Irish Labour Party, the Catholic hierarchy, the 'Irish Peace Conference' (a group of businessmen and aristocratic nonentities) and the newly arrived British Labour Party delegation. That a member of the Dáil should make such a proposal without any reference to the body of which he was a member surely demonstrated at least some weakening in its ranks. RIC reports for November and December noted a decline in support for Sinn Féin.

It was also at this point that some unnamed IRA leaders decided to get involved. Fredrick Dumont reported on 6 December that he was an intermediary in arranging a meeting between IRA and British army representatives. The position of the IRA men was that it was their army 'alone which makes and has made opposition to the British rule in Ireland practical' and that 'no one except themselves can bind them and their army to a settlement of any kind'. As a result of the meeting, a proposal was forwarded to Hamar Greenwood for a truce between the two forces. Dumont's report continues: 'An effort was then made to get the Dáil Éireann to join with the Irish Republican Army, allowing the latter to speak for them in any negotiations which took place between the leaders of the two armies.' The burning of Cork city and other British military actions brought an end to this development.

On 3 December six (of thirty-two) members of Galway County Council met and agreed on a statement; it could not be called a resolution, as the meeting lacked a quorum (eight members). Notice of a special meeting had been made, and James Haverty, the mover of the motion, had written to the *Irish Independent* beforehand of his intention. Haverty's resolution called for negotiations, adding that 'any side refusing to accept these proposals would be held by the world responsible for any further shootings or burnings that may take place'. Copies of the statement were sent to the other county councils, Dáil Éireann, the British Prime Minister and the Irish bishops, Catholic and Anglican. On the following day the Galway Urban District Council passed a similar resolution, arguing that since the members of the Dáil were either in jail or 'on the run', it was necessary for other supporters to take the initiative.

There was also some wavering in the allegiance of other local government bodies to Dáil Éireann. Westmeath County Council was to consider a motion to submit its accounts to the Castle's Local Government Board at its next meeting. A few days later it was withdrawn, probably at pistol point.

It was at this time that Father Michael O'Flanagan decided to intervene. On 5 December he sent a telegram to Lloyd George:

> You state you are willing to make peace at once without waiting till Christmas. Ireland is also willing to make peace. What first step do you propose?

He signed this message as Acting President of Sinn Féin. O'Flanagan had played an important role in the rise of Sinn Féin, but since the creation of the Dáil he had been relegated to the sidelines. With the arrest of Griffith and upon the fulsome urgings of James O'Connor, Lord Chief Justice, and Andy Cope, he decided to take what must have seemed to him to be the historic decision to step into the breach.[42]

The evidence of these developments convinced Lloyd George that he had seen the tip of the white flag. He decided to toughen his requirements for a truce. This was the substance of his statement to the House of Commons on 10 December; on the same day martial law was imposed on Cork, Kerry, Tipperary and Limerick. According to 'Watchman' (Darrell Figgis), writing in the *Irish Independent*, 'A cock-a-whoop cry of triumph went up at once in Downing Street, and we received martial law in four counties and two cities as a beginning, while Lloyd George assured his pack in Parliament that these were the voices of a nation.' Collins believed that Lloyd George's speech, together with the actions of British forces, 'has thrown everybody — even, I think, Roger Sweetman — in our Camp now'. These developments had shown 'what exactly the purrings of the previous weeks were intended for'.

Now was the time for some damage control on the other side. In order to deal with the local government situation, Griffith asked Diarmuid O'Hegarty on 6 December to get Brugha and Collins to issue a manifesto 'to prevent Local Bodies or individuals putting their "foot in it"'. He also wanted the Local Government Department 'to tackle these bodies and prevent any further cowardice'. Various members of the Galway County Council denounced the action of the half dozen members who had proposed appeasement. All of the county councils that addressed the matter supported Dáil Éireann as the sole authority to negotiate any agreement. The Clare County Council ordered that a copy of the Galway resolution should be burnt. Roger Sweetman was criticised by Seán Etchingham in a public letter and got further censure at the next Dáil meeting.

Then there was the matter of Father O'Flanagan. Pádraig O'Keeffe, the party secretary, declared that O'Flanagan's telegram 'is simply a statement of personal opinion and has not the sanction of the Sinn Féin Executive'. In New York de Valera stated that O'Flanagan's action was unofficial. A similar statement was issued by the cabinet. Stephen Gwynn commented that O'Flanagan 'has promptly and harshly been disavowed. A layman who spoke in the same sense would have been in grave danger, and Mr Sweetman is the only one who has been found to incur it.' On 13 December the Roscommon priest decided he could go no further until he had conferred with the 'two leading spokesmen of the Irish people'. The next day Collins suggested to Griffith that he ask O'Flanagan 'to give over these communications altogether', but 'I suppose Fr Michael thinks nobody is just quite able to handle things like he is himself'. Despite his statement, O'Flanagan resumed his correspondence with Lloyd George and travelled to London several times from late December well into the next year. By this time, however, it was clear that he did not represent the people that mattered.

There was also a need to shore up the position of the Dáil government. From prison Griffith promptly issued a statement: 'Let Ireland recall to-day George Washington's message to our ancestors: "Patriots of Ireland, stand fast." Today is Ireland's Valley Forge. Tomorrow will be Ireland's Yorktown.' 'Watchman' (Darrell Figgis) wrote two letters that appeared in the *Irish Independent* urging discipline and unity. Michael Collins also sent a message:

> At the present moment there is very grave danger that the country may be stampeded on false promises and foolish ill-timed actions. We must stand up against that danger. My advice to the people is 'Hold Fast'.

The *Irish Independent* printed his letter on 7 December; a police raid on its offices that night prevented it from printing another letter from Collins at that time; it appeared a few days later, its gist being 'Let us drop talking and get on with the work.' Collins also told Gavan Duffy on 9 December: 'There are a lot of foolish people here talking of peace — or rather well-intentioned people talking in a foolish manner. The English are certainly anxious for a truce. It is they who are raising the clamour.' 'Stand fast' posters and leaflets were distributed around the country.

There was a further problem concerning the leadership of the Dáil government. On 2 December Collins asked Griffith to 'send out a personal message to the Ministry to carry on the Departmental duties with increased vigour. It seems to me there are signs of slackness appearing, and this tendency must be combated.' Griffith apparently saw no problem in maintaining his leadership from jail. At the first two cabinet meetings following his arrest, those of 27 November and 4 December, J. J. O'Kelly, as Ceann Comhairle of the Dáil, presided. At both meetings requests were made for Griffith to nominate a successor. Finally, on 9 December, he did so, and his selection was confirmed at the meeting of 11 December. According to O'Kelly, Griffith's first choice was Brugha, who declined because of the pressure of army work; the second choice was Stack, who said he could not serve because of his preoccupation with the courts and police. The third nominee was Collins, and he accepted. Perhaps Griffith hoped all along that Collins would take his place; earlier he is said to have wanted Collins to step in if anything happened to him. Collins's time as substitute Acting President was to be short — from 11 December, the day of his appointment, to 24 December, the day de Valera returned to Dublin. Indeed, at the time of his appointment the Dáil leadership was aware that de Valera was on his way back from America.[43]

There was a lot more excitement to come in December. On 11 December the centre of Cork city was burnt down by the Auxiliaries and Black and Tans. Members of a British Labour Party commission on Ireland were on hand to view the destruction. On the following day Bishop Cohalan excommunicated all Catholics in his diocese involved in acts of murder. 'Even leaving aside the moral aspect of the question for the moment,' he demanded, 'what had the country gained politically by the murder of policemen?. . . When you come with an army able to fight the enemy and defend the weak and unprotected, I will act as Chaplain.' The bishop had earlier praised Sinn Féin's capacity for government and had submitted a case to a Dáil court. In a joint statement Lord Mayor O'Callaghan and J. J. Walsh, TD, attacked his assumption that 'there is no such thing as an Irish Government, and that the English invaders have a moral right in this country'. Professor Alfred O'Rahilly tackled him on theological grounds.

Bishop Cohalan responded to his critics in a pastoral letter on the following Sunday in which he said that the gutting of the centre of Cork was simply punishment for murder. He also rejected as 'false teaching' the assertion 'that Ireland is at the moment a sovereign independent State' and that consequently 'Irishmen have authority to kill England's forces and to burn English property in Ireland'. He clearly thought he was doing a public service. In a letter to Shane Leslie he declared: 'This ought to be a help to the Irish leaders; for though the ordinary young boy of the Irish Republican Army may believe that Ireland is a republic, the leaders know that a republic will not be recognised.' He acknowledged, however, that his point of view 'is anything but popular at the moment'. Another clerical correspondent of Leslie's, Canon Patrick Lyons of Ardee, told him that Cohalan 'is now without a particle of influence with his own people owing to his precipitancy and flippancy. . . . His chief contribution was an excommunication which miss fire[d].' Michael Collins commented that Cohalan's pronouncement 'does him no credit' and added that he had been told that 'the populace there were enraged with him and his tirade'. *Old Ireland* concluded bitterly: 'If Ireland is defeated after its heroic struggle, after the agony of its heroes, it will be defeated by men like Dr Cohalan and Dr Gilmartin.' None of the other bishops rose to defend Cohalan, nor did they follow his example of excommunication.[44]

With the truce episode apparently at an end, Collins expressed his satisfaction at the turn of events. He told Art O'Brien on 6 December:

My own opinion of these negotiations is that they are entirely dishonest . . . an effort to put us in the wrong with the world and particularly with our own people. . . . Some well-intentioned people here at home seem to think that if our acts of self-defence are discontinued we will get anything we liked from England.

He told Griffith on 14 December:

Let Lloyd George make no mistake, the IRA is not broken. The events of the week and these days are more eloquent on that question than all his Military advisers. Neither is the spirit of the people broken.

On 15 December Griffith informed him that a new formula for a truce had been developed. But this also proved abortive. Apparently General Macready was asking for three more months to crush the rebellion. Now the surrender of arms was demanded. The purpose of this last-minute demand, said Collins, was 'to show weak spots in our personnel. Of course nobody would dream of entertaining such a proposition.' By this time the British government and its agents were no longer interested in an immediate truce. At a meeting at the end of December the army commanders in Ireland and Sir John Anderson agreed that such a development would be a disadvantage to their side. The generals assured Lloyd George that they could defeat the opposition in four more months. This was the end of any truce negotiations at this time, but throughout the period until July 1921 confidential contacts and discussions on the matter took place. An encouraging development at the end of December 1920 was the report of the British Labour commission which denounced British policy in the country, urged the withdrawal of the British military, and proposed the formation of an Irish constituent assembly. And so the pivotal year in the struggle for Irish self-government came to an end.[45]

4

War of Wills

(1) DE VALERA TAKES COMMAND

De Valera returned to Ireland from the United States on 23 December 1920. he had been away for eighteen months, during which time a great deal had happened. A Dáil administration had come into being and was now enduring an effort to destroy it. The IRA had uprooted British authority in most of the country and was now subjected to a determined effort by its opponents to regain lost ground. A major political development was the emergence of Michael Collins as the driving force in the underground government and army.

The President arrived in the middle of the decisive period of the struggle. For two years the combatants had done battle both politically and militarily. Given the political facts of life in both Ireland and Britain, the conflict could not go on in its present form much longer. A majority of the Irish people had demonstrated not only that they supported self-government but that they were prepared to stand fast to that position during a period of prolonged adversity. But how much longer were they prepared to endure and resist? The Irish people had had a great deal of historical experience in these matters, but they had their limits. British public opinion was beginning to turn decisively against the British government policy of shooting and burning. In addition, European and American opinion was increasingly critical of the British campaign in Ireland. Within the context of the Western democracies, counter-terror could only be effectively employed for a short period of time, and time was running out. Despite all ethnic stereotypes, antipathies and hatreds, Ireland was not Zululand. The crucial consideration was: what would be the relative standing of the two sides when this phase of the conflict drew to a close? — and who would have, or could claim to have, the upper hand?

There had been considerable discussion in the British press and government circles about de Valera's return to Ireland. Noting that he was not a British subject by birth, some London newspapers demanded his exclusion. The President had his own view on the matter: 'I did not seek Mr Lloyd George's permission to come to the United States, and I shall not ask for it when the time of my return to Ireland comes.' The British cabinet initially decided that he should be kept out, but then reversed this position after several ships had been searched. Now he was 'to be allowed to slip in'. Thus he was left alone initially. General Macready was soon impatient about this arrangement. He wrote to Sir John Anderson on 11 January 1921 that the 'immunity of de Valera should have a definite term, and personally I think he has been here quite long enough to make up his mind'. Ignoring the presence of the rebel leader was having a demoralising effect on the commanders of the British forces.[1]

De Valera returned to take charge of a government. He was to prove to be a much more active and forceful executive than Griffith. Even before the arrest of the Acting President in November, the administration of the counter-state had been losing vitality. It was very much a matter of style and personality. Now de Valera wanted to know everything that had been happening. He was not there to edit a newspaper but to run an administration. The first thing he did was to set up a President's Office, something that apparently Griffith never did. De Valera called for equipment, supplies, books. Then he requested reports from all concerning activities and expenditures. He was obviously very serious about galvanising his administration. A laggard department was quickly brought to task: 'Urge the Language Department for their statement, or we will not wait for it.' He also ordered all departments to draw up standing orders, which would be sent to all missions abroad. He also proposed an early meeting of the Dáil, and immediately after it ordered the preparation of a press statement of the proceedings. Things were beginning to stir. Diarmuid O'Hegarty suddenly found he was swamped with work from the President's Office. He told Mulcahy: 'Since the President's return my duties as Secretary of the Ministry have become perhaps not more onerous but certainly more various and irksome, necessitating almost constant personal attention.' He requested the appointment of an Assistant Director of Organisation for the IRA; he had already received an Assistant Secretary to the Ministry in the previous summer. The problem, indeed contradiction, of the doubling-up of offices was becoming apparent. No proper government, underground or not, could have one person who was both the Director of Administration as well as a headquarters staff officer at the same time.

The Dáil leadership had weathered well all British efforts to destroy it. Capable replacements had been found for arrested ministers. At the time of de Valera's return there were two gaps in the cabinet. Joseph McGrath, Acting Minister for Labour, had been arrested on 2 December, and W. T. Cosgrave was absent from his department. McGrath was replaced by Joseph McDonagh at the end of January, and Cosgrave returned to work at that time. A more serious matter was that some departments — Fisheries, National Language and Trade and Commerce — had been brought to a near standstill. Some other departments — Home Affairs and Local Government — had been seriously restricted in their activities. Only Labour and Defence were able to carry on in a generally effective manner. But, at least, all the departments were able to maintain an administrative presence in the capital throughout the period.

The President made a variety of administrative changes. There were to be monthly, rather than weekly, cabinet meetings. The Dáil was to meet at least every two months. Correspondence dealing with cabinet matters was to sent to the Secretary to the Ministry, not to others, like Collins, who told Art O'Brien to communicate with O'Hegarty: 'I am trying to arrange to pass a good many of the details of our correspondence on to him.'

Nevertheless, O'Brien continued to write to Collins about almost everything. In addition, de Valera issued a ban on smoking (poorly observed) in government offices and established formal holiday provisions for employees. He began attending meetings of the army general staff and revived the Sinn Féin executive, which had not met since October.

He clearly understood the need for security. He instructed all departments to keep files to a minimum, with duplicates kept in safe storage. Further, 'when any communication from any Army department reaches a Civil Office it should receive priority . . . and be destroyed immediately when dealt with'. Whenever a office was raided, 'the head needs to communicate at once this information to other offices. . . . Carelessness in this matter must be regarded as a very definite neglect of duty.' On one occasion in February, when O'Hegarty was arranging for de Valera and the director of the Land Bank to meet an important American visitor, de Valera told him: 'Do not inform [them] until the last minute where they are to meet me.' On another occasion he instructed O'Hegarty: 'Our men are so important now that we ought never run the risk of two where one can do.' Yet the leaders of the Dáil government continued to travel publicly as required. Frank Gallagher saw this as an advantage: 'This careful openness, running counter, as it did, to the whole British idea, proved a great protection. Members of the Government and high army officers went wherever it was necessary to go. They did not court arrest, but they did not let the chance of it immobilise them.' De Valera found that the administration could proceed despite all the difficulties. He informed James O'Mara in New York: 'We are able to function here far more freely and effectively than anyone at the other side for a year or two can imagine.' The major difficulty was overseas communications: 'This lack helps to give our representatives in other countries the feeling that we are completely cut off and hemmed in, and so give them a wrong perspective.' He ordered the preparation of new ciphers and the formation of a regular courier service to London and the continent.

Collins had long been critical of inadequate attention to security. He told Art O'Brien in April: 'As for this kind of casual talk that goes on, it is positively dreadful. Some of my best places have been discovered in this fashion, and it is a miracle that one can keep going at all.' In his view, the lack of security was part of a pattern of administrative slovenliness:

> It is simply heartbreaking the way in which little things are neglected — little things which, put together, help very materially. I have noticed with unfailing consistency that it is the departments which are responsible for these neglects [that] are doing the most grumbling about delays.

To O'Brien's complaint that lack of co-ordination within the government was demonstrated by the failure of many officials to travel through London without contacting O'Brien's office, Collins said he would ask the President 'to specifically instruct all Departments that any person travelling to the Continent through London should be given a note of introduction to your office'.[2]

A serious difficulty within the underground government was internal communications. De Valera was conscious of this problem from the time of his arrival in Ireland. Almost immediately he requested a courier to link his office with the Propaganda Department. Four months later the situation had not improved. On 4 May he complained to O'Hegarty that contact between the two offices 'are so slow as to be about useless'. Yet the departments in Dublin, serviced by a corps of messengers, had much better communication with each other than they did with their representatives in the rest of the country. All the civil departments used the IRA network, which often was overloaded. The heaviest users were Agriculture, Home Affairs and Local Government. The Volunteer leadership bemoaned the fact that, while it was struggling for existence, the departments expected it to distribute routine correspondence and circulars.

The first attempt to deal with this problem took place in October 1920, when the army staff wrote to Sinn Féin requesting its assistance. W. T. Cosgrave called for a conference of civil heads and the Adjutant-General. Various departments had suggestions, one being that Cumann na mBan should be employed. Nothing was done, however, until April 1921, when Gearóid O'Sullivan decided he had had enough. He wrote to O'Hegarty: 'I am being overburdened at present with letters . . . marked "by hand".' He urged that only the most important messages should be sent through the Volunteer network. 'At the moment the enemy is striving hard to cut our communications and thus segregate us from our units in the country. Anything which facilitates the enemy in this respect is hurtful to our Army.' At the urging of de Valera, Sinn Féin finally agreed in June to set up a network, but it took six months for even a test of the service to be carried out.

De Valera was aware of the pressures under which the personnel of the counter-state operated. He told O'Brien in March: 'How you managed to keep all the irons hot which you were expected to in the past is more than I know. M.C. was in the same boat here. You are paying the penalty with your health, and M.C. ran it very close more than once too.' He advised pacing of effort for the long run: 'This fight isn't a question of a mere "spurt", so we must not run ourselves out in the early part of the race.'[3]

De Valera had returned from America with a clear conception in his mind about how the military campaign should proceed. He believed that the IRA should shift away from small-scale operations to bigger ones. This would ease the burden on the people of British counter-measures. He felt deeply the suffering of the people, and in a public letter of 21 January he declared: 'The armed bully is in your streets and with cowardly insolence he taunts you with your powerlessness.' Moreover, he believed this shift would change what he saw as the foreign perception of the IRA as a small group of terrorists to that of a real army. The publicity value would be considerable — and his American experiences had taught him the importance of achieving public attention and had given him plenty of practice in the art. Richard Mulcahy later said that de Valera 'attempted to make suggestions about a situation that he had no real knowledge of'. When he presented this proposal to the Dáil at its meeting of 25 January, de Valera stressed that it was based on an external view of the situation. It met with a hostile reception. It seemed to several deputies that easing off would be viewed by their opponents as giving in. This was a bruising re-entry into Irish politics for de Valera, and he backed down from his proposal.

An outspoken opponent of violence, Roger Sweetman, was subjected to a barrage of criticism for his advocacy of peace talks in December. After this meeting he resigned his seat, declaring in a letter to the press that he was 'in radical disagreement' with a majority in the Dáil on a 'vital matter of policy'. Although he did not say what this matter was, most informed people could have guessed. Sweetman thus was the second deputy to resign his seat (the first being Diarmuid Lynch in mid-1920); there were no further resignations.

Another belief de Valera brought back with him was that the Dáil should assume clear responsibility for the IRA and its actions. This met with complete support at the Dáil meeting of 11 March. The President was given discretion to make the position public, which he did a fortnight later. He also attended some meetings of the general staff and met individually with Volunteer leaders from the provinces.

Then there was his proposal that Collins should be sent to America. He had a long list of reasons why this was a good idea: Collins could try to mend the rift in the Irish camp in the USA, examine the state of financial support, prepare the ground for a new loan campaign, launch a boycott of English goods, and improve communications and the shipment of military supplies. An overriding consideration was that if Collins was safe outside Ireland, then the Dáil government would not have 'all our eggs in one basket', that 'whatever the coup the English may attempt, the line of succession is safe and the future provided for'. De Valera's statement clearly recognised the reality of Collins's position within the organisation, and the fact that Collins had become a major force. On the other hand, it was a serious matter to send away the person who was the most effective administrator. De Valera claimed that the cabinet unanimously approved this proposal at its meeting of 9 January, but the minutes do not indicate this. Two days before the meeting Collins wrote to Boland that he was not very keen on going to America and that he intended to make his position clear. Nevertheless, he was prepared to go; in fact he would already have left had there not been problems in arranging safe transportation. Three months later he still had not departed. Obviously he had dug in his heels on the matter. Finally, on 15 April de Valera informed Collins that he should not go, as serious initial contacts with British agents were about to take place.[4]

There is a considerable background to this proposal, and it centres around the intensifying conflict between Collins on one hand and Cathal Brugha and Austin Stack on the other. Collins, of course, was an aggressive, dynamic and outspoken leader, with strong opinions about everything, particularly about the performance of other people. He let Stack and others know that he considered Stack to be an administrative incompetent. There is no doubt that Stack was out of his element as head of an important department, but it was natural for Stack to hate Collins for taking it upon himself to make this apparent to everyone in the leadership. Another factor was that although Collins was, like Brugha and Stack, a cabinet member, he was also a Volunteer headquarters staff officer, serving as Director of Intelligence and, for most of the time, Adjutant-General, while also taking on many other duties unofficially. Brugha resented the power that Collins held within his (Brugha's) department, while Collins let no one else have any authority in his own department. Here again was the problem of doubling up, but in a much more serious situation. A complicating factor was that Collins was the head of the Irish Republican Brotherhood, an organisation that claimed supreme political power, and whose Supreme Council had, in fact, until very recently claimed to constitute the legitimate government of the Irish Republic. The position of the IRB within the Volunteers was bound to cause problems — as indeed it eventually did. No one was prepared to attack directly the anomaly of the IRB; such action could shatter the army. Griffith certainly could not do it; he was already suspect for his non-republican views. Moreover, to its supporters the organisation was simply a bulwark of republicanism within the Volunteers and Sinn Féin. Moreover, the IRB constitution had been amended in September 1919 to recognise the position of the Republic as ratified by Dáil Éireann.

Brugha had had problems keeping Collins in check as early as 1918 when Brugha was the Volunteer Chief of Staff. The conflict within the cabinet seemed to have really heated up in mid-1920 and continued apace. Just a month before de Valera returned to Ireland a new issue arose, and this time Brugha had the initiative. At that time Liam Mellows, newly returned from the United States, was appointed Director of Purchases, taking over from Collins, who had been unofficially in charge of this work. A lot of the army purchases of arms and ammunition had been made through the IRB network, and Volunteer and IRB accounts were often mixed together. Now Brugha demanded a complete accounting of all arms transactions. Mellows supported this measure for a time, before he realised what the game was really about. All purchases were suspended while the matter was dealt with. Because of the tangled accounts, Collins had great difficulty in rectifying them. Stack was in the happy position of acting as both judge and jury of the inquiry. Meanwhile the Volunteers were being denied the arms they urgently needed.

The dispute developed into a major row and landed in de Valera's lap soon after he returned. When Brugha told him about the overreaching activities of Collins, the President replied that he could hardly complain, as he had refused to take Griffith's place in December. After Brugha had employed the dangerous expedient of calling together the whole headquarters staff to rehash his version of the controversy, Mulcahy decided that he had to act. He went to the President and told him that 'Cathal was behaving in a way that would break the Staff and that if he was allowed to continue to behave as he was I could no longer accept the responsibility for the morale and *esprit de corps* of the Staff'. De Valera replied: 'Do you know, I think that Cathal is jealous of Mick.' He had no solution to the problem, however; he told Mulcahy that he would simply have to stick it out and make the best of things. Collins later told a journalist that de Valera did restrain Brugha from taking action against him. The Defence Minister frequently plotted extreme actions, such as assassinating the entire British cabinet, but nothing came of them. In any case, by the spring of 1921 Brugha began to turn against his Chief of Staff. Mulcahy relates that he became the channel through which Brugha 'would direct his attacks on Collins. I was a bad contact for the transmission of these attacks, and in that way Cathal became somewhat antagonistic to myself.'

On his return from America, de Valera had heard from all sides about various differences within the government and army. His only substantial recommendation for a change in personnel was his proposal to send Collins to America. Everyone else was to be left in place. Although he quelled the most obvious disputes at cabinet meetings, Art

O'Connor observed that he usually agreed with Brugha and Stack, and not with Collins.[5]

At first Collins looked upon de Valera as one who shared his views about how things should be run. After he told the President about all his trials and tribulations, de Valera replied: 'I would be sorry to think that your feeling discontented and dissatisfied and fed-up was due to anything more than natural physical reaction after the terrible strain you have been subjected to.' At the first cabinet meeting after de Valera's return Collins seemed distracted, troubled. Perhaps he already knew about de Valera's plan to sent him to the United States. He soon became impatient with de Valera's stories of his exploits in America; concerning these, he told Griffith: 'The President himself went into matters connected with his wanderings at some length.' He also became exasperated with de Valera's diffidence about the written word. Collins told a friend: 'I never met such a bloody man.' He was scornful of de Valera's initial lack of knowledge about the military situation. At the Dáil meeting in March he voiced his doubts about the position of the American funds, his concern undoubtedly being based on his lack of control of the money. Collins's remark to the assembly was a direct jibe at de Valera, who justified his long stay in America largely on the basis of having raised a huge amount of money. De Valera's reply was that Collins 'was not taking too rosy a view of affairs in America when he said that he hoped the expenditure there would be covered by receipts'. Collins apparently concluded that de Valera lacked effectiveness in pushing the movement forward, or at least that he was not as effective as himself.

It is difficult to assess de Valera's perception of Collins at this time. He obviously recognised Collins as a vital factor in both the government and army. In the beginning they were in constant communication, and it was obvious that Collins was the most involved and energetic of the ministers. De Valera was later to say that Collins was one of the two men he had worked with who always wanted to take immediate action once a decision had been reached (the other was Seán Lemass). It was Collins who found a secure place for him to live, provided the office equipment, and who, at de Valera's request, informed the available deputies of the January meeting. De Valera apparently did not like to hear the term 'Big Fellow' used; he is said to have remarked that now that he had returned to Ireland there was no such person as the Big Fellow. De Valera told one of his biographers that from April 1921 Collins no longer took heed of his direction. British intelligence reported that the two men had quarrelled and that Collins had emerged as the leader of the movement, yet there is no specific evidence of overt friction between the two leaders during this period.[6]

Despite all the difficulties, the Dáil government continued its growth, with employees being added to the Local Government and Foreign Affairs

Departments. The staff of the general secretariat had been expanded to seven. On a visit to the capital, Ernie O'Malley observed this development:

> The movement was now becoming respectable, success had drawn in many who had not even a half belief. I saw a new paid bureaucracy being built up in Dublin, and I heard the comments of some, who looked down on the fighting men and others who were bearing their share of the dirty work.[7]

(2) Crisis in Local Government

The Dáil department that probably was most embattled at the beginning of 1921 was the Department of Local Government. The great majority of local bodies had shifted their allegiance to the government of Dáil Éireann in mid-1920, but the cost of the action was now being felt. Grants from Dublin Castle had ceased. The department decided that the gap of a million pounds could best be met by reductions in local government spending and a bridging loan fund provided by the Dáil.

The department had another problem as well — a missing minister. Robert Barton was later to say of W. T. Cosgrave that that he 'was so elusive that he could hardly ever be found by his colleagues'. Cosgrave had experienced a period of imprisonment and illness from March to July 1920, during which time Kevin O'Higgins acted as substitute minister. The full blast of British repression in the autumn obviously had an effect on him. He was not at his post from November to January. The cabinet minutes, always cryptic, stated for 4 December: 'Authorise K. O'H. to carry on Department. Summon him to next meeting.' According to one account, Cosgrave had ceased going to his office to avoid arrest. Upon receiving complaints, Collins 'sent a message to Cosgrave to open the offices. Cosgrave told the messenger: "Tell Collins that I am not going to be shot for him."' Collins then sent for O'Higgins. The messenger found O'Higgins in Davy Byrne's, a well-known Dublin pub. Another account had Cosgrave fleeing to Manchester, where he stayed with a priest. He was said to have returned decked out with glasses, dyed hair and a soft tweed hat with fishing flies. In fact he stayed at the Glencree monastery in the Dublin mountains for about six weeks from December to January. Soon after de Valera's arrival in Ireland he got Cosgrave to resume his position. According to Richard Mulcahy, O'Higgins had a low opinion of his chief's capacity for leadership at this time. This view was obviously shared by Collins. In comparing Cosgrave and O'Higgins, Stack later gave it as his opinion that O'Higgins was 'the abler and stronger man of the two'.[8]

Cosgrave did not attend the first cabinet meeting after de Valera's return — that of 9 January — but was at his desk at the end of January. The problems his department faced were daunting. Among these were the financial crisis created by the withdrawal of British grants, the breakdown in the collection of rates, and the need to supervise the local bodies in a time of tumult. The £100,000 loan fund established by the Dáil in January 1921 helped to bridge the financial gap. The problem of rate collection was difficult, as the rate-collectors were caught between two governments. In December 1920 Kevin O'Higgins had issued a warning:

> The Department has done everything possible to meet the collectors. After this circular it will appeal no more but will act sternly and swiftly as a Government and as a Government in a state of war.

In the following month the cabinet decided that negligent collectors should be fired. Volunteers and Republican Police were widely used in their place. Some ratepayers decided to take a tax holiday until the situation clarified. Arrest of unco-operative rate-collectors and pressure on recalcitrant taxpayers kept money coming in; nevertheless, collection of rates came 'very near the point of closing down, but . . . never actually reached that point'. County council income plummeted, and when the councils struck new rates in April local finance was in dire straits. The *Weekly Summary*, no friendly observer, predicted that financial chaos was inevitable, but somehow the local bodies muddled through.

Getting the local bodies to follow the instructions of the Dáil department proved to be difficult. Three-quarters of them had pledged allegiance to the revolutionary government, but some of them believed that their declaration did not actually entail obeying that entity. O'Higgins later said that 'many members of local authorities did not act up to the mandate which they received from the people' and 'in some cases they definitely voted against carrying out instructions of this Department'.

One definite instruction was that the local bodies were to have no further contact with the Custom House board. The Dáil department had ways of finding out who was not following this order. When the department informed the Kilkenny Board of Guardians that its minutes were still being sent to the Custom House, the board's clerk responded that 'the minutes are being sent to the L. G. Board. He had no instructions to send them to Dáil Éireann, but he had them copied and would send them if the guardians wished. Consideration was left over to the next meeting.' On 11 March O'Higgins took firm action. He informed all available deputies that many local officials, if not councils, 'continue to correspond with that institution [the Custom House board], to forward minutes, and to interview its Auditors and Inspectors'. He enclosed a message from the Home Affairs Department which declared that any contact with the

Custom House board 'will be deemed treasonable practice and dealt with accordingly', adding: 'This struggle to maintain control of the Local Government machine is second only in importance to the activities of the Republic[an] Army.' Another problem was that although most bodies ceased contact with the rival board, many of them 'are not communicating with this Department, forwarding minutes or falling in with instructions issued by us'.[9]

O'Higgins told the Dáil in March that the situation was improving and cited the recent decision of the Kilkenny County Council to sever its ties with the Custom House board. The struggle, however, continued: 'It was a question of a trial of strength between two Governments.' The *Irish Bulletin* also believed the Dáil government was winning through. On 7 March it proudly announced: 'Despite the fact that from many Councils the Republican majorities have been removed to prison or internment camps, not one per cent of all the public bodies which declared their allegiance to Dáil Éireann have rescinded that declaration.' Only a few small bodies submitted to the audit of the Custom House board: Dundalk Urban District Council, Callan Board of Guardians, Enniscorthy Asylum Committee, and Galway County Council. One way to prevent an audit was to make off with the records. The *Irish Independent* in December reported a general condition: 'In several case[s] the books have been seized and carried off by some person or persons unknown, and in others this has been done by the forces of the Crown (and in Co. Dublin by both) with the result that many public bodies are unable to transact even routine business.' The Dublin County Council faced a serious situation:

LADY DOCKRELL asked which lot took the minute books.
MR WALSHE — I understand it was some person or persons unknown.
LADY DOCKRELL — The minute books were taken by some person or persons unknown, and when the steed was stolen the other persons arrived on the scene.

A huge financial sword hung over local government — ten million pounds in claims that had been imposed under the Malicious Damages Act. The Dáil department ordered the county councils not to pay any of these claims — an order which was, needless to say, complied with by the councils without objection. Moreover, on 2 April the department sent out a stern warning to anyone contemplating submitting such a claim:

Those who act as agents and instruments of the enemy in this attempt, and take part in this despicable and infamous war, are guilty of the highest crime against the State, and all who by Decrees obtained in enemy Courts, by garnishee orders, or other enemy device, are thus guilty are hereby warned that they will be dealt with accordingly and proceeded against with all the forces that the people's government can command.

Any settlement with Britain would have to include the provision that all damages caused by crown forces would have to be met by that government, while in the case of damages 'caused by the necessary operations of the National Army, the Home Government will see at the proper time that the loss is distributed over the nation as a whole'. The department claimed that this warning 'has had excellent results'. As a result of a meeting of the solicitors involved, almost all of the garnishee orders were withdrawn.

The department also arranged for local councils 'to resume normal relations with their Bank Treasurers' which 'has solved the difficulties that many Councils were experiencing with their rate-collectors'. Furthermore, 'the destruction of the Customs House has finally eliminated the British Local Government Board as a serious factor in the situation'. By May the local government situation was improving. The department proceeded to increase the number of its inspectors from fourteen to twenty.

Reporting to the Dáil in August, Cosgrave affirmed that 'the constructive side had been confined almost exclusively to the abolition of the workhouse'. The aged and infirm 'who could not be boarded out' were being provided for in district hospitals and county homes. 'The Department had set up a new institution under the Dáil', he said, 'which would free people for ever from the taint of pauperism.'[10]

(3) Problems in Home Affairs

In mid-1920 the Department of Home Affairs had been riding high. At that time a whole new court system and police force had been created, for both of which the department had been responsible. The formation of neither of these bodies, however, had been initiated by the department. The creation of the courts was due to local, popular initiative, while the Republican Police force was established from the ranks of the Volunteers by order of the Chief of Staff. When the British counter-offensive took place in the autumn of that year, neither body was able to withstand the pressure.

Beyond the difficulty of operating in a period of intense repression was the administrative failure of Austin Stack and his department. In the short period of time from the emergence of the new courts and police until the counter-offensive they failed to organise and solidify these bodies as systems capable of maintaining themselves in adversity. Michael Collins had clearly stated his view of Stack's competence — or rather lack of it — a position shared by the army headquarters staff. Given this problem of

leadership, it is curious that nothing was done to strengthen the administration of the department. Some other departments had assistant
ministers, but Stack was left to flounder on his own. He was also joint
national secretary of Sinn Féin and Assistant Chief of Staff of the
Volunteers, but he was completely inactive in these positions. Richard
Mulcahy told Brugha some time in 1920 that 'Even the most elementary
conception of what is to be the Unit of Organisation Socially or Politically
within the Republic has not been yet evolved.' The situation, he said, was
'that of a people looking for the Republic and its institutions and finding
only the Volunteers'. He blamed Stack's department for failing to
consolidate the civil departments at the local level. He also pointed to the
failure of the Sinn Féin organisation, of which Stack was joint national
secretary, effectively to sustain these bodies. The party's position was that
the IRA had drawn away party activists at the local level, thus leaving it
incapable of reinforcing the civil bodies. In July 1921 Brian Fagan, a
member of the party executive, declared:

> One of the main reasons for the disorganisation on the civil side of
> the movement has been the failure of the IRA rank and file to grasp
> the importance of civil activity. This inability to see beyond the end
> of a gun, even where the guns are used, has resulted in the wholesale
> lapsing of Cumainn.[11]

Courts

The courts situation was serious. The RIC reported a decline in Dáil court
activity beginning in the autumn of 1920. Frederick Dumont reported in
January 1921: 'Sinn Féin courts, as far as any public knowledge of them is
concerned, have ceased to exist, and I learn from private sources that this
is actually the case except that one is held in secret occasionally to
maintain the fiction that these courts continue.' According to Stack, the
only areas that maintained the courts throughout the period were North
and South Longford, North Dublin City, Cork City and parts of Co. Cork,
East Limerick and East and West Clare. The police force established in
June 1920 had almost completely disappeared.

The situation had reached a low ebb at the beginning of 1921. At the
January session of the Dáil Stack admitted that 'the position of the
Courts generally speaking is not satisfactory'. The principal reason for
this, he said, was the arrest of many of the judges and registrars, but
also 'to some extent diffidence on the part of persons to carry on in the
face of enemy aggression'. He hoped to turn the situation around soon,
and he asked the deputies to assist him in monitoring court activity. He
seemed uncertain whether he would be able to do very much: 'I shall
try to send out a few additional Organisers, but these are difficult to
find — good ones at any rate.'

In February Lloyd George expressed his deep satisfaction with the turn of events: 'The Police have recovered their authority. The Courts of the Crown have recovered their authority. Jurors are appearing. Magistrates who never functioned are coming back. . . . Sinn Féin patrols, military and police, are gone. The Sinn Féin Courts have disappeared into cellars.' The *Irish Bulletin* (18 Feb.) would have none of this. The Republican Police remained active, it claimed, and the Dáil courts 'still sit and hold many busy sessions. Less publicity is, of course, given to them because members of these Courts have been arrested.'

For his part, Stack sent out a couple of circulars to deputies and a few organisers, requested reports from judges and registrars and then awaited results. But there were no results. After several of the organisers had been arrested, he later explained, 'he saw no good in sending out others in places where the courts were established but allowed to fall through by the local people'. He told Mulcahy on 6 April: 'The North City Judges are attending to their work fairly well. I wish things were as good all over as they are in your "Bailiwick".' There is no evidence that de Valera prodded Stack or took any other action to revive the courts. At the May session of the Dáil Stack complained that his appeal to the deputies had met with a very poor response. He remained hopeful that 'given a fair opportunity' (a British withdrawal?), moribund courts would be back in business 'soon'. Mulcahy saw a lack of initiative on the part of Stack: 'The Organisers sent out by the Belfast Boycott Department had been very successful, and there was no reason why organisers from the Department of Home Affairs should not be sent to districts where the courts were not functioning.' Art O'Connor declared that many more land tribunal sittings would have been held if the local court officials had carried on their responsibilities. De Valera adopted the inspirational approach: 'The enemy Government were afraid of the renewal of the Republican Court activities. . . . The day they got the Courts working again all over the country they had the British beaten.' Stack proceeded to send a message to all local police chiefs in which he urged them to give their active support to the courts, adding that 'our Tribunals are sitting regularly and that we have to see that no cases are litigated in the English Courts, that the enemy has done his worst to destroy the Republican Courts and that he has failed in spite of the murders of several Registrars, Justices and Police'.

At the end of the month Stack's office was raided and its entire contents were seized. In considering the appointment of four provincial organisers in June, the Sinn Féin executive decided that one of their duties would be 'to see that all cases as far as possible are brought in to the Republican Courts'. During the truce Collins was characteristically outspoken about the courts situation: 'During the war there was no proper effort made to keep them going. There was not enough work done locally or at headquarters. He would like to know how many courts were held.' When other deputies joined in a chorus of criticism, de Valera provided a solution — decentralisation of the Republic's administration. 'If they adopted such a scheme,' he declared, 'there would be no complaints about the working of the Home Affairs Department.'[12]

Police

There were also severe problems in the Republican Police. This force was born out of the necessity to fill the gap caused by the retreat and collapse of the RIC in the first half of 1920. At first the Volunteers simply provided some policing, but in June Mulcahy ordered every army unit to appoint a police officer and called for recruits to man the force. Simon Donnelly, de Valera's lieutenant at Boland's Mills in 1916, was appointed national police chief. On 1 November the force was declared an organisation separate from the IRA. Officers appointed to the force 'would be placed on the army reserve and relieved of all routine army service'. Having been placed under the authority of the Home Affairs Department, the newly incorporated body soon foundered. Mulcahy later said that twice the GHQ formed a police force and both times it faded away in the hands of Austin Stack. It was Mulcahy's understanding that the upper ranks of the police force would be provided by the Volunteers, while the Sinn Féin Clubs would provide the lower ranks. It would appear that the Home Affairs Department expected the IRA to set up a complete police force that would run itself, except for the communications service and additional support to be provided by the army. Mulcahy held that Home Affairs did not issue specific instructions and regulations to police supervisors. For his part, Stack blamed the army for not doing enough for the police. Collins later said that the basic problem with the police force was 'the awful personnel that was attracted to its ranks'.

The debate about who did what to whom dragged on into 1921, while the courts and police faded from the scene and the IRA battled on against extermination. In May Mulcahy complained to Brugha about the situation; Brugha, while acknowledging Stack's inertia, counselled patience. By this time Mulcahy recognised that the present circumstances were too serious for the army to do much to assist the police force. In acknowledging that police chiefs had not been appointed in the Donegal brigades as late as April, he complained: 'We are not in a position to put a separate Police Organisation into force in an area like this.' The IRA Director of Organisation was also well aware of the absence of the police, but could offer nothing in the way of co-operation. When Stack asked him for information in March 1921, he replied: 'The Police Organisation when brought into being must use its own Intelligence.' Mulcahy later summed up his view of the situation: 'The whole police question shows a serious attitude towards civil administration on the part of military authorities, and a very irresponsible one in the civil department.' Stack continued to complain that the Volunteers never did enough to help him. At both the March and May sessions urgent pleas were made not to call upon the services of the army except in extreme circumstances. In August Brugha told the Dáil that he 'was tormented trying to get Volunteers to do police work. They had their own special work to do. . . . Police work was the work of the Department of Home Affairs and he did not want to have anything to do with it.' He announced that the Chief of Staff and himself were setting up a new police force which would be handed over to Home Affairs.[13]

Exit Permits

Another problem faced by Stack's department was the rise in emigration. In 1919 less than 3,000 persons had left Ireland, but this figure jumped to 30,000 (half to America and half to Britain) in the following year. From America de Valera in June proposed that an anti-emigration pledge should be taken by all young people at home. 'If we could only get them to stick it out for a year or two . . . .', he sighed, adding: 'The effect here of a large number of young people coming from Ireland will be very bad.' The cabinet responded by asking the President to appeal to the Irish in the United States not to buy tickets for intending emigrants. On 24 July the Home Affairs Department issued a decree prohibiting emigration without a permit from the department. The edict was aimed at 'men of military age'; members of the Volunteers would have to secure a signed statement from their brigade commandant. The Dáil confirmed the decree at its August meeting, although an amendment which stated that it should 'not be enforced pending the formulation of a scheme for providing employment in Ireland for intending emigrants' was defeated by 23 votes to 16, a surprisingly close result for the revolutionary Dáil.

In September 1920 Stack announced that he was tightening up the issuing of exit permits. In the following month his department sent out letters to Irishmen living abroad requesting their assistance in stemming emigration. It urged them not to pay for transportation or provide employment. As for IRA members who left without permission, 'treat them as having evaded the laws of the Republic and fled the country'. The problem of Volunteers who left without authority continued into the following year. In January the department noted that in Britain 'there are hundreds of young Irish men "on the run" at the present moment. Most of these men have gone to centres where there are large Irish populations, and as they have been able to tell pitiful tales of ill-treatment at the hands of the enemy they have succeeded in obtaining aid and comfort from our friends and supporters.' Frederick Dumont noted the outflow in March: 'The raids by armed bodies of Sinn Féiners at Liverpool and Queenstown during the last two months on the boarding houses in which Irish emigrants stop while waiting for boats are only a continuation of the tactics which have been carried on on the line from Galway to Dublin for many months.'

In April the department decided to deal with the problem by ordering shipping companies and agents not to take money from anyone who did not have a permit. Then it was a matter of getting the companies and agents to obey the order. Dumont estimated that the order would have little effect in the cities, where British forces were in control; yet 'Sinn Féin eventually punishes, however, and the agents' business houses will be raided or burned if they carry their disobedience of the order too far'. In June Simon Donnelly, the national chief of police, proposed that where travel agents refused to sign a form pledging them to abide by the order, the Republican Police should be given permission to seize 'all books, correspondence and literature on the premises'. As for the firms that attempted 'to defy the authority of the Republic or adopt a treacherous attitude in informing the enemy, I suggest that the destruction of their premises be carried out'.[14]

Michael Collins told Art O'Brien that the requirement of a permit for anyone leaving Ireland 'is another step in establishing the acceptance of the Government of Ireland'; an IRA man who left without authority 'is a deserter, or what is sometimes worse, an interferer'. O'Brien explained that 'our people here' did not look upon the orders of 'An Dáil as positive or definite. Their mental attitude towards them is probably the same as that which they would assume to the Regulations of a Society.' Despite all the problems, Stack told the Dáil in August that his department's efforts 'have had a very good effect', with the emigration agents 'being made to comply with the law of the Republic' and emigration itself having declined in the previous three months.

A clear but negative achievement of Stack's department was the prevention of the census of 1921. In this matter the Dáil government was determined to show who was boss in Ireland. At its session of March 1921 the Dáil unanimously passed a decree prohibiting the census, which it viewed as 'a usurpation of the rights of the Irish people'. When the British authorities decided not to proceed with the census 'because it would be impossible to obtain complete and accurate returns', the *Irish Bulletin* (8 Apr.) responded with a yelp of triumph: 'This is an ingenuous admission by Dublin Castle of the popular sanction given to the decrees of Dáil Éireann.' Sir John Anderson could only grumble: 'If the Irish people do not want the British Treasury to spend £90,000 in providing them with what other civilised communities think necessary, the money may as well be saved.'[15]

(4) Labour, Boycotts and Agriculture

The Labour Commission

The labour movement and the Dáil government worked in close co-operation throughout the period. Both Labour and Sinn Féin grew together in leaps and bounds after 1916. The leaders on both sides had established a relationship based on trust, mutual self-interest and a body of common objectives. At the time of the establishment of the Dáil the Labour leaders had secured the passage of the Democratic Programme. Thereafter they asked for nothing. Irish unions were involved in a series of strikes and other actions which supported the goal of independence, although in very few cases were these measures initiated by the Labour leaders. In this the situation was comparable to that of the Dáil leaders and ordinary Sinn Féiners. It was the grassroots who took the initiative and the leaders who responded, in apparent surprise and ill-humour.

The growth of organised labour continued to excite speculation about Labour's future actions, particularly in regard to its relationship with the independence movement. In September 1920 Frederick Dumont asserted that 'Sinn Féin's greatest triumphs have been possible only because of the whole-hearted support given Sinn Féin by organized Irish Labor.' Noting the domination of the Transport Union and its attachment to syndicalism, he commented that 'Sinn Féin acknowledges tacitly, if not officially, the One Big Union idea, the probable reason being that Sinn Féin must have the support of Irish Labor at any price.' In view of the continued contacts between Irish Labor and Russian representatives in London, he proposed that 'the American Consuls make a list of persons of Bolchevik [*sic*] tendencies in Ireland in order that visas may be refused these persons should they wish to go to the United States'.

Until the beginning of 1921 everything seemed to be going well for the labour movement. The number of members in unions affiliated to the ILP and TUC had risen to 300,000. Possibilities seemed almost unlimited. Then came the economic disruption caused by repression, the beginning of recession and, with the decline in agricultural prices, a reaction of the farmers against the farm labourers newly organised by the Transport Union.

The Labour leaders were anxious to meet with de Valera upon his return from the United States. They requested a meeting even before he had called together the cabinet. De Valera decided not to meet them personally at this time ('It is always best to keep something in reserve'), but appointed Collins, FitzGerald and Stack as his representatives to meet with William O'Brien, Thomas Johnson and Thomas Farren. At the meeting, held on 16 January, the Labour men had much to say. Johnson reported on his contact with M. Krassin, the Russian Soviet representative in London, and of the campaign of public meetings organised by the British Labour Party which began at that time. The Labour leaders had several suggestions for improving the propaganda campaign in Britain. Most importantly, they requested that the Dáil government adopt a general economic policy.

The proposal apparently met with a favourable response, and the matter was handed over to Joseph McDonagh when he became Minister for Labour at the end of the month. In February he decided to establish a labour commission composed of Johnson, O'Brien, Louie Bennett of the Irish Women Workers' Union, George Russell, Dr Coffey of Maynooth, Alfred O'Rahilly of University College, Cork, Hanna Sheehy-Skeffington, Ernest Blythe and Art O'Connor. On 2 March McDonagh submitted an 'Industrial Scheme' to the cabinet. He told the March Dáil session that the commission had the task of making proposals for a labour policy for the state. It was to produce its report in two months, and he 'thought that the Report should be published throughout Ireland'.

At the beginning of April the ILP and TUC issued a manifesto, *The Country in Danger*, in which it warned that growing unemployment would lead to a violent response by hungry workers. It pointed particularly to farmers who were reducing tillage and labourers' wages. The Irish Farmers' Union wrote to de Valera that the Labour statement 'appears to us to be nothing short of an attempt on the part of a minority of the Irish people to assume functions and powers which even the strongest and most settled Government might well hesitate to use'. The cabinet, determined to 'see what can be done to prevent anything like a class-war developing', called for a conference of the two sides. The President told the farmers' organisation that he was confident 'that the common patriotism of all sections will prove superior to all special class interests'.

At a conference held on 22 April the farmers' representatives declared that 'nothing more could be done for the present year' in regard to tillage. There was agreement 'to give all possible aid' to a turf-cutting scheme. The IFU provided £10,000 for the scheme and appealed to its members not to reduce the area under cultivation and 'only in the very last extremity to disemploy labour'. The Labour representatives could hardly have been satisfied with the results of the conference.

Meanwhile the labour commission had been meeting, and on 9 April McDonagh submitted to de Valera a synopsis of 'a labour scheme for the Irish state' which advocated the development of a 'distributive or co-operative commonwealth'. The guiding spirit behind the proposal was clearly Tom Johnson, for the contents of the document reiterated ideas he had expounded for years. Accepting the need to end 'the present intolerable abuse of Capital Ownership', the proposal argued that a shift to co-operative structures

> would not precipitate an Economic Crisis and it would reinstate the long-ignored Christian Conception of Ownership as a responsible Stewardship, in place of the prevailing Pagan idea as Ownership as

an Absolute, Arbitrary and Irresponsible Power over the World's Sources of Human Sustenance.

There is no record of the response of either de Valera or the cabinet. Together with the labour commission, the scheme disappeared without a trace.

The ILP and TUC made no public objection to the failure of the Dáil government to proceed in this matter. Undoubtedly the Labour leaders were told that the matter of labour policies, and social and economic matters in general, would best be left to more settled times. Despite inviting opportunities to do otherwise, the Labour leadership remained steadily behind the demand for self-government. Curiously, in 1921 — at the height of British repression — there was almost no strike activity in support of the independence movement. Perhaps growing unemployment had made many trade unionists reluctant to endanger their employment, national cause or not.[16]

More Boycotting

In lieu of other duties, the Department of Labour was in charge of the Belfast boycott. Under Joseph McDonagh the campaign against Belfast goods was pursued vigorously. A dozen boycott organisers were appointed, and local boycott committees, with power to impose fines and seize goods, were formed; there were 360 of them by the middle of May; by the summer there were 600. A million circulars and 50,000 posters were distributed. *Old Ireland* (15 Jan.) held that the boycott would have the desired effect: 'Economic partition of Ireland means that the limb lopped off withers away; as Belfast has chosen political partition, she must accept the logical consequences.' In March McDonagh told the Dáil: 'At least seventy per cent of the volume of goods that was leaking through up to three weeks ago has now been stopped and in another month Belfast should be almost altogether cut off.' He believed that 'politically the boycott should react very favourably in connection with the enforcement of Partition in North East Ulster'. One of the difficulties he had to deal with was that of Belfast goods that were transhipped through northern towns not included in the boycott and through British ports. 'The Belfast merchants used every ruse to break the boycott, and a number of cross-channel firms helped them,' he said in August, but a black-list of offending firms effectively dealt with this stratagem. The RIC Inspector-General reported in May that 'English firms are now yielding to [the boycott] and promising to obey the orders of Dáil Éireann'. It was, he said, 'useless to pretend that this is not extremely serious'.

Annoyed by the boycott, General Macready told Sir John Anderson on 12 March: 'It would be a good thing for the Government to say they have had enough of this nonsense and that unless it ceases they will put an embargo on coal for Southern Ireland.' Anderson reminded him that the action began in response to the expulsion of Belfast Catholics about which the British government did nothing effective. McDonagh had said that the boycott of the Belfast-based banks was the most difficult part of the campaign, a view shared by Anderson, who believed it to be 'a most futile proceeding'. The effort against the northern banks was renewed in June when the Dáil government issued an order, copies of which were 'prominently displayed in Dublin and the Provinces declaring notes and cheques on these Banks illegal'. According to the RIC, civilians in Kildare were 'threatened with their houses being burnt unless they withdrew their money from the Ulster Bank, which they did in most cases'. In Tyrone it was said that Belfast cheques and notes were 'to be confiscated after June 7'. Collins contemplated extending the boycott to the Post Office Savings Bank.

The boycott received wide support. The Catholic Bishop of Down and Connor (the diocese in which Belfast is situated) allowed two priests to visit 'all the priests in Ireland in the interests of the Boycott'. There seemed to be an abundance of people who were willing, indeed eager, to investigate the affairs of shopkeepers and others. Discovering contraband and seizing it was, of course, valuable preparation for those who eventually became customs officials. The British directorate of intelligence admitted in May that the boycott 'is growing in intensity and is seriously affecting the trade of the city'. Also noting its effectiveness, Frederick Dumont told the US State Department: 'Bundles of Belfast papers are seized and burned. Freight trains containing Belfast goods are held up at lonely places and the goods taken out and burned. If there is not sufficient time to search the train, cars holding them are burned.' McDonagh told the Dáil that Belfast goods had been destroyed in Gort and Clifden in Co. Galway and 'that shopkeepers dealing with the boycotted firms had their shop fronts decorated'. McDonagh claimed there were more bankruptcies in Belfast in the first six months of the year than in living memory. Seán MacEntee recalled that many prominent Unionist businessmen came to the Belfast committee seeking permits to send goods to the rest of the country.[17]

The cabinet also decided to impose a boycott of British goods. This was a logical extension of the Belfast campaign — and, after all, the government of Dáil Éireann had declared a state of war with the British government. The idea of such a scheme had been around for a long time: it was first considered in May 1919. In September 1920 Ernest Blythe had proposed such a measure. His 'Act for Protection of Irish Industries' stated that when a suitable Irish product was available, his department could 'prohibit retailers from taking into stock any foreign makes of such goods'. When five deputies raised objections about the burden this would place on shopkeepers and the lack of public preparedness, the proposal was handed over to a committee. In January 1921 Blythe told the Dáil that he believed a British boycott would not work, as the decrees might not be obeyed. He favoured a propaganda campaign to get the traders themselves to exclude British goods. It was de Valera's view that a revived Sinn Féin organisation should be asked to mount the propaganda effort.

As in other instances, it was outside agitation that prepared the way for action by the Dáil government. On 15 January *Old Ireland* strongly supported the idea. Other advocates were Maud Gonne MacBride and Kevin O'Shiel, who wrote a series of articles demonstrating the economic effects. McDonagh strongly urged such action in his report to the March session of the Dáil.

By this time the government had decided to act, and the Dáil accordingly passed a decree. Blythe's department was given the task of listing the goods to be banned, a matter he approached with caution and diffidence. He decided to stay away from the obvious items — alcoholic beverages and tobacco. (Ex-publican W. T. Cosgrave thought it would be wrong to exclude Bass ale, as it was 'a medicinal drink'.) Up to the truce of July 1921 Blythe issued five prohibition orders. The first of these, on 23 March, excluded English farm tools and machinery. Frederick Dumont believed that 'The order will cause considerable damage to English trade, as no dealers, for fear of Sinn Féin raids, and no farmers will stock or purchase such articles for the time being, or long enough to gauge the effectiveness of Sinn Féin opposition.' Sinn Féin opposition proved to be effective. Other exclusion orders followed: on biscuits, boot polish, soap, margarine, pictorial calendars, fruit preserves, medicated wines and proprietary ointments. Altogether a total of twelve classes of goods were excluded. De Valera asked the department to see about getting American substitutes for these.

As in the case of the Belfast boycott, enforcement was carried out by the Labour Department, the local Belfast committees and the IRA. As far as the general public was concerned, the Dáil had decreed the prohibition of all English goods. In May Stephen Gwynn observed 'a new form of Republican activity' — the holding up of people to inspect their cigarettes and matches. 'If these are of English make,' he said, 'the owner is liable to have a leg cut off his trousers.' 'These', he noted, 'are some of the steps on the way to freedom.' At the March session of the Dáil McDonagh declared the boycott would require a 'big publicity campaign'; already he had got an understanding from the three Dublin morning newspapers not to print advertisements for Belfast or prohibited British goods.

This boycott also irritated General Macready, who frequently gave attention to matters other than military. He told the British cabinet's Irish Situation Committee on 15 June how to handle the matter: 'He would summon a meeting of the Heads of [Irish] Soap and Biscuit firms and tell them that if they do not tell Dáil Éireann to stop the boycott, they would be closed down.' His own self-respect was involved:

'For instance, it put him in an absurd position to be unable to buy English goods in Dublin, although he was C-in-C of the British forces.' The simple answer to that, of course, was that he was not in Britain. Hoping to cause alarm and dismay, some wag in Dublin Castle issued a bogus prohibition order that excluded all (not just British!) tea, coffee, sugar, motor tyres and rubber goods.

The British boycott appeared to be successful. Art O'Brien reported from London that 'it is creating consternation in the city'. He had been told that wholesalers reported that 'their orders from Ireland, outside Belfast, had gone off completely'. He concluded that 'this economic pressure is going to have an enormous effect'. By August Blythe was enthusiastic about the results. Irish manufacturers of the excluded goods all reported increased orders. Even producers of goods not banned saw an increase— 'as regards cigarettes, the manufacturers have been snowed under'. The scheme had demonstrated that 'a policy of progressively excluding British goods would work a complete industrial transformation'. Moreover, 'if the war is resumed, we will be able to strike a vital blow at the enemy with this policy'.

The Agriculture Department Makes an Appointment
The Agriculture Department, under the circumstances, maintained reasonable activity. Land courts were held and the Land Bank continued to finance land purchases. Art O'Connor was involved in a variety of matters. In June he proposed the establishment of the office of Arbitrator-General and Inspector-General in land matters. To fill this position he nominated Crompton Llewelyn Davies, whom he described as 'an expert in all matters concerning Irish land tenure'. Under the name 'Dalta', Davies had written two pamphlets on the subject and, because of his involvement in the national movement, had been dismissed from his government position in London. O'Connor proposed that Davies receive the highest salary in the Dáil administration (£1,000 per annum), which found no objection from the Finance Minister. Michael Collins, who took a keen interest in Davies and in his Irish-born wife, Moya, strongly supported the appointment: 'It seems to me that we have to take things now on a permanent basis. This is a time when precedents are being made and when much thinking ahead is necessary. . . . I want to get hold of the services of every possible man. I want to bring them all back and have all their work and talent for ourselves.' Although he noted that the salary was high, de Valera approved the appointment.[18]

(5) Childers and the Propaganda Campaign

The arrest of Desmond FitzGerald in February 1921 brought about the necessity for an immediate replacement as head of the Propaganda Department (soon to be renamed the Publicity Department). De Valera wrote to Diarmuid O'Hegarty on 11 February: 'Is there anybody ready to take F's place in his office without disturbing B[ob] B[rennan]? It is most important that there should be no indication of a disorganisation in our propaganda.' The man eventually selected by de Valera was Erskine Childers. From the beginning of 1919 Childers had been actively involved in the creation of the alternative government — first as a press aide in Paris, director of the Land Bank, judge in the Dáil courts, and finally propagandist extraordinaire. His articles in the British press, later published in booklet form, were very effective in their indictment of Dublin Castle policies and practices. The United States consul in Cork told Washington in May 1919 that the statements in one of Childers's letters to the London *Times* (entitled 'A Free Choice for Ireland') 'are worthy of very careful consideration'. Just days before FitzGerald's arrest de Valera again proposed sending Childers to the USA.

Ernie O'Malley observed that the members of the Dáil government 'were very anxious and willing to have his advice and judgment, and to use his psychological knowledge of the British bureaucratic caste'. Childers had been recommended to de Valera by Collins, and the President was deeply impressed; he later said that Childers was the model of what he himself would like to be. Here was a man who was courteous and patient, but also fearless and idealistic; to him principle meant everything.

The appointment was not welcomed by everyone. Griffith viewed Childers as a valuable recruit to be employed in a subordinate position, but he opposed his appointment to a position of power, and specifically this position. He viewed Childers as an Englishman, and he did not believe that Englishmen should hold positions of standing in the organisation. This view was not fully logical, as Childers was a cousin of Robert Barton, who had been accepted as Director of Agriculture, though Barton had much closer connections with Ireland and, despite service in the British army during the war, had had no ties with England, unlike Childers. However, Griffith was now in prison and was therefore not in a position to block the Childers appointment. Another minister who had grave reservations about Childers was Brugha, who on this point found himself in unaccustomed agreement with Griffith. Brugha's distrust of Childers was due to the latter's wartime service as a British intelligence officer. But de Valera had his way, and Childers was appointed.

When Childers's appointment was presented to the Dáil in March, there were objections by Pádraig O'Keeffe and Seán MacEntee that Childers was not a member of the Dáil, to which de Valera replied that there was no necessity that he should be so, as his appointment was that of head of a department, not a minister. The fact of the matter was that there had been a fuzzy line between directors, of whom there were three, and ministers. The directors were for all intents and purposes ministers and attended cabinet meetings. This was the first appointment of a person who was not a member of the Dáil. Moreover, this man was seen by some as a johnny-come-lately to republicanism. Where was he, it was asked, in 1916, in 1917, in 1918?

Some people were disturbed by Childers's manner. Piaras Béaslaí, editor of *An tÓglach*, later commented: 'I was amazed at the impression of fussy, feverish futility he conveyed to me. He displayed the mind, outlook and ability of a capable British civil servant, but no understanding of Ireland or Irishmen, and no adequate appreciation of the situation with which he was dealing.' Béaslaí gives no examples to support this negative assessment, and all his judgments of men and events at that time — just after the civil war — were completely dominated by that event. What he said at the time about the Publicity Department under Childers's direction was most favourable. Another of Childers's colleagues, Robert Brennan, observed that Childers was extremely meticulous, wanting to check and re-check facts and figures, and this could be exasperating at times. De Valera, of course, was the same way.[19]

Collins joined Gavan Duffy in welcoming the change: 'Yes, I think the appointment of E.C. is very happy — I don't know whether you have noticed the change.' Art O'Brien told Childers that the department needed 'someone like yourself to put matters in order there. . . . Up to the present there has been nothing but misunderstanding between this office and the Prop. Dept., and with D.F.'s peculiar ideas of carrying on business there never could be anything but misunderstanding.' Seán T. O'Kelly also applauded the appointment.

In announcing Childers's appointment as Director of Publicity to the Dáil, de Valera asserted that the move would result in the strengthening of the activities of the propaganda campaign: the department was to be reorganised, the scope of activity broadened, and the *Irish Bulletin* was to be expanded and improved. Childers, he said, 'was completely overhauling the Department, and they hoped to extend its work out of all proportion to what it had been doing, especially in foreign countries'.[20]

The major change in the government's policy that Childers sought was for it to state clearly that the Volunteers were the army of the Republic. By not facing this issue squarely, the cabinet was playing into the hands of its opponents — 'a fatal failure because the propaganda of the enemy was that the Army was a "murder gang" and it was only by insisting that it was waging a legitimate war and by basing propaganda on that principle that one could meet the torrent of defamation'. Within a month of Childers being placed in charge of publicity the Dáil accepted de Valera's proposal to issue such a statement. It seems likely that Childers had a hand in bringing about this change.

There were no immediate alterations in the department's publications during his tenure. The *Irish Bulletin* remained largely unchanged, although de Valera told the Dáil that it 'would be got out in better and more extended form'. It was in great demand in England. O'Brien believed 'there are many who would pay a subscription' to get it; Mrs Bernard Shaw asked to put on its mailing list. At the beginning of the year separate foreign editions of the publication began to appear, beginning with a French edition, edited by Seán T. O'Kelly, launched in January. The most important work done by Childers was to write a series of reports summarising the administrative achievements of the Dáil government. Co-ordination with Béaslaí's military propaganda office was improved, and the circulation of *An tÓglach* was expanded to include newspapers, journalists and others. At the same time the IRA Chief of Staff urged all units to ensure the speedy dispatch of reports of all actions so that these could be passed on to the press. Mulcahy told a brigade commander on 13 February: 'Detailed and systematic reports of our operations form the best propaganda and is the stuff most readily accepted by American journalists who are eager to get any word regarding our work in this matter.'[21]

As well as preparing material to be sent to the United States, Childers was also responsible for writing questions to be asked of ministers in the British parliament. He sent the questions to Art O'Brien, who forwarded them to sympathetic MPs, particularly Commander J. M. Kenworthy. Collins, who took an active interest in Childers's work, also sent questions via O'Brien. Another of Childers's activities was 'to induce Irish authors to produce poems and ballads of national interest while representing the culture of Ireland'. The results of this effort are not apparent. Griffith had had the same idea in January 1919: 'Mobilise the poets. . . . Perhaps Yeats [*sic*] would use his muse for Ireland now.' In the summer of 1921 Mulcahy took the artistic and literary communities to task for not fully supporting the national movement, though many literary people did in fact publicly oppose the actions of the British administration and military.

There was strong dissatisfaction within the Dáil about how the nationalist press presented the news. Too often these reports adopted the assumptions of the Castle administration about its legitimacy and failed to take any cognisance of the existence of its rival. The United States consul in Dublin saw the situation from a completely different point of view. In his opinion, the nationalist press consistently employed a hostile view of the Castle administration and failed to provide accurate reports of the violent actions taken by the IRA. This failure was based on both fear and ignorance: 'Little of the real truth of such incidents is known to the Irish Press of Sinn Féin sympathies or to the American correspondents who congregate at these newspaper offices.' Any favourable news from the United States was given exaggerated treatment so that 'every uneducated person of Sinn Féin sympathies or affiliations is convinced thereby that

America is almost ready to take over Ireland's cause in its entirety, financing and supporting her'.

Childers was soon experiencing some of the same problems that confronted FitzGerald. He urged members of the Dáil to collect signed statements from 'the victims of enemy aggression, especially in the case of murders, floggings and attacks on women'. There was very little response from the deputies; at one point Seán MacEntee remarked that it was not their job to go around collecting affidavits. At the next Dáil session — in May — Béaslaí reported that Childers had complained to him that the departments were not supplying him with information for publication. As Volunteer Director of Intelligence, Collins, of course, sent along a lot of material, but he also often provided specific advice as to how the information should be employed. For a report of torture of an IRA prisoner, he suggested that 'it should be taken point by point . . . and rubbed in from day to day. . . . There will be other statements of torture to follow this one when it has had time to sink in.' Material in captured files about problems in the opposing forces 'could be used in the *Óglach* also showing the rotten state of the enemy forces even towards each other'. De Valera was also keenly interested in Childers's work. He instructed all departments to send information on their activities to the Publicity Department and laid down the rule that all official information was to be issued to the public only through that department. In May he asked for an additional messenger to improve communication with Childers's office. At the same time Childers requested each department sending reports to his office for publication to provide four typed or twenty-five duplicated copies in order to speed the delivery of the material into the hands of journalists.

There was also the difficult matter of how to treat some of the actions of the IRA and other agents of the underground government. In February 1921 Mrs Georgina Lindsay, a Cork Unionist, had been captured as a hostage to be exchanged for some IRA men under sentence of death; when the men were executed, Mrs Lindsay was killed. A young woman named Kitty Carroll had been executed as an informer by a local IRA unit at Aughnameena, Co. Monaghan, on 17 April. Childers knew nothing about these matters. Speculation soon arose in the daily press, and Childers saw the necessity to respond. Seeking to get to the bottom of these episodes, he wrote to Collins on 2 May:

> Shall we say (a) the execution of women spies is forbidden, and Kitty Carrol[l] was not killed by the IRA? or (b) Kitty Carrol[l] was killed in contravention of orders by the IRA, and that (c) Mrs Lindsay is now in prison for giving information to the enemy?

It took him a long time, but he eventually dragged the unpleasant facts out of Collins and published them in the *Bulletin*.[22]

There was also the familiar problem of security; the forces of the other side were constantly on the prowl. When Robert Brennan declared that a group of journalists would not be a 'security threat in a certain matter', de Valera commented: 'I am not pleased with Bob's taking it for granted that journalists can be trusted in this way.' On 26 March the Publicity Department's offices were discovered and all contents seized, including the printing-press. The President ordered O'Hegarty to get another printing machine at once: 'Do not let the enemy feel that he has completely disorganised us. We should be out with something to show business as usual.' Although Childers was not on hand when the raid took place, de Valera advised him to keep away from his office for a time, commenting that Childers was 'so easy to track down — a man on the run is far safer'. Frederick Dumont believed the raid had 'dealt a very heavy blow to Sinn Féin'; nevertheless, the next edition of the *Irish Bulletin* appeared on schedule.[23]

Among the things carted away to Dublin Castle were the typewriters and duplicating machine, and one of the British propagandists decided that it would be a clever idea to produce bogus issues of the *Bulletin*. The ploy failed, as the content was obviously not something a convinced Sinn Féiner would write, and, furthermore, Childers's staff secured the testimony of an expert who concluded that the bogus issues were produced on the seized equipment. The Castle's effort was condemned by, among others, the London *Times*. The Castle propagandists found another use for the bogus *Bulletins* — it drew on the spurious reports contained in them in order to provide the basis for the false statements it had posted around the south and midlands. To the genuine *Irish Bulletin* the lesson of the episode was clear: 'That the Headquarters of the British Government should be forced by circumstances to adopt forgery in an attempt to sustain its authority is an evidence of how completely that authority is repudiated by the people.'

There were some serious problems in Britain. At the Dáil session of September 1920 Joseph McDonagh declared that the Irish Self-Determination League there had achieved negligible results and that 'the leaders there seem to approach all questions with an air of hopelessness'. Griffith was instructed to inform the ISDL of the Dáil's desire for a more vigorous campaign. The organisation certainly was small — 27,000 members at its height. At its annual conference later in that month the body voted for the development of a propaganda scheme, but nothing came of this. When Childers requested a report on propaganda activities for the previous three months, O'Brien's reply was that the London office was completely out of all literature and that repeated requests for further supplies had been ignored. If the British organisation could not reprint pamphlets on its own, then it was almost totally useless.[24]

O'Brien had long been operating under great pressure. In October 1920 his health broke down, and he had long bouts of illness over the next few months. On 17 November he received a message from 'Black and Tan' to clear out of London in twenty-four hours: 'We won't allow you to live a free life in London at the price of the blood of Irish police.' Two weeks later his office was raided by Scotland Yard and all its records were impounded. January saw the beginning of the the arrest and deportation to Ireland of about a hundred supposed ISDL leaders. O'Brien wrote to his Dublin correspondent: 'Nobody knows two-thirds of the names on the list. The secret service men must be very rotten.' De Valera recognised the need to shore up the London office. On 24 April he told O'Brien: 'I am afraid we have been "Penny wise and Pound foolish" in overworking our representatives.' Collins also recognised the problems of the campaign in Britain. The appropriation for the London office was increased to £4,000. Although O'Brien evaded arrest, his office was disrupted; yet he resisted attempts to shift him to Spain. But the ISDL's efforts were effectively crippled. By the summer of 1921 its membership had declined to 20,000.

The propaganda campaign on the continent appeared to be gaining strength. The Paris office, under Seán T. O'Kelly's direction, became a centre for the publication of literature in various European languages. With the financial and editorial assistance of the Paris staff, a book by Yann Goblet (pseudonym of Louis Trequiz), *Ireland and the Universal Crisis*, was published in French in 1920 and republished in the following year. Another useful book to appear in both French and English at this time was Roger Chauvire's (pseudonym of Sylvain Briollay) *Ireland in Rebellion*. When in June Seán O'Faolain volunteered his services, O'Kelly commented: 'I am sure I shall find useful work for him to do in a quiet way.' The French edition of the *Bulletin* was followed by German, Swiss and Spanish editions in the spring. Hungarian and Czech translations were prepared, and there were plans to produce Bulgarian, Serbian, Greek Croatian and Romanian editions, with the work for central Europe to be co-ordinated from an office in Vienna. Maura O'Brien became press representative in Madrid. In February the Irish Republican Association of South Africa began producing a fortnightly review, *The Republic*. In Denmark the department's press agent, Gerald O'Loughlin, was ordered by the police to cease propaganda work; at the same time the cabinet provided him with a grant to publish a book in Danish on the Irish struggle.[25]

De Valera's Spanish background was employed to gain public attention. In February the *Weekly Summary*, quoting a British propaganda sheet, the *Western News*, declared that 'Valera belongs to a race of treacherous murderers and he has inducted Ireland into the murderous treachery of his race.' The President quickly informed the Spanish ambassador of this statement and instructed Maura O'Brien to 'have a number of Spaniards ready to follow it up by protests against the insult', while he also told Art

O'Brien to contact all Spanish-language journalists in London. Gavan Duffy found broad support for Irish self-government during his visit to Spain, and there was speculation there that de Valera was the grandson of the novelist and literary critic Don Juan Valera.

On 9 May Childers and Frank Gallagher were arrested in Childers's home and taken to Dublin Castle. Following the intervention of Alfred Cope, both were released that night. Collins was correct in reporting that 'There was a regular "action" inside [the Castle] between the military and civil chiefs, the former wanting to hold him, the latter insisting on release.' Art O'Brien wanted to know 'Why were the civil people so anxious to let him go? Were they afraid of consequences? And if so in what direction?' , to which Collins replied: 'I cannot say I properly understand what the reason for the release was. Their ways are very extraordinary. I fancy myself that the civil forces took a longer and more incisive view.' After this episode Childers 'went on the run', but the *Irish Bulletin* continued to appear on schedule.

Childers told the Dáil in the summer that he had strong evidence of mounting support for Irish self-government in the European press: 'In one batch 117 papers were taken. They came from practically every nation in Europe. Only eight of these could be definitely described as hostile to Ireland. Forty-eight could be described as definitely in favour of Ireland, and the remainder, about sixty, were neutral, but gave great emphasis to Irish news and, on the whole, acted fairly.' Of course, this broad press support was not due solely to the efforts of the Publicity Department. The country had a just case for self-government. But the case had to be made, and the department and its overseas agents were effective in making it.[26]

(6) FOREIGN FIELDS

Developing Diplomatic Organisation

De Valera was convinced that the government needed to expand its diplomatic network in Europe to such a degree as to match the organisation it had in the United States. The first thing he sought to do was to strengthen its administration in Dublin. Diarmuid O'Hegarty reported: 'The President is anxious to set up something that might correspond to a real Department of Foreign Affairs.' George Gavan Duffy, late of Paris and Brussels, was instructed to make a wide tour of European countries and submit 'as full a report as you can give on the whole European situation from which our general foreign policy with respect to continental groups, no less than our propaganda in several countries, might be determined'.

The need to improve administration was obvious. Count Plunkett, demoted to Associate Foreign Secretary while Griffith was in charge, was not a vigorous executive. Up to this point 'the work of the department was done in the office of the General Secretary', who could only give the department a fraction of his time. There were constant complaints from the overseas representatives about the long delay in getting responses to their messages. De Valera decided to fill the gap with Robert Brennan, the Sinn Féin Director of Propaganda, who was given the (American) title of Under-Secretary of State. Brennan was appointed in February 1921 and gathered together a staff of five. The President urged him to work closely with the Director of Propaganda: 'It is as much his department as yours. It is in fact what I have called the "Statistical" or permanent-value department of propaganda.' He instructed Brennan to attend all cabinet meetings.

A month later Brennan informed the foreign representatives that the President requested 'information immediately to enable the Department of Foreign Affairs to know exactly the activities of the Missions'. This was going to be a businesslike operation. All of the overseas offices were to submit monthly reports and accounts. In addition, they were to respond promptly to communications from the head office. The casual ways of communications were to cease: all messages from abroad were to be sent to Brennan's office. Security was tightened: 'Communication on matters of state with unauthorised persons is strictly forbidden. Discussion of policy or criticisms must be addressed to the Ministry direct.'

Brennan was soon having problems. He failed to maintain a numbering system for his correspondence. He used the Post Office, rather than secure couriers, for London communications. Before six months had passed he had a recurrence of nervous exhaustion and could not work effectively. Nervous breakdowns were an occupational hazard in the Dáil administration.[27]

The reports from all of European representatives declared that there was growing public, political and press support for Irish self-government. In terms of organisation, the major problem on the continent continued to be Germany. Attempts to set up a proper organisation remained unfulfilled. After his run around Europe at the beginning of 1921 Gavan Duffy reported on the position in Germany: 'I found the Germans exceedingly friendly, but the agencies are bad and knowledge scanty. There is a certain amount of admiration here, as everywhere else, for the magnificent bravery of our fight, but I think the predominant factor in sustaining interest is a lively sense of our potential value to the enemies of England.' At that time Thomas St John Gaffney was nominated to be head of the Berlin office, but because of his difficulties with the United States government he could not immediately go to Germany. Later, in March, he took over the office in Switzerland.

The man who was finally appointed to head the German mission was John Chartres, a puzzling figure. Born in England, the son of a British army officer, Chartres had for years been in charge of the London *Times* index. During the war he served as an intelligence officer in the Ministry of Munitions, and in 1919 he came to Dublin to work as an 'intelligence and statistical officer' in the British Ministry of Labour. At the same time his wife, Annie Vivanti, was working for the Irish mission in Paris. He made it known to certain Sinn Féin leaders, some of whom he had known previously, that he was now committed to Irish national- ism. Neither his wife or himself had any Irish connection, but both were readily accepted by the leadership; others were deeply suspicious of Chartres. It seems apparent that he was a British intelligence agent, but from now on he would be (also?) helping the other side. Robert Brennan had met him in Griffith's office several times and considered him to be 'a very valuable under-cover agent for Sinn Féin'. Chartres became a close acquaintance of Collins, and Piaras Béaslaí later reveal- ed that he did 'much valuable work of a confidential nature' for Collins. He apparently was well known to others in the Dáil govern- ment. In July 1920 Gavan Duffy in Paris assumed that Chartres would be appointed to head the press bureau in Geneva that was under con- sideration. After the killing of the group of British intelligence agents in Dublin on 'Bloody Sunday' in November 1920 Chartres resigned from his government position and left Ireland, probably going to Italy to see his wife. Collins began a search for him in February 1921, at one point declaring: 'He is a man whom we ought to be able to make good use of somewhere.' He was in Rome in May and did not take up his appointment in Berlin until the end of June 1921.

Georges Chatterton Hill, despite the cloud over him, continued to do propaganda work, probably because there was no one else there to do it. In approving Chartres's appointment, de Valera told Collins that 'Hill's reputation is so bad that I am afraid to leave the arrangements loose in any way.' Dr Nancy Wyse Power was appointed head of the press office. At the same time a Colonel Emerson was appointed financial director and Thomas Gaffney rejoined the staff. At last there was an adequate Irish mission in Germany.[28]

The Anglo-Irish struggle continued to be waged in one of its principal European battlegrounds — Rome. Here Gavan Duffy remained in vigilant opposition to all British efforts to secure a Vatican condemnation of the independence movement in general and the IRA in particular. In January he found out that there appeared to be a real threat of Vatican action. Duffy contacted Archbishop Clune, who was then in Rome, and Clune almost immediately had an audience with the pope. Mrs Gavan Duffy later reported that from various sources she had learned that Benedict XV 'was immensely impressed by Dr Clune, the murder of his nephew, his admira- tion for our leaders, in particular Mick Collins, his testimony of the religious faith of our Republicans'. Collins told O'Brien on 28 January: 'I have been, in a vague way, aware that the English were making every effort to secure such a pronouncement. It is, after all, their age-old way of doing things.' De Valera decided that, if the reports he was receiving were correct, he would see the Archbishop of Dublin. At the same time he was wary of issuing any threats against the church: 'The suggestion about Peter's Pence and Dues no good — that would not be the way to win if this contest is before us. That would follow as a matter of course from the people themselves.' Collins agreed entirely with this position.

At this point the President decided to take advantage of one of his American contacts. On 2 February he wrote to Archbishop Hayes of New York, who was about to visit Rome, of the consequences of such action. While in Rome Hayes 'warned the Vatican of an explosion among Catholics in the States if any pronouncement is made against Ireland'. Meanwhile the Irish bishops, through Bishop O'Doherty of Clonfert, sent a message to the effect 'that the Papacy and Ireland will not stand another Parnell pronouncement'. On 17 February Mrs Gavan Duffy reported that the British agents were conducting a 'filthy campaign against us': 'Roger [Casement]'s supposed "diary" has been sent over here to show the Vatican the type of leaders we follow.' Now, however, there was a much more friendly view of the Irish struggle in the church headquarters. When Archbishop Mannix met with the pope in May, Benedict extolled the Catholicism of the Irish people and contributed to a collection for Irish relief.[29]

The Dáil representatives continued to have regular contact with a variety of European and Asian nationalist groups. The Dáil government provided a subsidy to a paper published by a Scottish independence movement, in exchange for which it got a page of Irish coverage. Art O'Brien told Seán T. O'Kelly: 'You should make a point of seeing all our Breton friends in Paris; they have a very much better appreciation of our position than any other group in France and are more likely to give their sincere help.' Gavan Duffy advised Dublin to steer clear of a conference of oppressed nationalities organised by Flemish nationalists, because participation would irritate the French and Belgian governments. He thought it was best to work with the nationalities within the British empire.

The Irish envoys, particularly O'Brien and O'Kelly, maintained their advisory services to these very groups. O'Brien developed a relationship with the Burmese independence organisation in London. One of the Burmese told him after the death of Terence MacSwiney: 'The more the British people persist in this brutal attitude, the better for Irish freedom.' He also was in contact with a group of Indian revolutionaries. He told Collins in March 1921: 'They asked us if we could do anything for them. Please go ahead with any questions that may suggest themselves to you. They may give us further ground to work on.' What the Indians wanted was direct IRA assistance; Collins, for one, was prepared to pursue the matter. In December Emmet Dalton and Liam Tobin joined O'Brien in London at a meeting with the Indians, the result of which was an agreement to send an IRA representative to India. In the end, however, no agent was sent.[30]

New ground was broken in Australia and South Africa at this time. Osmond Grattan Esmonde, who was appointed counsellor in the Washington legation in the autumn of 1920, travelled to Australia in the following February and later went on to New Zealand. A support organisation was in existence in Australia, but did not succeed in raising much money. In August 1921 the Australian group had £20,000 on hand, but was not sure how it should be sent to Ireland. The Bishop of Melbourne, Dr Barry, suggested putting it in a bank and using the interest to produce publicity material. Robert Brennan thought this was 'a ridiculous proposition'. Collins responded that the funds could be transmitted by cable. The Dáil was told at that time that things were going well in Australia: 'Press extracts go to show that the League is gaining ground in support despite big opposition.' In New Zealand the Labour Party endorsed the demand for Irish self-determination.

In the spring of 1921 Esmonde travelled to Canada, where on his arrival at Vancouver he was arrested on a charge of sedition and was ordered to be deported. The Dáil department commented: 'We have been officially informed through the United States that the allegation contained in the charge was faked — that Mr Esmonde gave no undertaking on arriving at Vancouver, and that he made no speech in public.' Of course, reports of his activities in Australia and New Zealand had preceded him. The Dáil government did not appoint a Canadian envoy, but there was an active self-determination organisation there, headed by the remarkable Lindsay Crawford.

Nothing was done to establish a presence in South Africa until a relatively late stage. According to American consular reports, efforts in 1919 to develop an Irish independence organisation and collect money 'met with such a cool response that nothing further was done in the matter'. The organisation, however, eventually took shape in the following year. In March 1921 the Irish Republican Association of South Africa proposed a world conference of Irishmen. De Valera immediately accepted the idea, pointing out that 'I have had that world conference of the race idea in mind for a long time,' but adding that he had wanted to wait until organisations had been formed in the various countries; now, he declared, the time was right. In the same month two Dáil representatives were dispatched. P. J. Little was a Sinn Féin journalist and politician, while Colonel Maurice Moore had fought in the Boer War and had many acquaintances in South Africa, including the Prime Minister, Jan Smuts. They quickly had problems with communications with Dublin. When in June they asked to whom funds should be sent to in Ireland, Michael

Collins commented: 'Surely to goodness an Envoy of ours ought to have this information.' A similar request about sending relief funds to Ireland also irritated the Finance Minister: 'It is nonsense that the White Cross funds should not be sent openly — this is the kind of mystery business that gets things banned.' Little reported that 'The Dutch papers are favourable to Ireland. The English papers are entirely Jingo.' Moore noted that 'The majority of Irish are favourable, but are followers of General Smuts. They are mostly quite ignorant on the Irish question, but may be redeemed by the present movement.'

South America also received more attention in 1921. In the previous year de Valera had proposed a speaking tour there. The consular and propaganda activities were increased, and Laurence Ginnell travelled from the United States as an envoy 'to the Argentine and the other South American Republics [and] was present by official invitation at the *Te Deum* to commemorate the Independence of Peru'.[31]

The American Mission in the Doldrums
As can be expected, affairs remained lively in the United States, and even from the other side of the Atlantic de Valera continued to make his contribution to the situation. The American commission of inquiry, after three months of hearings, issued its first report in April 1921 in which it condemned the actions of British forces in Ireland. The American Committee for Relief in Ireland (ACRI), set up in December 1920, began a nationwide collection of funds in March. Another influential organisation was the American Association for the Recognition of the Irish Republic (AARIR), launched in November, which scheduled a national convention in April. To complete this extensive programme of activity, the Dáil government planned a second loan effort in the USA for the autumn of the year.

With the development of these organisations, de Valera believed it was now possible and necessary to reduce the expenses of the Irish mission. On 8 April, while offering James O'Mara the position of official representative in the United States, de Valera advised him that the cost of the Irish mission would have to be reduced to $150,000 for the fiscal year ending in June 1921 and $100,000 annually for the next year. To some in the Irish mission this two-sided message was seen as a 'well-thought-out plan to provoke O'Mara into resigning', to be followed by shifting Boland, leaving Diarmuid Fawsitt, the 'only person remaining and very much *persona grata* with Chief', as the principal link with Dublin. O'Mara had had some difficulties with Fawsitt and de Valera in the preceding year, as a result of which he almost resigned. Now O'Mara took de Valera's offer under advisement, although he made clear his view that the budget reductions ordered by de Valera would render ineffective the organisation of a new loan campaign.

The AARIR duly held its convention in April. It received an unexpected message from de Valera: he requested that the organisation pledge itself to provide a million dollars a year to the Dáil government; specifically he called for each member to contribute five dollars annually (with the organisation claiming 500,000 members, this would amount to $2,500,000 a year). De Valera had brought the proposal before the cabinet on 6 April, but obviously it came as a bolt from the blue to O'Mara and the convention. O'Mara immediately voiced his total rejection of the proposal in a heated telegram in which his anger and contempt spilled over:

> There are nearly $3,000,000 lying idle here to the credit of the American Trustees and at the disposal of your Government. . . . Your appeal now makes impossible any attempt later this year to raise the $20,000,000 loan which was contemplated. To use your own words, 'Crops will not grow on trampled land'. I would advise you to promptly send someone to this country who has your confidence, if such a person exists; and having done so, don't constantly interfere with his work.

Cable activity between Dublin and New York was heavy for the next few days. On 30 April O'Mara sent the President a terminal message: 'Your dispatches indicate your final decision to force through your policy which last December received the almost unanimous condemnation of the Irish Mission here.' To bridge over the matter, de Valera appointed O'Mara's brother, Stephen, the new Lord Mayor of Limerick, to replace him. At the same time he hoped that James O'Mara would remain as financial agent for the new loan. Despite many requests that he continue this work, O'Mara refused. He sent a circular letter explaining his view of what happened to Collins, O'Kelly, Bishop Fogarty and others. He declined to stand for election to the second Dáil or as a trustee of Dáil Loan funds and returned to Ireland in early July.

The national executive of the AARIR on 25 May sent de Valera a message pledging the people of Ireland 'its fullest support, moral and financial', but there is no record of the organisation sending any money to Ireland. Why did de Valera request a million dollars annually when $3,000,000 was at hand and a major relief fund was just under way? Was O'Mara right in coming to a negative conclusion concerning de Valera's judgment of American affairs and his executive ability? Probably the President saw this as a good opportunity to get the new organisation to make a specific commitment. In fact the AARIR was a financial drain. It had borrowed $10,000 from the Irish mission initially, and de Valera wanted it to raise money on its own. He wrote to Collins on 21 May: 'Spoon feeding has to stop; they should be able to get the money from their own organisation.' In requesting the pledge of a million dollars, however, he certainly did nothing to co-ordinate his action with the members of the Irish mission.[32]

On several occasions in 1921 de Valera felt the need to explain the heavy expenditures and the disposition of funds collected in the United States. He told the Dáil in March that of the $1,400,000 spent in the USA, a large proportion 'was really chargeable to world propaganda' and for 'preparing the ground work for a new loan'. His awareness of criticism on this score was a major factor in his decision to reduce American expenditure. Despite these reassurances, Collins remained dubious about the position of the American funds. He told de Valera on 30 May: 'Between ourselves I may say that I have a very nervous feeling about our American accounts.'

The President remained under attack from the enemies he had made during his time in America. A prominent member of the Friends of Irish Freedom stated openly in January that de Valera should send all the loan money to Ireland rather than leave millions in American banks under his control. As the membership of the FOIF collapsed, its national president, Bishop Gallagher fired off a desperate salvo in April. The AARIR, he declared, was spending

> thousands upon thousands of dollars trying to wipe out the Friends of Irish Freedom. Anyone who suggests that De Valera is not master of the people of Irish blood everywhere; or that, like ordinary mortals, he ever made a mistake in his whole life, is overwhelmed with billingsgate and foul abuse in the De Valera press.

John Devoy used his *Gaelic American* to broadcast the idea that de Valera's leadership in Ireland was under serious challenge and that Collins was the real leader. To refute these charges, all members of the cabinet and army general staff signed a 'statement of solidarity' on 24 June which declared that 'the Republican policy as set forth by the President is our policy'.

There were some indications that the campaign for Irish self-government in America was beginning to falter in 1921. The public was apparently losing interest. Yet support activities were at their height. Referring to this campaign in March, Frederick Dumont commented: 'It can be seen how dangerous this propaganda has become.' Several resolutions were introduced in Congress to recognise the Irish Republic. Senator Robert LaFollette launched a public campaign with this objective in April. The British government was told by its ambassador of the mounting condemnation of British actions. In January Sir Auckland Geddes sent 'a most gloomy account of the situation in America'. President Harding was informed by a visitor in June that 'England is irritated continually by the pro-Irish attitude of much public expression in this country.' Harry Boland was brimming with optimism when at the end of March he wrote to de Valera predicting that a new loan drive 'would be most popular' and noting that 'as the struggle in Ireland grows, so the spirit of approval in America grows with it'.

Irish-American backing remained strong, and the British government had to live in fear of outbursts in American public opinion and the actions of American politicians. In terms of international perceptions, the proponents of Irish freedom in America won the battle hands down. The Irish had a fully integrated existence in the country. There was substantial anglophile sentiment, but this could not be effectively mobilised as a counter-force in the face of the public perception of what the British forces were doing in Ireland. It ultimately occurred to some people in Britain that its government would have to choose between trying to keep control of Ireland and trying to maintain good relations with the USA. It could not have it both ways. Given the industrial, financial and political supremacy of America, the choice was obvious.[33]

The American Committee for Relief in Ireland

In late 1920 the Irish mission in the United States was considering some sort of American-based relief campaign. Both the American Red Cross and the Knights of Columbus were approached. Harry Boland believed that the latter 'was a wonderful organisation and have plenty of money. . . . Between the Commission [of inquiry] and the securing of the K. of C. to go to Ireland, it will make it very awkward for the British to keep up their atrocities.' In order to provide immediate relief and have effective control of the body, the idea of Dr William Maloney that a separate relief organisation be set up was adopted. It was established in December 1920, with the enthusiastic support of a group of wealthy Irish-Americans.

The strategy was clear and simple: it was based on the principle of the double punch. First the commission of inquiry would build a case against the British forces; this would then be followed by a relief effort to make good the harm done by those forces. The relief organisation was to operate hard on the heels of the commission, which would provide the ammunition for the relief publicity campaign. The commission began its work in November and amassed evidence of serious British misconduct, evidence that would convince anyone who wanted to be convinced. Now came their chance to do something about it. This would be an operation without any direct political identification. The loan drive, of course, provided support for the rebel republic; the new campaign, by contrast, would have every appearance of a non-partisan, humanitarian effort. It would have the further advantage of collecting donations, not loans to be repaid.

The relief scheme, in fact, was largely a political ploy. The funds raised would be used to help refugees and unemployed and to repair damaged or destroyed facilities and houses. No one claimed that the IRA was responsible for this destruction; it had damaged and destroyed some police stations, government offices and roads, but little more than that. Almost all the harm done to people and property was done by the agents of the British government. The rationale behind the relief fund was that the damage was so extensive that it would require international aid. The Irish themselves, with some real effort could have easily provided for the unemployed and the refugees; in fact they were largely doing that. The property damage was extensive, but this too could have been made good out of Irish resources. The relief scheme had the political impact of drawing American attention to the actions of British forces in the country and thus putting pressure on the British government. In addition, it drew Americans and America directly into the Anglo-Irish conflict.

The American Committee for Relief in Ireland (ACRI) was established with a temporary committee on 16 December 1920 at the Bankers' Club in New York; an executive committee was formed two weeks later. Included in those appealing for help were the Catholic Archbishops of Cashel, Dublin and Tuam, Lord Mayor O'Callaghan of Cork, and James Douglas, a prominent Dublin Quaker. The executive committee soon grew to include leaders of government, religion, labour and just about everything else; it was 'the most eminent collection of patrons ever assembled by an Irish-American organisation'.

Clement J. France, a Seattle lawyer with experience in wartime relief programmes, was appointed administrator of the scheme. His family was already strongly committed in the Anglo-Irish conflict. One of his brothers was a United States senator who was a strong advocate of Irish independence, while another was on the executive committee of the American commission of inquiry. France proposed sending a group of relief workers, but the executive decided to begin by collecting money. Edward L. Doheny, a wealthy oilman (who later went to prison as a result of the Teapot Dome scandal) and already president of the AARIR, contributed $10,000 and provided a guarantee for $250,000 in contributions. On 4 January the committee voted to send $50,000 to Ireland immediately; this money was paid over to James Douglas in Dublin.

The next move was the dispatch of France, Samuel J. McCoy, the secretary of ACRI, and six prominent American Quakers to Ireland, where they arrived on 12 February. They were given a frosty reception by Frederick Dumont, who told them that they were only there through the permission of the British government, 'which, as far as the American Government was concerned, was the only recognized authority in Ireland'. Nevertheless, one of the first things they did was to request an interview with President de Valera, who received them cordially on 17 February. The delegation declined a luncheon invitation from General Macready and would only meet secretly with Sir John Anderson and himself, explaining that they could not contact them openly as this would have destroyed their usefulness. Macready told them there could be no question of relief distribution in martial law areas, owing to the fact that the people in those areas were in a state of rebellion; financial aid would not help to 'bring these people to their senses'. Both Macready and Anderson were opposed to the payment of doles, since these would go to 'relieve the IRA war chest', but did approve of funds being used for reconstruction of damaged or destroyed plant and equipment. During the forty-three days the group was in Ireland it visited ninety-five communities in twenty-two counties.

At the same time an Irish relief organisation, the Irish White Cross, was established to receive the American aid. Founded on 1 February, it had Cardinal Logue as President, Lord Mayor O'Neill as chairman, and as members of the executive committee Michael Collins, Arthur Griffith, W. T. Cosgrave and Erskine Childers, among others; James Douglas served as honorary treasurer. In the eyes of Macready, the inclusion of Collins, who took an active interest in the organisation's affairs, proved that it was nothing more than a Sinn Féin front. Anticipating that it would use at least a substantial part of the relief money for rebuilding, the White Cross, with Dáil cabinet approval, appointed a Reconstruction Commission in April. In fact most of the money was used for personal assistance.[34]

As the delegation studied conditions in Ireland, the publicity campaign was being cranked up in the United States. A *Proposed Outline of Publicity*, which looks like the work of Dr Maloney, advised that the appeal should be geared 'to show that the people are worthy of help and that Ireland, standing alone, is a going concern'. Maloney produced a sixteen-page illustrated booklet, *A Summons to Serve from the Women and Children of Ireland*. The fund-raising effort was launched on St Patrick's Day, with the objective of raising $10 million. The campaign received the support of President Harding, Vice-President Coolidge and Secretary of Commerce Herbert Hoover, who had made his reputation in distributing aid to Belgium during the world war. The American Red Cross, which at first had resisted, was pressured into contributing $100,000.

When the campaign drew to a close five months later, $5,250,000 had been collected. The money was sent to Ireland in instalments several times a month. Some of the initial supporters soon drew back when they discovered its essentially political purpose, but these defections did little to blunt the public perception that a major campaign was under way to help a suffering people. The Irish White Cross also received £62,000 directly from supporters in the United States, another £62,000 in Ireland, £29,000 from other countries, and £5,000 from Pope Benedict XV.

At the end of March ACRI issued its first report, following closely on the interim report of the commission of inquiry, stating that there were 100,000 Irish people 'who are in pitiful need of instant help' and that 'material damage to Irish shop-buildings, factories, creameries and private dwelling houses inflicted by British forces in the last twelve months amounts approximately to $20 million'. The British embassy quickly labelled the statement as 'inaccurate and unfounded', adding that 'every case of distress and destitution is directly due to the effects of the Sinn Féin rebellion'. The *Manchester Guardian* had a different perception: 'It is to be hoped that the English people will realise the full ignominy of this charitable movement. It is as though Ireland were Armenia and we the Turks.'

In April Dublin Castle prohibited Irish donations to the relief fund. De Valera quickly told the Publicity Department that the proclamation should be used to demonstrate 'an effort to prevent aid to sufferers'. Then the Castle decided that it would refuse to have the funds distributed through the White Cross. ACRI sent Samuel J. McCoy to ask the US State Department to administer the relief. When this proposal was laid before the British government, Lord Curzon joined with Hamar Greenwood in rejecting the idea. Charles Evans Hughes, the new US Secretary of State, told the British ambassador that if the British government tried to prevent the distribution of relief funds, this action 'would rebound seriously on American opinion and hence on Anglo-American relations'. Ultimately Dublin Castle backed down and the White Cross distributed the money.

Only a small portion of the funds was handed out before the truce of July 1921. The White Cross explained that until that time 'it was virtually impossible for any person to travel about Ireland and report accurately on the need for relief'. While the campaign of reprisals was being continued, 'the Military looked with suspicion on any who might be attempting to repair their work of destruction'. Yet the fact that substantial resources were on hand and soon to be dispersed was a source of encouragement to both those who had suffered and those who were working for national independence.

Of the £1,374,795 that was distributed from the truce to August 1922, £804,000 went towards personal relief. Belfast got almost half of this amount, with a street being renamed 'ACRI Street' in honour of the organisation, while Cork got £170,000. The White Cross's Reconstruction Commission provided 650 loans totalling £243,000, almost all of it for rebuilding houses. Hopes that a substantial sum would be available for industrial reconstruction were not fulfilled.[35]

(7) Terrorists and Freedom Fighters

At the brief Dáil session of 21 January Frank Fahy asked two disconcerting questions about the position of the Volunteers: were they being cowed, and what chance did they have of holding out for another year? That a deputy minister should ask such questions demonstrates either that he was completely out of touch with the affairs of his government, or that he was reflecting a public perception that the British forces were getting the upper hand. This was the view of General Strickland, who declared at that time that the IRA was in a state of dissolution and that it was only a matter of a short time before it would cease to be an organised military body.

The first major measure de Valera took in regard to the army after his return from America was to acknowledge publicly that it was the official army of the Irish Republic. The President secured Dáil approval for this position on 11 March and made his public announcement of it at the end of the month. In doing so, he presented the matter as simply a reaffirmation and clarification of a relationship that had existed since the establishment of Dáil Éireann and the consequent oath of allegiance taken by all members of the Volunteers. This public affirmation was obviously reassuring to many volunteers. Even before de Valera's statement, in January, Oscar Traynor, commandant of the Dublin Brigade, told the leaders of the active service units: 'The Government of the Republic will accept full responsibility for your operations against the enemy and for your future welfare.' At the March Dáil session Mulcahy made the interesting point that such acknowledgment was timely, as the Volunteers had demonstrated that they would fight; with their effectiveness apparent, the Dáil would be on safe ground acknowledging them.

The Volunteers operated with severe difficulty during the British counter-offensive, but they did nonetheless operate; in fact, once the initial effect of British repression wore off, the IRA became more vigorous, initiating more actions. If the low point came in early November, the revival was well under way by March. In that month Lord Midleton told the British cabinet: 'No civilian that I have met will admit that we have gained in the last six months. If the resistance in last July is indicated by 100, then the resistance can now be put at 300. . . . Things have gone back since last November.' Thomas Jones, the British Cabinet Secretary, noted in April that Hamar Greenwood 'has dropped his optimism of six months ago and talks of pacification in years rather than months', adding his own comment: 'The tenacity of the IRA is extraordinary.'

There was always the danger that enemy intelligence would penetrate the organisation. British agents had attempted this, but with little success. A new approach was introduced in 1921. In February Art O'Brien passed on a report to Collins that the British authorities 'have sent 250 lady spies to Ireland'. In Collins's view, 'The number you give is an understatement altogether. I think there are probably ten times as many.' He held that these agents might have been Irish, but not Irish patriots: 'They will not and cannot get Irish girls to do this class of work for them.' There is no evidence that Irish Mata Haris or *femmes fatales* had any measurable influence on the course of events; on the other hand, women agents passed on lots of information to the IRA and the Dáil authorities. In April Sir John Anderson agreed with the idea of General Macready that agents of British insurance companies should be used to provide information, although he warned: 'The thing would have to be very carefully worked to avoid exposing individuals to risk.' Nothing further was heard of the idea. At the beginning of July Collins informed William O'Brien of the Transport Union that British agents, posing as trade union officials, were being sent out to regional offices.

There are many instances of persons informing to the British forces being quickly known to the other side. Liam Deasy cites an example in West Cork. After some Volunteers on a mission had taken her bicycle a seventeen-year-old girl wrote a letter to Bandon barracks giving the names of sixteen members of local Volunteer companies. This was quickly known to a local unit, and the girl's family was ordered to leave the country within twenty-four hours.

Another difficulty was the propensity of some Volunteers to depart without permission in order to pose as men on the run in Britain and America. Collins frequently railed against this. In May he told Art O'Brien: 'We find many cases of Deserters from Ireland being looked after and helped by our friends in England. If this sort of thing were stopped it would do immense good here.' He added that such action would also be a protection to members of the Irish Self-Determination League, as 'you will know very well that there has been many cases of imposters and frauds'. The next month he wrote to Seán Nunan in New York: 'I don't know what is the matter with our people abroad in cases of this kind. It is a disgraceful thing, for instance, that a man who deserted from here should be given a position in my office in New York.'

Then there was the vital matter of IRA relations with the general population. Commandeering of goods created strained relations. In May a Dublin building supply company which advertised itself as 'Contractors to His Majesty's Government' wrote to the Secretary to the Ministry to report that £81 worth of goods 'were taken away by members and under the authority of the IRA, and we wish to know if we can look to you for payment'. After determining that the goods were taken by Volunteers, Mulcahy made it clear that he wanted prompt action. He wrote to the O/C Dublin on 12 July: 'The delay in this matter . . . is rather discreditable. . . . I want to dispose of this case without any further delay.' To deal with this situation, Mulcahy at the beginning of August issued General Order No. 28, 'Commandeering of Stores', which set out the procedures to be followed. In March Mulcahy had issued a directive that a different procedure was to be followed concerning captured moneys. Since 'the finance day of reckoning will come sooner or later', it was ordered that all such funds should be sent to the Minister for Finance.[36]

Two notable incidents were the Robbie typewriter case and the Curragh cattle-stealing case. Both of them also figure in the continuing conflict between Collins on one hand and Brugha and Stack on the other. In the Robbie case a Dublin manager of a typewriter company fired a secretary whom he suspected of informing the IRA about machines which were to be delivered to the British army and were confiscated by the Volunteers. Without further ado, a local unit ordered Robbie to leave the country immediately. Brugha believed that this action was taken with insufficient evidence, and Mulcahy agreed with him. In the Curragh case someone stole some cattle. In June Collins received complaints about the matter which he passed on to the Home Affairs Department. Stack believed he was being ignored, however, and charged that Collins was somehow holding back information. The matter dragged on for an inordinate length of time, and Collins finally wrote to Mulcahy: 'This Curragh cattle-stealing case has got to finish. There have been more letters written and answered about this than on any other subject I know.'

The army needed popular support in order to survive. A serious development was a tendency of some people to distance themselves from the IRA. At the end of December 1920 the O/C of the West Clare Brigade told Mulcahy: 'The civil population, especially the farmers, in a great many districts have become from sheer dread of the enemy side . . . hostile towards the Volunteers.' Moreover, 'I find of late in a great many companies that the Volunteers themselves are rather inclined to fall in with the views of the old people to remain quiet.' Headquarters replied that it would issue instructions to deal with any lagging, adding: 'We must not have our machine encumbered at the present moment with people who do not intend to be soldiers of the Republic.' In January an RIC report from Cork claimed that Volunteers were no longer welcome in houses in which they have formerly been billeted.

When the IRA began collecting money from the population in May, Frederick Dumont reported that 'many small farmers who have had men of this army quartered on them without compensation have protested violently to Sinn Féin leaders'. A convention of the Ancient Order of Hibernians in Dundalk on 15 May rejected the imposition of involuntary contributions in threatening language. A further problem was caused by the action of Mr Ed Buckley, a farmer and shopkeeper in Newmarket, Co. Cork. In defiance of an IRA order, he posted a British army proclamation outside his shop; he was thereupon fined, an action approved by Mulcahy, who advised the area commandant to confiscate appropriate goods to the value of the fine. Despite these instances, there was no general pattern of declining support.

Modern weapons were always in short supply, but the IRA had enough to keep up the fight. Germany provided a new outlet. As early as April 1920 the British government suspected that supplies were coming from that source. The principal arms procurer was 'Mr Jetter', who was in fact John T. Ryan, an Irish-American lawyer, who had been charged with German ties during the war and had fled from the USA in 1918. The colourful Charles McGuinness of Derry transported a load of arms to Ireland. Collins dispatched the sixteen-year-old Seán MacBride to purchase arms in Germany in 1921.[37]

At the end of December 1920 the British government called together its commanders in Ireland for an estimate of the prospects of suppressing the rebellion. The general view of the military men was that this could be achieved in about three or four months. They had already employed or were about to employ a variety of measures to achieve this aim. These included the use of special forces (the Black and Tans and Auxiliaries), martial law, internment, massive sweeps and intensive searches, the taking of hostages, and reprisals against property. The scenario they envisaged would include the disruption and collapse of their guerrilla opponents, the waning of public support for the rebellion, and the crumbling of the underground government under relentless pressure. When these things had happened, then the Irish people would be prepared to accept the new Home Rule Act.

Dublin Castle held many beliefs about its opponents that were unfounded. One of these was that the 'gunmen' were hired assassins, some of whom had been imported from the bar-rooms of New York and Chicago. This belief was frequently voiced. Sir Edward Carson had made this assertion in parliament, and Frederick Dumont regularly informed Washington that this was the view of the British commanders. In March 1921 he claimed: 'Men of the flying columns are paid monthly wages, the "gunmen" special amounts, depending upon whom they kill . . .' Collins was aware that Dumont used British sources almost exclusively in his reports. On 3 May he asked de Valera what should be done about these 'damaging reports'. In any case, there were no imported hired gunmen, although Harry Boland stated that there were a hundred volunteers ready to proceed to Ireland. A small number of Irishmen did return from Britain and America to join the fight. One of these returned from the United States in April with a trunk of de Valera's clothes.

Nor were members of the active service units paid, although, since they were full-time soldiers, they were given subsistence. The British officials simply could not fathom people working without pay. In fact not more than 300 of the persons employed in the entire underground government service received pay, and most of these received very little. In addition, British officials were deeply suspicious of many of the people collecting unemployment benefit. General Macready asked in May: 'What about the continued payment of unemployment pay to gentlemen belonging to the IRA who are out of civil work, but employed on their particular Military duties against us?' The difficulty, however, was proving that these gentlemen were members of the IRA.

Another belief of British officials was that their opponents were running out of money. Frederick Dumont reported in March: 'The British hopes of overcoming the movement are partially based on the idea that as the Sinn Féin funds run low, peace must be made. This is one of the reasons that they are so suspicious of American relief.' At the same time Macready told him that, because of 'the drain upon the revenues of the United Kingdom due to the necessity of keeping British troops in various parts of the world', no reinforcements could be expected in the near future. In May the British intelligence directorate twice reported that Sinn Féin was facing a lack of funds. It cited as evidence de Valera's cable requesting a million dollars a year from the AARIR. Collins had told the Dáil that month that the government for the last six months of the year would be operating on an internal deficit. Of course, there was the $3 million in the United States, $100,000 of which was received that month. The expenses of the rebel republic had increased, but it did not face a financial crisis. The local units of the IRA had been self-financed all along; the levies they were imposing were probably needed to pay for the added expenses of the flying columns. A new loan campaign in the United States, about which Boland was very optimistic, was planned for the autumn.[38]

Although resignations from the RIC were reduced to a trickle by the end of 1920, the force had almost totally lost its effectiveness in combating the revolutionary movement. In order to shore up the police, the British government had begun to employ special forces — British recruits for the RIC and ex-army officers for an Auxiliary Division — in mid-1920. In the public mind they were collectively known as the 'Black and Tans'. By early 1921 there was no evidence that they had been effective in their mission; indeed, their impact was ultimately counterproductive. They earned the hatred of many Irish people. Their indiscipline, looting and casual violence eventually discredited them with British public opinion. General Macready attempted to curb their abuses. In November he urged General Tudor, the head of the RIC, 'to try and put a check on promiscuous firing in the air of lorry loads of RIC. It does not do any good, and is very subversive to discipline, and annoys the Army people extremely.' In February he demanded that police in martial law areas be placed under army authority. He would not have 'wild men treating the Martial Law Area as a special game reserve . . . [for] their amusement'. After a rampage by the Black and Tans in March he proposed that either the army should intervene to stop such actions or withdraw from the areas involved. He told Anderson: 'I will not have this sort of thing going on under the eyes of young soldiers.' The resignation of General Frank Crozier, head of the Auxiliary Division, following a outbreak of violence by his men at Trim, Co. Meath, in February roused a demand in the British press for Hamar Greenwood's resignation.

Another of the British government's new forces was, however, an immediate success. On the suggestion of Winston Churchill, a Special Constabulary was established, supposedly for the whole of Ireland, but in fact for the Unionist-dominated areas of Ulster. With the rise of IRA activity, members of the pre-war Ulster Volunteer Force had demanded counter-action, and some units had been revived. In September 1920 the Special Constabulary force was established and drew its member-ship almost entirely from the UVF. Rising to nearly 20,000 by July 1921, this auxiliary force was effective in maintaining British control within most of north-east Ulster.

A further measure to stifle rebellion was the imposition of martial law in the most disturbed counties. The British forces already had the power to try captured rebels by court martial since the spring of 1920. The effect of this was to drive hundreds of Volunteers from their homes into full-time guerrilla activity. This was the origin of the active service units or flying columns, which made the IRA a much more effective force. How martial law for whole counties would improve the situation for the other side is difficult to understand, but General Strickland, the British commander in Munster, believed it would prove effective in four months. On 10 December martial law was declared in Cork, Kerry, Limerick and Tipperary; on 4 January it was extended to Clare, Kilkenny, Waterford and Wexford. The problem with martial law was that no one was clear about exactly what it meant. Appeals from convictions handed down by courts martial were made to the civilian courts, and by the summer of 1921 the whole matter of martial law was in a legal tangle.[39]

The British forces had the power of internment since January 1920, but did not employ it extensively until after the shock of 'Bloody Sunday' in November. By the beginning of 1921 1,478 men had been interned and this figure grew to 4,454 (including 19 brigade and 93 battalion commanders) by July. That internment was not a panacea was clear to the RIC chief inspector in Limerick. He declared in January that Volunteers against whom there was no evidence had nothing to fear: 'They are aware of this and consequently their morale is high, for they know that if not actually taken with arms they will at most suffer internment. We are thus in the position of an army fighting an enemy and taking all prisoners.' In May General Macready requested that accommodation be provided in England for 2,000 internees. He had two reasons for his request: there was no further room for them in Ireland, and their transfer would release five battalions from guard duty. At the same time he sought to make clear that the internees were not prisoners of war. There is no evidence that internment had any serious impact on the effectiveness of the IRA; rather, the fact that it could carry on without obvious impairment was striking testimony to its resilience and strength.

In order to counter an anticipated IRA offensive against military and police vehicles, the British forces decided to carry hostages in vehicles in the most dangerous areas. On 19 December 1920 General Strickland issued an order to his units: 'In future a Sinn Féin Prisoner is to be taken handcuffed in the front of each lorry which comes or leaves their areas.' In January this order was extended to the whole country. The Dáil cabinet on 6 February decided to respond with a proclamation that all members of the British cabinet would be held responsible for the death of any hostage. The hostage order was withdrawn a few days later, but the practice was continued occasionally. The army put wire netting over open lorries to prevent bombs from being thrown in. One observer commented: 'It has been said that it took the Boers to put the British Army in khaki, the Germans to put them in tanks, and the IRA to put them in hen-coops.'[40]

Reprisals were also used. The Black and Tans had been attacking property around ambush sites for months when the British command decided on a policy of 'official reprisals' at the end of December. Dublin Castle had hoped that this approach would end unofficial, random destruction of property, but it did not do so. The IRA responded with counter-reprisals against the property of supporters of the crown. In May General Macready concluded that reprisals had not worked: 'If the military burned a cottage, then the Sinn Féiners burned two, then the military four, and so on. Guinness pointed out in the House last night that the military having burned a cottage, the Sinn Féiners had burned a mansion.' This was Tom Barry's recollection too, and he also referred to an additional tactic employed by the IRA against their perceived enemies:

> We sent a message to them that for every house of ours they burned we'd burn two of the big houses, the Loyalist mansions. We didn't let them just sell up their lands and run back to England. We put a ban on all sales of this property because we weren't going to have them leave Ireland with money in their pockets from land they'd stolen from the people.

The method of which the British command was most hopeful was that of massive search operations. Several of these were undertaken in country areas in 1921, though in fact none of them proved to be fruitful. There also were large-scale intensive searches in Dublin. Some arms and other military materials were found, but nothing that would cripple the IRA. After a search had turned up a few rifles and some revolvers in March, Macready observed privately: 'I could not help thinking how Michael and Co. would laugh, in view of the thousands of arms that they have at their disposal in Dublin itself without this one little consignment, which worked its way to Dublin in fish barrels from Sligo or somewhere.'

Military raids on specific targets were more productive. At the end of February a raiding party found the IRA Chief of Staff's office, though not Mulcahy himself. Collins declared that 'some very important papers' had been seized, but O'Hegarty, as Director of Organisation, immediately dispatched messengers to the areas effected, 'so unless they [the British forces] got to work very quickly the damage will not be great'. At about the same time the office of the Propaganda Department was raided and Desmond FitzGerald was arrested. In the next month the office underwent another raid and Childers was briefly detained. These actions, however, did not seriously disrupt the propaganda campaign. On 22 April de Valera's office was raided and a copy of the seal of the Republic and some official stationery were confiscated; the President commented: 'We shall be interested in the new series of forgeries.' A few days later a raid was conducted on the Dáil government's central secretariat, but the damage done seems to have been minimal.

The British forces actively pursued Collins, but although they sometimes came close, they never got him. There were reports, not confirmed, that they were offering a reward of £10,000 for information leading to his arrest. At the beginning of April a raiding party waited in one of Collins's offices for him, but the landlady had sent him a warning. He told de Valera: 'They waited to "interview me" all day. The old lady says they were so frightened that they certainly would not have hit me in any case.' After the Volunteers' attack on the Custom House on 28 May the British command made a desperate attempt to capture him. On one occasion he was almost apprehended in a raid on one of his offices; he related: 'The information was good, and I ought to have been there at the time. . . . It was the most providential escape yet. It will probably have the effect of making them think that I am even more mysterious than they believe me to be, and that is saying a good deal.' The pursuit went on. On 31 May he wrote to Art O'Brien: 'They have kept up a very raging offensive during the weekend for me. They are continuing today. It is a pretty close tug of war this time — one man and a few helpers would not appear on the face of things to have very much chance against many men and a big Empire, but somehow there must be some other equalising force.' A week later he reported: 'They cannot get very much nearer and they certainly did keep close to me for four days, and they have kind of contact with me still. I am writing this under what you might call "war conditions".' His opponents kept up their pressure to the end, and he was forced to the conclusion that there was an informant within his operation, whom he later privately identified.

The position concerning de Valera was not entirely clear. Until the end of January the British government had decided to leave him alone. This policy apparently was continued. Sir John Anderson told the cabinet's Irish Situation Committee in June that Dublin Castle 'had continually received information regarding meetings which de Valera attended personally in company with other rebels who were badly wanted'. Because of cabinet instructions not to arrest de Valera, these meetings had been allowed to take place: 'A raid would have meant shooting, and de Valera might have been shot.' Anderson undoubtedly had been receiving information about meetings, but it seems likely that this was provided *ex post facto*. Macready had for a long time been urging the arrest of all of the rebel leaders, to be promptly followed by trials. 'The Government must begin at the beginning,' he declared, 'and de Valera when caught must be tried for his life, otherwise the troops and the police would look at the proceedings as a farce.' However, in spite of his advocacy of such action, until the summer of 1921 Macready was prepared to go along with the policy of leaving de Valera at liberty. Some of his subordinates apparently were not. A few days after he moved out of an office in mid-April it was raided. At the end of the month he decided that it would be safer to move out of central Dublin; Collins arranged the purchase of a house for him in Blackrock. When British forces by chance did capture the President on 22 June, it was too late; negotiations for a truce were already under way. He was released on the following day.[41]

In March Dublin Castle decided to offer major rewards for the capture of the leaders of the insurgents. Macready proposed £10,000 rewards for information leading to the capture of Collins, Brugha and Mulcahy, and £3,500 for Cosgrave, McDonagh, Gearóid O'Sullivan (IRA Adjutant-General) and Stack. Anderson was doubtful about the idea — it would make greater heroes out of the wanted men and would show a lack of confidence in British intelligence; moreover, rewards had been tried before — for the arrest of Dan Breen, Seán Treacy and others — with 'absolutely no result'. There was absolutely no result this time as well, although luck seems to have been a factor. In order to encourage people to provide information, the British government provided a mail drop in London. Handbills were distributed throughout the country urging participation. This scheme did not work any better than the others.[42]

The propaganda weapon continued to be employed. Claims were made that the crown forces were getting on top of things. Anderson realised that this was a double-edged weapon: the immediate effect of such assertions 'must be to stimulate the enemy to further exertions'. His complaints about the propaganda effort would have been very familiar to Desmond FitzGerald and Erskine Childers. He urged the departments to supply information to Basil Clarke: 'I do not think he or anyone ought to be expected to create propaganda out of his own inner consciousness.' He also complained that the police were slow in supplying information to the army, and that by the time it got to the press other and often hostile versions had been printed. Official investigations of reprisal incidents certainly were not good for public relations. Indeed, 'the sooner the police machine can consume its own smoke the better we shall all be pleased'.

The British government thought it still had some arrows left in its quiver. There was talk about actions that could be taken to counter the Belfast and British boycotts. Another idea, proposed by Ormonde Winter, was to photograph everyone in the country and issue identity cards. There was an obvious need to improve efforts to prevent arms smuggling. One of the problems was that there were no customs barriers between Britain and Ireland. Furthermore, the British navy was equipped to fight wars, not patrol the coast. Searches of American ships allowed incidents to occur that could be used to manufacture anti-British propaganda. The cabinet considered imposing a blockade around Ireland. There was talk of withdrawing British forces to the coastal cities and starving the people into submission. As a foretaste of what might be coming, British forces temporarily cut off the Tralee peninsula in Kerry and the Greenore peninsula in Donegal during the spring; both blockades were overcome by local fishermen who brought in basic necessities. The Dáil government took the precaution of asking the American relief committee to secure adequate food supplies to meet such a possibility. Although the matter was discussed in the British cabinet as late as 15 June, the blockade proposal and its ramifications were, in fact, an acknowledgment of the failure of British policy. London had been reduced to bluster.

A basic problem with the British campaign was that it lacked sufficient manpower — fewer troops were employed in the eight-county martial law area than were used in the six counties of Northern Ireland in the 1970s. Macready had only 32,000 soldiers and the 13,000 members of the RIC (including 5,000 Black and Tans and 1,000 Auxiliaries) in March 1921. He believed he would need 100,000 soldiers 'to restore Ireland to its pre-war condition'. At this time the Volunteers had an active strength of about 5,000, with ten times that number involved on an occasional basis.

The British command often voiced the belief that both the IRA and the Dáil government were near breaking-point. On 24 December 1920 it informed the British cabinet that, in response to a British army proclamation, 'arms were being surrendered in some quantities. . . . Stress was laid on the importance of doing nothing to check the surrender of arms at a time when the forces of the Crown had at last definitely established the upper hand.' In fact there was no substantial surrender of arms. General Strickland believed that the Volunteers would, at best, bury their arms. A month later he confessed that 'the formations of the Republican Forces were almost as well organised as those of the British Army. . . . The number of arms personally surrendered could be counted on one hand.' On 29 January *The Kerryman* published, 'by request', the names of thirty-one persons who had 'voluntarily resigned from the IRA'; these resignations, however, were not duplicated elsewhere. At this time 'Colonel X' told an American journalist that the IRA was in fine fettle: 'The men are all well fed and are in good health and their continued resilience is amazing. . . . We hit them without being hit. We have kept on for a year, and the boys are still full of ginger and eager to continue.'

There were some in the British command who continued to believe that progress was being made. A secret general order was issued on 12 May that the troops were to observe a policy of friendliness to civilians owing to the fact that the IRA had been broken up and the crown forces were only dealing with 'wandering bands'. This policy probably had more to do with the need for a peaceful setting for the Home Rule elections than it did with the supposed defeat of the IRA. The *Irish Bulletin* believed that 'The main point deducible from the text of the Order is that the military terror in Ireland has failed.'[43]

The IRA's tactics and emphasis shifted according to circumstances; the position of headquarters was generally to confirm the changes that had already taken place. The flying columns grew out of the need for wanted men to 'go on the run'. Soon every battalion wanted an 'active service unit'. At the beginning of 1921 the army shifted from attacks on police barracks and ambushes to the destruction of roads, bridges and communications. The 'campaign against communications' provided targets that were undefended and plentiful. The shift to 'small jobs' showed a marked increase in total Volunteer activity, which grew month by month in 1921. In addition, the IRA came up with a brand new weapon — the Thompson sub-machine-gun that was just coming into production in the USA during the spring. What it lacked in accuracy it made up for in noise and volume of fire. Although only about fifty of the new weapons had arrived by the time of the truce, they gave the IRA a boost and caused concern on the other side.

One change initiated by headquarters was the creation of a divisional structure for the army. It terms of organisation it made little sense to try to co-ordinate a hundred units from one headquarters. In April the first three divisions were created. The commander of the 2nd Southern Division, Ernie O'Malley, was informed that his adjutant and himself would have to accept salaries; acceptance of this order was viewed by GHQ as a 'disciplinary measure'. Headquarters was at last exerting some control.

In this period of adversity the Volunteer leadership took an inspirational approach. Mulcahy broadcast ringing statements to his force: 'The stand you have made, that you are making now and that you mean to make right through . . . [is] one of the most memorable things in the history of the world.' As other countries realise what is happening in Ireland, 'many a tyranny in many a land will begin to tremble and totter. Ireland will once again be the teacher of nations.' To individual units he applied the carrot and the stick. Piaras Béaslaí was firmly optimistic. On 24 June *An tÓglach* announced: 'The steady advance in efficiency and effectiveness of the Irish Republican Army in every part of Ireland is paralleled by a steady decline in enemy morale.'[44]

The IRA also took action in England. There were a number of arson attacks in Liverpool in November 1920, and then, after a mass of arrests, a quiet interlude. Activity was renewed in February, when the Liverpool docks were again the target. There were a few other actions in England, but the police, obviously aware of whom to hold accountable, again responded with widespread arrests. There was a substantial Volunteer network in Scotland, but this concerned itself with sending weapons and ammunition to Ireland. There was a series of police raids for weapons in Scotland in December 1920. Cathal Brugha had a long-standing plan for an operation in Britain — the assassination of political leaders. His proposal to shoot members of the British cabinet in November was sidetracked by the Dáil cabinet. In the spring of 1921 he revived the idea, and the practicality of the scheme was investigated. Liam Tobin of GHQ spent some time in London studying the situation. Collins joined him in March, and also devoted attention to Mrs Llewelyn Davies, who was arrested after his departure. Scotland Yard found out about his visit too late, and as rumours circulated he urged Art O'Brien to fan the flames: 'Give them to understand I am there. You would know how to do the "wise intelligen[ce]" on a point like this.' Collins concluded that the London operation would not be effective — England could always get another cabinet. But Brugha was still committed to the idea, and at some point he actually led a group of gunmen to London, but nothing came of it. In March he summoned Seán Mac Eoin, the commandant of the Longford Brigade, to ask him to join the proposed London strike force. While returning from Dublin, Mac Eoin was arrested, and that ended the London assassination caper.

De Valera also had his favourite idea about military operations — occasional large-scale efforts that would attract international attention. He had first broached this subject both to a meeting of military leaders and Dáil Éireann in January 1921. He revived the idea in April. After a proposal to attack the Beggars' Bush barracks had been rejected, the Custom House was selected. It was one of the great public buildings, headquarters of the Local Government Board and other agencies, and was as yet unprotected. An attack on 25 May set the building blazing, but the quick response of the British military resulted in a toll of five dead and more than eighty arrested among the attackers. It was a costly victory, but in propaganda terms it was worth the price. The event made headlines in the world press, and the building burned for a week.[45]

What was the overall condition of the IRA in the spring of 1921? It was certainly under a great deal of pressure, but it was surviving; after all, this was the climax of the conflict. Neither had it lost its capacity to carry on guerrilla warfare. As late as June Collins proposed an all-out assault on the Dublin Castle civil administration. When an attempt was made to revive crown courts in Sligo in early June, the battalion commandant asked GHQ: 'Are we justified in shooting these men?' He was told to wait until the offensive against the enemy civil administration had been organised. According to Frank Thornton, one of Collins's leading intelligence directors, the entire IRA apparatus in Dublin was in place ready to launch such an assault when the Dáil cabinet suddenly sent an order to cancel the operation owing to the progress being made for a truce. Nor was there any slackening of effort in the countryside. Seán MacBride, then a training officer in south Leinster, believed that at that time 'we were just in a position to mount bigger and more widespread attacks'.

Yet there is evidence of severe strain within the army. On 30 March Mulcahy warned that it might be necessary to use the death penalty to stiffen morale. The commanders of both the 1st Southern and 1st Northern Divisions reported that their men were feeling the effects of British sweeps, but Ernie O'Malley said later that his division was in good shape: 'We were willing to keep up the pressure which had been increasing steadily; soon, in a month or more, the division would begin operations in the towns and use columns by sections.' When asked by de Valera how long his brigade in Cork could hold out, Tom Barry replied five years. Frank Thornton believed that 'we would have found ourselves very hard set to continue the fight with any degree of intensity owing to the very serious shortage of ammunition' at this time, but ammunition was always in short supply. Because of the weight of British activity in Dublin, Mulcahy and Collins probably took a more pessimistic view of the situation than did most of the field commanders. Moreover, there were no obvious signs that the Volunteers were falling apart. They could not hold out for ever — but neither could the British forces.

If the situation was very difficult in the rank of the IRA, what was the condition of its opponent? In a plea for reinforcements on 28 March General Macready stressed that 'the strain is very great, especially on young soldiers, of which the Army is at present composed'. He added that he could not guarantee that 'increased activity during the Summer months will result in the total suppression of Rebel activities'. Two months later he was more emphatic: 'Unless I am entirely mistaken, the present state of affairs in Ireland, so far as regards the troops serving here, must be brought to a conclusion by October, or steps must be taken to relieve practically the whole of the troops together with the great majority of the commanders and their staffs.' Even if reinforcements were provided, the new troops would have to be trained in counter-insurgency tactics. Sir Laming Worthington-Evans, the Secretary of State for War, took an even more alarming view: 'The position of the military forces in Ireland is anything but satisfactory.' In his opinion, the troops were being worn down: 'Fatigue and discomfort and the necessity for constant vigilance will not be without effect'; furthermore, 'there is no back area into which they can be withdrawn'. If the military stalemate continued through the summer and autumn, then 'winter will be a time of decisive advantage to the rebels'. There were various other negative assessments of the situation, and no positive ones. The only thing that could change the picture would be a mass of reinforcements. These finally started arriving in June, but by then the real action had shifted to the political field.[46]

(8) WEATHERING THE STORM

The Dáil Government's Darkest Hour

The underground government of Dáil Éireann was under extreme pressure in the first half of 1921. To provide for emergencies, the Dáil at its session of 11 March agreed to a procedure to ensure the survival of a voice for Irish independence. De Valera told the deputies that 'their numbers would not be increasing for some time and a situation might arise if their numbers went very low'. Richard Mulcahy proposed that each member be allowed to nominate a substitute 'to be ratified by the local Comhairle Ceanntair'. The idea of substitute members had been brought up from time to time, and a committee had been appointed to look into the matter, but nothing was ever done. Even now, when a majority of members were absent through imprisonment or work abroad, the proposal was not accepted. Perhaps it had something to do with reluctance to share power, the desire to maintain the prestige of being a Teachta Dála. In fact a few deputies had unofficially nominated substitutes, but one of the problems with the Dáil government all along was that there were few deputies available to represent the alternative administration to the people, particularly outside Dublin.

Both de Valera and Count Plunkett suggested that if the number of deputies at liberty sank to a very low figure, then the power of government should be transferred to the IRA. In the end the Dáil agreed to the proposal that if the number of deputies free to attend meetings was reduced to five, then these deputies should constitute a provisional government. No one explained how the power of authority of such a government would differ from what presently existed. The Dail fortunately did not have to face this situation. Twenty-five deputies attended the March session, and twenty-one were present in May.

Despite great pressure from enemy searches, the Dáil administration remained in being; its departments continued to operate, even if some of them no longer functioned effectively. Although several offices were raided, no ministers were arrested in 1921. The only director to be arrested was Desmond FitzGerald. According to Collins, the Department of Labour 'works in continuous fear of a raid. Nobody seems to be there.' There were enough deputies available to hold Dáil sessions. In order to provide for its continued authority should there be a total breakdown in communication — or worse — the Dáil government considered plans to decentralise administration. It apparently gave no serious consideration to using the unit of the province, which would have seemed the most logical basis of decentralisation. Perhaps it feared this might set a precedent. Aodh de Blacam certainly overstated the case when he declared in a propagandist work published during the truce: 'Centralisation is not the Dáil's permanent policy, and it has initiated a system by which its various works would stand by themselves if the central authority were smitten out of existence.'

The leaders of the counter-state maintained what might be viewed as a surprisingly positive attitude through it all. In January 1921 Collins wrote to Gavan Duffy: 'Everything goes on well, and, as you will see, certain elements in England are becoming very restive at the non-appearance of the success which was so lightly promised them by our latest Governors here.' A month later he told Art O'Brien: 'It seems to me that we are winning. I am more hopeful in a general way than I have been for many a month past.' De Valera found the situation not as bad as he had anticipated. He told James O'Mara in February: 'Operations here are much more extensive than you can imagine, and expenditure is correspondingly heavy.' The Dáil could still meet, and despite the crushing pressure that the British were bringing to bear, 'I think the worst is past'. Robert Brennan was positively bubbling with confidence when he told Gavan Duffy in April: 'The position here continues excellent. The savage military regime has failed to cow the people, who are more than ever determined not to flinch.' In May de Valera told the Dáil that 'he felt they had now come to the point in which they had turned the corner. It was only a question now of keeping up the constructive effort and keeping the country with them.' Perhaps this optimism was justified. At least some political observers had picked up an important signal — self-government was on its way, and the men of the rebel government would continue to hold political power. In May the members of the Royal Dublin Society voted to rescind a resolution of January 1917 calling upon Count Plunkett to resign.[47]

Home Rule Elections

The Government of Ireland Act had committed the British government to the staging of elections to the two parliaments provided under the act. As in the local government elections, the proportional representation method of voting would be employed. Polling was to take place on 24 May, and as this time approached the reassurance given by military leaders in Ireland that order would be restored by that time proved to be ill-founded. In April the British cabinet considered delaying the elections until a semblance of public peace was achieved. It faced the dilemma of wanting the six-county elections to proceed as planned in order to get a Unionist government in place promptly, yet seeking to prevent Sinn Féin from achieving a sweeping victory in the twenty-six counties. It concluded that it was in a legal trap, and that it was impossible to avoid holding both elections on the same date. Putting the best face on the decision to proceed, Winston Churchill argued that the elections would at least force their opponents to shift from a campaign of violence to constitutional, political activity. The elections, after all, were taking place as a result of British legislation.

The British authorities also considered the possibility of a truce during the elections to allow the appearance, at least, of a free choice of the voters. The military men strongly opposed this idea, as it would be of advantage to their opponents. Lloyd George concluded that because of the peace feelers that had been extended to the other side, a truce offer would 'give them the idea we are on the run.' Alfred Cope continued to work for a truce right up to the elections. On 21 May a message from him to the Dáil government urged great speed on the matter, as the British military 'are grasping for "real Martial Law"'. Diarmuid O'Hegarty's comment was that 'If Mr Cope wants a truce by the 24th it looks like a fairly good tip that the threat of the military grasping is three parts bluff.'

The opponents of the underground government could only approach the matter of elections with grim foreboding. In January Mark Sturgis noted that the leaders of Sinn Féin did not share Hamar Greenwood's view that if the elections were held, they would lose seats; on the contrary, 'they confidently expected to sweep the lot. When a Dr Ash came looking for money in April to fight Sinn Féin with ex-soldier candidates who would support the Home Rule Act, Sturgis was doubtful: 'Apparently his sup-porters did not include patriots of means, or else their patriotism does not reach to their pockets.'

The Dáil government on 6 February decided to treat the contests in the two areas as an election for a new Dáil. On 1 May it declared that it 'has decided to recognise the popular elections in order that the will of the people may once more be demonstrated'. As in 1918, Sinn Féin made an agreement with Joseph Devlin's Nationalist Party organisation in Ulster to prevent the two parties from contesting the same seats. De Valera did not have unrealistic hopes about the election in Northern Ireland. He estimated that Nationalist candidates would win eleven to fifteen out of fifty-two seats. On the positive side, the election would provide an opportunity 'to consolidate Nationalist opinion in Ulster and draw it into Republicanism'. On the other hand, there was a problem concerning election expenses. The new electoral arrangements required a deposit of £150 per candidate (the better to drain Sinn Féin resources?). If Sinn Féin put forward 140 nominees, £21,000 would have to be provided — and, because successful Sinn Féin candidates would refuse to take their seats in Home Rule parliaments, none of it would be returned. The Home Affairs Department asked the Dáil for £4,000 for election contingencies; the cabinet had originally planned to ask for £30,000 as a loan to Sinn Féin, but the appearances of separation between party and state had to be maintained. The requested £4,000 was obviously intended as deposit money for northern candidates, and Pádraig O'Keeffe from Cork was having none of it: 'While the rest of Ireland was fighting, Ulster was sitting down.' With 80,000 Catholic families in the north, local supporters 'should be easily able to raise £20,000 for the election'. He urged the government to 'intimate to Ulster that if they were not prepared to finance the elections they would wash their hands of them'. Sean MacEntee pointed out that 'no money could be got in Belfast because Republicans there were in a state of destitution since July last'.

One of the concerns of Austen Chamberlain regarding the elections was that they would require Sinn Féin once again to affirm its commitment to the Republic, 'and that will make fresh negotiations more difficult'. Frederick Dumont arranged the visit to Mountjoy of a 'peaceful Shinner named Keating', who urged that some arrangement be made before the elections that would not force the party to take such a firm position. In fact there was no mention of the word 'republic' in de Valera's statement of 1 May. Neither did it appear in the only election address — that of Collins in Armagh — that this writer has been able to find. Dublin Castle observed that de Valera's statement was 'less bellicose and uncompromising' than the Sinn Féin manifesto of 1918.

Already, on 28 April, the Home Affairs Department had instructed local government bodies not to participate in the election of members of the senate to be created by the Government of Ireland Act. Stack did this to counter the advice tended by W. T. Cosgrave to the secretary of the General Council of County Councils: 'I do not think it likely that advice on the subject would be given by the Dáil Ministry.'[48]

The most interesting feature of de Valera's public announcement about the election was that the Dáil government was prepared to accept Ulster home rule within the Irish state. He declared that 'Provided the unity and independence of Ireland is preserved, we are ready to give such local autonomy to Ulster, or to any other part of Ireland . . . if it will make for the contentment and satisfaction of the citizens resident there.' Going further, he voiced his certainty that his government was prepared to give more power to a subordinate parliament than did the British act. Special treatment for Ulster had been a matter of public discussion since February, when Professor Alfred O'Rahilly of Cork had made the proposal. Alex McCabe revealed he had tried to get the Dáil interested in federalism, but without success. Since his return from America de Valera had been telling foreign journalists that he would, if necessary, support autonomy for the Unionist part of Ulster. He did not direct this message directly to the Belfast area or to the Irish people as a whole; when the matter of making an offer to the northern Unionists was broached in the Dáil in March, he cut off discussion with the comment that it was not the time for such an offer, although 'he was not against such a policy'. It is obvious that neither did he think it was the place. De Valera's statements were, in fact, part of his strategy to bring pressure on the British government for a settlement by showing international opinion how reasonable he was. He was addressing world opinion, not Ulster opinion. World opinion could be swayed, but not Ulster Unionist opinion.

As was its wont, Sinn Féin offered nothing specific in terms of social and economic proposals; in its view, independence was the solution to every problem. That the party completely lacked an attraction for Protestant workers is revealed in Seán MacEntee's comment that the election pact with the Devlinites 'would mean polling a large number of Protestant labour votes'. In parliament Joseph Devlin voted with the Labour Party on almost every matter; in this manner he served his working-class constituents. The Sinn Féin campaign paper, *The Unionist*, edited by James Good, stressed the virtues of self-determination and the harm that would be done to the north by partition.

When nomination day arrived on 13 May, only Sinn Féin candidates were proposed for 124 of 128 seats in the twenty-six counties of 'Southern Ireland'. Four Unionists were similarly unopposed in the Dublin University constituency. Not a single Home Ruler decided to stand. To some observers this was due to fear and intimidation. A publican in Blackrock named McCabe announced that he would be a candidate, but after a visit by some Volunteers he changed his mind. One RIC county inspector asserted that 'the gunman rules the politician' and 'any prospective candidate not to their liking would have to live in a Police or Military Barracks'. The Labour Party decided to stand aside once again, although it had surveyed the political scene before doing so.[49]

The situation in Northern Ireland was quite different. The Special Constabulary, together with the RIC and the British army, had succeeded in keeping the IRA under control. The Unionist Party was well prepared for the contest. As in 1918, Sinn Féin was forced to come to an accommodation with the remnant of the Irish Parliamentary Party that had survived in Ulster under the leadership of Joseph Devlin. This time it took no intervention of the Catholic Church to divide up the seats; having agreed on the principle of self-determination and abstention from the proposed parliaments, both parties were committed to giving their second preferences to the other; they both put forward twenty-one candidates. There had been a lot of unfounded optimism in Sinn Féin ranks about what would happen in these elections. Robert Brennan told Gavan Duffy in April: 'If the elections under the Partition Act are held we shall sweep the board in "the rest of Ireland" and cripple the northern Parliament by taking a very large number of seats for the abstentionists.' Collins predicted that if only Sinn Féiners stood against Unionists, as he anticipated might happen, 'then we can at the very outset give Partition what ought be an almost fatal blow'.[50]

The results in the north were disappointing to Sinn Féin. For the forty-eight popularly elected seats (there were four university seats), it won six, while the Nationalist Party also won six and the Unionists thirty-six. An unusual feature of the result was that none of the Sinn Féin winners lived in the north; the only ones who had roots in the six-county area were Eoin Mac Néill and Ernest Blythe, both of whom had left the north many years before. The only Belfast man in the Dáil, Seán MacEntee, was elected for Monaghan. One Sinn Féin candidate, Seán O'Mahony, who had been returned for a constituency of the Northern Ireland parliament, never took his seat there, but was subsequently admitted as a member of the Dáil on the strength of this election. But with these exceptions, and despite the fact that there were twice as many seats involved in comparison with 1918, there were no additional representatives from the six counties in the Dáil. It is little wonder that the matter of partition figured so little in the Treaty controversy at the end of the year.

The Sinn Féin press charged that the election had been plagued by Unionist violence, intimidation, personation and gerrymandering. *Old Ireland* (11 June) pointed out that although Republican/Nationalist candidates polled 30 per cent of the total vote, they won only twelve seats, fewer than they were entitled to. A considerable degree of gerrymandering or intimidation (or both) must have been present in Belfast, where the Unionists won fifteen of sixteen seats. Sinn Féin, of course, won none; Joe Devlin was the victor. The same situation prevailed in Tyrone and Fermanagh. Despite the fact that the Nationalist/Republican candidates outpolled the Unionists by 44,791 to 37,718, the seats won were evenly divided. On the other hand, Unionists could point to Armagh, where their candidates got 25,718 votes to their opponents 20,814, yet both sides got two seats.

As far as Sinn Féin itself was concerned, although it received 104,000 votes to the Nationalist Party's 60,000, its percentage of the total vote in the six counties was below that of 1918. The great men of Dublin did not loom very large in north-east Ulster. Perhaps the root cause of Sinn Féin's failure there was the reluctance of northern nationalists to give up the security and confidence in the party they had — led by an able man — for the more flamboyant and dangerous attraction of Sinn Féin. The northern nationalists were every day locked in struggle with the Unionists. They could not afford to take chances. The contest in the rest of the country was completely different. Basically the rest of Ireland was seeing off the British administration, the British forces and the tattered remnant of Unionism (and their lackeys, agents, touts and others). There were no easy victories or vast cheering crowds for republican heroes in Belfast; the Sinn Féin leaders concentrated on the easy pickings, not the hard ground of the north. In fact no Sinn Féiner resident in the six counties won a seat there either in 1918 or 1921.[51]

Although he believed he had won over a couple of thousand Protestant votes in Armagh (why would they vote for him?), Michael Collins was depressed about the whole northern business. He told Art O'Brien that the working of the partition act had opened the eyes of many people. 'They are beginning to see', he wrote, 'that what they have always known as Ulster is nothing more than a handful of people in one corner of the country, whose material interests depend upon the maintenance of their foreign ascendancy, and who are bent on securing their material interests at all costs.' They had no love for Kathleen Ni Houlihan.[52]

The overall results of the two 'Home Rule' elections showed that of the 168 popularly elected seats at stake, Sinn Féin won 126, Ulster Unionists 36, and northern Nationalists 6. There also were twelve university seats; Sinn Féin won the four for the National University, while the Unionists gained four each in Dublin University (Trinity College) and Queen's University, Belfast.

At the May session of the Dáil the government, or rather de Valera, prepared the way for the new Dáil to be inaugurated two weeks later. Ministers would remain in power until the new Dáil met and then would 'resign their portfolios through the President'. It would also be the President, rather than the Ceann Comhairle, who would summon the new Dáil. Cathal Brugha saw this as entirely appropriate 'since it would be the President who would be in charge until the new Dáil assembled'. This was a curious reading of the as yet unpublished constitution. In de Valera's view, the President, not the cabinet, held executive power; in practice, the Dáil was there to receive his pronouncements.

Although Sinn Féin had won 124 seats in the new Dáil, many of the successful candidates were in prison or on the run. There was a security risk in trying to assemble the eighty-odd persons who were free to attend the meetings of the Dáil. As Diarmuid O'Hegarty commented, 'The task of bringing together ninety members including several well-known ladies will be a big one.' De Valera suggested that after an inaugural meeting the Dáil could be divided up into committees of twenty. Collins proposed that only half the members should meet at any one time. The cabinet finally decided on a grand committee of thirty-one members, with proportional representation for each province. By the time the second Dáil met three months later, however, the transformed political situation made such considerations irrelevant.

A small problem created by the elections was that several people who held paid positions in the Dáil administration won seats. They wanted to hold on to both positions. Anticipating charges of jobbery, Collins declared they would have to give up their paid employment. Although it was in agreement that the holding of two posts was undesirable, the cabinet came to no definite decision on the matter. A general exception was made for those who worked in the Department of Defence; there were a lot of young commandants among the new deputies.[53]

The Reluctant Church

With a sweeping victory at his back, de Valera decided that the time had come to make a formal request to the Catholic hierarchy to issue a public statement acknowledging the legality of the Republic of Ireland. The idea of asking for such recognition goes back to at least December 1920. For long there had been a felt need among the supporters of the counter-state that their church should make some open gesture of recognition. The bishops felt differently. Most of them were opposed to all abrupt or radical political change; their loyalty and responsibility was to their own institution.

The idea of seeking such recognition was proposed to the Dáil government in December 1920 by 'certain well known Catholic theologians'. Both Arthur Griffith and Alfred O'Rahilly, the Cork lay theologian, wrote drafts of the request. Collins, who had 'very grave doubts as to timing', consulted Bishop Fogarty, and nothing more was done about the proposal at that time. The timing was not right in December. Bishop Cohalan had just excommunicated Volunteers who had killed members of the crown forces. There was no indication of growing support for the Republic among the hierarchy. The underground government was subjected to intense pressure; some thought it would go under.

In February 1921 W. T. Cosgrave forwarded to de Valera a suggestion that had been sent to him that 'there should be a sort of "upper house" to the Dáil consisting of a Theological Board which would decide whether any enactments of the Dáil were contrary to Faith and Morals or not'. In return, 'the Holy Father will be asked to recognise the Dáil as a body entitled to legislate for Ireland'. Cosgrave himself did not like the idea, which he thought 'might lead to very grave trouble'; moreover, 'for the Dáil to admit that there existed the necessity for such a check on their legislation would, I think, be a fatal error'. De Valera did not like the idea either, commenting that 'There is no necessity at the moment to consider it further.'

For their part, the bishops, singularly and in conference, continued to denounce British repression and call for national self-determination, adding always, with differing emphasis, censure of violence. If most of the people wanted a republic, this had little effect on the bishops: they did not have to stand for election; they had jobs for life. The *Irish Bulletin* commented on 23 March: 'The Catholic Bishops of Ireland are one of the most conservative bodies in the country. The majority are not in agreement with the more forward elements in the Republican movement. Some are numbered among its strongest opponents.'

In April Lord Derby arrived on the scene as an emissary of the British government. He met not only de Valera but also Cardinal Logue. The President was gravely concerned that Derby would draw Logue into supporting some sort of dominion status by the offer of fiscal autonomy or other means. Logue was no republican, and on different occasions and by different means he let it be known that he thought a moderate settlement would be for the best. After seeing Derby, Logue declared that 'an Irish Republic they would never achieve so long as England had a man left to fight'. De Valera told Collins privately: 'The old man up North has given them his views. I would like to use bad language, but I won't.' Archbishop Mannix, who was still in England, urged de Valera to respond publicly, but the President thought otherwise. The *Irish Bulletin* (2 May) commented that Logue was 'not at any time regarded as a wise statesman, and with advancing years he has become more and more a stranger to the ideals of his own people'.

Denunciations of violence by Archbishop Gilmartin of Tuam, Bishop Cohalan and other church dignitaries were repeatedly responded to by *Old Ireland*. On 26 March it insisted:

> If the Irish Republic today could count on the allegiance of even half the Irish bishops, the intrigues would be checked, the enemy's hope of our surrender ruined, and peace would undoubtedly follow rapidly. But the record of Irish bishops has always been so faulty from an Irish standpoint that one is hardly disappointed when they do not rise in their actions to the standards of plain Irishmen.

Three weeks earlier the same journal had declared that the time had arrived 'when An Dáil should put it to the Irish Hierarchy to declare their attitude towards An Dáil'. In June de Valera decided that the time had come to bring this matter to a head. On the 21st the President addressed the hierarchy at Maynooth. In what must have been a dramatic scene, he urged the bishops to recognise the Republic. This they would not do, but they did approve yet another statement supporting self-determination and denouncing British repression. There the matter was left.[54]

Controversy in Britain

By the spring of 1921 the British government was under sustained attack for its Irish policy from a wide range of forces at home. These included not just the opposition parties — the Asquith Liberals and the Labour Party — but also the press, church leaders, intellectuals, writers and other influential people and, in the end, a number of members of the government. Moreover, it had very few supporters. By that time it was obvious that British public opinion had rejected the argument that the methods used to suppress rebellion in Ireland were either necessary or effective.

From the beginning of 1919 there was criticism of the government's approach to Irish affairs. The dissatisfaction centred on the government's refusal to come to terms with the Irish demand for self-government. The Government of Ireland Act failed to assuage public opinion, and this measure was opposed by almost all political groups in Ireland. With increased efforts to repress the Sinn Féin movement, opposition in Britain mounted. By the spring of 1921 it had become a veritable torrent. No democratically elected government can resist this sort of opposition for long, and the Lloyd George government was a coalition nearing the end of its existence. Its resistance to negotiations was stiffened by the Conservative members of the government and the Conservative Party in the Commons, but there was no evidence of popular support for continued coercion.

The abuse the government was subjected to in the press was staggering, and it had few supporters. One of these was the extreme right-wing *Morning Post*, which declared on one occasion that the Irish independence movement was 'inspired by the anti-Christ, which seeks political aggrandisement by murder and every other form of violence, which scoffs at authority and which derives its inspiration from Moscow and not from Rome'. It its view, the pope was no longer the fount of all evil. The London *Times* had long been opposed to the government's policy. On 29 January it even admitted: 'Deeds have unquestionably been done in Ireland which have lastingly disgraced the name of Britain in that country.' The *Daily News* (26 Jan.) asserted that Hamar Greenwood 'has failed to a point that even his opponents did not foresee a few months ago. He did not intimidate the Volunteers, but he intimidated nearly everyone else. His tactics were directed against the morale of the civilian population rather than against the morale of armed men.'

The general press onslaught was deeply disturbing to the British forces in Ireland. General Strickland commented in March that every soldier he met complained about the situation that 'while nearly every paper at home is full of the atrocities committed against the patriotic IRA, yet the Government avail themselves of no propaganda on the other side'. General Macready emphatically agreed with this complaint. Sir John Anderson recognised that British public opinion did not back his government's policy:

The broad fact is unfortunately that the section of the public which opposes the Government is ready to seize hold of anything to the prejudice of the administration, while the other section, large though it may be in numbers and influence, regards Ireland as a plague-spot, of whose existence it hates to be reminded.

In April Lloyd George said he believed public opinion could be swung around in support if MPs would actively carry the government's point of view to the people; however, this did not happen, and his remarks did not convey the conviction that he really thought it would happen — he admitted that the people were 'a little unhappy' about what was going on in Ireland.[55]

The Labour Party conducted an effective campaign against the government's Irish policy. It was not until November 1920 that the party firmly rejected the 'Home Rule' approach. At that time it changed to supporting the withdrawal of British troops and the forming of a constituent assembly to decide the country's political future, qualified by the protection of minority rights and Britain's security interests. The party sent two delegations to examine the situation in Ireland — one at the beginning of 1920, and the other at the end of the year. The first delegation issued a report which condemned British policy and advocated self-determination, but no action was taken by the party. The report of the second delegation (a Labour commission) got results. Of course, conditions in Ireland had deteriorated considerably during the year, and the commission was in Ireland during one of the most violent periods — from 30 November to 14 December. It travelled around the country, ably assisted by Thomas Johnson. It viewed the smouldering ruins of the centre of Cork city; in Mark Sturgis's view, it was 'rampaging all over the place'.

A special Labour Party conference held on 29 December endorsed the commission's report. In addition to supporting self-determination, with protection for minorities and British security, the conference demanded the withdrawal of British forces. Beginning in January, the party staged a series of public meetings to rouse public opposition to the government's policies.

The trade union side of the labour movement provided less direct but perhaps greater indirect support than did the political side. Although the British TUC had protested against the government's Irish policy and had supported self-determination as early as September 1919, the unions declined to take any specific action in support of this position. During the Irish industrial action against the movement of military supplies and armed troops, the National Union of Railwaymen executive provided no support. J. H. Thomas tried every means possible to get the railwaymen to abandon their action. At the time of the Belfast expulsions only one British union took action against the deeds of its Belfast members. Following the killing of some members by British soldiers at Mallow in February 1921, the Amalgamated Society of Locomotive Engineers and Firemen threatened to call a general strike if an open government inquiry was not held by 15 February. It settled for having a legal representative at a closed military inquiry. To Sinn Féiners this was simply additional evidence that British trade unionists would not do anything effective in support of Irish self-government.

British trade unions did, in fact, play an important, if indirect and unintentional, role in weakening the capacity of the British government to resist Irish independence. A series of strikes and the threat of a general strike by the triple alliance of railwaymen, transport workers and dockers required the British army to keep more soldiers at home than was normal. In addition, troops from Ireland had to be transferred to England on several occasions to deal with the threat of industrial disorder. These were the very troops that were needed to suppress the rebellion in Ireland. Mark Sturgis noted in April that the English coal strike had made Sinn Féin 'very bobbery' and that its leaders would not negotiate as long as it continued. Yet there is no evidence that any effort was made to co-ordinate action between the leaders of the Irish movement and British Labour. Of course, Irish Labour leaders were well informed about what was happening in the British movement, and they passed this information on to the Dáil government.[56]

The burning of the centre of Cork in December had caused a public outcry, and the British government immediately initiated an inquiry into the affair. After anguished deliberations, however, the cabinet announced in January that it would not make the inquiry report public. The British Labour Party commission had already placed the blame on the crown forces. On the day the government report failed to appear, the Irish Labour Party published an account, *Who Burnt Cork?*, written by Alfred O'Rahilly, which was conveniently packaged in an illustrated booklet that was distributed widely by the British Labour Party.

The growing public opposition began to be felt within the cabinet. In February Churchill admitted that 'our friends are unhappy about the Irish position', but he believed they would still support the government. With no end of the rebellion in sight, Greenwood told the cabinet in April: 'I was much too optimistic last December than I ought to have been.' At a cabinet meeting on 12 May, which heard a report from Anderson that 'the position of the Crown forces is stronger and is improving every day', three ministers — Addison, Munro and Fisher — voiced strong opposition to the government's policy. Thomas Jones, who as Cabinet Secretary was not without influence, privately promoted the idea of a settlement. He had already told Bonar Law in January that 'the ghastly things that were being done were enough to drive one to join the Republican Army'.

During the spring the Prime Minister considered the consequences of a truce and negotiations. He told cabinet meetings in April and May of his concerns. Any offer to the Irish side would only open the door to further claims. He held that to meet the public demand for conciliation and settlement would result in initial relief, but 'the ultimate feeling would be disgust that we gave in so easily'. A settlement could result in cheap beer, tobacco and tea for the Irish working man, while Britons would be paying higher income taxes. The Irish could erect a tariff barrier to British goods. He also recalled his past negotiations with Irish politicians and looked to the future with apprehension:

> I think these people will force you to fight. They will fight on cash. There is a hard side to the Irish nature. They are greedy beyond any other part of the United Kingdom. . . . They will drive a hard bargain.

Another reason for avoiding negotiations that several cabinet members proffered was that it was Collins, not de Valera, who was the strong man on the other side. The assumed supremacy of Collins was probably based on reports received from Dublin Castle in March and April, which were eagerly seized upon by the cabinet hardliners. Any offer would be seen as a victory for the revolutionary army. Lloyd George told a cabinet meeting on 27 April:

> De Valera and Michael Collins have quarrelled. The latter will have a Republic and he carries a gun and he makes it impossible to negotiate. De Valera cannot come here and say he is willing to give up Irish independence, for if he did, he might be shot.

Austen Chamberlain argued that there could be no truce until the gunmen had been broken, and this could not be done 'as long as de Valera is at the mercy of Michael Collins'. Edward Shortt, the Home Secretary (and former Chief Secretary for Ireland), agreed that 'it would be fatal to offer a truce to gunmen'.[57]

(9) Negotiating a Truce

Despite the breakdown of the movement towards negotiations in December, both sides continued to put out feelers for peace. One of the first things de Valera wanted to know about after his return from America were the events in the abortive truce negotiations. In an effort to damage the public image of its opponents, the British government in January finally published its account of the 'German plot' of 1918. De Valera's response was that the British government's distortions in that document would be kept in mind 'when estimating the probable honesty of so-called offers and proposals emanating from them'. Even in January Father O'Flanagan continued to meet with British ministers in London; and the President wanted to be informed about what had occurred at these meetings. Lloyd George finally tired of doing business with minions. He told O'Flanagan that he 'must deal with someone who could deliver the goods', whereupon O'Flanagan and James O'Connor, who had been involved in December, saw Sir John Anderson, who 'told them to sound de Valera'. The President stated that he was prepared to meet the Prime Minister provided no conditions were laid down. At the cabinet meeting of 30 January Lloyd George was strongly in favour of proceeding; Bonar Law was equally strongly opposed, and no action was taken.

De Valera was not interested in verbal messages about the prospects of negotiations. He told Father O'Flanagan that the best way to deal with telephone messages of this sort was to hang up. When James MacMahon, the Joint Under-Secretary, phoned him, he would only talk about other things. Andy Cope got the same treatment. If the British government was serious about negotiations, it would have to communicate this message openly and directly. De Valera's caution in this matter is understandable in the light of the events of December 1920, when the British government had pulled back from offering a truce when the other side gave the appearance of being eager for it.

Art O'Brien believed that Lloyd George was playing a waiting game. O'Brien wrote to Collins on 29 February saying that he believed that the Prime Minister 'is purposely letting things get as bad as possible, so that he may step in as the Saviour and cry a halt and then suggest his new measure with a flourish of trumpets'. O'Brien saw this as being only 'another stage in the game, but every such stage brings the general position more and more forward'.

In mid-March Lord Derby arrived incognito ('Arthur Vincent') as an unofficial emissary; he had an interview with de Valera on the 13th. De Valera later dismissed the meeting as being without importance; he told the Dáil in May that he regarded Derby as a mere political scout, and he 'spoke to him as he would to a Press Man'. The President had certainly been excited about the meeting before it took place; he must have been hoping for the first substantial indication that the British government was ready to treat. Disappointment turned to alarm when Derby proceeded to meet with Cardinal Logue, but de Valera's fear that the British government might succeed in driving a wedge between the Catholic Church and Sinn Féin proved to be unfounded.[58]

At this point the leaders of the Irish labour movement got involved. At a meeting on 16 January Labour's Thomas Johnson, William O'Brien and Thomas Farren told a ministerial team of Collins, Stack and FitzGerald that the ILP and TUC held the same views on a truce as did the Dáil government. According to William O'Brien, Thomas Foran, the General President of the Transport Union, received a telegram on 11 March from a British railway executive who urged Foran to come to London. On the following day, after a failed effort to confer with de Valera, the Labour leaders O'Brien, Foran and Johnson travelled to London. There they met with Edward Shortt, the British Home Secretary, who told them he believed the British cabinet was prepared to offer full Dominion Home Rule for twenty-six counties, but with restrictions on defence and foreign policy as well as no coercion of 'Ulster'. According to Shortt, the Labour men declared that they would support a settlement that included fiscal autonomy. If such an offer was made, they would issue a manifesto accepting the terms. According to the account given to the British cabinet, 'The Transport Workers had made an arrangement with Sinn Féin that if the Transport Workers came out with this manifesto the Sinn Féiners would denounce it but would allow the elections to be worked. One of the difficulties is that you have Sinn Féin who want to save their faces and get an excuse to get out of the Republic pledge and do not know how to begin.' Because of pending executions of members of the IRA, the Labour men refused to confer with other ministers. On their return to Ireland, Johnson and O'Brien met with de Valera. The only record of this meeting — a letter from the President to Collins — says nothing about the Labour proposal. De Valera did observe, however, that 'feelers are being thrown out in all directions just now'.

This was not quite the end of the affair. Mark Sturgis noted that J. J. Parkinson, a Dublin coal merchant who was involved with setting up the London meeting, told him that Sinn Féin would welcome what would look like a threat from organised labour in order 'to skip off the Republican platform upon which they find themselves so unfortunately fixed'. According to Sturgis, Foran also met with de Valera, and Parkinson conferred with Bishop Fogarty around 20 March. On the 23rd Parkinson held a meeting with O'Brien, Foran and at least one Dáil minister, Joseph McDonagh. On 25 March Foran called a meeting of the Transport Union executive to consider another deputation to London. Because of the failure to halt executions during the previous visit and a great reluctance to proceed 'without knowing they will get something', no action was taken. Sturgis met Foran alone on 26 March, and O'Brien on Easter Monday (28 March), by which time he had a message from Sir John Anderson in London, which, he said, impressed them. The episode drew to a close at the beginning of April when Sturgis was informed that 'Sinn Féin had vetoed any direct dealings with Labour and the Government'.

Both the Dáil government and Labour records are silent about anything beyond the meeting between the Labour representatives and Edward Shortt; no mention is made of any offers of settlement or manifestos. There were other meetings, however, and it seems most unlikely that the Labour leaders would have taken any initiative without the approval of de Valera at this time. It is probable that the Dáil leadership was trying to entice the British government into action with the lure of a division between Labour and Sinn Féin. Both Shortt and Sturgis said that it was the Labour leaders who initiated the contacts that led to the meeting, and they were certainly very quick to go to London after the telegram arrived. They might have talked with Shortt about fiscal autonomy and other matters, but the careers of Foran, O'Brien and Johnson give no indication that they would have attempted to get ahead of the Dáil government concerning either negotiations or terms of settlement.[59]

There were now a variety of people in motion claiming to be in receipt of peace offers from the British government. In order to reduce visitor congestion in Mountjoy, Arthur Griffith on 13 March announced that 'Any peace proposals between the British Government and Ireland should be addressed not to the Government's prisoners but to Dáil Éireann.' At the end of March Art O'Brien was told by a London friend that Basil Thompson, the head of Scotland Yard, was willing to act as an intermediary; O'Brien found this to be 'a good joke'. Parkinson and James Cuffe, a Dublin auctioneer, met with Lloyd George on 4 April. Later that month a certain Barney Daly, who had ties with W. T. Cosgrave, got in on the act. Sturgis found him to be 'terribly cocked up and thinks he is going to live in history'. John Steele, the American journalist, found a new contact partner in Seán O'Connell of Tralee, and the two of them made the rounds in London at the end of April. O'Brien reported that O'Connell 'is very much in the same category as our old friend Mr M[oylett]. He has limitless language and is inclined to regard his own importance as being of the greatest import in the whole world. . . . I wonder if Steele is wilfully malicious.'

In fact the Dáil's former intermediary Patrick Moylett did not remain inactive in the peace business and returned to the hustings in May, this time as a solo act; Diarmuid O'Hegarty called him 'a conceited ass'. At that time Frederick Dumont asked him to arrange a meeting between de Valera and Anderson or Andy Cope. Moylett contacted W. T. Cosgrave, who told him to see Cope. According to his later account of the meeting of 30 May, Cope told him: 'We are willing to acknowledge that we are defeated militarily; there is nothing for us to do now but exterminate the whole population of the country, and that we are not willing to do.' Moylett passed on the message. Father O'Flanagan also resumed his activities at this time.

By late March Collins had grown impatient with the involvement of the unofficial emissaries: 'May God help these poor people and their trust in silly souls. Yet they are a nuisance, and they have a way of getting themselves into the papers and into all sorts of things.' *Old Ireland* (5 Mar.) took a sterner view of their actions: 'These people do not realise that by keeping the door of intrigue open, that by encouraging the enemy's hope that the Irish claim may be compromised, they are making the existence of the Black and Tans and Auxiliaries possible.'[60]

The evidence is clear that the British government was generating a variety of peace feelers at this time. In late April Sir John Anderson declared that he 'could not understand why contact could not be established with the responsible persons in the movement', especially as Lloyd George 'was prepared to go to extreme limits to make a settlement'. The Prime Minister, in fact, complained in cabinet about the unreliability of some of the intermediaries. Why did the British government not use the direct approach? Undoubtedly it wanted to draw out the other side's position on a settlement without officially committing itself. Moreover, it did not want to be seen acknowledging the Dáil government's authority. If it could encourage unofficial contact, then it could try to make it appear that it was the other side that was asking for negotiations.

However, the other side did not bite at the bait. De Valera finally decided to simplify the process; on 14 June he made it known that if the British government sent his government a message, it would receive a reply.

From the beginning of the year the President employed the deliberate approach of public moderation in order to advance the feasibility of negotiations. Through interviews with foreign newsmen, he directed his message at world and British opinion. He offered Britain military security and Unionist Ulster autonomy — if the British government would only recognise what was political reality: the Republic of Ireland. De Valera explained his approach to Art O'Brien in May:

> I am keen personally . . . as the best way to lead on those Britishers who are anxious to come to terms. The main thing about it is that it leads them to accept the Republic as a fact from which all endeavours at compromise must proceed. . . . To those who are groping for some way out, we ought, I think, let them see a glimmer of light in the direction of an *independent friendly* state, with at least a guarantee of neutrality from us.

He found it necessary to respond to the objections of some of his colleagues to this approach. He informed Harry Boland at the end of February:

> There is no use in saying that Dáil Éireann cannot negotiate on account of the mandate which is given it, that simply means that Lloyd George will be put in a position of being able to force an Irish Party into existence to oppose us at the next elections on the platform of freedom to negotiate.

Seán T. O'Kelly was alarmed by de Valera's approach. He wrote from Paris on 17 April:

Lest you should have to say later, why did not people protest in time,
I hold seriously — and I shall be astonished if some others will not be
found who think as I — I hold that the firm stand we take 'on an
Irish Republic or nothing' needs not *change* but *development*.

De Valera's response was that he had been misunderstood, but he made
clear to O'Kelly that official representatives abroad 'must carry out the
instructions of the Department, whether they personally agree with
policy or not'. If they did not agree with a major policy decision, then
they should resign.

Did de Valera at this time think he could wrest recognition of the
Republic from the British government? When the Labour leaders told
him in March that British ministers were offering Dominion Home Rule,
he commented, according to William O'Brien, that they would have to
come another bit. Thomas Casement recorded in his diary on 14 June
that 'De Valera frankly told me he knew that a Republic was out of the
question. All he wanted was a Treaty between two Nations.' Years later de
Valera said Casement's statement was not accurate, that what he might
have said was that acceptance of the republican position was not a
necessary preliminary to negotiations. The British government had said
over and over again that it would not agree to a republic — but then, it
had said it would not do a lot of other things, and had then done them. In
any case, the President was evolving a plan to make a republic palatable to
the British.[61]

The British government was in a constitutional trap, one of its own
making. According to the Government of Ireland Act, if either of the two
parliaments provided for in the legislation failed to function by the end of
June, then crown colony status would follow on 14 July. One cabinet
member, Edwin Montagu, warned his colleagues of this possibility
in April: 'It would be an awful irony if our Bill results in Crown Colony
Government.' A further complicating factor was the forthcoming Commonwealth conference, due to be held in London in early July. Some
representatives of the dominions were sure to be critical of the government's Irish policy. Jan Smuts for one made this clear. Arriving in
London in mid-June, the South African Prime Minister informed Lloyd
George of his vehement opposition to that policy; it was his strongly
expressed opinion that 'the present situation is an unmeasured calamity'.

Alfred Cope, Lloyd George's personal agent in Dublin Castle whom
Sturgis believed had got to the point of accepting the enemy claims,
never stopped trying to encourage contact between the two sides. He
managed to convince both de Valera and Sir James Craig, the Ulster
Unionist leader, that each wanted to meet the other. A meeting was
arranged on 4 May, with Craig coming to Dublin and being driven
round and round by an IRA escort. The two quickly established the fact
that they had been brought together under a false assumption, and

nothing at all came from the meeting. Craig's version of the two hours they spent together was not flattering to de Valera. Craig said he met a man of haggard appearance, dry lips and an excitable manner. De Valera admitted that he delivered a history lecture. The two departed without any plans to confer again, and they never did.

Events began to move quickly in June. Seán Ó Muirthile later declared that the IRB approved of a truce at this time as it believed that 'the military campaign against the British could have no further success, and that perhaps terms could be obtained that would put Ireland in a position from which she could develop on lines that would enable her to achieve complete independence'.

Direct contact was established between the rebel state and Downing Street. On 14 June de Valera announced: 'If the British Government send a *written communication* to me *directly* I will reply.' A minor problem occurred when de Valera was arrested on 22 June; he was released the following day. He immediately wrote to Diarmuid O'Hegarty: 'I was released, of course, unconditionally, but for reasons of high British policy I expect. . . . I am going to move about freely for a few days, going only where no harm will come of it.' He called a meeting for the next day with Collins, Brugha and Stack. King George V made a plea for peace at the opening of the Northern Ireland parliament on 22 June. On the 24th Lloyd George invited de Valera and the associates of his choice to confer in London with representatives of his government. Sir Henry Wilson, the Chief of the Imperial General Staff, was furious at the Prime Minister's action. Wilson told his cabinet superior that the invitation was an act of 'pure cowardice, and if a man committed a sufficient number of murders he was qualified to be asked to breakfast at 10 Downing Street'. Two days later the President established his office in the Dublin Mansion House. Arthur Griffith was released from prison the same day.[62]

De Valera replied to Lloyd George on 28 June that before accepting the Prime Minister's invitation to a conference, he was going to confer with Unionist representatives. He invited Craig, now Prime Minister of Northern Ireland, and four southern Unionists to meet him. This time Craig did not come, but the others held a consultation with him on 4 July. To remind the other side of its American support, Sinn Féin staged an American Independence Day celebration in Dublin; British troops and police were dispatched to pull down some of the American flags. Then de Valera informed Lloyd George that there could be no meeting until a truce was arranged; the Prime Minister reluctantly agreed to this condition. Meanwhile Jan Smuts arrived from the Commonwealth conference in London on 5 July to inform de Valera of the advantages of dominion status.

On the same day, 5 July, negotiations for a truce began. The crowd around the Mansion House was so great that the President's messenger could not fight his way through. On 7 July de Valera met with Brugha, Collins, Stack, Griffith, Count Plunkett and Eoin Mac Néill 'to consider a very important decision to be made'. On the 8th he warned the other ministers of the 'danger of committing to paper any of our plans or views on the present negotiations'. Greeted by a cheering throng, about which he must have had mixed feelings, General Macready joined the negotiations taking place that same day at the Mansion House. When general terms had been agreed upon, de Valera sent a message to Lloyd George that he would come to London on 14 July.

The truce terms were announced on Saturday 9 July. They provided for a ceasefire and no provocative actions on either side. They said nothing about Dáil Éireann or the political situation, but these would be matters for the London meeting. Douglas Duff, then serving as a Black and Tan in Galway, was stunned by the news; he related: '"Of course", we argued, "this talk of a truce is all moonshine, not even Lloyd George would be fool enough to stop when victory is within his grasp." But it *was* so . . .'. Looking back on the event, Leo Amery, a member of the British cabinet, commented: 'Once their first surprise was over, the Irish leaders realised that their opponents' nerve had gone, and that they could afford to behave as the victors in an open war between two nations. It was a magnificent and well-sustained bluff.'

The ceasefire was to come into effect at noon on Monday 11 July. This left the weekend open, and the IRA made the most of it. In Dublin there was widespread relief, and the two days before the truce passed without serious incident. Outside the capital things were different. Almost every provincial unit, including those who had never fired a shot, sprang into action. Police barracks and British army posts suffered an onslaught. The Clare RIC inspector reported: 'There was evidently an intention to murder as many police and other Crown Forces as possible before the truce came on.' His colleague in Waterford observed that the two days' notice 'seems to have spurred the local patriots to redouble [their] exertions, doubtless to let the world see what dashing fellows they are'. While the Volunteers blazed away, a different kind of assault occurred in Belfast. Angered by the truce announcement, Unionist mobs attacked nationalist areas, as a result of which fifteen people were killed, sixty-eight wounded and 161 houses burnt.

At noon on the 11th the firing ceased. People poured into the streets. The men of the flying columns came down from the hills to be greeted as conquering heroes. *Old Ireland* described the scene:

> The towns and the hills were ablaze, not now with the residences of women and children, but with innumerable bonfires. On the night of the 11th and 12th few of the people remained indoors. National songs were sung in the streets; the flag of the Republic was publicly honoured.

In Leix 'there was jubilation on the part of the Sinn Féiners during the evening of the 11th and on the following days over the victory they had gained'. In the popular view, come what may, the cause of Irish self-government had triumphed; and that perception proved to be correct.[63]

From Truce to Civil War

(1) The Dáil Government during the Truce

The truce transformed the political situation. By its terms the administration and army of the underground government had been put on a position of equality with its counterpart. The leaders could now come out into the open. They sought to gain an understanding of what it all meant and what the future would hold. They also faced the problem of openly operating a government while its rival was still on the scene. The Castle administration, on the other hand, was in a state of trauma; its days were clearly numbered. In the early days of the truce both sides moved diffidently.

The American vice-consul in Dublin, Charles Bay, observed that the suspension of hostilities had an important political effect. He noted that the failure of Dublin Castle to control events 'has given the masses a sense of victory. With the realization of the truce, and the opportunity to organize and co-ordinate governing departments which function, the masses have had their aspirations visualized, in leaders, "cabinets", conferences, meetings, speech-making, etc., and their enthusiasm does not stop short of an absolute republic.' This view was generally shared by the RIC.

Public celebration of the truce was expansive and extended. The men and women of the counter-state and its army were treated to a near-orgy of public gratitude. Nothing was too good for them. Some IRA men clearly got carried away, strutting about in new uniforms and conspicuously accepting alcoholic tributes. In some places Volunteers commandeered vehicles. The Kerry RIC inspector said that this was done 'for the purpose of going to watering places. They say they are entitled to some consideration for having fought for the freedom of Ireland.' In Meath a car commandered on 10 July was found by its owner two days later, who 'naturally took it home'. On the 29th some Volunteers again seized the vehicle, alleging that 'he broke truce . . . by taking back his car'. At a more refined level, the new mood of euphoria even had its effects in the cultural and artistic sphere. When Kevin Barry's old unit in October asked Augusta Gregory's permission to stage a production of 'your beautiful little drama, *The Rising of the Moon*' for a fund-raising event, she quickly agreed. She also offered the Prisoners' Dependants' Fund the use of the Abbey Theatre and its cast for a production of Terence MacSwiney's *The Revolutionist.* On the night of the performance Richard Mulcahy took the stage to inform the audience: 'It seems to me that we have been deserted at the present time, and all through the struggle put up in the country, by our poets and by our literary people.' This seemed a bit rum to Lady Gregory: 'I wonder if he has seen Yeats's poem, and AE's on Brixton Prison, and his pamphlets (my *Nation* articles, not being signed, don't count).'

Tom Barry was appalled by what he saw when he visited Dublin:

> I could see the way the headquarters was carrying on in Dublin — big carpeted suites of rooms in the Gresham Hotel and bottles of whiskey and brandy all around. I went in and told them they should be ashamed of themselves.

The Shelbourne Hotel housed the IRA liaison office. P. J. Matthews, a staff member, observed that the office became 'a centre of entertainment' for Volunteers up from the country, as well as being besieged by job-hunters and people trying to sell things 'to the new rulers of Ireland'. Visitors charged bills for food and drink, totalling £20,000, to the office. Alfred Cope, the British agent, was a frequent visitor who 'often had late sittings with high IRA officers'. Matthews concluded that Cope knew 'nearly everything that was to be known about the IRA organisation'.

It was with difficulty that the work of the revolutionary government was resumed. De Valera found it necessary to issue a warning against excess. On 16 July Collins was able to tell him: 'Although there was a little more relaxation than I should have liked, everybody is working fairly hard again.' Characteristically, Collins put the interlude to good use: 'I have made millions of discoveries, and have been confirmed absolutely in certain things.' He was not concerned about personal security. 'I hadn't the slightest doubt', he declared, 'that no street members of their Forces would touch me.'

Some of the Dáil deputies had to be reined in. They were suddenly in demand for endorsements of financial schemes. The names of some deputies 'have been prominently displayed in advertisements as directors and patrons of various financial ventures'. To deal with the problem, Collins secured Dáil approval for the appointment of a registrar/ supervisor of societies. 'We are starting now what is a new order in Ireland,' he announced, 'and one of the first duties of the national Government is to secure that thrifty people shall not be deprived of their savings by any kind of schemer, or any kind of society, or group of individuals.' De Valera requested that until the registrar's office was functioning deputies would not allow their names to be used to promote investment schemes. Collins commented privately: 'I never did allow my name for any such and never intend to.'

Three days after the beginning of the truce de Valera had his first of several meetings with Lloyd George in London. These were followed by a lengthy correspondence, principally about the terms of the proposed conference. De Valera was not optimistic about a settlement. He wrote to Collins from London on 19 July: 'Things may burst up here suddenly, so all should be prepared.' Collins anxiously sought to find out what was going on in London. He wrote to Art O'Brien on 27 June asking him to 'find out what is being thought in well-informed circles'; on 11 July he urged O'Brien to keep in close touch with Crompton Llewelyn Davies, adding: 'You know how highly I value his advice and his judgment.' On the preceding day O'Brien had written desperately of his 'need for instructions immediately'. On the 28th he again pleaded for information: 'I have no indication from anyone as to how things are going or what may be expected.'[1]

The new Dáil, in existence since May, still had not met, which would appear to demonstrate a cavalier attitude on the part of the executive towards its legislature. The leaders probably did not want over 120 deputies milling around and asking questions while the initial steps in negotiations were taking place. O'Hegarty informed each deputy on 18 July that the meeting of the assembly 'must be delayed for a fortnight' owing to developments in negotiations. Then the government decided that the new Dáil would not assemble until all members were free to attend; this would require the release from prison of thirty-eight members. At the beginning of August the British government agreed to release all but Seán Mac Eoin, who had been convicted of murder. Michael Collins urged the Dáil cabinet to take a firm position on the matter: 'There can, and will be, no meeting of Dáil Éireann unless and until Commandant Seán MacKeon is released. The refusal to release him appears to indicate a desire on the part of the English Government to terminate the Truce.' Some cabinet members saw this as being too truculent, and de Valera's public statement on the matter only stated that without Mac Eoin's release he could no longer assume responsibility for further negotiations. Obviously dissatisfied with the President's statement, Collins brought his own statement to the *Irish Times*, which printed it on 8 August. This was followed by a press release from Erskine Childers pointing out that Collins's statement was 'wholly unauthorised'. With the release of Mac Eoin on the very day that Collins's statement appeared, the evidence of disagreement was generally viewed as having little significance. The country gave its attention to much more important matters than a minor cabinet tiff.

When the assembly finally met in mid-August, de Valera was elected President of the Republic, a position which had not existed before then. What this new position meant in terms of power was unclear, but at the least it meant an increase in status. De Valera certainly did not under-estimate his position. He told the Dáil: 'I more or less concentrate in myself the whole Executive responsibility.' This elevation caused some unease. W. T. Cosgrave is said not to have liked it, but did not give it much thought. One of the new deputies, Michael Hayes, believed this was the position of many of the members. George Gavan Duffy specifically objected to the provision stipulating that the President 'shall also be Prime Minister', which he saw as a 'dangerous precedent'. While Seán T. O'Kelly agreed that the President should not also be Prime Minister, he pointed out that the constitution (which he had helped to write) was only provisional and that there should be an understanding that the creation of a dual position did not set a precedent.

De Valera also took the opportunity to pour cold water on excited political expectations. He did this in small but sharp doses. At the first Dáil session, that of 16 August, he seemed to do some prevaricating about the Republic. He asserted that the 1918 election had demonstrated a clear demand for self-government, but 'I do not say that that answer was for a form of government so much, because we are not Republican doctri-naries, but it was for Irish freedom.' Two days later, in a private session, he swept away many illusions. The Irish in America had no political influence in national politics. No American President would recognise the Irish Republic at present. 'He himself would refuse to recognise it, for it could be imagined that he was elected President of the United States, because the American people would not back him, and would turn him down at once if he dared to do it.' Thus, 'as far as getting recognition was con-cerned, they might put it out of their heads'. On 22 August he told the assembly that 'if they were determined that they would only make peace on the basis of the recognition of the Republic, they were going to face war'. There was no use facing war again 'unless they in Ireland were pre-pared for a Sherman's march'. He also told the deputies that 'if the Republic were recognised, he would be in favour of giving each county power to vote itself out of the Republic if it so wished'. However, as we have seen, he had already stated his firm belief that the Republic would not be recognised.

In a private session on the following day he warned that negotiations with the British government probably would result in 'sharp differences' concerning the terms of settlement. He anticipated that 'we will, there-fore, have proposals brought back which cannot satisfy everybody and will not'. It was to be his role 'that when such a time comes I will be in a position, having discussed the matter with the Cabinet, to come forward with such proposals as we think wise and just'. This, in fact, is exactly what he did five months later. Finally, on 14 September he informed the Dáil that 'as far as he was concerned his oath of allegiance was to do the best he could for the Irish nation. That was the only allegiance he acknowledged.' After the euphoria of the early days of the truce, these were sobering statements.

De Valera took advantage of the truce to reorganise the executive. Its structure was changed to a cabinet of six major ministries, with seven minor ministries outside the cabinet. Those included in the cabinet were Foreign Affairs, Home Affairs, Defence, Finance, Local Government, and — a new ministry — Economic Affairs, with Robert Barton as minister. For the first time Publicity (formerly Propaganda) was made a ministry. The Department of the National Language was changed to Education, with J. J. O'Kelly remaining as minister. Count Plunkett was shifted to the new Ministry of Fine Arts. De Valera took pains to emphasise the value of the undertaking: 'It was very important . . . that the constructive work of the Government in literature and arts should get attention. It gave the appearance of stability and progressiveness to their affairs if they set up a Ministry of Fine Arts.' At the same time the Belfast boycott organisation was detached from the Labour Department and set up on its own, with Joseph McDonagh continuing as director.

There was very little change in personnel. On his release from jail in August, Desmond FitzGerald returned to his position as head of Publicity. He seemed to harbour some resentment towards his erstwhile replacement. Erskine Childers, after all, had been critical of the operation he took over in February. In any case, FitzGerald informed Frederick Dumont, the United States consul, that Childers had been left out in the reorganisation for good reasons. In the version relayed by the newly appointed Lord Lieutenant, Viscount Fitzalan, to Lloyd George, 'They have left Childers out of the Government altogether. This is good as he was dangerous, and I believe they make no secret that this is the reason, though they excuse it by saying that he is overwrought.' Yet de Valera told the Dáil that 'The Cabinet proposed asking Mr Childers to retain sectional work either in that Department or in Foreign Affairs Department. They could not lose Mr Childers's services as they were of extreme value to them.' The result of Childers' labours that summer was a series of persuasive booklets, *The Construction Work of Dáil Éireann*, which presented details of the administrative successes of the counter-state.[2]

The Dáil sessions of August allowed for full reporting of all departments, indeed a general review of their activities of two and a half years. Ministers explained what they had accomplished and why, and what they had not accomplished and why not. The department that attracted the most criticism was Home Affairs. The point of controversy was the failure of the courts to be sustained during the British counter-offensive and the lack of resilience of the Republican Police force. At one point de Valera remarked that he 'did not like to see Cabinet Ministers showing divided counsels before the Dáil'. In his view, 'they could not expect from that Department as much efficiency as from the military'. His solution was the decentralisation of civil administration: 'If they adopted such a scheme there would be no complaints about the working of the Home Affairs Department.' He did not address the matter of the executive ability of the minister of that department.

Another source of controversy was the working of the Foreign Affairs Department. In a bitter statement George Gavan Duffy dismissed the department's report as vague and misleading. His criticism centred on the communications system, which he claimed 'was as bad as bad could be'. He also brought up the matter of his expulsion from France as a result of his protest to the French President during Terence MacSwiney's hunger strike. Arthur Griffith asserted that Duffy's action was 'a grave error of judgment'. To rub it in, he added: 'The fault was with Mr Gavan Duffy. It was their [the Dáil's] envoy made the mistake and not the French Government.' De Valera put a stop to the recrimination by declaring that 'the thing was done and finished with'.

De Valera wanted to take full advantage of the opportunity provided by the truce to galvanise the activities of his government. On 23 July he pointed out: 'There are many activities of ours which ought to be carried on at increased pressure and which in no sense violate the spirit of the Truce.' The only activity precluded, of course, was that of guerrilla warfare. 'The heads of all Departments', he ordered, 'should therefore be at work feverishly to make the very most of the short time that may be available. To rest on their oars at this time would show a total want of appreciation of the situation.' On 25 August the Dáil approved a budget of £144,000 for the second half of the year. Employees were added to the police force, the foreign service and the Land Commission. On the other hand, the Dáil passed no legislation during this period.

There was a general revival of the Dáil courts. Austin Stack informed district court registrars that 'there must be no relaxation in our efforts to empty the enemy Courts, but the work should go on quietly and unostentatiously.' There should be no public notices of court sittings, and newspaper reports should be avoided. In addition, decrees and orders should 'be executed with as little display as possible'. This also was de Valera's position. He told the Dáil on 18 August: 'The courts should go on, but should go on quietly as before. This was a time for reorganising and doing work.' Some court officials took a more casual view of the matter. Stack told the court registrars that 'in very few cases have the necessary returns been made for the month of August'. Eamonn Duggan, the chief liaison officer, said that his British counterparts objected to court activity because 'we wanted to do things now that we could not do during the war. That was, justices who were afraid to sit before were now anxious to sit publicly.' The way forward, he believed, was to get an understanding that 'the courts could be held in private, as they were previous to the Truce, and do their work efficiently in such a way that the enemy police might pretend they did not know anything about them'. The position of the British authorities, which they had held all along, was that arbitration courts were lawful. If there was any doubt about the nature of any court, 'a senior Police Officer will attend and assure himself a Court is Arbitration only'. If it proved to be otherwise, 'inform those present that it is a breach of the truce and cannot proceed. Allow, say, half an hour for dispersal, then act in accordance with previous instructions, and notify HQ and local Sinn Féin.'

Stack also asserted that the Republican Police force had been established throughout the country, and he proposed that local police chiefs should be paid. Collins, always quick to take issue with Stack, held that paid police chiefs were not necessary. The British position on the Republican Police was that 'Sinn Féin Police are tolerated as IRA men'. On the other hand, 'RIC men must not submit to any interference in carrying out their duties'. De Valera recognised that there would be a difficulty in Republican Police officers enforcing judgments of Dáil courts. His advice was to go easy: 'He did not see the necessity of enforcing decrees overnight and they could be deferred for the time being.' Stack took the same approach: 'He did not think there would be many Decrees to be enforced, but he would prefer to hold over any case that would be likely to be tough.' When Duggan sent a message from London that decrees were not to be enforced, both Stack and de Valera rejected the proposal.[3]

The Local Government Department had its hands full dealing with difficult local authorities. Kevin O'Higgins reported in October that after the general release of deputies in August some members who had been imprisoned or interned for upwards of a year and were consequently out of touch with local affairs 'immediately began to criticise and obstruct the schemes of reform and economy'. Many of these local representatives 'have no appreciation of how near we were to a total collapse of this front last winter and in the spring of this year'. Although there was a 'certain amount of free-lance opposition by the Mayo Teachtaí', the problem centred in Wexford, where Deputies Etchingham, Ryan and Corish resisted efforts to close down county hospitals and workhouses. Corish was defiant: 'The Local Government Department is not An Dáil, and so its ruling need not be accepted as final.' Because of the loss of Dublin Castle grants of about a million pounds a year, local rates had soared. O'Higgins argued that 'This year's collection will only be successful if the general body of ratepayers are convinced that substantial economics are taking place.'

Some of the other departments launched initiatives. The Department of Education set up a commission on secondary education, with Michael Hayes as chairman, whose task was 'to draft a programme which would meet the national requirements, while allotting its due place to the Irish language'. The commission held its first meeting on 24 September, and a preliminary proposal was distributed to teachers, headmasters 'and others interested in education' at the end of November with the request that comments and responses be received by 15 January. In addition, the cabinet on 2 December instructed the minister to prepare a proposal on the serious matter of school attendance.

The Department of Trade and Commerce initiated action to deal with rising food prices. Dublin Corporation had earlier passed a resolution proposing that local food committees establish reasonable prices. Ernest Blythe thought this idea was extreme, but did propose that stores be required to list the prices of stipulated goods, principally food. He also proposed the establishment of a national food committee to investigate the problem of profiteering. The cabinet approved these measures in October and issued an appropriate decree on 11 November.

Art O'Connor was strongly in favour of allowing republican representatives to appoint nominees to the Council of Agriculture. The refusal of the Dáil government to allow this in May meant that the mandate of the existing council had expired. T. P. Gill of the Dublin Castle agriculture department was trying to reconstitute the council in November. O'Connor argued that grants totalling £190,000 to local committees of agriculture and technical education would probably be lost if the council could not be revived. Moreover, the council was an all-Ireland body whose nominees were selected by popularly elected representatives. The cabinet decided that participation would be granting recognition to the other administration, and that if a settlement with Britain was achieved, then every department of that administration would come 'to a rapid end'. The executive also concluded that confiscated lands should be returned 'as an act of grace on the part of Ireland'. At the same time it declared its opposition to the British scheme to grant land to ex-soldiers by compulsory purchase. The Defence Minister was directed 'to take the matter in hands', and the British were to be told through the liaison office that such action would be viewed 'as an incitement to a breach of the Truce'. The cabinet was not averse to taking control of existing bodies. On 18 November it instructed the Director of Fisheries to prepare a plan 'for the capture of the Inland Fisheries machinery at present in the hands of the Conservators'. According to a special correspondent of the *Manchester Guardian* (12 Oct.), the truce gave the Dáil government 'an opportunity to pursue the tasks which it has been attempting for more than two years such as it has never enjoyed before'. If agreement could be reached with the British government, he declared, 'the Irish people will have already in existence something more than the skeleton of a system of government according to their national aspirations'.

As part of a reorganisation of the Publicity Department, the cabinet in November proposed the publication of a 'weekly gazette', whose principal purpose would be 'to show how active the Republican Government really is, as well as keeping the various Departments informed of each other's work'. It added: 'All matter for publication to be censored by Secretary to Cabinet'; clearly this was not to be just propaganda for foreign consumption. Nothing more was heard of this proposal. But the foreigners were not overlooked. In order to swing American opinion to the Irish side in the pending negotiations, a cadre of deputies and other supporters was assembled for dispatch to the United States in September. Another consideration was the new loan which had been authorised by the Dáil on 26 August with the objective of collecting £500,000 in Ireland and $20 million (£5,250,000) in the United States). Collins complained that the group was composed solely of orators: 'Practical men will get the money; the speakers will not.' De Valera replied that 'Speakers to draw the crowds is part of the practical work.'[4]

The cabinet also took care to prepare for a renewal of hostilities. Even before the truce went into effect, it asked Clement France of the American Committee for Relief in Ireland 'to urge on importers of food to provide supplies against a blockade'. On 25 August the Dáil voted to allow the cabinet to make a provisional order which would have the effect of a decree until the next meeting of the assembly. Because the new Dáil was almost twice as large as the first Dáil, there would be great difficulty in assembling the full body in event of a renewal of war. De Valera proposed that the Dáil create a grand committee, with one deputy from each of the constituencies, to be available to meet in such circumstances. He argued that this arrangement would provide for some legislative review and supervision even if the full body could not meet. Several deputies objected to the idea, but it was approved, with the amendment that the membership of the grand committee would consist of thirty deputies, who would be elected from the four provinces in proportion to existing Dáil membership. This is the only time that the revolutionary Dáil passed any legislation that took into consideration, or was based on the reality of, the provinces.

Austin Stack wanted a law he could use to strike at the officials of the other government should hostilities resume. His proposed decree was specifically aimed at judges and others involved in Dublin Castle's judicial system, but 'the Ministry might think it necessary to deal with all kinds of English civil servants in the country'. De Valera announced that if fighting began again, the government intended 'to root out every enemy Department of civil administration in the country'; the cabinet 'was going to issue orders forbidding enemy civil functions step by step, and they would declare them enemies and traitors'. He believed, however, that the provisional orders decree would provide the executive power to achieve this objective, and Stack's proposal was withdrawn.

The principal means for preparing for a new onslaught was the establishment of locally based administrative committees — one for each county and county borough. These bodies would supervise the operations of the Dáil administration at that level. This would bring the Dáil government down to the grassroots and provide a nexus of administration should contact with Dublin be broken. Local people would have a local body to turn to when they had matters of government to be dealt with. Decentralisation, therefore, would deal with the problems experienced during the conflict of the Home Affairs Department. De Valera had told the Dáil on 18 August that he 'could see no way to get efficiency in civil matters unless they decentralised'. Two days later a special decentralisation conference met to construct the plan, and in the following week the Dáil approved the proposal. Deputies were asked to volunteer to serve, and thirty-five did so.

De Valera was serious about the scheme. He told Stack that he wanted 'the very best men in the county — those who still stick through thick and thin'. He realised that the process of creating about forty committees 'will necessarily be a slow one, but now would be the best time to get going on it'. Stack met with Cosgrave and Pádraig O'Keeffe of Sinn Féin on 2 September to frame the structure of the committees. They proposed that the committees have six to nine members, with paid secretaries. The President believed that smaller committees — restricted to three members each initially — would be more effective. He held a special conference with representatives of Home Affairs, Local Government and Economic Affairs on 26 September at which it was agreed that the three departments would nominate members for the committees. In addition, those deputies who had volunteered to serve would be *ex officio* members of the committees in their counties. Local councils could also make nominations. The names of nominees were circulated for examination to deputes, local councils and Volunteer commandants on 7 October; since the matter was urgent, a reply was requested by 17 October. On 11 November the cabinet directed Stack to draw up a draft decree defining the authority of the administrative committees; he did so, and this decree was passed a week later. These committees never went into operation, as there was no resumption of hostilities. It seems likely, however, that they would have filled the gap between Dublin and the rest of the country that had proved such a problem before the truce.[5]

(2) The Northern Question

The Northern problem was obviously pressing. The six-county Home Rule government of Northern Ireland had been established in June and was busily organising its administration. Authorised in mid-1920, a huge Special Constabulary had been developed. A Northern Unionist enclave had become a fact.

The truce was greeted in Belfast with another spate of sectarian conflict, which was renewed periodically through the autumn. As far as Northern Unionists were concerned, the truce was a victory for Irish nationalism. Eoin O'Duffy, as the IRA liaison officer for Ulster, set up headquarters in Belfast. The Northern units of the Volunteers were reorganised and the Republican Police were established in nationalist areas of Belfast. At a meeting on 12 August the Northern members of the Sinn Féin executive supported the continuation of the Belfast boycott. Several representatives supported both passive and active resistance to the Northern parliament.

At the August meeting of the Dáil de Valera made what appeared to be a conciliatory statement about the North. He declared that if the Republic was recognised, 'he would be in favour of giving each county power to vote itself out of the Republic if it so wished'. This statement was consistent with the position he had taken during the first half of the year. He added, however, that 'otherwise they would be compelled to use force'. Eoin O'Duffy believed that only force would be effective: 'The Ulster people have very little force themselves if unaided by British armed forces. So far as Ulster was concerned, they could not meet them by concession. He had dealt with them by force in Monaghan, Fermanagh and Tyrone, and these people were now silent.' Alex McCabe declared that he 'would not exchange Irish unity for an Irish Republic for a portion of Ireland'. The President was aware of the need to accommodate the Ulster Unionists if a united Irish state could be achieved through agreement with the British government:

> His attitude would be that the minority in Ulster had a right to have their sentiments considered to the utmost limit. He believed the minority in this country were devotedly attached to certain connections and it was their duty so far as they could to go to the utmost limit without sacrificing the interests of the majority.

The boycotts of Belfast and selected British goods continued during the truce, as did sectarian violence in Belfast. On 17 August Joseph McDonagh told the Dáil: 'The Truce does not mean that the Belfast boycott is off, but only that drastic measures cannot be taken at present.' Indeed, British units were instructed to prevent the destruction of Belfast goods and to arrest anyone who did this, 'using force if necessary'. Belfast merchants had used 'every ruse to break the boycott and a number of cross-channel firms had helped them', McDonagh said, but when his organisation prepared a black-list of the British firms involved, the managing directors 'asked them for God's sake to take off the boycott, professing to have great sentimental as well as business interests in Ireland'. There also had been resistance in Dublin, but this was too broken: 'Some of the firms in Dublin with the biggest names saw fit to trade with Belfast, but every one of those had in the end to pay a fine of £100 . . . and to sign an apology.' At least one prominent company did not conform. On 2 December 1920 the cabinet was asked to stop the trams in Dublin because the Dublin United Tramway Company (William Martin Murphy's firm) had not paid a fine of £300 and continued to carry advertisements for banned Belfast goods. The cabinet passed the matter on to the Defence Minister and the liaison officer. At the same time it instructed the boycott director to appoint a travelling investigator 'to examine the whole question of infliction and collection of fines'.

The management of the boycott ran into controversy as a result of the action of the Limerick committee in boycotting goods from all over the six counties. The Dáil decree had limited the boycott to five towns: Belfast, Lisburn, Dromore, Banbridge and Newtownards. Arthur Griffith held that the Limerick committee 'was acting in defiance of the Dáil. It was no use for the Dáil to pass a Decree against Belfast if Limerick decreed a boycott against the Six Counties'. In October the cabinet considered placing Portadown on the boycott list.

In September Collins made a tumultuous appearance in his constituency in Armagh. In the same month a special Ulster committee, headed by Eoin Mac Néill and Seán Milroy, was established. This was to be another propaganda body, to promote the cause of Irish unification. In November the cabinet instructed the committee to prepare a comprehensive publication on the Ulster question. Diarmuid O'Hegarty directed that 'The booklet should be so drawn up as to admit of the inclusion of our concrete proposals regarding Ulster at the Conference when their final form has been settled.' The conference, of course, was over before the booklet was ready. Dr James Gillespie of Cookstown, Co. Tyrone, wrote to de Valera in November to warn that the transfer of executive power to the Northern state was continuing while negotiations were proceeding in London. The head of St Columb's College in Derry asked the cabinet if his institution should recognise the Northern state for the purpose of securing grants. De Valera was to deal with the matter on 8 December, when he had arranged to meet a delegation from the six counties.

The government decided not to add to the list of prohibited English goods, because such action 'would be used as an argument by the English to show how well-founded their fears of the imposition of protective tariffs by the Irish against themselves are'.[6]

(3) THE UNDERGROUND ARMY ON THE SURFACE

The terms of the truce of July 1921 were almost wholly concerned with military matters. An uneasy relationship existed from the first between the guerrilla fighters and their old opponents. Problems soon arose. There were thousands of men still interned and imprisoned. The young men of the IRA walked the streets, with their counterparts hovering nearby, full of anger and resentment. As one RIC inspector glumly noted, his men 'are hard put to it to look on and do nothing'. The IRA began an expanded training programme and also collected money in many parts of the country. Tom Barry, the IRA liaison officer in Munster, quickly came into conflict with British authorities concerning protocol and practice. On a visit to Dublin he was disgusted by the subservience of Eamonn Duggan, the chief liaison officer, towards Dublin Castle. Barry took the opportunity to tell General Macready he was a flat-foot bastard and a few other things. Another RIC inspector commented that 'The persons who seem to be the most active in organising breaches of the so-called truce are the "liaison officials." On a trip to his native Cork in mid-July, Collins found British soldiers acting in a manner that was 'arrogant and provocative.' Overall, however, the truce was generally observed by both sides because both sides wanted it to work. Probably the most serious incident occurred in Galway during October when a group of British soldiers invaded a fund-raising dance sponsored by the Republican Prisoners' Defence Fund. During a resulting brawl a British officer was killed.

There were a lot of loose ends that needed to be dealt with. The British authorities wanted to know what happened to British officers who had been kidnapped during the conflict. A request from Thomas Jones to Art O'Brien for a list of burial places of executed officers met with response that in the case of the 1916 leaders and Kevin Barry 'the demand of the relatives to have the bodies handed over to them, for the purposes of decent burial, has never been listened to'. O'Brien proposed that both sides should let the matter rest for the time being. In October Mulcahy ordered all units to 'give enemy no information about missing agents'. Collins had to deal with two difficult cases. One concerned the fate of Mrs Georgina Lindsay of Cork, who, in fact, had been executed as an informer; the other dealt with the effort of the mother of one of the British officers shot on Bloody Sunday to prove that her son had been killed on mistaken information.[7]

Both military forces kept a close watch on the activities of the other side. British forces observed that the IRA continued to collect funds by means of levies and that some of the money collected 'was spent in buying beer at the nearest public house'. An intelligence report declared that one such collection 'has caused such a lot of ill-feeling amongst all classes in Co. Clare (Sinn Féiners included) that they discontinued the practice. . . . It will be noticed that this ill-feeling was noticed after the damage was done.' At the end of August the Dáil government decided that the imposition of all levies would cease, but did allow uncoerced collection of funds under 'the greatest possible supervision'. Referring to a request from a unit commander about the position, Diarmuid O'Hegarty told Brugha: 'There is no doubt a lot of truth in what the O/C says regarding people who want a Republic and not prepared to give anything for it.' In mid-October the cabinet members available in Dublin decided against all collection of funds by the Volunteers. They based their decision on the fact that such collections had not been given government sanction and that it would work against the planned new loan campaign and the principle that the army should be supported by the national treasury. From London Collins voiced his opposition to the decision, arguing that they should not make it too convenient for the other side and that they should not give up the principle of the thing. The army turned to other fund-raising activities — boxing matinees and other sports events.

The British army noted that the IRA was working hard to increase its armaments. It claimed that 'the arrival of a number of Thompson sub-machine-guns has been followed by the organisation of machine-gun squads'. These weapons were 'the most important new adjunct in the Sinn Féin armory.' It drew this conclusion: 'There is little doubt that the IRA is far better equipped than it was prior to the Truce.' Seán MacMahon, the Quartermaster-General, later revealed that the number of machine-guns on hand increased from a mere six before the truce to fifty-one. He also observed that the cessation of hostilities 'brought with it no facility for this Department, which had to carry out the greater portion of its work as under war conditions'. From the beginning of the truce GHQ ordered an intense accumulation of war materials; there was to be no vacation time. The Department of Defence loaned £1,000 to the 1st Western Division for the establishment of arms factories. Moreover, the British forces were not able to prevent the smuggling of arms or their manufacture within the country.[8]

One of the serious problems faced by the Volunteers in the summer of 1921 was the flood of recruits; it seemed that everyone wanted to be one of the brave boys of the IRA. These were the 'Trucileers', who, commented Michael Hayes, 'by dint of drilling and parading . . . persuaded themselves they were soldiers and actually felt the need of doing some fighting against somebody. Places where there had been no fighting against the British now found that they had an enormous number of Volunteers.' There were so many men available that Brugha could not accept a group of military specialists that Harry Boland had recruited in the United States at Brugha's request. Mulcahy argued that 'Our experience is that we cannot very well succeed in absorbing these men and that we get a very much better return from money spent upon our own men.'

Lacking in weapons and training facilities, it was difficult to maintain discipline in such a large civilian-based force. Mulcahy later referred to 'the Truce excesses of many, who without being useful politically were only on the fringe of the Volunteers, and came in for the sun of the summer and the Truce'. A recurrent problem was that of public drunkenness. A British intelligence report observed that at an IRA dance in Co. Limerick 'many were drunk and brandished revolvers and automatics, causing a certain amount of consternation'. Máire Comerford recalled that heavy responsibilities had suddenly been placed on young officers 'who had proved themselves in the flying columns, but had not established their ability to keep their heads when flattered, or to hold their drink. The more exuberant of our young heroes were soon to be seen around in their new uniforms, plus the latest thing in green leather coats and fast sports cars.' As late as 21 October the cabinet voted that a general instruction concerning intemperance be issued to all units.

The army leadership was also concerned to keep the military from intervening in civil affairs. At the beginning of the truce Mulcahy made the position clear:

> Volunteers as Volunteers are under their ordinary military control shall not interfere or order interference in any matter of civil administration except in so far as such interference is covered by the definite order or permission of their superior officer.

Inevitably there were incidents. On 21 October the Chief of Staff ruled that 'no member of the Police Force shall be removed from Police work without the authority' of the national police chief. At the same time, however, he annulled as invalid an order issued to an officer to resign his position as a court registrar: there was 'no prohibition preventing a Volunteer occupying any position on the Civil side of our Administration'. When he heard about a Volunteer 'sworn inquiry' into alleged irregularities in a Dáil court, he responded by insisting: 'There must be no direct interference on the part of Volunteers, as such, in matter of Civil Administration.' After a group of Volunteers forced a civilian to repay money to one of their members, Austin Stack told Mulcahy that someone deserved a 'severe reprimand, at least'.

A notable case arose in Bray in September when three former Volunteers who were members of the local prisoners' dependants' committee were charged with neglect and were arrested by a group of Volunteers. Then Gearóid O'Sullivan, the Adjutant-General, ordered the three men off the committee. After an investigation by Judge Cahir Davitt, the cabinet concluded on 24 November that 'Government forces, Civil or Military, should not be used on work of this kind without order of Court-Martial or Civil Court.'

Mulcahy decided to use the truce period to try to resolve some of the problems that had arisen between the military and civil organisations.

The major difficulty, of course, was between the army and the Home Affairs Department. He asked a leading staff officer, Lieutenant-General J. J. O'Connell, 'to review the difficulties the Army had been suffering under in its work, by reason of the fact that there was not a proper organisation of the civil side in the country'. In sending the report to Brugha, Mulcahy 'suggested that he would look at this, not as a statement of things that were supposed to exist, but rather, with the question in his mind, that if these difficulties and weaknesses did exist, what ought to be done to remedy them'. Brugha objected to this line of inquiry: 'The person who made these allegations should be made prove them.' Mulcahy later commented: 'That was the end of that, even though the attitude then of the [Minister] for Defence was that we were to be fully prepared for a return to war.'

Another matter Mulcahy had to deal with at that time was the army's relationship with Sinn Féin. In July Brian Fagan, of the party executive, wrote to Austin Stack blaming the army for the withering away of Sinn Féin over the previous two years:

> This inability to see beyond the end of a gun, even where the guns are used, has resulted in the wholesale lapsing of Cumainn. Even those who are physically unfit for military service have been influenced by this view, and have ceased to take any interest in Sinn Féin as such.

Fagan wanted the military to issue a general circular, 'pointing out that the two arms of the Government, military and political, should work together and supplement each other'. Of course, the party organisation was not part of the government, but Fagan did not see it that way. When the proposal reached Brugha, he handed it over to Gearóid O'Sullivan, whose response was that 'The army officers have had thrown upon them practically all the work of the Government. . . . Sinn Féin Cumainn have died because there was no source from which they could derive continued inspiration and direction in activity.'

Mulcahy later pointed out that Stack, as joint secretary, had done nothing to maintain the vitality and organisation of the party. In any case, in his weekly memorandum of 21 October he noted that there were complaints that Volunteers were 'standing aloof' from the party and that 'this is not right'. He declared that 'the ultimate object of the Army work is the building up of the Social and Civil life of our country' and 'that the Sinn Féin Clubs are the medium through which proper Republican representatives in the Civil sphere are selected and secured'. This statement probably placated the party executive. Already Sinn Féin had been assigned a specific task, something it could get its teeth into — the creation of a nationwide communications system for the Dáil government. The network was almost ready for a test run when the Anglo-Irish Treaty was signed.

While negotiations were proceeding in London during the autumn there were few incidents between the two forces. The British government did object, however, to the public announcement in October that the Dáil courts were to hold sessions. On the 12th de Valera had written to Collins in London to stress that it was 'very important that you stipulate that our civil functions — police, courts, etc. — go on'. He argued that 'their work can be carried on *unostentatiously* . . . but they cannot be given up, otherwise the truce if continued long enough would mean that we had gone out of business'. Collins' reply was heated: 'If the unostenticity part of it had been maintained we would not have been let down like we have been. It is just a damn shame, that's what it is, and cheap bravado at that.' A week later Mulcahy instructed all units not to allow 'interference by the Enemy of our Civil Administration'.[9]

There was always a danger of a breakdown in negotiations and the consequent resumption of hostilities. Lloyd George agreed with Art O'Brien that termination of the truce should be subject to a week's notice on either side, but he failed to put this in writing. On 23 September *An tÓglach* warned its readers: 'At all times since the Truce started it was the duty of every Volunteer to consider himself liable to be called back on active service at a moment's notice, but at no time was this more obviously the case than at present.' As negotiations reached a critical stage de Valera issued a directive on 24 November 'to prepare for an immediate breakdown in the Peace Negotiations. Plans for safeguarding documents, etc. should be taken in hands at once and only the necessary minimum kept in the working office.' If hostilities were resumed, the army planned a general onslaught on all of the offices of the other government; such an attack had in fact been about to take place and was prevented only by the agreement of the truce. In any case, there was no breakdown of negotiations, but there was a near breakup in the leadership of the Volunteers.

Cathal Brugha and Michael Collins had been engaged in a lengthy tug-of-war concerning authority within the army and other matters. Brugha issued orders through Mulcahy to get at Collins, and Mulcahy objected. This was going on before the truce, and the situation got worse after that. Twice during the truce Brugha dismissed Mulcahy from his position, then reversed his decision. More than once Mulcahy threatened to resign. In addition, the Irish Republican Brotherhood continued to constitute a problem and a source of division. As a former member, Brugha was aware that this organisation claimed to be a power unto itself. Four of the members of the headquarters staff (Collins, Mulcahy, O'Sullivan and O'Duffy) and several unit commanders were in its leadership. A new and deep source of conflict arose in Brugha's decision to recommission the army. The army, of course, predated the existence of the state and was only brought under the authority of the Dáil as a result of an agreement between the army executive and the

Defence Minister. A recommissioned army would make the civil control of the military officially absolute.[10]

The idea of a recommissioned army first surfaced in September when the cabinet voted on the 15th that the force was 'to be put on [a] regular basis'. It also decided that Austin Stack, who had been nominally Deputy Chief of Staff, should attend GHQ meetings and that Brugha should 'get an office of his own'. There apparently was no consultation with the military leaders concerning the proposal. Brugha insisted that the reorganisation was necessary 'in view of the possibility of further fighting and in order to put the Army in an unequivocal position as the legal defence force of the Nation, under the control of the Civil Government'. One 4 November the cabinet reaffirmed the decision and ordered that the recommissioning should proceed forthwith. All staff members and divisional commanders would be offered the impressive rank of commandant-general, and the new commissions would take effect on 25 November. Collins, busy with negotiations, did not get directly involved in the matter. He kept at an amused distance; Brugha, he said, was carrying on somewhat like Napoleon. At this time Brugha and Mulcahy were at daggers drawn. Mulcahy wrote to de Valera informing him that 'The continuance of the present relationship between the Minister for Defence and myself must, I fear, lead to the destruction in a very short time of the vigour and discipline of the Staff.' He declined to attend any further staff meetings. De Valera patched up the quarrel somehow, but ill-will persisted. When on 4 October Brugha appointed J. J. O'Connell to be in charge of the commission of defence (organised in conjunction with the London negotiations) Mulcahy inquired: 'What will be the role of GHQ in Defence Proposals?' Brugha's reply was 'None'.

Later that month, on the 22nd, Mulcahy sought to find out what was happening with the army recommissioning and presented Brugha with his recommendations for the staff; they did not include Stack. Brugha wanted Stack as Deputy Chief of Staff, but Mulcahy would not have him. He wanted Eoin O'Duffy, who had been acting in this position, to be formally appointed as his deputy. He wrote to Brugha on 1 November: 'If the Ministry decide to make an appointment to such an important Staff position against my judgment, I cannot accept the responsibility attaching to any position on the Staff.' Nevertheless, three days later the cabinet once again approved the recommissioning scheme. Mulcahy and Brugha resumed their tussle. Offered the enhanced rank of commander-in-chief, Mulcahy asked on 16 November if he would have the authority to select the staff; Brugha replied that this would be the responsibility of the minister. As far as Mulcahy's recommendations were concerned, Brugha made two changes: Stack would be Deputy Chief of Staff, and O'Duffy would be Director of Organisation. Mulcahy again threatened to resign, sent the correspondence to Collins in London, and requested a meeting between the staff and the cabinet. Brugha then became conciliatory: 'I intend recommending to the Cabinet that the personnel of the new Staff shall be the same as the old one that worked so well.' O'Duffy specifically objected to the position offered him, which he viewed as 'a personal slight and a grave dishonour'. At least one of the proposed generals was swelling up in his new uniform.

The simmering ill-feeling and resentment boiled over at a meeting with de Valera on 25 November. First there was a long and exhausting cabinet meeting at which terms of the proposed treaty with Britain were debated. Then, before meeting with the staff, de Valera took Mulcahy aside to tell him a compromise had been arranged. O'Duffy would be Deputy Chief of Staff acting for Mulcahy, and Stack would also be a Deputy Chief of Staff, acting as 'Cathal's ghost on the Staff'. This arrangement apparently was not transmitted to the staff, who proceeded to complain about the recommissioning. Besides the inclusion of Stack, what they had to complain about is unclear, but their response was one of pouting emotionalism. This was their organisation; they had built it, they had made it. In objecting to any changes, J. J. O'Connell declared that the staff 'had been a band of brothers.' They certainly were — brothers in the Brotherhood. O'Duffy asserted that his proposed appointment as Director of Organisation was 'an insult and a criticism to himself'. De Valera had had enough of these uniformed prima donnas. Responding to the emotional tone of the meeting, the President, according to Mulcahy, 'rose excitedly in his chair, pushed the small table in front of him and declared in a half-scream, half-shout: "Ye may mutiny if ye like, but Ireland will give me another army" and he dismissed the whole lot of us from his sight.'

Five days later Brugha had Mulcahy send out a letter to unit commanders that all was well and that they should formally accept the new commissions. One divisional commandant (and IRB member), Liam Lynch, protested that Mulcahy and his staff 'cannot do their duty when they are not placed in a position to do so'. The IRB group at headquarters seized upon questions concerning subordinate rank and titles to delay the reorganisation until the whole matter was swallowed up by the Treaty controversy. Brugha had waited too long to act.

That members of the staff could carry on as they did was entirely due to their substantial political influence. Mulcahy and Collins had been deputies and ministers from the beginning; Béaslaí was a deputy. O'Duffy, O'Sullivan and Mellows were elected to the Dáil (as were many other IRA leaders) in May. Thus six of the thirteen members of the general staff were also deputies. The mixing together of political and military, political and administrative, positions was a flaw in the system that had caused problems all along, but it now became a much more serious matter. The incident did not become public knowledge, but certainly it was not the way to prepare for the possibility of war. The whole episode was apparently nothing more than a storm in a teacup, as there were no substantial changes in staff positions. What was so terrible about having Stack included? He had been nominal Deputy Chief of Staff all along. Would he really show greater interest in military matters than in the past? Was there some special reason that the staff feared that Brugha would have an informant at the meetings? Apparently the members of the staff had grasped the reality that there was not going to be any resumption of hostilities with the British. They had turned their attention to matters of rank and prestige and to any presumed threat to the positions they believed they had justly earned. In effect, the lines of division were being drawn.[11]

(4) Negotiating the Treaty

In looking forward to negotiations with the British, the leaders of Dáil Éireann could reasonably anticipate that they soon would be the governing authority in at least three-quarters of Ireland. Any agreement, no matter what its terms, would result in the closing down of the other administration. The Government of Ireland Act of 1920 at least provided for that.

The Dáil sessions of August demonstrated that the executive was not going to hold out for a fully independent state. The British government simply would not have this. There was a general recognition within the counter-state that a return to guerrilla warfare would not change this position. What was needed was an arrangement with Britain that would satisfy Irish nationalist aspirations as well as British defence concerns. A formula was evolved — a scheme of external association, which would allow for Ireland to be a republic and have full powers in internal matters, yet be associated for some external affairs with Britain and her empire. It was de Valera who conceived this ingenious answer to a major political dilemma. The idea first surfaced around June, and, according to Cosgrave, it was introduced to the cabinet but not explained. According to Griffith, de Valera asked him to get him out of the strait-jacket of the republic; this was, in fact, precisely what the external association device was intended to do.

Now came the task of selling the idea to the British government, which was prepared to offer a limited form of dominion status, but nothing more. There was also the need to provide for British security concerns (military bases, for example), but this did not seem to be a major difficulty for the Dáil government. Finally, there was the Northern situation, which, owing to partition and the entrenched position of Ulster Unionism, was now recognised as constituting a major problem. Art O'Brien forwarded some subtle advice from London:

We must use our strength to get what we want, not to 'score off them' or merely to show they are in the wrong. We can even let them save their face, their *amour propre*, or get out of it without appearing to surrender, as long as the surrender is there. For instance, the Partition Act. If they said let us frame on to it together a Statute which will satisfy you, and to which we can agree, and which can be ratified by both countries: if it gave us all we want — our freedom, because it had once been the Partition Act, and they could say it had once been it — we are too strong, and would be, to my mind, grudging them their hollow 'triumph'. Our ultimate act of independence must, I think, come by some such process of evolution. It will come into existence like a volcanic eruption.[12]

De Valera's direct involvement in negotiations was preliminary and largely ceremonial. He met with Lloyd George a few times, presented his proposals, rejected the British terms, and then withdrew to a campaign of correspondence. A British intelligence report in August declared that he 'is the typical example of an Irishman who has already made up his mind to buy a horse or cow at a certain price, but will argue around the price for some time, simply because it is his nature to do so'. It also reported that the 'merchant, farmer and shopkeeper class . . . consider the terms offered as generous and are quite willing to accept them. However, should negotiations fail, there is no doubt that they are such "rabbits" that they would assist the IRA as hitherto through intimidation.' On the other hand, it reported that 'The loyalists view with horror the present terms, and have decided, in the event of these being accepted, to clear out of the country. . . . They will only be allowed to live in the country as long as it pays the local inhabitants to keep them.' Bishop Fogarty also reported a favourable reaction to the British terms by nationalists. He wrote to Collins: 'Apart from Partition, which may be remedied in whole or in part, the people feel that there is in the proposals something very substantial to negotiate and work upon.' Collins forwarded the message to de Valera with the comment 'I don't like sending you this, but I suppose it is the proper thing for me to do.' The proposed settlement drawn up by the Dáil government at the end of August puzzled Mark Sturgis: 'The Shinns themselves confess that after days of public and private deliberation they have succeeded in producing a document which no ordinary brain can interpret.'

If an agreement could be hammered out, it would have to be through a conference. This was arranged for October. Now came the business of deciding who would do the negotiating for the Irish state. De Valera immediately decided that he should not be part of the team. It was better, he believed, that he should be held in reserve, as a symbol of the Republic. He had observed that Woodrow Wilson had failed at Versailles, but Wilson's failure at the Peace Conference was not due to his personal involvement. The negotiating team would refer back terms to the President and, of course, the cabinet. De Valera's position split the cabinet, and it was only by his casting vote that he remained at home. Griffith, Collins and Cosgrave were opposed. The matter was not allowed to rest there. At the Dáil session of 14 September Cosgrave declared that 'They were leaving their ablest player in reserve. . . . The reserve would have to be used some time or other, and it struck him now was the time they were required.' Gavan Duffy and Collins also urged de Valera to go. The President again explained why he thought he should remain behind: 'To be in the very best position for the possibilities of a breakdown and to be in the best position to deal with those questions as they would arise and not to be involved in anything that might take place in those negotiations — to be perfectly free . . . ' De Valera later said that he believed that if external association was accepted, he would be in a stronger position to secure approval from hardline republicans — both in the army and the Dáil — if he was not a direct party to the agreement.

Then who would go? An obvious choice was Griffith, but he was no republican and could be expected to work for no more than a moderate agreement. De Valera later said that he considered Griffith as bait for Lloyd George, leading him to the Irish position. What he said to Griffith at the beginning, however, was that 'there may have to be scapegoats', and Griffith said he was willing, if necessary, to play that role. Collins was not an obvious choice. He was a man who really could be kept in reserve — the publicly acclaimed guiding force behind the underground army. Collins himself did not want to go, but de Valera pushed him into it. The President told the Dáil why he believed Collins was a good choice: 'It was from the personal touch and contact he had with his mind that he felt and he knew the Minister for Finance was a man for that team. He was obviously vital to the delegation.' Neither Stack nor Brugha would go, and no one expected them to go. Neither man had demonstrated intellectual subtlety or even capacity; they were simple men with simple ideas. Stack later declared: 'It consoles me to feel that from the outset I instinctively and openly set my face against negotiations in London; so did Cathal.' Here was a recipe for conflict: whatever terms — short of heaven and earth — Collins and company brought back, Stack and Brugha would not be able to resist the opportunity to attack their arch-rival. Did no one see this probability? The other negotiators were Robert Barton, the widely respected Minister for Economic Affairs who had carried on a long struggle with the authorities in Dartmoor; Eamonn Duggan, an almost silent member of the Dáil and accommodating chief liaison officer during the truce; and George Gavan Duffy, an international lawyer and Dáil diplomat. Erskine Childers was appointed as the delegation's secretary. John

Chartres was brought from Germany to advise on constitutional law and the workings of British government.

The members of the delegation were given the status of plenipotentiaries, that is, having full powers of negotiate and sign an agreement. De Valera argued that they needed this status for purposes of prestige and moral standing. Yet they were instructed to refer all important matters to the cabinet before making any agreement. So back and forth they went, and their reports too, and in the end this arrangement broke down. If de Valera had been in London with them, there would have been no need for all the shuffling back and forth, which contained no real advantage, yet had the potential for misunderstanding, and more.[13]

At the September Dáil session de Valera took the opportunity privately to prepare the deputies for a compromise settlement. He informed them that 'As far as he was concerned, his oath of allegiance was to do the best he could for the Irish nation.' He stressed the necessity for pragmatism: 'He again warned them of the fact they were sending men to do a thing a mighty army and navy could not do. They had got to face facts no matter how high their ideals were and to deal with a practical situation as they found it.'

The Dáil government anticipated lengthy negotiations. On 3 October it instructed Joseph McGrath to rent a house in London for at least two months. The conference began on 11 October. Cabinet decisions were forwarded to ministers in London, who would have a week after receipt to indicate if they wanted to decisions reconsidered after they returned. Progress concerning negotiations was reported by Griffith and Childers to the cabinet in Dublin. Back and forth went the files.

Political rhetoric was reined in for the duration. The Minister for Labour was advised that she could speak strongly about the mistreatment of political prisoners, but should not demand their release or mention a report which condemned their living conditions. The Sinn Féin executive proposed an amendment to the party constitution which pledged support to Dáil Éireann but said nothing about the Republic.

What was the popular anticipation about the outcome of the negotiations? A British army intelligence report dated 17 November noted: 'The people seem optimistic, but most feel that they will get whatever they want without any more bloodshed. All people seem to think that peace will finally be attained.' A week later a similar report commented: 'An early settlement is expected is expected in the area, and the IRA are boasting about what they will do when they get Home Rule.' When Charles Bay, the American vice-consul in Dublin, peered into the future, he saw a sordid picture:

> Whatever settlement is arrived at of the Irish situation, the new phase will be the breaking up into political divisions, for the national psychology exemplified in an intense national egotism, attempts to

rejuvenate an all but extinct and useless language, and a world-wide agitation, will disintegrate into an individual effort to obtain rewards and benefits of office. In the latter, the Irishman is characteristically excellent, and aided by a climate which does not impose the exercise of prudential faculties, he universally tries to supply his few needs by means of cunning or subterfuge rather than hard work.

As an agreement loomed the delegation returned to Dublin on 24 November. At a meeting the next day the cabinet agreed that the Irish state would have a link with Britain through the crown:

> The following formula was unanimously approved: 'That Ireland shall recognise the British Crown for the purposes of the Association as symbol and accepted head of the combination of Associated States'.

This was in keeping with the external association approach, but the British government would insist on more imperialistic terminology. Despite Brugha's objection, the cabinet also agreed to the provision of an 'annual voluntary sum to Civil list'. The British would insist on more substantial financial ties than that.

The delegation again returned to Dublin on 2 December and went into session with the cabinet on the following day. The meeting demonstrated that the only remaining major stumbling-block to an agreement was the form of the oath of allegiance. It also revealed that the delegation was split. Barton and Duffy, as well as Childers, believed more could be extracted from the British, while Griffith, Collins and Duggan basically did not. Both Brugha and Collins objected to the wording of the proposed oath of allegiance, but Collins pointed out that it would not come into effect for twelve months, and he asked if it 'would be worth while taking that twelve months and seeing how it would work'. De Valera and Brugha objected to the provisions for the North, which included a Boundary Commission. In his characteristically blunt fashion, Brugha addressed the matter of the division in the delegation. He wanted to know 'who was responsible for the splitting of the Delegation so that two members (Messrs Griffith and Collins) did most of the work and that the other members were not in possession of full information'. He was told that 'the British Government was responsible for the arrangement but that it had the approval of the whole Delegation'. Brugha's response was that 'the British Government selected its men'.

De Valera chose to ignore the reality of a deep division within the cabinet. He proposed an amended oath of allegiance:

> I, ... , do solemnly swear true faith and allegiance to the Constitution of the Irish Free State, to the Treaty of Association and to recognise the King of Great Britain as Head of the Associated States.

In his view, the document was close to being acceptable: 'With modifications, however, it might be accepted honourably, and he would like to see the Plenipotentiaries go back and secure peace if possible.' Griffith made it clear that he would not break on the question of the crown 'and thereby hand to Ulster the position from which she had been driven'. He argued that the document 'would practically recognise the Republic'. He warned that 'the country would not fight on the question of allegiance and there would be a split'. What he wanted was to have the plenipotentiaries sign the agreement and 'leave it to [the] President and Dáil to reject'. He made it plain that 'When as many concessions as possible [were] conceded and when accepted by Craig [?], he would go before the Dáil. The Dáil was the body to decide for or against war.' So Griffith was all for agreement, including this agreement, and he was prepared to circumvent the cabinet in securing its acceptance by the assembly. Collins also indicated that he was ready to settle. He warned that 'non-acceptance of [the] Treaty would be a gamble as England could arrange a war in Ireland within a week'. He was prepared to recommend that the Dáil 'go to [the] country on [the] Treaty'. Collins too would not be stopped by de Valera or the cabinet.

That Griffith and Collins, at least, were prepared to act before receiving cabinet consent can be seen in the matter of the contribution to the civil list, which was proposed to the British side before the cabinet voted on it. Moreover, there was another party to the negotiations — the Supreme Council of the Irish Republican Brotherhood. According to Seán Ó Muirthile, Collins kept this group informed and it approved the form of the oath that appeared in the final agreement.

At this crucial cabinet meeting of 3 December the President was once again asked to join the delegation, and once again declined. He later said that once he had secured Griffith's commitment not to sign any agreement before referring it back to the cabinet, he decided not to go. Negotiations were obviously at a critical juncture. If there ever was a time for calling in the reserve, it was then. If there was a split, as now appeared likely, the supposed dignity of his office, which he was so concerned to protect, would count for nothing. Or was he really protecting himself from the unpleasant business of making a compromise settlement with Britain? Here was a man who agonised over words. How could he ever be satisfied with the wording of the proposed agreement, if he did not have a direct hand in its composition?

So ended the last cabinet meeting before the signing of the Anglo-Irish agreement. Griffith had to hurry for the mail boat; he had to be back in London the next morning. But what was he planning to do in London on a Sunday? No negotiating sessions were arranged for that day. Similarly, on the night of 25 November both Griffith and Collins had to leave before the session with the headquarters staff to catch the mail boat. What was the rush? Mail boats often leave late; could not the sailing have been held up for a couple of hours while they concluded critical consultations about their country's future? Why not wait and take the morning boat? Or was it that they wanted to get away quickly?

The delegation was supposed to go back to London, try to extract better terms, and then send them back to Dublin. It did not happen that way. Lloyd George obviously believed that five months was long enough to achieve an agreement. Using threats as well as persuasion, he succeeded in forcing the matter to a decision, demanding that all the delegates should sign the proposed treaty. Why did the delegates not contact Dublin by telephone? For reasons of security, they had never communicated with de Valera in that way; even if they had telephoned at that time, the President was not in Dublin. Instead of remaining at his post in readiness for the final confrontation, de Valera was far away, ineffectually reviewing Volunteer units on the west coast.

A further complication was the threat of a British onslaught if negotiations failed. This danger, however, had hung over the conference all along, and it is hard to believe that the Irish team was intimidated by it on the night they signed the Treaty. The threat of a renewal of the conflict had earlier been used by de Valera and others to get the Dáil in the proper frame of mind for compromise. With both sides so close to agreement, the British government lacked political support for a sustained military effort. According to John W. Dulanty (subsequently the Irish representative in Britain), the British government never intended to renew hostilities. During the negotiations Winston Churchill told him that 'whatever else might be the outcome of the treaty negotiations, England would not embark on further military operations in Ireland', that the War Office was entirely opposed to the renewal of the campaign. Dulanty said he reported this to the Irish delegation and to Dublin. Gavan Duffy later concluded that Griffith accepted the terms because if force did not follow rejection, then Lloyd George 'would appeal over our heads to the country', which was 'likely to expose the weakness of the really national elements and perhaps to reveal an insistent yearning for peace'.[14]

(5) THE TREATY AND AFTER: REPUBLIC OR FREE STATE?

The articles of agreement signed by the Irish and British negotiators on 6 December 1921 immediately sparked controversy in Ireland. At the last cabinet meeting on 3 December Griffith had agreed to send back to the cabinet the results of the final negotiating session. De Valera was depending on this. During the course of negotiations all the members of the cabinet had agreed to some form of compromise with the British. De Valera was poised to intervene in the negotiating process at the end, but the Treaty was signed before he could do so. That all of the Irish negotiators signed the agreement is testimony to the fact that the negotiations had taken on a life of their own. On the other hand, it was only natural for de Valera to be offended and angry by Griffith's failure to send back the terms one more time. A week later the President told the Dáil: 'I was captaining a team, and I felt that the team should have played with me to the last and that I should have got the last chance which I felt would have put us over and we might have crossed the bar in my opinion at the high tide.' Moreover, the two sides in London agreed to the publication of the terms even before de Valera and the cabinet had seen them; that was, at least, sharp practice. In addition, both Griffith and Collins made press statements extolling the agreement before they left London. So the conflict about the agreement started off with charges of bad faith and dereliction of duty.

Some of the leaders, Desmond FitzGerald for example, were surprised that de Valera opposed the agreement. At the meeting between the cabinet and the negotiators on 8 December supporters of the Treaty urged de Valera to endorse it. Those opposed urged the signatories not to do more than present and recommend the document to the Dáil. The meeting failed to achieve agreement. According to Erskine Childers, Collins argued 'that in a contest between a great Empire and a small nation, this was as far as the small nation could get. Until the British Empire was destroyed Ireland could get no more.' Brugha warned that there would be opposition in the army, but he was prepared to accept the judgment of the Dáil. De Valera would not discuss army opinion: 'The Army as such was the instrument of the Civil Government and must obey the decision of the Dáil.' One of the leading military men, Liam Lynch, also believed at this time that the army would not divide on the issue.

The agreement contained many great benefits to Ireland: British recognition of Irish autonomy, complete control of affairs within the country, the takeover of the Dublin Castle administration, its bureaucracy and resources, and the obvious potential for further constitutional development. One of the negative aspects, felt by everyone in the Dáil, was the fact that the agreement required the maintenance of some constitutional linkage with Britain, including an oath of allegiance. Members of the Irish legislature would be required to swear 'true faith and allegiance to the Constitution of the Irish Free State', as well as declaring to 'be faithful' to the British monarch — although the latter was, at best, a vague commitment. The problem of the Unionist North was dealt with by the Boundary Commission provision, which Griffith, Collins and just about everyone else assumed would result in the transfer of large amounts of territory to the Free State, leaving the Unionists with a pathetic enclave. Only Seán MacEntee gave serious attention to the impact of the Treaty on Ulster, which he saw as being disastrous.

De Valera had wanted external association and failed to get it. Now he wanted the Dáil to reject the Treaty and allow the cabinet once again to propose external association. But the British government had made it clear that it would not agree to this. What would have happened if the Dáil had rejected the agreement (as it almost did)? The most likely result is that there would have been further negotiations, but it seems unlikely that London would have agreed to substantial changes in terms. New negotiations would have provided the opportunity to examine more carefully all of the provisions of the agreement, particularly the Boundary Commission clause — which subsequently turned out to be the most contentious of all. Yet the Irish negotiators would have been in a relatively weak position. Both public opinion and a large number of deputies supported the Treaty. Furthermore, there was every indication that most politically conscious Irish people were willing to accept the Treaty on the grounds that it provided for peace, stability and the opportunity to look to the future. Meanwhile, however, the Dublin Castle administration and British forces would have remained in place; Ireland would have continued to exist in a political limbo, except in the six north-eastern counties, where the Unionist administration continued to take root.

In the debates of the Treaty, which raged from December to January, opponents concentrated on the objectionable symbolism insisted on by the British government. Supporters of the agreement admitted that they did not like the symbolism either, but argued that it was one of the distasteful parts of the package that nevertheless provided enormous benefits. They privately put forward the persuasive argument that the Free State could be used as a stepping-stone to the Republic. To counter this argument, de Valera issued a proclamation on 4 January which declared: 'Be bold enough to say NO to those who ask you to misrepresent yourselves. If there were not a gun nor an ounce of lead in Ireland you should say it.' Many opponents declared they could not break the oath they had taken to uphold the Irish Republic. In practical, concrete terms, what was the difference between the Republic and the Free State? Sinn Féin would control the Irish government. There would be no British authority within its territory. The dominions already had effective independence: the British government had no power in Canada. Building on the basis of the Free State, the nation would be in a position to move on to a Republic if it chose. Taking into consideration the intervening Commonwealth constitutional development, how little difference there was between the two statuses can be seen when in 1949 Ireland did cease to be a dominion and became officially termed a republic. No change in coinage, postage stamps, or anything else except the official description of the state.

The concentration on symbolism by the opponents of the Treaty may have been due, in part, to the fact that they could not find much else that was objectionable. The Treaty split was the surface manifestation of an internal division that had been developing. Any agreement made by Griffith and Collins, whatever its content, would be met by opposition from Brugha, Stack and others. This was their great opportunity to put Collins in the wrong. Everyone knew that the agreement with the British would involve compromise, but this simply provided ammunition to the enemies of Griffith and Collins. De Valera had managed to keep a semblance of co-operation between the two sides, but with the Treaty this was no longer possible. Since he himself had not negotiated the Treaty, he opposed it, specifically because of the oath of allegiance.

The principal reason why symbolism was so important in the Treaty controversy was because Sinn Féin, indeed Ireland, had been living in a world of political theatre. The whole thrust of the political movement was based on activism, dramatic gestures, manifestos and posturing. All of this had been most effective. The British were being stripped of control of the country largely by these means. There had been a lot of concrete, practical administrative work done, but that was not nearly as exciting or popular. The glorification of the IRA, especially since the truce, re-emphasised the attractions of gestures, drama, action. There were many who wanted to continue to live in an atmosphere of revolutionary fervour. Liam Ó Briain has described what they had lived through:

A highly emotional experience, an escape from hum-drum sordid existence, happy days in internment camps, exciting meetings, intimate committees, delightful Sunday evening causeries, writing articles and poetry, wonderful public funerals, praying outside prisons, patriotic concerts and the grand feeling of superiority, of being a hero.

Then there was the membership of the Dáil, elected the previous May in an atmosphere of defiance and rabid nationalism. Many of its members were unsophisticated young men who had a few fixed political ideas. At best, they had only the haziest notion about how the social and economic life of the country should be developed. Suddenly they were being asked to make a serious decision on a very practical but mixed proposition — the Treaty. Many of them decided to stick to their few fixed ideas. The practical, mundane benefits of the Treaty were too much for them; they contained no political excitement, no opportunities for heroic posturing.

There were many people in Ireland who shared this enthusiasm for political theatre. They recognised the great progress that had been achieved by militant nationalism. Sinn Féin and the Dáil government could both rightly claim mass political support. Some people wanted to maintain the Republic at any cost. Others were indifferent and even hostile to the Republic. Most people, however, were prepared to accept a good bargain when they saw it. They viewed the Treaty as an opportunity to consolidate many of the gains that had been made. They also knew that more could come later on.

This raises the question as to how real the rebel Republic was perceived by the Irish people. Some of them saw it as merely a sham, play-acting, an empty imposture. Others viewed it as a living, effective reality in their lives. Most people had to recognise that it was at least one of the governing forces in the country. What was said about it during the Treaty debates? Many anti-Treaty speakers maintained that they had taken an oath to uphold the Republic and intended to keep it, but no one talked about the achievements of the republican government. The response, of course, would be that all those things could be done on a bigger scale and with adequate resources under the Free State. Griffith pointed out that the Republic did not have effective control during the struggle with the British:

> You have been spoken to as if you had a Republican Government functioning all through Ireland, and that you were asked to give up this Government and functioning Republic for this Treaty. You all know here that, instead of governing through Ireland, the most we could do was to hold, and to barely hold, the position we were in.

Desmond FitzGerald made basically the same point: 'The Republic has been spoken of as if it were a thing existing unchallenged. If that is so, I don't know what we were fighting for.' Joseph McGrath argued that the alternative state was not an effective government because it was incapable of achieving any progress towards the fulfilment of the Democratic Programme, which declared it was the first duty of the Irish Republic to provide for the children of the nation. Lorcan Robbins, one of the new deputies, added that 'The Republic of Ireland is only two years old, and it was a very weak infant all the time. I was working for it, and I know how it was able to function.'

While the great debate proceeded, an attempt was made to avoid a divisive vote. The pro-Treaty leadership privately argued that the Dáil need not vote on the agreement. This could be done by the 'Southern Ireland Parliament', provided for in the Government of Ireland Act. With the Treaty ratified, the British would withdraw their army and hand over control of its administration. Then the question of Free State *versus* Republic could be fought out at a general election. The anti-Treaty leadership would not agree to this device. After the Treaty was approved the Dáil continued to meet. Griffith was now President, and he agreed to maintain the Republic until the voters had decided on the Treaty. At the same time Collins became head of the Provisional Government which had the task of taking over the Dublin Castle administration. Anti-Treaty deputies were adamant in asserting that the Republic was still in being; they viewed with suspicion the activities of the Provisional Government, which was not responsible to the Dáil. Most importantly, the anti-Treatyities continued to participate in the assembly. For a time it looked as if the Treaty would be put into effective operation without violent opposition. It seemed as if Collins's proposition to his former colleagues might be accepted: oppose the Treaty but not the Treaty position.

Acceptance of the Treaty was urged by most of the press, business organisations, the Catholic hierarchy, local government bodies and the leaders of the labour movement. In its manifesto of April 1921 the ILP and TUC had asserted that the country was facing an economic crisis. After an unsuccessful effort by the Labour executive to get the Dáil to accept an agreed plan of action before voting on the Treaty, Thomas Johnson lobbied for acceptance of the Treaty. Immediately after the Treaty vote he led a Labour delegation into the Dáil to urge the deputies to put political discord aside in order to confront the deepening recession. The Labour Party congress issued a statement that said, in effect, that the agreement should be worked for the sake of the social and economic welfare of the nation. As the split within the national movement widened, the Labour executive took further action. On 24 April 1922 it staged a widely observed general strike against the growth of militarism. At the same time, in order to bridge the political gap, it proposed a plan, which included the principles that the Irish people held all political power and that Dáil Éireann would continue to be the sole legislative authority in the country. It further suggested that a plebiscite on the Treaty issue be held, thus separating the question from the election of a new national assembly. Why these sensible proposals did not secure acceptance from both sides is testimony to the poisoned relations within a riven Sinn Féin.[15]

Hopes for a peaceful transition in government were dashed by the intervention of the military. This might not have happened — or at least not decisively — if the opposition to the Treaty in the Dáil had not been so great, but the membership of the assembly was now split almost right down the middle. The Treaty was supported by a majority of the army headquarters staff (nine for, four against), as well as the executive of the IRB. The principal argument that swayed both bodies was that the agreement could be worked for all it was worth and would be a stepping-stone to the republican objective. Many commanders and ordinary Volunteers were not impressed by the staff's endorsement. The men in the localities, having little political experience, preferred a clearly defined, simple position on the matter. Ringing reaffirmations of the Republic appealed to them. This was appropriate to their truce-time elevation as selfless and heroic soldiers; local opinion expected them to stand fast. Many of them, who had done no fighting before the truce or had joined afterwards, had to demonstrate that they were true to their oath to the Republic. Moreover, the weapons and supplies accumulated during the truce were on hand.

As the new Minister for Defence, Mulcahy had promised that the IRA would remain the official army, and many military men hoped that

Collins, de Valera and the other political leaders might yet come up with a solution to the conflict. In addition, they anticipated that an army convention, called for March, would clarify the situation for the rank and file. A peaceful transfer of barracks and military bases to IRA began in February. Then the army split. Foreseeing an anti-Treaty majority, the Dáil cabinet voted to ban the convention, whereupon the anti-Treaty group established its own executive, which seized control of several public buildings in Dublin, including the Four Courts, on 13 April. Was this to be a re-run of 1916? The Irish people certainly had demonstrated a dramatic shift of position when a small group took action on that occasion. The leaders of the executive obviously hoped that history would repeat itself, but the situation in 1922 was quite different — this time there was a new Irish government in formation, led by two widely respected men. Nevertheless, O'Connor, O'Malley, Mellows and the others pushed ahead with their plans to prevent the displacement of the Republic. As British and police units withdrew from provincial posts, conflict, sometimes violent, broke out between the two factions within the Volunteers. At the same time both forces covertly co-operated in a campaign against Unionist authority in the six counties.

For a time the politicians simply watched the slide to chaos. De Valera, the most important of them, did not oppose the actions of the anti-Treaty military men. In fact some of his public statements offered them cleverly phrased encouragement and support. Emerging in his role of abusive combatant, Kevin O'Higgins attacked de Valera's statements in the Dáil as well as in the new pro-Treaty newspaper; in the latter he characterised de Valera's pronouncements as being those of a 'fury-ridden partisan of the wild words and bitter taunts, the leader of men whose methods are rapidly degenerating into emulation of the "Black and Tans" '.

The anti-Treatyites in the IRA, in any case, were not looking to de Valera for leadership. He was shortly afterwards to write to a colleague: 'The old contempt for civil or semi-civil work apparently persists.' For a time it looked as though the Collins–de Valera agreement concerning the election might avert civil war. The agreement provided for a united slate of Sinn Féin candidates, with the two sides having nominees in proportion to their existing strength in the Dáil. Other parties and candidates would be free to participate, although various methods were used to discourage them. After the election a coalition government would be formed. Collins had held out the hope that many of the objections to the Treaty would be remedied in the draft constitution. When the British government insisted on a document which used terminology objectionable to republicans, public release of its contents was withheld until the eve of the election, thus denying the voters time to consider the document. Gavan Duffy believed that its publication 'on the morning of the election, too late to be studied or even to be seen by many electors, was a shock to men of good will'. Speaking in Cork just before the election, Collins urged voters to support whatever candidates they wanted, thus undermining the election pact.

Griffith did nothing to head off civil war; he rigidly stood by the Treaty and opposed all attempts to bring the two sides together. He certainly did not support the Collins–de Valera agreement, although, with extreme reluctance, he consented to it. He readily agreed to the British demands for changes in the draft constitution. Although he was only fifty-one, Griffith's health was in rapid decline, and he died of a cerebral haemorrhage only a month after the election to the third Dáil. During the Treaty negotiations Griffith had been drinking heavily, perhaps to relieve extreme tension. (Collins was also drinking, but he was a young man and in excellent health.) During the Treaty debates Griffith displayed the impatience and temper of a person suffering from hypertension. Of course, he was not solely responsible for the Treaty split and the civil war, but his unfortunate physical and mental state was a factor in these developments.

The election results showed that the voters in the twenty-six counties wanted peace and were willing to accept the Treaty. Among the Sinn Féin candidates, 56 of 66 pro-Treaty and only 35 of 59 anti-Treaty nominees were elected. Some well-known republicans were defeated. Moreover, all of the others elected — Labour (17), Farmers' Party (7) and independents (6) — were prepared to work the Treaty. The way was now clear for the meeting of the new Dáil, announced for 1 July, and for the formation of the much-discussed coalition government.

As an adjunct to the election pact, an effort was made to reunite the army. Already the two sides were co-operating in a secret campaign against the Northern regime. For a time it looked as if reunification might take place, but a convention of the anti-Treaty forces held on 18 June was hopelessly split, with some in favour of accepting an agreement with the pro-Treaty side, and others supporting a pre-emptive attack on the remaining British troops.

Six days after the election, on 22 June, Sir Henry Wilson, former British army chief and rabid supporter of Ulster Unionism, was murdered in London. The anti-Treatyites had no hand in this; the act was committed by members of the London Brigade of the IRA, probably acting under an order from Collins. The British government took the opportunity to demand that the armed opposition of the Four Courts forces be terminated. In any case, the Four Courts executive decided that it now had to act if it was not to be left behind when the political wheels rolled forward. Its seizure of vehicles and the capture of General J. J. O'Connell, Deputy Chief of Staff of the Free State army, was one of the precipitating events in setting off civil war. On the other hand, the Free State forces were preparing to attack even before these actions took place.

The attack on the Four Courts seemed to disorientate the Provisional Government. It seemed as if Collins and his colleagues wanted a crushing military victory before resuming the political game. The resort of physical force, which Collins had earnestly sought to avoid, would stifle the maddening criticism of those who had accepted the British bargain; more denunciation could be expected concerning the constitution, about which Collins had held out such fond hopes. As early as 4 July de Valera declared his belief that Collins had initiated the attack 'to cover up the killing of Henry Wilson'. Militarism was in the air. Collins gave up his position as head of the Provisional Government in order to become commander-in-chief. Now he could be a real soldier, not the leader of back-alley guerrillas. Kevin O'Higgins and some others like him, who had never had anything to do with the Volunteers, 'joined the army' with high rank. The fine new uniforms could be put to use. Although the opening session of the new Dáil was due to take place on 1 July, it did not in fact meet for another two months; Collins and Griffith made no public statements about the next constitutional step; nothing further was heard of the coalition government. The members of the political opposition were left to join the military opponents. De Valera, for one, was prepared to attend the July meeting.

After repeated postponements, the Dáil finally met in September, but by then the damage had been done. Henceforth political debate in the Free State would centre around who caused the civil war and who shot whom. This suited many political people, as it was vivid, simple-mined grist for small mills; it demanded no serious thought about the building of a new Ireland.[16]

The continuing split so weakened the Free State government that it was unable to avoid the fiasco of the Boundary Commission. Many of the 'pure republicans' who preoccupied themselves in debating the oath and other remnants of arcane imperialism bore considerable responsibility for this outcome, which continues to be a source of violent contention seventy years later. They refused to accept the argument that these English trappings could be disposed of once effective Irish self-government had been established. Some of the anti-Treatyite political leaders were moving in this direction, but by then they had lost control of their military allies. Their revolution turned on itself. As the violent factions of nationalism clashed, Ireland completed the process of becoming an independent nation.

6

Conclusion

The essential idea of Sinn Féin — achieving self-government by action and self-reliance rather than by entreaty and agitation — led to the formation of the counter-state. The preconditions for such action were the excited democratic expectations generated by the European war, Irish frustration concerning self-government, and the 1916 rebellion.

The major difficulty facing the movement for Irish self-government in the immediate wake of the European war was that it sought to achieve this from one of the most powerful states in the world, one that had just emerged victorious from that conflict. Surely Britain could deal with a small-scale rebellion on the adjacent island which had a population of a mere four million. Yet Britain's strength was more apparent than real. The United Kingdom was weakened and exhausted by the war. As time was to show, the British people were not prepared to support a sustained, exasperating and apparently fruitless operation which they did not believe involved vital national interests. Moreover, after a long political agitation, the British government was committed to providing at least some measure of Irish self-government, although there was the assumption that it would not go as far as many Irish nationalists wanted.

The immediate post-war period, in fact, was a most opportune time to strike for Irish self-government. British public opinion wanted to get the Irish question settled, one way or another, and at last off the political agenda. The wartime propaganda of the Allies — that they were fighting for democracy and the rights of small nations — provided Sinn Féin with irrefutable arguments. Woodrow Wilson's plea for national self-determination gave Irish separatists a platform to demand the application of this principle to the Irish people. Sinn Féin used these arguments not only with its own people but also with the British, and in doing so struck at a sensitive spot in the imperial power. By focusing on the contradiction between democracy and imperialism, the Irish movement exposed an embarrassing conflict of values within British political thinking.

The movement which conducted the drive for full self-government was a coalition of moderates and radicals. In October 1917 those who had been seeking a peaceful evolution of self-government in Sinn Féin were joined by those who advocated more vigorous methods and an absolutely independent state. The party, in turn, was effectively in coalition with the Irish Volunteers, the popular militia that evolved into a guerrilla army. It is not surprising or unusual that there were conflicts and rivalries within the movement, but these did not impair the efficiency of the two organisations, and were largely unknown outside of the leadership, until their goals had been essentially achieved.

Sinn Féin employed a radical method but did not have a radical ideology. It presented no grand vision of reform of Irish society; rather, it promised renewal, by the sole means of having Irish people make decisions about Irish matters. Yet it had clear objectives. The first of these was the establishment of self-government and the creation of an Irish state. It had a cultural goal — the revival of the Irish language as the vernacular of the country — and, growing out of that, the re-creation of a distinctively Irish culture. The third objective was to impose national direction, if not state control, of the development of the country's resources. The achievement of the last two objectives were dependent on the use of state power, which could only happen if the first objective was attained. The recognition that the instrument of government would be necessary is evidence that Sinn Féin had a practical and, indeed, progressive concept of how it could attain its ends. Of course, the Irish people had long been conditioned to state direction in a wide range of matters. The party also accepted as given the prevailing ideas about parliamentary government, economics and social organisation. This position was politically advantageous in that Irish opinion also accepted the conventional ideas of the day. Time was to show that these ideas were lacking in the thrust and incentive necessary to move a backward country to overcome its deficiencies, but they seemed promising to young political zealots at the time.

One of the undoubted benefits of long inclusion in the United Kingdom was the experience in representative government gained by the Irish people before the country became independent. It also meant that the country already had many of the institutions needed for a functioning nation-state. Based on a popular mandate, the opportunity for which was provided by the 1918 general election, Sinn Féin proceeded to establish Dáil Éireann as the national legislature. Irish nationalists had no objection to the parliamentary system of government as such; they simply wanted to have their own assembly. But the revolutionary government was more democratic than the parliamentary system it was breaking away from. A republic replaced a monarchy; a unicameral assembly was substituted for a parliament which included an hereditary second chamber; there were no social distinctions based on law. This is further evidence of the essentially progressive and democratic nature of the Irish independence movement.

The leaders of the new government set out with determination tempered by caution in their effort to make the alternative administration the effective governing force in Ireland. Their success in doing so undoubtedly exceeded their most sanguine expectations. The principle reason for this achievement was that the methodology employed appealed to the Irish imagination. Here was a unique way to achieve the desired end. It contained all the necessary ingredients — novelty, theatre, self-dramatisation, duplicity and a degree of danger.

In its initial period the rebel state relied on gestures and propaganda while it made its plans and gathered the resources that would make an effective, if small, administration possible. Where the Dáil government failed to take the initiative, ordinary supporters forced the issue. Believing in the basic tenet of Sinn Féin, they were prepared to act, rather than wait for a signal from Dublin. This was the creative part of the Irish revolution. The most vivid example of this — and the most important test of the counter-state — was the land agitation in the western counties during the spring of 1920. The Dáil itself had set the stage for this development by its grand gesture of June 1919 in passing a decree which stated that land for the landless was now the law of the Republic. At that time it made a modest beginning towards achieving that objective with the establishment of the National Land Bank. If the agitation had been allowed to continue without check, Dáil Éireann's claim to be the governing authority in the country would have been discredited. The Dáil government was slow enough to respond, but, forced to act by the pressure of events, its response was effective. Rather than stifling the agitation, it channelled it into a responsible mode through the formation of the land tribunals and, later, the Land Commission. It also held out the probability of further action when full self-government had been achieved.

A similar pattern can be seen in the creation of the courts. First the Dáil ordained that courts should be created, but left implementation to local initiative. While the Dáil cabinet occasionally set up a tribunal to deal with a few Dublin squabbles, first a committee and then Austin Stack considered what to do next and came to the conclusion that the difficulties were daunting. In the spring of 1920 local initiative quickly devised a court system, and the Dáil government finally caught up with this development.

The revolutionary government gained a wide measure of effective authority in the country. There is no example where its clearly stated policy was rejected by the mass of the people. On the other hand, Dáil Éireann acted with calculated restraint in what it tried to do. It claimed the allegiance of the people, but did not put that loyalty to an unduly severe test. For example, it did not demand that the people transfer income tax and land annuity payments to the counter-state; indeed, it did not even say these payments should no longer be made to its rival.

The Dáil government initially had an ambiguous relationship with the revolutionary military force, but it gradually and effectively asserted its authority over it. Only in the supreme crisis of the Treaty controversy did this authority break down. Right at the beginning there was the embarrassing situation where a handful of Volunteers attacked policemen on the very day on which the Dáil was inaugurated. It should be noted, however, that there was no repetition of this sort of incident. Given the need for local initiative and autonomy, the IRA followed the main lines of policy as dictated by its executive and the Dáil government. The guerrilla organisation needed this authority and direction. As Tom Barry has noted, 'Without [it] there would, most likely, have been no sustained fight with moral force behind it.'

It its contest with the Dublin Castle regime, the underground republic held most of the advantages. It was popular, dynamic and innovative; yet at the same time people did not expect too much of it, at least initially. The old regime bore the burden of its record, which, in the eyes of many people, was one of failure, repression and, indeed, criminality. Everyone knew that there were going to be major changes in Irish government, so they viewed the Castle as an expiring authority. The counter-state was new and therefore not responsible for past failures, and it could hold out glowing promises. The best testimony to the popular acceptance of the underground government is that it operated in the middle of the Irish metropolis. According to one authority on revolutionary movements, having a subterranean presence in the very centre of the enemy base of operations 'is probably the most advanced form of revolutionary development, and the most difficult to achieve'. The Dáil government was able to do this because of the crucial decision of Michael Collins and the underground army to destroy the effectiveness of the existing police force and its auxiliary of spies and informers. Just as important, of course, was popular support, as well as the obvious pleasure in the fact that the counter-state functioned under the nose of the old regime.

The British administration was playing with a losing hand from the beginning. It demonstrated no political ability in dealing with the situation, and its military measures were, in fact, counterproductive. Previous administrations had been more successful, implementing reforms in land transfers, education, local government and other important matters. At the same time Irish control of Irish affairs was expanding. Sinn Féin and the IRA simply provided the culminating thrust to this movement.

Perhaps a more fundamental reason for the British failure is provided by Hannah Arendt's exposition on revolution. She argued that the object of rebellion is liberation, while that of revolution is the foundation of freedom. Rebellion without the creation of the framework of freedom can only lead to futility. Ireland had its rebellion in 1916, which was suppressed, but what was launched in 1919 was much more than a revolt. In Arendt's terms, it was a revolution, as it sought to create the conditions of freedom in the new state. It established a republic and a democratically based parliament. In the Democratic Programme it adopted a set of progressive social and economic objectives. It did not go as far as to frame a fully developed constitution for the new state, but there were many more pressing and less contentious matters to be dealt with at that time. The great stumbling-block to the British campaign in Ireland in 1919–21 was that it was trying to suppress not a rebellion but the birth of a nation.

In social and economic matters the party generally was cautious and conservative. It had no specific programme for the development of public education. By leaving that matter largely in the hands of the Catholic Church, it demonstrated political sagacity. The Dáil government maintained a close and effective relationship with the labour movement and, in the Democratic Programme, was prepared to make a general commitment to the improvement of social conditions, but it did not share Labour's socialist vision of a new Ireland. Sinn Féin held to the position that economic policy was a matter that should be decided upon after self-government was achieved, but Griffith plainly assumed that the country would develop within a capitalist framework. The Dáil government took several steps — the commission of inquiry, the fisheries programme, the Land Bank, the land tribunals and the economic council — that showed a disposition towards an active role for the state in economic development, but, given the conditions of the time, that was as far as it could and would go. This also was politically wise. Being an underdeveloped country, with most people rural and agricultural, Ireland had little understanding of the possibilities of new economic ideas. There was not a single person in the Dáil leadership who was an economist. Apparently there was no new school of radical economic thought in the country. With the exception of Alfred O'Rahilly and possibly a couple of his colleagues at University College, Cork, the academics of the National University who supported Sinn Féin were of no use in this matter; their concerns were cultural and political, with a conservative orientation. Trinity College might as well have been located in the highlands of Scotland. Sinn Féin had a simplistic idea about economic development — build a tariff wall around the country and the Irish people would do the rest.

The Dáil government effectively utilised international support, particularly in the Commonwealth and the United States. Given the mass of Irish people living in these countries, it is hardly surprising that it was able to do so. The public brawl in which de Valera became involved while in the United States did damage to the movement and was a forerunner to the disastrous split at home which did so much to discredit the Irish independence movement internationally. On the other hand, the conflict in the United States was probably unavoidable. Having controlled the movement there for so long, the Irish-American politicians and professional revolutionaries simply could not grasp the reality that the movement at home had suddenly achieved vigour and effectiveness.

The revolutionary government certainly demonstrated little understanding of the dimensions of the problem of the Northern Unionists. Sinn Féin had won and was seeking to consolidate political backing in nationalist Ireland. One of the main attractions of the counter-state was its full commitment to the cultural programme — the revival of a Gaelic Ireland. The party would have to change its recipe for success in coming to terms with the contrary cultural, sectarian and political orientation of the Ulster Unionists. Dáil Éireann had declared a republic for all of Ireland; a serious effort to accommodate the Northern Unionists, especially after 1920, obviously would require considerable modification of that claim. By means of the Treaty and the 1922 constitution it was so modified, but not as part of any rapprochement with Ulster Unionism.

As British public opinion turned decisively against its policies and practices in Ireland, the British government was forced to retreat to positions it could defend — constitutional protection for Ulster Unionists, the security needs of Britain, and the maintenance of the empire. What it had to surrender was effective control of most of Ireland. Because of the deep reluctance of Britain to grant this, the Anglo-Irish Treaty of December 1921 must be viewed as a British defeat and an Irish victory. What the Irish nationalist movement gained was British recognition of an Irish nation-state, albeit with substantial limitations. Yet because the settlement did not fulfil all the objectives of Irish republicanism, Sinn Féin was not able to take full advantage of its success. The controversy that erupted over the Treaty of 1921 divided the forces of Irish nationalism, thereby costing them a major opportunity to deal an effective blow against the partition arrangement.

When the Treaty terms were brought back from London, the dimensions of the Irish political landscape became fully illuminated. Sinn Féin was only the leading element within the political spectrum, and many within that movement did not believe in the necessity of immediate and absolute independence, or, at least, they quickly shifted to this position when confronted with the advantages contained in the agreement. Included in the body politic, whose views had been muted or silenced during the fight against the British, were those who were indifferent or hostile to Irish nationalism and were prepared to accept any kind of settlement as long as it provided for peace and stability. There were others who viewed the agreement as providing opportunity for themselves — government jobs, money, patronage, prestige, contracts. A sizeable element in the population was tired of the whole thing — the violence, the upheaval, the personal danger — and wanted to turn from the waning intoxication of public affairs to the proper pursuit of their own lives and fortunes.

After years of unremitting propaganda, the Treaty settlement was too great a shock of reality for many Irish republicans. There was also the inability of de Valera to accept the position that his ingenious idea of external association did not form the basis of the settlement. Another difficulty was that to many Irish people the achievement of national freedom was just a matter of wilfulness; they had neither the time nor the experience to see that self-government also required responsibility and restraint. What followed certainly must have been a sobering experience. The division in the political leadership allowed military activists to take the initiative; and thus the Irish revolution lost control of its army. Many of the guerrilla leaders believed that through their devotion and sacrifice they had earned the right to be at least a part of the decision-making process in determining the acceptability of a settlement with Britain. As in 1916 and 1919, an active minority decided to take the initiative, in this case by opposing the settlement by force of arms. Its venture failed, largely because it was confronted by a native government, headed by respected political and military figures and supported by a popular mandate.

It has often been observed that but for the division caused by the Treaty the evolution of Irish politics would have been quite different, that it would have, among other things, given greater attention to social and economic matters. On the other hand, Sinn Féin essentially was seeking a political objective, and the Irish electorate had little expectation that its chosen government would assume an important role in these other matters. In presenting a great constitutional question, the Treaty was an entirely appropriate issue to cause the dissolution of the coalition of forces that had come together in 1917. Furthermore, the conflict and rivalries within the leadership were bound eventually to cause division, and the Treaty simply brought this about. Whatever the constitutional status of Ireland, it was most unlikely that Griffith and Collins on the one hand, and Brugha and Stack on the other, would have continued to work together. The Irish public took readily to the Treaty dispute: here was the kind of question with which they had considerable experience, one that brought forth their capacity for discussion, debate and oratory. The problem of Northern Unionism was beyond their grasp. The tragedy was that the Treaty controversy could not be contained within the political sphere and ended in violence. As in the case of upheavals elsewhere, the institutions of the revolutionary government were not yet strong enough to limit the conflict.

The terrible irony of the civil war was that many of those who fought for the pro-Treaty side did not intend to keep the provisions of the agreement. The conflict shattered nationalist Ireland, leaving it in such a weakened condition that it put the British government in a position to adopt an interpretation of the Boundary Commission clause that was very different from that of Collins, Griffith and just about everyone else in Sinn Féin. If the opponents of the Treaty had directed some of the energy and time they lavished on the question of the oath to the boundary provision, its pitfalls could at least have been identified, if not rectified. Because of the bitterness generated by the civil war, de Valera and the other anti-Treaty politicians, now outcasts, could only use the fiasco of the Boundary Commission for partisan advantage, thereby seeking to evade their responsibility for the situation. The failure of nationalist Ireland to maintain essential unity was the principal reason why partition took root. The Northern Unionists had a relatively easy time in creating their sectarian enclave.

The Irish civil war could be viewed simply as a victory of conservatives over radicals, and shortly after the end of that conflict Kevin O'Higgins declared that his colleagues of 1919–21 had been the most conservative revolutionaries in history. In saying that, he was blocking from his singular mind the full record of what had happened since the beginning of 1919. Moreover, he was not speaking for many, if not most, of the people who had supported and sustained the revolutionary government in Dáil Éireann. If those in the first Free State government were basically conservative in most matters, their successors were much more radical and populist, supporters of state action to address social and economic problems. And this leadership drew its inspiration and example from the principles of Sinn Féin and the policies and actions of the first Dáil.

Thus Ireland did not make the transition to self-government without a bitter and humiliating internal conflict. The civil war was a demonstration of political immaturity; but, of course, other new nations also went through the trauma of domestic division on the road to achieving stable and responsible representative government, no easy task. Nevertheless, the civil war was a political and moral setback for the Irish political nation. One of its effects was to obscure the many achievements of the revolutionary government. Yet in the longer view it can be clearly seen that the government of Dáil Éireann was an imaginative and effective vehicle that carried most of Ireland to self-government. In that, it moved according to the primary principle of Sinn Féin — forging the future by self-action, achieving by doing. It transferred control of Ireland into Irish hands.[1]

Appendix 1
The Leadership of the Revolution

(A) Ministers (11)

Eamon de Valera (President)
Arthur Griffith (Home Affairs; subsequently Acting President; Foreign Affairs)
Michael Collins (Finance)
William T. Cosgrave (Local Government)
George Noble, Count Plunkett (Foreign Affairs; subsequently Fine Arts)
Eoin Mac Néill (Industry)
Cathal Brugha (Defence)
Seán Etchingham (Fisheries)
J. J. O'Kelly (National Language/Education)
Austin Stack (Home Affairs)
Constance Markievicz (Labour)

(B) Substitute and assistant ministers (6)

Joseph McDonagh
Thomas Kelly
Joseph McGrath
Kevin O'Higgins
Francis Fahy
Joseph McGuinness

(C) Directors and substitute directors (7)

Ernest Blythe (Trade and Commerce)
Desmond FitzGerald (Propaganda)
Laurence Ginnell (Propaganda)
Robert Barton (Agriculture; subsequently Economic Affairs)
Art O'Connor (Agriculture)

Erskine Childers (Publicity)
Michael Staines (Belfast boycott)

(D) Senior officials and other important persons (42)

(i) Civil administrator (1)
Diarmuid O'Hegarty, Secretary to the Ministry, chief of administration

(ii) Military (16)
Tom Barry, Cork IRA leader
Dan Breen, Tipperary IRA leader
Michael Brennan, Clare IRA leader
Liam Lynch, Cork IRA leader
Seán Mac Eoin, Longford IRA leader
Seán McGrath, London arms procurer
Dick McKee, IRA Dublin Brigade leader
Terence MacSwiney, TD, Lord Mayor of Cork, IRA leader
Sam Maguire, arms procurer in England
Seán Milroy, Cork IRA leader
Richard Mulcahy, IRA Chief of Staff
Rory O'Connor, IRA headquarters staff
Eoin O'Duffy, Ulster IRA leader
Ernie O'Malley, IRA training officer
Gearóid O'Sullivan, IRA headquarters staff
Seán Tracey, Tipperary IRA leader

(iii) Support activities: propaganda, fund-raising, foreign service (20)
Piaras Béaslaí, IRA Director of Publicity
Harry Boland, US mission
Robert Brennan, publicist; Under-Secretary, Foreign Affairs
Cornelius (Con) Collins, TD, supporter of loan and land programmes
John Devoy, Clan na Gael leader
George Gavan Duffy, envoy to France and Italy
Darrell Figgis, Secretary, Commission of Inquiry into Resources
Frank Gallagher, publicist, *Irish Bulletin*
Patrick J. Little, Dáil representative in South Africa and South America
Seán MacEntee, Dáil link with Belfast
Joseph McGarrity, Clan na Gael leader
Maurice Moore, Chairman, Commission of Inquiry into Resources;
    Dáil representative in South Africa
Liam Mellows, US mission
Art O'Brien, Dáil representative in Britain
Rev. Michael O'Flanagan, Vice-President of Sinn Féin
Pádraig O'Keeffe, Sinn Féin administrator
Seán T. O'Kelly, envoy to France and Italy

James O'Mara, US mission
Hanna Sheehy-Skeffington, active in US
Frank P. Walsh, head of US loan campaign

(iv) Judicial (5)
Arthur Clery, Dáil court judge
Diarmuid Crowley, Dáil court judge
Conor Maguire, Dáil court judge
James Creed Meredith, Dáil court judge
Kevin O'Shiel, land commissioner

(E) Key outside supporters (8)
Eamonn Donnelly, Ulster organiser
James Douglas, White Cross organiser
Michael Fogarty, Bishop of Killaloe
Thomas Johnson, Secretary, ILP and TUC
Dan McCarthy, Sinn Féin organiser
William Maloney, US propagandist and organiser
William O'Brien, General Treasurer, Irish Transport and General
   Workers' Union
Laurence O'Neill, Lord Mayor of Dublin

Appendix 2
Sessions of Dáil Éireann,
21 January 1919 – 8 June 1922

First Dáil Éireann (January 1919–May 1921)

The first Dáil Éireann met on twenty-one days: fourteen in 1919, three in 1920, and four in 1921. The paucity of meetings in 1920–21 was due to the extremely adverse conditions under which the Dáil Éireann government operated. Four of these meetings were public and seventeen were private; the large number of private meetings was due to the fact that the Dublin Castle administration had declared Dáil Éireann an illegal assembly in September 1919.

Before the first formal meeting of An Dáil Éireann on 21 January 1919, a number of preparatory meetings were held by some of the twenty-six Sinn Féin members who had been elected and were at liberty. There were six such gatherings — on 1, 2, 7, 14, 17 and 19 January 1919.

The first three formal sessions (eight days) were held in the Dublin Mansion House, with the public sessions being held in the Round Room and the private meetings in the Oak Room. According to Piaras Béaslaí (*Michael Colllins and the Making of a New Ireland*, i, 28), the three private meetings of June 1919 were held in Fleming's Hotel in Gardiner Place (owned by Seán O'Mahony, TD). When the Dáil was declared an illegal assembly by the Dublin Castle authorities in September 1919, secure locations were required. The remaining eight sessions of the first Dáil were held in a variety of places: the Oak Room in the Mansion House, Fleming's Hotel, Alderman Walter Cole's house in Mountjoy Square, and possibly at 86 Harcourt Street, a building owned by the Dáil government.

There were sixty-nine Sinn Féin candidates elected in 1918 (four of whom were elected for two constituencies). Owing to imprisonment, less than one-third of the members attended the initial meetings. With the release of political prisoners in March 1919, the next Dáil meeting had fifty-two members in attendance — the highest number at any meeting of the first Dáil. With the exception of the first meeting after the banning of Dáil Éireann in the autumn of 1919, Dáil attendance averaged approximately forty-five members. The number was kept down by about a dozen members who were overseas on various diplomatic and propaganda activities. At the height of British repression — in the first half of 1921 — an average of only twenty-three members attended the three sessions held in that period.

The information in the following list is derived from *Minutes of Proceedings of the First Parliament of the Republic of Ireland.*

Opening session

1. 21 January 1919 (public)
   Attendance: 29 (Two of those listed as attending, Michael Collins and Harry Boland, were not present: see *Minutes of Proceedings,* corrigenda.)
   Location: Round Room, Mansion House, Dublin
2. 22 January 1919 (private)
   Attendance: 24
   Location: Oak Room, Mansion House

2nd session

3. 1 April 1919 (private)
   Attendance: 52
   Location: Oak Room
4. 2 April 1919 (private)
   Attendance: no listing
   Location: Oak Room
5. 4 April 1919 (private)
   Attendance: no listing
   Location: Oak Room
6. 10 April 1919 (public)
   Attendance: no listing
   Location: Round Room
7. 11 April 1919 (public)
   Attendance: no listing
   Location: Round Room

3rd session

8. 9 May 1919 (public): reception of Irish-American delegation
   Attendance: 50
   Location: Round Room

4th session

9. 17 June 1919 (private)
   Attendance: 40
   Location: Fleming's Hotel
10. 18 June 1919 (private)
    Attendance: no listing
    Location: Fleming's Hotel

11. 19 June 1919 (private)
    Attendance: no listing
    Location: Fleming's Hotel

5th session
12. 19 August 1919 (private)
    Attendance: 42
    Location: Oak Room (?)
13. 20 August 1919 (private)
    Attendance: no listing
    Location: Oak Room

6th session
14. 27 October 1919 (private)
    Attendance: 28
    Location: probably Oak Room

7th session
15. 29 June 1920 (private)
    Attendance: 46
    Location: Fleming's Hotel

8th session
16. 6 August 1920 (private)
    Attendance: 48
    Location: Fleming's Hotel

9th session
17. 17 September 1920 (private)
    Attendance: 47
    Location: (?)

10th session
18. 21 January 1921 (private)
    Attendance: 24, including Erskine Childers, Substitute Director of
    Publicity, who was not then a Dáil member
    Location: Walter Cole's house, Mountjoy Square
19. 25 January 1921 (private): de Valera's first appearance since his
    return from the USA
    Attendance: 25, including Childers
    Location: Cole's house

11th session
20. 11 March 1921 (private)
    Attendance: 25
    Location: Cole's house (see Béaslaí, *Michael Collins*, ii, 200)

12th session
21. 10 May 1921 (private)
   Attendance: 21
   Location (?)

Second Dáil Éireann (August 1921–June 1922)

The first Dáil was not dissolved before the 'Home Rule' general election of May 1921 out of concern that the election might be cancelled. De Valera informed the meeting of 16 August 1921: 'Until the moment the Speaker left the Chair the old Dáil was in session. The new Dáil is in session now.' This procedure was not followed in 1922, although there was an agreement that a final session would be held after the general election of June 1922, thus creating a point of contention in the civil war. Owing to the fear of invasion, the original prodedure was observed during the period of the 1943 general election. (*Official Report*, 200 (16 Aug. 1921); information from Dr T. P. O'Neill)

The second Dáil Éireann met on forty-two occasions. After a flurry of meetings (nine in all) in August, in the wake of the beginning of the truce declared on 11 July, the Dáil met only one other time — on 14 September — during the period leading up to the signing of the Anglo-Irish Agreement of December 1921. Thirty of its meetings were public and twelve were private.

Fifteen of the meetings were devoted to consideration of the Treaty, which was narrowly approved on 7 January. After its adjournment on 10 January following the conclusion of the Treaty debate, the Dáil held fifteen further meetings in the period from February to June 1922.

All of the meetings of the second Dáil were held at University College, Dublin, in Earlsfort Terrace, and all 125 members were available to attend.

The information in the following list is derived from *Official Report, 16–26 August 1921 and 28 February–8 June 1992; Private Sessions of Second Dáil; and Debate on the Treaty between Great Britain and Ireland.*

1st session
22. 16 August 1921 (public): first meeting after beginning of truce
23. 17 August 1921 (public)
24. 18 August 1921 (private)

2nd session
25. 22 August 1921 (private)
26. 23 August 1921 (private)
27. 25 August 1921 (private)
28. 26 August 1921 (private)
29. Same day: 26 August 1921 (public)
30. 27 August 1921 (private)

3rd session
31. 14 September 1921 (private)

4th session
32. 14 December 1921 (private): consideration of Treaty begins
33. Same day: 14 December 1921 (public)
34. 15 December 1921 (private)
35. 16 December 1921 (private)
36. 17 December 1921 (private)
37. 19 December 1921 (public)
38. 20 December 1921 (public)
39. 21 December 1921 (public)
40. 22 December 1921 (public)

5th session
41. 3 January 1922 (public)
42. 4 January 1922 (public)
43. 5 January 1922 (public)
44. 6 January 1922 (private)
45. Same day: 6 January 1922 (public)
46. 7 January 1922 (public): vote on Treaty
47. 9 January 1922 (public)
48. 10 January 1922 (public)

6th session
49. 28 February 1922 (public)
50. 1 March 1922 (public)
51. 2 March 1922 (public)

7th session
52. 26 April 1922 (public)
53. 27 April 1922 (public)
54. 28 April 1922 (public)

8th session
55. 3 May 1922 (public)
56. 5 May 1922 (public)

9th session
57. 10 May 1922 (public)
58. 11 May 1922 (public)

10th session
59. 17 May 1922 (public)
60. 18 May 1922 (public)
61. 19 May 1922 (public)
62. 20 May 1922 (public)

11th session
63. 8 June 1922 (public): last meeting before civil war

References

Abbreviations

BMH	Bureau of Military History, Dublin
cab. minutes	Minutes of Dáil Éireann cabinet, 1919–22
Dáil papers	Correspondence, memoranda and reports of the Dáil Éireann government, 1919–22
Dáil procs	Dáil Éireann, *Minutes of Proceedings of the First Parliament of the Republic of Ireland, 1919–1921: Official Record* (Dublin [1921])
Dáil off. rep.	Dáil Éireann, *Official Report for periods 16th August 1921 to 26th August 1921, and 28th February 1922 to 8th June 1922* (Dublin [1922])
Dáil priv. sess.	Dáil Éireann, *Private Sessions of Second Dáil, 18 August to 14 September 1921, and Report of Debates, 14 December 1921 to 6 January 1922* (Dublin [1972])
FJ	*Freeman's Journal*
IB	*Irish Bulletin*
IG	Inspector-General, Royal Irish Constabulary (monthly reports)
IT	*Irish Times*
Ir. Ind.	*Irish Independent*
NAI	National Archives of Ireland
NLI	National Library of Ireland
SFSC	Sinn Féin Standing Committee, minutes, 1918–21
TCD	Trinity College, Dublin, Library
Treaty deb.	Dáil Éireann, *Debate on the Treaty between Great Britain and Ireland signed in London on 6th December 1921* (Dublin [1922])
UCD	University College, Dublin, Archives
USNA, DS	United States National Archives, Department of State

Preface (pp ix–xii)

1. Irish MP quotation: Horace Plunkett letter, London *Times*, 2 May 1919.
2. *Nation*, 2 August 1920; for a leaflet about the controversy see the anonymous pamphlet, *The Case for the Republic* (copy in NLI, LO p117 (67)).
3. One of the few participants to write about his experiences was Seán T. O'Kelly. He wrote a series of articles in *The Nation* in 1930 and published an autobiography in Irish, *Seán T.*, in 1963.

Introduction (pp 1–3)

1. *Arthur Griffith: A Study of the Founder of Sinn Féin* (pamphlet, Dublin, 1918).
2. Michael Laffan, 'The Development of Sinn Féin, 1916–17', (MA thesis, UCD, 1978); Mitchell, *Labour in Irish Politics*, 65–7, 78–9, 91–103; H. M. Pim, 'Sinn Féin: Past, Present and Future', *Nineteenth Century*, lxxxvi (June 1919), 1165–74.
3. Votes cast in 1918 (excluding university seats):

	Sinn Féin	*Others*	*Total*	*% Sinn Féin*
Ulster	109,835	358,641	468,476	23.45
Munster	87,609	39,650	127,259	68.84
Leinster	193,346	114,913	308,259	62.72
Connacht	104,409	30,626	135,035	77.32
Total	495,199	543,830	1,039,029	47.66

Source: Cronin, *Irish Nationalism: A History of its Roots and Ideology*, 319.

T. P. O'Neill, 'The General Election, 1918', *Capuchin Annual* (1968); *Irishman*, 21 Dec. 1918, 4 Jan. 1919; SFSC minutes, 9 Jan. 1919; Rumpf and Hepburn, *Nationalism and Socialism in Twentieth-Century Ireland*, 22–3; Phillips, *The Revolution in Ireland*, 152–3; UCD, Hayes Papers, P53/1443–4. The UK vote register in 1918 'was notoriously bad' owing to wartime conditions. Butler, *Electoral System in Britain*, 8, 171–2; J. L. McCracken, *Representative Government in Ireland*, 80; *Ir. Ind.*, 31 Dec. 1918; *Treaty deb.*, 24, 246, 340.

Chapter 1: The Establishment of Dáil Éireann (pp 5–42)

1. Lyons, *John Dillon*, 457; *FJ*, 4, 9, 20 Jan. 1919; *Catholic Bulletin*, Jan. 1919; *Evening Telegraph* (Dublin), 2, 8 Jan. 1919; *Ir. Ind.*, 31 Dec. 1918, 1, 2, 8, 9 Jan. 1919.
2. *New Ireland*, 11 Jan. 1919; *Catholic Bulletin*, Feb. 1919; SFSC minutes, 19 Dec. 1918; Ó Ceallaigh, *Seán T.* (Dublin 1972), ii, 59–62; Collins to Stack, 15 Jan. 1919 (NLI, Stack Papers, MS 5843); *Ir. Ind.*, 6, 7 Jan. 1919; *Evening Telegraph* (Dublin), 3, 14, 15, 18 Jan. 1919. 'Dáil Éireann' was the name given to a future national assembly in the Gaelic League journal in 1906 (Garvin, *Nationalist Revolutionaries in Ireland*, 114, and Seán Ó Lúing interview). It was probably first used within Sinn Féin at the 1918 *ard-fheis*. *FJ*, 30 Oct. 1918, *Saoghal Gaedhealacht* (*Irish World*), 4, 11 Jan. 1919. For petitions see NLI, ILB 300 p5 and LO p114, no. 103 and *Belfast Newsletter*, 10 Mar. 1919.
3. Anon., *Voice of Ireland*, 4; SFSC minutes, Jan. 1919; *Nationality*, 4 Jan. 1919; *Ir. Ind.*, 2 Jan. 1919; *FJ*, 7 Jan. 1919. The two MPs who replied were Robert Woods, Independent Unionist from Trinity College, and Thomas Harbinson, from North-East Tyrone. A writer in *The Irishman* (11 Jan.) argued that the four Nationalist members from Ulster who were elected as part of the campaign pact should have come into the Dáil because they were elected, in part, by Sinn Féin voters. *Cork Examiner*, 18 Jan. 1919; *Voice of Labour*, 25 Jan. 1919.
4. Brennan, *Allegiance*, 176–80; Lavelle, *James O'Mara, a Staunch Sinn Féiner*, SFSC minutes, 19 Dec. 1918, 1 Jan. 1919; 'An urgent preliminary note for

the information of the President of the USA with regard to Ireland and the Peace Conference', Dec. 1918 (NAI, Duffy Papers); *Evening Telegraph*, 3 Jan. 1919; organisation of the assembly: NLI, O'Kelly Papers, MSS 8385 (3), 8469 (2); NLI, Plunkett Papers, MS 11404; *FJ*, 13–21 Jan. 1919.

5. *FJ*, 30 Oct. 1918; A Parliament of Felons in FitzGerald (ed.), *Voice of Ireland*, 140–2; UCD, Hayes Papers, P52/1552,1556; Chubb, *Constitution of Ireland*, 9; Figgis, *Recollections*, 219–20, 228–33. The term 'democratic programme' was first used by Joseph Devlin in 1917 when he advocated a 'new democratic programme'. In March 1918 the Dublin Trades Council urged the inclusion of a 'democratic programme' in the constitution of the future Irish state (Farrell, *Founding of Dáil Éireann*, 57–61; Lynch, 'The Social Revolution That Never Was' in Williams (ed.), *The Irish Struggle*, 45–8.

6. *Catholic Bulletin*, Feb. 1919; Máire Comerford memoir, ch. 12, p. 1 (UCD); Comerford, *First Dáil*, 52; *Irishman*, 1 Feb., 1919; *Ir. Ind.*, 22 Jan. 1919; Cathal O'Shannon interview, 1 June 1964; article by Piaras Béaslaí, *Ir. Ind.*, 24 Jan. 1962; Holmes, *Little Field Marshal*, 348; *New Ireland*, 25 Jan., 1919; *Leader*, 1 Feb. 1919; opening day: UCD, Hayes Papers, P53/1550; *Nationality*, 25 Jan. 1919; Hathaway to US Secretary of State, 1 Feb. 1919 (USNA, DS, 841.d.00/22); see also *Irish World*, 1 Feb. 1919.

7. *Dáil procs* (22 Jan. 1919), 26–7. Robinson later wrote: 'What I feared was that the Government, once formed being our moral superiors, a state of stalemate would be inevitable unless war was begun before the Dáil could take responsibility' (NLI, Robinson Papers, MS 21265); Breen, *My Fight for Irish Freedom*, quoted in Townshend, *British Campaign in Ireland*, 16–17; *Ir. Ind.* 22, 24, 27 Jan. 1919; Richardson Evans, 'Ireland and the Realm', *Nineteenth Century*, lxxxix (Apr. 1921), 574–86; Hathaway to US Secretary of State, 1 Feb. 1919 (USNA, DS, 841.d.00/22); Holmes, *Little Field Marshal*, 34; *Nationality*, 22 Feb. 1919; *FJ*, 22, 23 Jan., 17 Feb. 1919; *Ir. Ind.*, 22, 23 Jan. 1919; London *Times*, 22 Jan. 1919; *An tÓglach*, 31 Jan 1919.

8. IG monthly reports, Jan., Feb. 1919 (PRO, CO 904/108); *FJ*, 19, 26 Feb., 1 Mar. 1919; Griffith memorandum to O'Kelly (UCD, Hayes Papers, P53/1018); *Ir. Ind.*, 9, 22, 27 Jan., 13 Feb. 1919; London *Times*, 21 Jan. 1919; *Evening Telegraph*, 5, 17 Feb. 1919; Healy, *Letters and Leaders*, ii, 644; Churchill, *World Crisis*, 282; Hathaway to US Secretary of State, 1 Feb. 1919 (USNA, DS, 841.d.00/22); Holmes, *Little Field Marshal*, 348–9; Jones, *Whitehall Diary*, iii: *Ireland*, 12–13.

9. Results of the two elections in North Derry:

1918 election	Hugh A. Anderson (U)	10,530
	Patrick McGilligan (SF)	3,951
1919 by-election	Hugh T. Barrie (U)	9,933
	Patrick McGilligan (SF)	4,333

Source: Walker (ed.), *Parliamentary Election Results in Ireland, 1801–1922*, 189, 191.

By election: *Dáil procs*, 37, 41, 116, 121, 196.

10. Comerford memoir, ch. 12, p. 2; Hathaway to US Secretary of State, 1 Feb., 15 Apr.1919 (USNA,DS, 841.d.00/22); SFSC minutes, 19 Dec. 1918, 6 Feb. 1919; ILP & TUC, *Ireland at Berne*, 40; ILP & TUC, *Annual Report, 1919*,

23–7; Mitchell, *Labour in Irish Politics*, 110–12; *Irishman*, 5, 12 Feb. 1919; *Irish World*, 21 Dec. 1918, 17 May 1919; O'Kelly to Dáil govt, 24 Aug. 1919 (NAI, Duffy Papers); O'Hegarty to O'Kelly, 1 Sept. 1919 (ibid.); British Labour Party, *The International at Lucerne* (copy in NLI, LO p24).

11. *Daily Mail*, 2, 7 Feb. 1919, *Ir. Ind.*, 10 Feb. 1919; *Nationality*, 22 Feb. 1919; NLI, Duffy Papers, MS 15439; *Irishman*, 25 Jan. 1919. The collection of signatures on petitions was considered as another method to draw attention to the Irish case (copies of petitions, TCD, Childers Papers, MS 7814, and NLI, LO p114); articles by O'Kelly, *Irish Press*, 27, 28 July 1961; *FJ*, 1 Mar. 1919; cab. minutes, 4 Mar. 1920 (NAI, DE 1/2); Figgis, *Recollections*, 249; MacWhite: O'Kelly to de Valera, 24 May 1919 (NAI, Duffy Papers); Duffy to Dáil govt, 27 Feb. 1920 (ibid).

12. A. E. Malone, 'Half a League', *New Ireland*, 8 Mar. 1919; *FJ*, 18 Feb., 1 Mar. 1919; *Irishman*, 15 Mar. 1919; *Nationality*, 8 Feb. 1919; *Voice of Labour*, 29 Mar. 1919; *Irishman*, 15 Mar. 1919; *Ir. Ind.*, 11 Feb., 8 Apr. 1919; Creel, *Rebel at Large*, 218–21; Carroll, *American Opinion and the Irish Question*, 124; Associated Press report, 7 Mar. 1919, quoted in *Sinn Féin and the Peace Conference* (pamphlet); Longford and O'Neill, *De Valera*, 87, 88; Béaslaí, *Collins*, i, 269–70.

13. *Evening Telegraph*, 5, 21 Feb., 13 Mar. 1919; *IT*, 8 Feb., 7 Mar. 1919; Brennan, *Allegiance*, 238–9; Figgis, *Recollections*, 243–5; Townshend, *British Campaign*, 15; IG monthly report, Mar. 1919; *Ir. Ind.*, 26 Mar. 1919; *An tÓglach*, 15 Apr. 1919; Collins to Stack, 26 Mar. 1919 (NLI, Collins Papers, MS 17090); Childers journal (TCD, Childers Papers, MS 7811); *Irishman*, 5 Apr. 1919; *Irish World*, 5 Apr. 1919; Longford and O'Neill, *De Valera*, 90; O'Hegarty, *Victory of Sinn Féin*, 38; Paris conference: pamphlet (NLI, ILB 300 p7); *FJ*, 5 Nov. 1918; Brennan, *Allegiance*, 181. The executive approved the candidacy of Harry Nichols for Trinity College, but he did not stand. Lyons, *Dillon*, 449; *FJ*, 6 Dec. 1918.

14. McCracken, *Representative Government in Ireland*, 32–4. For my list of the leadership see Appendix 1. Tom Garvin, *Nationalist Revolutionaries in Ireland* examines a larger leadership group and comes to somewhat different conclusions. Standing orders and constitutional amendment: *Dáil procs* (1 Apr. 1919), 32–4; League: ibid. (12 Apr. 1919), 32–4, 45–7, 53–69, 76–8; *Irishman*, 19 Apr. 1919; IG monthly reports, Mar., Apr., June 1919; *Irishman*, 12 Apr. 1919; *FJ*, 9 Apr. 1919; Figgis, *Recollections*, 245–7; Collins to Stack, 1 July 1919 (NLI, Collins Papers, MS 5848); *Leader*, 3 May 1919.

15. *Nation*, 22 Feb., 1 Mar. 1930; Boylan, *Dictionary of Irish Biography*, 96; Figgis, *Recollections*, 249; Duffy to Dáil govt, 15 June 1919 (NAI, Duffy Papers); Oliver Snoddy, 'Ireland and the Paris Peace Conference, 1919', *Capuchin Annual* (1969), 389–400; Childers journal (TCD, MS 7811); Vivanti: Paris delegation to Dáil govt, 15 June 1919 (NAI, Duffy Papers); Duffy to Mrs Chartres (i.e. Vivanti), 30 June 1919 (ibid.,); Duffy to Dáil govt, 15 July 1919 (ibid.); Griffith to O'Kelly, 23 Jan. 1919 (UCD, Hayes Papers, MS P53/1018); Lynch, *The IRB and the 1916 Insurrection*, 197–8; Carroll, *American Opinion*, 131; O'Kelly to Art O'Brien, 20 Apr. 1919 (NLI, O'Brien Papers MS 8422).

16. London *Times*, 21 Apr., 13, 14 May 1919; Carroll, *American Opinion*, 132–3, 254; SFSC minutes, 212–14; Dáil govt, to Paris delegation, 28 Apr. 1919 (NAI, Duffy Papers); *IT*, 5, 9 May 1919; Irish-American delegates'

addresses: *Dáil procs* (9 May 1919), 99–108; expenses: ibid., 125; UCD, Hayes Papers, MS P3/1550; Healy, *Letters and Leaders*, ii, 611–12; McCartan, *With de Valera in America*, 115; *FJ*, 19 May 1919; Comerford, *First Dáil*, 60; Longford and O'Neill, *De Valera*, 91; Figgis, *Recollections*, 250–1.

17. *Nationality*, 17 May 1919; *FJ*, 15, 16 May 1919; IG monthly report, May 1919; O'Kelly to de Valera, early June (?) (NAI, Duffy Papers); Ryan problem: *Dáil procs* (17 June 1919), 116–17; American Commission on Irish Independence, *Report on Conditions in Ireland, with Demand for Investigation by the Peace Conference*, 8–9, 12; *The Republic*, 28 June 1919; O'Kelly to Art O'Brien, 27 June 1919 (NLI, O'Brien Papers, MS 8422); Carroll, *American Opinion*, 256–7; London *Times*, 18 June 1919; James P. Walsh, 'Woodrow Wilson: Historians *versus* the Irish', *Éire–Ireland* (summer 1967), 55–66.

18. Pakenham, *Peace by Ordeal* (1972 ed.), 35;; Bullit statement in *Old Ireland*, 25 Oct. 1919; de Valera's comment on delegates: *Dáil procs*, 83; James Carty, 'The Riddle of the New Wilson', *New Ireland*, 7 June 1919; Creel, *Rebel at Large*, 219; Duffy report to Dáil govt, 15 June 1919 (NAI, Duffy Papers); *Irishman*, 7, 28 June, 5 July 1919; Carroll, *American Opinion*, 136; Childers in Paris: Childers journal (TCD, MS 7811); Figgis, *Recollections*, 251; *Hibernian Journal*, Apr. 1920; *Sinn Féin and the Peace Conference* (pamphlet) (copy in NLI); IG monthly report, June 1919; Hathaway to Secretary of State, 11 July 1919 (USNA, DS, 341.d. 00/22).

19. G. Ward Price, 'An Englishman on the Irish Problem', *Century Magazine* (July 1919), 242; O'Kelly to Art O'Brien, 24 June 1919 (NLI, O'Brien Papers, MS 8422); O'Kelly to de Valera, 24 May 1919 (NAI, Duffy Papers); *Ir. Ind.*, 1, 4 July 1919.

Chapter 2: Building the Counter-State (pp 43–119)

1. O'Flaherty, *Life of Tim Healy*, 303; article in *Sunday Express*, quoted in *Evening Telegraph*, 3 Feb. 1919; *Ir. Ind.*, 3 Mar. 1919: *Catholic Bulletin*, Apr. 1919; *Irish World*, 25 Jan., 15 Feb., 22 Mar., 3 May 1919; *Irishman*, 26 Apr. 1919; *FJ*, 12, 13 May 1919; IG monthly report, Aug. 1919 (PRO, CO 904, 109); London *Times*, 30 May 1919; Irish Unionist Alliance, *Ireland of Today: Sinn Féin and Bolshevism* (pamphlet) (copy in NLI).

2. David Fitzpatrick, 'Strikes in Ireland, 1914–21', *Saothar*, 6 (1980), 26–39; *IT*, 2 May 1919; IG monthly report, June 1919; de Blacam, *Towards the Republic*, 58, 64–7; *Irish World*, 25 Jan., 15 Feb., 8, 15, 22 Mar. 1919; *Nation*, 19 Apr. 1919; *New Ireland*, 15 Feb., 5, 26 Apr. 1919; *FJ*, 30 Apr. 1919; *Irish Citizen*, May 1919.

3. J. J. Walsh to Hanna Sheehy-Skeffington, 5 May 1919 (NLI, Hanna Sheehy-Skeffington papers, MS 22689; Walsh motion: *Dáil procs* (19 June 1919), 131; cab. minutes, 23 June, 18 July, 15 Aug. 1919 (NAI, DE 1/1). Walsh again raised the matter of a formal committee structure on 18 Sept. 1920, but received no support. *Dáil procs*, 213–14; Figgis, *Recollections*, 254–8, 264.

4. Co-operatives: *Dáil procs*, 113, 116, 120, 175; *New Ireland*, 23 Aug. 1919; SFSC, programme of Oct. 1917 convention, minutes, 23 Apr. 20, 22 May, 12, 19 June, 3, 10 July 1919; *New Ireland*, 5, 12, 19 Apr., 3 May 1919; Dept Finance report, Aug. 1919; *Ir. Ind.*, 4 July 1919; IG monthly report, June 1919; O'Flanagan at co-operative store meeting, *FJ*, 27 June 1919.

5. SFSC minutes, 22 May, 6 June, 3 July 1919; Sinn Féin and co-operatives: pamphlet (NLI, ILB 300 p5); cab. minutes, 18 July, 26 Sept. 1919; IG monthly report, June 1919; 'Gaillimuh' to Collins, 29 Feb., 3, 10 Mar. 1919 (NAI, DE 2/25); Cosgrave statement on state-run insurance: *Dáil priv. sess.* (18 Aug. 1921), 16; *Ir. Ind.*, 17 Mar., 2 Sept. 1919; O'Hegarty to Duffy, 14 July, 27 Aug. 1919 (NAI, Duffy Papers); government programme: *Dáil procs* (17 June 1919), 114–15, 121–3; *Irish World*, 16 Aug. 1919.

6. Dumont to Secretary of State, 2 Jan., 12 Mar. 1920 (USNA, DS, 841.d.00/119/163); Comerford memoir, ch. 21, pp. 1–2A (UCD).

7. Comerford memoir ch. 21, p. 8 (UCD); Macready, *Annals of an Active Life*, ii, 430; Saorstát: Tierney, *Eoin MacNeill*, 276; Liam Gogan claimed he first proposed the use of *saorstát* instead of *poblacht*. Ó Dochartaigh, *Cathal Brugha*; Francis J. Byrne, 'Saorstát Éireann meant the Irish Republic', *Ir. Ind.*, 18 Feb. 1959; Brennan, *Allegiance*, 216–17; Comerford memoir, ch. 31, 21; de Valera on name, *Dáil priv. sess.* (14 Dec. 1921), 115; Longford and O'Neill, *De Valera*, 72; Green, *Government of Ireland*, 14–15.

8. Richard Mulcahy, 'Conscription and the General Headquarters Staff', *Capuchin Annual* (1968), 382–95; Pakenham, *Peace by Ordeal* (1972 ed.), 102; O'Malley, *On Another Man's Wound*, 115; Kathleen McKenna, 'The *Irish Bulletin*', *Capuchin Annual* (1970), 514; Fr Dermot Hegarty interview, 15 Aug. 1983.

9. Martin, *Ireland in Insurrection*, 39–40; cab. minutes, 11, 18 July, 19 Sept. 1919 (NAI, DE 1/1); premises known as 'Irish Club' to post office (ibid., DE 2/48); purchase: *Dáil procs* (19 Apr. 1919), 139; McKenna, 'The *Irish Bulletin*'.

10. Nineteen members did not attend; cab. minutes, 17 Oct. 1919; *Ir. Ind.*, 10 Dec. 1919; McKenna, 'The *Irish Bulletin*'; IG monthly report, Dec. 1919 (PRO, CO 904/11); Dept of Defence, CID to Intelligence Dept, 'Offices used in Black and Tan period', 28 Mar. 1923 (NLI, microfilm DD pos 919); Comerford memoir, ch. 26; P.J. Matthews memoir, 36–41 (NLI, MS 9873).

11. Bicycles: McKenna, 'The *Irish Bulletin*'; Comerford memoir, ch. 18, p. 9; de Valera and bicycle: de Valera to O'Hegarty, 18 Feb. 1921 (NAI, DE 2/1–3 (99)); Briollay, *Ireland in Rebellion*, 23; Griffith and O'Grady (ed.), *Curious Journey*, 80, 208.

12. Ward, *Unmanageable Revolutionaries: Women and Irish Nationalism*, 119–55; Brennan, *Allegiance*, 298; McKenna, 'The *Irish Bulletin*'; Griffith and O'Grady (ed.), *Curious Journey*, 149–50; Comerford memoir, chs 16, 17; NLI, Plunkett Papers, MS 11404; Dáil messenger, precuations, May 1921 (NAI, DE 2/22); Mac Eoin (ed.), *Survivors*, 151–3, 340–2.

13. McDonagh to O'Hegarty, reply, 17 Feb. 1920 (NAI, DE 2/234 A); cab. minutes, 17 Oct. 1919; NLI, Barton Papers, MS 16888; *Dáil procs*, 115, 142, 236–7; *Irish Bulletin*, 9 Mar. 1920.

14. *Dáil procs*, 41, 234, 128–9, 162; cab. minutes, Feb.–June (NAI, DE 1/1); Comerford, *First Dáil*, 58; Comerford memoir, ch. 12, p. 8; *Ir. Ind.*, 5 Nov. 1918; *Leader*, 21 Dec. 1918; IG monthly report, May 1919 (PRO, CO 904/109); SFSC minutes, 1 Jan. 1919; *FJ*, 10 Feb. 1919.

15. Anti-conscription funds: *Dáil procs*, 36; *Nationality*, 1 Mar., 17 May 1919; *Evening Telegraph*, 31 Jan. 1919; *Ir. Ind*, 1 Mar. 1919; *Irishman*, 5 Apr. 1919; *FJ*, 19 May 1919; IG monthly report, May 1919.

16. American funds: *Dáil procs*, 151, 135, 146; Lynch, *IRB*, 222–3; McCartan, *With de Valera in America*, 94–5; Duffy to Dáil govt, 15 June, 12 Aug. 1919 (NAI, Duffy Papers).

17. De Valera in USA and loan: *Dáil procs*, 139, 150, 155, 133–4; Collins to Stack (NLI, Collins Papers, MS 5848); *Observer*, 30 Apr. 1919; Forester, *Collins*, 107; Béaslaí, *Collins*, i, 347; Dept Finance report, 30 Aug. 1919; ibid., 31 Oct. 1919 to 30 Apr. 1920; de Valera to Frank Walsh, Sept. 1919, reply, 2 Oct. 1919 (NLI, McCartan Papers, MS 17681 (1)). The phrase 'wonder man' is that of William O'Brien. MacLysaght, *Changing Times*, 128. The de Valera comment is from T. P. O'Neill interview, 10 Feb. 1982.

18. Comerford memoir, ch. 29; Dept Finance report, Aug. 1919; USA and domestic loan: *Dáil procs* (20 Apr. 1919), 150–1; progress of loan: NLI, McKenna Napoli Papers, MS 22600; Forster, *Collins*, 108–9. Some insurance agents solicited subscriptions (New Ireland Assurance Co., *New Ireland Comes of Age, 1918–1939*, 11).

19. Expenditures for loan campaign: cab. minutes, 29 Sept. 1919; *Evening Herald*, 6 Nov. 1965; Dept Finance report, 31 Oct. 1919 to 30 Apr. 1920 (NLI, Duffy Papers, MS 15439); IG monthly report, Oct. 1919; *IB*, 8 Nov., 1 Dec. 1919; O'Hegarty to Duffy, 27 Aug. 1919 (NAI, Duffy Papers); Figgis, *Recollections*, 269; London *Times*, 22 Sept. 1919; Macpherson to Bonar Law, 13 Sept. 1919, in Townshend, *Political Violence in Ireland*, 344.

20. Griffith statement on Dáil suppression (NLI, McKenna Napoli Papers, MS 22738); Griffith and Collins loan appeal (NLI, Duffy Papers, MS 15439); London *Times*, 15, 22, 23, 25, 27 Sept. 1919; *Ir. Ind.*, 22, 23 Sept. 1919; *Old Ireland*, 15, 29 Nov. 1919; O'Hegarty to O'Kelly, 9 Oct. 1919 (NAI, Duffy Papers); Collins to all TDs, 9 Aug. 1919 (NLI, McCartan Papers, MS 17681); *Observer*, 30 Nov. 1919; MacLysaght, *Changing Times*, 112.

21. *Old Ireland*, 15 Nov. 1919; Sinn Féin, report of officers and directors, 16 Oct. 1919 (NLI); Collins to TDs (NLI, Plunkett Papers, MS 11404); Forester, *Collins*, 109; *IB*, 27 Jan. 1920; *Ir. Ind.*, 27, 28 Jan. 1920; Collins to Stack, 20 July 1919 (NLI, Collins Papers, MS 5848; Béaslaí, *Collins*, i, 358–9; cab. minutes, 25 Mar. 1920 (UCD, O'Hegarty Papers, P8).

22. Collins to Alex McCabe, 7 Jan., 10 Feb. 1920 (NLI, Art O'Brien Papers, MS 8430); UK govt opposition to loan (NLI, Duffy Papers, MS 15439); Winter, *Winter's Tale*, 299–300; IG monthly report, June 1920 (PRO, CO 904/112); *Observer*, 30 Nov. 1919; Griffith on *Chicago Tribune*, *Dail procs* (27 Oct. 1919), 159; cab. minutes, 10, 24 Oct. 1919, 25 Mar. 1920 (NAI, DE 1/2); O'Kelly to O'Brien on poor response to advert, 7 Nov. 1919 (NLI, O'Brien Papers, MS 8426); MacLysaght, *Changing Times*, 112; Collins to MacSwiney, in Forester, *Collins*, 110; poor response in Britain: O'Brien to Collins, 22 Mar. 1920 (NAI, DE 2/321); Dept Finance report (NLI, Duffy Papers MS 15439); Béaslaí, *Collins*, i, 413.

23. *IB*, 24 Feb., 9 Mar. 1920; *Ir. Ind.*, 8, 11, 23 Mar. 1920; Dept Finance report, June 1920 (NAI, DE 2/7); Dumont to Secretary of State, 19 Nov. 1920; Sturgis diary (NLI, MS P7498); audit by D. O'Connor of Dept Finance, 1 May–31 Dec. 1920 (NAI DE 2/7); Collins on repayment, *Treaty deb.* (9 Jan. 1922), 381; Diarmaid O'Crowley article, *An Phoblacht*, 23 Feb. 1935.

24. Cab. minutes, 16 June 1920; closing the campaign: *Dáil procs* (29 June 1920), 182; Griffith statement, ibid., 171; Dept Finance reports, 21 Jan.,

24 Oct. 1919, 5 Aug. 1920; O'Connor *With Michael Collins in the Fight for Irish Independence,* 117–18. O'Connor gave the gold to the Irish Provisional Government set up under the Treaty in 1922. Diarmaid Ó Cruadhlaoich (O'Crowley), *Step by Step: From the Republic back into the Empire* (pamphlet), 8.

25. Ryan, *Séan Treacy and the Third Tipperary Brigade,* 55; Breen, *My Fight for Irish Freedom* (1924 ed.), 32–3; Séamus Robinson's account of Soloheadbeg (NLI, Frank Gallagher Papers, MS 21265); Mulcahy to Dr Fogarty, 12 Jan. 1925 (UCD, Mulcahy Papers, MS P74/51). As Mulcahy said, his statement did not appear in the *Dáil procs.* Brugha ratified as Minister for Defence, *Dáil procs* (1 Apr. 1919), 31.

26. Mulcahy, 'The Irish Volunteer Convention, 27 October 1917', *Capuchin Annual* (1967), 400–20; de Valera statement on relations with IRA, *Dáil procs* (10 Apr. 1919), 47, 51–2; oath, ibid. (20 Aug. 1919), 151–2, 158 (29 June 1919), 168; O'Malley, *On Another Man's Wound,* 115–16; O'Donoghue, *No Other Law,* 43; *Dáil off. rep.* (28 Apr. 1922), 327–9; *Ir. Ind.,* 22 Oct. 1920; cab. minutes, 31 May, 24 July 1920.

27. O'Hegarty, *Ireland under the Union,* 742; Dept of Defence microfilm (NLI, DD, 914, 6 June, 9 Aug. 1919); IT, 22 Oct. 1920; on affiliation fees (NLI, DD 919–20; ILB 300 p2 (71)); Ó Broin, *Revolutionary Underground,* 181–3; 'J. Woods' (Boland) to 'W. Field' (Collins), 4 Nov. 1920 (T. P. O'Neill, manuscript biography of de Valera).

28. Circular of Clerk of the Dáil, 24 Apr. 1919 (NAI, DE 2/175); *Ir. Ind.,* 19 Feb. 1919; O'Shiel memoir, 622; Colum, *Ourselves Alone,* 156–7; Neligan, *Spy in the Castle,* 75; NLI, ILB 300, p5 (106); NAI, DE 2/175; *Irishman,* 9 Aug. 1919; O'Shiel memoir, 873; on RIC: *Dáil procs* (10 Apr. 1919), 67; IG monthly report, Mar. 1919 (PRO, CO 904/198).

29. O'Shiel memoir, 875–6; IG monthly report, Aug. 1919 (PRO, CO 904/109); *IB,* 16 Dec. 1919; *Ir. Ind.,* 23 Sept., 14, 15, 23 Dec. 1919; *Irish Statesman,* 3 Jan. 1920; Frank Barrett to Collins, 4 Nov. 1919, Collins to Barrett, 8 Nov. 1919 (NLI, DD 915); Dumont to Secretary of State, 2, 14, Jan. 1920.

30. Breen, *My Fight* (1964 ed.), 48; *Ir. Ind.,* 1 Oct. 1919; Townshend, *British Campaign,* 22; Hathaway to Secretary of State, 15 Apr., 11 July 1919; *Ir. Ind.,* 23, 29 Aug., 17, 22 Sept., 9 Oct. 1919; London *Times,* 17 Sept. 1919.

31. IG monthly reports, July, Aug. 1919; Figgis, *Recollections,* 262–4; Mulcahy, 'Chief of Staff, 1919' *Capuchin Annual* (1969), 350–1.

32. *Ir. Ind.,* 16, 20 Aug., 21 Oct., 26 Nov., 1, 22 Dec. 1919; *Old Ireland,* 17 Jan. 1920; IG monthly report, Aug. 1919; *Ir. Ind.,* 17 Oct. 1919; Ryan, *Seán Treacy,* 88–9; Breen, *My Fight,* 53–4; O'Malley, *On Another Man's Wound,* 119.

33. *Ir. Ind.,* 27 Oct. 1919; Comerford memoir, ch. 12, p. 9 (UCD); Macardle, *Irish Republic* (1968 ed.), 270; Mitchell, *Labour in Irish Politics,* 117–18; Ryan, *Seán Treacy,* 90–107, 139; Bell, *Secret Army,* 20; IG monthly report, Aug. 1919.

34. Mulcahy 'Chief of Staff, 1919', *Capuchin Annual* (1969), 350–1; Fitzpatrick, *Politics and Irish Life,* 208; Hayes commentary (UCD, Hayes Papers, P53/1551, 1568); Ryan, *Séan Treacy,* 115–24; *Ir. Ind.,* 19 Dec. 1920; O'Donoghue, *No Other Law,* 48, 86.

35. *Old Ireland,* 29 Nov. 1919; *IT* 2, 13 Feb. 1920; NLI, O'Brien Papers, MS 8427; O'Hegarty, *Victory of Sinn Féin,* 47; Figgis, *Recollections,* 259–60; O'Connor, *Big Fellow* (1966 ed.) 55; Griffith on Fenians: UCD, Hayes Papers, P53/1547; UCD, Mulcahy Papers, P7D/96; Virginia Glandon, 'Arthur Griffith and

the Ideal Irish State', *Studies* (spring 1984), 35; de Valera, *Ireland and India* (pamphlet, New York 1920); O'Malley, *On Another Man's Wound*, 285.

36. O'Malley, *On Another Man's Wound*, 102, 219, 294; O'Connor, *Big Fellow*, 28, 59, 114–16; Béaslaí, *Collins*, ii, 99; Forester, *Collins*, 123; Younger, *Ireland's Civil War*, 113–14; Mulcahy on relations with Brugha: UCD, Hayes Papers, P53/1445.

37. Cab. minutes (NAI, DE 1/1); Dept Finance report, 24 Oct. 1919 (NLI, Duffy Papers, MS 15440); Dept Finance reports, July–Dec. 1920 (NAI, DE 2/7); Dept Finance report Jan.–Mar. 1921 (NLI, Plunkett Papers, MS 11404); Dept Finance report, 14 Aug. 1921 (NLI Duffy Papers, MS 15439); *Dáil procs*, 169, 172–3, 270.

38. Resources commission: *Dáil procs*, 117, 112–3, 138, 142; Figgis, *Recollections*, 266, 270; *Ir. Ind.*, 15 Oct. 1919; Boylan, *Dictionary of Irish Biography*, 106; Brennan, *Allegiance*, 204–6; O'Malley, *On Another Man's Wound*, 77; Colum, *Ourselves Alone*, 160.

39. *The Republic*, 21 June–20 Sept. 1919; Figgis ratification; *Dáil procs* (19 Aug. 1919), 142–3; *Ir. Ind.*, 20 Sept., 25, 26 Nov. 1919, 26 Jan. 1920; Figgis, *Recollections*, 267–8, 300–7; Dáil Éireann [Erskine Childers], *The Constructive Work of Dáil Éireann*, no. 2, 26; Sylvain Briollay, *Ireland in Rebellion*, 54–5; *IB*, 5 Dec. 1919, 26 Jan. 1920; Jones, *Whitehall Diary*, iii, 34 (4 Aug. 1920).

40. Commission of inquiry, report of meeting (NAI, DE 2/82); *Dail procs*, 174–7; Collins to Griffith, 11 Dec. 1920 (NAI, DE 2/242); Wells, *Irish Indiscretions*, 130–1; Dept of Trade and Commerce report, 11 Aug. 1921; problems with commission: *Dáil procs* (10 May 1921), 282–7; Blythe: *Dáil priv. sess.* (22 Aug. 1921), 38–40; *Constructive work*, no. 2, 27–30; inquiry report (NAI, DE 2/18); cab. minutes, 21, 26 Oct., 4 Nov. 1921.

41. Land bank: *Irishman*, 8 Feb., 5 Apr., 31 May 1919; *Dáil procs* (20 Aug. 1919), 146–8, (27 Oct. 1919) 159–66; Boylan, *Irish biography*, 19–20; Dept Home Affairs, 'Explanatory statement' on land scheme and bank (NLI, Duffy Papers, MS 15440); National Land Bank booklets (NLI, Ir. 300 p46); Barton on bank proposal: TCD, Childers Papers, MS 7833; Dept Finance report, Aug. 1919.

42. Dept Agriculture report, 26 June 1920; explaining the land act: NLI, Duffy Papers, MS 15440; directors: NLI, Barton Papers, MS 16888; Childers involvement; TCD, Childers Papers, MSS 7811, 7833; Dept Finance report, 31 Oct. 1919–30 Apr. 1920; Collins to de Valera, 9 Feb. 1920 (NAI, DE 2/245); *Ir. Ind.*, 17, 27 Mar. 1920; Dept Finance report, 1 Jan.–30 June 1921; Lionel Smith Gordon, 'Ireland's Official Bank' in FitzGerald (ed.), *Voice of Ireland*, 327–8.

43. Childers and bank: TCD, Childers Papers, MS 7811; Barton and Art O'Connor statements: *Dáil priv. sess.* (23 Aug. 1921), 47–50; Griffith on bank expansion: *Dáil procs.* (29 June 1920), 170, 180–1; land commission and bank: ibid., 201, 232; Dept Finance report, 5 Aug.–14 Sept. 1920; *Dublin Directory and Calander for 1921*, advertisement section, p. 21; National Land Bank, report of directors, 30 June 1921 (NLI, Ir. 332 p5); Con Collins to O'Hegarty, 4 Mar. 1920 (UCD, O'Hegarty Papers, P8); Dept Fisheries report, June 1920; cab. minutes, 18, 25 Mar., 9 Apr. 1920; Dept Agriculture report, Jan. 1921 (NLI, Duffy Papers, MS 15440; article by Smith Gordon, *Irish Year Book, 1921*; *Dáil off. rep.* (1 Mar. 1922), 150–3.

44. Forestry: Griffith statement, *Dáil procs* (17 Apr. 1919), 114, 121–2, 148–9, 159, 165–6, 203; Forestry report (NAI, DE 2/127); SFSC minutes, 20 May 1919; Sinn Féin Arbour Day circulars (NLI, ILB 300 p2 (28), p5).

45. Fisheries: Griffith statement, *Dáil procs* (18 June 1919), 114; Dáil decree, ibid., 122, debate on report, ibid., 141, report summary, ibid., 163; fisheries committee report, Oct. 1919, and Etchingham to ministers on fish distribution, n.d. (NLI, Plunkett Papers, MS 11404); report, June 1919 (NLI, Duffy Papers, MS 15440; report, June 1920 (ibid., MS 15439); NLI, Tomás O Máille Papers, MS 20855; article by Dan Walsh, *Enniscorthy Echo*, 3 Aug. 1984; Brennan, *Allegiance*, 64–79; cab. minutes (NAI, DE 1/2, 1/3); Collins to Jerome Harrington, Skibbereen, 12, 17 May 1920 (NLI, McKenna Napoli Papers, MS 22767); report on summary, *Dáil procs* (6 Aug. 1920), 205; captured Griffith memo: Macready to Anderson, 5 Aug. 1920 (PRO, CO 904/188).

46. Problems with fishing co-operatives: NAI, DE 2/25; sub-committee on food and fisheries report, fragment, n.d. (UCD, Blythe Papers, P24/17A, 17B); testimony on fisheries: *Old Ireland*, 18 Dec. 1920; Dept Agriculture report, 14 Jan.–14 Apr. 1922 (NLI, O'Brien Papers, MS 8425); discussion on report, *Dáil priv. sess.* (23 Aug. 1921), 44–7, 73, 65; *Dáil off. rep.*, 45–52, 148.

47. Brugha on Irish-speaking districts, *Dáil procs* (20 Aug. 1919), 153–4, 162–3; Hickey and Doherty, *Dictionary of Irish History*, 440: Aireacht na Gaedhilge, report, June 1920 (NLI, Duffy Papers, MS 15440); ratification of J. J. O'Kelly as minister. *Dáil procs* (29 June 1920), 185; cab. minutes, 27 Aug. 1920; Hayes manuscript, 'Ministers of Education' (UCD, Hayes Papers, P53/1398); *Dáil off. rep.* (17 Aug. 1921), 49; Mortimer O'Kelly interview; *Ir. Ind.*, 6 Aug. 1920; Pádraigín Ní Cheallaigh, 'An Ghaeilge sa Choras Oideachais, 1919–1929', *Teagasc na Gaeilge*, iv (1984–5), 113–32; P. J. Matthews memoir, 34–43 (NLI, MS 9873). Matthews was an official in the department.

48. Séamas Ó Buachalla, 'Education as an Issue in the First and Second Dáils', *Administration* (spring 1977), 57–75; *Ir. Ind.*, 7, 9, 11, 13 Feb. 1920; cab. minutes, 4 Mar. 1920; Secetary of Ministry to Dept. Finance, 5 Mar. 1920 (NAI, DE 2/7, Dept Finance file); Aireacht na Gaedhilge report, Jan. 1921 (NLI, Duffy Papers, MS 15440); Titley, *Church, State and the Control of Schooling in Ireland*, 75–82.

49. Cab. minutes, 20 Feb., 4 Mar. 1920; department's language publications: Best, *Bibliography of Irish Philology and Manuscript Literature: Publications, 1912–1941*; Gaedhilge report, Mar. 1921 (NAI, DE 2/54); Gaedhilge report, Aug. 1921 (NLI, Duffy Papers, MS 15440); O'Connell, *History of INTO*, 243–5; arrest of O'Kelly: *Dáil procs* (11 Mar. 1921), 265; funds for publications: ibid., 273–4; Collins to O'Brien, 12 Jan. 1921 (NLI, O'Brien Papers, MS 8426); Dáil papers (NAI, DE 2/3 (49, 91, 11)); discussion of report, *Dáil priv. sess.* (22 Aug. 1921), 40–1; estimate for department, ibid. (25 Aug. 1921), 65–6.

50. Propaganda/Publicity: Brennan, *Allegiance*, 162–3; SFSC minutes, 19 June, 3 July 1919; *Nationality*, 14 June 1919; cab. minutes, 12 Sept. 1919; Ginnell to Dáil govt, 17 Mar. 1920, O'Hegarty to Ginnell, 10 June 1920 (NAI, DE 2/29); cab. minutes, 10 June 1920; Ginnell's illness: *Dáil procs* (29 June 1920), 186.

51. *Evening News*, quoted in *Weekly Summary*, 7 Jan. 1921; Dumont to Secretary of State, 28 Sept. 1920; Wells, *Irish Indiscretions*, 138; Pakenham, *Peace by Ordeal* (1972 ed.) 102; Childers's work: TCD, Childers Papers, MS 7833; Kathleen McKenna 'The *Irish Bulletin*', *Capuchin Annual* (1970); Joyce M. Nankivell and Sydney Loch, *Ireland in Travail*, 172–3; Sheila Humphries statement in Mac Eoin (ed.), *Survivors*, 339–40.

52. Dumont to Secretary of State, 28 Sept. 1920; O'Malley, *On Another Man's Wound*, 212; Wells, *Irish Indiscretions*, 139; Fitzgerald to O'Brien, 10 Sept. 1919, (NLI, O'Brien Papers, MS 8426).

53. Secretary of Ministry to Minister for Finance, 19 Mar. 1920 (NAI, DE 2/7); O'Brien to Collins, 17, 31 Aug. 1920 (NAI, DE 2/324); Brennan, *Allegiance*, 274–5; O'Brien to Dept Finance, 7 Sept. 1920 (NLI, O'Brien Papers, MS 8426); Joseph Cassell interview, 29 Dec. 1965; Propaganda Dept report on interviews with journalists, n.d.; O'Brien to de Madariaga, 8 Aug. 1921 (NLI, O'Brien Papers, MS 8427); Publicity Dept reports, 31 Oct. 1919, 1 Jan. 1920 (NAI, DE 1/10:6, 2/10:11).

54. Dept Finance to Duffy, 18 May, 16 June 1920 (NAI, Duffy Papers); Duffy on *Bulletin: Dáil priv. sess.* (23 Aug. 1921), 53.

55. Propaganda Dept report, 25 June 1920 (NLI, McKenna Napoli Papers, MS 22606); Duffy to Dáil govt, 16 Apr. 5, 6 May 1920 (NAI, Duffy Papers); cab. minutes, 13 Nov. 1920.

56. SFSC minutes, 19 June 1919; cab. minutes, 4 July, 13, 15 Aug., 5, 19 Sept., 3 Oct. 1919; Propaganda Dept report, Aug. 1919; Brennan, *Allegiance*, 164–5; Secretary of Ministry to Director of Propaganda, 14 Feb. 1920 (NAI, DE 2/10); Dumont to Secretary of State, 5 Apr. 1920; O'Brien to Fitzgerald, 30 Dec. 1919 (NLI, O'Brien Papers, MS 8428).

57. Secretary of Ministry to Dept Finance, 14, 15 May 1920 (NAI, DE 2/19:9); O'Brien to Secretary of Ministry, 12, 30 July 1920 (NAI, DE 2/11); O'Brien to Collins, 16 Sept. 1920 (NLI, O'Brien Papers, MS 8425); O'Brien to Collins, 16, 20, 22 Dec. 1920 (ibid., MS 8430).

58. O'Hegarty to Duffy, 5 July 1920, Duffy to O'Hegarty, 24 Aug. 1920 (NAI, Duffy Papers); Collins to Director of Propaganda, 20 Sept. 1920 (NLI, O'Brien Papers, MS 8430); Collins to O'Brien, 14, 29 Sept. 1920 (NAI, DE 2/324); Collins to O'Brien, 2, 21 Dec. 1920, 5 Jan. 1921 (NAI, DE 2/326); Collins to O'Brien, 28 Jan. 1921 (NLI, O'Brien Papers, MS 8426); Fitzgerald statement: *Dáil procs* (17 Sept. 1920), 225–6.

59. *Irish World*, 14 June, 21 Sept. 919; *Nation*, 1 Mar. 1920; O'Kelly to de Valera, June 1919 (NAI, Duffy Papers); Griffith statement: *Dáil procs* (17 June 1919), 117.

60. Dáil govt to Paris delegation, 25 June 1919 (NAI, Duffy Papers); O'Brien to O'Kelly, 12 May 1919 (NLI, O'Brien Papers, MS 8422); O'Brien to Plunkett, 26 June 1919 (ibid., MS 8426); cab. minutes, 25 July 1919; statement attached to Foreign Affairs report dated 25 July 1919 (NLI, O'Brien Papers, MS 8426); Brennan to Duffy, 25 May 1920 (NAI, Duffy Papers); Dept Foreign Affairs report, June 1920; O'Hegarty to Duffy, 15 July, 13 Aug. 1920 (NAI, Duffy Papers); O'Brien to O'Hegarty, 16 June 1920 (NAI, DE 2/403); Duffy to Dáil govt, 30 Mar. 1920 (NAI, Duffy Papers); Briollay, *Ireland in Rebellion*, 52.

61. Duffy to Dáil govt, 30 Jan. 1920, Duffy to O'Kelly, 19 Mar. 1920, Paris office to Dáil govt, 27 Mar. 1920 (NAI, Duffy Papers); O'Brien to Collins, 12 Sept. 1920 (NAI, DE 2/324); Duffy to Dáil govt, 9 July 1920 (NAI, Duffy Papers); *Old Ireland*, 10, 14 July, 25 Sept., 2 Oct. 1920; Rashid to O'Brien, 19 Aug. 1920 (NAI, DE 2/323).

62. De Valera, *Ireland and India*; Paris office to Dáil govt, 27 Feb. 1920 (NAI, Duffy Papers); O'Brien to Collins, 23 Oct. 1920, Collins to O'Brien, 25 Oct. 1920 (NAI, DE 2/325); Secretary of Ministry to Paris office, 17. Jan. 1921, Paris office to O'Hegarty, 18 Jan. 1921 (NAI, DE 2/1:2(33)); O'Brien to Collins, 10 Sept., 29 Nov. 1921 (NLI, O'Brien Papers, MS 8430); cab. minutes, 6 June, 9, 25 Nov. 1921; Childers contacts with Egyptians: TCD, Childers Papers, MS 7788; O'Brien correspondence, Nov. 1921 (NLI, O'Brien Papers, MS 8428).

63. Duffy to Dáil govt, 15 June 1919 (NAI, Duffy Papers); Dept Finance file, 6 Feb. 1920 (NAI, DE 217); cab. minutes, 18 Mar. 1920; Duffy to O'Kelly, 3 Sept. 1919, Duffy to Dáil govt, 16 June 1920 (NAI, Duffy Papers).

64. Dept Foreign Affairs report, June 1920; Duffy to C.B., 8 Feb. 1920, O'Kelly to Duffy, 10 Mar. 1920, Duffy to Dáil govt, 19 Mar. 1920 (NLI, O'Brien Papers, MS 8426); Duffy to de Valera, 5 July 1920 (NAI, Duffy Papers); O'Brien to Duffy, 10 July 1920 (NLI, O'Brien Papers, MS 8426); Brennan to Duffy, 25 May 1920 (NAI, Duffy Papers); Dept Foreign Affairs report, June 1920; O'Hegarty to Duffy, 15 July, 23 Aug. 1920 (NAI, Duffy Papers); O'Brien to O'Hegarty, 16 June 1920 (NAI, DE 2/403); Duffy to Dáil govt, 30 Jan., 27 Feb., 30 Mar. 1920, O'Hegarty to Duffy, 15 Apr. 1920 (NAI, Duffy Papers); Briollay, *Ireland in Rebellion*, 54.

65. McCartan, *With de Valera in America*; Cronin, *The McGarrity Papers*; O'Brien and Ryan (ed.), *Devoy's Post-Bag*, ii; Lynch, *IRB*; Carroll, *American Opinion*.

66. *New Ireland*, 21 June 1919; *Irishman*, 5 July 1919; Duffy to Dáil govt, 15 June 1919, Seán Dunne to O'Kelly, 29 May 1919 (NAI, Duffy Papers); O'Kelly to Devoy, 2 July 1919 (*Devoy's Post-Bag*, ii, 534–5).

67. Collins to Seán Nunan, 6 Oct. 1919 (NAI, DE 2/292); McCartan, *With de Valera in America*, 135–6, 141; O'Hegarty to Paris office, 25 June 1919 (NAI, Duffy Papers); Longford and O'Neill, *De Valera*, 97, 98.

68. NLI, McCartan Papers, MSS 17688, 17681(1); correspondence between F. P. Walsh and E. F. Dunne, Aug. 1919 (NAI, DE 2/245); McCartan to Secretary of Ministry (ibid.,); Nunan to Collins, 3 Sept. 1919 (NAI, DE 2/292); *An Poblacht*, 8 Oct. 1932; Ryan, *The Phoenix Flame*, 312–13; O'Kelly to O'Brien, 7 Nov. 1919, O'Brien to O'Kelly, 15 Nov. 1919 (NLI, O'Brien Papers, MS 8426); Béaslaí, *Collins*, i, 4.

69. De Valera to Dáil govt, 21 Aug. 1919 (NAI, DE 2/235); *Nationality*, 26 July 1919; *Boston Post*, 30 July 1919; *Ir. Ind.*, 15 Aug. 1919; London *Times*, 24 June 1919; *Ir. Ind.*, 14 Oct. 1919; *Daily Mail*, 15 Nov. 1919; Dept Foreign Affairs report, Oct. 1919 (NLI, Duffy Papers 15440); Sinn Féin, *Report of Officers and Directors, Ard-Fheis*, 16 Oct. 1919; *Ir. Ind.*, 17 Oct. 1919; Griffith statement: NLI, McKenna Napoli Papers, MS 22729; Briollay, *Ireland in Rebellion*, 27; article by Brailsford in *Nation*, quoted in *Ir. Ind.*, 22 Nov. 1919.

70. NLI, James O'Mara Papers, MSS 15548, 21548(1); Lavelle, *James O'Mara*; Monteith, *Casement's Last Adventure*, 238–40; Nunan correspondence (NAI,

DE 2/292); *IT*, 7 July 1920; London *Times*, 14 July 1920; Collins to O'Brien, 16 July 1920 (NLI, O'Brien Papers, MS 8426); Collins to O'Brien, 17 Oct. 1919 (ibid., MS 8430); Collins to de Valera, 3 Jan. 1921 (NAI, DE 2/244; Dennis M. Sullivan, 'Eamon de Valera and the Forces of Opposition in America, 1919–1920', *Éire–Ireland* (summer 1984), 100–10; *Ir. Ind.* 30 Dec. 1919; *Young Ireland*, 10 Jan. 1920; *Ir. Ind.*, 22 July 1919; *Sunday Express*, 28 Sept. 1919.

71. *Ir. Ind.*, 20, 24, 27 Nov. 1919; London *Times*, 8 Dec. 1919; extract from letter of Rev. T. Maguire, Clogher (NAI, DE 2/245); Blythe statement, *IB*, 9 Dec. 1919; *Kerryman*, 3 Jan. 1920; *Gaelic American*, 14, 21 Feb. 1920; *Ir. Ind.*, 17 Sept., 3, 30 Dec. 1919, 9 Feb. 1920; *IT*, 16 Feb. 1920; Boland to Collins, 5 Mar. 1920 (NAI, DE 2/245); *Old Ireland*, 17 Apr. 1920; American Commission on Conditions in Ireland, *Interim Report*, 113n; Collins to Griffith, 21 Apr. 1920 (NAI, DE 2/242); Collins to O'Brien, 28 June 1920 (NLI, O'Brien Papers, MS 8426); Dunnico to O'Brien, 17 Sept. 1921 (NAI, DE 2/442); NAI, DE 2/332; Wilson, *Irish Case*, 4.

Chapter 3: The Year of Revolution (pp 120–224)

1. *Nationality*, 24 May 1919; Sinn Féin organisation: *Dáil procs* (19 Aug. 1919), 143–4; *Ir. Ind.*, 22 Aug. 1919, 19 Jan. 1920; *IT*, 29 Jan. 1919; *Irish World*, 12 Apr. 1919; Figgis, *Recollections*, 290; *Ir. Ind.*, 9, 14 Oct. 1919; *IB*, 14 Jan., 17 May 1920; Dept Local Govt reports, Aug., Oct. 1919 (NLI, Duffy Papers, MS 15440); SFSC minutes, 31 Oct. 1919; Sinn Féin circulars (NLI, ILB 200 p5 (39, 42, 99)); cab. minutes 31 Oct. 1919.

2. Mitchell, *Labour in Irish Politics*, 122–7; *Old Ireland*, 13 Dec. 1919; SFSC minutes, 14 Aug., 20 Nov. 1919; *IB*, 17, 25, 19 Jan. 1920; *IT*, 25 Feb., 20 Jan. 1920; *Ir. Ind.*, 19, 30 Jan., 25 Feb. 1920.

3. *IT*, 20, 30 Jan. 1920; Dept Local Govt report, June 1920 (NAI, Duffy Papers); *Ir. Ind.*, 23 Jan., 17 Feb., 29 Apr., 26 Mar. 1920; Dumont to Secretary of State, 15 June 1920 (USNA, DS 841.d.00/209); local govt elections, June 1920: cab. minutes, 21 May 1920; *Ir. Ind.*, 5–14 June 1920; Kee, *Ourselves Alone*, 92; NLI, ILB 300 p4 (103).

4. *Ir. Ind.*, 22 Sept., 13, 18 Dec. 1919; *Young Ireland*, 3 Jan. 1920; *IT*, 5 Jan. 1920; *Ir. Ind.*, 3, 5, 6 Feb., 30 Mar. 1920; USNA, DS, 841.d.00/152/178; *Daily Herald*, 30 May 1920; *IT*, 5, 14 Apr. 1920; Townshend, *British Campaign in Ireland*, 65; Mitchell, *Labour in Irish Politics*, 119–20; *IT*, 14, 15, 26–9 Apr. 1920; *Morning Post*, quoted in *Ir. Ind.*, 5 May 1920; Wormwood Scrubs situation: NLI, O'Brien Papers, MS 8427; Stack to Seán McGrath, 27 May 1920 (ibid., MS 8430); Collins to O'Brien, 1 May 1920 (ibid., MS 8426); local govt elections, June 1920: cab. minutes, 21 May 1920; *Ir. Ind.*, 5–14 June 1920.

5. Land agitation: D. R. O'Connor Lysaght, *Soviets in Ireland* (forthcoming), ch. 2; SFSC minutes, 15, 21 Feb., 10 Mar. 1918; Art O'Connor, *Brief Survey*, 7–10, 12–14; *IT*, 6, 15, 16, 24, 29 Apr. 1920; IG monthly report, Aug. 1920; Jones, *Whitehall Diary*, iii, 17; SFSC minutes, 23 Feb. 1918, 4, 13 May 1920; Sawyer to Griffith, 25 Oct. 1921 (NAI, DE 1/485); *Dáil off. rep.* (10 May 1922), 395; *Sunday Times* report, disputed in *Ir. Ind.*, 22 June 1920; O'Shiel memoir, 909–10, 933, 936–97; Figgis, *Recollections*, 291–2; Maguire on origin of land courts: NLI, Gallagher Papers, MS 21244; RIC: *IB*, 19 May 1920; IG

monthly report, June 1920; Hoctor, *Department of Agriculture*, 115; O'Shiel memoir, 907–8; Dept Agriculture report, 26 June 1920 (NLI, Duffy Papers, MS 15439); cab. minutes, 25 Apr. 13, 31 May 1920.

6. O'Shiel memoir, 937–47, 974–1066; article by Gwynn, *Observer*, 23 May 1919; Figgis, *Recollections*, 295–6; Maguire to Gallagher, 26 Dec. 1959 (NLI, Gallagher Papers, MS 21244); O'Connor to cabinet, 30 Sept. 1920 (NAI, DE 2/8:32); establishment of Land Commission: *Dáil procs* (6 Aug. 1920), 199–202; warning about land agitation: ibid. (29 June 1920), 178–9; Dáil Éireann, *Constructive Work of Dáil Éireann*, 8–13; *Old Ireland*, 22 May 1920.

7. J. P. Casey, 'The Genesis of the Dáil Courts', *Irish Jurist*, ix (1974), 326–38; O'Brien and Ryan (ed.), *Devoy's Post-Bag*, ii, 22–4; *FJ*, 30 Oct. 1918; SFSC minutes, programme of Oct. 1917 convention, 21 Feb. 1918; *Irishman*, 8 Feb., 31 May 1919; *Nationality*, 19 Apr. 1919; establishment of Dáil courts: *Dáil procs* 40, 114, 122, 138–9, 163–4; 'Courts of Justice' (Dept Defence microfilm, NLI, pos 915); cab. minutes, 30 June, 4, 11, 8, 25 July, 1, 15 Aug., 31 Oct., 7, 14 Nov. 1919, 11, 18 Mar., 16 Apr., 13 May, 10, 16, 22 June 1920 (NAI, DE 1/2); courts committee reports (NAI, DE 2/38/5, 6, 17); Dept Home Affairs report, 27 Oct. 1919 (NLI, Duffy Papers, MS 15440); Dept Home Affairs report, n.d. [post-Jan. 1920?] (NLI, Plunkett Papers, MS 11404); *Irish Law Times and Solicitors' Journal*, 6 Nov. 1920.

8. Gaughan, *Austin Stack*, *Dáil procs*, 171; Stack to O'Hegarty, 20 Feb. 1920 (NAI, DE 2/64); 'National Arbitration Courts Report', 4 Mar. 1920 (NAI, DE 2/38/17); Dept Home Affairs report, June 1920 (NAI, DE 2/51); *Daily News*, reported in *Ir. Ind.*, 5 July 1920; *Kerryman*, 12 June 1920; cab. minutes, 18 Mar., 2 Apr., 2, 13 May, 10 June 1920; see also NAI, DE2/51 and DE 2/64.

9. Kilmaine statement in BMH chronology, iii, 269; *Church Times*, quoted in *Old Ireland*, 11 Dec. 1920; Jones, *Whitehall Diary*, iii, 24–5; Dumont to Secretary of State, 15 June 1920 (USNA, DS 841.d.00/209); J. P. Casey, 'Republican Courts in Ireland, 1919–1922', *Irish Jurist*, v (1970), 321–42; Queenstown notice: *Ir. Ind.*, 19 June 1920; BMH chronology, iii, 159; Seán O'Duffy interview; Lynd report: *Ir. Ind.*, 5 July 1920; *Manchester Guardian*, 1 July 1920; *IB*, 3 July, 27 June 1920; BMH chronology, iii, 215; *IB*, 24 June 1920; Griffith on land courts: *Dáil procs* (29 June 1920), 170; O'Farrell, *Seán Mac Eoin Story*, 37; Comerford memoir, ch. 22 (UCD); London *Times*, 28, 4 June 1920; Gaughan, *Austin Stack*, 124, 144–5. For court cases see *Ir. Ind.*, 12, 19 June, 1920; Stack on judges and courts: *Dáil priv. sess.* (25 Aug. 1921), 67.

10. Dept Home Affairs report, Aug. 1920 (NAI, DE 2/51); Anderson to cabinet, 25 July 1920 (PRO, CO 904/188); Ó Cruadhlaoich (O'Crowley), *Step by Step*; Cahir Davitt, 'The Civil Jurisdiction of the Courts of Justice of the Irish Republic, 1920–1922', *Irish Jurist*, iii (1968), 112–27; cab. minutes, 3 Sept. 1920; *IB*, 14, 20 July 1920; total number of courts: NAI, DE 25/16; Maguire to Gallagher, 19 Jan. 1960 (NLI, Gallagher Papers, MS 21144); cab. minutes, 22 July 1920; *IB*, 23 Aug. 1920; London *Times*, 4 June 1920; Dumont to Secretary of State, 15, 21 June, 28 Sept. 1920 (USNA, DS, 841.d.00.243/209); *Ir. Ind.*, 6, 10 Aug. 1920; Conor A. Maguire, 'The Republican Courts', *Capuchin Annual* (1969), 378–88; Irish Situation Committee meeting, 6 Aug. 1920 (PRO, CAB 27/107).

11. RIC: *IT*, 8 Jan., 16, 28 Apr. 1920; IRA proclamation: Dumont to Secretary of State, 12 Mar. 1920; O'Shiel memoir, 877–9; Adj.-Gen. to Acting Brigade Commandant, Mid-Clare, May 1920 (Dept Defence microfilm, NLI, pos 911); 'Resignations and Retirements from Irish Police Force' (NAI, DE 2/87); Collins to O'Brien, 20 Sept. 1920 (NLI, O'Brien Papers, MS 8426); Collins on no employment promises, 20 Sept. 1920 (NAI, DE 2/324); Boland to O'Hegarty on jobs in USA, 19 Nov. 1921 (NAI, DE 2/245); E. F. Kinkead, 8 Mar. 1921, in Dumont to Secretary of State, 21 July 1921; Mee matrial (NAI, DE 2/87; DE 2/161); Óglaigh na hÉireann proclamation (NLI, ILB 300 p3); cutting off hair: O'Shiel memoir, 876; London *Times*, 11 May 1920; Macardle, *Irish Republic*, 326; decline of DMP: UCD Hayes Papers, P52/1551; *Birming-ham Post*, 18 Jan. 1920; Athlone meting: PRO, CO 904 1881/1; Townshend, *British Campaign*, 109: Tudor statement: NAI, DE 2/234B; Boyce, *British Public Opinion*, 55; IG monthly report, June 1920 (PRO, CO 904/112); Sturgis diary, 4 Aug. 1920 (NLI MS P7498); *Ir. Ind.*, 10 Aug. 1920; RIC resignations pamphlet (NLI, ILB 300 p8 (78)).

12. Republican police: cab. minutes, 25 Apr., 16 June, 17, 24 July 1920; police activities and policies: Dept Defence microfilm, NLI, pos 916–17; Seán Condran memoir in Comerford memoir, ch. 22, pp 1–14 (UCD); *Ir. Ind.*, 27, 29 Apr., 3 May, 16 June 1920; *IB*, 16 June 1920; London *Times*, 26, 11 May, 29 June, 7 July 1920; 'Republican Police' (Dept Defence microfilm, NLI, pos 917, 919); Mulcahy statement: UCD, Hayes Papers, P53/1547; O'Malley *On Another Man's Wound*, 168; Mulcahy twice created a force but Stack's department failed to maintain it: UCD, Mulcahy Papers, P7D/96 (2); reorganisation, Nov. 1921: ibid., P7A/37; Macready to Greenwood, 17 July 1920 (PRO, CO 904/188); London *Times*, 14, 15, 22 May 1920; Brugha on policing: *Dáil procs*, 169–70; distilling: 207–8, 196; *IB*, 19 June 1920; O'Shiel memoir, 902–3; Croke Park police: Patrick O'Daly memoir (NLI, MS 4548); excessive policing: NLI, ILB 300 p12; BMH chronology, iii, 145; Neligan, *Spy in the Castle*, 128, 143; *Ir. Ind.*, 5 July, 19 June, 31 May, 6 Sept., 19 Nov. 1920.

13. Macready to Anderson 11, 12 Oct. 1920 (PRO, CO 904/188); Dumont to Secretary of State, 15 June 1920; C. Grasty, 'Irish Realities', *Atlantic Monthly*, Sept. 1920, 383–94; James Carty, 'Ireland's Republican Government', *Nation* (USA), 28 Aug. 1920; Collins to O'Brien, 18, 30 June 1920, O'Brien to Duffy, 10 July 1920 (NLI, O'Brien Papers, MS 8426); de Valera on administration: NAI, DE 2/58; proposed committee system: *Dáil procs* (17 Sept. 1920), 213–14; Collins statement: ibid., 247; number of employees: Colm Gallagher interview; information from Dept Public Service; McCartan to Secretary of Ministry (?) (NAI, DE 2/245); O'Brien to Collins, 21 May 1921 (NAI, DE 2/8 (27)).

14. Dept Local Govt reports, Oct. 1919, June 1920 (NLI, Duffy Papers, MSS 15439–40); report, Sept. 1920 (NAI, DE 2/243); planning the break: *Dáil procs* 184–5, 203–4, 219–22, 253–5; local govt allegaince: NAI, DE 2/444; *Dáil off. rep.* (17 Aug. 1921), 35, (3 May 1922), 356; Commission Local Govt, interim report, 6 Aug. 1920 (NAI, DE 2/243); Comerford memoir, ch. 27 (UCD); Fitzpatrick, *Politics and Irish Life*, 84–97; BMH chronology, iii, sec. 2, 252; O'Higgins on resistant local officials, 19 Nov. 1920 (NAI, DE 2/155); *Ir. Ind.*, 7 Aug. 1920; O'Higgins circular, 20 Dec. 1920 (NLI, Plunkett Papers,

MS 11404); Dept Local Govt report, Jan. 1921 (NLI, Duffy Papers, MS 15440); Michael Hayes on Dept Local Govt (UCD, Hayes Papers, P53/1547).

15. Labour: Boylan, *Dictionary of Irish Biography*, 220; Van Voris, *Constance de Markievicz*, 255–98; M. J. Lennon, manuscript biography of Griffith, (NLI, Lennon Papers, MS 22293); response to UK employment insurance legislation: O'Hegarty to Markievicz, 9 Nov. 1920 (NAI, DE 2/5(5)); Comerford memoir, ch. 18, p. 5 (UCD); Kathleen McKenna, 'The *Irish Bulletin*', *Capuchin Annual* (1970), 509; Sturgis diary, 27, 29 Sept. 1920; Dumont to Secretary of State 12 Nov. 1920 (USNA, DS, 841 d.00/259); cab. minutes, 17, 22 July, 15 Sept. 1920; new union: cab. minutes, 7 May, 16 June 1920; Minister for Labour to Depts, 21 May 1920 (NAI, DE 2/116); Dept Labour report, June 1920, (NLI Duffy Papers, MS 15439); transport action: Secretary of Ministry to Minister for Finance, 11 June 1930, audit to 31 Dec. 1920 (NAI, DE 2/7); cab. minutes, 16, 24 June, 24 Sept., 16 Oct., 30 Nov., 4 Dec. 1920, 9 Jan. 1921 (NAI, DE 1/3); Trade and Commerce: UCD, Blythe Papers, P24; Boylan, *Dictionary*; Walsh, *The Invincible Irish*, 44; *Dáil off. rep.* (17 Aug. 1921), 37, 41; cab. minutes, 27 Feb., 11 Mar., 2 Apr., 26 June, 15, 24 Sept. 1920 (NAI, DE 1/2). Dept Trade and Commerce reports: Oct. 1919 (NLI, Duffy Papers, MS 15440); Jan. 1921 (ibid., MS 15439); Aug. 1921 (UCD, Blythe Papers, P24/16): *Dáil procs*, 209, 223, 229–32.

16. Finance: *Dáil procs*, 219, 222–3, 181–2; SFSC minutes, 10 May 1918; Collins to Duffy, 22 July 1920 (NAI, Duffy Papers); Cork Corporation resolution, MacSwiney and Collins statements (UCD, Mulcahy Papers, P7A/12): Dept Finance reports: 24 Oct. 1919 (NLI, Duffy Papers, MS 15440); 4 Aug. 1920, 14 Sept., 31 Dec., 1920 (NAI, DE 2/7); NLI, ILB 300, 3 (118); *Dáil procs*, 189, 259; cab. minutes, 2, 30 May, 23 June 1919, 27 Feb., 9 Oct. 1920; *Irish World*, 30 Sept. 1922; O'Connor statements: *Dáil off. rep.* (17 Aug. 1921), 24–5, (10 May 1922), 394; Dept Finance report, Aug. 1921 (NLI, Duffy Papers, MS 15439; de Valera to Collins, 14 June 1921, reply, 16 June 1921 (de Valera Epitome, PRO, CO 904/23 (7)).

17. SFSC minutes, 9 Jan., 29 May 1919; *Evening Telegraph*, 6 Jan. 1919; Griffith memorandum, 23 Jan. 1919 (UCD, Hayes Papers, P53/1018); Forbes Patterson: *New Ireland*, 11 Jan., 12, 26 Apr. 1919; *Young Ireland*, 4 Oct. 1919; *Irish World*, 19 Apr. 1919; SFSC minutes, 2 June, 4 Sept., 30 Oct. 1919; cab. minutes, 7, 21, 28 Nov. 1919; Patterson's report (NAI, DE 2/89); *Red Hand*, Sept.–Dec. 1920; Ulster Information Bureau, see Carty, *Bibliography of Irish History, 1912–1921*, 155, 133; Bew, Gibbon and Patterson, *The State in Northern Ireland*, 48; *Catholic Bulletin*, Jan. 1920; *Ir. Ind.*, 30 Jan. 1920; SFSC minutes, 26 Aug., 12 Oct. 1919, 5 Feb., 10 Aug. 1920; *Old Ireland*, 21 Feb. 1920; Belfast Expelled Workers' Fund: NLI, Hanna Sheehy-Skeffington Papers, MS 22693 (1); *Dáil procs* (6 Aug. 1920), 190–4; cab. minutes, 11 Aug. 1920; *Dáil procs* (17 Sept. 1920), 212–13, 228, 233; ILP & TUC, *Annual Report, 1920*, 100; *Ir. Ind.*, 4, 8, 10, 11, 15, 20, 29 Sept., 14, 16 Dec. 1920; Childers's opposition: NLI, Plunkett Papers, MS 11404; *Dáil procs* (25 Jan. 1921), 258, 257; BMH chronology, iii, sec. 3, 390.

18. D. S. Johnson, 'The Belfast Boycott, 1920–22' in Goldstrom and Clarkson (eds), *Irish Population, Economics and Society*; O'Hegarty, *Victory of Sinn Féin*, 49–53, 183–5; Gaughan, *Jeremiah Mee*, appx 12, 338–45; McDonagh to local

authorities, Mar. 1921 (NAI, DE 2/110); Macready to Anderson, 12 Mar. 1921, reply, 14 Mar. 1921 (PRO, CO 904/188); Patterson, *Class Conflict and Sectarianism in Northern Ireland,* 115–31; *Old Ireland,* 15 Feb., 18 June 1921; de Valera on election agreement: *Dáil procs* (11 Mar. 1921), 266; Anon., 'Ulster in 1921', *Blackwoods Magazine,* Oct. 1922.

19. Catholic Church: London *Times,* 12 May, 26 June 1919, 27 Jan. 1920; NLI, O'Brien Papers, MS 8419; BMH chronology, iii, sec. 2 (20 Oct. 1920); Rev. W. McDonald, *Some Ethical Questions;* O'Brien to O'Hegarty, 16 June 1920 (NAI, DE 2/402); *Old Ireland,* 31 July 1920, 12 Feb. 1921; see also *Irish World,* 3, 24 May 1919.

20. Catholic Church: P. S. Ó Broin to President, spring 1921 (NAI, DE 2/402); *Ir. Ind.,* 12 Apr. 1920; Dumont to Secretary of State, 12 Nov. 1920; NAI, DE 2/85; *Ir. Ind.,* 24 July, 20 Aug., 24 Sept. 1920; *Nationality,* 3 May 1919; Miller, *Church, State and Nation in Ireland,* 426–86.

21. *Star,* 16 Feb. 1929; D. R. O'Connor Lysaght, introduction to Connolly, *Socialism Made Easy; Ir. Ind.,* 22 Oct., 15, 22 Nov. 1919; London *Times,* 2 May 1919, 24 May, 9 Aug. 1920 article by Fr Finlay, in *Studies,* Feb. 1919; *Ir.Ind.,* 3 Oct., 2 Feb., 4, 10, 18 Mar. 1920; London *Times,* 21 Jan. 1920; David Fitzpatrick, 'Strikes in Ireland, 1914–21', *Saothar,* 6 (1980), 26–39; Dumont to Secretary of State, 27 Jan., 15 June, 15 Oct. 1920; Griffith interview, *Ir. Ind.,* 10 Apr. 1920; de Valera statement: Ruth Russell, *What's the Matter with Ireland?* 65; Labour standards: *Dáil procs,* 198, 229; *Evening Telegraph,* 10 Jan. 1919.

22. Mitchell, *Labour in Irish Politics,* 117–22; J. W. Davis to Secretary of State, 19 Apr. 1919 (USNA, DS, 841.d.00/48); motor permits strike: *Ir. Ind.,* 3, 17 Dec. 1919; Minister for Finance to Dáil trustees, 6 Dec. 1919, 6 Feb. 1920 (NAI, DE 2/7); Dumont to Secretary of State, 14, 27 Jan. 1920; *Blackwood's Magazine,* July 1920; *Ir. Ind.,* 10 Feb. 1920; bacon and pigs: *Ir. Ind.,* 16, 17, 21 Apr. 1920; *IT,* 23 Apr. 1920; Belfast consul to Secretary of State, 30 Apr. 1920 (USNA, DS, 841.d.00/196); SFSC minutes, 11 May 1920; political prisoners: *Pall Mall Gazette,* 27 Apr. 1920; Bennett, *The Black and Tans,* 36; *Ir. Ind.,* 27 July, 23 Aug. 1920; munitions strike: *Ir. Ind.,* 31 May, 10, 21 June 1920; Jones, *Whitehall Diary,* iii, 167–8;Macready, *Annals of an Active Life,* ii, 472; London *Times,* 5, 7, 21, 25 June, 29 July 1920; *Old Ireland,* 5, 24 July 1920; SFSC minutes, 22 June 1920; cab. minutes, 10 June 1920; Dumont to Secetary of State, 15 June, 28 Sept, 12 Nov. 1920; Collins to James Burns, 9 Nov. 1920 (NLI, MS 22456); *Irish World* (NY), 29 Jan. 1921; James W. Good, 'British Labour and Irish Needs', *Studies,* Dec. 1920; Charles Townshend, 'The Irish Railway Strike of 1920: Industrial Action and Civil Resistance in the Struggle for Independence', *Irish Historical Studies,* xxi, no. 83 (Mar. 1979), 265–83.

23. Dept Foreign Affairs, consuls: *Dáil procs* (17, 18 June 1919), 114, 121, 123–4, (29 June 1920), 172–4; cab. minutes, 30 May, 29 Aug., 5, 27 Sept., 31 Oct. 1919; Boland to Griffith, 11 Aug. 1919 (NAI, DE 2/245); de Valera to Dáil govt, 30 Jan. 1920 (NAI, Duffy Papers); Dunne to O'Brien, 30 Oct., 4, 6 Nov., 12 Dec. 1920 (NLI, O'Brien Papers, MS 8421); Duffy to Dáil govt, 15 June 1919, 10, 12, 18 Aug. 1920, 12 Apr. 1921 (NAI, Duffy Papers); O'Brien to Collins, 16 June 1920 (NLI, O'Brien Papers, MS 8426); *Ir. Ind.,* 4 Sept. 1920.

24. Rome: Duffy to Dáil govt, 21 May 1920 (NAI, Duffy Papers); Dept Foreign Affairs report, June 1920; Duffy to O'Kelly, 18 June 1920 (NLI, O'Brien

Papers, MS 8426); *Ir. Ind.*, 4, 5 June, 1 July, 7, 23 Dec. 1920; *Nation,* 8 Mar. 1930; O'Brien to O'Hegarty, 24 June (NLI, O'Brien Papers, MS 8427); de Valera to Dáil govt, 6, 21 May 1920, O'Kelly to Dáil govt, *c.* Sept. 1920 (NAI, Duffy Papers); Keogh, *The Vatican, the Bishops and Irish Politics,* 41–5.

25. France: Duffy to Dáil govt, 3, 8 July, 1, 24 Aug., 1920 (NAI, Duffy Papers); *Ir. Ind.,* 9 Sept. 1919; Duffy to Blythe, 20 June 1920, Duffy to O'Kelly, 19 Mar. 1920 (NAI, Duffy Papers); Briollay, *Ireland in Rebellion,* 52; Duffy to O'Hegarty, 9 Sept. 1920, O'Hegarty to Duffy, 13 Sept. 1920, O'Brien to O'Hegarty, 4 Sept. 1920 (NLI, O'Brien Papers, MS 8427); O'Brien to Duffy, 4, 12 Sept. 1920 (NAI, Duffy Papers); Duffy expulsion: *Dáil priv. sess.* (18 Aug. 1921), 13–14; *Dáil procs* (17 Sept. 1920), 21–6; Dáil govt to O'Kelly, Sept. 1920 (NLI, O'Brien Papers, MS 8426); *Ir. Ind.,* 6, 9 Sept. 1920; Dept Foreign Affairs report, Jan. 1921 (NLI, Duffy Papers, MS 15440); O'Kelly to O'Brien, 2 Nov. 1920 (NLI, O'Brien Papers, MS 8421); 'Pat' to Duffy, 14 Jan. 1921, O'Brien to Duffy, 26 Feb. 1921 (NAI, Duffy Papers).

26. Germany: cab. minutes, 29 Aug., 5, 27 Sept., 31 Oct. 1919; Ward, *Ireland and Anglo-American Relations,* 143; O'Kelly to Dáil govt, 24 Aug. 1919 (NAI, Duffy Papers); Secretary of Ministry to Minister for Finance, 28 Feb. 1920 (NAI, DE 2/7, Dept Finance file); Collins to O'Brien, 18 May, 16 Aug. 1920, O'Kelly to O'Brien, 7 Nov. 1919, O'Brien to Collins, 24 June 1920 (NLI, O'Brien Papers, MS 8426); Stanhope to de Valera, 21 Jan. 1920, O'Hegarty to Duffy, 9 July 1920, Duffy to O'Hegarty, 7 Aug. 1920, Duffy to Dáil govt, 17 July, 15 Aug. 1920 (NAI, Duffy Papers); Gaffney to Collins, 19 May 1920 (NAI, DE 2/401); Collins to Duffy, 3 Sept. 1920, O'Hegarty to Duffy, 15 Apr. 1920, de Valera to Dáil govt, 16 Apr. 1920 (NAI, Duffy Papers); Carroll, *American Opinion,* 103, 238n; Brennan, *Allegiance,* 327; Dept Foreign Affairs report, June 1920; Plunkett on problems in Germany: *Dáil procs* (29 June 1920), 184; O'Hegarty to O'Brien, 16 Dec. 1920 (NLI, O'Brien Papers, MS 8428); see also Ernst Rowohlt, *Irische volksmarchen* (Berlin 1920) (copy in NLI).

27. Russia: ILP & TUC, *Ireland at Berne;* Duke of Northumberland, *International Revolutionary Propaganda: The Situation in Ireland* (pamphlet, 1920) (copy in NLI); McCartan, *With de Valera in America,* 2–4, 106–7, 201; *American Monthly,* June 1919; McCartan to Duffy, 10 May 1919 (NAI, Duffy Papers); *Voice of Labour,* 30 Aug. 1919; *Ir. Ind.,* 30 Apr. 1919; O'Brien to Collins, 14 Jan. 1920 (NLI, O'Brien Papers, MS 8426); McCartan, *With de Valera in America,* 201, 272–4; Cronin, *McGarrity Papers,* 203–8; 'crown' jewels: According to James O'Mara, de Valera told him that Harry Boland brought the jewels back to Ireland, who gave them to Collins, who threw them back after the Treaty split. Boland gave them to his mother to keep safe until de Valera returned to power. She gave them to the new government in 1932. Patrick McGilligan, Minister for Finance, said in 1948 that the jewels were given to the Department of the Taoiseach in 1938 and transferred to the Department of Finance in 1948. Wesley Boyd has written that the Russian government repaid the loan and the jewels were returned in the following year. See Harry Boland diary, 14, 15 Apr. 1920 (cited in T. P. O'Neill, manuscript biography of de Valera); T. P. O'Neill interview; Lavelle, *James O'Mara;* NLI, O'Mara Papers, MS 21552; *Dáil Debates* (1948), cxiii, 1526; Boyd article, *IT,* 5 June 1967.

28. Russia: cab. minutes, 2 Apr., 5 June 1920; *Dáil procs,* 174, 184; Dept Foreign Affairs report, June 1920; Duffy to Dept Finance, 8 July 1920, Duffy to Dáil govt, 7 Aug. 1920 (NAI, Duffy Papers); O'Kelly to O'Brien, July 1920 (NLI, O'Brien Papers, MS 8426); O'Brien to Collins, 19 July 1920 (NAI, DE 2/322); O'Brien to Collins, 29 July 1920 (NLI, O'Brien Papers, MS 8424); de Valera to cabinet, 9 July 1920 (NAI, DE 2/245); Steffens: O'Brien to Collins, 16 Oct. 1920 (NLI, O'Brien Papers, MS 8426); most friendly towards Ireland: *Dáil procs* (17 Sept. 1920), 217; Connolly and McAlpine: NAI, DE 2/119, DE 8/17; *Dáil procs* (25 Jan. 1921), 250–1; mission to Moscow: NLI, McCartan Papers, MS 17682; *Intercourse between Bolshevism and Sinn Féin* (Cmd 1326) (HMSO, 1921); *Weekly Summary,* 24 June 1921; Dept Foreign Affairs report, 6 June 1921 (NLI, Plunkett Papers, MS 11404); Secretary of Ministry to President, 9 May 1921 (NAI, DE 2/1 (109)).

29. United States: *Ir. Ind.,* 3 Feb. 1920; *IT,* 2, 9 Feb. 1920; NAI, DE 2/245; *Dáil procs,* 267; Leon Ó Broin, *The Prime Informer: A Suppressed Scandal* (London 1971); de Valera to Fawsitt, 23 Nov. 1921 (NAI, DE 2/478); NLI, O'Mara Papers, MS 21548 (3) (4); cab. minutes, 27 Feb. 1922 (NAI, DE 1/4); Ward, *Ireland and Anglo-Irish Relations,* 225–6; de Valera to cabinet, 5 Mar. 1920 (NAI, DE 2/245); Collins to Seán Nunan, 20 Mar. 1920 (NAI, DE 2/292); *Ir. Ind.,* 10 May, 15 June 1920; London *Times,* 25 June 1920; *IT,* 21 Apr. 1920; Dumont to Secretary of State, 2 Jan. 1920 (USNA, DS 841.d.00/119); *Old Ireland,* 18 Mar. 1920; see also Donal McCartney, 'De Valera's Mission to the US, 1919–20' in Cosgrove and McCartney (eds), *Studies in Irish History presented to R. Dudley Edwards,* 304–22.

30. *IT,* 30 Jan. 1920; State Dept records, correspondence, 16 Jan. 1920, memo, 27 Jan. 1920 (USNA, DS, 841.d.01); *Ir. Ind.,* 8 Jan., 3, 9 Feb., 5 Mar. 1920; McCartan, *With de Valera in America,* 153; O'Flanagan to Collins, 15 Mar. 1920 (NAI, DE 2/234A); de Valera to cabinet (NAI, DE 2/245); cab. minutes, 15 Mar. 1920; US Senate: *Ir. Ind.,* 22, 23 Mar. 1920; Briollay, *Ireland in Rebellion,* 28.

31. O'Mara's resignation: O'Mara to O'Brien, 18 Mar. 1920 (NLI, O'Mara Papers, MS 21548); McCartan on O'Mara situation (NLI, McCartan Papers, MS 17688); Collins to de Valera, 9 Feb. 1920, Fawsitt to O'Mara, 24 Mar. 1920, de Valera to O'Mara, 4 Mar. 1920 (NLI, O'Mara Papers, MS 21548); Collins to Seán Nunan, 29 Apr. 1920 (NAI, DE 2/292); Collins to Boland, 19 Apr. 1920 (NAI, DE 2/245); finance: Collins to de Valera, 9 Feb. 1920 (ibid.); Collins to Seán Nunan, 29 Apr. 1920 (NAI, DE 2/292); cab. minutes, 5 June 1920; Boland to Collins, 22 Sept. 1920 (NAI, DE 2/245); Taylor, *Collins,* 110; conventions: Nunan to Collins, 17 May 1920 (NAI, DE 2/292); Cronin, *McGarrity Papers,* 83; Collins to O'Brien, 22 June, O'Brien to Collins on Lynch, 13 July 1920 (NLI, O'Brien Papers, MS 8426); Griffith to Devoy and Cohalan in support of de Valera, 23 June 1920, de Valera to Boland, 21 Oct. 1920 (NLI, Gallagher Papers, MS 18375 (15)); Lynch, *IRB,* 210–12; Lynch's resignation: *Dáil procs* (6 Aug. 1920), 188–90, 195; T. P. O'Neill, manuscript biography of de Valera.

32. Cronin, *McGarrity Papers,* 84–5; *Ir. Ind.,* 6 Sept. 1920; Dan Foley to Frank P. Walsh concerning Cardinal O'Connell interview (NLI, O'Mara Papers, MS 21548 (3)); Boland to de Valera, 29 Oct. 1920 (ibid.); Ellen O'Connor

to Hanna Sheehy-Skeffington on de Valera–FOIF conflict, 24 Sept. 1920 (NLI, Sheehy-Skeffington Papers, MS 22693 (v); Ó Broin, *Revolutionary Underground*, 190–1; *Dáil procs*, 250, 289; cab. minutes, 9 Oct. 1920 (NAI, DE 1/3); *Irish World* (NY), 11 Dec. 1920.

33. Cab. minutes, 23 Oct. 1920; inquiry commission: McCartan, *With de Valera in America*, 210–11, 235–9; de Valera to Boland, 21 Oct. 1920 (NLI, Gallagher Papers, MS 18374 (15); Ward, *Anglo-American Relations*, 238–41; *Ir. Ind.*, 16 Oct. 1920; collecting evidence: O'Hegarty to Fitzgerald, 2 Nov. 1920, reply, 20 Nov. 1920 (NAI, DE 2/118); Dumont to Secretary of State, 12 Nov. 1920 (USNA, DS, 841.d.00/259); American Commisson on Conditions in Ireland, *Interim Report*, v–vi, 3–14, 106–14; Francis M. Carroll, 'The American Commisson of Inquiry on Conditions in Ireland', *Éire–Ireland* (winter 1981), 59–74; relief commission: cab. minutes, 6 Nov. 1920.

34. Money: NLI, O'Mara Papers, MS 21548 (3), (4); Dept Finance report, 5 Aug.–14 Sept. 1920 (NAI, DE 2/7); Cronin, *McGarrity Papers*, 92; Collins on US loan total, *Dáil procs* (11 Mar. 1921), 267; Béaslaí, *Collins*, ii, 353–6; O'Kelly statement, *Dáil off. rep.* (22 Feb. 1922), 113.

35. Figgis, *Recollections*, 307–8; Holmes, *Little Field Marshal*, 38–9, 348–9; flyer on French (NLI, ILB 300, p6 (14)); Townshend, *British Campaign*, 73–82; Sturgis diary, 3 Sept. 1920, 30 Apr. 1921, 22 Aug. 1920 (NLI, MS P7498); Wheeler-Bennett, *John Anderson, Viscount Waverly*; Cope in Sturgis diary, 4 Oct. 1920; O'Brien to Collins, 2 Sept. 1920 (NLI, McKenna Napoli Papers); Townshend, *British Campaign*, 55–82; *Morning Post*, cited in *Ir. Ind.*, 19 July 1920; *IT*, 21 Apr. 1920; *Ir. Ind.*, 30 Mar. 1920; A. J. P. Taylor, *Beaverbrook* (London 1972), 187; Irish Situation Committee, 15 July 1920 (PRO, CAB 27/107); Jones, *Whitehall Diary*, iii, 16–17 (31 May 1920); Gaughan, *Jeremiah Mee*, 364–5.

36. *IT*, 29 Apr. 1920; Townshend, *British Campaign*, 106–31; *Ir. Ind.*, 8 Mar. 1920; London *Times*, 2 June 1920; Macardle, *Irish Republic*, 368; Dumont to Secretary of State, 28 Sept. 1920; transport action: Mitchell, *Labour in Irish Politics*, 120–1; Townshend, 'Railway Strike', 265–82; audit to 31 Dec. 1920 (NAI, DE 2/7); Sturgis diary, 11 Nov. 1920 (NLI, MS P7498); cab. minutes, 30 Nov., 4 Dec. 1920; Dumont to Secretary of State, 15 June 1920; British army pamphlet, *Sinn Féin* (1919) (PRO, WO 32/4308); Dumont to Secretary of State, July 1920 (USNA, DS 841.d.00/214); London *Times*, 19 July, 15 Sept. 1920; British army suppression of Sinn Féin courts (Dept. Defence microfilm, NLI, pos 918); Sturgis diary, 20 Sept., 22 Aug. 1920 (NLI); Anderson comment: PRO, CO 904/188; IG monthly report, Aug. 1920; Dáil Éireann Courts of Justice (Dept Defence microfilm, NLI, pos 917); O'Shiel memoir, 902; Collins to O'Brien, 10 Nov. 1920 (NAI, DE 2/325); Sturgis diary, 6 Dec. 1920 (NLI); Connaught Rangers: Pollock, *Mutiny for the Cause*; Hickey and Doherty, *Dictionary of Irish History*, 87–8; Mitchell and Ó Snodaigh, *Irish Political Documents, 1916–1919*, 78–81; Duffy to Dáil govt, 9 July 1920 (NAI, Duffy Papers); Collins to O'Brien, 25 Nov. 1921 (NLI, O'Brien Papers, MS 8430); Maurice Moore circular letter, 18 Oct. 1922 (NAI, Duffy Papers); *Irish Weekly Independent*, 21 Feb.–18 Apr. 1925; Collins and portable planes: O'Brien to Collins, 29, 30 July, 1–3, 10, 20 Sept. 1920 (NLI, O'Brien Papers MS 8426, also MS 8430); Collins to

O'Brien, 21 Aug., 13, 17 Sept. 1920 (NAI, DE 2/323); Collins to R.M.G., 25 June 1921 (NLI, O'Brien Papers, MS 8430).

37. Townshend, *British Campaign*, 113–14, 116–17; *IB*, 16 July, 5 Oct. 1920; Dept Defence microfilm, NLI, pos 918; memo, 7 Aug. 1920 (PRO, CO 904/188/1); Sturgis diary, 9, 13, 19 Aug., 3, 20 Sept., 31 July, 4, 11 Nov., 22 Aug. 1920 (NLI, MS P7498); Dumont to Secretary of State, 28 Sept. 1920; Collins to Nunan, 30 Sept. 1920 (NAI, DE 2/292); Collins to O'Brien, 10 Nov. 1920 (NAI, DE 2/325); Brind statement (NLI, O'Brien Papers, MS 8430); Collins to Duffy, 3 Oct. 1920 (NAI, Duffy Papers); Collins to O'Brien, 17 Nov. 1920 (NLI, O'Brien Papers, MS 8426); Mulcahy conclusion (UCD, Hayes Papers, P53/1568); RIC: SFSC minutes, 14 Oct. 1920; monthly report, Nov. 1920; *IB*, 22 Dec. 1920; O'Shiel memoir; Conor Maguire, 'The Republican Courts', *Capuchin Annual* (1969); Collins to O'Brien, 2 Dec. 1920 (NLI, O'Brien Papers, MS 8426; Dáil Éireann, *Constructive Work of Dáil Éireann, No. 1: The National Police and Courts of Justice*, 31; Dept Home Affairs report, 16 Aug. 1921 (NAI, DE 2/51); McCabe statement, *Dáil priv. sess.* (18 Aug. 1921), 21; Dumont to Secretary of State, 12 Nov. 1920.

38. Griffith charge: Dumont to Secretary of State, 12 Nov. 1920 (USNA,DS, 841. d.00/197, 163); Wells, *Irish Indiscretions*, 135, 138; Dept Defence microfilm, NLI, pos 918; Montmorency, *Sword and Stirrup*, SFSC minutes, 9 Jan. 1919; handbill (NLI, ILB 300, p8); Macready, *Annals*, ii, 465, 456, 495; Bowden, *The Breakdown of Public Scrutiny*, 112–14; Boyce, *Englishmen and Irish Troubles*, 86–8; Childers, *Military Rule in Ireland*, 34n; *Young Ireland*, cited in *Ir. Ind.*, 20 Aug. 1920; Hogan, *Four Glorious Years*, 290, 107; Duff, *Sword for Hire*, 77; *IB*, 8 Dec. 1920, 27 Jan. 1921; Sturgis diary, 24 Sept., 1, 13, 17 Oct., 23 Dec. 1920 (NLI, MS P7498); Macready to Under-Secretary, 11 Oct. 1920 (PRO, CO 904/118).

39. MacSwiney: Dumont to Secretary of State, 12 Nov. 1920; Sturgis diary, 4 Sept., 1 Nov. 1920 (NLI, MS P7498); London *Times*, 28 Aug. 1920; Collins to O'Brien, 29 Sept. 1920 (NLI, O'Brien Papers, MS 8426); O'Brien to Collins, 9 Oct. 1920 (ibid.); O'Brien to Collins, 30 Dec. 1920 (ibid., MS 8430); capture of Mulcahy papers: Sturgis diary, 18 Nov. 1920 (NLI, MS P7478); Bishop Cohalan: *Ir. Ind.*, 18 Dec. 1920; Bloody Sunday: *IB*, 1–2 Dec. 1920; Sturgis diary, 21 Nov. 1920 (NLI, MS P7478); Colum, *Ourselves Alone!*, 238; Dumont to Secretary of State, 12 Nov. 1920; Charles Townshend, 'Bloody Sunday: Michael Collins Speaks', *European Studies Review*, ix (1979), 377–85; *Ir. Ind.*, 25 Nov. 1920; London *Times*, 22 Nov. 1920; Dumont statement, Consulate Weekly Report, 23 Nov. 1920 (USNA, DS, record 800, correspondence).

40. Griffith arrest: Jones, *Whitehall Diary*, iii, 46; UCD, Hayes Papers, P53/1547; statement of Mrs Griffith (NAI, DE 2/356); Griffith to Secretary of Ministry, 3 Dec. 1920 (NAI, DE 2/234A); Mac Néill poem: NLI, McKenna Napoli Papers, MS 22744; aftermath: Sturgis diary, 27, 28 Nov. 1920 (NLI, MS P7498); Brady, *Ireland's Secret Service in England*, 33; British army memorandum, 27 Nov. 1920 (Dept Defence microfilm, NLI, pos 918); *Ir. Ind.*, 28, 29, 30 Nov. 1920; see also Celia Shaw memoir (NLI, MS 23409).

41. Feelers for peace; Sturgis diary, 2 Nov. 1920 (NLI, MS P7498); Cope: O'Brien to Collins, 8 July, 2 Sept. 1920 (NLI, O'Brien Papers, MS 8426); Cope's pursuit of J. J. O'Kelly (Sceilg): P. J. Matthews memoir, 56 (NLI, MS 9873); Collins to O'Brien, 4 Sept. 1920 (NAI, DE 2/323); Dumont to Secretary of

State, 14 May 1920 (USNA, DS 841.d.00/197); O'Brien to Collins, 23 July 1920 (NAI, DE 2/234A); O'Brien to Collins, 8, 15, 16, 23, 30 July 1920 (NLI, O'Brien Papers, MS 8420); Jones to Anderson, 10 Aug. 1920 (PRO, CO 904/118/1); MacMahon telegram, 2 Aug. 1920 (ibid.); Griffith's denial: *Dáil procs* (6 Aug. 1920), 190; BMH chronology, iii, sec. 2 190; September: Colum, *Ourselves Alone!*, 233–4; Sturgis diary, 26 Sept. 1920 (NLI, MS P7498); October: Colum, *Ourselves Alone!*, 233, Moylett: *IT*, 15–17 Nov. 1965; Steele to O'Hegarty, 10 May 1928 (NAI, DE 2/251); Collins's comment on Moylett: Collins to O'Brien, 15 Dec. 1920 (ibid.); O'Brien to Griffith, 2 Dec. 1920, Griffith to Secretary of Ministry, 3 Dec. 1920 (NAI, DE 2/2344); Gilmartin and others: *FJ*, 5 Nov. 1920; *Ir. Ind.*, 26 Nov. 1920; letters to Churchill (NLI, Shane Leslie Papers, MS 22841); *Ir. Ind.*, 29, 30 Nov., 1, 3, 4, 6 Dec. 1920.

42. Clune: O'Brien to Griffith, 2 Dec. 1920, McDonagh to Collins, 29 Nov. 1920, Griffith to Secretary of Ministry, 3 Dec. 1920 (NAI, DE 2/234A); cab. minutes, 4 Dec. 1920 (NAI, DE 1/3); IRA: Dumont to US embassy, London, 6 Dec. 1920, telegram, Dumont to Secretary of State, 21 Jan. 1921 (USNA, DS 841.d.00.262/314); Galway County Council: *Ir. Ind.*, 4, 6, 8, 13–16 Dec. 1920; *Connaught Tribune*, 11, 18, 25 Dec. 1920; Brennan, *The War in Clare*, 65; Westmeath County Council: *Ir. Ind.*, 6, 13 Dec. 1920; Fr O'Flanagan: *Ir. Ind.*, 6, 7, 14 Dec. 1920, *Observer*, 5 Dec. 1920; Collins to Griffith, 14 Dec. 1920 (NAI, DE 2/234B).

43. Lloyd George's reaction: 'Watchman', *Old Ireland*, 18 Dec. 1920; Collins to O'Brien, 14 Dec. 1920 (NAI, DE 2/234B); Dáil govt: *Young Ireland*, quoted in *Ir. Ind.*, 3, 7, 13 Dec. 1920; *Old Ireland*, 18 Dec. 1920; Collins to Duffy, 9 Dec. 1920 (NAI, Duffy Papers); local govt: Griffith to O'Hegarty, 6 Dec. 1920 (NAI, DE 2/234B); leadership: Collins to Griffith, 2 Dec. 1920 (ibid.); cab. minutes, 27 Nov., 4, 11 Dec. 1920; Griffith to Secretary of Ministry, 9 Dec. 1920 (ibid.); O'Kelly, *Stepping Stones*, 13; Béaslaí, *Collins*, ii, 81.

44. ILP & TUC, *Who Burnt Cork City?*; *Ir. Ind.*, 13, 15, 18, 28 Dec. 1920; Cohalan to Leslie, 29 Dec. 1920, Lyons to Leslie, 9 Mar. 1921 (NLI, Leslie Papers, MS 22838); Collins on Cohalan: Collins to J. McDonagh, 16 Dec. 1920 (NAI, DE 2/234B); Celia Shaw memoir (NLI); Mac Eoin (ed.), *Survivors*, 239–40; *Old Ireland*, 8 Jan. 1921.

45. Final negotiations: Griffith to Collins, 15 Dec. 1920, Collins note, 18 Dec. 1920, Collins to O'Brien, 21 Dec. 1920 (NAI, DE 2/234B); Deasy, *Towards Ireland Free*, 180; *Irish Press*, 18 Jan. 1966.

Chapter 4: War of Wills (pp 225–299)

1. *Ir. Ind.*, 17 Dec. 1920; Longford and O'Neill, *De Valera*, 115; *Irish World* (NY), 8 Jan. 1921; Sturgis diary, 21 Dec. 1920 (NLI, MS P7498); Jones, *Whitehall Diary*, iii, 46; Macready to Anderson, 10 Jan. 1921 (PRO, CO 904/188).

2. Correspondence of President with O'Hegarty and ministers, Jan. 1921 (NAI, DE 2/3 (22)); de Valera Epitome (PRO, CO 904/23(7); O'Hegarty to Mulcahy on increased duties 'more various and irksome', n.d. (UCD, Mulcahy Papers, P7A/17 (97–8)); Collins to O'Brien, 31 Jan. 1921 (NLI, O'Brien Papers, MS 8426); SFSC minutes, 15 Feb. 1921; Collins to de Valera, 12 Apr. 1921 (NAI, DE 2/244); President to several depts (PRO, de Valera Epitome); de Valera to O'Hegarty, 17 Feb. 1921 (NAI, DE 2/3

(91); de Valera to O'Hegarty, 10 Mar. 1921 (NAI, DE 2/14); Hogan, *Four Glorious Years*, 271; de Valera to O'Mara, 8 Apr. 1921 (NLI, O'Mara Papers, MS 21552); Collins to O'Brien, 8 Apr. 1921, reply, 25 Apr. 1921, Collins to O'Brien, 4, 14 May 1921 (NLI, O'Brien Papers, MS 8430).

3. President to Secretary of Ministry, Jan., 2 May 1921 (NAI, DE 1 (93)); Cosgrave to Secretary of Ministry, 5 Oct. 1920, Griffith to O'Hegarty, 2 Apr. 1920, Secretary of Ministry to all depts, 5 Apr. 1921 (NAI, DE 2/58); cab. minutes, 6 Apr. 1921; SFSC minutes, 31 May, 7 June, 6 July, 2, 9 Dec. 1921, 16 Jan. 1922; Béaslaí on improved contact between military and civil organisations, *Dáil procs* (10 May 1921), 283; O'Hegarty to Mulcahy, 8 June 1921 (NAI, DE 2/2 (15)); de Valera to O'Brien, 19 Mar. 1921 (NLI, O'Brien Papers, MS 8429).

4. Mulcahy on de Valera's proposals (UCD, Hayes Papers, P53/1293); de Valera's statement, *Dáil procs* (25 Jan. 1921), 240–50; *FJ*, 25 Jan. 1921; *Ir. Ind.*, 28 Jan. 1921; de Valera to O'Hegarty, 23 Mar. 1921 (NAI, DE 2/14); proposal to send Collins to USA: de Valera to Collins, 18 Jan. 1921 (UCD, Hayes Papers, P53/1552); Béaslaí, *Collins* ii, 141–7; O'Connor, *Big Fellow*, 109; Colum, *Ourselves Alone!*, 243–5; Dumont to Secretary of State, 22 July 1921 (USNA, DS, 841.d.00/402); Longford and O'Neill, *De Valera*, 119; O'Neill, *De Valera*, i, 197–8.

5. O'Connor, *Big Fellow*, 89–90, 114–16; conflict between Brugha and Collins in 1918: Brennan, *Allegiance*, 166, 180; M. J. Lennon, manuscript biography of Griffith (NLI, Lennon Papers, MS 22293); Greaves, *Liam Mellows*, 223–4, 231; T. P. O'Neill interview; Mulcahy on Collins and Brugha: UCD, Hayes Papers, P53/1443, P53/1568); Hayden Talbot, *Michael Collins's Own Story*, 80; Gaughan, *Stack*, 174.

6. Longford and O'Neill, *De Valera*, 118, 42, 148; O'Connor, *Big Fellow*, 24, 108–9; relation between de Valera and Collins: NAI, DE 2/14; O'Connor, *Death in Dublin*, 76; Collins to Griffith, 26 Jan. 1921 (Béaslaí, *Collins*, ii, 149); O'Malley, *On Another Man's Wound*, 294; Butler, *Barry's Flying Column*, 159; de Valera and Collins on US funds: *Dáil procs* (11 Mar. 1921), 267; T. P. O'Neill interview.

7. Dáil govt chronology: NAI, DE 2/14; O'Malley, *On Another Man's Wound*, 291.

8. *Republican Leader*, 26 Aug. 1923; TCD, Childers Papers, MS 7925; Comerford memoir, ch. 31, 14–15 (UCD); not going to be shot and Manchester: NLI, M. J. Lennon Papers, MS 22293; Rory O'Connor on Cosgrave: UCD, O'Malley Papers, P17/E/18; T. P. O'Neill interview; Brother Doyle statement, *Sunday Independent*, 21 Nov. 1965; Mulcahy statement (NLI, Hayes Papers (P53/ 1546); Gaughan, *Stack*, 276, 163; Matthews memoir, 37 (NLI, MS 9873); Collins on Cosgrave: Feehan, *Shooting of Michael Collins*, 91.

9. Cosgrave statement, *Dáil procs.* (25 Jan. 1921), 253–5; *Weekly Summary*, 14 Jan., 4 Mar. 1921; Dept Local Govt report, Aug. 1921, *Dáil priv sess.* (22 Aug. 1921), 35–8; Hayes narrative (UCD, Hayes Papers, P53/1549); report, Jan. 1921 (NLI, Duffy Papers, MS 15440); Fitzpatrick *Politics and Irish Life*, 185–97; failure of some local officials to follow Dáil policies: O'Higgins to O'Keeffe, 4 Sept. 1921 (NLI, ILB 300 p2 (21)); *Ir. Ind.*, 13 Dec. 1920; O'Higgins to local officials (no further relations with UK department), 15 Mar. 1921 (UCD, Mulcahy Papers, P7A/17 (28)).

10. O'Higgins on gaining ground, *Dáil procs* (11 Mar. 1921), 269; IG monthly report, 1 Feb. 1921 (PRO, CO 904/114); *Ir. Ind.*, 6 Dec. 1920; Duke of Cumberland's Fund, *Plight of Southern Irish Loyalists*, (pamphlet, n.d., *c.* May 1921); O'Hegarty to de Valera, 2 Apr. 1921 (NAI, DE 2/1); *IB*, supplement, 27 Apr. 1921; Dept Local Govt report, July 1921; report, Aug. 1921, *Dáil off. rep.* (17 Aug. 1921), 33–6.

11. O'Connor, *Death in Dublin*, 135; Mulcahy statements: UCD, Hayes Papers, P53/1547; *Dáil off. rep.* (17 Aug. 1921), 22; Dept Home affairs report, Jan. 1921 (NLI, Duffy Papers, MS 15440); Fagan: UCD, Mulcahy Papers, P7A/17 (152–7) and Hayes Papers P53/1547.

12. IG monthly reports, Oct. 1920–Mar. 1921 (PRO, CO 904/113, 114); Dumont to Secretary of State, 28 Jan. 1921 (USNA, DS 841.d.00/314); Dept Home Affairs report, Jan. 1921 (NLI, Duffy Papers, MS 15440); report, May 1921 (NAI, DE 2/51); Stack to TDs urging support, 1 Apr. 1920 (UCD, Mulcahy Papers P7A/17 (152–6)); O'Higgins on courts, *Dáil Debates* (24 July 1923), 1325–8; de Valera on need to get courts 'working again', *Dáil procs* (10 May 1921), 292, Mulcahy on same, ibid. (11 Mar. 1921), 284; Art O'Connor on courts, ibid., 273; raid on office: Stack to O'Hegarty, 30 May 1921 (NAI, DE 2/51); SFSC minutes, 7 June 1921; operation of courts and police reviewed: *Dáil priv. sess.* (18 Aug. 1921), 22–6.

13. Bishop Cohalan's praise of Republican Police: *Ir. Ind.*, 18 Dec. 1920; Mulcahy on double failure: UCD, Mulcahy Papers, P7D/96 (92); Mulcahy on how many Volunteers viewed appointment as police officers: *Dáil priv. sess.* (25 Aug. 1921), 68; appointment of police officers in each Donegal battalion: Chief of Staff to Director of Organisation, 25 Apr. 1921 (UCD, Mulcahy Papers, P7A/17 (332)); Director of Organisation to Dept Home Affairs, 24 Mar. 1921 (NAI, DE 2/421); Collins on police performance, Aug. 1922: Hopkinson, *Green Against Green*, 91; Brugha tormented: *Dáil priv. sess.* (25 Aug. 1921), 68; Mulcahy on need for civil offences code: *Dáil procs* (10 May 1921), 284.

14. *Thom's Official Directory of Great Britain and Ireland for the year 1922*, 642; de Valera to cabinet, 10 June 1920 (NAI, DE 2/245); prohibition of emigration: *Dáil procs* (6 Aug. 1920), 206–7; Stack on emigration permits, ibid. (17 Sept. 1920), 215; letter, 12 Oct. 1920 (NLI, O'Brien Papers, MS 8429); Dept Home Affairs report, Jan. 1921 (NLI, Duffy Papers, MS 15440); Dumont to Secretary of State, 22 Mar., 23 Apr. 1921; order to shipping agents, 1921 (UCD, Mulcahy Papers, P7A/17 (2–282)); Dept Home Affairs report, May 1921 (NLI, O'Brien Papers, MS 8429); Chief of Police to Minister for Home Affairs, 28 June 1921 (NLI, Plunkett Papers, MS 11404).

15. Collins to O'Brien, 29 May, 13 June 1921, reply, 21 May 1921 (NAI, DE 2/8 (37)); Dept Home Affairs report, Aug. 1921 (NAI, DE 2/51); prohibiting census: *Dáil procs.* (11 Mar. 1921), 275–6; Anderson to Macready, 21 Mar. 1921 (PRO, CO 904/188/1).

16. Dumont to Secretary of State, 15 Sept. 1920 (USNA, DS, 841. d. 00/237); Blythe to Secretary of Ministry, 5 Jan. 1921 (NAI, DE 2/56); NAI, DE 2/5 (456) (42); report of meeting, 16 Jan. 1921 (NAI, DE 2/56); Mitchell, *Labour in Irish Politics*, 140–1; IFU to President, 7 Apr. 1921 (NAI, DE 2/102); cab. minutes, 6 Apr. 1921; Dept Labour report, Mar. 1921 (NAI, DE 2/5); Dumont to Secretary of State, 22 July 1921; McDonagh on labour commission, *Dáil procs* (11 Mar. 1921), 268; response to labour manifesto: ibid. (10 May 1921), 285.

17. Boycotting: Dept Labour reports, Mar., Aug. 1921 (NAI, DE 2/5); *Dáil procs* (11 Mar. 1921), 256–8, 268; ibid. (10 May 1921), 290; cab. minutes, 27 Apr., 20 June 1921; 'Belfast Trade Boycott' (NAI, DE 2/11); Forester, *Collins*, 194; *Dáil off. rep.* (17 Aug. 1921), 27–33; *Dáil priv. sess.*, 17–19; Macready to Anderson, 12 Mar. 1921; Anderson to Macready, 14 Mar., 16 June 1921 (PRO, CO 904/188); Directorate of Intelligence, 'Report on Revolutionary Organisations in the UK', 5 May 1921 (PRO, CP 2916, CAB 24/123); Dumont to Secretary of State, 9 June 1921; Seán MacEntee interview.

18. Buy Irish proposal: *Dáil procs* (17 Sept. 1920), 229–31; proposed British boycott: ibid. (25 Jan. 1921), 255–7; *Old Ireland*, 21 Feb. 1921; British boycott: *Dáil procs* (11 Mar. 1921), 271–3; Dumont to Secretary of State, 25 Mar. 1921; *Dáil off. rep.* (17 Aug. 1921), 42; *Observer*, 15 May 1921; progress of British boycott: *Dáil procs* (10 May 1921), 286–8; Irish Situation Committee report (PRO, CAB 27/107); bogus order: Brother Allen Papers, O'Connell Schools museum; O'Brien to Collins, 5 July 1920 (NLI, O'Brien Papers, MS 8430); *Dáil off. rep.* (17 Aug. 1921), 37–43; agriculture: O'Connor to de Valera, 11 June 1921, reply, 14 June 1921 (PRO, CO 904/23 (7)); Collins to O'Brien, 28 May 1921 (NLI, O'Brien Papers, MS 8430).

19. Propaganda Dept: de Valera to O'Hegarty, 12 Feb. 1921 (NAI, DE 2/10: 19); Hathaway to Secretary of State, 19 May 1919 (USNA, DS, 841.d.00/54); cab. minutes, 6 Feb. 1921 (NAI, DE 1/3); O'Malley, *Singing Flame*, 193; Longford and O'Neill, *De Valera*, 119; Boyle, *Childers*, 260–2, 269, 323; Childers appointment: *Dáil procs* (11 Mar.), 274–5, (10 May) 283; Béaslaí, *Collins*, ii, 168–9; Brennan, *Allegiance*, 245–6, 252–4.

20. De Valera on appointment, *Dáil procs* (11 Mar.), 265, 274; Collins to Duffy, 24 Mar. 1921 (NAI, Duffy Papers); O'Brien to Childers, 10 Mar. 1921 (NLI, O'Brien Papers, MS 8421 (42)); O'Kelly to O'Brien, 24 Mar. 1921, O'Brien to Duffy, 1 Apr. 1921 (NAI, Duffy Papers; DE 2/10:58); report, Mar. 1921 (NLI, McKenna Napoli Papers, MSS 22610, 22782, 22783)

21. O'Brien to Childers, 18 Mar. 1921, Childers to O'Brien, 2, 6 May 1921, O'Brien to Childers, 31 May 1921 (NLI, O'Brien Papers, MS 8432(11)); Boyle, *Childers*, 257; O'Brien to Collins, 4 Feb. 1921 (NLI, DE 2/327); O'Brien to Collins, 4 Feb. 1921 (NLI, O'Brien Papers, MS 8430); O'Brien to Duffy (ibid., MS 8421); *Dáil procs* (10 May 1921), 283; Dumont to Secretary of State,   22 May 1921.

22. Boyle, *Childers*, 271; Collins material to Propaganda Dept (NAI, DE 2/436); Childers and propaganda campaign: NLI, O'Brien Papers, MS 8429); Dumont to Secretary of State, 23 Apr., 9 June 1921; *Dáil off. rep.* (17 Aug. 1921), 76; Griffith memorandum, 23 Jan. 1919 (UCD, Hayes Papers, P53/1018); *Dáil procs* (11 Mar. 1921), 274–5; Propaganda Dept report, 10 Mar. 1921 (NLI, McKenna Napoli Papers, MS 22620); MacEntee on TDs and propaganda, *Dáil procs*, 259; Béaslaí on need for more information, ibid., 290; Collins to Propaganda Dept, 11 Oct. 1920, 13 May 1921 (NAI, DE 2/436); President to all departments, 9 Mar 1921; President to Secretary of Ministry, 15 Mar. 1920 (NAI, DE 2/14); Carroll and Lindsay: Dumont to Secretary of State, 17 Apr. 1921; UCD, Mulcahy Papers, P7/821 (155); P7A/33 (7–9).

23. President to O'Hegarty, 24 May 1921 (NAI, DE 2/10: 78, 79); President to O'Hegarty, 29 Mar. 1921 (NAI, DE 2/14); Dumont, weekly consular report, 29 Mar. 1921; Childers to O'Brien, 3 May 1921, reply, 6 July 1921 (NLI, O'Brien Papers, MS 8421).

24. Kathleen McKenna, 'The *Irish Bulletin*', *Capuchin Annual* (1970), 523–4; *IB*, 7 Apr., 1 June 1921; *Dáil procs*, 226; Childers to O'Brien, 10 Feb. 1921, O'Brien to Propaganda Dept., 21 Feb. 1921 (NLI, O'Brien Papers, MS 8426); organisation of ISDL: ibid., MSS 8421, 8427; O'Brien to Collins, 21 Feb. 1921 (ibid., MS 8430).

25. President to O'Brien, 24 Apr. 1921, Collins to O'Brien, 6 June 1921 (NLI, O'Brien Papers, MS 8430); O'Brien to Childers, 6 July 1921 (ibid., MS 8421); Dept Foreign Affairs report, June 1921; *Dáil off. rep.*, 20; cab. minutes, 12 July 1920; Duffy to Dáil govt, 28 May 1921 NAI, Duffy Papers; O'Faolain: O'Kelly to O'Brien, 15 June 1921 (NLI, O'Brien Papers, MS 8421).

26. De Valera to O'Brien, 21 Feb. 1921 (NLI, O'Brien Papers, MS 8429); O'Brien to Maura O'Brien, 3 Aug. 1921 (ibid., MS 8421); Boyle, *Childers*, 272–3; Collins to O'Brien, 12, 17 May 1921, reply, 13 May 1921 (NLI, O'Brien Papers, MS 8430); release of Childers: NLI, McKenna Napoli Papers, MS 22785; Childers on purpose of *Irish Bulletin*: ibid., MS 22783; report, Aug. 1921, *Dáil off. rep.* 16–21 and UCD, Blythe Papers, P24/19).

27. O'Hegarty to Duffy, 23, 29 Nov. 1920, Brennan to Duffy, 18 Mar. 1921 (NAI, Duffy Papers); Brennan, *Allegiance*, 297–9; de Valera to Brennan, 28 Feb. 1921 (NAI, DE 2/526); Dwyer, *De Valera's Darkest Hour*, 69–70; Brennan and communications: NLI, O'Brien Papers, MS 8426; Dept Foreign Affairs report, June 1921 (NLI, Plunkett Papers, MS 11404).

28. Germany: cab. minutes, 8 Mar. 25 May 1921 (NAI, DE 1/3); Chartres: President to Collins, 2 Apr. 1921 (NAI, DE 2/244); Brennan, *Allegiance* 270, 326; *Dáil off. rep.*, 19; Comerford memoir, ch. 26, pp 7–8 (UCD); arms from Germany: Briscoe, *For the Life of Me*, 80–83, 93–107; Seán MacBride interview; *Dublin Directory and Calander for 1921*, 95; Béaslaí, *Collins*, i, 221; Duffy to Fitzgerald, 8 July 1920, O'Kelly to Duffy, 5 Aug. 1920 (NAI, Duffy Papers); Feehan, *Shooting of Michael Collins*, 33, 42–3; Mac Eoin (ed.), *Survivors*, 499–507, 516; O'Brien to Collins, 28 Feb. 1921, reply, 4 Mar. 1921 (NAI, DE 2/327); President's Dept, 7 Mar 1921 (NAI, DE 2/14); Nancy Wyse Power: O'Neill, *From Parnell to de Valera: A Biography of Jennie Wyse Power*, 115–16, 126, and her articles in *Irish Press*, Oct.–Nov. 1935; O'Brien to O'Kelly, 24 Apr. 1921, reply, 25 Apr. 1921 (NAI, Duffy Papers).

29. Vatican: Collins to O'Brien, 28 Jan. 1921, de Valera to Collins, 28 Jan. 1921 (NLI, O'Brien Papers, MS 8426); O'Brien to Collins, 17 Feb. 1921 (ibid., MS 8430); O'Brien to P., 17 Feb. 1921 (NAI, DE 2/411); de Valera to Hayes, 2 Feb. 1921 (NLI, Gallagher Papers, MS 18375 (15); Collins to de Valera, 23 May 1921 (NAI, DE 2/411, also 2/444); Brennan to Duffy, 14 Apr. 1921, Duffy to Dáil govt, 30 June 1921 (NAI, Duffy Papers).

30. Nationalist groups: NLI, O'Brien Papers, MS 8427; O'Brien to O'Kelly, 1 Nov. 1919, 16 July 1920 (ibid., MS 8426); Duffy to Dáil govt, 17 Mar 1920 (NAI, Duffy Papers); Asia: Ba Pe to O'Brien, 22 Oct. 1920 (NLI, O'Brien Papers, MS 8427); Collins to O'Brien, 23 Mar. 1921 (NAI, DE 2/329); Collins to Mulcahy, 15 Sept. 1921 (NAI, DE 2/332); O'Brien to Collins, 21 Apr. 1922 (NAI, DE 2/344).

31. Australia (Esmond): NLI, O'Brien Papers, MS 8427; McCartan, *With de Valera in America*, 212; *Dáil off. rep.* 21; Brennan to Collins, 19 Aug. 1921, Collins to Brennan, 24 Aug. 1921 (NAI, DE 3/287); New Zealand: H. E. Holland to O'Brien, 28 July 1921 (NLI, O'Brien Papers, MS 8424); South Africa: Little to Brennan, 21 Mar. 1921 and n.d., Collins to Brennan, 3 June 1921 (NAI, DE 2/282); US consular reports, 23 Oct. 1919 (USNA, DS 841.d.00/104); *Dáil off. rep.*, 19; de Valera to O'Brien, 13 May 1921 (NLI, O'Brien Papers, MS 8428); *Old Ireland*, 2, 23 July 1921; *The Republic* (publication of Irish Republican Association of South Africa, 1920–22) (copy in NLI); Maurice Moore reports (NLI, Moore Papers, MS 10581); South America: *Dáil off. rep.*, 16–17; Laurence Ginnell, 'A Glance Back at the Time of Our Harmony', *Catholic Bulletin*, Dec. 1922.

32. 'Correspondence to and from the US', Dumont to Secretary of State, 22 July 1921; O'Mara's objections and resignation: NLI, O'Mara Papers, MSS 21548, 21549, 21552; cab. minutes, 6 Apr. 1921; Dwyer, *De Valera's Darkest Hour*, 60; de Valera to Collins, 21 May 1921 (NAI, DE 2/244).

33. De Valera's statement on US expenditures, *Dáil procs.* (11 Mar. 1921), 290; Collins to de Valera, 30 May 1921 (NAI, DE 2/244); *Weekly Summary*, 21 Jan., 4 Feb. 1921; Tansill, *America and the Fight for Irish Freedom*, 394; 'Statement of Solidarity' (NAI, DE 2/2 (52)); Carroll, *American Opinion*, 175–6, 280; BMH chronology, iii, 3; Dumont to Secretary of State, 22 Mar. 1921; Jones, *Whitehall Diary*, iii, 49; Division of European Affairs, State Dept records, 841.d.01; Boland to de Valera, 30 Mar. 1921 (NAI, DE 2/245); Dumont to Secretary of State, 22 July 1921.

34. ACRI: Boland to Secretary of Ministry, 4 Nov. 1920 (NAI, DE 2/245); NLI, McCartan Papers, MS 17683; ACRI report, 48–54, 62–4; Ward, *Ireland and Anglo-American Relations*, 242; France and McCoy to ACRI executive committee, 15 Mar. 1921 (NAI, DE 2/298); cab. minutes, 12 Feb. 1921 (NAI, DE 2/3 (65, 91); BMH chronology, iii, 3; *Dáil procs.* (11 Mar. 1921), 267; Sturgis diary, 12 Mar. 1921 (NLI, MS P7498); cab. minutes, 6 Apr. 1921.

35. NLI, McCartan Papers, MS 17683; Ward, *Ireland and Anglo-American Relations*, 241–5; McCartan, *With de Valera in America*, 223–9; ACRI report (NLI, Duffy Papers, MS 15440); Dumont to Secretary of State, 29 Apr., 9 June 1921 (USNA, DS, 841 d.00/353/381); Division of Western European Affairs to Secretary of State, 10 June 1921 (ibid., 841 d.01); de Valera to Cabinet Secretary, 5 Apr. 1921 (NAI, DE 2/3); PRO, CP 2921, CAB 24/123 (9 May 1921); Alan Ward, 'America and the Irish Problem, 1899–1921' in L. J. McCaffrey (ed.), *Irish Nationalism and the American Contribution*, 88; Irish White Cross, *Report*, 38; NLI, Maurice Moore Papers, MS 10558; Carroll, *American Opinion*, 165–70, 274–8; Irish White Cross, *Report*, 13–15, 38–9, 42, 86–9, 101.

36. *Dáil procs* (21 Jan. 1921), 237, (11 Mar.), 264, 278–89; *Irish World* (NY), 12 Feb. 1921; Macardle, *Irish Republic*, 401–3; Ryan, *Seán Treacy*, 117; Jones, *Whitehall Diary*, iii, 54–5; O'Brien to Collins, 20 Feb. 1921, reply, 26 Feb. 1921 (NLI, O'Brien Papers, MS 8429); Macready to Anderson, 4 Apr. 1921, reply, 5 Apr. 1921 (PRO, CO 904/188); O'Brien, *Forth the Banners Go*, 216–18; Deasy, *Towards Ireland Free*, 210; Collins to O'Brien, 17 May 1921 (NLI, O'Brien Papers, MS 8430); Collins to Nunan, 29 June 1921 (NAI, DE 2/292); Secretary of Ministry to President, 23 Mar. 1921 (NAI, DE 2/14); J. Pullar

Phibbs to Secretary of Dáil, 26 May 1921; Chief of Staff to O/C Dublin, 12 July 1921; Adjutant-General's memo, 7 July 1921 (NAI, DE 2/421).

37. Robbie and Curragh: UCD, Mulcahy Papers, P7 A/1; P7 A/22 (39–47), P7A/ 20 (86–8, 293); another example of conflict between Collins and Stack (concerning the boycott of a Cork draper): NAI, DE 2/509; Dumont to Secretary of State, 22 Mar., 9 June 1921 (USNA, DS, 841.d.00/339, 381); Cork RIC report, Jan. 1921 (PRO, CO 904/114); Dumont to Secretary of State, 22 Mar. 1921; German arms report: *Ir. Ind.*, 13 Apr. 1920; O'Hegarty to Duffy, 15 Apr. 1920 (NAI, Duffy Papers); Brennan, *Allegiance*, 327; McGuinness, *Nomad*; Seán MacBride interview.

38. Townshend, *British Campaign* 140–1; J. W. Davis to Secretary of State, 21 June 1920 (USNA, DS, 841.d.00/205A); Collins to Griffith, 3 Nov. 1920 (NAI, DE 2/242); Dumont to Secretary of State, 22 Mar. 1921; Collins to President, 3 May 1921 (NAI, DE 2/244); Boland to de Valera, 30 Mar. 1921 (NAI, DE 2/ 245); Dumont to Secretary of State, 22 July 1921; Collins to President, 17 Apr. 1921 (NAI, DE 2/244); Macready to Anderson, 7 May 1921 (PRO, CO 904/ 188); Director of Intelligence, 5, 12 May 1921 (PRO, CP 29216, CAB 24/123).

39. Gaughan, *Jeremiah Mee*, 205; Macready to Anderson, 3 Nov. 1920, 14 Feb., 28 Mar. 1921 (PRO, CO 904/188); Townshend *British Campaign*, 163. Beginning in the summer, Crozier asked the Dáil government for employment and a loan: Crozier to de Valera, 2 July 1921 (PRO, DE 2/2 (78)); Special Constabulary: Townshend, *British Campaign*, 124; Farrell, *Arming the Protestants*, 7–29, 32–50, 58; martial law: Macardle, *Irish Republic*, 381; Townshend, *British Campaign*, 113–14; 141–2, 150, 193–4; 'Trial and Execution of Rebels' (PRO, CO 904/ 188); 'Areas under Martial Law' (Dept of Defence microfilm, NLI, pos 918).

40. Townshend, *British Campaign*, 114, 223; Chief Inspector, Limerick, monthly confidential report, Jan. 1921 (PRO, CO 904/114); Secretary of State for War, memo to cabinet, 31 May 1921 (PRO, CP 2996, CAB 24/123); hostages: *IB*, 2, 6, 10 Feb. 1921; Dumont to Secretary of State, 28 Jan. 1921 (USNA, DS 841.d.00.314); NAI, DE 2/23; Macardle, *Irish Republic*, 383, 406.

41. Townshend, *British Campaign*, 149–50, 185; IG monthly report, June 1921; Jones, *Whitehall Diary*, iii, 72; Griffith and O'Grady, *Curious Journey*, 221; Macardle, *Irish Republic*, 861–2; searches: Townshend, *British Campaign*, 155–7; Macready to Anderson, 28 Mar. 1921 (PRO, CO 904/188); raids: Dept Finance to President, Secretary of Ministry to President, 21 Feb. 1921 (NAI, DE 2/3 (91) (108); President to Secretary of Ministry, 22 Apr. 1921, reply, 26 Apr. 1921 (NAI, DE 2/1 (61)); Collins: Mac Eoin (ed.), *Survivors*, 132n.; Béaslaí, *Collins*, ii, 205; Collins to de Valera, 5 Apr. 1921 (NAI, DE 2/244); Collins to O'Brien, 28, 31 May, 6 June 1921 (NLI, O'Brien Papers, MS 8430); Collins to President, 1 June 1921 (NAI, DE 2/244); Ó Broin, *Collins*, 75, 79, 85, 80; de Valera: Irish Situation Committee meeting, 15 June 1921 (PRO, CAB 27/107); President to Secretary of Ministry, 28 Apr. 1921 (NAI, DE 2/1 (61)); Longford and O'Neill, *De Valera*, 124–5.

42. Rewards: Macready to Anderson, 5 Mar. 1921, reply, 8 Mar. 1921 (PRO, CO 904/188); Ó Broin, *Collins*, 56; handbill urging information (TCD, Childers Papers, MS 15444 (2)); Neligan, *Spy in the Castle*; Forester, *Collins*, 134, 201, 220; *Irish World* (NY), 12 Feb. 1921.

43. Anderson to Macready, 29 Mar. 1921 (PRO, CO 904/188); Macready to Anderson, 9 Mar. 1921 (ibid.); Mulcahy on Tralee blockade (UCD, Mulcahy Papers, P7A/21 (95–7)); Jones, *Whitehall Diary*, iii, 77; cab. minutes, 1 July, 23 Sept. 1921 (NAI, DE 2/2); *Observer*, 24 June 1921; *Morning Post*, 14 June 1921; Townshend, *British Campaign*, 205, 175, 179; Dumont to Secretary of State, 22 Mar. 1921; Macready to Army Council, 28 Mar. 1921 (PRO, CO 904/188); Jones, *Whitehall Diary*, iii, 47; *Manchester Guardian*, 20 Jan. 1921; *Irish World* (NY), 12 Feb. 1921; *IB*, 20 May, 17 June 1921.

44. Charles Townshend, 'The Irish Republican Army and the Development of Guerilla Warfare, 1916–21', *English Historical Review*, xciv (1979), 330–42; Townshend, *British Campaign*, 177–80; Dumont to Secretary of State, 9 June 1921 (USNA, DS, 841.d.00/381); O'Malley, *On Another Man's Wound*, 329; J. Bowyer Bell, 'The Thompson Submachine-Gun in Ireland', 1921', *Irish Sword*, viii, no. 31 (1967), 98–108; inspirational: UCD, Mulcahy Papers, P7A/19 (53, 54, 198, 178), P7A/20 (232).

45. Greaves, *Liam Mellows*, 231; Walter Kendall, *The Revolutionary Movement in Britain, 1900–21* (London 1965), 290, 430n; Directorate of Intelligence report, 26 May 1921 (PRO, CP 2979, CAB 24/123); Dept Engineering report, June 1921 (UCD, Mulcahy Papers, P7A/21 (107)); Brugha's scheme: Robert Brennan claimed he originated the idea: *Allegiance*, cab. minutes, 6 Nov. 1920 (NAI, DE 1/3); Ó Broin, *Collins*, 75–6; O'Brien to Collins, 22, 23, 24 Mar. 1921, replies 8, 21, 30 Apr. 1921 (NAI, DE 2/329); Custom House: Townshend, 'Irish Republican Army', 341–2; Hogan, *Four Glorious Years*, 275–6; Bennett, *Black and Tans*, 172, 175; Forester, *Collins*, 196.

46. IG monthly reports, Apr.–June 1921; Collins to de Valera concerning 'onslaught' on UK departments, 27 June 1921 (NAI, DE 2/296); Mulcahy on condition of IRA: UCD, Mulcahy Papers, P7A/19, 42, P7A/20 (49–51), 37); Ó Broin, *Collins*, 85; MacBride lecture; Mac Eoin (ed.), *Survivors*, 113–14; Townshend, 'Irish Republican Army' 340–1; Townshend, *British Campaign*, 180–2; execution of British agent: UCD, Mulcahy Papers, P7A/19 (159); O'Donoghue, *No Other Law*, 174–6; O'Malley, *On Another Man's Wound*, 342; Butler, *Barry's Flying Column*, 159; British forces: Macready to Army Council, 28 Mar. 1921 (PRO, CO 904/188); memo by Secretary of State for War, 24 May 1921 (PRO, CP 2964, CAB 24/123); Townshend, *British Campaign*, 182, 190.

47. De Blacam, *What Sinn Féin Stands For*, 134; Collins to de Valera, 7 June 1921 (PRO, De Valera Epitome, CO 904/23); Collins to Duffy, 14 Jan. 1921 (NAI, Duffy Papers); Collins to O'Brien, 22 Feb. 1921 (NLI, O'Brien Papers, MS 8426); de Valera to O'Mara, 3 Feb. 1921 (NLI, O'Mara Papers, MS 21552); Brennan to Duffy, 8 Apr. 1921 (NAI, Duffy Papers); de Valera 'turned the corner': *Dáil procs* (10 May 1921), 292; London *Times*, 20 May 1921.

48. British govt: Jones, *Whitehall Diary*, iii, 53–70; Sir James O'Connor to James O'Connor, in Secretary of Ministry to President, 21 May 1921 (NAI, DE 2/1 (147); Sturgis diary, 13 Jan., 9 Mar. 1921, 22 Apr. 1921 (NLI, MS P7498); *IB*, 4 May 1921; *Dáil procs* (11 Mar. 1921), 165–7, 291–2; PRO, CP, 2915, CAB 24/123; 'Elections to "Southern Ireland" Senate' (NAI, DE 2/96, DE2/98).

49. De Valera interview, 2 May 1921: see Macardle, *Irish Republic*, 855–6; Bowman, *De Valera and the Ulster Question*, 43–6; de Valera on Ulster: *Dáil procs* (11 Mar.

1921), 266; *Old Ireland*, 15 Feb., 26 Mar. 1921; McCabe: statement by Padeen O'Keeffe (UCD, Hayes Papers, P53/1438–40); Labour: President to Secretary of Ministry, 26 Apr. 1921 (NAI, DE 2/1 (70)); President to Secretary of Ministry, 19, 21 May 1921 (NAI, DE 2/1 (152, 153)).

50. SFSC minutes, 10 Feb., 19 Mar., 13 Apr., 4, 9, 31 May 1921; cab. minutes, 6 Feb., 6, 27 Apr. 1921; Dept Home Affairs report, May 1921 (NAI, DE 2/51); PRO, de Valera Epitome, CO 904/23; Brennan to Duffy, 8 Apr. 1921 (NAI, Duffy Papers); Collins to Griffith, 1 May 1921 (NAI, DE 2/242).

51. *Daily Herald*, 13 May 1921; PRO, CP 2915, 2948, CAB 24/123; *Old Ireland*, 11 June 1921.

52. Padeen O'Keeffe on Sinn Féin organisation in six counties: UCD, Hayes Papers, P53/1438–40, 1548; SFSC minutes, 26 Aug., 1, 14 Oct. 1920; cab. minutes, 27 Aug., 30 Sept., 3, 15 Sept. 1920; *Evening Telegraph*, 6 Jan. 1919; Collins to O'Brien, 29 May, 6 July 1921 (NLI, O'Brien Papers, MS 8430).

53. De Valera on election of second Dáil: *Dáil procs* (10 May 1921), 291–2; O'Hegarty to de Valera, 9 May 1921 (NAI, DE 2/1 (109); DE 2/445); cab. minutes, 25 Aug. 1921; O'Higgins to Collins, 18 May 1921, reply, 24 May 1921 (NAI, DE 2/443); cab. minutes, 25 May (NAI, DE 1/3).

54. Dec. 1920 proposals: NAI, DE 2/85; Cosgrave on theological board: NAI, DE 2/296; Miller, *Church, State and Nation in Ireland*, 481–3, Longford and O'Neill, *De Valera*, 122; O'Brien to de Valera, 3 May 1921 (NAI, O'Brien Papers, MS 8429); *Old Ireland*, 5 Mar. 1921.

55. Boyce, *Englishmen and Irish Troubles*, 83–141; *Morning Post*, 2 Dec. 1920; Macready to Anderson, 7 Mar. 1921, reply, 8 Mar. 1921 (PRO, CO 904/188); Jones, *Whitehall Diary*, iii, 68.

56. Mitchell, *Labour in Irish Politics*, 132–5; *IT*, 21 Jan. 1920; *Ir. Ind.*, 21 Feb. 1920; British Labour Party, *Report of the Labour Commission to Ireland*, 103, 110–13; *Old Ireland*, 8 Jan. 1921; O'Brien to Collins, 11 Feb. 1921, reply, 17 Feb. 1921 (NAI, DE 2/329); Sturgis diary, 10 Apr. 1921 (NLI, MS P7498).

57. Jones, *Whitehall Diary*, iii, 59–62; *Ir. Ind.*, 17 Dec. 1920, 19 Jan. 1921; Mitchell, *Labour in Irish Politics* 134; Jones, *Whitehall Diary*, iii, 70, 60–1, 65–8; de Valera and Collins: Chief Secretary's report, 14 Apr. 1921 (PRO, CP 2838); Dumont to Secretary of State, 22 Mar. 1921 (USNA, DS 841.d.00/339); Jones, *Whitehall Diary*, iii, 60, 68, 70.

58. *IB*, 11 Jan. 1921; Collins to O'Brien, 8, 12, 15 Jan., 9 Feb. 1921 (NLI, O'Brien Papers, MS 8426); James O'Connor: O'Hegarty to de Valera, 15, 19 Feb. 1921, de Valera to O'Flanagan, 19 Feb. 1921 (NAI, DE 2/3 (70, 102)); Jones, *Whitehall Diary*, iii, 49, 52; Cope: UCD, Hayes Papers, P53/1553); Longford and O'Neill, *De Valera*, 117; Sturgis diary, 23 Mar. 1921 (NLI, MS P7498); O'Brien to Collins, 28 Feb. 1921 (NLI, O'Brien Papers, MS 8430); de Valera on Derby visit: *Dáil procs* (10 May 1921), 292; de Valera to O'Hegarty, 13 Mar. 1921 (NAI, DE 2/14); de Valera to O'Brien, 24 Apr. 1921 (NLI, O'Brien Papers, MS 8429).

59. O'Brien, *Forth the Banners Go*, 111–15; Labour cab. conference, 16 Jan. 1921 (NAI, DE 2/234B); Sturgis diary, 17, 20, 23–6, 28 Mar., 4 Apr. 1921 (NLI, MS 7498); Jones, *Whitehall Diary*, iii, 57–60, (27 Apr. 1921); de Valera to Collins, 18 Mar. 1921 (NAI, DE 2/244).

60. BMH chronology, iii, 3 (13 Mar. 1921); O'Brien to Collins, 31 Mar. 1921 (NAI, DE 2/329); O'Hegarty to de Valera, 4 Apr. 1921 (NAI, DE 2/364); Sturgis diary, 18, 26 Apr. 1921 (NLI, MS P7498); O'Brien to Collins, 21 Apr. 1921 (NAI, DE 2/329); O'Hegarty to de Valera, 12 May 1921 (NAI, DE 2/1 (122)); *Irish Press*, 5 Nov. 1936; O'Flanagan to O'Hegarty, 27 May, 28 June 1921 (NAI, DE 2/262); Collins to O'Brien, 24 Mar. 1921 (NAI, DE 2/234B).

61. Dumont to Secretary of State, 23 Apr. 1921; de Valera to Collins, 14 June 1921 (NAI, DE 2/244); de Valera to O'Brien, 4 May 1921 (NLI, O'Brien Papers, MS 8429; de Valera to Boland, 28 Feb. 1921, in Dumont to Secretary of State, 22 July 1921; Dwyer, *De Valera's Darkest Hour*, 57–60; de Valera and republic: O'Brien, *Forth the Banners Go*, 214; Sarah G. Millan, *General Smuts*, ii, 319–33.

62. Jones, *Whitehall Diary*, iii, 62, 75; Sturgis diary, 3 Mar. 1921 (NLI, MS P7498); de Valera's Dáil statement on meeting with Craig: *Dáil procs*, 383; Jones, *Whitehall Diary*, iii, 65, 68; Longford and O'Neill, *De Valera*, 122–3; IRB: UCD Mulcahy Papers, P7C/13; de Valera to Collins, 14 June 1921 (NAI, DE 2/244); arrest of de Valera: Griffith and O'Grady, *Curious Journey*, 230–1; Longford and O'Neill, *De Valera*, 124–5; de Valera to O'Hegarty, n.d. (NAI, DE 2/2 (53)), 27 June 1921 (ibid. (60)), 28 June 1921 (ibid. (63)); BMH chronology, 24 June 1921; Collins to de Valera, 29 June 1921 (NAI, DE 2/244).

63. Macardle, *Irish Republic*, 432–3; Smuts's visit: O'Hegarty to de Valera, 28 June 1921, Smuts to de Valera, 29 June 1921 (NAI, DE 2/262); O'Hegarty to de Valera, 5 July 1921 (NAI, DE 2/2 (no number)); Townshend, *British Campaign*, 197–8; de Valera to O'Hegarty, 5 July 1921 (NAI, DE 2/2 (92)); de Valera to O'Hegarty, 6, 8 July 1921 (NAI, DE 2/2 (94, 96)); Jones, *Whitehall Diary*, iii, 77–85; Ó Muirthile: UCD, Mulcahy Papers, P7C/13; Macardle, *Irish Republic*, 434–7; Duff, *Sword for Hire*, 84; L. S. Amery, *My Political Life* (London 1953–5), ii, 1230; Plunkett to Brugha on danger of truce, 9 July 1921 (NLI, ILB 300 p3 (59)); article by Denis Gwynn, *Observer*, 17 July 1921; *Old Ireland*, 30 July 1921.

Chapter 5: From Truce to Civil War (pp 300–333)

1. Weekly consular report, 11 Oct. 1921; IG monthly report, July, Aug. 1921; literari: Griffith to O'Kelly, 23 Jan. 1919 (UCD, Hayes Papers, P53/1018); Gregory, *Journals*, i, 302–3; *Irish World*, 19 Mar. 1921; A. Norman Jeffares, *W. B. Yeats: Man and Poet*, (London 1949), 328 n. 40; Costello, *The Heart Grown Brutal*, 185–6; Griffith and O'Grady, *Curious Journey*, 241, 244; Andrews, *Dublin Made Me*, 201; Mac Eoin (ed.), *Survivors*, 358, 366; P. J. Matthews memoir (NLI, MS 9873); Collins to President, 16 July 1921; President to Collins, 19 July 1921 (NAI, DE 2/244); O'Farrell, *Seán Mac Eoin Story*, 65–7; *IT*, 8, 9 Aug. 1921; *Dáil off. rep.*, 85; election of de Valera as President of Republic: *Dáil priv. sess* (28 Aug. 1921), 57–9; O'Hegarty to TDs, prohibiting commercial endorsements, 17 Oct. 1921 (NAI, DE 2/477); Collins to O'Brien, 27 June (NLI, O'Brien Papers, MS 8430); Collins to O'Brien, 11 July 1921 (NAI, DE 8/329); Stack to registrars, n.d. (NAI, DE 25/1A); O'Brien to Collins, 10, 28 July 1921 (NAI, DE 2/331).

2. O'Hegarty message (NAI, DE 2/236); *Dáil off. rep.* (26 Aug. 1921), 77–80, 9, 12; Cosgrave's view concerning President of Republic: UCD, Hayes

Papers, P53/1442); *Dáil priv. sess.*, 13, 29, 33–4, 54–8, 60, 86, 96; *Dáil off. rep.*, 9, 82–3; Fitzgerald and Dumont: Boyle, *Childers*, 279; Younger, *Ireland's Civil War*, 154, 158.

3. *Dáil priv. sess.*, 20–6, 67–8, 9–14, 73; President to Secretary of Ministry, 23 July 1921 (NAI, DE 2/2); Stack instructions, 18 Oct. 1921 (NAI, DE 8/18); Dept Home Affairs report, Aug. 1921 (NAI, DE 2/51); Dáil discussion: *Dáil priv. sess.*, 20–6; Divisional Commissioner Barron's diary, Limerick (UCD, Mulcahy Papers, P17A/9); Gaughan, *Stack*, 164.

4. O'Higgins to Secretary of Ministry, 5 Oct. 1921 (NAI, DE 2/468; see also DE 2/475); Education: NAI, DE 2/473; cab. minutes, 2 Dec. 1921; Trade and Commerce: NAI, DE 2/417; cab. minutes, 18 Nov. 1921; Agriculture: NAI, DE 2/418; cab. minutes, 13, 18, 25 Nov. 1921; Fisheries and Publicity: cab minutes, 18 Nov. 1921; *Dáil off. rep.*, 84–5; cab. minutes, 23 Sept. 1921; Collins to President, 15 Oct. 1921, reply, 16 Oct. 1921 (NAI, DE 2/244).

5. Preparations for hostilities: cab. minutes, 1 July 1921; *Dáil priv. sess.*, 62–4, 83–4, 75–8, 288; 'on guard' order: UCD, Mulcahy Papers, P7A/24 (22); *An tÓglach*, 9 Sept. 1921; administrative committees: *Dáil priv. sess.*, 24, 26, 60–2, 79; county organisation, Sept.–Nov.: NAI, DE 2/465; Dept Home Affairs preparations: UCD, Mulcahy Papers, P17A/135; Mulcahy narrative (UCD, Hayes Papers, P53/1547); cab. minutes, 23 Sept., 11 Nov. 1921; Collins to O'Hegarty, 24 Nov. 1921 (NAI, DE 2/8 (36)); NLI, ILB 300 p2 (26).

6. UCD, Mulcahy Papers, P7A/22 (5–6), P7A/24 (80–2); Farrell, *Arming the Protestants*, 63–5; SFSC minutes, 12 Aug., 15 Nov. 1921; *Dáil priv. sess.* (22 Aug. 1921), 29–32; *Dáil off. rep.* (17 Aug. 1921), 2, 7–8; cab. minutes, 10 Sept., 3, 5, 21 Oct., 9 Nov., 2 Dec. 1921; *Gaelic American*, 10 Sept. 1921; Secretary of Ministry to ministers on Ulster booklet, 10 Nov. 1921 (NAI, DE 2/434); development of Northern Ireland govt: Gillespie to President, 23 Nov. 1921 (NAI, DE 2/424).

7. IRA: Griffith and O'Grady, *Curious Journey*, 240–4; IG monthly reports, Aug., Sept. 1921; Collins to President, 20 July 1921 (NAI, DE 2/244); conflict between British forces and IRA: UCD Mulcahy Papers, P7A/286; Duff, *Sword for Hire*, 88; O'Brien to Jones, 22 Sept. 1921 (NLI, O'Brien Papers, MS 8429); Óglaigh na hÉireann, weekly memo no. 16, 7 Oct. 1921 (UCD, Mulcahy Papers, P17A/2).

8. Truce terms: UCD, O'Malley Papers, P17A/2; Mulcahy opposition to appointment, 1 Nov. 1921, Brugha to Mulcahy, 16 Nov. 1921, reply, 16 Nov. 1921 (UCD, Mulcahy Papers, P7A/135); British army report, 18th Infantry Brigade, Limerick, 20 Aug. 1920 (ibid., P7A/23 (7–13); cab. minutes, 17 Oct. 1921); Collins to de Valera, 15 Oct. 1921, reply, 19 Oct. 1921, Collins to de Valera, 21 Oct. 1921 (NAI, DE 2/244); British army, GHQ narrative, *Ireland*, 36–7 (UCD, Mulcahy Papers, P7A/37); Mulcahy's orders, 1 Oct. 1921 (ibid., P17A/2); Quartermaster-General to Minister for Defence, 19 Dec. 1921 (ibid., P7A/21 (53–4), P7A/23 (7–13)); cab. minutes, 9 Nov. 1921 (NAI, DE 1/3); Seán MacBride lecture and interview.

9. Hayes on 'trucileers' (UCD, Hayes Papers, P53/1552); Boland to Mulcahy on US volunteers, 23 Sept. 1921 (UCD, Mulcahy Papers, P7A/37); activities of police and courts: UCD, O'Malley Papers, P17A/12; Hayes on second Dáil composition (UCD, Hayes Papers, P53/1549); Comerford memoir, ch. 35

(UCD) ; cab. minutes, 21 Oct. 1921; Hopkinson, *Green Against Green*, 15–16; Bray case, Sept.–Nov. 1921 (NAI, DE 2/419); cab. minutes, 24 Nov. 1921; see also Dept Defence microfilm, NLI, pos 911, on land dispute in Raheen; Mulcahy on relations between IRA and civil administration and Sinn Féin (UCD, Hayes Papers, P53/1547); President to Collins, 12 Oct. 1921, reply, 15 Oct. 1921 (NAI, DE 2/244).

10. O'Brien to Collins, 23 Sept. 1921 (NLI, O'Brien Papers, MS 8430); O'Hegarty to all departments, 24 Nov. 1921 (NLI, McKenna Napoli Papers, MS 22796); UCD, Mulcahy Papers, P7A/24 (22); UCD, Hayes Papers, P53/1547; Béaslaí, *Collins*, ii, 290–91.

11. Army reorganisation: cab. minutes, 15 Sept., 4, 25 Nov. 1921; Mulcahy's comments on reorganisation (UCD, Mulcahy Papers, P7A/37; P7A/2, 4, 5, 14); Mulcahy on 25 Nov. meeting (ibid., P7D/96 (2); Mulcahy letter, *IT*, 15 Oct. 1962; Gaughan, *Stack*, 141–3; O'Donoghue, *No Other Law*, 199–200; P. J. Matthews memoir, 71–3 (NLI).

12. Negotiations: T. P. O'Neill interview: O'Hegarty, *Victory of Sinn Féin*, 86–7; *Dáil off. rep.* (27 Apr. 1922), 303; Cosgrave on external association (UCD, Hayes Papers, P53/1442); NLI, O'Brien Papers, MS 8427; British army report, Limerick, on public opinion on prospects of a settlement (UCD, Mulcahy Papers, P7A/23 (7–13)); Collins to de Valera, 1 Sept. 1921 (NAI, DE 2/244); Sturgis diary, 25 Aug. 1921 (NLI, MS P7498).

13. Cab. minutes, 9 Sept. 1921; Griffith and O'Grady, *Curious Journey*, 251; *Dáil priv. sess.*, 94–8; *Dáil off. rep.*, 304; Gallagher, *Anglo-Irish Treaty*, 74; Sceilig [J. J. O'Kelly], *Trinity of Martyrs*, 111.

14. *Dáil priv. sess.*, 96; Secretary of Ministry to Minister for Labour, 26 Nov. 1921 (NAI, DE 2/5); SFSC minutes, 27 Oct. 1921; (UCD, Mulcahy Papers, P17A/9); Bay's US consular reports, 4 Oct. 1921; ministers in London and cabinet decisions: NAI, DE 2/418; cab. minutes, 3 Oct., 25 Nov., 3, 7, 8 Dec. 1921; *Dáil priv. sess.* (14 Dec. 1921), 105; Gaughan, *Stack*, 166, 169; Duffy statement, BMH transcript (NAI, Duffy Papers); Seán MacBride lecture and interview; Ó Muirthile memoir (UCD, Mulcahy Papers, P7/52): de Valera's instruction of 7 Sept. 1921 (NLI, Plunkett Papers, MS 14404); note on Churchill conversation with Dulanty, 1935 (NLI, O'Brien Papers, MS 8427).

15. Childers's notes of cabinet meeting (TCD, Childers Papers, MS 7814 (6); O'Donoghue, *No Other Law*, 191; *Dáil priv. sess.*, 101, 110; *Treaty deb.*, 154–8, 229, 342, 234, 305–6, 207, 324, 318, 343; Collins's statement, *Dáil off. rep.*, 365, 435; Gaughan, *Stack*, 172–4; de Valera's proclamation on eve of vote (NLI, McKenna Napoli Papers, MS 22611); Liam Ó Briain typescript (UCD, Hayes Papers, P53/1547); Mitchell, *Labour in Irish Politics*, 144–52, 156–7.

16. O'Higgins on de Valera: *The New de Valera*, repr. from *An Saor Stát*, 25 Mar. 1922 (copy in NLI); 'old contempt': Longford and O'Neill, *De Valera*, 207; Duffy statement (BMH transcript); Duffy to Collins, 25 May 1922, Duffy to Griffith, 19 June 1922 (NAI, Duffy Papers); Griffith's health and excessive drinking in London: Seán MacBride interview; T. P. O'Neill interview; Mac Eoin (ed.), *Survivors*, 131–2; Feehan, *Shooting of Michael Collins*, 83; Andrews, *Dublin Made Me*, 209–13; O'Donoghue, *No Other Law*, 208,

249–54; NLI, ILB p14 (10), p16 (13); de Valera's willingness to attend: Comerford memoir (NLI); de Valera to O'Brien, 4 July 1922 (NLI, O'Brien Papers, MS 8460).

Chapter 6: Conclusion (pp 334–341)

1. Hannah Arendt, *On Revolution* (Harmondsworth 1965 ed.), 140–1; Fitzpatrick, *Politics and Irish Life*, 185; Barry, *Guerilla Days in Ireland*, 61–2; M. Elliott-Bateman, 'The Conditions for People's War' in T. Bowden, M. Elliott-Bateman and J. Ellis, *Revolt to Revolution*, 304: Ronan Fanning, *Independent Ireland*, 53.

Bibliography

1. Interviews

Brother Allen, O'Connell Schools, Dublin
Joseph Cassell
Máire Comerford
Michael J. Costello
Colm Gavan Duffy
Colm Gallagher
Rev. Dermot F. Hegarty
Sheila Humphries
Seán MacBride
Joseph McDonagh
Seán MacEntee
Leon Ó Broin
Seán O'Duffy
Mortimer O'Kelly
Seán Ó Lúing
Thomas P. O'Neill

2. *Manuscript Sources*

(a) Collection of personal papers and unpublished memoirs

For reports of Dáil departments preserved in collections of personal
papers see pp 399–401 below.

Robert Barton (NLI)
Earnest Blythe (UCD)
Erskine Childers (TCD)
Michael Collins (NLI; Kilmainham Jail Museum)
Máire Comerford (UCD and privately held)
John Dillon (TCD)
George Gavan Duffy (NLI; NAI (National Archives of Ireland), for-
    merly privately held)
Frank Gallagher (NLI)
Michael Hayes (UCD)
Thomas Johnson (NLI)
M. J. Lennon (NLI)
Shane Leslie (NLI)
Patrick McCartan (NLI)
Joseph McGarrity (NLI)
Kathleen McKenna Napoli (NLI)
P. J. Matthews (NLI)
Maurice Moore (NLI)
Richard Mulcahy (UCD)
Art O'Brien (NLI)
William O'Brien (NLI)
M. O'Carroll (NLI)
Patrick O'Daly (NLI)
T. A. O'Donoghue (NLI)
Seán M. O'Duffy (NLI)
Diarmuid O'Hegarty (UCD)
Patrick O'Keeffe (NLI)
J. J. O'Kelly (NLI)
Seán T. O'Kelly (NLI)
Ernie O'Malley (UCD)
James O'Mara (NLI)
Kevin O'Shiel (UCD)
George Noble Plunkett (NLI)
Séamus Robinson (NLI)
Celia Shaw (NLI)
Hanna Sheehy-Skeffington (NLI)
Austin Stack (NLI)
Mark Sturgis (NLI)

(b) Party records: Sinn Féin

Sinn Féin Standing Committee, minutes, 5 June 1919–23 March 1922 (NAI (National Archives of Ireland), 999/40)

(c) Works in manuscript

Lawless, Lauri, 'The Story of Art O'Connor' (typescript, private ownership)

Lysaght, D. R. O'Connor, 'Soviets in Ireland, 1919–23' (forthcoming publication)

MacBride, Seán, 'The Civil War to the Death of Michael Collins'(lecture, MacGill Summer School, Glenties, Co. Donegal, 1985)

Moore, Fergus, 'Republic, 1919–1921: Ideal or Reality?' (UCD, Hayes Papers, P53/1341–7)

Ó Muirthile, Seán, 'History of the Irish Republican Brotherhood' (UCD, Mulcahy Papers, P7A/201)

O'Neill, T. P., Biography of Eamon de Valera

3. Newspapers and journals

An tÓglach 1918–21, 1925–6
Belfast News-Letter 1918–19
Belfast Strike Bulletin Jan.–Feb. 1919
Belfast Telegraph 1918–19
Catholic Bulletin 1918–19
Cork Examiner 1918–19
Dublin *Evening Mail* 1918–19
Dublin *Evening Telegraph* 1918–19
Freeman's Journal 1918–22
Gaelic American (New York) 1919–20
Galway Express 1919–20
Irish Bulletin 1919–22
Irish Catholic 1919–20
Irish Citizen 1915–20
Irish Commonwealth Mar. 1919
Irish Independent 1918–22
Irish Nation 1916–19
Irish News (Belfast) 1918–19
Irish Statesman 1919–20
Irish Times 1918–22
Irish World (Dublin) 1918–19
Irish World (New York) 1920–21
The Kerryman 1920
The Leader 1918–19
Nationality 1917–19
New Ireland 1919–20
News Letter (Friends of Irish Freedom) 1919–20
Notes from Ireland (Irish Unionist Alliance) 1918–21

Old Ireland 1920–21
The Red Flag 1919
The Red Hand (Belfast) Sept.–Dec. 1920
The Republic 1919
Saoghal Gaedhealacht, see *Irish World* (Dublin)
The Unionist May 1921
Voice of Labour 1918–19
Watchwork of Labour 1921–2
Young Ireland 1918–21

4. Books, pamphlets and articles

(a) By contemporaries

Acland, Mrs Francis, *The Sinn Féin Fellowship* (pamphlet, n.p.; repr. of article in *Westminster Gazette*, 29 Apr. 1921)

American Commission on Conditions in Ireland, *Interim Report* (Washington, DC, Mar. 1921)

——, *Evidence on Conditions in Ireland, comprising the Complete Testimony, Affidavits and Exhibits presented before the* . . . *Commission* (Washington, DC, Nov. 1921)

American Commission on Irish Independence, *Report on Conditions in Ireland, with Demand for Investigation by the Peace Conference* (Paris 1919)

American Commission for Relief in Ireland, *Report* (New York 1922)

Andrews, C. S., *Dublin Made Me* (Cork 1979)

Anon., *Arthur Griffith: A Study of the Founder of Sinn Féin* (pamphlet, Dublin, 1918)

Anon., *Sinn Féin and the Peace Conference: Promises and Performances* (Dublin 1919)

Anon., *Irish Soldiers Appeal to Peace Conference* (petition, [Dublin] 1919)

Anon., *The Voice of Ireland* (pamphlet, [Dublin 1919])

Anon., *Louise to Lord French* (leaflet, n.p. Mar. 1920) (NLI, ILB 300 p6 (14))

Anon., 'History of the Dáil', *Freeman's Journal*, 16 Aug. 1921

Anon., *The Case for the Republic* (pamphlet, n.p. [1922])

Anon., *Protestantism at Stake: Moderator's Views: The Truth about the Irish Situation* (leaflet, repr. from *Belfast News-Letter*, 12 Sept. 1922)

Barry, Tom, *Guerilla Days in Ireland* (Dublin 1949)

Béaslaí, Piaras, *Michael Collins and the Making of a New Ireland* (2 vols, London 1926)

Belfast Telegraph reprint, *The Terror in Ireland* (n.p. 1921)

Birmingham, George A. [J. O. Hannay], *An Irishman Looks at his World* (London, 1919)

Blythe, Ernest, *The Ulster Question* (Glór na Fiann booklet, Dublin 1919)

Boland, Harry, *Last Letters of Harry Boland* (leaflet, Dublin 1922)

Brady, Edward M., *Ireland's Secret Service in England* (Dublin 1928)

Breen, Dan, *My Fight for Irish Freedom* (Dublin 1924: revised ed. 1964)

Brennan, Michael, *The War in Clare, 1911–1921: Personal Memoirs of the Irish War of Independence* (Dublin 1980)

Brennan, Robert, *Allegiance* (Dublin 1950)

Briollay, Sylvain [Roger Chaurive], *Ireland in Rebellion* (London 1922)

Briscoe, Robert, *For the Life of Me* (Boston 1958)

Burke, James A., *The Foundations of Peace* (Dublin 1920)

Carty, James, 'The Riddle of the New Wilson', *New Ireland*, 7 June 1919

——, 'Ireland's Republican Government', *Nation* (USA), 28 Aug. 1920

Childers, Erskine, *A Strike-Breaking Army at Work* (pamphlet, Dublin 1919; repr. of article in *Daily Herald*, 26 May 1919)

——, *Military Rule in Ireland* (pamphlet, Dublin 1920)

——, *The Constructive Work of Dáil Éireann* (series of pamphlets, Dublin 1921)

Churchill, Winston S., *The World Crisis, 1911–14* (London 1923)

Collins, Michael, *The Path to Freedom* (Dublin 1922)

Colum, Pádraic, *Ourselves Alone!: The Story of Arthur Griffith and the Origin of the Irish Free State* (New York 1959)

Comerford, Máire, *The First Dáil* (Dublin 1969)

Creel, George, *The War, the World and Wilson* (New York 1920)

——, *Rebel at Large: Recollections of Fifty Crowded Years* (New York 1947)

Crowley, Diarmaid, *Step by Step: From the Republic back into the Empire* (Dublin [1933–4])

Crozier, Frank P., *Impressions and Recollections* (London 1930)

'Dalta' [Crompton Llewelyn Davis], *An Irish Commonwealth* (pamphlet, Dublin 1920)

Darling, William Y., *So It Looked To Me* (London 1952)

Davis, Crompton Llewelyn, *see* Llewelyn Davis

Davitt, Cahir, 'The Civil Jurisdiction of the Courts of Justice of the Irish Republic, 1920–1922', *Irish Jurist*, iii (1968), 112–30

Dawson, Richard, *Red Terror and Green* (London 1920)

de Blacam, Aodh, *Towards the Republic: A Study of New Ireland's Social and Political Aims* (Dublin 1918; revised ed. 1919)

——, *What Sinn Féin Stands For* (Dublin 1921)

de Valera, Eamon, *The Foundation of the Republic of Ireland* (pamphlet, New York 1919)

——, *Ireland and India* (pamphlet, New York 1920)

Dillon, Thomas, 'Birth of the New Sinn Féin', *Capuchin Annual* (1967), 394–9

Duff, Douglas V., *Sword for Hire: The Saga of a Modern Free Companion* (London 1934)

——, *The Smooth and the Rough* (London 1939)

Duggan, George C., 'The Royal Irish Constabulary' in Edwards and Pyle (eds), *1916: The Easter Rising*

Duke of Northumberland's Fund, *Plight of Southern Irish Loyalists* (pamphlet, London [1921])

Dunne, Edward F., *What Dunne Saw in Ireland* (pamphlet, New York 1919)

Evans, Richardson, 'Ireland and the Realm', *Nineteenth Century*, xix (Apr. 1921), 574–86

Ewart, Wilfred, *A Journey to Ireland, 1921* (London 1922)

Figgis, Darrell, *The Gaelic State in the Past and Future* (pamphlet, Dublin 1917)

——, *The Historic Case for Irish Independence* (pamphlet, Dublin 1918)

——, *The Economic Case for Irish Independence* (pamphlet, Dublin 1920)

——, *Recollections of the Irish War* (London 1927)

FitzGerald, Desmond, *Preface to Statescraft* (London 1939)

FitzGerald, William G. (ed.), *The Voice of Ireland* (London 1924)

Friends, Society of (British), *Report on Ireland* (London 1920)

Gaffney, Thomas St John, *Breaking the Silence: England, Ireland, Wilson and the War* (New York 1930)

Gallagher, Frank, *The Anglo-Irish Treaty* (London 1965)

Gallagher, Michael J., *Matters Arising out of de Valera's Visit* (pamphlet, New York 1920)

Geary, R. C., 'The Oneness of Ireland', *Studies*, lxx, no. 277 (spring 1981), 17–34

Ginnell, Laurence, 'A Glance Back at the Time of Our Harmony', *Catholic Bulletin*, Dec. 1922

Gordon, D. J., *The Truth about Ireland: An Exposé of the Sinn Féin Lie* (pamphlet, Oakland, Calif., [1920])

Green, Alice Stopford (Mrs J. R.) *The Government of Ireland* (pamphlet, London 1921)

——, *The Irish Republican Army* (pamphlet, Chicago 1921)

Gregory, Augusta, Lady, *Journals*, ed. Lennox Robinson (New York 1947)

Griffith, Arthur, *The Resurrection of Hungary: A Parallel for Ireland* (Dublin 1904; 3rd ed. 1918)

——, 'Important Letter of 1919', *Capuchin Annual* (1969), 330–5

Hackett, Francis, *Ireland: A Study in Nationalism* (New York 1920)

Hayes, Michael, 'The Importance of Dáil Éireann', *Capuchin Annual* (1969), 336–9

Headlam, Maurice, *Irish Reminiscences* (London 1947)

Healy, Timothy M., *Letters and Leaders of My Day* (2 vols, London 1928)

Hogan, David [Frank Gallagher], *Four Glorious Years* (Dublin 1953)

Horgan, J. J., *From Parnell to Pearse* (Dublin 1948)

Hughes, Katherine, *English Atrocities in Ireland* (pamphlet, New York 1920)

Irish Labour Party and Trade Union Congress, *Annual Reports* (Dublin 1918–30)

——, *Ireland at Berne,* (Dublin 1919)

——, *Who Burnt Cork City?* (Dublin 1921)

Irish Republican Army, Publicity Department, *The Responsibility* (pamphlet, Dublin 1922)

Irish Unionist Alliance, *Ireland of Today: Sinn Féin and Bolshevism* (pamphlet, Dublin 1919)

——, *Further Sidelights on Bolshevism, Sinn Féin and the Irish Trades Congress* ([Dublin 1919])

Irish White Cross, *Report of the Irish White Cross to 31 August 1922* (Dublin 1922)

Irish Year Book, 1921, ed. Alex McCabe (Dublin 1921)

Johnson, Thomas, *A Handbook for Rebels: A Guide to the Successful Defiance of the British Government* (pamphlet, Dublin 1918)

Jones, Thomas, *Whitehall Diary,* vol. iii: *Ireland, 1918–25,* ed. Keith Middlemas (London 1971)

Labour Party (British), *The International at Lucerne* (London 1919)

——, *Report of the Labour Commission to Ireland* (London 1921)

Lawson, Henry, *A Report on the Irish Situation* (Peace with Ireland Council, London 1920)

Llewelyn Davis, Crompton, *National Land Policy* (pamphlet, Dublin 1920)

Lynch, Diarmuid, *The IRB and the 1916 Insurrection,* ed. Florence O'Donoghue (Cork 1957)

Lynd, Robert, *Ireland a Nation* (London 1919)

McCabe, Alex (ed.), *Irish Year Book* (Dublin 1921)

McCartan, Patrick, *With de Valera in America* (Dublin 1932)

McCormick, Wright, *Irish Republican Arbitration Courts* (pamphlet, New York 1920)

McDonald, Walter, *Some Ethical Questions of Peace and War* (London 1919)

Mac Eoin, Seán, *With the IRA in the Fight for Freedom: 1919 to the Truce* (Tralee 1955)

McEvatt, R. M., 'Arthur Griffith and his Early Sinn Féin Policies', *Capuchin Annual* (1971), 232–8

McGuinness, Charles J., *Nomad* (London 1934)

McKenna, Kathleen, 'The *Irish Bulletin*', *Capuchin Annual* (1970), 503–27

MacLysaght, Edward, *Changing Times: Ireland since 1898* (London 1978)

Macready, Nevil, *Annuals of an Active Life* (2 vols, London 1924)

Maguire, Conor, 'The Republican Courts', *Capuchin Annual* (1969) 378–89

Martin, Hugh, *Ireland in Insurrection* (London 1921)

Mellows, Liam, *Notes from Mountjoy Jail* (pamphlet, London 1966)

Montmorency, Hervey de, *Sword and Stirrup* (London 1936)

Monteith, Robert, *Casement's Last Adventure* (Dublin 1953)

Mulcahy, Richard, 'The Irish Volunteer Convention, 27 October 1917', *Capuchin Annual* (1967), 400–10

——, 'Conscription and the General Headquarters Staff', *Capuchin Annual* (1968), 382–95

——, 'Chief of Staff, 1919', *Capuchin Annual* (1969), 340–53

——, 'The First Dáil', *Hibernia,* 17 Jan. 1969

Neligan, David, *The Spy in the Castle* (London 1967)

New Ireland Assurance Company, *Achievements: The Twenty-Eight Years' Story of New Ireland Assurance Company* (Dublin 1947)

Nunan, Seán, 'President Eamon de Valera's Mission to the United States of America', *Capuchin Annual* (1970), 236–49

O'Brien, William, *Forth the Banners Go* (Dublin 1969)

—— and Ryan Desmond (ed.), *Devoy's Post-Bag, 1871–1928* (2 vols, Dublin 1948–53)

Ó Ceallaigh, Seán T., articles on his experiences in Paris and Rome, *The Nation*, 15 Feb.–15 Mar. 1930

——, *Seán T.* (Galway 1963 (in Irish); transl., 2 vols, Dublin 1972)

O'Connor, Art, *Notes on National Economy* (pamphlet, Dublin 1925)

O'Connor, Batt, *With Michael Collins in the Fight for Irish Independence* (London 1929)

O'Connor, Frank, *The Big Fellow: A Life of Michael Collins* (London 1937)

——, *An Only Child* (London 1961)

Ó Cruadhlaoich, Diarmaid, *see* Crowley

O'Doherty, Kathleen, *Assignment America: de Valera's Mission to the United States* (New York 1957)

O'Donnell, Peadar, *There Will Be Another Day* (Dublin 1963)

O'Donoghue, Florence, *No Other Law: The Story of Liam Lynch and the Irish Republican Army, 1916–1923* (Dublin 1954)

——, *Tomás MacCurtain: Soldier and Patriot* (Tralee 1971)

O'Faolain, Seán, *Vive moi!* (Boston 1964)

O'Flaherty, Liam, *Life of Tim Healy* (London 1927)

O'Flanagan, Michael, *Co-operation* (pamphlet, Dublin 1921)

O'Hegarty, Patrick S., *The Victory of Sinn Féin* (Dublin 1924)

——, *A History of Ireland under the Union* (London 1952)

O'Higgins, Kevin, *The New de Valera* (pamphlet [Dublin 1922], repr. of article in *An Saor Stát*, 25 Mar. 1922)

O'Kelly, J. J., *see* 'Sceilg'

O'Kelly, Seán T., *see* Ó Ceallaigh

O'Malley, Ernie, *On Another Man's Wound* (London 1936; repr. Dublin 1979)

——, *The Singing Flame* (Dublin 1979)

O'Rahilly, Alfred, *Who Burnt Cork City?* (pamphlet, published under the name of ILP & TUC, Dublin 1921)

O'Shiel, Kevin, 'Memories of My Lifetime', *Irish Times*, 7–23 Nov. 1966

'Periscope' [G. C. Duggan], 'The Last Days of Dublin Castle', *Blackwood's Magazine* (Aug. 1922), 137–90

Phillips, W. Alison, *The Revolution in Ireland, 1906–1923* (London 1924)

Pim, Herbert Moore, 'Sinn Féin: Past, Present and Future', *Nineteenth Century*, lxxxv (June 1919), 1165–74

Pollard, H. B. C., *The Secret Societies of Ireland* (London 1922)

Price, G. Ward, 'An Englishman on the Irish Problem', *Century Magazine*, xcviii (6 June 1919), 241–6

Rashid, Ibrahim, *An Egyptian in Ireland* (London 1921)

Russell, George (AE), *The National Being* (Dublin 1916)

——, *Ireland and the Empire at the Court of Conscience* (Dublin 1921)

——, *The Inner and the Outer Ireland* (pamphlet, Dublin 1921)

——, 'Twenty-Five Years of Irish Nationality', *Foreign Affairs*, vii (Jan. 1929), 204–20

Ryan, Desmond, *Remembering Sion* (London 1934)

——, *Benevolent Dictator: A Study of Eamon de Valera* (London 1936)

——, *The Phoenix Flame* (London 1937)

——, *Seán Treacy and the Third Tipperary Brigade* (Tralee 1945)

——, 'Sinn Féin Policy and Practice' in Williams, *The Irish Struggle*

'Sceilg' [J. J. O'Kelly], 'Austin Stack: Some Recollections and Associations', *Catholic Bulletin* (June 1929), 533–49

——, *A Trinity of Martyrs* (pamphlet, Dublin 1929)

——, *The Republic of Ireland Vindicated* (pamphlet, Dublin 1931)

——, *Stepping Stones* (pamphlet, Dublin [1939?])

Street, Cecil J. C. [pseud. 'I.O.'], *The Administration of Ireland, 1920* (London 1921)

——, *Ireland in 1921* (London 1922)

Thom's Dublin Directory and Calendar for 1921 (Dublin 1920)

Ulster Unionist Labour Association, *Labour Party Commission on Ireland: Analysis and Criticism* (Belfast 1921)

Walsh, J. C, *The Invincible Irish* (New York 1919)

Walsh, J. J, *Recollections of a Rebel* (Tralee 1944)

Wells, Warre B., *Irish Indiscretions* (Dublin 1923)

Wilson, P. Whitell, *The Irish Case* (New York 1920)

Winter, Ormonde, *Winter's Tale* (London 1955)

Women's International League, British section, *A 'Sort of War' in Ireland: Report of the Mission to Ireland* (pamphlet, London 1920)

(b) Later works

Barrett-Brown, M., *After Imperialism* (London 1963)

Bell, J. Bowyer, *The Secret Army: A History of the IRA, 1916–1970* (London 1970)

——, 'The Thompson Submachine-Gun in Ireland, 1921', *Irish Sword*, viii, no. 31 (1967), 98–108

——, *On Revolt: Strategies of National Liberation* (Cambridge, Mass. 1976)

Bennett, Richard, *The Black and Tans* (London 1959; repr. 1961)

Bew, Paul, 'Sinn Féin, Agrarian Radicalism and the War of Independence, 1917–21' in Boyce (ed.), *The Revolution in Ireland*

——, Gibbon, Peter, and Patterson, Henry, *The State in Northern Ireland, 1921–72: Political Forces and Social Classes* (New York 1977)

Bolger, Patrick, *The Irish Co-operative Movement: Its History and Development* (Dublin 1977)

Bowden, Tom, 'Bloody Sunday — A Reappraisal', *European Studies Review*, ii, no. 1 (1972), 25–42

——, 'The Irish Underground and the War of Independence, 1919–21', *Journal of Contemporary History*, viii, no. 2 (1973), 3–23

——, *The Breakdown of Public Security: The Case of Ireland, 1919–1921, and Palestine, 1936–1939* (London 1977)

——, Elliott-Bateman, M., and Ellis, J., *Revolt to Revolution: Studies in the Nineteenth and Twentieth Century Experience* (Manchester 1974)

Bowman, John, *De Valera and the Ulster Question, 1917–1973* (Oxford 1982)

Boyce, D. G., *Englishmen and Irish Troubles: British Public Opinion and the Making of Irish Policy, 1918–1922* (Cambridge, Mass. 1972)

——, *Nationalism in Ireland* (London 1982)

—— (ed.), *The Revolution in Ireland, 1879–1923* (Dublin 1988)

Boyle, Andrew, *The Riddle of Erskine Childers* (London 1977)

Brindley, Ronan, 'Woodrow Wilson, Self-Determination and Ireland, 1918–19: A View from the Irish Newspapers', *Éire–Ireland*, xxiii, no. 4 (winter 1986), 62–80

Butler, David, *The Electoral System in Britain since 1918* (Oxford 1963)

Butler, Ewan, *Barry's Flying Column* (London 1971)

Byrne, Francis J., 'Saorstát Éireann meant the Irish Republic', *Irish Independent*, 18 Feb. 1959

Carroll, Francis M., *American Opinion and the Irish Question, 1910–23* (Dublin 1978)

——, 'The American Commission of Inquiry on Conditions in Ireland', *Éire–Ireland*, xvi, no. 4 (winter 1981), 59–74

——, (ed.), *American Commission on Irish Independence, 1919: The Diary, Correspondence and Report* (Dublin 1985)

Casey, James P., 'Republican Courts in Ireland, 1919–1922', *Irish Jurist*, v (1970), 321–42

——, 'The Genesis of the Dáil Courts', *Irish Jurist*, ix (1974), 326–38

Chorley, Katherine, *Armies and the Art of Revolution* (1943; repr. Boston 1974)

Chubb, Basil, *The Government and Politics of Ireland* (Stanford/London 1970)

——, *The Constitution of Ireland* (Dublin 1970)

——, *The Constitution and Constitutional Change in Ireland* (Dublin 1978)

Clarkson, Jesse Dunsmore, *Labour and Nationalism in Ireland* (New York 1925)

Cohan, A. S., *The Irish Political Elite* (Dublin 1972)

Coogan, Tim Pat, *Ireland since the Rising* (Dublin 1966)

——, *The IRA* (Dublin 1966)

Corish, P. J. (ed.), *Radicals, Rebels and Establishments* (*Historical Studies, XV*) (Belfast 1985)

Costello, Francis J., 'Irish Representatives to the London Anglo-Irish Conference in 1921', *Éire–Ireland*, xxiv, no. 2 (summer 1989), 52–78

Costello, Peter, *The Heart Grown Brutal: The Irish Revolution in Literature, from Parnell to the Death of Yeats, 1891–1939* (Dublin 1977)

Counahan, Geraldine, 'The People Backed the Movement, *Capuchin Annual* (1970), 250–4

Cox, Tom, *Damned Englishman: A Study of Erskine Childers (1870–1922)* (Hicksville, NY 1975)

Cronin, Seán, *The McGarrity Papers* (Tralee 1972)

——, *Irish Nationalism: A History of its Roots and Ideology* (Dublin 1980)

Curran, Joseph M., *The Birth of the Irish Free State, 1921–1923* (University of Alabama 1980)

Davis, Richard P., *Arthur Griffith and Non-Violent Sinn Féin* (Dublin 1974)

——, 'The Advocacy of Passive Resistance in Ireland, 1916–1922', *Anglo-Irish Studies*, iii (1977), 35–55

Deasy, Liam, *Towards Ireland Free: The West Cork Brigade in the War of Independence, 1917–1921* (Cork 1973)

Delany, V. T. H., *The Administration of Justice in Ireland* (Dublin 1965)

Dwyer, T. Ryle, *Michael Collins and the Treaty: His Differences with de Valera* (Cork 1981)

——, *De Valera's Darkest Hour: In Search of National Independence, 1919–1932* (Cork 1982)

Edwards, Owen Dudley, 'Frank Talking in the Era of the Provisional Government', *Irish Times*, 21 Apr. 1976

——, *Eamon de Valera* (Washington, DC 1987)

—— and Pyle, Fergus (eds), *1916: The Easter Rising* (London 1968)

Fanning Ronan, *The Irish Department of Finance, 1922–1958* (Dublin 1978)

——, *Independent Ireland* (Dublin 1983)

Farrell, Brian, *The Founding of Dáil Éireann* (Dublin 1971)

——, 'The Legislation of a "Revolutionary" Assembly: Dáil Decrees, 1919–1922', *Irish Jurist*, x (1975), 112–27

Farrell, Michael, *Arming the Protestants: The Formation of the Ulster Special Constabulary and the Royal Ulster Constabulary, 1920–27* (London 1983)

Feehan, John, *The Shooting of Michael Collins* (Cork 1981)

Fitzpatrick, David, *Politics and Irish Life, 1913–1921: Provincial Experience of War and Revolution* (Dublin 1977)

——, 'The Geography of Irish Nationalism', *Past and Present*, no. 78 (1978), 113–44

——, 'Strikes in Ireland, 1914–21', *Saothar*, 6 (1980), 26–39

Forester, Margery, *Michael Collins: the Lost Leader* (London 1971; repr. Dublin 1989)

Garvin, Tom, *The Evolution of Irish Nationalist Politics* (Dublin 1981)

——, *Nationalist Revolutionaries in Ireland, 1858–1928* (Oxford 1987)

Gaughan, J. Anthony, *Memoirs of Constable Jeremiah Mee, RIC* (Dublin 1975)

——, *Austin Stack: Portrait of a Separatist* (Dublin 1977)

——, *Alfred O'Rahilly* (2 vols, Dublin 1986–9)

Glandon, Virginia E., 'Arthur Griffith and the Ideal Irish State', *Studies*, lxxiii, no. 289 (spring 1984), 26–36

——, *Arthur Griffith and the Advanced Nationalist Press: Ireland, 1900–1922* (New York 1985)

——, 'John Dillon's Reflections on Irish and General Politics, 1919–1921', *Éire–Ireland*, xi, no. 3 (autumn 1974), 30–41

Goldring, Maurice, *Faith of Our Fathers: The Formation of Irish Nationalist Ideology, 1890–1920* (Dublin 1982)

Greaves, C. Desmond, *Liam Mellows and the Irish Revolution* (London 1971)

Griffith, Kenneth, and O'Grady, Timothy, *Curious Journey: An Oral History of Ireland's Unfinished Revolution* (London 1982)

Hachey, Thomas E., *Britain and Irish Separatism: from the Fenians to the Free State, 1867–1922* (Chicago 1978)

Hancock, W. K., 'Problems of Nationality, 1918–1936' in *Survey of British Commonwealth Affairs*, vol. i (London 1937)

Hawkins, Richard, 'Dublin Castle and the RIC' in Williams (ed.), *The Irish Struggle*

Hoctor, Daniel, *The Department's Story: A History of the Department of Agriculture* (Dublin 1971)

Holmes, Richard, *The Little Field Marshal: Sir John French* (London 1981)

Hopkinson, Michael, *Green Against Green: The Irish Civil War* (Dublin 1988)

Johnson, D. S., 'The Belfast Boycott' in J. M. Goldstrom and L. A. C. Clarkson (eds), *Irish Population, Economy and Society: Essays in honour of the late K. H. Connell* (Oxford 1982)

Kee, Robert, *The Green Flag: A History of Irish Nationalism* (London 1972)

Keogh, Dermot, *The Vatican, the Bishops and Irish Politics: Church and State in Ireland, 1919–1939* (Cambridge 1986)

——, *Ireland and Europe, 1919–1948* (Dublin 1988)

Kilfeather, T. P., *The Connaught Rangers* (Tralee 1969)

Kotsonouris, Mary, *Retreat from Revolution: The Dáil Courts, 1920–24* (Dublin 1994)

Laffan, Michael, *The Partition of Ireland, 1911–1925* (Dublin 1983)

Lavelle, Patricia, *James O'Mara, a Staunch Sinn Féiner, 1873–1948* (Dublin 1961)

Lawlor, Sheila, *Britain and Ireland, 1914–23* (Dublin 1983)

Lee, Joseph J., 'Irish Nationalism and Socialism: Rumpf Reconsidered', *Saothar*, 6 (1980), 59–64

Longford, Earl of, and O'Neill, T. P., *Eamon de Valera* (London 1970)

Lynch, Patrick, 'The Social Revolution That Never Was' in Williams (ed.), *The Irish Struggle*

Lyons, F. S. L., *John Dillon: A Biography* (London 1968)

——, *Ireland since the Famine* (London 1971; repr. 1973)

Lysaght, D. R. O'Connor, *The Republic of Ireland* (Cork 1970)

——, Introduction to James Connolly, *Socialism Made Easy* (pamphlet, repr. Dublin 1971)

——, *The Story of the Limerick Soviet* (pamphlet, Limerick 1979)

——, *The Communists and the Irish Revolution* (Dublin 1993)

Macardle, Dorothy, *The Irish Republic* (London 1937; repr. New York 1968)

McCartney, Donal, 'De Valera's Mission to the United States, 1919–20' in Art Cosgrove and Donal McCartney (eds), *Studies in Irish History presented to R. Dudley Edwards* (Dublin 1979)

McColgan, John, *British Policy and the Irish Administration, 1920–22* (London 1983)

McCracken, J. L., *Representative Government in Ireland: A Study of Dáil Éireann, 1919–48* (Oxford 1958)

MacDonagh, Oliver, *States of Mind: A Study of Anglo-Irish Conflict, 1780–1980* (London 1983)

Mac Eoin, Uinseann (ed.), *Survivors: The Story of Ireland's Struggle as told through some of her outstanding living people* (Dublin 1981; repr. 1987)

McEvett, R. M., 'Arthur Griffith and his Early Sinn Féin Policies', *Capuchin Annual* (1971), 232–8

McInerney, Michael, *The Riddle of Erskine Childers* (Cork 1971)

McManus, Sheila, *Britain and Ireland, 1914–1923* (Dublin 1986)

Mansergh, Nicholas, *The Irish Question, 1840–1921* (London 1965)

Marreco, Ann, *The Rebel Countess* (Philadelphia 1967)

Martin, F. X., '1916: Myth, Fact and Mystery', *Studia Hibernica*, no. 6 (1967), 7–126

——, 'The 1916 Rising — *Coup d'État* or "Bloody Protest"?', *Studia Hibernica*, no. 8 (1968), 106–37

Miller, David, *Church, State and Nation in Ireland, 1898–1921* (Dublin 1973)

Milotte, Mike, *Communism in Modern Ireland* (Dublin 1985)

Mitchell, Arthur, *Labour in Irish Politics, 1890–1930* (Shannon 1974)

——, 'Thomas Johnson, 1872–1963: A Pioneer Labour Leader', *Studies*, lviii, no. 232 (winter 1969), 396–404

——, 'William O'Brien, 1881–1968, and the Irish Labour Movement', *Studies*, lx, no. 239 (winter 1971), 311–31

——, 'The Economic Philosophy of George Russell', *Irish Times*, 17 Apr. 1967

——, 'Revolutionary Government in Ireland: Dáil Éireann, 1919–21', *Proceedings of the South Carolina Historical Association* (1983), 66–75

—— and Ó Snodaigh, Pádraig (eds), *Irish Political Documents, 1870–1916* (Dublin 1989)

—— and Ó Snodaigh, Pádraig (eds), *Irish Political Documents, 1916–1949* (Dublin 1985)

Mulcahy, Risteárd, 'Michael Collins and the Making of a New Ireland', *Studies*, lxvii, no. 267 (autumn 1978), 187–200

Neeson, Eoin, *The Civil War in Ireland* (Cork 1966)

Nowlan, Kevin B., 'Dáil Éireann and the Army: Unity and Division, 1919–1921' in Williams (ed.), *The Irish Struggle*

O'Brien, Conor Cruise, *The Shaping of Modern Ireland* (London 1960)

Ó Broin, Leon, *Revolutionary Underground: The Story of the Irish Republican Brotherhood, 1858–1924* (Dublin 1976)

——, *Michael Collins* (Dublin 1980)

Ó Buchalla, Séamas, 'Education as an Issue in the First Dáil and Second Dáil', *Administration* (spring 1977), 57–75

O'Connor, Emmet, *Syndicalism in Ireland, 1917–1923* (Cork 1988)

Ó Dochartaigh, Tomás, *Cathal Brugha* (Dublin 1969)

O'Farrell, Patrick, *England's Irish Question: Anglo-Irish Relations, 1534–1970* (New York 1972)

O'Farrell, Pádraic, *The Seán Mac Eoin Story* (Cork 1981)

O'Halpin, Eunan, *The Decline of the Union: British Government in Ireland, 1892–1920* (Dublin 1987)

Ó Lúing, Seán, 'The German Plot', *Capuchin Annual* (1968), 377–81

——'Arthur Griffith, 1871–1922: Thoughts on a Centenary', *Studies*, lx, no. 238 (summer 1971), 127–38

O'Neill, Marie, *From Parnell to de Valera: A Biography of Jennie Wyse Power, 1858–1941* (Dublin 1991)

O'Neill, Thomas P., *Eamon de Valera* (2 vols, Dublin 1968) (in Irish)

——, 'The General Election, 1918', *Capuchin Annual* (1968), 396–404

—— and Longford, Earl of, *Eamon de Valera* (London 1970)

Ó Snodaigh, Pádraig, *see* Snoddy, Oliver

O'Sullivan, Donal, *The Irish Free State and its Senate* (London 1940)

Pakenham, Frank, *Peace by Ordeal: The Negotiation of the Anglo-Irish Treaty, 1921* (London 1935; repr. 1972)

Patterson, Henry, *Class Conflict and Sectarianism: The Protestant Working Class and the Belfast Labour Movement, 1868–1920* (Belfast 1980)

Pimley, Adrian, 'The Working-Class Movement and the Irish Revolution, 1896–1923' in Boyce (ed.) *The Revolution in Ireland*

Pollack, Sam, *Mutiny for the Cause* (London 1971)

Ranelagh, John O'Beirne, 'The IRB from the Treaty to 1924', *Irish Historical Studies*, xx, no. 77 (Mar. 1976), 26–39

——, 'The Irish Republican Brotherhood in the Revolutionary Period, 1879–1923' in Boyce (ed.), *The Revolution in Ireland*

Rumpf, Erhard, and Heburn, A. C., *Nationalism and Socialism in Twentieth-Century Ireland* (Liverpool 1977)

Snoddy, Oliver [Pádraig Ó Snodaigh], *Cómhghnaillithe na Réabhlóide, 1913–16* (Dublin 1966)

——, 'National Aid, 1916, 1917, 1918', *Capuchin Annual* (1968), 331–9
——, 'Ireland and the Paris Peach Conference, 1919', *Capuchin Annual* (1969), 389–400
——, 'The Truce', *Capuchin Annual* (1971), 298–304
——, 'From the Bridge to the Abyss', *Capuchin Annual* (1972), 315–50
—— and Mitchell, Arthur (eds), *Irish Political Documents, 1870–1916* (Dublin 1989)
——, —— (eds), *Irish Political Documents, 1916–49* (Dublin 1985)
Sullivan, Dennis M., 'Eamon de Valera and the Forces of Opposition in America', *Éire–Ireland*, xix, no. 2 (summer 1984), 100–10
Tansill, Charles C., *America and the Fight for Irish Freedom* (New York 1957)
Taylor, Rex, *Michael Collins* (London 1958; repr. 1961)
Tierney, Michael, *Eoin MacNeill: Scholar and Man of Action, 1867–1945* (Oxford 1980)
Titley, E. Brian, *Church, State and the Control of Schooling in Ireland, 1900–1944* (Montreal 1983)
Townshend, Charles, *The British Campaign in Ireland, 1919–21* (Oxford 1975)
——, 'The Irish Republican Army and the Development of Guerrilla Warfare, 1916–21', *English Historical Review*, xciv (1979), 318–45
——, 'Bloody Sunday: Michael Collins Speaks', *European Studies Review*, ix (1979), 377–85
——, *Political Violence in Ireland: Government and Resistance since 1848* (Oxford 1983)
Ussher, Arland, *The Mind and Face of Ireland* (London 1949)
Valiulis, Maryann G., *Almost a Rebellion: The Irish Army Mutiny of 1924* (Cork 1985)
Van Voris, Jacqueline, *Constance de Markievicz in the Cause of Ireland* (Boston 1967)
Wall, Maureen, 'Partition: The Ulster Question' in Williams (ed.), *The Irish Struggle*
Walsh, James P., 'Woodrow Wilson: Historians *versus* the Irish', *Éire–Ireland*, ii, no. 2 (summer 1967), 55–66
Ward, Alan, *Ireland and Anglo-American Relations, 1899–1921* (London 1969)
——, *The Easter Rising: Revolution and Irish Nationalism* (Arlington Heights, Ill. 1980)
Ward, Margaret, *Unmanageable Revolutionaries: Women and Irish Nationalism* (Dingle 1983)
Wheeler-Bennett, John, *John Anderson, Viscount Waverley* (London 1962)
White, Terence de Vere, *Kevin O'Higgins* (Tralee 1967)
Williams, T. Desmond (ed.), *The Irish Struggle, 1916–26* (Dublin 1966)
—— (ed.), *Secret Societies in Ireland* (Dublin 1973)
Younger, Calton, *Ireland's Civil War* (London 1968; repr. 1972)

5. *Official publications and departmental reports*

(a) Official publications: Dáil Éireann

Cabinet minutes, 1919–21 (NAI (National Archives of Ireland), DE 1/1–1/3)

Dáil Éireann, *Miontuairisc on Chéad Dála, 1919–21: Minutes of Proceedings of the First Parliament of the Republic of Ireland, 1919–1921: Official Record* (Dublin [1921])

Dáil Éireann, *Tuairisg Oifigiúil (Official Report) for periods 16th August 1921 to 26th August 1921, and 28th February 1922 to 8th June 1922* (Dublin [1922])

Dáil Éireann, *Suíonna Príobhóideacha an Dara Dála: Private Sessions of Second Dáil, 18 August to 14 September 1921, and Report of Debates 14 December 1921 to 6 January 1922*, ed. and introd. T. P. O'Neill (Dublin [1972])

Dáil Éireann, *Tuairisg Oifigiúil: Díosbóireacht ar an gConnradh idir Éire agus Sasana: Official Report: Debate on the Treaty between Great Britain and Ireland, signed in London on 6th December 1921* (Dublin [1922])

Department of Propaganda (after Feb. 1921, Department of Publicity), *Irish Bulletin* (1919–22)

The Authority of Dáil Éireann (pamphlet, Dublin 1919)

Presidential Statement of Policy, delivered at the Public Session of Dáil Éireann, April 10, 1919 (pamphlet, Dublin, 1919)

The Constructive Work of Dáil Éireann (series of pamphlets, Dublin 1921)

(b) Departmental reports: Dáil Éireann

Agriculture
June 1920 (NLI, Duffy Papers, MS 15439)
Jan. 1921 (NLI, Duffy Papers, MS 15440)
Aug. 1921 (NAI, DE 2/418)
Jan.–Apr. 1922 (NLI, O'Brien Papers, MS 8425)

Belfast boycott, see Labour (p. 400 below)

Commission of Inquiry into Ireland's Industrial Resources, 1919–22
Eight reports, 1922 (NAI, DE 2/18)

Defence
This department issued no reports, but the Mulcahy Papers (UCD) contain a near-complete record of the activities of the department and the army. See also Department of Defence microfilm (NLI, pos 914, 917, 918).

Óglaigh na hÉireann Irish Republican Army, General order: boycott of RIC [1919] (NLI, ILB 300 p31)

Engineering Department, Telephone tapping memoranda, Apr. 1921 (NLI, Ir. 94109 p61)

Earthing lines memorandum, Apr. 1921 (ibid.)

Destruction of enemy motor transport memorandum, Apr. 1921 (ibid.)
'Enemy aeroplane observation in guerrilla warfare with suggestions for
   ground defence tactics' (pamphlet, [1921]) (copy ibid.)
General Headquarters, 'Dealing with Enemy Deserters and Danger of
   Spies' (memorandum, 17 Oct. 1921)

Finance
Aug. 1919 (NAI, DE 2/7)
Oct. 1919 (NLI, Duffy Papers, MS 15440)
Oct. 1919–Apr. 1920 (NLI, Duffy Papers, MS 15439)
June 1920 (NAI, DE 2/7)
Aug. 1920 (NAI, DE 2/7)
Sept. 1920 (NAI, DE 2/7)
Dec. 1920 (NAI, DE 2/7)
Jan.–Mar. 1921 (NLI, Plunkett Papers, MS 11404)
Aug. 1921 (NLI, Duffy Papers, MS 15439)

Fisheries
Committee report, June 1919 (NLI, Duffy Papers, MS 15440)
June 1920 (NLI, Papers, Duffy MS 15439)

Foreign Affairs
June 1919 (NLI, O'Brien Papers, MS 8426)
Aug. 1919 (NLI, Duffy Papers, MS 15440)
June 1920 (NAI, DE 2/7)
Jan. 1921 (NLI, Duffy MS 15440)
June 1921 (NLI, Plunkett Papers, MS 11404)

Home Affairs
'National Arbitration Courts', report, early 1920 (NLI, Plunkett Papers,
   MS 11404)
Judiciary: rules and forms, parish and district courts, 1921 (NLI, Seán
   M. O'Duffy Papers, MS 21658)
Courts (winding-up) Commission, 1924–6, report (NAI, DE 149)

June 1920 (NAI, DE 2/51)
Aug. 1920 (NAI, DE 2/51)
Jan. 1921 (NLI, Duffy Papers, MS 15440)
May 1921 (NLI, O'Brien Papers, MS 8429)
Aug. 1921 (NAI, DE 2/51)

Labour
June 1920 (NLI, Duffy Papers, MS 15439)
Mar. 1921 (NAI, DE 2/5)
Aug. 1921 (NAI, DE 2/5)
Belfast boycott, Aug. 1921 (Dáil Éireann, *Official Report*, 27–33; Dáil
   Éireann, *Private Sessions*, 17–19)

Local Government
Aug. 1919 (NLI, Duffy Papers, MS 15440)
Oct. 1919 (NLI, Duffy Papers, MS 15440)
June 1920 (NLI, Duffy Papers, MS 15439)
Jan. 1921 (NLI, Duffy Papers, MS 15440)
Aug. 1921 (Dáil Éireann, *Official Report*, 33–6)

National Language/Education
Aug. 1921 (NAI, DE 2/473)

Propaganda/Publicity
Oct. 1919 (NAI, DE 1/10/6)
Jan. 1920 (NAI, DE 2/10/11)
Mar. 1921 (NLI, McKenna Napoli Papers, MS 22610

Trade and Commerce
Oct. 1919 (NLI, Duffy Papers, MS 15440)
Jan. 1921 (NLI, Duffy Papers, MS 15439)
Aug. 1921 (NAI, DE 2/417; UCD, Blythe Papers, P24/16)
Industrial Resources Inquiry, *see* Commission of Inquiry into Ireland's
    Industrial Resources (p. 399 above)

(c) British and US reports and publications
British
RIC, monthly reports, 1919–21 (PRO, CO 904)
Chief Secretary's reports, 1919–21 (PRO, CO 904)
Weekly Summary, 13 Aug. 1920–1 July 1921
Intercourse between Bolshevism and Sinn Féin, 1921 (Cmd 1326)
Epitome of de Valera Material, seized June 1921 (PRO, CO 904/23) PRO,
    London
Documents relative to the Sinn Féin Movement, 1918 ['German plot'
    material], 1921 (Cmd 1108)

USA
Consular reports, 1919–21 (National Archives, Department of State
    files)

6. Reference works

Best, R. I, *Bibliography of Irish Philology and Manuscript Literature: Publica-
    tions, 1913–1941* (Dublin 1969)
Boylan, Henry, *A Dictionary of Irish Biography* (Dublin 1978)
Carty, James, *A Bibliography of Irish History, 1870–1912* (Dublin 1940)
——, *A Bibliography of Irish History, 1912–1921* (Dublin 1936)
Crone, J. S., *A Concise Dictionary of Irish Biography* (Dublin 1937)
Eager, A. R., *A Guide to Irish Bibliographical Material* (London 1964)

Flynn, William J., *Oireachtas Companion and Saorstát Guide* (Dublin 1928)

Hayes, Richard J. (ed.), *Manuscript Sources for the History of Irish Civilisation*, 11 vols (Boston, Mass. 1965)

——, *Sources for the History of Irish Civilisation: Articles in Irish Periodicals*, 9 vols (Boston, Mass. 1970)

Hickey, D. J., and Doherty, J. E., *A Dictionary of Irish History since 1800* (Dublin 1978)

O'Farrell, Pádraic, *Who's Who in the Irish War of Independence* (Cork 1980)

Walker, Brian M. (ed.), *Parliamentary Election Results in Ireland, 1801–1922* (Dublin 1978)

—— (ed.), *Parliamentary Election Results in Ireland, 1918–92* (Dublin/Belfast 1992)

Index

Sub-headings run in chronological order.